financial accounting, reporting & analysis

financial accounting, reporting & analysis

second edition

jennifer maynard

OXFORD
UNIVERSITY PRESS

OXFORD
UNIVERSITY PRESS

Great Clarendon Street, Oxford, OX2 6DP,
United Kingdom

Oxford University Press is a department of the University of Oxford.
It furthers the University's objective of excellence in research, scholarship,
and education by publishing worldwide. Oxford is a registered trade mark of
Oxford University Press in the UK and in certain other countries

Published in the United States of America by Oxford University Press
198 Madison Avenue, New York, NY 10016, United States of America

British Library Cataloguing in Publication Data
Data available

Library of Congress Control Number: 2017934845

ISBN 978–0–19–874531–0

Printed in Great Britain by
Bell & Bain Ltd., Glasgow

To my late mother, Monica.

CONTENTS IN BRIEF

CONTENTS

Who the textbook is for

This textbook on financial accounting, reporting and analysis is principally aimed at Level 2 and 3 undergraduate students on specialist accounting and finance degree programmes, although it may be relevant for postgraduate courses in financial statement analysis. It is assumed that all readers will have completed an introductory financial accounting course, and may go on to study more advanced financial reporting courses. There is, however, an introductory chapter, which revises the main topics covered in introductory financial accounting courses and textbooks, and this provides a foundation on which the remainder of the textbook's material is built. The textbook's basis is international financial reporting standards (IASs and IFRS) issued by the International Accounting Standards Board (IASB).

New to the second edition

This second edition has been substantially updated for all changes in IFRS and the regulatory environment. In addition two new chapters have been added.

Chapter 7 *Revenue from contracts with customers* is now based entirely on IFRS 15 *Revenue from contracts with customers*, although implementation of this standard is not required by companies until accounting periods beginning on or after 1 January 2018.

Chapter 15 *Leases* maintains details of IAS 17 *Leases* since companies will still be reporting under this standard for a few more years. It also covers the new replacement standard IFRS 16 *Leases*. This is not required to be implemented by companies until accounting periods beginning on or after 1 January 2019.

There are no real-life application examples of these two new standards yet; however, some of the financial reporting in practice illustrations are from companies that make reference to the future impact of the standards on their financial statements.

Chapter 2 *The financial reporting system* includes discussion of the proposals contained in the IASB's 2015 Exposure Draft (ED) of the *Conceptual Framework for Financial Reporting*. This significant IASB project has been in progress for some years, and is hopefully nearing conclusion, with the final *Conceptual Framework* expected to be issued in early 2017. Amongst other changes, the ED places more explicit emphasis on stewardship as an objective of financial reporting, prudence is back as an underpinning concept in certain circumstances and measurement principles are fully updated. All these issues are discussed in detail in the chapter.

The two new chapters cover more advanced financial reporting topics and are included at the request of reviewers.

Chapter 14 *Financial instruments* addresses the important topic of financial instruments and is based on the latest and final version of financial reporting standard IFRS 9 *Financial Instruments* and the related presentation and disclosure standards IAS 32 *Financial Instruments: Presentation* and IFRS 7 *Financial Instruments: Disclosures*. Financial instruments are held by many companies, not only financial institutions, and encompass some fundamental items such as cash, receivables and payables. The chapter does not cover the more complex instruments—derivatives and hedging instruments. As for other recently issued financial reporting standards there are few full practical examples available of the application of IFRS 9, as companies have until accounting periods beginning on or after 1 January 2018 to implement the standard; however its expected impact is fully discussed.

Chapter 16 *Employee benefits and share-based payments* concerns all forms of employee remuneration, and concentrates on how companies account for post-retirement benefit plans (pension schemes) and all forms of share-based payments. The applicable standards are IAS 19 *Employee Benefits* and IFRS 2 *Share-based Payment*.

The technical nature of financial reporting

One key issue with a second year undergraduate course in financial reporting is how to take students from Level 1 basic financial accounting, which focuses on the preparation of the main financial statements, to an understanding of the complexities and many subtleties of financial reporting. Financial reporting is about communicating financial information about a business entity to its users. This is mirrored by this textbook's main aim—to enable readers to understand and interpret the financial statements of business entities—mainly companies. Inevitably and unapologetically this requires understanding of detailed technical material and terminology, and the use of judgement in situations where there are often no right or wrong answers. However, the textbook explains the technicalities and complexities in a clear manner, so that students become familiar with and confident in the use of this material and language, and are able to develop use of their own judgement as necessary. However, in all this complexity, the overarching objective of financial reporting should not be lost.

The textbook also seeks a balance between the sometimes conflicting needs of financial reporting courses. On the one hand these may seek to attract professional accountancy body exemptions, but on the other they need to be theoretical enough and include sufficient critical perspective to meet the demands of academic benchmarking requirements. Thus the technical material is current and comprehensive, but not so much so that the main points are swamped in a mass of detail. The financial accounting and reporting methods are discussed in relation to underpinning frameworks and principles and always in the context of what they mean for the user.

Approach taken by the textbook

The textbook takes as its foundation the IASB's decision-usefulness objective of financial reporting, which is to provide financial information about a reporting entity that is useful to users in making decisions. Discussion of the more technical topics then uses a model which addresses three questions:

- How is the financial accounting done?
- Why is the accounting done in the way that it is?
- What does this mean for the user?

(So that material is not presented in an artificial manner, the explanations and discussions of the topics integrate these questions.)

How the financial accounting is done, is the technical, preparing element, essential for professional accountancy body requirements. The textbook discusses the significant aspects of international financial reporting standards using clear explanations, which are supported by short explanatory examples and longer worked examples, and backed up by a comprehensive glossary.

Why the accounting is done in the way that it is, is the understanding element. Accounting methods are linked back to underpinning concepts and principles, and this provides the more critical perspective. It is set in the context of the financial reporting governance framework, and chapters in the textbook examine why this takes the form it does today, and also consider what future developments there are likely to be.

What it means for the user is the key interpretation theme of the textbook and, in addition to this question being addressed in individual chapters, there are two chapters devoted to interpretation. Chapter 5 provides details of basic interpretative tools, which are used in subsequent chapters when considering the effect of a particular accounting method or requirement. However, a full interpretation can only be achieved properly by understanding the interrelationships of all financial statements taken together and of the basis of individual figures, so the final chapter pulls together much of the material covered by all previous chapters. It illustrates this by the use of a detailed case study—an interpretation of the financial statements of J Sainsbury plc.

Sequence of chapters

The interrelationship of financial statements creates questions over the most appropriate order of material in a textbook on financial reporting. Further, there are questions over which topics should be included. In response to the latter question, this edition includes those topics which research indicated were the ones users and potential users of the book wanted, given the intended audience. The topics also include those in the syllabuses of the intermediate levels of the main UK professional accountancy bodies.

All topics within chapters are sectioned by number, and so if material is not covered in a course or module, it should be easy to indicate the relevant sections to students.

The sequence of the chapters is loosely based on the following approach:

- Revision of level one financial accounting—Chapter 1
- The framework for and context of financial reporting—Chapters 2 and 3
- Published financial statements—Chapter 4
- Interpretative techniques used in financial reporting—Chapter 5
- Topics principally relating to the statement of profit or loss—Chapters 6, 7 and 8
- Taxation—Chapter 9
- Topics principally relating to the statement of financial position—Chapters 10, 11, 12, 13, 14, 15 and 16
- Consolidated financial statements—Chapters 17 and 18
- Interpretation of published financial statements—Chapter 19.

The interrelated nature of the material results in all chapters including many cross-references to other chapters.

Financial reporting in real life

The final objective of this textbook is to show its readers that financial reporting is a real, live subject. Business entities have to address questions about how they account for and present the results of their increasingly complex financial and other transactions, and what information the users of their financial reports will want. Thus the information disclosed by entities is discussed in all chapters, and illustrated by the financial reporting in practice examples. Readers will be able to understand how the detailed material they have studied is ultimately reported by entities.

Jennifer Maynard
August 2016

ACKNOWLEDGEMENTS

Firstly, I should like to thank the development team at OUP for their encouragement throughout the rewrite and the suggestions they have made. They have organised and produced summaries of all the reviews of draft chapters, and so, secondly, I should like to thank all academic staff at other universities who have given their time and energy in this process and who made helpful and constructive comments.

Thirdly, I should like to thank former and present colleagues who, through conversations about financial accounting and reporting and how to best teach and deliver the subject, have provided inspiration, ideas and examples.

Finally, I must thank anyone who recognises examples I have used in this textbook as their own and whom I have not acknowledged. In over 20 years of teaching financial accounting and reporting I have inevitably accumulated and adapted examples, the original source of which has now been lost.

How to use this book

ACKNOWLEDGEMENTS

Chapter introduction

> ➤ **Introduction**
>
> As defined in Chapter 1, financial reporting
> mation about an entity to interested users.
> financial information provided needs to be of
> applicable to non-listed companies whose s
> ter discussed various characteristics that a

Each chapter opens with a concise outline of the chapter contents, including key definitions.

Learning objectives

> ★ **Learning objectives**
>
> After studying this chapter you will be able to
> ● appreciate the importance of appropriate
> ● explain the main elements of the regulator
>   in the UK, both listed and unlisted, and des

A bulleted outline of the main concepts and ideas indicates what you can expect to learn from each chapter.

Key issues checklist

> ✔ **Key issues checklist**
>
> ❏ Definitions of, and issues covered by, corp
> ❏ Stewardship and agency theories.
> ❏ The consequences of poor corporate gov
> ❏ The UK's approach to regulation of corpor

Use this checklist for each chapter to chart your progress with the accounting issues—great for helping you to plan your revision.

Terminology

> **Accrual accounting/accruals principle** The effects of t
> actions and other events and circumstances on a busi
> economic resources and claims are accounted for i
> periods in which those effects occur, even if the res
> cash receipts and payments occur in a different peri
>
> **Accumulating compensated absences** Compensate
> sences by an employee that are carried forward and c

Accounting concepts are highlighted where they are first explained and definitions are collated in a convenient glossary at the back of the book along with a handy 'Terminology converter' that clarifies equivalent terms.

Reminder

> ⓘ **Reminder** *The criteria for recognition*
> *Framework are:*
>
> ● *There is a probable inflow or outflow of re*
> ● *The asset or liability has a cost or value th*
>
>   *The proposed criteria in the ED of the new*
> *liabilities should be recognised if such recogn*

Refresh your memory of essential financial accounting terms and concepts with these short reminder points.

Financial reporting in practice

> **Financial reporting in practice 1**
>
> Rolls-Royce plc, a major manufacturing company,
> 2015 statement of financial position. The compar
>
> **(a)** Uses various financial instruments to manag
>   rates.
>
> **(b)** Uses commodity swaps to manage its expo

Understand how the theory relates to financial reporting in practice with frequent extracts from real-world annual reports from organisations such as Sainsbury's, Rolls-Royce, British Airways and Lloyds TSB.

Illustrative examples

Regular examples of how to account for particular transactions
and items, as well as example statements, help support your
learning.

📌 **Example of** where offsetti...

A company acquires a non-current asset under
company has a resource, an asset and a liabili
Even though they are associated, the asset and
on the statement of financial position as both h

Worked examples

Detailed worked examples walk you through the calculation
and presentation of figures required for financial statements.

Worked example 14.3: to
financial asset

Westwood plc acquires a zero coupon bond wit
£94,500. Broker's fees of £1,500 were incurred
active market, and is redeemable on 31 Decem
interest on the bond is 7.04%.

Summary of key points

Linked to the learning objectives, each chapter concludes with a
summary of the most important concepts you need to take away
from it.

🔑 **Summary of key points**

An assessment of the liquidity of a company re
assets that a company holds. Inventories vary
particularly important for this asset. Companies
that the quantities of inventories on hand are
addresses the measurement of inventories is IA

Further reading

Extend your knowledge with this annotated further reading
section.

📕 **Further reading**

IASB (International Accounting Standards Board
Discontinued Operations. London: IASB.
IASB (International Accounting Standards Board
IASB (International Accounting Standards Board)

Graded questions

Test and consolidate your knowledge with end-of-chapter
questions graded into 3 levels of difficulty:

- do a quick test of your ability;
- then develop your understanding as you build confidence
  with the accounting methods;
- finally, take it further by applying everything you have
  learned in the chapter to more complex scenarios.

**Check your progress by accessing the full set of
answers available on the Online Resource Centre
where you can also watch walk-through solutions
to key questions.**

 Questions

● **Quick test**

1   Comment on why corporate governance inf
2   Discuss the view that sustainability reportir

●● **Develop your understanding**

3   Discuss how current developments in the
     relate to issues of accountability.
4   What role do ethics play in corporate gover
5   Sustainability reporting is one issue in c
                                          al with s
7   Identify some common barriers to the su
     practice.

●●● **Take it further**

8   Obtain the GRI's 2013 *Sustainability Re*
     globalreporting.org. Discuss to what extent
     report (available from www.j-sainsbury.co.u

How to use the Online Resource Centre

Make the most of this package by accessing your online supplementary learning materials at:

www.oxfordtextbooks.co.uk/orc/maynard/2e/

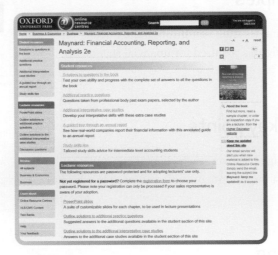

Student resources

Free and open-access material available:

Complete set of solutions to the questions in the book

Test your own ability and progress with the complete set of answers to all the questions in the book.

Walk-through solutions to key questions in the book

Watch the author walk you through step-by-step practical demonstrations of more complex accounting tasks.

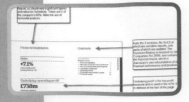

A guided tour through an annual report

See how real-world companies report their financial information with this annotated guide to an annual report.

Additional practice questions

Go that extra mile in consolidating your understanding by
practising these higher-level additional questions.

Additional interpretative case studies

Develop your interpretative skills with these extra case studies.

Study skill tips

Read the author's tips for success in your accounting studies.

Lecturer resources
Free for all registered adopters of the textbook:

PowerPoint slides

Accompanying each chapter is a suite of customisable slides, fully
integrated with the textbook, to be used in lecture presentations.

Outline solutions to the additional interpretative case studies

The outline answers to the additional case studies can be used in assignments
and seminar preparation.

Discussion questions for seminar use

A set of stimulating questions to help lecturers plan group discussions.

**Don't forget that all of these resources can be uploaded to your
institution's Virtual Learning Environment to allow students
to access them directly!**

Part 1
Introduction

1

Financial reporting and accounting

> **Introduction**

Financial reporting is concerned with the reporting of financial information about an entity to interested users. For profit-making entities, users require information about their financial position, including liquidity, and about their financial performance, which results in changes in the financial position. For companies and, in particular, public limited companies, financial reporting regulations are complex and onerous.

Financial accounting is about the systems and methods used to produce the financial statements. For all entities the basis of financial accounting is the double-entry bookkeeping system from which the key financial statements—the statement of financial position and statement of profit or loss—are derived. These two statements alone are insufficient to provide all the financial information that users will require, and so other financial statements are also produced for users, such as the statement of cash flows and the statement of changes in equity.

This chapter is a revision chapter, and provides a summary of the main issues covered in introductory financial accounting texts and courses, which are concerned with the preparation of these main financial statements. The chapter focuses on limited companies. This will provide a sound foundation on which the complexities of financial reporting can be built in later chapters.

★ Learning objectives

After studying this chapter you will be able to:

- understand who the main users of financial information are and the type of information they require to help them make decisions
- explain the characteristics of financial information which makes it useful
- carry out double-entry bookkeeping for simple transactions
- produce a trial balance from the nominal ledger
- understand the main period-end accounting adjustments required and account for these
- draw up in good form from trial balance, including the main period-end adjustments, a statement of financial position and a statement of profit or loss for a sole trader and limited company, and, in addition, for a company, a statement of changes in equity.

✔ Key issues checklist

- ☐ Financial reporting as the provision of decision-useful information to users—who the users are, what needs they have, and how the financial information is used.
- ☐ Qualitative characteristics of financial information.
- ☐ Financial accounting as the preparation of the financial reports.
- ☐ Underpinning concepts—business entity, historic cost, accruals and prudence.
- ☐ Accounting systems, including double-entry bookkeeping and the trial balance.
- ☐ Share capital and accounting for dividends.
- ☐ Accounting for accruals and prepayments, depreciation, and irrecoverable debts and allowances for receivables.
- ☐ The preparation of the main financial statements—the statement of financial position, the statement of profit or loss and, for companies, the statement of changes in equity—from trial balance and including adjustments for accruals and prepayments, depreciation, and irrecoverable debts and allowances for receivables.

1.1 Financial reporting

Financial reporting in practice 1.1 — Tesco plc, 2014

The importance of reliable financial reporting.

Tomorrow, Tesco will reveal its latest results. Sales and profits are likely to be down again. Grim enough. But these are also the restating of the results Tesco was meant to release last month—until it stumbled across a £250m accounting problem in its profit forecasts. I'll just repeat that. A £250m accounting problem in its profit forecasts. For a business that was predicting it would make £1.1bn profits for the first half of this year, a mis-statement of £250m is a significant number. So significant that a series of former executives from the business I have spoken to simply don't believe it. They say it is likely that Tesco will announce a lower figure tomorrow. That is just a wrinkle. If you cannot trust a business's accounts, then there is not much left to trust.

They [investors] are voting with their wallets. Since the announcement that Tesco could have been booking profits from suppliers before costs—flattering Tesco's bottom line—the retailer's share price has fallen by 10%. Warren Buffett is the highest-profile seller, saying his 4.1% investment stake in Tesco was a 'huge mistake' which has cost him £465m in a year. This is a man who runs an investment fund—Berkshire Hathaway—so successful and popular it costs £200,000 to buy one top-graded share.

Now, a share price that drops by 50% may not mean very much to the shopper in the street. Until he or she realises that Tesco's profits and dividends—slashed by the retailer—make a vital contribution to all of our pension funds. The business is also one of Britain's largest corporate tax payers. If too many major British businesses fail, then that not only means bad news for UK Plc and, in this case, the supply of groceries—it also means bad news for our savings and the government's tax income.

Extracted from Kamal Ahmed's Business Blog, BBC, 22 October 2014

Financial reporting is concerned with the reporting of financial information about an entity to external interested parties. Entities can take many forms. Generally, there are business entities deemed to be concerned with making profits, which range from sole traders, through partnerships and small **companies** to large and complex multinational corporations; and there are entities less concerned with profit-making, such as government organisations, charities, clubs and societies. Whatever form a business takes, or whatever its legal status, it reports the financial affairs only of itself; this is one of the underpinning concepts of financial reporting—that of the **separate business entity**.

Business entities started as fairly simple affairs funded and run by an individual or small group of individuals, and, in this context, the reporting of financial information needed to satisfy the requirements of the owners only. The owners required information about the financial results and position of the business in which they had invested in order for them to assess their investment and make decisions about future investment. As businesses grew, more investment was required, ownership widened and management of the business was devolved to others. In this context the owners needed to be able to assess whether this was being carried out satisfactorily. Financial reporting therefore assumed a role of assessment of **stewardship**.

Investment provided by others can be on a perpetual basis (share ownership in companies) or on a fixed-term basis. This latter lender/creditor group also requires financial reports about their investment. Their principal needs differ, however, from the owners, as they mainly require information about the security of their loan—will it be repaid when it is due, will the business pay the servicing charges when due, what security is there if the business defaults on any part of the agreement?

In today's global environment, with the many different types of business entity, there is a wide range of external groups of people who are interested in businesses' financial information. The financial reports the external users can obtain are generally backward-looking, reporting on what has happened in the past. The external user will have to use these historic financial reports to try to predict what may happen in the future. Contrast this with the management of a business, the internal user, who will require financial information in order to run and control their business effectively and efficiently. In addition to financial information about what has happened management will need information which is forward-looking, concerning planning for the future.

So who are the external users and what information do they want? The answer to this lies in asking who deals with business entities and *for what purpose* these users want the information—what are they going to do with it, what course of action will they take having obtained the information, what decisions will they take? This is the key issue that drives financial reporting today—the **decision-usefulness** of financial information.

1.1.1 User groups

Figure 1.1 shows the main external groups of people who are likely to be interested in the financial statements provided by a business entity.

The main decisions they will take using financial information and the information needed to take these decisions are shown in Table 1.1.

1.1.2 Main financial statements

Although it can be seen that different users require different information, by considering the needs of the investors, lenders and other creditors, many of the needs of other users will be satisfied. The common requirements of this primary group of users concern making investment decisions, and information needed for these is of the financial position and **liquidity** (the ability to have cash available to pay amounts due) of the business, and information about the financial performance, which results in changes in the financial position. Thus, businesses provide financial information in three key financial statements to satisfy these information needs. These financial statements need to be produced regularly, and so entities will draw them up at least annually.

Statement of financial position

This statement, also called a balance sheet, shows the resources a business has (**assets**), the claims against those resources (**liabilities**) and the residual ownership interest (**capital**) at a particular point in time.

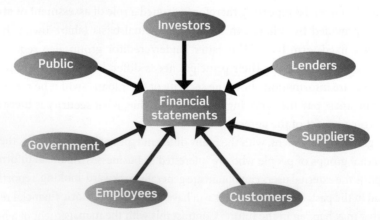

Figure 1.1 The external users of financial statements

Table 1.1 External users' decisions and the financial information they require

User group	Decisions	Financial information required
Investors	Continuation of investment? Withdrawal of investment? Increase investment?	Return from investment Ability to pay returns to investors Value of investment Performance of management Risk in investment
Lenders	Lend or not? Interest rate to be charged? Security required?	Ability to repay loans when due Ability to pay interest when due Security for loans
Suppliers	Sale of goods or services to the business? Prices to be charged?	Ability to pay amounts owing when due Future of business for further supply
Customers	Purchase of goods or services from the business?	Whether the business is a secure source of supply for repeat purchases and after-sales care
Employees	Continuation of employment?	Long-term future and stability of business Ability to provide appropriate level of remuneration Retirement and other benefits Employment opportunities
Government	HMRC—has the business paid the appropriate taxes it owes? Other departments/agencies—has the business carried out its business in accordance with regulation and made appropriate information available?	Business profits Employee details Various reports and statistics
The public	Variety of decisions, including whether the business should be contributing to the local economy or whether it should be investigated because its practices are harmful to the environment	Various reports and statistics

An asset is an **economic resource** controlled by the business as a result of past events (in other words, the event giving rise to the control of the resource must have happened before the date at which the statement is drawn up).

A liability is a present obligation of the business to transfer an economic resource as a result of past events.

An economic resource is a right that has the potential to produce economic benefits for the business. For example, the economic benefit may be a flow of cash into the business, or something that enables a business to produce a product.

Capital (termed **equity** for a company) is the residual interest in the assets of the business after deducting all its liabilities and represents the owners' investment in the business. Capital of a business increases if the entity makes profits and reduces if the entity makes losses. If the owner invests more in the business or takes resources out of the business for personal use, then the capital will also increase and decrease respectively.

These three **elements** are linked by the basic accounting equation:

ASSETS = CAPITAL + LIABILITIES

The **statement of financial position** can help users identify the business's financial strengths and weaknesses, its liquidity and solvency, its needs for additional investment and how successful it will be in obtaining this financing. Information about different types of asset and liability, for example distinguishing those that are continuously circulating as **working capital** from those used in the entity's long-term operations, will assist in this analysis. Thus, the statement of financial position usually shows different types of assets and liabilities under four main categories:

Non-current assets	Those assets held for long-term use.
Current assets	Those assets continuously changing as business is conducted.
Current liabilities	Where the obligation is due for **settlement** within a short time frame, usually taken as one year.
Non-current liabilities	Where the obligation is due for settlement usually after one year.

The basis of valuation (termed measurement in financial accounting) of many assets and liabilities is **historic cost**, i.e. for an asset the purchase price, although, as seen in later chapters, certain assets and liabilities are or may be (where a business has a choice) valued using alternative methods.

 ## Example statement

Business XXX	
Statement of financial position at accounting period end date	

	£
ASSETS	
Non-current assets	
Property, plant and equipment	XX
Intangible assets	XX
	XX
Current assets	
Inventories	XX

Receivables	XX
Prepayments	XX
Bank and cash	XX
	XX
TOTAL ASSETS	XX
CAPITAL	XX
LIABILITIES	
Non-current liabilities	
Long-term loans	XX
	XX
Current liabilities	
Bank overdraft	XX
Payables	XX
Accruals	XX
	XX
TOTAL LIABILITIES	XX
TOTAL CAPITAL AND LIABILITIES	XX

Statement of profit or loss

This statement, also called the income statement or profit and loss account, shows the financial performance of a business over an accounting period by depicting the effects of transactions and other events when they occur, even if the resulting cash receipts and payments occur at a different time or in a different accounting period. This is termed **accrual accounting**. The **statement of profit or loss** includes **income** earned net of **expenses** incurred over the accounting period, resulting in net profit.

Income is defined as increases in the economic benefits during the accounting period arising from **revenues** from, for example, sales, fees, interest and rent, and from other **gains**, such as those arising from the sale of a non-current asset.

Expenses are decreases in economic benefits during the accounting period and encompass expenses that arise in the normal course of business, such as cost of sales, salaries and wages, heat and light, and insurance and other losses, such as those resulting from flood damage or changes in exchange rates. Expenses are usually grouped under categories such as cost of sales, overhead expenses and finance costs, with a subsidiary profit being calculated after each category of expenses has been deducted so that different levels of return from differing groups of activities can be ascertained.

Information about the financial performance helps users understand the return that the business has generated from its resources, and provides an indication of how effectively and efficiently these have been managed. Financial performance measured on the accrual basis provides a better basis for assessing the business's past and future performance than information about cash receipts and payments.

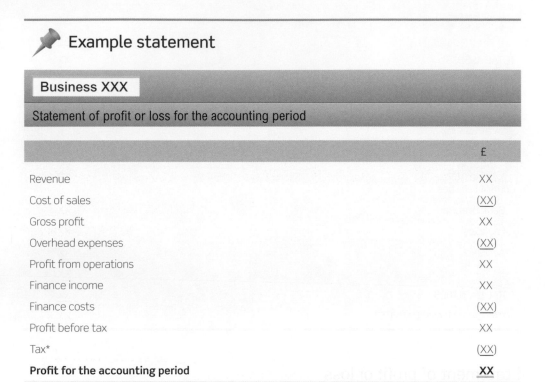

Example statement

Business XXX

Statement of profit or loss for the accounting period

	£
Revenue	XX
Cost of sales	(XX)
Gross profit	XX
Overhead expenses	(XX)
Profit from operations	XX
Finance income	XX
Finance costs	(XX)
Profit before tax	XX
Tax*	(XX)
Profit for the accounting period	**XX**

* Note it is only companies, as separate legal entities from their owners, which show the tax charged on their profits in the statement of profit or loss, as it is the company that is liable for this.

For limited companies the statement of profit or loss forms part of the **statement of comprehensive income**, which is discussed in Chapter 4.

Statement of cash flows

This statement provides information about the financial performance of a business measured solely in terms of cash receipts and payments. It shows the inflows and outflows of cash, and monetary assets deemed to be equivalent to cash (such as short-term deposits) over the accounting period. The inflows and outflows are classified under different types of activity, resulting in an increase or decrease in **cash and cash equivalents**. The different activities that a business conducts include those related to its main operations, acquiring or selling non-current assets, borrowing or repaying debt, receiving additional investment and distributing cash to the owners.

Information about cash flows helps users assess the ability of the business to generate future net cash inflows, and evaluate its liquidity or solvency.

The preparation and presentation of a **statement of cash flows** for a company is covered in Chapter 4.

1.1.3 Statement of changes in equity

Limited companies are required to produce an additional financial statement—a **statement of changes in equity**—which provides information about changes in the equity (**share capital** and **reserves**) balances over the accounting period.

 Example statement

Company XXX					
Statement of changes in equity for the accounting period					

	Share capital £	Share premium £	Other reserves £	Retained earnings £	Total £
Balance at start of period	XX	XX	XX	XX	XX
Issues of share capital	XX	XX			XX
Profit/(Loss) for the period				XX/(XX)	XX
Dividends paid				(XX)	(XX)
Other changes			XX	XX	XX
Balance at end of period	XX	XX	XX	XX	XX

1.2 The difference between profit and cash flow

As indicated in the previous section, financial performance can be measured either in terms of profits according to accrual accounting or in terms of cash flows. For many transactions the difference between the measures is one of timing, in other words in which period the effect of the transaction is included.

 Worked example 1.1: to show the difference between profit and cash flows

On 1 January 20X7 Giles starts his own business by investing £8,000 of his own money and getting a business contact to lend the business £2,000 for 5 years, on which interest will be paid at 5% p.a. Giles rents an office space and pays £1,000 for furniture and equipment. During the first year the business purchases goods for resale for £6,000, of which £5,500 had been paid by 31 December

20X7. The business makes sales of £5,000 on credit and £1,500 for cash, and Giles's credit customers have paid £4,000 by 31 December 20X7. Office running costs paid during the year total £2,200, and Giles takes £1,000 out of the business for personal expenses. At the year end goods which had cost £2,000 are still on hand.

Required:

Draw up financial performance statements for Giles's business for the year ended 31 December 20X7:

(i) On the accruals basis

(ii) On a cash basis.

(i) Giles's business statement of profit or loss for the year ended 31 December 20X7

		£
Sales	(5,000 + 1,500)	6,500
Cost of sales	(6,000 − 2,000)	(4,000)
Gross profit		2,500
Overhead expenses		(2,200)
Profit from operations		300
Loan interest	(5% × 2,000)	(100)
Net profit		200

Notes

1   The office furniture and equipment is not included in the statement of profit or loss as this is an asset (**depreciation**—see section 1.6.2—has been ignored in this example).

2   The cost of sales is the cost of the goods that have actually been sold.

3   The loan interest is included in the statement of profit or loss even though it has not been paid because it is an expense that has been incurred in the year.

(ii) Giles's business statement of cash flows for the year ended 31 December 20X7

		£	£
Cash receipts			
Owner's investment			8,000
Loan			2,000
From sales	(1,500 + 4,000)		5,500
			15,500

Cash payments

Furniture and equipment		1,000
Goods for resale		5,500
Office running costs		2,200
Owner's personal expenses		1,000
		(9,700)
Net cash inflow		£5,800

Notes

1 This statement includes all the year's transactions on a cash basis. The resulting net cash inflow is equivalent to the cash balance at 31 December 20X7, as, in this example, there is no opening cash balance at 1 January 20X7.

2 A company would group cash receipts and payments according to the activity type.

It can be seen that net profit and net cash flow result in very different figures because they are providing different measures of performance and resulting changes in different resources. The statement of financial position summarises all resources of the business at the end of the year.

Giles's business statement of financial position at 31 December 20X7

	£	£
Assets		
Furniture and equipment		1,000
Inventory		2,000
Receivables	(5,000 – 4,000)	1,000
Cash		5,800
		£9,800
Capital		
Initial investment		8,000
Net profit		200
Withdrawals		(1,000)
		7,200
Liabilities		
Loan	2,000	
Loan interest	100	
Payables	(6,000 – 5,500) 500	2,600
		£9,800

1.3 Qualitative characteristics

There are many important principles and concepts that underpin the nature of financial information included in financial statements and which provide the basis for accounting methods. These are set out in *The Conceptual Framework for Financial Reporting*, which is produced by the **International Accounting Standards Board (IASB)**. The *Conceptual Framework* and the IASB are discussed in detail in Chapter 2. Although applicable for listed companies, these principles and concepts are relevant for all reporting businesses.

As discussed previously, users of financial statements need financial statements to help in making their decisions. So an important principle is that the information contained in the statements needs to be **relevant** to their decisions and it must **faithfully represent** what it purports to represent. Without these two **fundamental qualitative characteristics**, the information will not be useful.

Some financial information is better than other financial information. For example, information about a business that can be meaningfully compared with another business will be more useful than information that is in a completely different form or prepared according to an alternative basis. Also, information that is supported by facts is more reliable than that based on estimates. So information that is **comparable**, **verifiable**, **timely** and **understandable** will improve the usefulness of relevant and faithfully represented financial information. These are termed **enhancing qualitative characteristics**. These are illustrated in Figures 1.2 and 1.3, and discussed in sections 1.3.1 to 1.3.6.

1.3.1 Relevant financial information

Relevant financial information can make a difference to decisions made by users. Users need information that confirms or changes their evaluations about a business, and that can also

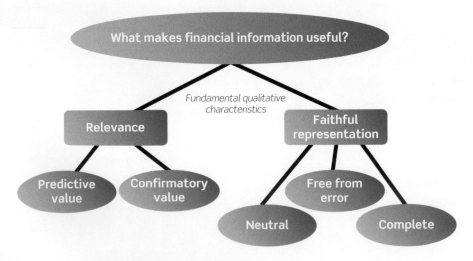

Figure 1.2 Fundamental qualitative characteristics

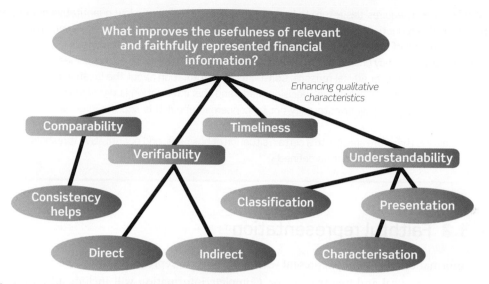

Figure 1.3 **Enhancing qualitative characteristics**

be used in making predictions about future outcomes. Thus, for information to be relevant it must have confirmatory value, predictive value or both.

 Example of relevant information

An investor wishes to invest in a growing company. Relevant financial information would include sales revenues. Revenue information for the past few years can be used for predicting revenues in future years. The current year's revenue can also be compared with revenue predictions that were made in the past for the current year. The results of the comparisons can help the investor correct and improve the processes that are used to make future predictions.

Information is material if its omission or misstatement influences the decision made by a user. So **materiality** is an aspect of relevance that relates to the nature or size, or both, of the information.

 Example of materiality

Relevant financial information for the investor interested in investing in a business that makes a certain level of return on sales will include sales revenues and profit. A business makes sales of £10 million and reports profits at £1,010,000. The return on sales for this business is 10.1% (1.01 million/10 million).

If the investor requires this return to be 10%, they would have a very low quantitative materiality threshold, as a reduction in profit of only £10,000 would change their decision. However, an investor requiring a return of only 5% or more would have a much higher materiality threshold.

Another investor may choose not to invest in businesses that trade with other businesses in certain countries for religious or ethical reasons. Consequently, information about the location of the trading partners will affect the investment decision made and this information is deemed material to this investor. However, another investor may not be concerned about this and the information is, therefore, not material.

Materiality is therefore specific to a certain situation or business, and quantitative thresholds or the nature of material items cannot be defined.

1.3.2 Faithful representation

For information to faithfully represent what it purports to represent it should be as complete as possible, neutral and free from error. Complete information will include all aspects of the item which enable the user to understand what is being depicted and may require some narrative explanations.

 Example of completeness

A complete depiction of a group of non-current assets would include, at a minimum, a description of the nature of the assets in the group (e.g. land and buildings, machinery, fixtures and fittings, motor vehicles), numerical values for each type of asset, and an explanation of what the numerical values represent (e.g. original cost, or depreciated cost or **fair value**).

Neutral information is without bias. In other words, it should not be slanted, weighted, emphasised, de-emphasised or otherwise manipulated to increase the likelihood that the information will be received favourably or unfavourably by users. There has been much debate in recent years about these characteristics excluding **prudence**. This is briefly discussed in section 1.7 and in more detail in Chapter 2.

Not all financial information can be completely accurate. Many areas of financial accounting require estimates to be made, for example the expected lives of non-current assets in order to calculate depreciation or the amount owed for electricity at the end of an accounting period. This is referred to as measurement uncertainty. The actual lives or amounts owed may turn out to be different from the estimates made, but this does not mean that the financial information is inaccurate. Users will require financial information to be as free from error as possible, and require information about where and how estimates have been made, and any limitations of the estimating process. Provided that the processes to derive the estimates are reasonable and applied without error, the information presented about these items is still faithful.

1.3.3 Comparable information

Users' decisions involve choosing between alternatives, for example in which company an investment should be made. Information is therefore more useful if it can be compared with similar information about another business. This does not mean that identical or uniform accounting methods have to be used from one business to another, for example all businesses having to depreciate their buildings over 50 years. However, a valid comparison will require the same basis of accounting to be used, and the same information and explanations about like items to be presented from one business to the next.

1.3.4 Verifiable information

Verifiability helps assure users that information faithfully represents what it purports to represent and relates to how sound the evidence for particular information is. The better the evidence, the more reliable the information. Information that is completely verifiable could be, for example, sales revenue for a simple business, where this could be verified by summing all sales invoices and deducting credit notes. Information that is estimated may not be able to be directly verified, and so users will require information about how the estimates have been made and any underlying assumptions.

1.3.5 Timely information

Generally, the older the information is, the less useful it is. However, there may be a trade-off between providing timely information and ensuring it is as verifiable as possible.

 Example of verifiability versus timeliness

A business may have incurred expenses for electricity and telecommunications during the accounting period, but not yet received the actual supplier invoices which would confirm the amounts incurred and owing at the end of the period. There may be pressure from users requiring information about the financial period as early as possible so that they can make decisions. To meet the users' demands, the business will have to make estimates of the expenses incurred—information which could be more verifiable if the business waited until the actual invoices had been received and accounted for.

1.3.6 Understandable information

Information should be classified, characterised and presented clearly and concisely in order to make it understandable. Financial information about some transactions and items is inherently complex and not easy to understand. Although exclusion of this information may make the financial statements easier to understand, it would also make them incomplete and misleading.

A basic premise in determining how understandable information is that it is assumed that the users have a reasonable knowledge of business and economic activities, and they will review and analyse the information diligently. However, it is acknowledged that even a well-informed user may need to seek expert advice to understand particularly complex financial transactions.

1.3.7 Cost constraint

The provision of financial information imposes costs on businesses, which are borne, ultimately, by investors through lower returns. These users want high quality, useful information to enable them to make the best decisions possible. In the context of investments in publicly traded companies on capital markets, this will result in more efficient functioning of these markets and a lower cost of capital for the economy as a whole. Hence, there has to be a trade-off between the benefits of businesses reporting particular information and thoroughly considering its qualitative characteristics with the costs incurred to provide and use such information.

1.4 Financial accounting

Financial accounting is concerned with the preparation of financial statements. Methods have been developed over centuries in order to record financial transactions and produce these statements in a systematic manner.

Figure 1.4 provides a representation of a simple accounting system. This type of system would not only produce two of the key financial statements, the statement of financial position and the statement of profit or loss, but also provide detailed information about some of the aggregate figures that would be included in these statements. This would aid management in running and controlling the business.

The heart of the accounting system is the **nominal ledger** from which the financial statements are drawn up. Every system will include a nominal ledger. Most basic accounting systems will also include receivables and payables ledgers, which provide details of the account

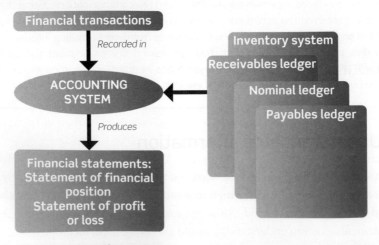

Figure 1.4 The financial accounting system

balances of all customers and suppliers, plus, if the business trades goods, some form of inventory control system.

1.4.1 The nominal ledger

The nominal ledger comprises all the accounts of the business in which are recorded all the individual financial transactions. Each account is effectively labelled as being one of five types of account, with the type of account determining whether its balance appears in the statement of financial position or in the statement of profit or loss. The types of account and examples of different accounts corresponding to the label are as follows.

Statement of financial position accounts

Account type	Examples of accounts
Asset	Property, plant and machinery; motor vehicles; computer software; inventory; accounts receivable; bank and cash
Liability	Bank overdraft, accounts payable, loan
Capital	Share capital, **share premium**, retained profits and losses, drawings, dividends paid

Statement of profit or loss accounts

Account type	Examples of accounts
Income	Sales, rent receivable, interest receivable
Expense	Purchases, wages and salaries, heat and light, telephone, insurance, motor expenses, depreciation, bad debts, loan interest

Each nominal ledger account has two sides—a **debit** side and a **credit** side:

DEBIT | CREDIT

1.4.2 Double-entry bookkeeping

Transactions are recorded in the accounts in the nominal ledger by **double-entry bookkeeping**. This method, which has been in existence for centuries, recognises that every transaction affects two (or more) accounts. If only two accounts are affected by the transaction, one account will be debited and the other account will be credited with the same monetary amount. If more than two accounts are affected, the total of the debit entries will equal the total of the credit entries. This ensures that the statement of financial position equation always balances:

$$ASSETS = CAPITAL + LIABILITIES$$

The rules of double-entry are shown in Figure 1.5.

Statement of financial position accounts

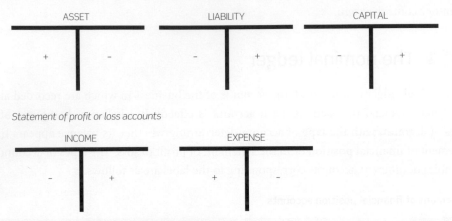

Statement of profit or loss accounts

Figure 1.5 The rules of double-entry bookkeeping
A '+' indicates an account *increases* as a result of the transaction. This will mean a debit or credit entry, dependent upon whether the '+' is on the debit or credit side of the account.
A '–' indicates an account *decreases* as a result of the transaction. This will mean a debit or credit entry, dependent upon whether the '–' is on the debit or credit side of the account.

 Example of double-entry bookkeeping

Transaction	Accounts increased or decreased	Resulting double-entry
1 The owner of a business pays £10,000 into the business bank account	Capital increases and bank increases	Debit: bank Credit: capital
2 The business purchases a motor vehicle on credit	Motor vehicles increase and accounts payable increase	Debit: motor vehicles Credit: accounts payable
3 The business sells goods on credit	Sales increase and accounts receivable increase	Debit: accounts receivable Credit: sales
4 The business pays wages	Wages increase and bank decreases	Debit: wages Credit: bank
5 The business pays a supplier from whom goods had been purchased on credit	Accounts payable decrease and bank decreases	Debit: accounts payable Credit: bank
6 The business receives a loan	Bank increases and loan increases	Debit: bank Credit: loan

1.4.3 The trial balance

When the financial statements are required to be prepared, businesses will determine the balance on each account in the nominal ledger—a net debit or a net credit. A listing of all account balances, which is called a **trial balance**, is drawn up.

The trial balance is a half-way house in the preparation process. If double-entry book-keeping has taken place, then the total of the debit balances will equal the credit balances, and businesses can review the balances to ensure they appear reasonable. However, the trial balance will not show whether the recording of transactions has been completely accurately done, for example a transaction may have been omitted entirely, or the wrong accounts may have been debited or credited.

1.4.4 Financial statements

As each account is labelled as either a statement of financial position account or a statement of profit or loss account, these financial statements can be drawn up from the trial balance.

 Worked example 1.2: to show the drawing up of financial statements from a trial balance

Suraya's business trial balance at 31 December 20X8 is as follows:

	Debit £	Credit £
Capital		101,177
Plant and machinery	56,152	
Fixtures and fittings	35,040	
Inventories at 1 January 20X8*	15,450	
Receivables	43,415	
Payables		29,327
Bank		10,526
Sales		296,483
Purchases*	175,962	
Rent	6,397	
Heat and light	26,730	
Wages and salaries	36,389	
Insurance	11,978	
Drawings	30,000	
	437,513	437,513

Inventories at 31 December 20X8 were counted and valued at £16,070*

* Note this business has recorded the inventories it purchased during the year in a purchases account, which is an expense account. A separate inventory account is maintained which is a statement of financial position account. The balance on this account in the trial balance represents inventories at the start of the accounting period. Inventories on hand at the end of the year have to be counted, valued and accounted for as an adjustment to the trial balance figures.

Required:

Draw up the statement of profit or loss for the year ended 31 December 20X8 and the statement of financial position at that date for Suraya's business.

Identifying each account in the trial balance as either a statement of profit or loss account (income and expense accounts) or a statement of financial position account (asset, liability and capital accounts) gives:

	Debit £	Credit £
Capital		101,177
Plant and machinery	56,152	
Fixtures and fittings	35,040	
Inventories	15,450	
Receivables	43,415	
Payables		29,327
Bank		10,526
Sales		296,483
Purchases	175,962	
Rent	6,397	
Heat and light	26,730	
Wages and salaries	36,389	
Insurance	11,978	
Drawings	30,000	
	437,513	437,513

Statement of profit or loss accounts

Inventories at 31 December 20X8 were counted and valued at £16,070.

	Debit £	Credit £
Capital		101,177
Plant and machinery	56,152	
Fixtures and fittings	35,040	
Inventories	15,450	
Receivables	43,415	
Payables		29,327
Bank		10,526
Sales		296,483
Purchases	175,962	
Rent	6,397	

Statement of financial position accounts

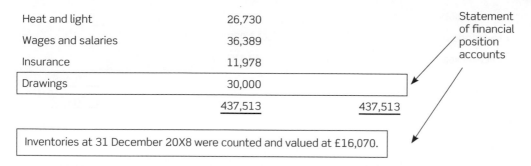

Heat and light	26,730	Statement of financial position accounts
Wages and salaries	36,389	
Insurance	11,978	
Drawings	30,000	
	437,513 437,513	

Inventories at 31 December 20X8 were counted and valued at £16,070.

The financial statements are drawn up as follows.

Suraya's business

Statement of profit or loss for the year ended 31 December 20X8

	£	£
Sales		296,483
Cost of sales		
Opening inventories	15,450	
Purchases	175,962	
	191,412	
Closing inventories	(16,070)	(175,342)
Gross profit		121,141
Expenses		
Rent	6,397	
Heat and light	26,730	
Wages and salaries	36,389	
Insurance	11,978	
		(81,494)
Net profit		£39,647

Suraya's business

Statement of financial position at 31 December 20X8

	£	£
Non-current assets		
Plant and machinery		56,152
Fixtures and fittings		35,040
		91,192

Current assets		
Inventories	16,070	
Receivables	43,415	
		59,485
Total assets		£150,677
Capital		
Opening capital		101,177
Net profit for year (from the statement of profit or loss)		39,647
		140,824
Drawings		30,000
		110,824
Current liabilities		
Bank overdraft	10,526	
Payables	29,327	
		39,853
Total capital and liabilities		£150,677

1.5 Limited companies' financial statements

Worked example 1.2 demonstrates financial statements for a sole trader. Many businesses start out in the form of a sole trader, but, as they grow, they incorporate as a **private limited company**. The word 'limited' or 'Ltd' will appear in the business name. This means the capital of the business will be in the form of share capital and there can be more than one owner, called **shareholders**, who will each hold a number of shares in the company.

There are many reasons why businesses incorporate, but the most important of these is probably the limited liability status. This means a company has a separate legal identity from the owners and the owners' liability is limited to the amount they have invested. One consequence of this is that if the company collapses with amounts owing, the **creditors** cannot pursue the shareholders personally to settle the company's debts.

If a private limited company wishes to raise capital on stock markets and have its shares traded publicly, it will need to fulfil certain statutory requirements, register as a **public limited company**, or 'plc', and then apply to be listed. This is an onerous undertaking, as there will be increased scrutiny of the company and additional information, financial and otherwise, will have to be made public.

The basic underpinning financial accounting for private and public companies is the same. In the following sections, unless specifically stated, references to companies apply, therefore, to both private and public companies.

1.5.1 Company financial accounting

Double-entry bookkeeping and the basic format of the financial statements is the same for companies as for sole traders. However, there are some important differences which arise from the limited liability status.

1 Companies issue shares to their investors. The statement of financial position becomes:

ASSETS = EQUITY + LIABILITIES

Equity consists of share capital and reserves, one of which is **retained earnings**, which accumulates the profits and losses the company makes.

(See further details of shares in section 1.5.2.)

2 There is separation of ownership and management. The shareholders are the owners and they appoint **directors** to run the company (although directors are often also shareholders in the company they are managing). The shareholders' return is in the form of **dividends**, which are paid out of retained earnings.

3 Directors are employees of company and receive remuneration, which is shown as an expense in the statement of profit or loss.

4 Companies have to pay tax on the profits they make which are chargeable to corporation tax. The tax is shown as a reduction of profits in the statement of profit or loss.

5 Companies have to prepare additional financial statements for reporting purposes—a statement of changes in equity and a statement of cash flows.

6 Companies' legislation is extensive and, in the UK, is covered by the Companies Act 2006 and related statutory regulations. Some of these relate to financial statements. In addition, all companies have to follow **accounting standards** when preparing their financial statements for reporting purposes. Private limited companies follow four UK financial reporting standards, **Financial Reporting Standards (FRSs)** 100, 101, 102 and 103; public listed companies follow international financial reporting standards which are called **International Accounting Standards (IASs)** or **International Financial Reporting Standards (IFRS)**. It cannot be emphasised enough how detailed and complex these financial reporting requirements are.

(See Chapter 2 for further details of what financial reporting standards are.)

1.5.2 Shares and share capital

There are two types of share capital: **equity (or ordinary) shares** and **preference shares**. A comparison of these two types can be summarised as shown in Table 1.2.

Table 1.2: Equity and preference shares

Equity shares	Preference shares
Ordinary shareholders are ultimate owners of company	There are two main types of preference share: • **irredeemable preference shares**, which are accounted for as part of equity • **redeemable preference shares**, which are accounted for as a non-current liability
A vote is attached to each share	No votes are attached to shares
There is no entitlement to a dividend—the amount of dividend is at the directors' discretion	Most preference shares give entitlement to a fixed rate dividend

The **authorised share capital** is the maximum amount of share capital that can be issued. It is disclosed in the financial statements.

When a company is first formed the initial value at which shares are issued is called the **nominal (or par) value**.

 Example of the nominal value of shares

Four friends decide to form a company. They each agree to supply £5,000 to provide the initial capital. What is the nominal value of the equity share capital?

The nominal value can be chosen as any amount, so it could be set at £5,000 per share. Each friend would therefore hold one share. However, this may not be the best nominal value to choose as the shareholders will be unable to sell part of their investment—it will be all or nothing. All new issues of (the same class of) shares will also have to be in units of £5,000, which is a large amount per investor. It is better to have share capital in small units, for example 20,000 shares of £1 nominal value, or 40,000 50p shares, or 200,000 10p shares, etc.

Once a company starts trading (and making profits), the value of shares at which they can be traded and issued may increase. This value is called the **market value**.

 Example of share premium

A company with 50,000 £1 equity shares, whose market value is £1.50, wishes to raise £300,000 by a new issue of the same class of share.

How many shares will the company issue, and how would this be accounted for?

$$\text{No. of shares issued} = \frac{£300,000}{£1.50}$$

$$= 200,000$$

Each share is issued at a premium of 50p:

	Per share £	Total £
Share capital	1.00	200,000
Share premium	0.50	100,000
Cash raised	1.50	300,000

Share premium is a reserve which is part of the equity in the company.

1.5.3 Dividends

Dividends are paid out of **distributable profits**. They may be paid in two stages—interim dividends are paid during the year, usually after half-year results become available, and final, or proposed, dividends are paid after the year end.

The description of preference shares indicates the level of fixed dividend to be paid, for example 6% £1 irredeemable preference shares means each preference shareholder will receive 6% × £1 = 6p per share for the year. Dividends on equity shares are paid at the directors' discretion and, for public companies, there are large policy implications surrounding this decision which may affect the market value of the company.

 Example of the calculation of equity and preference dividends

A company whose issued share capital is:

   £200,000 in 50p equity shares

   £100,000 in 8% £1 irredeemable preference shares

proposes the following dividends:

- the preference dividend
- a dividend of 5p per equity share.

What are the total dividends proposed?

	£
Preference dividend	
8% × £100,000	8,000
Equity dividend	
No. of equity shares × 5p	
(200,000 × 2 = 400,000) × 5p	20,000
Total dividend	28,000

Dividends paid during a financial year are shown as a reduction in retained earnings in the statement of changes in equity.

Redeemable preference shares are, in essence, the same as a long-term loan, as the amount invested in the company will eventually have to be paid back to the shareholder (in other words, redeemed) and there is a fixed rate of dividend. They are therefore accounted for as a liability on the statement of financial position and, to match this classification, dividends on these shares are accounted for as a finance cost in the statement of profit or loss according to the accruals principle (see section 1.6).

1.6 Accruals principle

1.6.1 Accruals and prepayments

As explained in the previous sections, the statement of profit or loss shows income earned net of expenses incurred over the accounting period, resulting in net profit. Income and expenses are included according to the accruals principle, that is when the underlying transaction occurs, and not on the basis of cash receipts and payments. The principle results in the expenses included in the statement of profit or loss being those which match with the revenues generated by them and which match to the relevant accounting period. This leads to some expenses having to be accounted for before they are actually paid (accrued expenses or accruals) or expenditure having to be carried forward to a subsequent accounting period (prepaid expenses or prepayments).

 Worked example 1.3: of an accrual

Steyn Ltd has a year end of 31 December. The company has paid electricity bills covering the period 1 January to 31 October 20X8 amounting to £450. On 8 February 20X9 the business receives a bill for £150 covering the period 1 November 20X8 to 31 January 20X9.

Required:

What is the electricity expense (incurred) in 20X8?

Steyn Ltd will have to estimate the proportion of the £150 bill that relates to the financial year ended 31 December 20X8, i.e. how much electricity was incurred in the two months November and December 20X8. Unless there is other strong evidence to suggest otherwise, a time apportionment is considered a reasonable estimate, hence 2/3 × £150 = £100 will be estimated as the electricity expense for these two months. Figure 1.6 shows this calculation.

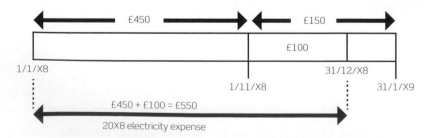

Figure 1.6 A timeline to time-apportion expenses (1)

This £100 is owed at 31 December 20X8 and is therefore a liability. It is an accrual and will be included in current liabilities on the statement of financial position.

It can be seen from Example 1.3 that the effect of accounting for an accrual is to increase the expense and to show a liability. This translates into double-entry bookkeeping as:

Debit   Expense account

  Credit   Accrual

 Worked example 1.4: of a prepayment

Steyn Ltd also makes rent payments of £5,000 during the year ended 31 December 20X8, which covers the period 1 January 20X8–31 March 20X9.

Required:

What is the rent expense for the year 20X8?

Steyn Ltd needs to determine how much of the total payment relates to 20X8. The total payment covers 15 months, of which 12/15 relates to 20X8: 12/15 × £5,000 = £4,000. Figure 1.7 shows this calculation.

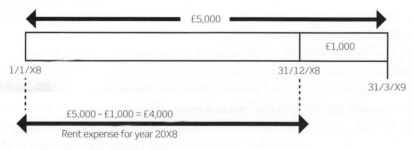

Figure 1.7 A timeline to time-apportion expenses (2)

£1,000 of the payment relates to 20X9 and needs to be carried forward as a prepayment. It is an asset as the business will gain future economic benefits from the occupancy of the premises and will be included in current assets on the statement of financial position.

This example shows that the effect of accounting for a prepayment is to decrease the expense and to show an asset. This translates into double-entry bookkeeping as:

Debit   Prepayment

  Credit   Expense account

1.6.2 Depreciation

The accruals principle applies to expenditure on non-current assets. Each time a non-current asset is used the cost of this is matched to the revenues it helps to generate. The accounting

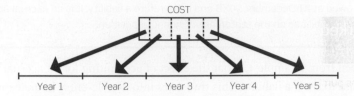

Figure 1.8 Depreciation: spreading the cost over the years a non-current asset is used

method used to do this is called depreciation and it can be thought of as spreading the cost of the asset over the years it is used, as shown in Figure 1.8.

The application of depreciation results in non-current assets' carrying amounts on the statement of financial position being reduced each accounting period. In the nominal ledger accounts, a statement of profit or loss depreciation account records the expense and an additional statement of financial position accumulated depreciation account is used to record the total depreciation written off each asset. The double-entry to record depreciation is therefore:

Debit   Depreciation expense
    Credit   Accumulated depreciation

At the end of an accounting period, the (credit) balance on the accumulated depreciation account is netted off with the (debit) balance on the asset's cost account to give the carrying amount, called the **net book value**. Note, the net book value does not represent any other value, such as market value or resale value—it is the residual **carrying amount** of the asset after deducting accumulated depreciation.

In order to apply depreciation a business needs to determine an asset's cost, and estimate its expected **useful life** and expected **residual value**. This has to be done for all assets except for freehold land, where the estimated life is deemed to be unlimited. Freehold land is therefore not depreciated and, where a business has freehold property as a non-current asset, the buildings and land costs have to be separated as the buildings are depreciated.

The next question is how the asset is going to be used, as this will determine the depreciation method to be applied. Although there are a number of methods of depreciation, the two main methods used by businesses are:

Straight-line   where the asset is used the same every year
Reducing balance   where the use of the asset reduces over the years

Less common methods include **sum-of-digits** and **units of production**. A business should select the method that best reflects the pattern of usage of an asset and, once selected, it should be applied consistently from one accounting period to the next unless altered circumstances justify a change.

1.6.3 Straight-line depreciation

A fixed amount is written off the carrying amount of the asset each year; in other words, the depreciation expense each year is the same.

Worked example 1.5: to show the calculation of straight-line depreciation

Rochford & Sons purchases a machine that costs £50,000. The business estimates it will use the machine for 10 years and, at the end of this time, the machine will be sold for £5,000.

Required:

Calculate the annual depreciation expense and the accounting effect of the depreciation.

$$\text{Annual depreciation expense} = \frac{\text{Cost} - \text{Estimated residual value}}{\text{Estimated life}}$$

$$= \frac{£50,000 - £5,000}{10}$$

$$= £4,500$$

Straight-line depreciation can also be expressed as a percentage, which is derived from the life. So this machine is depreciated at 10% straight-line:

$$\text{Annual depreciation expense} = 10\% \times (£50,000 - £5,000)$$

$$= £4,500$$

Statement of financial position balances will be as follows:

	Cost	Accumulated depreciation	Net book value
	£	£	£
Year 1	50,000		
Depreciation expense		4,500	45,500
Year 2			
Depreciation expense		4,500	
		9,000	41,000
Year 3			
Depreciation expense		4,500	
		13,500	36,500
Year 10			
Depreciation expense		4,500	
		45,000	5,000

1.6.4 Reducing balance depreciation

Under this method a fixed percentage is written off the reduced carrying amount (net book value) of the asset each year. This results in the annual depreciation expense reducing each year.

A business requires the cost and estimates of the expected life and residual value in order to calculate the fixed percentage from the formula:

$$1 - \sqrt[n]{(r/c)}$$

Where c is the cost, r is the estimated residual value and n is the estimated life.

Once the percentage has been derived and applied to calculate each period's depreciation, the accounting is the same as for straight-line depreciation.

Worked example 1.6: to show the calculation of reducing balance depreciation

Rochford & Sons also purchases a motor vehicle for £20,000. Depreciation is to be charged at the rate of 25% on the reducing balance.

Required:

Calculate the annual depreciation expense and the accounting effect of the depreciation.

	Cost £	Accumulated depreciation £	Net book value £
Year 1	20,000		
Depreciation expense (25% × 20,000)		5,000	15,000
Year 2			
Depreciation expense (25% × 15,000)		3,750	
		8,750	11,250
Year 3			
Depreciation expense (25% × 11,250)		2,813	
		11,563	8,437

Note the annual depreciation expense reduces each year.

1.6.5 Disposal of non-current assets

If a non-current asset is disposed of, the difference between the sale proceeds and the net book value of the asset gives rise to a profit or loss on sale, which is included in the statement of profit or loss.

The double-entry bookkeeping requires a disposals account, to which is transferred the net book value (cost and accumulated depreciation) of the asset disposed of and the sales proceeds. The balance on this account will be the profit or loss on disposal. The detailed bookkeeping steps are as follows:

1   Transfer original cost of asset to a disposals account

Debit   Disposals   } with original cost

  Credit   Asset cost   }

2   Transfer accumulated depreciation to disposals account

Debit   Accumulated depreciation   } with accumulated

  Credit   Disposals   } depreciation at date of disposal

3   Account for proceeds (if any)

Debit   Bank

  Credit   Disposals

Worked example 1.7: to show the accounting for the disposal of a non-current asset

The balances on the machinery account and machinery accumulated depreciation accounts of Haslam Ltd at 1 January 20X9 were £58,000 and £32,000 respectively. The business scraps a piece of machinery on 31 October 20X9 and sells the parts for £1,000. The machinery had originally cost £6,000 on 1 January 20X3. The business's depreciation policy for machinery is straight-line at 10%, with a full year's depreciation charged in the year of acquisition and none in the year of disposal.

Required:

Show the double-entry bookkeeping for the disposal of the machinery and the resulting figures that would appear in the financial statements of Haslam Ltd for 20X9.

The double-entry bookkeeping for the disposal is as follows:

1   Transfer original cost of asset to a disposals account

		£	£
Dr	Disposals	6,000	
Cr	Asset cost		6,000

2   Transfer accumulated depreciation to disposals account

		£	£
Dr	Accumulated depreciation	3,600	
Cr	Disposals		3,600

Accumulated depreciation at date of sale = 6 years × (10% × £6,000)

3   Account for proceeds

		£	£
Dr	Bank	1,000	
Cr	Disposals		1,000

The balance on the disposals account is the profit or loss on disposal—in this case a loss of £1,400—which is an expense in the 20X9 statement of profit or loss.

Disposals account

Cost	6,000	Accumulated depreciation	3,600
		Proceeds	1,000
		Loss on disposal	1,400
	6,000		6,000

Assuming there are no further transactions in machinery in 20X9, the remaining machinery is depreciated in the usual way:

		£	£
Dr	Depreciation expense	5,200	
Cr	Accumulated depreciation		5,200

Depreciation = 10% × Cost of remaining assets
= 10% × 58,000 − 6,000

The resulting balances on the machinery cost and accumulated depreciation accounts are as follows:

Cost				Accumulated depreciation			
Bal. b/f	58,000	Disposal	6,000	Disposal	3,600	Bal. b/f	32,000
		Bal. c/f	52,000	Bal. c/f	33,600	Deprecn.	5,200
	58,000		58,000		37,200		37,200
Bal. b/f	52,000					Bal. b/f	33,600

The net book value of the machinery at 31 December 20X9 = 52,000 − 33,600 = £18,400.

1.7 Prudence

A business that overstates its profits or the value of its net assets does not provide useful information to users. For many years the fundamental concept of prudence underpinned financial accounting in order to counter the excessive over-optimism of some owners or managers in reporting financial results and positions. Broadly, this stated that where estimations were made, or choices existed, businesses should choose lower values when considering assets and profits, and higher values when considering losses and liabilities.

However, businesses have used the prudence concept in certain situations to undervalue net assets and profits, and, in the same way that overvaluation of business results and financial positions is undesirable, undervaluation of these amounts does not provide useful information to users.

Prudence has not been included in the characteristics that make financial information useful earlier in the chapter as, essentially, it is considered that it creates bias and is therefore not neutral. However, for financial information to be represented faithfully, the values placed on assets and liabilities should be realistic and honest—in certain circumstances this may mean that being conservative, or prudent, about estimates could provide more useful information to some users. The inclusion of prudence in the *Conceptual Framework* is discussed in more detail in Chapter 2.

1.7.1 Receivables, irrecoverable debts and allowances for receivables

One application of where prudence may be considered necessary is in the measurement of accounts receivable. For accounts receivable to be represented faithfully, a business needs to consider that the amount does not only represent an amount owed by a customer or other party, but also that it represents the actual economic benefit expected to flow to it in the future, in other words how much cash is expected to be received. If there is any question over this amount then the business will need to adjust the amount shown as receivables.

Firstly, any debts that are definitely not going to be received are written off—these are termed irrecoverable debts (or bad debts) and are included as an expense. The double-entry bookkeeping is:

Debit   Irrecoverable debts expense

    Credit   Accounts receivable

Secondly, the business must then take an honest review of its remaining receivables and, if there is doubt about whether any amounts will be collected, the accounts receivable figure must be reduced to reflect this. In practice, a business will identify specific customers and/or invoices over which there is doubt, and also consider its history of debt collection from particular customers in order to determine the receivable balances that may not be collected. A doubtful receivable is a subjective judgement.

Doubtful receivables are not written off receivables. Instead, the accounting requires the creation of an allowance for receivables account, which records the specific allowances, and whose balance is netted off with accounts receivable in the statement of financial position. The balance on the allowance for receivables account is maintained at the required amount, with any changes passing through the statement of profit or loss irrecoverable debt expense. The double-entry bookkeeping is as follows:

1   To create an allowance for doubtful receivables

    Debit   Irrecoverable debts expense

       Credit   Allowance for receivables

2   To increase the allowance for receivables in subsequent accounting periods

    Debit   Irrecoverable debts expense   } with increase only

       Credit   Allowance for receivables   }

3   To decrease the allowance for receivables in subsequent accounting periods

Debit	Allowance for receivables	} with decrease only
Credit	Irrecoverable debts expense	}

Worked example 1.8: to show the accounting for irrecoverable debts and allowances for receivables

(a) Barney starts trading on 1 January 20X2 and, during the year ended 31 December 20X2, makes total credit sales of £110,000 and collects cash from credit customers amounting to £95,900. The following debts are found to be irrecoverable and are written off on the dates shown:

30 April	Customer A	£220
31 August	Customer B	£130
31 October	Customer C	£50

On 31 December 20X2 the schedule of receivables, amounting to £13,700, is examined and it is decided to make an allowance for doubtful receivables of £440.

(b) During 20X3 Barney makes credit sales of £205,600 and receives payments from credit customers of £192,400. The business also writes off irrecoverable debts totalling £1,200. At 31 December 20X3 accounts receivable total £25,700. Barney has identified customers owing £1,760 in total as doubtful and decides to make an allowance against these.

Required:

Show the accounting for Barney's irrecoverable and doubtful receivables, and the resulting figures which will appear in the year's financial statements for the years 20X2 and 20X3.

(a) <u>20X2</u>

On the dates the business identifies the irrecoverable debts it will record the write-offs as follows:

		£	£
Debit	Irrecoverable debts expense	400 (in total)	
Credit	Accounts receivable		400

At 31 December 20X2, the business will create an allowance for receivables as follows:

		£	£
Debit	Irrecoverable debts expense	440	
Credit	Allowance for receivables		440

The resulting figures in the financial statements at 31 December 20X2 relating to receivables, irrecoverable debts and allowances for receivables will be as follows:

Statement of profit or loss

	£
Irrecoverable debts written off	400
Allowance for receivables	440
Total irrecoverable debts expense	840

Statement of financial position

Current assets:	£	£
Inventory		X
Accounts receivable	13,700	
Less: allowance for receivables	(440)	
		13,260
Prepayments		X
Bank		X

The amount expected to be collected from customers

(b) 20X3

The irrecoverable debts will be written off as follows:

		£	£
Debit	Irrecoverable debts expense	1,200	
Credit	Accounts receivable		1,200

At 31 December 20X3 the business determines whether the allowance for receivables increases or decreases the allowance already maintained.

	£
Allowance for receivables required at 31 December 20X3	1,760
Allowance for receivables at 31 December 20X2	440
Increase in allowance	1,320

This increase will be recorded as follows:

		£	£
Debit	Irrecoverable debts expense	1,320	
Credit	Allowance for receivables		1,320

The resulting figures in the financial statements at 31 December 20X3 relating to receivables, irrecoverable debts and allowances for receivables will be as follows:

Statement of profit or loss

	£
Irrecoverable debts written off	1,200
Increase in allowance for receivables	1,320
Total irrecoverable debts expense	2,520

Statement of financial position

Current assets:	£	£
Inventory		X
Accounts receivable	25,700	
Less: allowance for receivables	(1,760)	
		23,940
Prepayments		X
Bank		X

1.8 Pulling everything together

The previous sections on accruals and prepayments, depreciation, and irrecoverable debts and allowances for receivables provide examples of accounting adjustments that businesses have to make every time they require a statement of profit or loss and statement of financial position to be drawn up. Many other adjustments will be required, some of which may result from correction of errors, and all will have to be posted to the nominal ledger by means of a journal entry (i.e. by double-entry bookkeeping), so that the financial statements are in accordance with the books and records. Other accounting adjustments will be explained in subsequent chapters as more detailed financial reporting requirements in specific areas are examined.

However, at this stage, in order to provide a sound basis for an understanding of how three of the main financial statements are prepared, a comprehensive example follows. This requires the preparation of a statement of profit or loss, statement of changes in equity and statement of financial position for a company from trial balance, and including main period-end accounting adjustments. Further examples are provided in the end-of-chapter exercises.

Worked example 1.9: to show the preparation of financial statements from trial balance including year end adjustments

The following trial balance was extracted from the books of Mayfield Ltd at 31 December 20X5:

	Dr	Cr
	£000	£000
Issued share capital:		
400,000 50p equity shares		200

100,000 10% £1 irredeemable preference shares		100
Share premium		40
Retained earnings		90
Equity dividend paid	48	
Preference dividend paid	4	
Administration expenses	150	
Selling and distribution expenses	170	
Interest expense	6	
Investment income		8
Accounts receivable	80	
Allowance for receivables at 1 January 20X5		6
Accounts payable		56
Short term investments	70	
Non-current assets cost:		
Premises	400	
Machinery	160	
Motor vehicles	64	
10% Loan		120
Accumulated depreciation at 1 January 20X5		
Premises		40
Machinery		48
Motor vehicles		24
Inventory at 1 January 20X5	42	
Cash and bank	32	
Purchases	144	
Sales		638
	1,370	1,370

Adjustments for the following are required at the year end:

1 The closing inventory was valued at cost at £48,000
2 Salesmen's commission, which is included in selling and distribution expenses, for December of £10,000 had not yet been accounted for
3 Administrative expenses included a payment of £12,000 for insurance for the period 1 September 20X5 to 31 August 20X6
4 The loan was taken out in 20X3 and is due for repayment in 20X8. Its interest rate is fixed at 10%
5 The company's depreciation policies are as follows:

Buildings	Straight-line over 20 years
Machinery	Straight-line at 20%
Motor vehicles	25% on reducing balance

The buildings cost is £200,000

6   £4,000 of receivables was considered doubtful at the year end, and it was decided that an allowance for these should be accounted for

7   The directors propose to:

   (a) Provide for £20,000 corporation tax

   (b) Pay the remaining preference dividend

   (c) Pay a final dividend on the equity shares of 10p per share.

Required:

Prepare Mayfield Ltd's:

 (i) Statement of profit or loss for the year ended 31 December 20X5

 (ii) Statement of changes in equity for the year ended 31 December 20X5

(iii) Statement of financial position at 31 December 20X5.

Solution

Step 1

Identify which accounts in the trial balance belong in which financial statement, for example share capital balances are statement of financial position balances and will be shown in equity. Note that the preference shares are irredeemable, so they will be part of equity.

Step 2

Work out what adjustments are required in respect of the additional information.

1   This is closing inventory and will be included in cost of sales in the statement of profit or loss and current assets in the statement of financial position.

2   This is an expense relating to the year which has not yet been paid—it is an accrual.

		£	£
Dr	Selling and distribution expenses	10,000	
Cr	Accruals		10,000

3   Part of the period covered by the insurance falls in the following financial year, hence this is a prepayment. The prepayment is calculated as 8/12 × 12,000 = £8,000. Insurance is an administration expense.

		£	£
Dr	Prepayments	8,000	
Cr	Administration expenses		8,000

4 Total loan interest for the year = 10% × 120,000 = £12,000. The trial balance interest expense account shows that only £6,000 has been paid and accounted for. Therefore, the remaining £6,000 must be accrued.

		£	£
Dr	Interest expense	6,000	
Cr	Accruals		6,000

5 Depreciation for the year needs calculating:

Buildings	200,000/20	= £10,000
Machinery	20% × 160,000	= £32,000
Motor vehicles	25% × (64,000 − 24,000)	= £10,000

The adjustment will be:

		£	£
Dr	Depreciation expense	52,000	
Cr	Accumulated depreciation		
	Premises		10,000
	Machinery		32,000
	Motor vehicles		10,000

6 Allowance for receivables adjustment:

	£
Allowance for receivables at 31 December 20X5	4,000
Allowance for receivables at 1 January 20X5	6,000
Decrease in allowance	2,000

The adjustment required is:

		£	£
Dr	Allowance for receivables	2,000	
Cr	Irrecoverable debts expense		2,000

7 (a) The corporation tax is a deduction from profits shown in the statement of profit or loss and, as it will not have been paid yet, it is also a liability to be shown in the statement of financial position:

		£	£
Dr	Tax expense	20,000	
Cr	Tax liability		20,000

(b) and **(c)** The equity and preference dividends proposed at the year end are not accounted for in the 20X5 financial statements. It is only the dividends paid in the year, and shown in the trial balance, that are included in the statement of changes in equity.

Step 3

Draw up pro-forma financial statements and insert the figures from the trial balance, adjusted, as necessary, by step 2.

Mayfield Ltd

Statement of profit or loss for the year ended 31 December 20X5

	£000	£000
Sales		638
Cost of sales		
Opening inventory	42	
Purchases	144	
	186	
Closing inventory	(48)	
		(138)
Gross profit		500
Expenses		
Administration expenses (150 – 8)	142	
Selling and distribution (170 + 10)	180	
Decrease in allowance for receivables	(2)	
Depreciation		
Premises	10	
Machinery	32	
Motor vehicles	10	
		(372)
Profit from operations		128
Investment income		8
Interest expense		(12)
Profit before tax		124
Corporation tax		(20)
Profit for the year		104

Mayfield Ltd

Statement of changes in equity for the year ended 31 December 20X5

	Equity share capital £000	Preference share capital £000	Share premium £000	Retained earnings £000	Total £000
Balance at 1 Jan 20X5	200	100	40	90	430
Profit for the year				104	104
Dividends paid					
Equity				(48)	(48)
Preference				(4)	(4)
Balance at 31 Dec 20X5	200	100	40	142	482

Mayfield Ltd

Statement of financial position at 31 December 20X5

	£000	£000	£000
Non-current assets	Cost	Acc depn	NBV
Premises	400	50	350
Machinery	160	80	80
Motor vehicles	64	34	30
	624	164	460
Current assets			
Inventory		48	
Accounts receivable	80		
Less: allowance for receivables	(4)		
		76	
Short-term investments		70	
Prepayments		8	
Cash and bank		32	
			234
Total assets			694
Equity			
Equity share capital			200
Preference share capital			100
			300

Share premium		40
Retained earnings		<u>142</u>
		482
Non-current liabilities		
Loan		120
Current liabilities		
Accounts payable	56	
Accruals	(10 + 6)	16	
Taxation	<u>20</u>	
		<u>92</u>
Total equity and liabilities		<u>694</u>

🔑 Summary of key points

Businesses report financial information to interested users in the form of standard financial statements, the main statements being:

- the statement of financial position, which shows the resources a business has, the claims against those resources and the residual interest of the investors at a particular point in time
- the statement of profit or loss, which shows the net profit the business has made over a period of time
- the statement of cash flows, which shows the cash inflows and outflows of a business over a period of time, resulting in a net increase or decrease in the cash or near-cash resources
- the statement of changes in equity (companies only), which shows the changes in the investors' interest over a period of time.

These statements provide most users with the financial information that they require in order to make decisions about their involvement with the business. In particular, they provide the principal users of company financial statements, in other words the investors (shareholders), potential investors, lenders and other creditors, with information to help them assess the returns that they can expect from their investment and changes in the value of their investment. In order for financial information to be truly useful, it should exhibit certain characteristics, the fundamental ones being that the information should be relevant to the decisions that need to be made and faithfully represent the underlying transactions or items. If the information is also comparable, verifiable, timely and understandable it will be more useful.

In order for businesses to produce financial statements regularly, all, except perhaps the very smallest, will maintain a financial accounting system. The heart of this is the nominal ledger, in which double-entry bookkeeping takes place. This system ensures that all financial transactions and items are recorded in a methodical manner and so that the two key statements—the statement of financial position and the statement of profit or loss—can be drawn up easily.

Financial statements are drawn up in accordance with various principles, such as accruals and historic cost. This requires the financial statements to include not only the financial transactions that have occurred throughout an accounting period, but also the effect of adjustments made at period-end, such as depreciation, accruals and prepayments, and changes to any allowance for doubtful receivables.

 ## Further reading

IASB (International Accounting Standards Board) (2010) *Conceptual Framework for Financial Reporting.* London: IASB (Introduction, Chapters 1 and 3).

 ## Bibliography

Ahmed, K., Tesco, what went wrong? Available from www.bbc.co.uk/news/business-29716885 (accessed 1 August 2016)

 ## Questions

● Quick test

1   For a sole trader, identify which nominal ledger accounts will be affected by the following transactions, and state whether the accounts will be increased or decreased as a result of the transaction:

		£
(a)	Owner started business by paying into a business bank account	15,000
(b)	Loan received	5,000
(c)	Motor car purchased for cheque	8,000
(d)	Goods purchased on credit from supplier Hall	2,250
(e)	Goods sold on credit to customer White	1,645
(f)	Cheque paid for office expenses	340
(g)	Goods sold for cash to customer Black	1,300
(h)	Goods purchased on credit from supplier Marks	1,200
(i)	Credit note issued for goods returned by White	245
(j)	Credit note received from Hall for return of faulty goods	300
(k)	Cheque paid for car insurance	195
(l)	Cheque paid to Hall	1,125
(m)	Wages paid in cash	250
(n)	Owner withdrawals to cover personal expenses	500
(o)	Cheque received from White	900
(p)	Cheque paid to Marks after deducting a £50 cash discount	1,150
(q)	Payment made on loan	1,500

(NB—loan of £5,000 has interest @ 10% p.a. and is being repaid in £1,000 instalments.)

2   Enter the transactions given in Question 1 in the nominal ledger accounts of the business using double-entry bookkeeping, balance off the accounts and extract a trial balance.

3   Draw up the statement of profit or loss for the year ended 30 June 20X4 and statement of financial position at that date for P. Glass's business from the following trial balance.

	Dr £	Cr £
Inventory at 1 July 20X3	2,368	
Sales		19,647
Purchases	13,874	
Returns inwards	205	
Returns outwards		322
Salaries and wages	4,206	
Rent	300	
Insurance	76	
Motor expenses	554	
Office expenses	328	
Heat and light	160	
General expenses	325	
Carriage inwards	250	
Discounts allowed	68	
Premises	5,000	
Motor vehicles	1,800	
Fixtures and fittings	450	
Trade receivables	3,704	
Trade payables		2,731
Cash at bank		1,710
Drawings	1,200	
Capital at 1 July 20X3		10,458
	34,868	34,868

(Note: inventory at 30 June 20X4 was valued at £2,946.)

●● Develop your understanding

4   The trial balance of Lytax at 31 December 20X2 is as follows:

	£	£
Capital at 1 January 20X2		68,000
Five-year loan		15,000
Land and buildings	67,000	
Plant and machinery	38,000	
Fixtures and fittings	21,300	
Accumulated depreciation at 1 January 20X2		
Land and buildings		12,000
Plant and machinery		8,100
Fixtures and fittings		5,300
Receivables	9,000	
Bank		1,000
Payables		8,400
Discounts allowed	700	
Purchases	79,500	
Heat and light	1,300	
Insurance	1,400	
Wages and salaries	24,200	
Inventory at 1 January 20X2	7,800	
General expenses	1,200	
Irrecoverable debts	700	
Allowance for receivables		300
Drawings	25,000	
Sales		159,000
	277,100	277,100

The following information needs to be taken into account before the financial statements can be finalised:

(a) Inventory was valued at £8,000 at the close of business on 31 December 20X2

(b) The owner took goods for his own use during the year. The cost of these was £1,500, and they have not been accounted for

(c) Interest on the loan at 8% p.a. has not been paid for the year ended 31 December 20X2

(d) Wages and salaries owing at 31 December 20X2 amounted to £400

(e) The figure for insurance includes a premium of £1,000 for the period 1 July 20X2 to 30 June 20X3

(f) £450 of receivables are considered doubtful at 31 December 20X2 and an allowance against these is required

(g) The business's depreciation policies are:

Buildings	Straight-line over 50 years

(Buildings element in the land and buildings cost is £40,000)

Plant and machinery	15% straight-line
Fixtures and fittings	5% reducing balance.

Required:

Prepare Lytax's statement of profit or loss for the year ended 31 December 20X2 and a statement of financial position at that date.

5 Porter Ltd is a company with total authorised share capital of £2,000,000 divided into £500,000 of 6% irredeemable preference share capital and £1,500,000 equity share capital.

Porter's trial balance at 31 May 20X6 has been extracted and is reproduced below:

	£000	£000
Preference share capital: £1 shares		500
Equity share capital: 50p shares		600
Retained earnings at 1 June 20X5		336
Inventory at 1 June 20X5	1,071	
Sales		4,377
Purchases	2,225	
Wages and salaries	808	
Motor expenses	164	
Rent	210	
General distribution costs	81	
General administration expenses	79	
Debenture interest	28	
Royalties receivable		42
Directors' remuneration	185	
Irrecoverable debts	31	
Plant and machinery at cost	1,750	
Motor vehicles at cost	320	
Accumulated depreciation at 31 May 20X5:		
Plant and machinery		504
Motor vehicles		145
Trade receivables	781	
Trade payables		498
Bank		43
Allowance for receivables		29

Preference dividend paid	30	
Equity dividend paid	89	
Corporation tax paid	76	
VAT payable		54
7% debentures	____	800
	7,928	7,928

The following information is also relevant:

(a) Included in general administration expenses is a £24,000 insurance premium for the year ended 31 December 20X6

(b) An electricity invoice for £6,000 for the quarter ended 30 June 20X6 was received on 6 July and has not yet been accounted for

(c) Inventory at 31 May 20X6 was valued at £1,123,000

(d) An allowance against doubtful receivables of £34,000 is required at 31 May 20X6

(e) Total corporation tax for the year ended 31 May 20X6 has been agreed with HM Revenue & Customs at £102,000

(f) The directors wish to provide for the following at 31 May 20X6:

    (i) Directors' bonuses of £36,000

    (ii) Auditors' fees of £12,000

    (iii) Any debenture interest due

(g) The company's depreciation policies are as follows:

Plant and machinery	10% straight-line
Motor vehicles	35% reducing balance

Required:

Prepare the statement of profit or loss and statement of changes in equity for Porter Ltd for the year ended 31 May 20X6 and a statement of financial position at that date.

●●● Take it further

6   Falmouth plc has an authorised share capital of £2,000,000 divided into 3,000,000 equity shares of 50p and 500,000 12% redeemable preference shares of £1.

The following trial balance has been extracted from the accounting records at 30 June 20X1:

	Debit £000	Credit £000
50p equity shares (fully paid)		500
12% £1 preference shares (fully paid)		200
8% debentures		400
Retained earnings 1 July 20X0		368
Freehold land and buildings (cost)	860	

Plant and machinery (cost)	1,460	
Motor vehicles (cost)	440	
Accumulated depreciation at 1 July 20X0:		
Freehold buildings		40
Plant and machinery		444
Motor vehicles		230
Inventory at 1 July 20X0	380	
Sales		6,590
Purchases	4,304	
Final dividends for year end 30 June 20X0:		
Equity	40	
Interim dividends for year end 30 June 20X1:		
Preference	12	
Equity	16	
Debenture interest	16	
Wages and salaries	508	
Light and heat	62	
Irrecoverable debts expense	30	
Other administration expenses	196	
Receivables	578	
Payables		390
Allowance for receivables		20
Corporation tax paid	112	
Bank	168	
	£9,182	£9,182

The following information needs to be dealt with before the financial statements can be completed:

(a) Inventories at 30 June 20X1 were valued at £440,000 (cost)

(b) Other administration expenses include £18,000 paid in respect of a machinery maintenance contract for the 12 months ending 30 November 20X1. Light and heat does not include an invoice of £12,000 for electricity for the quarter ending 3 July 20X1, which was paid in August 20X1

(c) The directors wish to provide for:

   (i)   any debenture interest due

   (ii) directors' bonuses of £24,000

   (iii) the year's depreciation

(d) The allowance for receivables required at 30 June 20X1 is £24,000

(e) During the year ended 30 June 20X1, a customer whose receivables balance of £8,000 had been written off in previous years as irrecoverable paid the full amount owing. The company credited this amount to receivables

(f) The debentures have been in issue for some years

(g) Corporation tax of £256,000 is to be charged on the profits

(h) During the year a piece of machinery, which had originally cost £320,000 and had been owned by the company for 6 years, was scrapped. Proceeds received were £40,000. These have been incorrectly credited to the plant and machinery cost account

(i) The buildings element of the freehold land and buildings cost is £400,000.

Depreciation methods and rates are as follows:

Buildings	Straight-line over 50 years
Plant and machinery	10% straight-line
Motor vehicles	33% reducing balance

Required:

Prepare the statement of profit or loss and statement of changes in equity of Falmouth plc for the year ended 30 June 20X1 and a statement of financial position at that date.

 Visit the Online Resource Centre for solutions to all these end of chapter questions plus visual walkthrough solutions. You can test your understanding with extra questions and answers, explore additional case studies based on real companies, take a guided tour through a company report and much more. Go to the Online Resource Centre at www.oxfordtextbooks.co.uk/orc/maynard2e/

Part 2
Financial reporting in context

2

The financial reporting system

As defined in Chapter 1, financial reporting is concerned with the reporting of financial information about an entity to interested users. For financial markets to function efficiently, the financial information provided needs to be of the highest quality, and this requirement is equally applicable to non-listed companies whose shares are not publicly traded. The previous chapter discussed various characteristics that are required to make financial information useful, such as relevance and faithful representation. However, on their own, these are insufficient to ensure that the information is of the highest quality, as corporate scandals over the years have demonstrated. Thus, rules and regulations governing how financial information is provided have evolved and are still evolving.

This chapter explains the accounting rules and regulations that govern published financial reports of companies, who sets and influences these rules and regulations, and the authority they have. The main player in this is the International Accounting Standards Board (IASB), which sets international financial reporting standards and the concepts and principles underpinning them. Its programme of work and acceptance of its standards are key to the development of global financial reporting systems that will produce high quality financial statements.

After studying this chapter you will be able to:

- appreciate the importance of appropriate regulation
- explain the main elements of the regulatory framework of financial reporting for all companies in the UK, both listed and unlisted, and describe who the bodies are that set the regulation
- understand what international financial reporting standards are, their importance, the processes by which they are produced, and to which companies they are applicable internationally
- discuss the concepts and principles that underpin international financial reporting standards
- discuss the work of the IASB in relation to the goal of achieving a set of high quality global financial reporting standards.

- ❑ Investors' and the capital markets' need for high quality financial information.
- ❑ The need for legislation and financial reporting standards to contribute to high quality information in the context of UK listed and non-listed companies.
- ❑ UK companies legislation.
- ❑ 'True and fair'.
- ❑ International financial reporting standards (generic term to include both International Accounting Standards (IASs) and International Financial Reporting Standards (IFRS)), and their development and use globally.
- ❑ The IASB—its development, authority and accountability.
- ❑ Financial reporting systems in the USA, and the convergence project between the FASB and IASB.
- ❑ The principles, judgement-based approach to international financial reporting standards.
- ❑ The IASB's underpinning *Conceptual Framework*, and the proposals in the 2015 Exposure Draft.
- ❑ The elements of financial statements, and recognition, derecognition and measurement principles relating to these.
- ❑ Fair value.
- ❑ Presentation and disclosure principles.
- ❑ The consequences of global adoption of international financial reporting standards.
- ❑ The future of global adoption.

2.1 High quality financial reporting

The objective of financial reporting, which was discussed in Chapter 1, is:

> …to provide financial information about the reporting entity that is useful to existing and potential investors, lenders and other creditors in making decisions about providing resources to the entity.
>
> *(IASB, 2010a)*

In today's global environment, most public listed companies will be operating in many different countries, and will probably have their shares listed on a number of international stock markets. The investors, lenders and other creditors will be multinational, and will require high quality financial information that they can compare easily across international boundaries.

High quality financial information will ensure that investors and lenders have trust in it, which will give them confidence to make good investment decisions, and thus enhance the liquidity and efficiency of capital markets. Efficient capital markets help reduce companies' costs of capital, and therefore improve returns and contribute to wealth creation for the economic good.

However non-listed companies and small- and medium-sized entities (SMEs) constitute approximately 95% of companies in the world, and the provision of high quality financial information about them is just as important as for publicly traded companies. These companies produce financial statements which are used by their investors, who may be venture capitalists, but, particularly, by lenders, such as banks and suppliers, and also by employees, government departments and others outside the company. All these users would lose confidence if information was not high quality. In addition, these companies' access to capital, which is vital to their continuance and growth, and the economies of the countries in which they reside, would become even more difficult.

The global financial crisis of 2008 placed a particular focus on the quality of financial information provided by companies, with popular sentiment calling for companies, in this case in the financial sector, and their auditors to improve financial reporting. This is nothing new—history is littered with examples of such calls following financial scandals or major company collapses. Some more recent examples of this include Maxwell, Barings Bank and Polly Peck in the UK in the 1980s and 1990s, and, more recently, Enron and WorldCom in the USA in the 2000s and Olympus in Japan in 2011. Heads of government at the G20 summit in April 2009 also called for transparency and accountability to be strengthened, sound regulation to be enhanced, integrity in financial markets to be promoted, and the reinforcement of international cooperation.

2.1.1 What ensures high quality financial reporting?

As discussed in Chapter 1, it is necessary for financial information to be relevant, and to faithfully represent the financial position and performance to enable quality decisions to be taken. The quality of financial reporting will be enhanced by the information being comparable, verifiable, timely and understandable.

However, these attributes are only part of the financial reporting system. For the system to be reliable, and to produce what the users require, regulation to govern this has had to evolve and, for financial reporting, this is both statutory (in the UK, companies legislation) and includes the **audit**, and mandatory (financial reporting standards). For companies which have public accountability, additional requirements are specified by listing rules.

Although the main purpose of financial reporting is decision-usefulness, it is also about showing the results of the stewardship of management, in other words the accountability of management for the resources entrusted to it. It may be argued that the financial statements and detailed breakdown of figures contained therein provide the information that users need to make decisions and to assess stewardship. However, many users are also concerned with *how* companies achieve wealth creation through how they are run, how relationships with investors are managed and with long-term sustainability matters, such as the impact of companies' affairs on the environment or local community. Thus, financial reporting extends to the areas of corporate governance, corporate social responsibility and ethical issues. Again, in these areas regulation to govern this has had to evolve. These issues are discussed in more detail in Chapter 3.

2.1.2 The regulatory framework of financial reporting

If the financial statements of UK publicly listed companies are considered first, Figure 2.1 illustrates the main sources of regulation of these.

For non-listed UK companies, the regulations are not very different, as Figure 2.2 illustrates.

IASB   International Accounting Standards Board
FASB   US **Financial Accounting Standards Board**
FCA   **Financial Conduct Authority**
FRC   **Financial Reporting Council**
IFRS   International Financial Reporting Standards

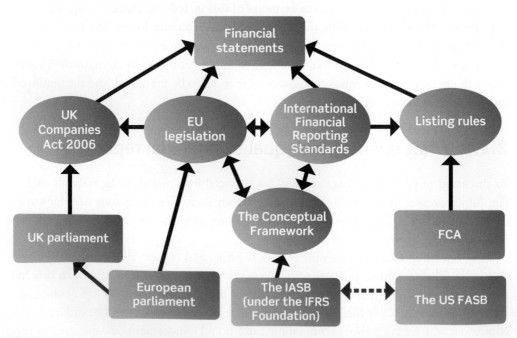

Figure 2.1 **Regulatory framework of financial reporting (UK listed companies)**

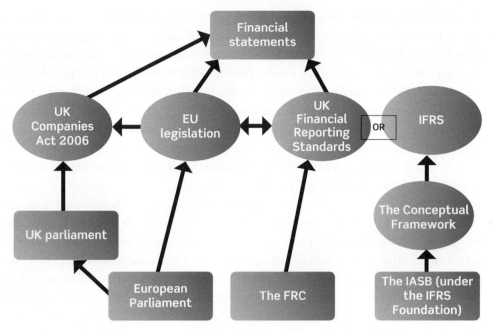

Figure 2.2 Regulatory framework of financial reporting (UK non-listed companies)

2.2 Companies legislation

In the UK statutory regulation is contained in Companies Acts and currently in directives of the European Parliament. The overriding requirement of Companies Act 2006 is that:

> …directors must not approve accounts unless they are satisfied that they give a true and fair view of the assets, liabilities, financial position and profit or loss…

(s.393, UK Companies Act 2006)

2.2.1 True and fair

The evolution of the company with its limited liability status gave rise to legislation governing its conduct and accountability. This included the requirement for companies to produce financial statements for its members (shareholders). From 1900 in the UK these financial statements (at this date a balance sheet only) were required to show a 'true and correct' view of the company's state of affairs. In 1947, following recommendations by the **Institute of Chartered Accountants in England and Wales** (ICAEW), one of the UK's professional accountancy bodies, the requirement was changed to 'true and fair' and was extended to apply to the profit and loss account. True and fair remains the overriding requirement of today's legislation concerning accounts in the Companies Act 2006 and it is on this that the external auditors ultimately provide their opinion.

A statutory definition of true and fair is not included in legislation; however, various statements as to its meaning have been produced—the most authoritative being legal opinions written by Lord Hoffmann and Dame Mary Arden in 1983 and 1984, respectively, and by Dame Mary Arden in 1993. A more recent opinion is that of Martin Moore QC, which was commissioned by the Financial Reporting Council (FRC) in 2008, and which endorsed the analysis in the opinions of Lord Hoffmann and Dame Mary Arden. The FRC produced its own document in 2014, confirming that the true and fair requirement remains paramount in the presentation of UK company financial statements. Legal opinion confirms that financial statements that have been prepared in accordance with relevant financial reporting standards will 'prima facie' give a true and fair view.

As indicated in Chapter 1, financial accounting is not an exact science; estimates are required to be made, such as in determining the expected useful life of a non-current asset or in judging whether a customer will pay its debts. As demonstrated in further chapters, there are many other areas which require judgements to be made, based on opinion, and, inevitably, differences exist between one person's opinion and another's. Financial statements cannot therefore be 'correct', but if they are true and fair they should be accurate and comprehensive to within acceptable limits; where estimates and opinions are required, professional, informed and reasonable judgement should be exercised; the transactions and items represented within them should reflect their commercial substance; and they should contain sufficient information in quantity and quality to satisfy the reasonable expectations of the users.

2.2.2 Other requirements

The Companies Act 2006 states that companies should prepare their financial statements in accordance with the applicable accounting framework, which, for listed companies and **groups**, is in accordance with international financial reporting standards, as specified by Article 4 of the 'IAS Regulation':

> …for each financial year starting on or after 1 January 2005, companies governed by the law of a Member State shall prepare their consolidated accounts in conformity with the international accounting standards … if, at their balance sheet date, their securities are admitted to trading on a regulated market of any Member State…

> *(Regulation (EC) no. 1606/2002 of the European Parliament and of the Council of 19 July 2002)*

For non-listed companies the applicable accounting framework is companies legislation, and the financial statements should consist of a balance sheet and profit and loss account with accompanying explanatory notes. Various provisions concerning whether group accounts should be prepared are also given—these are discussed in more detail in Chapter 17.

All financial statements must be approved by the board of directors and signed on behalf of the board by a director of the company on the company's balance sheet.

2.3 International financial reporting standards

Mandatory regulation governing financial statements is in the form of financial reporting standards and most of the chapters of this textbook are based on the detail contained in these.

2.3.1 Terminology

Clarification is needed in this area in relation to terminology, much of which is very similar. Firstly, international accounting standards (IASs) and international financial reporting standards (IFRS) have the same meaning, and reference to either term will encompass both IASs and IFRS. The reason for the different terms is explained later.

Secondly, international financial reporting standards are the standards issued by the International Accounting Standards Board (IASB). The IASB has also issued an IFRS for small and medium-sized entities (the IFRS for SMEs), which is a set of international financial reporting standards tailored for smaller companies. As referred to earlier, different financial reporting standards are used by different types of company and in different countries. Those used by non-listed companies in the UK are issued by the UK's Financial Reporting Council (FRC) and are called Financial Reporting Standards (FRSs). In the USA financial reporting standards are called financial accounting standards (FASs) and are issued by the US Financial Accounting Standards Board (FASB). Other developed countries will also have their own version of an accounting standards board and their own domestic standards.

Thirdly, a generic term—**generally accepted accounting principles (GAAP)**—is often used. This is used to refer to the standard framework of accounting guidelines used in any given jurisdiction. GAAP includes legislation, financial reporting standards and any other conventions and rules followed in the preparation of the financial statements.

This is summarised in Figure 2.3.

2.3.2 Financial reporting standards

Financial reporting standards are the 'instruction manual' of accounting. They are authoritative statements of how particular types of transaction and other events should be reflected in financial statements, and are there to answer the question 'how' should something be accounted for? As mentioned previously, compliance with financial reporting standards is necessary for financial statements to show a true and fair view.

Accounting methods have to evolve constantly to cope with, for example, changing opinions on relevant valuation methods, or new financial transactions or items such as complex financial **derivatives**, or changes in emphasis in what makes financial information really useful. Thus, financial reporting standards are constantly being withdrawn or revised, or new standards are issued. The last 15 years have seen an unprecedented level of change in financial reporting standards, particularly international standards, as discussed in the following sections.

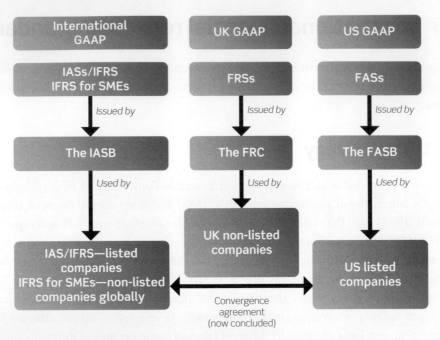

Figure 2.3 Accounting frameworks

2.3.3 UK financial reporting standards

In the UK, financial reporting standards have been in issue since 1970 when the first body to produce them was formed, the Accounting Standards Steering Committee. Prior to this, accounting practice was considered a matter for the accounting profession, which also oversaw auditing firms. From 1942, the ICAEW produced its *Recommendations on Accounting Principles* for the information of its members. However, these were not binding and during the 1960s there was growing disquiet over UK companies publishing audited financial statements which were subsequently found to be materially incorrect.

Two particular cases triggered calls for action to be taken—GEC's takeover of AEI Ltd in 1967 and Pergamon Press Ltd's 1968 audited accounts.

In the AEI takeover, AEI produced a forecast profit figure of £10 million for 1967, on which its auditors provided assurance that it was reasonable and fair. After the takeover, GEC produced the actual accounts for AEI for 1967, largely from the same information, which showed a loss for the year of £4.5 million. £5 million of the difference of £14.5 million in the two profit figures was attributed to a change in facts, but the remaining £9.5 million, some of which related to inventory and work-in-progress valuations, arose from differences in judgement of the two teams of accountants.

Pergamon Press's 1968 audited accounts showed a profit of approximately £2 million. However, an independent investigation by another professional firm of accountants suggested that the profit should be reduced by £1.5 million as a result of differences in opinion over valuations.

The obvious question of how different accountants could arrive at such different profit figures was raised and, as a result, the Accounting Standards Steering Committee (ASSC) was formed from the main professional accounting bodies in the UK and Ireland:

- The Institute of Chartered Accountants in England and Wales (ICAEW)
- The Institute of Chartered Accountants of Scotland (ICAS)
- The Institute of Chartered Accountants in Ireland (ICAI)
- The Association of Certified Accountants (now the **Association of Chartered Certified Accountants** or ACCA)
- The Institute of Cost and Management Accountants (now the **Chartered Institute of Management Accountants** or CIMA).

The Chartered Institute of Public Finance and Accountancy (CIPFA) joined later.

The Committee's objective was 'to develop definitive standards for financial reporting' and it issued the first Statement of Standard Accounting Practice (SSAP 1) on Accounting for the Results of Associated Companies in January 1971. Companies and auditors were required to apply the standards or explain any departures from their application. For the next 19 years the Accounting Standards Committee (ASC—the 'Steering' was dropped from its title) issued 25 SSAPs until, in 1990, the Accounting Standards Board (ASB), a subsidiary body of the newly established Financial Reporting Council (FRC), took over its work. The ASB adopted the existing SSAPs, but any new standards that it issued were given the title Financial Reporting Standards (FRSs).

As a result of the adoption of international financial reporting standards by listed companies, many SSAPs and FRSs were reissued to bring them into line with international requirements. A separate UK accounting standard setter therefore was considered no longer necessary, and in 2012 the FRC assumed responsibility for issuing FRSs. At this time, work began in earnest on the consolidation of all extant SSAPs and FRSs into one overriding standard, and the clarification of financial reporting frameworks applicable to different companies. The result, applicable from 1 January 2015, is six FRSs, numbered from FRS 100 to FRS 105, which explain both the accounting reporting frameworks applicable to different sized companies and to those which are part of a group, and set out the actual accounting requirements. The new FRSs are broadly consistent with international standards, but allow for UK legal requirements.

2.3.4 International Financial Reporting Standards (IASs) and the International Accounting Standards Board (IASB)

A discussion of international financial reporting standards and their use can only be carried out in the context of a discussion of the development of the body that issues them.

IASs have been in issue since 1973 when the International Accounting Standards Committee (IASC) was formed as a result of an agreement by accountancy bodies in nine countries—Australia, Canada, France, Germany, Japan, Mexico, the Netherlands, the UK and Ireland, and the USA—and these countries constituted the board of IASC at that time. The original intention of the IASC was to issue accounting standards with which the members should use 'best endeavours to ensure compliance'. External auditors were encouraged to report cases of non-compliance. The IASC issued its first standard, IAS 1 *Disclosure of Accounting Policies*, in 1974.

Although, over the next 15 years or so, the IASC expanded as accountancy bodies from other nations joined the organisation, and it began to hold discussions with national standard-setters, the accounting standards issued by local setters always took precedence. However, IASs were useful to companies in countries that did not have fully established financial reporting systems. Research in the early 1980s demonstrated that IASs had not changed national standards in developed countries and were only really codifying generally accepted practice. Pressure from these countries, particularly the USA and the UK, ensured that by 1982 there was agreement that IASs would not override national standards.

Significant events that triggered a greater acceptance of IASs globally were German reunification following the collapse of the Soviet Union in 1989, and the agreement of a list of core IASs by the International Organisation of Securities Commissions (IOSCO) in 1993. Following these events a number of Continental European companies started to adopt IASs for **consolidated financial statements** purposes and, in 1998, laws were passed in Belgium, France, Germany and Italy to permit large companies to use IASs domestically.

2.3.5 US acceptance of IASs

While Europe was moving swiftly towards acceptance of IASs in 2000, with the European Commission announcing plans to require IASC standards for all European Union (EU) listed companies from no later than 2005, the key global player, the USA, was hesitating over the development of a set of financial reporting standards which would attract widespread international support. Possibly, the USA perceived that the EU wanted a politically based financial reporting structure, whilst the EU may have been concerned that the USA wanted to fashion IASs on US GAAP. The impasse was broken as a result of a number of events.

Firstly, the IASC restructured itself in 2000 with a new constitution and wider membership, and the IASB became the body with responsibility for setting financial reporting standards, which were designated IFRS. Sir David Tweedie, formerly the Chair of the UK's ASB, became Chairman of the new IASB, and immediately instituted a thorough review and update of all inherited IASs, which, he admitted, were second-rate. Secondly, in 2000 IOSCO, which includes the USA's Securities and Exchange Commission (SEC), recommended that its members allow multinational issuers to use 30 IASs in cross-border offerings and listings.

Finally, the commitment to the use of IASs by all EU listed companies was a clear message to the whole world of the significance of IASs for the future. From 1 January 2005 more than 7,000 companies were required to prepare their financial statements in accordance with IASs as opposed to their national GAAP.

These events had enormous significance. The New York Stock Exchange (NYSE) is the largest capital market in the world, which leads to it being very attractive to companies wishing to raise capital and for their global profile. In order to list on the NYSE or NASDAQ (National Association of Securities Dealers Automated Quotations, the USA's electronic screen-based equity securities trading market), foreign companies were required to either produce a set of financial statements prepared in accordance with US GAAP, which would be in addition to the financial statements prepared under their national GAAP, or to produce reconciliations of net profit and shareholders' equity from their national GAAP to US GAAP, with full details of differences. Either of these requirements imposed a large costly burden on companies.

Although this requirement remained for the time being, a major step forward was taken in 2002 with the IASB and the FASB signing the 'Norwalk Agreement', which committed the boards to work together to remove differences between IFRS and US GAAP, and to coordinate their future work programmes. Then, in 2006, a 'Memorandum of Understanding' was drawn up between the two bodies, which set out a joint work programme to be completed by 2011. This was based on three principles:

1   Convergence was to be achieved by the development of high quality, common standards over time

2   Rather than eliminating differences between a FAS and an IAS, a new common standard should be developed

3   If standards needed replacing, new standards should be developed jointly.

Short-term projects to remove the variety of individual differences between US GAAP and IASs were agreed, with target completion dates by the end of 2008. In 2008 the two boards identified a series of priorities and milestones to complete the remaining major joint projects by June 2011, emphasising that the goal of joint projects was to produce common, principle-based standards.

As a result of progress on the Memorandum of Understanding, and also acceptance that the EU move to IAS in 2005 had generally been successful, in November 2007 came the (earlier than expected) decision of the US SEC to remove the requirement of reconciliation from home GAAP, which, in many cases, meant IFRS, to US GAAP for non-US companies listing in the USA.

Finally, in August 2008, the SEC produced a roadmap which would permit US companies to use IFRS domestically by 2014, with a decision to be taken by 2011 on whether the use of IFRS was 'in the public interest'.

Since then, events have intervened, such as the financial crisis and global recession, the Obama administration taking power in the USA, changes in the leadership at the SEC, and companies themselves hesitating because of the large costs of conversion to IFRS. Consequently, there has been a fall in the momentum towards full acceptance of the adoption of IFRS.

However, pressure on the USA for adoption remains. In 2009, the G20 leaders called on 'international accounting bodies to redouble their efforts to achieve a single set of high quality, global accounting standards within the context of their independent standard setting process …'. Since 2001, almost 140 countries have required, or permitted, the use of IFRS, or use their own national standards which are substantially converged with IFRS. All major economies, including significant emerging ones, such as China and India have established timelines to converge with, or adopt, IFRS in the near future. (The status of IFRS in different jurisdictions is available from the IFRS website.)

The position is now that US GAAP is used only by domestic US companies. All foreign companies listing on the US markets can choose IFRS, which has broad global acceptance. Indeed, US companies are *required* to use US GAAP—at present they cannot even elect to use IFRS!

In 2012 the SEC published a report entitled *Work Plan for the Consideration of Incorporating International Financial Reporting Standards into the Financial Reporting System for US Issuers: Final Staff Report*, which analysed the issues relating to the possible incorporation of IFRS into the US financial reporting system. No recommendations were included in this report, and the SEC has not made any subsequent determination about whether and, if so, how and when to take this matter further.

Many involved consider that the decision to fully adopt IFRS for US companies will be taken eventually, but it will be a prolonged, cautious and incremental process.

2.4 The International Accounting Standards Board (IASB)

Although an explanation of how the predecessor body, the IASC, was formed has been provided in section 2.3.4, it is important to understand what the current IASB is and what authority it has. It is an independent accounting standard-setting board, part of the IFRS Foundation, and overseen by a geographically and professionally diverse body of trustees, who are publicly accountable to a Monitoring Board. The structure is shown in Figure 2.4.

The IFRS Foundation is a not-for-profit, private sector body that raises funds to support the operations of the IASB as an independent accounting standard-setter. It is funded by a wide range of market participants from across the world's capital markets through the establishment of national financing regimes, proportionate to a country's relative Gross Domestic Product, that charge a levy on companies or provide an element of publicly supported financing.

There are currently 12 members of the IASB, who are experts with an appropriate mix of recent practical experience in setting financial reporting standards, in preparing, auditing or using financial reports, and in accounting education. The board has been chaired since 2011 by Hans Hoogervorst from the Netherlands. The board aims to have broad geographical diversity with members currently from Europe, the USA, South America, Asia and Africa.

The mission of the IFRS Foundation is:

> to develop international financial reporting standards (IFRS) that bring transparency, accountability and efficiency to financial markets around the world.

(IFRS Foundation, About Us)

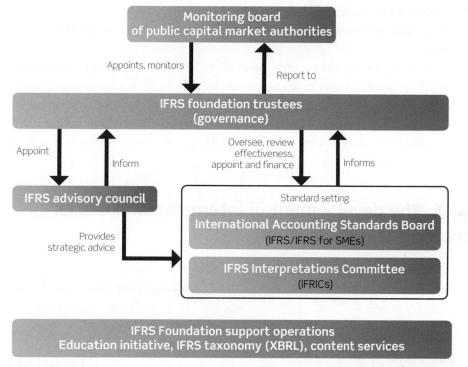

Figure 2.4 International Financial Reporting Standards (IFRS) Foundation, International Accounting Standards Board (IASB), *How we are structured,* **2016. Reproduced with the kind permission of IASB.**

The mission statement goes on to state that the Foundation's work serves the public interest by fostering trust, growth and long-term financial stability in the global economy. The use of IFRS:

● brings transparency by enhancing the international comparability and quality of financial information, enabling investors and other market participants to make informed economic decisions.

● strengthens accountability by reducing the information gap between the providers of capital and the people to whom they have entrusted their money. The standards provide information that is needed to hold management to account. As a source of globally comparable information, IFRS is also of vital importance to regulators around the world.

● contributes to economic efficiency by helping investors to identify opportunities and risks across the world, thus improving capital allocation. For businesses, the use of a single, trusted accounting language lowers the cost of capital and reduces international reporting costs.

The IASB engages closely with its stakeholders around the world, including investors, analysts, regulators, business leaders, accounting standard-setters and the accountancy profession. It claims to follow thorough, open and transparent processes in standard setting with the publication of consultative documents, such as discussion papers and exposure drafts, for public comment. All meetings of the IASB are held in public and via webcast.

The IFRS Interpretations Committee (formerly called the IFRIC) is the interpretative body of the IASB. Its mandate is to review, on a timely basis, widespread accounting issues that have arisen from the practical application of current IFRS and to provide authoritative guidance, through the publication of IFRICs, on those issues. The Interpretation Committee follows the same transparent, thorough and open due process, with its meetings open to the public and via webcast.

2.4.1 The development of international financial reporting standards (IFRS)

IFRS are developed through an international consultation process, the 'due process', which involves interested individuals and organisations from around the world. The due process comprises six stages:

1 Setting the agenda

2 Planning the project

3 Developing and publishing the discussion paper (DP)

4 Developing and publishing the exposure draft (ED)

5 Developing and publishing the standard (IFRS)

6 Procedures after an IFRS is published, including meetings with interested parties and post-implementation reviews.

Round-table discussions are held in locations around the world while the project is being developed, with comment periods allowed after stages 3 and 4.

The IASB sets itself an annual work plan with target dates for publication stages. In practice, these often differ, particularly if there are numerous comments from stakeholders which question the proposals. For example, an unprecedented number of comment letters was received following the publication of the ED on *Leases* in August 2010 and, although this was one of the key convergence projects due for completion by June 2011, a new accounting standard was not published until 2016.

2.4.2 International Financial Reporting Standard (IFRS) for small and medium-sized entities (SMEs)

There is general agreement that many IFRS are long, very detailed and complex, and are suitable mainly for listed companies. This is inevitable, as they have to address accounting for the type of tough and complex matters in which these companies engage. Small companies and their users have complained for years that many IASs and IFRS are not relevant for the type of business transactions and decisions that they make. The IASB undertook a major project to address this starting in 2003 and, in 2009, finally issued its IFRS for SMEs.

This is a self-contained standard, containing accounting for all areas considered applicable for smaller companies. It excludes some of the topics not relevant for SMEs, simplifies many of the principles and choices contained in full IFRS and significantly reduces disclosure requirements. It is designed for any size company globally that is required to produce financial statements and that does not have public accountability (publicly accountable companies should be using full IFRS), and focuses on ensuring that key information about cash flows, liquidity and solvency is provided.

According to the IASB, over 95 per cent of companies globally are eligible to use the IFRS for SMEs, and 77 jurisdictions require or permit use of the standard. A further 11 jurisdictions are considering its adoption.

The UK now has its own financial reporting framework for non-listed companies, which includes UK FRSs (see section 2.3.3 above).

2.5 Principles based international financial reporting standards (IFRS)

The objective of the IASB is to produce high quality financial reporting standards, and some discussion has been included at the start of this chapter as to how high quality financial reporting can be achieved. One of the main features of IFRS, which contributes to their high quality, is that they are considered to be **principles based** and consistent with an underpinning conceptual framework.

Financial reporting in practice 2.1 — Enron

One issue which came to light in the Enron case was the accounting treatment of special-purpose entities (SPEs) in which Enron had invested and in which the company had 'hidden' much of its debt. The SPEs were 'off balance sheet', in other words they did not appear in the company's consolidated financial statements and, therefore, neither did the debt.

Enron, in agreement with its auditors, Arthur Anderson, had accounted for these SPEs in accordance with a specific 'rule' contained within US financial reporting standards relating to ownership interest and, as the 'rule' appeared to have been applied appropriately, the debt was not disclosed.

Even though financial statements in the USA are signed off as 'presenting fairly' the financial position and results, financial reporting systems in the USA accept that this essentially means that all accounting rules set out in the financial reporting standards have been followed correctly. Whether the financial statements reflected the economic substance of Enron's investment in the SPEs—the company essentially controlled them—was considered less important.

There has been much discussion over the past decade or so of what is meant by principles based financial reporting standards, mainly in comparison with so-called **rules based financial reporting standards**. Broadly speaking, the US financial reporting standards are said to be rules based and the perceived superiority of the IASB's principles based standards came to the fore particularly after the collapse of the US energy giant, Enron.

Claims that an 'Enron-type' corporate collapse could not happen in jurisdictions that had principles based financial reporting systems were really expressing the point that the financial statements produced under these systems are required to faithfully represent the economic reality of businesses and their transactions. Faithful representation is discussed in Chapter 1—it is one of the fundamental characteristics of financial information that makes it useful. This concept, together with the idea that accounting should be in accordance with the economic or commercial reality of a transaction, is very much tied to the themes also discussed previously in relation to the meaning of true and fair.

⦿ **Reminder of true and fair** *Accurate as far as reasonably possible, with professional, informed and reasonable judgement exercised.*

IFRS encompass the principle of **substance over form**, in other words accounting for a transaction according to its commercial substance rather than its legal form.

 Example of substance over form

A business leases a machine. The business does not legally own this asset, as title is held by the leasing company. However, the business will use the machine to produce goods in the same manner as any machine which it legally owns.

The commercial substance of the **lease** arrangement is that the business has a resource—an asset—from which it will generate revenues; therefore, the financial statements should reflect the asset, together with all other assets, on its statement of financial position, even though it does not legally own the asset.

Note: accounting for leases is discussed in detail in Chapter 15.

Also key to a principles based system is the exercise of professional judgement rather than the identification of the rule that directs how a transaction should be recorded. Judgement should be reasonable in the light of the facts and circumstances present at the time it is made. It is suggested that this can lead to inconsistency and lack of comparability, which is one of the enhancing characteristics of financial information. Concerns are also expressed that subjective judgement rather than the application of rules could increase the risk of lawsuits. (Perhaps the litigious nature of US society has, in part, contributed to the numerous rules that comprise US financial reporting standards.) However, a robust and mature financial reporting system should ensure that accountants and auditors making these judgements are highly trained and experienced. Sufficient disclosure of the nature and effects of the judgement that has been exercised should also enable users to understand how it has influenced the financial information; although this does lead to additional length of corporate reports.

Principles based financial reporting standards address broader areas than rules based standards, which are therefore more numerous, as rules for each specific element of accounting need to be provided. This latter system creates complexity and lack of clarity.

Although there are currently 41 financial reporting standards (25 extant IASs and 16 IFRS), 14 IFRICs and 7 further statements of interpretation (SICs), this compares with approximately 90 financial accounting topics covered in the FASB's Accounting Standards Codification. IASs and IFRS cover broad areas of accounting (see list in section 2.5.1), and all follow the same format:

- the objective and scope of the standard are outlined
- terms used in the standard are defined
- the accounting methods are explained
- required disclosures are specified
- if necessary, implementation guidance and illustrative examples are provided
- the basis for conclusions is given.

Principles based standards are also more flexible and adaptable. If a standard does not deal with a specific item or transaction, preparers of financial statements are able to refer to the underpinning principles and exercise judgement. This contrasts with rules based standards which create 'bright lines', and the use of them can determine or influence the actual transaction entered into in order to achieve a particular result.

From this discussion it can be appreciated why there have been difficulties in the convergence programme between the IASB and the FASB, and why the time frame to produce a new standard under the programme has been so long.

2.5.1 Current international financial reporting standards

The following is a list of current international accounting and financial reporting standards at the time of publication. Up-to-date lists can be found on the IFRS website (www.ifrs.org).

IAS 1	Presentation of Financial Statements
IAS 2	Inventories
IAS 7	Statement of Cash Flows
IAS 8	Accounting Policies, Changes in Accounting Estimates and Errors
IAS 10	Events after the Reporting Period
IAS 12	Income Taxes
IAS 16	Property, Plant and Equipment
IAS 19	Employee Benefits
IAS 20	Accounting for Government Grants and Disclosure of Government Assistance

IAS 21	The Effects of Changes in Foreign Exchange Rates
IAS 23	Borrowing Costs
IAS 24	Related Party Disclosures
IAS 26	Accounting and Reporting by Retirement Benefit Plans
IAS 27	Consolidated and Separate Financial Statements
IAS 28	Investments in Associates and Joint Ventures
IAS 29	Financial Reporting in Hyperinflationary Economies
IAS 32	Financial Instruments: Presentation
IAS 33	Earnings per Share
IAS 34	Interim Financial Reporting
IAS 36	Impairment of Assets
IAS 37	Provisions, Contingent Liabilities and Contingent Assets
IAS 38	Intangible Assets
IAS 39	Financial Instruments: Recognition and Measurement
IAS 40	Investment Property
IAS 41	Agriculture
IFRS 1	First-time Adoption of International Financial Reporting Standards
IFRS 2	Share-based Payment
IFRS 3	Business Combinations
IFRS 4	Insurance Contracts
IFRS 5	Non-current Assets Held for Sale and Discontinued Operations
IFRS 6	Exploration for and Evaluation of Mineral Resources
IFRS 7	Financial Instruments: Disclosures
IFRS 8	Operating Segments
IFRS 9	Financial Instruments
IFRS 10	Consolidated Financial Statements
IFRS 11	Joint Arrangements
IFRS 12	Disclosure of Interests in Other Entities
IFRS 13	Fair Value Measurement
IFRS 14	Regulatory Deferral Accounts
IFRS 15	Revenue from Contracts with Customers
IFRS 16	Leases

2.6 The conceptual framework

One feature of a principles based financial reporting system is that it is underpinned by a conceptual framework to provide the broad principles on which financial reporting standards can be built. Without the guidance provided by an agreed framework, standard setting could end up being based on individual concepts developed for each standard separately and therefore lack coherence. The USA has a number of 'Concepts Statements' providing a theoretical underpinning to its standards and, in 1989, the IASC, the predecessor committee of the IASB, published its underpinning conceptual *Framework for the Preparation and Presentation of Financial Statements*. As the IASB and FASB began to work together to converge their standards it became apparent that having two frameworks was causing difficulties, even though they were fairly similar. So, from 2004, the two boards started on a long-term convergence project to develop a common conceptual framework. The objective of this project was to create a sound foundation for future financial reporting standards that are principles based, internally consistent and internationally converged.

The project was split into eight phases but, by the end of the convergence programme, only one stage had been completed, as more urgent issues took precedence. In September 2010, the IASB issued two replacement chapters dealing with the objectives of financial reporting and the qualitative characteristics, while the FASB replaced two of its 'Concepts Statements'. This 2010 version of the *Framework* retained other chapters from the 1989 *Framework*. Following a review of its work programme in 2012, the IASB undertook to prioritise the revision of the *Conceptual Framework*. An Exposure Draft (ED) was issued in May 2015, and the IASB aims to finalise the final version in 2017.

The *Conceptual Framework* describes the objective of, and the concepts for, financial reporting. Its purpose is to:

(a) assist the IASB to develop standards that are based on consistent concepts;

(b) assist preparers to develop consistent accounting policies when no standard applies to a particular transaction or event, or when a standard allows a choice of accounting policy; and

(c) assist all parties to understand and interpret standards.

(IASB, Conceptual Framework ED, 2015)

The *Conceptual Framework* thus contributes to the transparency, accountability and efficiency of financial markets as it enhances comparability and quality of financial information, enabling investors and other market participants to make informed decisions. It is not an accounting standard and the requirements of any standard will always override the contents of the *Conceptual Framework* should there be a conflict.

The proposals in the ED fill gaps in the 2010 *Framework*, such as providing guidance on presentation and disclosure of financial information. It also updates parts which are now out of date, for example, definitions of assets and liabilities, plus clarifies certain areas, such as how to deal with **measurement** uncertainty. It also puts more emphasis on stewardship, reintroduces prudence and incorporates specific reference to substance over form; issues which many have called on to be addressed. These are discussed in more detail in the following sections.

2.6.1 Objectives of financial reporting

The objectives of financial reporting are largely discussed in Chapter 1. The ED includes some proposals for amendments to the 2010 *Framework*. The objectives state the decision-usefulness objective of financial reporting:

> … to provide financial information about the reporting entity that is useful to existing and potential investors, lenders and other creditors in making decisions about providing resources to the entity. Those decisions involve buying, selling or holding equity and debt instruments, and providing or settling loans and other forms of credit.
>
> *(IASB, 2015, 1.2)*

Note that the **primary user group** is defined as investors, lenders and creditors; the reason for this is that these are the resource providers in capital markets, and have the most critical and immediate need for the information in financial reports. Other users, as set out in Chapter 1, are acknowledged, but the *Conceptual Framework* sets out that financial reporting is not directed primarily towards these other groups, as otherwise 'the *Conceptual Framework* would risk becoming unduly abstract or vague' (IASB, 2010, BC1.14).

As mentioned previously, the ED includes more emphasis on stewardship, in other words, the importance of providing information to assess the management of the entity's resources:

> To help existing and potential investors, lenders and other creditors make assessments of the amount, timing and uncertainty of (the prospects for) future net cash flows, they need information about:
>
> (a) the resources of the entity, claims against the entity, and changes in those resources and claims; and
>
> (b) how efficiently and effectively the entity's management and governing board have discharged their responsibilities to use the entity's resources.
>
> *(IASB, 2015, 1.4)*

Past information about stewardship is useful in predicting how well management will use the entity's resources to generate cash flows in the future. Examples of management's responsibilities given in the *Framework*'s objectives include protecting the entity's resources from unfavourable effects of economic factors such as price and technological changes, and ensuring that the entity complies with applicable laws, regulations and contractual provisions. In addition, information about management's discharge of its responsibilities is also useful for decisions by those users who have the right to vote on or otherwise influence management's actions.

This quote also identifies the main need of the primary user group—that of being able to assess an entity's future net cash inflows. This will determine the returns they receive from, and market price increases in, their investment, which, in turn, will assist them in decisions about providing resources to the entity. Information about the resources of the entity, claims against the entity and changes in the resources and claims refer to the type of financial statement that entities produce (the statement of financial position, statement of comprehensive income, statement of cash flows and statement of changes in equity), as discussed in Chapter 1, although they are not defined as such in the objectives chapter. This information will help the users assess the entity's future net cash flows.

The principles basis of financial reporting is emphasised in the objectives chapter by the statement that, to a large extent, financial reports are based on estimates, judgements and models, rather than exact depictions, with the concepts underlying these being established in the *Conceptual Framework*.

2.6.2 Qualitative characteristics of financial reporting

The qualitative characteristics of useful financial information included in the 2010 *Framework* are those discussed in Chapter 1.

🛈 **Reminder of qualitative characteristics** *The fundamental characteristics, without which the information would be useless, are relevance and faithful representation. Information is enhanced by the characteristics of comparability, verifiability, timeliness and understandability.*

However, so many respondents to the Discussion Paper issued prior to the ED called for prudence to be reintroduced as an underpinning principle, that the ED now contains explicit reference to the notion of prudence in certain circumstances.

Prudence is a concept that has always played a major role in financial reporting. In essence it means that assets and income are not overstated and that liabilities and expenses are not understated, and this can result in users having more confidence in reported financial information. However, the application of prudence can cause asymmetry in accounting as it requires a higher degree of certainty before **recognition** of assets than of liabilities—assets and gains are reported only if they are highly probable or reasonably certain, whilst liabilities and losses are recognised as soon as they are identified. Because of this, reference to prudence was removed from the 2010 *Framework* as it was considered inconsistent with the characteristic of neutrality. However, many consider that prudence is needed to counteract management's natural bias towards optimism, with investors more concerned with downside risk than upside potential. They also point to the financial crisis where the need for prudence when making estimates was clearly demonstrated. Prudence is also inherent in many current financial reporting standards.

The IASB has acknowledged that prudence can mean different things to different people, and the ED makes reference to two views:

1   **Cautious prudence**—the need to exercise caution when making judgements under conditions of uncertainty

2   **Asymmetric prudence**—losses are recognised at an earlier stage than gains are.

The three characteristics of completeness, neutrality and freedom from error are still required for faithful representation to be exhibited, but the ED now states that neutrality is supported by the exercise of prudence. The use of cautious prudence will help preparers, auditors and regulators to counter management's natural bias towards optimism. For example, the need to exercise care in selecting inputs used in estimating a fair value that cannot be observed directly would be required.

The question of whether asymmetric prudence is compatible with neutrality is debatable, and the IASB has chosen to focus on two aspects of neutrality to counter this:

1   The selection of neutral accounting policies, i.e. policies which are not slanted, weighted, emphasised, de-emphasised or otherwise manipulated to affect how the financial information is received by users

2   Neutral application of accounting policies.

The basis for conclusions to the ED specifies that accounting policies that treat gains and losses asymmetrically would not be inconsistent with neutrality if the above two aspects were followed and the result was relevant information that faithfully represents what it purports to represent. However, the IASB states categorically that the application of asymmetric prudence should not be considered a *necessary* characteristic of useful financial information. So the recognition of all unrealised gains should not be prohibited, as in some circumstances, for example, the measurement of financial instruments, this does provide relevant information to users.

One further key amendment proposed to the qualitative characteristics chapter introduces substance over form as an aspect of the definition of faithful representation. The ED suggests that a faithful representation would not result if information were provided only about the legal form of a transaction or item and this differed from the economic substance of the transaction or item.

This chapter of the *Conceptual Framework* also acknowledges that cost imposes a constraint on useful financial reporting, with the necessary costs of financial reporting having to be justified against the benefits, and that this is a subjective assessment.

2.6.3 Other chapters of the *Conceptual Framework*

The remaining text of the 2010 *Framework* consists of the same chapters of the IASB's 1989 *Framework for the Preparation and Presentation of Financial Statements*, and these are the chapters which principally require updating and where gaps need to be filled. The ED in doing this proposes three additional new chapters which deal with financial statements and the reporting entity, derecognition, and presentation and disclosure.

2.6.4 Financial statements and the reporting entity

This proposed new chapter names the required financial statements as:

● A statement of financial position
● Statements of financial performance
● Notes to the financial statements.

They include monetary information about recognised assets, liabilities, equity, income and expenses.

Financial statements are normally prepared on the assumption that an entity is a **going concern** and will continue in existence for the foreseeable future. If the entity intends to liquidate or materially curtail the scale of its operations, the financial statements may have to be prepared on a different basis, possibly by valuing the assets and liabilities on a break-up basis.

The chapter goes on to define the boundaries of the reporting entity as this has been referred to in the Objectives chapter. The definition of a reporting entity is proposed as:

> An entity that chooses, or is required, to prepare general purpose financial statements.

(IASB, 2015, 3.11)

It is not necessarily a legal entity (a limited company is a legal entity), and encompasses single entities, a portion of a single entity, and two or more entities. It is bound up with the issue of whether one entity controls others. If the reporting entity does control other entities, directly or indirectly, then consolidated financial statements are required in order to give a faithful representation of the economic activities included within the reporting entity. This is discussed further in Chapters 17 and 18.

2.6.5 The elements of financial statements

The elements, or broad classes of financial effects and transactions, are next defined, with principles setting out when they can be included in the financial statements, when they should be excluded, plus the value at which they can be recognised (see Figure 2.5).

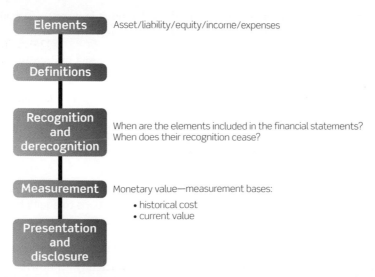

Figure 2.5 The IASB's *Conceptual Framework for Financial Reporting:* **the elements of financial statements. Reproduced with the kind permission of IASB.**

Definitions of an asset, a liability and equity, as given in the ED, have been provided in Chapter 1 and are as follows:

> An asset is a present economic resource controlled by the entity as a result of past events
>
> A liability is a present obligation of the entity to transfer an economic resource as a result of past events
>
> Equity is the residual interest in the assets of the entity after deducting all its liabilities

(IASB, 2015, 4.4)

Note that the definitions of both an asset and a liability include reference to an economic resource. This is further defined as a right that has the potential to produce economic benefits. A right is usually established by a legal contract, but it could arise from a constructive obligation of another party, in other words, from customary practices or published policies, or the entity may have the potential to receive future economic benefits that are not available to other parties, such as from know-how that is not in the public domain. The resource also only needs to have the potential to produce economic benefits. This needs to be neither certain, nor even probable—all this requires is at least one circumstance in which it would produce economic benefits.

The word 'control' is important in all of financial reporting, and is taken here, in the definition of an asset, to mean that the entity has the ability to direct the use of the economic resource and prevent other parties from doing so.

In the definition of a liability, the words 'present obligation' mean that another party has the right to receive that economic resource. So again it does not need to be certain, nor probable—just one circumstance need exist.

The definitions of income and expenses in the ED, as in the 2010 *Framework*, are in terms of changes in assets and liabilities:

> Income is increases in assets or decreases in liabilities that result in increases in equity other than those relating to contributions from holders of equity claims.
>
> Expenses are decreases in assets or increases in liabilities that result in decreases in equity, other than those relating to distributions to holders of equity claims.

(IASB, 2015, 4.4)

These definitions flow from the effect of changes to the fundamental accounting equation:

$$Assets = Equity + Liabilities$$

which can be expanded to:

$$Assets = (Opening\ equity +/- contributions\ from/distributions\ to\ equity\ holders + Income - Expenses) + Liabilities$$

Some question whether these definitions imply undue primacy of the statement of financial position over the statement of profit or loss, and do not sufficiently acknowledge the importance of matching income and expenses. However the IASB confirms that it is not designating information about financial position or about financial performance as the primary focus. It has found over the years that it is more effective, efficient and rigorous to define assets and liabilities first, rather than recognising income and expenses first with assets and liabilities becoming by-products of this approach. Assets and liabilities are real economic resources and obligations, and have to meet their definitions and recognition criteria. Indeed the ED generally places more emphasis on profit or loss as being the measure of financial performance of key importance to users than the 2010 *Framework* did.

2.6.6 Recognition and derecognition

Recognition is the process of capturing an item that meets the definition of an element for inclusion in the statement of financial position or the statement of financial performance. It relates to both the depiction of the item in words and by a monetary amount.

The ED proposes new recognition criteria, which link back to the fundamental qualitative characteristics of financial information, as follows:

> An entity recognises an asset or liability if such recognition provides users of financial statements with:
>
> (a) Relevant information about the asset or the liability and about any income, expenses or changes in equity;
>
> (b) A faithful representation of the assets or the liability and of any income, expenses or changes in equity;
>
> (c) Information that results in benefits exceeding the cost of providing that information.
>
> *(IASB, 2015, 5.9)*

In other words, information that is useful to users should be recognised. This will depend on the item and the specific facts and circumstances, and require judgement to be applied. In some circumstances the recognition of an item that meets the definition of the particular element can provide information that is not useful, for example, the recognition of asset when expenditure is incurred may not be useful, so the transaction should result in an expense being recorded, which may be more useful.

The recognition criteria may not always be met when one or more of the following applies:

(a) it is uncertain whether an asset or liability exists

(b) future inflows or outflows of economic benefits from the asset or liability are very unlikely; or

(c) the measurement is so uncertain that the resulting information has little relevance.

Derecognition is a new section in the ED. It is about when the removal of all or part of a previously recognised asset or liability from an entity's statement of financial position should be accounted for. This usually occurs for an asset when the entity loses control of all or part of the asset; and for a liability when the entity no longer has a present obligation for all or part of the liability. Ultimately the aim of the principles for derecognition are that the assets and liabilities retained after the transaction giving rise to the derecognition and the resulting changes in the assets and liabilities should be faithfully represented.

Discussion of how recognition and derecognition are applied to specific areas of accounting will be discussed in subsequent chapters.

2.6.7 Measurement

Measurement refers to the valuation methods applied to the elements. The 2010 *Framework* provides very little guidance on measurement, so the ED proposes a more extensive measurement chapter to discuss the different measurement methods that might be used, and the factors that should be considered when selecting an appropriate measurement method to apply in any given situation. There are many different ways assets and liabilities can be measured, and the choice affects the measurement of profit and users' opinions on the financial performance and position. Which are the best and most appropriate measurement methods to use have been debated for decades, and this will no doubt continue. All methods have their own particular conceptual and practical issues. A mixed measurement approach has evolved over the years as financial reporting standards have developed and been refined. This means that the method of measurement differs for different assets and liabilities. There are critics of this approach, who contend that when aggregating assets and liabilities, the resulting totals and subtotals can have little meaning if different measurement methods are used. Similarly, profit or loss may lack relevance if it reflects a combination of flows based on different measurement bases. Those that advocate a single measurement method tend to favour the use of **current values**. However, it is generally accepted by many that a single measurement basis for all elements may not provide the most relevant information to users of financial statements. Different measurement bases can be easier to understand and implement, be more verifiable and less prone to error or uncertainty, and be less costly to implement. Investors indicate that their detailed analytical methods are consistent with a mixed measurement approach.

In the ED two measurement bases have been proposed—historical cost and current value.

Historical cost measures use information derived from the transaction or event that created the element. It may seem easy to determine the historical cost of an asset or liability, and in simple situations it is easy to determine initial cost—it is the cash paid or received. However complications arise if, for example, a deferred payment is considered, where the time value of money needs to be taken into account. Another example is a payment with consideration other than cash—what is the historical cost of this transaction? In addition, determining historical cost after initial recognition is not straightforward. Historical cost relies on rules and conventions to specify whether and how it should subsequently be adjusted (for example, for depreciation and impairment). The need for these rules and conventions causes complexity and makes it challenging for investors to interpret the output.

Current value measures use information that is updated to reflect conditions at the measurement date and incorporate both positive and negative changes. The base includes:

- **fair value**
- **value in use** for assets and **fulfilment value** for liabilities.

Fair value generally means prices quoted in a market, and is discussed in more detail in section 2.6.8. Value in use and fulfilment values are entity-specific values, and are the **present value** of the cash flows that an entity expects to derive from the use of an asset or to incur as it fulfils a liability. Whilst current values for certain assets and liabilities are often considered more relevant for meeting the decision-usefulness objective of financial reporting, the values are generally more subjective than historical values, and thus verifiability may be reduced.

The ED provides discussion of factors which should be considered in selecting which measurement basis should be used for an asset or a liability and the related income and expenses. The overriding requirements are that it should be relevant and faithfully representative and be selected after consideration of the effect on all financial statements. Consideration should be given to how the asset or liability contributes to future cash flows, which in part will depend on the nature of the business activities being conducted. For example, if land and buildings are held by different businesses for different purposes (e.g. the property is the place where business is conducted, or the property is held for investment reasons), it may be more informative for different measurement bases to be used by the different business. Another factor is measurement uncertainty, but this has to be balanced with how relevant the measurement basis is. For example, it would have to be weighed up whether an unlisted investment should be measured at current value, which was considered more relevant to users, even if this was unverifiable because there were no available market values.

 Example of relevance

A business holds property for investment purposes. Which measurement basis would be more relevant for the users of the business's financial statements—the purchase price or the current market value (fair value)?

Current market values would provide information about whether the investment strategies were providing adequate returns. If the properties were valued at historic cost, this information would not be available.

As for recognition and derecognition, the applicable measurement basis will be discussed in relation to a particular area and the different elements in later chapters.

2.6.8 Fair value

Many recent IFRS require the use of fair value which, before the publication of the ED of the proposed *Framework*, was not defined specifically in this document. The IASB/FASB convergence project had addressed this in one of its projects with the publication of IFRS 13 *Fair Value Measurement* in 2011. The proposed *Framework*'s ED does now include a section relating to fair value.

Fair value is a measurement basis that has become extremely important over the past decade and has received much publicity, some not particularly favourable. The growth of its use can be explained partially by the emphasis on decision-usefulness as the main objective of financial reporting, with fair value being considered more applicable for, for example, many **financial assets and liabilities**, and providing more relevant information to users than historical cost.

Many IFRS require some elements to be measured at fair value; however, its use has been added to IFRS piecemeal and inconsistently over the years, leading to diversity in practice. The 2008 financial crisis (which some critics claim was exacerbated by the use of fair values by financial institutions) highlighted the need for clear guidance in this area and added impetus to the convergence project. IFRS 13 does not specify when fair value is to be used—the particular standard on a certain area of accounting will state this—but it establishes a single source of guidance for how fair value should be measured and it sets out the enhanced disclosures about the degree of subjectivity in the methods used. This adds relevant information for users, as it helps them to assess the reliability of the resulting values.

The IFRS defines fair value as:

> The price that would be received to sell an asset or paid to transfer a liability in an orderly transaction between market participants at the measurement date.
>
> *(IASB, 2011)*

Fair value is therefore an 'exit price' and is a market-based measurement, taking into account market conditions at the measurement date. Because of this it makes assumptions about how market participants would price the asset or liability, which are not necessarily the same as those the entity would choose. This approach also presumes that all transactions between participants in the same market would result in the same fair value. In many circumstances the price would depend on the particular seller and buyer.

> A fair value measurement assumes that the transaction to sell the asset or transfer the liability takes place either:
>
> (a) in the *principal market* for the asset or liability; or
>
> (b) in the absence of a principal market, in the most advantageous market for the asset or liability.
>
> *(IASB, 2011, para. 16)*

The principal market is the market with the greatest volume and level of activity for the particular asset or liability, in other words the most liquid market. The most advantageous market is the market that maximises the amount that would be received to sell the asset or that minimises the amount that would be paid to transfer the liability, after taking into account **transaction costs** and transport costs.

 Example of fair value in the principal or most advantageous market

An asset is sold in two **active markets**, Market A and Market B at £26 and £25 respectively. Cronshaw plc can access both markets. At the measurement date, costs associated with the sale of the asset in the two markets are as follows:

	Market A	Market B
	£	£
Transaction (selling) costs	3	1
Transportation costs to that market	2	2

If Market A is the principal market for the asset, the fair value of the asset would be £24 (selling price of £26 less transportation costs of £2). Transaction costs would be ignored.

If neither market is the principal market, Cronshaw must measure the fair value in the most advantageous market. This is the market which would maximise the net amount received from the sale of the asset, after deducting both transaction and transportation costs. This would be from Market B.

Market A: 26 – 3 – 2 = £21

Market B: 25 – 1 – 2 = £22

However transaction costs would be ignored in determining the fair value which would be £23 (25 – 2).

For non-financial assets the fair value measurement looks at the use to which the asset can be put. It takes into account the ability of a market participant to generate economic benefits by using the asset in its highest and best use. In other words, the market participant should consider the use that maximises the value of the asset.

When determining fair value the characteristics of the asset or liability should be considered. This could include, for example, the age and condition of the asset, such as the number of miles an aircraft has flown. Any restrictions on the sale or use of the asset or liability also need to be evaluated, for example, in a sale of equity shares whether there are any legal or contractual restrictions for a specified time period. Fair values can be determined for a stand-alone asset/liability, or a group of assets/liabilities, or a **cash-generating unit**. The particular IFRS requiring use of fair value measurement will provide guidance as to which is more appropriate.

The use of fair value does make an assumption that observable and up-to-date market prices are available—if so, 'mark to market' is possible. However, this is not always the case, and so some form of alternative 'mark to model' will be necessary. The assumptions used in arriving at a fair value (referred to in the standard as the 'inputs') are classified in a hierarchy that categorises the data they are based on, and whether this is observable or non-observable. The higher the level, the less subjective and therefore the more reliable fair value can be said to be.

Level 1 inputs	Quoted prices in active markets for identical assets and liabilities that the entity can access at the measurement date, e.g. the market price of a traded security.
Level 2 inputs	Inputs other than quoted prices included in level 1 that are observable either directly or indirectly, e.g. the quoted price of the shares in a listed company which is similar to the shares in the unlisted company for which the fair value is required.
Level 3 inputs	Inputs not based on observable market data (unobservable inputs), but which should reflect the assumptions the market participants would use when pricing the asset or liability, including assumptions about risk, e.g. a cash flow model to value the shares in an unquoted company.

As discussed above, where fair value is not directly observable, it should be estimated using valuation techniques. These valuation techniques should be appropriate in the circumstances and should maximise the use of observable inputs and minimise the use of unobservable inputs. They may be combined to measure fair value in a given situation. IFRS 13 describes three valuation techniques, as follows:

Income approach	Converts future amounts (e.g. cash flows or income and expenses) to a single current (i.e. discounted) amount. The future amounts are based on current market expectations about the amounts.
Market approach	Uses prices and other relevant information generated by market transactions involving identical or similar assets, liabilities or a group of assets and liabilities, such as a business.
Cost approach	Reflects the amount that would be currently required to replace the service capacity of an asset (i.e. the current replacement cost).

Entities are required to make full disclosure of the levels and valuation approaches for all assets and liabilities which use fair value as the measurement model. For recurring fair value measurements using significant unobservable inputs (Level 3), the effect of the measurements on profit or loss or other comprehensive income should also be disclosed. Examples of disclosures relating to fair value in the measurement of financial instruments are included in Chapter 14.

To sum up, current values are considered more relevant to users' decisions than historic values, and they also assist in predicting future cash flows. There may be more consistency between companies using this measurement method. However, the values are far more subjective, particularly if fair value is used and there is no active market for the asset or liability, and they can also be misleading if markets are volatile. There is also a greater cost involved in obtaining the values. The required disclosures add to the length and complexity of financial reports.

2.6.9 Presentation and disclosure

This is the final new proposed chapter in the ED of the *Framework*. Since detailed disclosures of transactions and items are contained in the relevant financial reporting standards, this chapter aims to set out the underlying principles on which these are based. It discusses, at a high level:

(a) the objective and scope of financial statements

(b) issues relating to achieving effective and efficient communication

(c) classification and aggregation

(d) conceptual guidance on whether to present income and expenses in profit or loss or in other comprehensive income.

The scope of financial statements is determined by their objectives, and so the ED's proposals in this area generally summarise the types of information financial statements normally contain. This includes reference to information about risks relating to both recognised and unrecognised elements, plus relevant forward-looking information.

As financial reports are an important communication tool between companies and users, they should enable companies 'to tell the story' and users 'to hear the story'. Communication principles are therefore concerned with classifying information in a structured manner, aggregating information so that it is not obscured by unnecessary detail, and permitting presentation and disclosures to be less mechanistic or boilerplate.

The question of which income and expenses are included in profit or loss and which in other comprehensive income is an issue on which many preparers and users have called for more clarification for some time. Although the specifics are addressed in IAS 1, the IASB is setting out the underpinning principles in this proposed chapter. They include confirmation that the statement of profit or loss, which incorporates a total for profit or loss for the period, is the primary source of information about an entity's financial performance for the period. Hence there is an assumption that all items of income and expense are included in this statement, which is only rebuttable if:

(a) the income or expenses (or components thereof) relate to assets and liabilities measured at current values—but this excludes components that are of the type which would arise if the related assets or liabilities were measured at historical cost, for example, interest income on a financial asset; and

(b) excluding the income or expenses (or components thereof) would enhance the relevance of this statement.

There is also a presumption that income and expenses included in other comprehensive income in one period are subsequently included in profit or loss, unless this would not enhance the relevance of the statement of profit or loss. This is referred to as recycling, and is discussed in more detail in Chapter 4.

The ISAB is currently undertaking a Disclosure Initiative, which is a collection of implementation and research projects aimed at improving disclosure in financial reporting. The result of this will provide additional guidance for the principles of presentation and disclosure contained in the Framework's ED. (Some aspects of this are discussed in Chapter 4.) The IASB is also considering whether to commence a project on performance reporting.

2.7 The consequences of global IFRS adoption

There is no doubt that as businesses operate increasingly in a global market, and with the internationalisation of capital markets, a common financial reporting language is needed so that communication with investors and other users is improved. The growing complexity of some financial transactions requires a strong financial reporting system to respond, so that the accounting is carried out in a consistent and understandable manner. Users require consistent and comprehensive financial reporting standards which are based on clear principles and sound professional judgement, rather than complex rules and guidance. This will enable the financial statements to reflect the underlying economic reality of companies' affairs.

Global adoption of IFRS should provide all these benefits, and, indeed, most research shows that the preparers and users of financial statements prepared under IFRS are benefitting. Companies are able to attract capital from a larger pool of investors, which drives down their cost of capital, and facilitates cross-border mergers and acquisitions activity and strategic investment.

Surveys of, and other research conducted into, EU listed companies following the 2005 move to IFRS have shown that, in general, adoption went well, with an improvement in the quality of financial statements and subsequent reductions in the cost of capital, although this is not uniform across all EU countries. It should be noted, however, that measures of 'quality' and 'cost of capital' are subjective and can be influenced by many other factors. Fears over the use of fair values appeared to be unfounded; although, again, it should be noted that prior to the switch to IFRS, the EU had negotiated that a modified version of IAS 39 *Financial Instruments: Recognition and Measurement* be adopted following many continental European banks' objections to the requirements for **hedging instruments**. A general criticism of IFRS was the volume and complexity of disclosures required—the average length of companies' annual reports increased significantly, which continues to be an issue. However, others counter this by suggesting that greater disclosure has enhanced the transparency of financial and risk exposure information.

Global adoption of IFRS does attract further criticism, particularly since the credit crisis. The use of fair values required banks to revalue downwards many of their **financial instruments**, with complainants claiming that these were then artificially low values which would recover in the future. Greater earnings volatility also results as changes in fair value from one year end to the next pass through profit or loss. There are also issues with alternative accounting treatments permitted by some standards (e.g. measurement models for **property, plant and equipment**, and **investment property**), which will be examined in more detail in later chapters. In addition, some critics claim that in creating a global monopoly for a single set of financial reporting standards, more harm than good will result for the efficient functioning of organisations and markets, and some competition in accounting standard setting would be beneficial. Quite how this might work in practice is questionable.

One common theme that has emerged from recent research is that the benefits of IFRS adoption depend on a country's enforcement mechanisms for ensuring proper application of IFRS. These vary from country to country; even in Europe they are delegated to a national level. In the UK, for example, the preparation of financial statements is only part of the financial reporting system, with the audit, listing rules, corporate governance and regulation of these playing their part in ensuring that the financial statements provide high quality information. Specifically, in relation to appropriate application of IFRS (and companies legislation), the **Financial Reporting Review Panel** (FRRP), a part of the FRC's **Conduct Committee**, examines the published annual reports of companies for compliance, either through its own selection procedures or following complaints from the public, press or City. Where it appears that requirements have not been followed and the financial statements are defective in some way, the panel has powers to require remedial action to be taken, which could be the company withdrawing the accounts and reissuing them. It should be stressed that in the UK this is fairly rare and a less extreme sanction could require correction of the error in the comparative figures in the next set of financial statements.

2.8 The future of IFRS

The year 2011 was crucial for the future of IFRS globally. The IASB/FASB nine-year convergence project came to an end with the publication of some major revised financial reporting standards in the areas of consolidated financial statements and financial instruments, and the issue of the fair value standard. The final major convergence projects on revenue recognition and leasing have recently been completed and standards issued. In 2011 Sir David Tweedie's tenure as Chair of the IASB came to an end and Hans Hoogervorst replaced him. After a period to enable implementation and review of the new standards, the IASB undertook a consultation on its future work programme. One of the key projects to emerge from this consultation was the *Conceptual Framework* which is nearing completion. Post-implementation reviews of and improvements to other financial reporting standards continue. The IFRS Foundation is committed to countries fully adopting IFRS, with convergence seen as an intermediary step. Working relationships with counties in convergence processes, including the USA, will reflect this aim. There have recently been developments towards IFRS adoption amongst the three largest Asian economies: Japan, India and China. All three currently have some form of convergence or acceptance in place.

The USA is still the major economy which does not permit IFRS for its domestic listed companies. IFRS will not be able to be a truly global system if the USA does not allow this.

However the IASB is continuing its work programme without the USA, and there is continued growth in the number of other countries engaging with IFRS. A consequence of the US position could be that its companies would become isolated, losing easy access to global capital markets, and the USA would no longer play the large influential role it has enjoyed. The result of the 2016 presidential election appears unlikely to change the US's position.

At the time of writing, the UK's 'Brexit' referendum has resulted in the UK voting to leave the European Union. No steps have yet been taken to start this process, nor are details available of the impact of the decision on financial reporting in the UK. As detailed, the use of IFRS for companies listing on the UK stock markets is required as a result of an EU directive, and much other UK accounting law is aligned with EU law. However, it seems unlikely that IFRS would be abandoned by the UK. IFRS use is increasing globally and is seen as the benchmark for reporting by listed companies around the world. For many years the UK government has been a strong supporter of IFRS, and evidence suggests that adoption of IFRS since 2005 has brought economic benefits. As a major global financial centre, the UK will probably wish to continue to adhere to internationally accepted financial reporting standards. In addition, any company wishing to list on an EU-regulated market would have to use IFRS for its financial statements.

What happens in the EU once the UK has left may be of more concern for international reporting and the IASB's standard-setting processes. The UK has been a strong voice in favour of adoption of unmodified IFRS in the EU, and the dynamics of future EU discussions may change. This may impact on the development of future IFRS.

 ## Summary of key points

In order for high quality financial information to be available which will assist the efficient functioning of global capital markets, high quality systems to produce this are required. These have evolved over time, with different countries developing their own methods based on their economies, legal systems, professional bodies and culture, etc.

Any financial reporting system needs to determine the overall aim of financial statements and the methods of accounting used in their preparation. In the UK the overriding concept of 'true and fair' has been required for financial statements since the middle of the twentieth century. Following a number of prominent accounting scandals, financial reporting standards, which specified methods of accounting for certain transactions and events, began to be developed by the ASC, an independent body set up for the purpose by the existing professional accounting bodies. Other capital economies also developed their own GAAP.

However, in today's global economy with multinational companies, international markets and cross-border listings, a common language to be used in financial accounting is increasingly necessary to ensure that users have the information they require for the type of decisions they make. Thus, the use of a set of global financial reporting standards, which are accepted by markets in different jurisdictions, has become increasingly important.

The IASC, an independent international body, had already produced some accounting standards for international use, although they were not widely accepted. The main impetus for more international use came from a reorganisation of the IASC in 2000, which became the IASB, acceptance of the use of IASs from IOSCO in the early 2000s, and then the requirement from 1 January 2005 for all listed European companies to use them. Since the global financial crisis of 2008 the leaders of the G20 nations have called for the use of high quality international standards. Although there are issues with the change, more and more countries have now switched to the use of international financial reporting standards. The IASB and the US FASB were engaged in a project to converge their two sets of standards from 2002 to 2011, and the final standards which were subject to this have recently been completed. The final key step in achieving a truly global set of standards requires the US markets to accept their use for all US domestic companies—they currently do accept cross listings prepared under IAS/IFRS—but this may still be some years away. The implications of the recent 'Brexit' vote by the UK on its financial reporting systems will also unfold over the next few years.

International financial reporting standards are principles based, where sound professional judgement in their application is vital, with an underpinning conceptual basis, and there has been much discussion about the relative merits of such a system over rules based standards, which is what US GAAP has tended towards. Since 2012 the IASB has been working hard to complete another project started under IASB/FASB convergence—that of amending the *Conceptual Framework*—and this is nearing completion with the issue of an ED in 2015. The proposals update the existing *Framework*, add some new sections and clarify many concepts and principles.

 ## Further reading

DiPiazza, S. A., Flynn, T., McDonnell, D., Quigley, J. H., Samyn, F. and Turley, J. S. (2008) *Principles-based accounting standards*. Presented at the 4th Global Public Policy Symposium, January 2008. Available at: http://wwwgrantthornton.com/staticfiles/GTCom/files/services/Audit%20and%20assurance%20services/Assurancepublications/PBAS-White_Paper.pdf (accessed 30 September 2012). Why read? A discussion of the importance of principles based financial reporting standards from the leaders of the top accountancy firms.

International Accounting Standards Board (IASB) (2015) Exposure Draft *Conceptual Framework for Financial Reporting*. London: IASB.

International Financial Reporting Standards (IFRS) Foundation. (2016) *About Us*. Available at: http://www.ifrs.org/About-us/Pages/IFRS-Foundation-and-IASB.aspx (accessed 14 January 2016).

 ## Bibliography

AccountingWeb (2010) *Dissidents Call for 'Rethink' on IFRS*. Available at: http://www.accountingweb.co.uk/ (accessed 30 September 2012).

ASB (Accounting Standards Board) (2010) *The Future of Financial Reporting in the United Kingdom and Republic of Ireland*. London: ASB.

Bruce, R. (2008) *Discussing the Credit Crunch*. Interview with Sir David Tweedie and John Smith, IFRS Foundation Insight Q1/Q2 2008. Available at: http://www.ifrs.org/Archive/INSIGHT-journal/Q1-and-Q2-2008/Documents/INSIGHT_Q1Q208_lowres.pdf (accessed 30 September 2012).

Bruce, R. (2011) *Europe and IFRSs: Six Years On*. London: IFRS Foundation.

Bullen, H. G. and Crook, K. (2005) *A New Conceptual Framework Project*. Available at: http://www.fasb.org/ (accessed 30 September 2012).

Cooper, S. (2015) *Taking a Measured Approach*. Available at: http://www.ifrs.org/Investor-resources/Investor-perspectives-2/Documents/Investor-Perspectives_Taking-a-measured-approach.pdf (accessed 19 January 2016)

DiPiazza, S. A., Flynn, T., McDonnell, D., Quigley, J. H., Samyn, F. and Turley, J. S. (2008) *Principles-Based Accounting Standards*. Presented at the 4th Global Public Policy Symposium, January 2008. Available at: http://wwwgrantthornton.com/staticfiles/GTCom/files/services/Audit%20and%20assurance%20services/Assurancepublications/PBAS_White_Paper.pdf (accessed 30 September 2012).

EFRAG (European Financial Reporting Advisory Group) (2013a) *Getting a Better Framework—Prudence*. Brussels: EFRAG.

EFRAG (European Financial Reporting Advisory Group) (2013b) *Getting a Better Framework—The Role of a Conceptual Framework*. Brussels: EFRAG.

FASB (Financial Accounting Standards Board) (2010) Exposure Draft *Conceptual Framework for Financial Reporting: The Reporting Entity*. Norwalk, CT: FASB.

FRC (Financial Reporting Council (2014) *True and Fair*. London: FRC.

FRC (Financial Reporting Council) (2015a) *Overview of the Financial Reporting Framework*. London: FRC.

FRC (Financial Reporting Council) (2015b) *FRS 100 Application of Financial Reporting Requirements*. London: FRC.

FRC (Financial Reporting Council) (2015c) *FRS 102 The Financial Reporting Standard Applicable in the UK and Republic of Ireland*. London: FRC.

Flint, D. (1982) *A True and Fair View in Company Accounts*. Monograph. Edinburgh: ICAS.

G20 (2009) *Declaration on Strengthening the Financial System*. London: G20.

Hoffmann, L., QC and Arden, M. H. (1983) *Legal Opinion Obtained by Accounting Standards Committee of True and Fair View, with Particular Reference to the Role of Accounting Standards*. London: Accounting Standards Committee.

Hoogervorst, H. (2015a) *Historical Cost versus Fair Value Measurement: Les Extrêmes se Rejoignent*. Speech to the IFRS conference, June 2015. Paris.

Hoogervorst, H. (2015b) *IFRS: 2015 and Beyond*. Speech to the AICPA conference, December 2015. Washington D.C.

Hoogervorst, H. (2016) *Introductory Comments to the European Parliament*. Speech to the European Parliament, January 2016. Brussels.

IASB (International Accounting Standards Board) (1989) *Framework for the Preparation and Presentation of Financial Statements*. London: IASB.

IASB (International Accounting Standards Board) (2010a) *Conceptual Framework for Financial Reporting 2010*. Introduction and Chapters 1 and 3. London: IASB.

IASB (International Accounting Standards Board) (2010b) Exposure Draft *Measurement Uncertainty Analysis Disclosure for Fair Value Measurements*. London: IASB.

IASB (International Accounting Standards Board) (2010c) Comprehensive Project Summary, *Developing Common Fair Value Measurement and Disclosure Requirements in IFRS and US GAAP*. London: IASB.

IASB (International Accounting Standards Board) (2010d) *A Guide to the IFRS for SMEs*. London: IASB.

IASB (International Accounting Standards Board) (2011) IFRS 13 *Fair Value Measurement*. London: IASB.

IASB (International Accounting Standards Board) (2015a) Exposure Draft *Conceptual Framework for Financial Reporting*. London: IASB.

IASB (International Accounting Standards Board) (2015b) Exposure Draft Basis for Conclusions *Conceptual Framework for Financial Reporting*. London: IASB.

IASB (International Accounting Standards Board) (2015c) Exposure Draft Snapshot *Conceptual Framework for Financial Reporting*. London: IASB.

IASB (International Accounting Standards Board) and FASB (Financial Accounting Standards Board) (2002). *The Norwalk Agreement*. Norwalk, CT: IASB and FASB.

IASB (International Accounting Standards Board) and FASB (Financial Accounting Standards Board) (2006) *A Roadmap for Convergence between IFRSs and US GAAP—2006–2008, Memorandum of Understanding*. London: IASB and FASB.

ICAEW (Institute of Chartered Accountants in England and Wales) (2010) *Business Models in Accounting: The Theory of the Firm and Financial Reporting*. London: ICAEW.

ICAEW (Institute of Chartered Accountants in England and Wales) (2015) *Moving to IFRS Reporting: Seven Lessons Learned from the European Experience*. London: ICAEW.

ICAS (Institute of Chartered Accountants of Scotland) (2006) *Principles not Rules, A Question of Judgement*. Edinburgh: ICAS.

IFRS (International Financial Reporting Standards) Foundation (2007) *The EU two years after the adoption of IFRSs*. IFRS Foundation Insight Q4 2007. London: IFRS.

IFRS (International Financial Reporting Standards) Foundation. *About the IFRS Foundation and the IASB*. Available at: http://www.ifrs.org/ (accessed 14 January 2016).

IFRS (International Financial Reporting Standards) Foundation. *IFRS application around the world*. Available at http://www.ifrs.org/Use-around-the-world/Pages/Jurisdiction-profiles.aspx (accessed 14 January 2016)

IFRS (International Financial Reporting Standards) Foundation and IASB (International Accounting Standards Board) (2016) *Who We Are and What We Do*. London: IFRS and IASB.

Li, S. (2010) Does mandatory adoption of international financial reporting standards in the European Union reduce the cost of capital?, *The Accounting Review*, 85(2): 607–636.

Moore, M. QC (2008) *The True and Fair Requirement Revisited: Opinion*. London: Financial Reporting Council.

Nobes, C. (2015) The Conceptual Framework: A Work in Progress, *By All Accounts*, July 2015. London: ICAEW.

Pijper, T. (2009) IFRS in Europe—not yet an unqualified success, *International Accountant*, 45(Feb/Mar): 6–7.

Pitt, H. (2010) Following the road to IFRS convergence, *Compliance Week*. Available at: http://www.complianceweek.com (accessed 3 October 2012).

Sleigh-Johnson, N. (2016) Brexit: *The Implications for Financial Reporting in the UK*. Available at https://ion.icaew.com/talkaccountancy/b/weblog/posts/brexit-the-implications-for-financial-reporting-in-the-uk (accessed 2 August 2016)

Singleton-Green, B. (2011a) Who calls the tune?, *Accountancy*, 147(1410): 104.

Singleton-Green, B. (2011b) *Fair Value: Six Impossible Things*. Available at http://www.icaew.com/~/media/corporate/files/technical/financial%20reporting/ifrs/fair%20value%20six%20impossible%20things.ashx (accessed 21 January 2016)

Soderstrom, N. S. and Sun, K. J. (2007) IFRS adoption and accounting quality: a review, *European Accounting Review*, 16(4): 675–702.

Tweedie, D. (2011) *The Future of Financial Reporting, Convergence or Not?* Speech to the US Chamber of Commerce, March 2011. Washington, DC.

UK Companies Act 2006 (2006) Available at: http://www.legislation.gov.uk/ (accessed 16 January 2016).

Questions

● Quick test

1   High quality financial information is important to everyone. Of the various reasons that support this conclusion which ones seem most important to you and why?

2   Explain why neutrality is a key ingredient of high quality financial reporting. How might non-neutral financial information be harmful to investors? Can financial information be both neutral and prudent?

●● Develop your understanding

3   Should usefulness in decision-making be the predominant objective of financial reporting or does stewardship (accountability) still have a role?

4   How important are financial reporting standards in ensuring the quality of financial information in the marketplace? What other functions or roles must be carried out for the financial reporting system to be considered high quality?

5   Discuss how the International Accounting Standards Board's *Conceptual Framework* contributes to high quality corporate reporting.

6   Critically evaluate whether the 'substance over form' concept, inherent in international financial reporting standards, results in financial statements that are fairly stated.

●●● Take it further

7   The IASB's *Conceptual Framework* sets out the concepts that underlie the preparation and presentation of financial statements that external users are likely to rely on when making economic decisions about an entity. Also contained within the *Framework* are the definitions of, and recognition criteria for, the five elements related to the financial position and performance of the entity, plus explanations of the qualitative characteristics which make the information provided in the financial statements useful to users.

(a) Discuss the purpose and authoritative status of the *Framework*.

(b) Using examples of items in an entity's financial statements, critically evaluate why the definitions and recognition criteria of the five elements and the details of the qualitative characteristics are of particular importance to the users of an entity's financial statements.

8   Carduus plc is preparing its financial statements for the year ended 30 September 20X5 and a number of issues need to be resolved.

(1) Accounts receivable at 30 September 20X5 total £69 million. Included in this balance is a debt owed by Pardew Ltd for £3 million. Pardew Ltd is now in administration. Not included in the balance are a number of debts by Greek customers totalling £7 million that have been factored for cash by a financial institution (in other words, Carduus plc sold the debts to

the financial institution). The factoring contract gives the financial institution recourse to Carduus plc in the event of the customers defaulting.

(2) Carduus plc has entered into an arrangement to lease a fleet of delivery vehicles over a number of years through a leasing company which would have legal title to the vehicles. The purchase price of the vehicles would be £20 million, and the lease payments over the contract life total £24 million.

(3) Carduus plc has undertaken a programme of staff training and incurred costs of £4 million in the year in relation to this. The Human Resources Director has asked if these can be capitalised and depreciated over the next 5 years.

(4) Carduus plc is currently being sued by a customer for the supply of faulty products in the year ended 30 September 20X5. The customer is claiming damages of between £5 million and £7 million. Carduus is disputing the claim and is seeking legal advice.

(5) Carduus plc has acquired a company with brand names valued at £75 million. The brand manager for Carduus plc states that this now brings the company's total brand values up to £500 million, and that this amount should be reflected in the statement of financial position. A hostile take-over bid for Carduus plc has been rumoured and the inclusion of this amount would be seen as a deterrent to a low priced bid.

(6) In emergency discussions at Carduus plc's board meeting in response to the take-over rumours, it was suggested that the statement of financial position undervalued the company and the market price of shares did not fully reflect this. This was due partly to the brands discussed above but also because of other factors such as employee expertise, customer loyalty and market position and that this goodwill asset should be valued and included in the financial statements.

Required:

Using the elements' definitions and recognition criteria set out in the IASB's *Conceptual Framework*, discuss how each of the above issues impact on the financial statements of Carduus plc. Where appropriate include in your answer the monetary values which would be accounted for.

9 Discuss whether the IASB's proposals for measurement in the 2015 Exposure Draft of its *Conceptual Framework for Financial Reporting* are justified in relation to relevance, faithful representation and comparability.

10 Haddon plc needs advice on how to value an asset and liability in accordance with IFRS 13 *Fair Value Measurement*. The company has an asset that is traded in different markets and Haddon currently only buys and sells the asset in the African market. Data relating to the asset are set out below:

Year to 31 March 20X4	North American market	European market	African market
Volume of market—units	4 million	2 million	1 million
Price	£19	£16	£22
Costs of entering the market	£2	£2	£3
Transaction costs	£1	£2	£2

Additionally, Haddon plc acquired an entity on 31 March 20X4 and is required to fair value a decommissioning liability. The entity has to decommission a mine at the end of its useful life, which is in three years' time. If Haddon plc were allowed to transfer the liability to another market participant, then the following data would be used:

Input	Amount
Labour and material cost	£2 million
Overhead	30% of labour and material cost
Third party mark-up—industry average	20%
Annual inflation rate	5%
Risk adjustment—uncertainty relating to cash flows	6%

Haddon plc's internal interest rate adjusted for risk is 6%.

Required:

Discuss, with relevant computations, how Haddon plc should fair value the above asset and liability under IFRS 13.

 Visit the Online Resource Centre for solutions to all these end of chapter questions plus visual walkthrough solutions. You can test your understanding with extra questions and answers, explore additional case studies based on real companies, take a guided tour through a company report and much more. Go to the Online Resource Centre at **www.oxfordtextbooks.co.uk/orc/maynard2e/**

3

Corporate governance, sustainability and ethics

➤ Introduction

Today, high quality financial information is more than just relevant and faithfully representational financial statements which are, principally, prepared for shareholders and lenders. A high quality financial reporting system needs to be transparent, to provide information about how the financial results and position have been achieved, and to enable the assessment of the long-term success of the business. Many other stakeholders, such as customers, suppliers and the public, as well as the shareholders and lenders, are increasingly interested in this information; therefore, issues such as who runs the company, how it is run and governed, what the company's environmental and social policies are, what steps the company is able to take to mitigate against changes in external factors, and how shareholders are involved in the company, need to be explained. This can be seen in a listed company's annual report, where approximately half of the report is devoted to narrative information, some of which explains the financial data, but much of which addresses the above issues of concern to this wider stakeholder group.

This chapter considers in further depth why this information is provided, the regulation, if any, that governs the information, and the principles that underpin it.

★ Learning objectives

After studying this chapter you will be able to:

- understand the wider issues that the provision of high quality financial information encompasses
- understand what corporate governance is, its significance, and the issues the subject covers
- explain the five key areas of corporate governance included in the Financial Reporting Council's (FRC) *UK Corporate Governance Code 2014*
- explain the reporting requirements with regard to corporate governance
- understand the increasing significance of corporate sustainability issues for companies and their stakeholders
- explain what, how and why corporate sustainability issues may be reported
- understand how ethical behaviour is integral to the financial reporting chain.

✔ Key issues checklist

- ❑ Definitions of, and issues covered by, corporate governance.
- ❑ Stewardship and agency theories.
- ❑ The consequences of poor corporate governance.
- ❑ The UK's approach to regulation of corporate governance—principles based on 'comply or explain'.
- ❑ The development of the FRC's *UK Corporate Governance Code 2014*.
- ❑ The board of directors and regulation that governs their actions.
- ❑ The five key areas of corporate governance included in the *UK Corporate Governance Code*—leadership, effectiveness, accountability, remuneration and relations with shareholders.
- ❑ The external audit and the relationship of the auditor to the audit committee.
- ❑ The reporting requirements with regard to corporate governance.
- ❑ The issues corporate sustainability encompasses, including environmental and social.
- ❑ The increasing significance of these issues for companies and their stakeholders.
- ❑ How corporate sustainability may be reported.
- ❑ Why ethical behaviour is important.
- ❑ Ethics in business—the link from the individual to the organisation.
- ❑ Ethics in professional accountancy bodies.

3.1 A wider financial reporting system

As discussed in Chapter 2, investors in and lenders to listed companies require high quality financial information on which to base their decisions and in which they can have confidence. Financial reporting systems in the UK therefore ensure that financial statements are prepared according to companies legislation and international financial reporting standards (IFRS) and are audited by a regulated firm of professional accountants in accordance with audit regulation. However, other issues, in addition to financial matters, are becoming increasingly important for investors, for example how a company is managed and run, whether its behaviour is ethical, the long-term sustainability of the business, and its attitude to the environment and local communities. Thus, reporting systems should be thought of in a wider sense as they need to provide information that encompasses these matters. As for financial statements, users need to have confidence in this information; thus, in the UK the result is the development of other regulation concerned with corporate governance and social responsibility matters.

Figure 3.1 represents the relationships of the interested parties in companies and the reports they produce.

If a typical UK listed company's annual report is obtained, the user will find that it contains, on average, well over 100 pages, with approximately half (usually the front half) being narrative reports. These might include the following:

● chairman's/chief executive's statement

● directors' report

● strategic report

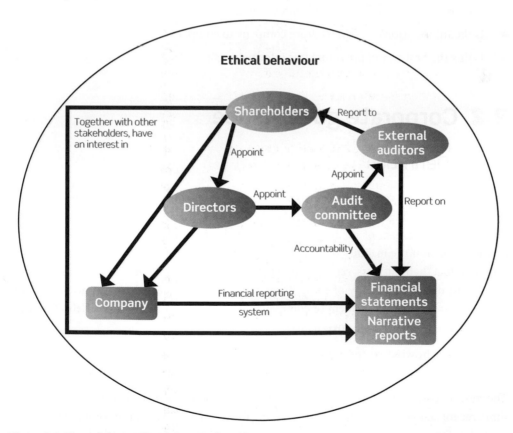

Figure 3.1 Financial reporting: interested parties

- directors' remuneration report
- statement of corporate governance
- statement of corporate responsibility.

(Note: Chapter 4 discusses the format and content of the actual financial statements contained in the second half of an annual report.)

Some of these narrative reports provide an analysis of the numbers in the financial statements; others deal with corporate governance and social and environmental issues—all have grown in length over the past two decades. Some of the narrative reports are required by statute; others from listing requirements; others contain information provided voluntarily. They will vary in style and approach from company to company, but one key feature is that most of this information is not audited, in other words there is no independent assurance that the information is 'true and fair'. (The external auditor of the financial statements is only required to ensure that the information does not conflict with the financial statements.)

All of this therefore raises a number of questions:

- Do these reports provide the information that users increasingly want?
- What, if any, regulations govern the information contained in these reports?
- Can users have confidence in this information?
- Is the information comparable from company to company?
- Is this the best way of providing this information?

3.2 Corporate governance

3.2.1 Definition

The significance of corporate governance has grown enormously over the last 30 years, driven mainly by high-profile corporate collapses and, more recently, the financial crisis. The continuous stream of media reports and articles have highlighted many issues, such as regulation and the inability of regulators to control how banks and other large corporations conduct their business, remuneration levels, risk, and the link between risk and reward, fraud, and dishonesty. Many of these issues stem from a perceived lack of accountability of, and trust in, the management of companies and can be summarised in a definition that encapsulates what corporate governance is about:

> The system by which companies are directed and controlled.
>
> *(Cadbury, 1992)*

The roots of corporate governance are in stewardship and the principal–agent problem, with more recent stakeholder theories underpinning the role and behaviour of companies in society today. Stewardship describes the role the management of a company (the board of directors) is delegated by the investors (the shareholders). The directors are accountable to the investors and are expected to provide them with open and honest reports about the direction in which the company is being taken, and whether they are discharging their duties properly. The assumption is that the directors are acting in the best interest of the shareholders, which traditionally is considered the maximisation of wealth.

However, this separation of ownership and control can result in the goals of the shareholders (the principal) and the directors (the agent) conflicting. The principal–agent problem assumes that the directors will pursue their own personal objectives, for example the maximisation of their own remuneration or short-term profits, rather than the long-term wealth of the company and its shareholders. To be able to do this, the directors can rely on the fact that they have information that is not available to shareholders, in other words, information asymmetry.

The relationship between the shareholders and directors is therefore key in corporate governance, as seen in updated definitions of the purpose of corporate governance following recent changes to regulation in this area:

> The role of corporate governance is to protect and advance the interests of shareholders through setting the strategic direction of a company and appointing and monitoring capable management to achieve this.
>
> *(Walker Review, 2009)*

> The purpose of corporate governance is to facilitate effective, entrepreneurial and prudent management that can deliver the long-term success of the company.
>
> *(FRC, 2014)*

3.2.2 The role of reporting in corporate governance

Good corporate governance therefore requires that shareholders have trust in the directors. This will come from the directors being properly accountable to the shareholders, in other words providing an account of how they have fulfilled their responsibilities so that the shareholders can evaluate their performance. Financial reporting systems that produce high quality financial statements are part of this system of accountability, but more information is needed than just the numbers. From the various definitions given in the previous section, it can be seen that corporate governance requires details of both how shareholders' wealth has been, and will be, created and how it is, and will be, protected:

> Through reporting and auditing, chartered accountants support transparency and the flow of reliable information between management, boards, shareholders, regulators and other stakeholders.
>
> *(ICAEW, 2007)*

3.2.3 The consequences of ineffective corporate governance

The past 30 years have seen a significant number of high-profile corporate collapses, including Maxwell (1991, UK), Barings Bank (1995, UK), Enron (2001, USA), Parmalat (2003, Italy) and Lehman Brothers (2008, USA). While these cannot be attributed to single issues, all exhibit some aspect of corporate governance failure. Of course, the consequences of these collapses do not just impact the company, its investors and employees—all stakeholders (including those in the supply chain, pensioners and customers) have suffered losses. Many of the more recent collapses have had worldwide implications.

Details of two of these cases are provided to illustrate their lack of effective corporate governance.

Financial reporting in practice 3.1 — Maxwell (1991, UK)

Robert Maxwell headed up a complex corporate media empire which was based around two key UK public companies: Maxwell Communication Corporation and Mirror Group Newspapers. The empire was built up through the 1970s through lavish spending on media companies and high levels of borrowings. In November 1991 Robert Maxwell's body was found floating in the Atlantic Ocean near his luxury yacht—a verdict of 'accidental drowning' was delivered. The loss of a key individual involved in running the companies made investors and lenders nervous and once the banks called in their loans, it was discovered that £272 million had been stolen from the two public companies' pension funds to prop up the business empire. As a result, the corporate empire collapsed, losing the shareholders an estimated £1 billion. Maxwell's sons, who held key positions in various companies, ended up in court, but the case against them collapsed through technical complexities.

Subsequently, the corporate governance issues were identified as follows:

- There was lack of segregation of positions of power—Maxwell (allegedly a bully) was both Chief Executive Officer (CEO) and Chairman.
- The non-executive directors did not perform a proper independent function.
- The pension fund trustees failed to examine Maxwell's financial affairs in sufficient detail.
- The auditors did not appear to observe the transfers of funds from the pension funds to the companies.
- Many years previously, in 1969, the then Department for Trade and Industry had considered that Maxwell was 'not to be a person who can be relied upon to exercise proper stewardship of a publicly quoted company', yet he remained in his position.

Financial reporting in practice 3.2 — Enron (2001, USA)

Enron was a Houston-based energy company, founded by Kenneth Lay, who became both CEO and Chairman. The company started as an oil and gas exploration business, but ended up as the world's largest energy trading company. By the time of its demise, it was involved predominantly in trading financial derivatives and energy contacts. The company exhibited phenomenal success and growth—in 1997 it reported sales of $4 billion; by 2000 sales had grown to more than $100 billion. By February 2001 its stock market value was $60 billion, which made it the seventh largest US company at the time. Enron pursued aggressive (and what were subsequently found to be fraudulent) earnings recognition policies, including **forward contracts**, financial derivatives, etc., and used US rules based financial reporting standards to avoid accounting for special-purpose entities, in which it had invested, to hide its debt and losses.

Once the energy markets fell, Enron's losses eventually caught up with the company, and it had to report some large write-offs. Then in August 2001 the chief operating officer, Jeff Skilling, resigned unexpectedly. In response to these events the financial markets started to get nervous and sell shares. Enron's share price fell and fell and its credit rating was soon cut to 'junk bond' status. Numerous class action lawsuits were filed against the company, whilst the company was also accused of insider trading. Enron finally filed for Chapter 11 bankruptcy in December 2001.

The collapse of Enron has had enormous repercussions globally, not least in that it triggered the demise of one of the world's largest professional accountancy firms, Arthur Anderson, which was the company's auditor. The USA's Sarbanes–Oxley Act, which governs all manner of internal and external financial accounting and reporting issues, was also a direct result of the scandal. The causes were numerous, but the following can be said to be related to corporate governance:

- There was unfettered power in the hands of the CEO—who was also the Chairman (and who, by some accounts, was a 'cult leader').
- The board of directors were shown to be of poor moral character.
- The non-executive directors did not detect the fraudulent activities.
- There were conflicts of interest involving members of the internal audit committee, which did not perform its functions of internal control and of checking the external auditing function properly.
- The external auditors' independence was compromised by the fact that they earned $millions from non-audit services.

The more recent credit crisis can also be considered to have its roots in poor corporate governance, with a lack of effective control mechanisms to curb excessive risk-taking by financial institutions. Remuneration schemes for bankers, on which there is much focus, are accused of encouraging short-termism, and failing to manage the interconnection between business risk and incentives. Boards of directors, non-executive directors and supervisory bodies have also been accused of comprehending neither the nature nor scale of the risks, and weaknesses have been identified in the reporting of risk. (There are parallels here between the credit crisis and the collapse of Barings Bank in the UK in 1995, when a 'rogue trader' was found to be responsible for bringing down the bank as a result of the risky trading in which he was involved, but which was not questioned by his superiors until it was too late.)

3.2.4 The UK's approach to corporate governance

Principally, the UK's approach to corporate governance has been reactionary, with the approach of the government or other authoritative bodies being to commission reports into corporate collapses or other prominent financial scandals, and then to draft or redraft regulation in the area. In 1992 the Cadbury Committee was set up by the FRC, the London Stock Exchange and the accountancy profession to 'help raise the standards of corporate governance in financial reporting and auditing by setting out clearly the responsibilities of those involved'. Since then there have been numerous reviews and reports into various corporate governance issues. The FRC's *UK Corporate Governance Code*, first issued in 2006, has pulled many of these together into one Code and has itself undergone a number of revisions subsequently.

A summary of the various reports is given in Table 3.1.

Table 3.1 Corporate governance reports in the UK since 1992

Date	Review/report	Focus of review
1992	Cadbury	Comprehensive: Operation of the main board of directors Audit and remuneration subcommittees Non-executive directors Auditing and the relationship with the external auditor Shareholder relations
1995	Greenbury	Directors' remuneration
1998	Hampel	Implementation of Cadbury and Greenbury Approach to corporate governance should be to *contribute* to business prosperity
1998	Combined Code	Amalgamated Cadbury, Greenbury and Hampel
1999	Turnbull	Internal controls (updated in 2005)
2003	Higgs	Non-executive directors
2003	Tyson	Recruitment and development of non-executive directors
2003	Smith	The audit committee (updated in 2008)
2004	A practical guide	Implementation of corporate governance
2006, 2008 and 2009	Combined Code	Revisions and updates
2009	Turner	Causes of global financial crisis Regulation and supervisory approaches Bankers' remuneration and risk-taking
2009	Walker	Banking sector Risk management Remuneration incentives Effectiveness of the board of directors—skills and expertise, performance of subcommittees Role of institutional shareholders. Turnbull and Walker reviews combined in FRC Guidance on Risk Management, Internal Control and Related Financial and Business Reporting (2014)
2010	UK Corporate Governance Code	Revision of Combined Code, incorporating Walker recommendations. Revised in 2012 and 2014
2010	UK Stewardship Code	Engagement between companies and institutional investors. Revised in 2012
2011	Davies	Gender diversity on boards of directors
2012	Sharman	Going concern and liquidity risks

The approach to corporate governance in all these reports has maintained the overriding one set out by Cadbury—that this should be principles based rather than rules based, with the reporting being based on a 'comply or explain' approach. The Financial Conduct Authority (FCA) listing rules require companies to include a statement on whether, and how, they have, complied with the latest set of corporate governance regulations or to explain why they have not complied. The *UK Corporate Governance Code* stresses that good corporate governance practices should be ingrained in businesses as an aspect of their codes of ethics. Detailed regulation may unnecessarily constrain business practice and innovation, and could lead to a 'tick-box' mentality. Businesses should pay more attention to the spirit of the code rather than its letter.

3.3 The UK Corporate Governance Code 2014

The *UK Corporate Governance Code* sets out corporate governance principles and recommendations (described as provisions). The context of the Code has not been changed from Cadbury:

> Corporate governance is the system by which companies are directed and controlled. Boards of directors are responsible for the governance of their companies. The shareholders' role in governance is to appoint the directors and the auditors and to satisfy themselves that an appropriate governance structure is in place. The responsibilities of the board include setting the company's strategic aims, providing the leadership to put them into effect, supervising the management of the business and reporting to shareholders on their stewardship. The board's actions are subject to laws, regulations and the shareholders in general meeting.
>
> *(FRC, 2014a)*

The five areas dealt with by the Code are:

A Leadership

B Effectiveness

C Accountability

D Remuneration

E Relations with shareholders.

3.3.1 The board of directors

Sections A and B deal with the board of directors, considered the 'apex of the internal control system' (Jensen, 1993). Directors are appointed by the shareholders and are therefore accountable to them (as discussed in section 3.2.1), but corporate governance principles require that they are responsible for the long-term success of the company, which will involve relations with all stakeholders. This principle ties in with directors' duties, as specified in the Companies Act 2006, section 172. The implication here is that directors' duties are no longer just about acting in the best interests of the company, but that they should act for the good of society at large—good corporate governance as part of a wider corporate social responsibility:

> Section 172: Duty to promote the success of the company
>
> 1 A director of a company must act in the way he considers, in good faith, would be most likely to promote the success of the company for the benefit of its members as a whole, and in doing so have regard (amongst other matters) to:
>
>   (a) the likely consequences of any decision in the long term,
>
>   (b) the interests of the company's employees,
>
>   (c) the need to foster the company's business relationships with suppliers, customers and others,
>
>   (d) the impact of the company's operations on the community and the environment,
>
>   (e) the desirability of the company maintaining a reputation for high standards of business conduct, and
>
>   (f) the need to act fairly as between members of the company.
>
> *(Companies Act, 2006, s. 172)*

The *UK Corporate Governance Code* attempts to address the classic disciplinary problem of constraining versus enabling as it relates to a board of directors, in other words how they are prevented from pursuing undesirable actions while, at the same time, given the appropriate encouragement to act productively. Thus, the Code deals with structural issues, how the board is managed and lead, how appointments are made and how it should operate. The provisions are classified as either leadership issues or effectiveness issues.

3.3.2 Leadership

The main principles of the Code are as follows:

- Every company should be headed by an effective board which is collectively responsible for the long-term success of the company.

- There should be a clear division of responsibilities at the head of the company between the running of the board and the executive responsibility for the running of the company's business. No one individual should have unfettered powers of decision.

- The chairman is responsible for leadership of the board and ensuring its effectiveness on all aspects of its role.

- As part of their role as members of a unitary board, non-executive directors should constructively challenge and help develop proposals on strategy.

(FRC, 2014a)

The chairman, required to be independent of the company on appointment (for example, has not been employed by the company recently, or had recent business relationships with the company), is considered to have an absolutely crucial role in ensuring good corporate governance. The chairman and CEO, who is responsible for the actual running of the company's operations, are required to be different people, to avoid the problems of Maxwell and Enron, and the chief executive should not move to the role of chairman. This is different from the typical US model, where there is still no such required separation of duties, despite Enron.

The structure of the board of directors of a typical UK company is unitary, with the **non-executive directors** being part of this main board, rather than comprising a second board. **Executive directors** are those whose role is to run the company on a day-to-day basis. Non-executive directors are engaged by the company to act in an advisory capacity. Cadbury first recommended that there should be at least three non-executive directors on a board and set out their role. The Higgs Report in 2003 (following the Enron and Parmalat scandals) raised the prominence of this role by making what were considered at the time quite radical proposals, but which are now incorporated into the *UK Corporate Governance Code*. The Code requires that for all FTSE 350 companies at least half the board should comprise independent non-executives.

The position of a non-executive director is tricky. There is inherent conflict in that the intention is for them to both contribute expertise, but, at the same time, be scrutinising the performance of the executive directors. Higgs recommended that they be remunerated adequately for their work. This, together with the fact that many non-executive directors are already executive directors of other companies, leads to the perception that their independence may be compromised. Research into whether, and how, non-executives have contributed to good corporate governance is mixed, with some showing that they act as effective monitors of management, with share prices reacting positively to their appointment, while other research has found a negative effect on financial performance. In spite of this they are generally considered a pillar of good corporate governance.

3.3.3 Effectiveness

The main principles of the Code are as follows:

- The board and its committees should have the appropriate balance of skills, experience, independence and knowledge of the company to enable them to discharge their respective duties and responsibilities effectively.

- There should be a formal, rigorous and transparent procedure for the appointment of new directors to the board.

- All directors should be able to allocate sufficient time to the company to discharge their responsibilities effectively.

- All directors should receive induction on joining the board and should regularly update and refresh their skills and knowledge.

- The board should be supplied in a timely manner with information in a form and of a quality appropriate to enable it to discharge its duties.

- The board should undertake a formal and rigorous annual evaluation of its own performance and that of its committees and individual directors.
- All directors should be submitted for re-election at regular intervals, subject to continued satisfactory performance.

(FRC, 2014a)

This section of the Code deals with the composition of the board, elections and re-elections to the board, and the development of the board as a body to take the company forward. A board should be of appropriate size so that it can discharge its duties properly; a balance has to be struck between one large enough to include all necessary expertise, but one that is not too large so that decision-making becomes cumbersome. One of the issues identified as a result of the financial crisis was that boards were insufficiently diverse, with women making up only 12.5 per cent of board members of FTSE 100 boards in 2010:

> Gender diversity strengthens board effectiveness by reducing the risk of 'groupthink', making fuller use of the talent pool …

(Baroness Hogg, Chair of FRC, 2011)

The 2012 Davies Report, *Women on Boards*, recommended a minimum target of 25 per cent female representation on FTSE 100 company boards by 2015. Although some companies had reached this target, not all have, and other FTSE 350 companies have only made progress towards it. However, the majority of female appointments have been to non-executive positions. The aim is to continue the increase to 33 per cent representation by 2020, with more women being appointed to executive or senior non-executive roles.

A nominations committee, comprising mainly independent non-executive directors, is required to lead the process for board appointments, and there should be appropriate procedures in place and provision of support to ensure both new and existing directors are properly introduced to, and receive up-to-date information about, the company and their role, and can refresh their skills. All directors of FTSE 350 companies are now subject to annual election by shareholders, which replaced a system where only some of the directors were re-elected each year by rotation. Annual performance evaluations should be conducted by an external facilitator at least once every three years.

The board of directors delegates some of its work to a number of standard committees, whose members are mainly non-executive directors. A listed company will typically have an audit committee, a remuneration committee and a nominations committee.

The chairman is encouraged to comment on the effectiveness of the board in his/her report, which is usually contained in the company's annual report.

3.3.4 Accountability

Accountability encompasses financial and business reporting, as well as risk management, internal control and audit-related matters. The main principles of the Code are as follows:

- The board should present a fair, balanced and understandable assessment of the company's position and prospects.

- The board is responsible for determining the nature and extent of the principal risks it is willing to take in achieving its strategic objectives. The board should maintain sound risk management and internal control systems.

- The board should establish formal and transparent arrangements for considering how they should apply the corporate reporting, risk management and internal control principles and for maintaining an appropriate relationship with the company's auditors.

(FRC, 2014a)

The requirement for a 'fair, balanced and understandable assessment of the company's position' is generally achieved by the statutory strategic report, whose aim is to ensure investors receive a complete and meaningful picture of its business model, strategy, development, performance and position. All companies, except those classified as small, have to include this strategic report in the company's annual report, the contents of which are set out by Companies Act 2006 (Strategic Report and Directors' Report) Regulations 2013, as follows:

(1) The purpose of the strategic report is to inform members of the company and help them assess how the directors have performed their duty under section 172 (duty to promote the success of the company).

(2) The strategic report must contain—

  (a) a fair review of the company's business, and

  (b) a description of the principal risks and uncertainties facing the company.

(3) The review required is a balanced and comprehensive analysis of—

  (a) the development and performance of the company's business during the financial year, and

  (b) the position of the company's business at the end of that year, consistent with the size and complexity of the business.

(4) The review must, to the extent necessary for an understanding of the development, performance or position of the company's business, include—

  (a) analysis using financial key performance indicators, and

  (b) where appropriate, analysis using other key performance indicators, including information relating to environmental matters and employee matters.

(5) In subsection (4), "key performance indicators" means factors by reference to which the development, performance or position of the company's business can be measured effectively.

(6) Where a company qualifies as medium-sized in relation to a financial year (see sections 465 to 467), the review for the year need not comply with the requirements of subsection (4) so far as they relate to non-financial information.

(7) In the case of a quoted company the strategic report must, to the extent necessary for an understanding of the development, performance or position of the company's business, include—

  (a) the main trends and factors likely to affect the future development, performance and position of the company's business, and

  (b) information about—

    (i) environmental matters (including the impact of the company's business on the environment),

    (ii)   the company's employees, and

    (iii) social, community and human rights issues, including information about any policies of the company in relation to those matters and the effectiveness of those policies.

If the report does not contain information of each kind mentioned in paragraphs (b)(i), (ii) and (iii), it must state which of those kinds of information it does not contain.

(8)   In the case of a quoted company the strategic report must include—

   (a)   a description of the company's strategy,

   (b)   a description of the company's business model,

   (c)   a breakdown showing at the end of the financial year—

    (i)   the number of persons of each sex who were directors of the company;

    (ii)   the number of persons of each sex who were senior managers of the company (other than persons falling within sub-paragraph (i)); and

    (iii) the number of persons of each sex who were employees of the company.

(9)   In subsection (8), "senior manager" means a person who—

   (a)   has responsibility for planning, directing or controlling the activities of the company, or a strategically significant part of the company, and

   (b)   is an employee of the company.

(10) In relation to a group strategic report—

   (a)   the reference to the company in subsection (8)(c)(i) is to the **parent** company; and

   (b)   the breakdown required by subsection (8)(c)(ii) must include the number of persons of each sex who were the directors of the undertakings included in the consolidation.

(11) The strategic report may also contain such of the matters otherwise required by regulations made under section 416(4) to be disclosed in the directors' report as the directors consider are of strategic importance to the company.

(12) The report must, where appropriate, include references to, and additional explanations of, amounts included in the company's annual accounts.

(13) Subject to paragraph (10), in relation to a group strategic report this section has effect as if the references to the company were references to the undertakings included in the consolidation.

(14) Nothing in this section requires the disclosure of information about impending developments or matters in the course of negotiation if the disclosure would, in the opinion of the directors, be seriously prejudicial to the interests of the company.

(Companies Act 2006, (Strategic Report and Directors' Report) Regulations 2013)

Alongside these requirements the FRC has issued guidance on the preparation of the strategic report, which should serve as best practice for companies to 'tell their story'. The emphasis of both the Companies Act legislation and the FRC guidance, however, is on the financial year that has passed, rather than providing an assessment of the company's 'future prospects', as also required by the Code.

3.3.5 Accountability: risk

At the time of the financial crisis many criticisms focused on the banks' poor reporting of the risks to which they were exposed, despite this being a requirement of the then required business review, which was the predecessor of the strategic report. Critics claimed that risks detailed in annual reports were often generic risks of merely being in business rather than an explanation of the factors that may affect the ability of the particular company to achieve its strategic objectives, or how the company manages its exposure to the risks it faces. Following the financial crisis, the UK's Department for Business, Innovation and Skills (BIS) consulted widely on the future of narrative reporting, including the reporting of risk.

Walker's 2009 report also addressed risk and many of his recommendations have been incorporated in the *UK Corporate Governance Code*. In addition Lord Sharman's 2012 review into going concern and liquidity risks produced a number of recommendations. The FRC pulled these reviews together with previous guidance issued in this area, and in 2014 produced an overall guide to risk management and internal control and their relationship to financial and business reporting. The emphasis in the reporting of risk is on 'what keeps the executives awake at night', with this approach being considered to deliver a more rigorous review of risk. The provisions recommend that discussion of risk and uncertainties should be linked to disclosures of the company's 'business model', and explain how they are managed or mitigated. Risk here encompasses more than financial risk—for example it could include strategic risk, technological risk, reputational risk, cyber security, theft of intellectual property, supply chain risk and risk from outsourcing.

Some financial reporting standards also have requirements for disclosures of the risks relating to the particular issue they deal with—for example, IAS 1 has requirements for a statement on going concern, as discussed in Chapter 4, and the IFRS 9 requirements for disclosures on the risks associated with financial instruments are fairly extensive, as discussed in Chapter 14. Non-financial business risks are also considered part of the sustainability agenda and will probably be included in a sustainability report (this is discussed in section 3.5). Thus risk reporting can be scattered in various places in an annual report, which can be seen as problematic for users who wish to understand the overall risks a company faces.

Financial reporting in practice 3.3 | Marks and Spencer plc, 2015

The high street retailer M&S plc incorporates a discussion of risk management within the strategic report in its 2015 annual report. Extracts from the discussion are reproduced here.

The company starts by explaining its approach to risk management and how it identifies its principal areas of risk:

Risk management

We believe that effective risk management is critical to the achievement of our strategic objectives' and the long-term sustainable growth of our business.

(continued)

(continued)

Approach to risk management

The Board has overall accountability for ensuring that risk is effectively managed across the Group and, on behalf of the Board, the Audit Committee reviews the effectiveness of the Group Risk Process. Each business area is responsible for identifying, assessing and managing the risks in their respective area.

Risks are identified and assessed by all business areas half-yearly and are measured against a defined set of criteria, considering likelihood of occurrence and potential impact to the Group. The Group Risk function facilitates a risk identification and assessment exercise with the Executive Board members. This information is combined to form a consolidated view of risk. The top risks (based on likelihood and impact) form our Group Risk Profile, which is reported to the Executive Board for review and challenge, ahead of final review and approval by the Group Board.

To ensure that our risk process drives continuous improvement across the business, the Executive Board monitors the ongoing status and progress of key action plans against each risk quarterly.

Key areas of focus

We continue to drive improvements to our risk management process and the quality of risk information generated, whilst at the same time maintaining a simple and practical approach. This year we have placed significant focus on developing our approach to risk appetite.

The objective of our risk management approach is to identify and assess all significant risks to the achievement of our strategic objectives. Risk appetite is an important consideration in strategic decisions made by the Board. It is an expression of the types and amount of risk we are willing to take or accept to achieve our plan and should support the definition of mitigating activities required to manage risk likelihood and impact to within acceptable levels. By defining our risk appetite we aim to support consistent, risk-informed decision-making across the Group.

This year we have taken steps to strengthen our approach to risk appetite, starting with the definition of draft, Group-level risk appetite statements. The purpose of these is to articulate the Board's desired risk-taking approach to the achievement of our strategic objectives, in the context of managing our principal risks. During the 2015/16 financial year we will further develop our approach to risk appetite, refining these statements and integrating them with our wider risk management processes.

These statements are accompanied by diagrammatic representations of risk likelihood versus impact, and what the company calls its risk radar, which identifies a number of key risk areas. These are described further together with the company's mitigating activities. M&S plc identifies the following principal risks and uncertainties:

Principal risks and uncertainties

As with any business, we face risks and uncertainties on a daily basis. It is the effective management of these that places us in a better position to be able to achieve our strategic objectives and to embrace opportunities as they arise.

Overleaf are details of our principal risks and uncertainties and the mitigating activities in place to address them. It is recognised that the Group is exposed to risks wider than those listed. However, we have disclosed those we believe are likely to have the greatest impact on our business at this moment in time and those that have been the subject of debate at recent Board or Audit Committee meetings.

To achieve a holistic view of the risks facing our business, both now and in the future, we consider those that are:

- External to our business;
- Core to our day-to-day operation;

- Related to business change activity; and
- Those that could emerge in the future.

The 'risk radar' below maps our principal risks against these categories. This tool is also used to facilitate wider Executive and Board level discussions on risk.

Brand and reputation

1 GM customer engagement

2 Food safety and integrity

3 Food competition

Day-to-day operation

4 GM margin

5 Information security

6 IT change

Selling channels

7 M&S.com business resilience

8 International expansion

People and change

9 Our people

10 Staff retention

11 Programme and workstream management

12 GM supply chain and logistics network

As an illustration of the information provided on mitigation, these are the details given on the principal risk of GM customer engagement:

Risk	Description	Mitigating activities
GM CUSTOMER ENGAGEMENT Continued loss of engagement with our customer	As we strengthen our brand recognition and reassert our GM quality and style credentials, it is important that we understand and address our customers' needs in an increasingly competitive market.	• Regular engagement with customers through data gathered by our Customer Insight Unit and focus groups. • Updated brand positioning and marketing approach with greater emphasis on product. • Continued focus on product quality and style, including adherence to our Clothing Quality Charter. • Continual updates to the M&S.com website to enhance the online customer shopping experience. • Ongoing improvements to store environment, addressing specific customer feedback. • Targeted marketing and promotional activity using customer loyalty data.

3.3.6 Accountability: internal controls

Although internal controls are often thought of in terms of financial controls, they serve a wider purpose—that of safeguarding shareholder value, as defined in Turnbull's updated 2005 report:

> Internal control facilitates the effectiveness and efficiency of operations, helps ensure the reliability of internal and external reporting and assists compliance with laws and regulations.
>
> *(FRC, 2005)*

Internal control therefore encompasses a company's policies, culture, organisation, behaviours, processes and systems, and should be embedded in all of these, and be able to respond to evolving business risks.

Financial controls are, of course, an important part of this, and incorporate policies and procedures to ensure:

- the safeguarding of assets
- the prevention and detection of fraud and error
- the accuracy and completeness of the accounting records
- the timely preparation of reliable financial information.

They include approval procedures, segregation of duties, the granting of appropriate authority for access to assets and records, checks on accuracy, the reviewing of control accounts and trial balances, and reconciliations.

The maintenance of a sound system of internal controls should assist the management of risk. The board of directors, through its audit committee, is required to ensure that there are effective internal controls in place. Many corporate collapses can be attributed in part to failures of internal controls.

3.3.7 Accountability: the audit committee

One of the main board's subcommittees, the audit committee has been identified as 'a cornerstone of effective corporate governance' (Spira, 2006). It was recommended by Cadbury in 1992 and widely adopted by UK companies. Audit committees have an extremely important and wide remit of overseeing the integrity of a company's financial affairs, encompassing financial reporting, risk management, internal controls and monitoring the audit and the independence of the auditors.

The *UK Corporate Governance Code* requires the composition of the committee to comprise at least three independent non-executive directors, at least one of whom has recent and relevant financial experience; for example, it is desirable they have a professional accountancy qualification. The composition of the committee has been shown to be critical to the reliability of financial reporting systems—the more independent non-executive directors, the less the likelihood of financial fraud or earnings management. However, this is recognised as creating some practical problems, as the pool of available, suitably qualified non-executives, who can commit sufficient time, is relatively small.

The work of the audit committee is required to be explained in a company's annual report.

3.3.8 Accountability: the audit

The audit committee has prime responsibility for monitoring the company's relationship with the external auditors. The external audit is part of the chain of corporate governance, as outlined by Cadbury in 1992:

> The annual audit is one of the cornerstones of corporate governance ... The audit provides an external and objective check on the way in which the financial statements have been prepared and presented.

It is a mechanism to increase shareholders' confidence in the financial statements, and contributes to the monitoring and control of directors. Failure of the audit function was a major contributor to the Maxwell and Enron collapses, and the 'big four' auditors of the UK's financial institutions were criticised in the March 2011 House of Lords Economic Affairs Committee report into the UK audit market, with their 'complacency' and 'dereliction of duty' said to have contributed to the financial crisis:

> We do not accept the defence that bank auditors did all that was required of them. In the light of what we now know, that defence appears disconcertingly complacent. It may be that the Big Four carried out their duties properly in the strictly legal sense, but we have to conclude that, in the wider sense, they did not do so.

(House of Lords Economic Affairs Committee, 2011, para. 198)

The objective of an audit is to enable the auditor to express an opinion whether the financial statements are prepared, in all material respects, in accordance with an applicable reporting framework, in other words, in the UK for listed companies, in accordance with IFRS and companies legislation. The opinion is expressed that the financial statements show a 'true and fair' view, and thus provides reasonable, but not absolute, assurance of this. A significant and ongoing problem for the auditing profession is the **expectations gap**—the role of the auditor often being misunderstood, even by financially sophisticated individuals. Investors frequently believe that the audit provides more assurance than is actually the case or that it provides assurance on different issues from those actually reported on. An audit is a complex procedure, and it is difficult to convey exactly what the auditor does and on what they have based their opinion in a clear, succinct manner that does not lead to further complexity and possible misunderstanding. The audit report has changed a number of times over the past 20 years as attempts to clarify this situation and provide transparency, with the auditors' responsibilities and those of the directors being set out in various forms. More recently, descriptions of the scope of the audit, the areas considered by the auditor to be principal risk areas and what impact this assessment had on the audit approach, and explanations of how the auditor has applied the concept of materiality, are required. The auditors are also required to consider the information given in the strategic report and other corporate governance statements, and report, by exception, if:

- the statement given by the directors that they consider the annual report and accounts taken as a whole to be fair, balanced and understandable and provides the information necessary for shareholders to assess the entity's performance, business model and strategy, is inconsistent with the knowledge acquired by the auditor in the course of performing the audit; and

- the section describing the work of the audit committee does not appropriately address matters communicated by the auditor to the audit committee.

The result is that the audit report is now fairly lengthy. However, standard worded, brief statements are a thing of the past, with auditors encouraged to be innovative in how they convey information about their work and how they have reached their opinions.

Extracts from a recent audit report is illustrated in *Financial reporting in practice 3.4*.

Financial reporting in practice 3.4 | Marks and Spencer plc, 2015

Parts of this actual report are set out in tabular form, with some use of diagrams. These have not been reproduced here.

Independent auditors' report to the members of Marks and Spencer Group plc

Opinion on financial statements of Marks and Spencer Group plc

In our opinion:

- The financial statements give a true and fair view of the state of the Group's and of the parent company's affairs as at 28 March 2015 and of the Group's profit for the 52 weeks then ended.

- The Group financial statements have been properly prepared in accordance with International Financial Reporting Standards (IFRSs) as adopted by the European Union.

- The parent company financial statements have been properly prepared in accordance with IFRSs as adopted by the European Union and as applied in accordance with the provisions of the Companies Act 2006.

- The financial statements have been prepared in accordance with the requirements of the Companies Act 2006 and, as regards the Group financial statements, Article 4 of the IAS Regulation.

The financial statements comprise the Consolidated Income Statement, the Consolidated Statement of Comprehensive Income, the Consolidated and Company Statements of Financial Position, the Consolidated and Company Statements of Changes in Equity, the Consolidated and Company Statements of Cash Flows, the reconciliation of net cash flow to movement in net debt note, and the related notes 1 to 28 and C1 to C7. The financial reporting framework that has been applied in their preparation is applicable law and IFRS as adopted by the European Union and, as regards the parent company financial statements, as applied in accordance with the provisions of the Companies Act 2006.

Going concern

As required by the Listing Rules we have reviewed the directors' statement contained within the 'Other disclosures' section on page 82 that the Group is a going concern. We confirm that:

● We have concluded that the directors' use of the going concern basis of accounting in the preparation of the financial statements is appropriate.

● We have not identified any material uncertainties that may cast significant doubt on the Group's ability to continue as a going concern.

However, because not all future events or conditions can be predicted, this statement is not a guarantee as to the Group's ability to continue as a going concern.

Our assessment of risks of material misstatement

The key risks we identified are:
1. Presentation of non-GAAP measures

2. Impairment of store assets

3. Inventory valuation and provisions

4. Revenue recognition—gift cards, loyalty schemes, returns and franchise arrangements

5. Supplier rebates

6. Retirement benefits

The assessed risks of material misstatement are those that had the greatest effect on our audit strategy, the allocation of resources in the audit and directing the efforts of the engagement team.

The Audit Committee has requested that, while not required under International Standards on Auditing (UK and Ireland), we include in our report any significant findings in respect of these assessed risks of material misstatement.

The description of risks below should be read in conjunction with the significant issues considered by the Audit Committee discussed on pages 48 and 49.

Our audit procedures relating to these matters were designed in the context of our audit of the financial statements as a whole, and not to express an opinion on individual accounts or disclosures. Our opinion on the financial statements is not modified with respect to any of the risks described below, and we do not express an opinion on these individual matters.

The audit report then describes each of the above six risks and how the scope of the audit responded to the risk. The information for one risk is shown in detail:

Presentation of non-GAAP measures

Risk description

The presentation of income and costs within non-GAAP measures (to derive 'underlying profit before tax') under IFRS is judgemental, with IFRS only requiring the separate presentation of material items. Judgement is required in determining the classification of items as non-underlying.

In calculating the reported non-GAAP measures, there are two risks which may result in the underlying profit measure being misstated and therefore not being reliable to users of the financial statements:

(continued)

(continued)

- Items may be included in the non-underlying adjustments which are underlying or recurring items, distorting the reported underlying earnings.
- Items may be omitted from the non-underlying adjustments which are material and one-off in nature.

Explanations of each adjustment to derive underlying profit from the reported profit before tax are set out in notes 1 and 5 to the financial statements.

How the scope of our audit responded to the risk

We evaluated the appropriateness of the inclusion of items, both individually and in aggregate, within non-underlying profits, including assessing the consistency of items included year-on-year and ensuring adherence to IFRS requirements and latest FRC guidance. We also agreed these items to supporting evidence.

We assessed all items, either highlighted by management or identified through the course of our audit, which were regarded as one-off but included within underlying earnings to ensure that these are not material either individually or in aggregate. For all adjustments recorded in calculating underlying profits, we discussed the appropriateness of the item with the Audit Committee and any disclosure considerations.

Findings We are satisfied that the items excluded from underlying earnings and the related disclosure of these items in the financial statements is appropriate.

The audit report continues by providing details of how the auditors have conducted their work:

Our application of materiality

We determined materiality for the Group to be £32.0m.

We reported all audit differences in excess of £1.0m.

We define materiality as the magnitude of misstatement in the financial statements that makes it probable that the economic decisions of a reasonably knowledgeable person would be changed or influenced.

We use materiality both in planning the scope of our audit work and in evaluating the results of our work.

We determined materiality for the Group to be £32.0m, which is approximately 5% of pre-tax profit and 1% of equity. The materiality used by the predecessor auditor in 2014 was £31.0m, which represented 5% of pre-tax profit adjusted for non-GAAP performance measures.

We agreed with the Audit Committee that we would report to the Committee all audit differences in excess of £1.0m (2014: the predecessor auditor reported on all differences identified above £1.5m) as well as differences below that threshold that, in our view, warranted reporting on qualitative grounds. We also report to the Audit Committee on disclosure matters that we identified when assessing the overall presentation of the financial statements.

An overview of the scope of our audit

Scope of audit

Our Group audit was scoped by obtaining an understanding of the Group and its environment, including Group-wide controls, and assessing the risks of material misstatement at the Group level. The

Group has retail operations in 59 countries, of which 17 are wholly-owned businesses, two are joint ventures, and 40 operate under franchise agreements (in addition to two wholly-owned businesses which also operate franchise agreements in those territories).

Based on that assessment, we focused our Group audit scope primarily on the audit work at eight wholly-owned locations: United Kingdom, Republic of Ireland, Czech Republic, Greece, Turkey, India, China and Hong Kong. All of these were subject to a full audit. These locations represent the principal business units and account for 99% of the Group's revenue and 95% of the Group's profit before tax and 76% of the Group's net assets. They were also selected to provide an appropriate basis for undertaking audit work to address the risks of material misstatement identified above. Whilst we audit the revenues received by the Group from franchise operations, which account for 3% of the Group's revenue, we do not audit the underlying franchise operations.

Audit components

We performed a full scope audit on components representing 99% of the Group's revenue and 95% of the Group's profit before tax and 76% of the Group's net assets.

At the parent entity level we also tested the consolidation process and carried out analytical procedures to confirm our conclusion that there were no significant risks of material misstatement of the aggregated financial information of the remaining components not subject to a full audit.

We visited all significant components during the year

The most significant component of the Group is its retail business in the United Kingdom, which accounts for 89% of the Group's revenue, 91% of the Group's operating profit and 50% of the Group's net assets. The Group audit team performs the audit of the UK business without the involvement of a component team. During the course of our audit, the Group audit team conducted 16 distribution centre and 27 retail store visits in the UK to understand the current trading performance and, at certain locations, perform tests of internal controls and validate levels of inventory held.

Since this was our first year as the Group's auditor, we visited each of the eight significant locations outlined above at least once. Each component was visited during our transition, planning and risk assessment process, in order for a senior member of the Group audit team to obtain a thorough understanding of the operations, risks and control environments of each component. For more significant or complex components, we conducted a second visit during the audit to review the component auditor's working papers and attend key meetings with component management.

Going forward, we will follow a programme of planned visits that has been designed so that a senior member of the Group audit team visits each of the locations where the Group audit scope was focused at least once every two years, and the most significant of them at least once a year. In years when we do not visit a significant component we will include the component audit team in our team briefing, discuss their risk assessment, and review documentation of the findings from their work.

In addition to our visits in these locations, senior members of each component audit team attended a two-day training programme hosted by the Group audit team covering topics which included understanding the business and its core strategy, a discussion of the significant risks and workshops on our planned audit approach.

Here is the opinion on matters other than the financial statements:

(continued)

(continued)

Opinion on other matters prescribed by the Companies Act 2006

In our opinion

- The part of the Directors' Remuneration Report to be audited has been properly prepared in accordance with the Companies Act 2006.
- The information given in the Strategic Report and the Directors' Report for the financial year for which the financial statements are prepared is consistent with the financial statements.

Matters on which we are required to report by exception

Adequacy of explanations received and accounting records

Under the Companies Act 2006 we are required to report to you if, in our opinion:

- We have not received all the information and explanations we require for our audit.
- Adequate accounting records have not been kept by the parent company, or returns adequate for our audit have not been received from branches not visited by us.
- The parent company financial statements are not in agreement with the accounting records and returns.

We have nothing to report in respect of these matters.

Directors' remuneration

Under the Companies Act 2006 we are also required to report if in our opinion certain disclosures of directors' remuneration have not been made or the part of the Directors' Remuneration Report to be audited is not in agreement with the accounting records and returns. We have nothing to report arising from these matters.

Corporate Governance Statement

Under the Listing Rules we are also required to review the part of the Corporate Governance Statement relating to the Company's compliance with ten provisions of the UK Corporate Governance Code. We have nothing to report arising from our review.

Our duty to read other information in the Annual Report

Under International Standards on Auditing (UK and Ireland), we are required to report to you if, in our opinion, information in the Annual Report is:

- Materially inconsistent with the information in the audited financial statements.
- Apparently materially incorrect based on, or materially inconsistent with, our knowledge of the Group acquired in the course of performing our audit.
- Otherwise misleading.

In particular, we are required to consider whether we have identified any inconsistencies between our knowledge acquired during the audit and the directors' statement that they consider the Annual

Report is fair, balanced and understandable and whether the Annual Report appropriately discloses those matters that we communicated to the Audit Committee which we consider should have been disclosed. We confirm that we have not identified any such inconsistencies or misleading statements.

Respective responsibilities of directors and auditor

As explained more fully in the Directors' Responsibilities Statement, the directors are responsible for the preparation of the financial statements and for being satisfied that they give a true and fair view. Our responsibility is to audit and express an opinion on the financial statements in accordance with applicable law and International Standards on Auditing (UK and Ireland). Those standards require us to comply with the Auditing Practices Board's Ethical Standards for Auditors.

We also comply with International Standard on Quality Control 1 (UK and Ireland). Our audit methodology and tools aim to ensure that our quality control procedures are effective, understood and applied. Our quality controls and systems include our dedicated professional standards review team and independent partner reviews.

This report is made solely to the Company's members, as a body, in accordance with Chapter 3 of Part 16 of the Companies Act 2006. Our audit work has been undertaken so that we might state to the Company's members those matters we are required to state to them in an auditor's report and for no other purpose. To the fullest extent permitted by law, we do not accept or assume responsibility to anyone other than the Company and the Company's members as a body, for our audit work, for this report, or for the opinions we have formed.

Scope of the audit of the financial statements

An audit involves obtaining evidence about the amounts and disclosures in the financial statements sufficient to give reasonable assurance that the financial statements are free from material misstatement, whether caused by fraud or error. This includes an assessment of:

- Whether the accounting policies are appropriate to the Group's and the parent company's circumstances and have been consistently applied and adequately disclosed.
- The reasonableness of significant accounting estimates made by the directors.
- The overall presentation of the financial statements.

In addition, we read all the financial and non-financial information in the Annual Report to identify material inconsistencies with the audited financial statements and to identify any information that is apparently materially incorrect based on, or materially inconsistent with, the knowledge acquired by us in the course of performing the audit. If we become aware of any apparent material misstatements or inconsistencies we consider the implications for our report.

Ian Waller (Senior statutory auditor) for and on behalf of Deloitte LLP
Chartered Accountants and Statutory Auditor
London, United Kingdom
19 May 2015

All audits are governed by regulation, which are legal (Companies Act 2006 and, currently, EU directives), mandatory (auditing standards issued by the FRC which are largely based on international auditing standards) and professional body requirements. Auditors must be members of a Recognised Supervisory Body (RSB) (e.g. the ICAEW is a RSB), which has procedures for monitoring auditors and codes of professional ethics. The FRC also issues ethical standards concerning independence, objectivity and integrity.

These last items are issues that are at the heart of corporate governance and its relationship with the audit and auditors, and are not new. Auditor independence—both actual and perceived—has been a recurring issue throughout the history of external audit. The fact that Enron's auditor, Arthur Anderson, earned $25m from the audit, and $27m from consulting services in 2000, is a clear illustration of perceived lack of independence. It was considered an important issue in the Cadbury report:

> The central issue is to ensure that an appropriate relationship exists between the auditors and the management whose financial statements they are auditing.
>
> *(Cadbury Report, 1992, p.38)*

The Co-ordinating Group on Audit and Accounting Issues in the post-Enron aftermath raised the issues it considered needed review and, more specifically, listed the following independence issues:

- audit partner rotation
- audit firm rotation
- auditor and client relationships
- auditor's economic dependence on a single client
- non-audit services for audit clients
- disclosure of audit/non-audit fees
- transparency of audit firms.

Since then, there have been many initiatives aimed at reforming the audit and the audit market in the UK and more widely in the EU, and some of these issues have been addressed. Other reforms are still in the pipeline. For example, audit engagement partners of listed companies are required to change every five years (APB Ethical Standard 3), although the firm does not change; auditors are required to ensure that any non-audit services they provide do not compromise their independence (APB Ethical Standard 5); and fees charged for audit and non-audit services have to be disclosed. As a result of an Order published by the Competition and Markets Authority on 2014, the *UK Corporate Governance Code* now requires FTSE 350 companies to put their audit out to tender every ten years. There is much more focus on the role of the audit committee, which plays a key role in managing these issues, and the overall relationship with the auditor. The committee is required by the *UK Corporate Governance Code* to review and monitor the auditor's independence and objectivity, and the effectiveness of the audit process, and report on how it has done this. This will require an evaluation of the quality of the audit, which, the FRC suggests, will include an assessment of, amongst other matters, the mind-set and culture of the auditor, their skills, character and knowledge, the exercise of professional judgement and the quality control the audit firm itself exercises.

The reforms, yet to come into force at the time of writing, stem from EU Regulation EU/537/2014 and Directive 2014/56/EU issued in April 2014, which were the result of a consultative process which was started after the financial crisis and which aimed at restoring investors' confidence in the financial statements of companies and their audits. Even with the recent referendum vote for the UK to leave the EU, these reforms are highly likely to be introduced in the UK by the end of 2016. The objectives set out during the consultations were to:

- eliminate conflicts of interest
- guarantee the independence of the auditor
- provide sound supervision capable of identifying early warning signs of problems; and
- encourage more diversity in the audit market.

The requirements of the Regulation and Directive will require changes to companies legislation, auditing standards and the *UK Corporate Governance Code*. The changes will further enhance governance by increasing the role of the audit committee and introducing a fair and transparent tendering process for the selection of the auditor; introduce a system of mandatory rotation of audit firms that encourages joint audits; provide a list of prohibited non-audit services (for example, all forms of tax advice) and a cap on permitted non-audit services provided by the audit firm; and require more detailed reporting by the auditor to the audit committee and the shareholders. Some of the provisions in the Regulation and Directive give member states of the EU some choices. The FRC and Department of BIS have consulted on the requirements, and final changes will be confirmed in due course.

3.3.9 Remuneration

Probably the most contentious and widely commented on area of corporate governance, remuneration levels of directors, achieved prominence in the mid-1990s with media reports of eye-wateringly large remuneration packages, which seemed unconnected to the financial successes of the companies.

 Examples of excessive remuneration levels

Cedric Brown of British Gas achieved notoriety in 1995 when a pig named Cedric was paraded outside the AGM as his large remuneration package was agreed.

Sainsbury's chairman, Sir Peter Davis, received a bonus of £2.4 million in 2004, a year when profits at the company fell.

Fred Goodwin, the subsequently de-knighted chairman of Royal Bank of Scotland, received a basic salary and bonuses totalling £15.5 million between 2003 and 2007, but what caused an outcry, in particular, was his pension pot of more than £16 million when he agreed to 'retire' from the bank in 2008 following a disastrous takeover of Dutch banking group ABN Amro.

The average pay reported for a FTSE 100 CEO in 2014 was £4.96 million. Average FTSE 100 CEO pay in 2014 was 183 times the earnings of the average full-time UK worker, up from 182 times in 2013, 160 times in 2010 and 47 times in 2000.

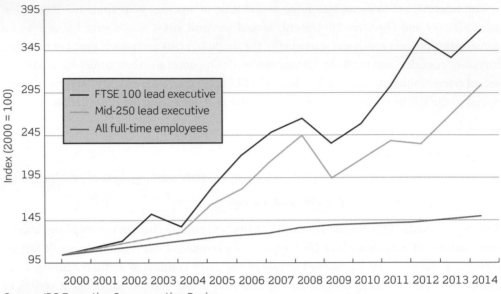

Source: IDS Executive Compensation Review

Figure 3.2 Comparison of FTSE executives' pay versus average workers' pay

The enormous increases in the compensation awarded to executive directors of FTSE companies compared to the average worker's pay is further illustrated by Figure 3.2.

It is perhaps no wonder that companies and, to a certain extent, institutional investors, complain that the corporate governance debate is often hijacked by questions about remuneration.

The debate over remuneration, stemming from the principal–agent problem, often centres on the balance between fixed and variable elements of remuneration, with the variable elements used as a mechanism to incentivise the directors to improve corporate performance. How much, and the level, of directors' remuneration should be in the form of basic salary (the fixed element) and how much in the form of bonuses and other incentives such as **share options** (short- or long-term variable elements) causes much debate. One view is that directors have been unduly incentivised to maximise their companies' profits in the short term because the focus of many institutional shareholders is on short-term results. This may be because the institutional shareholders themselves are incentivised by short-term aspects of their own remuneration systems. This is clearly counter to the spirit of corporate governance. However, evidence shows that, from the mid-1990s, changes in the balance of directors' remuneration towards more long-term performance-related pay has resulted. This can be partly attributed to Greenbury's report into directors' remuneration in 1995 which set out principles which have guided boardroom remuneration strategies ever since.

The linkage between pay and performance, clearly articulated by Greenbury, has led to currently on average only one-fifth of executives' remuneration being from a basic fixed salary, with the remainder from a myriad of short-term bonus and complex long-term incentive performance schemes, where rewards are based on many different criteria which could have overlapping aims and targets. Since the early 2000s there has been an increasing trend in maximum incentives and payouts under these arrangements.

The principles of the *UK Corporate Governance Code* relating to remuneration are as follows:

- Executive directors' remuneration should be designed to promote the long-term success of the company. Performance-related elements should be transparent, stretching and rigorously applied.

- There should be a formal and transparent procedure for developing policy on executive remuneration and for fixing the remuneration packages of individual directors. No director should be involved in deciding his or her own remuneration.

(FRC, 2014a)

The performance-related elements should be in line with the company's objectives and risk policies. If a long-term incentive scheme is a share option scheme, the options should not be exercisable for at least three years. Since 2013, shareholders have had a binding vote on remuneration policy at least every three years, but they do not have legal power over the actual level of directors' remuneration as they have an advisory vote only at a company's AGM. Recent research by the UK's High Pay Centre has found that acceptance of a pay for performance culture has spread beyond the boardroom, with investors and all the main political parties agreeing that generous rewards are justified where a company has shown strong long-term performance. However, the research further demonstrates that increases in all the key elements of FTSE 350 directors' remuneration have far outstripped a range of corporate metrics, with little discernible link between directors' earnings and corporate performance.

 Examples of shareholders' advisory votes against directors' remuneration

A number of high-profile UK companies faced a significant proportion of their shareholders voting against the directors' remuneration packages at spring 2016 AGMs. These were advisory votes only. The companies included:

- Engineering firm, Weir Group plc, where a proposed pay policy was rejected by 72 per cent of shareholders.

- Online payment services company, Paysafe Group plc, where 51.7 per cent voted against the remuneration report.

- BP, where 59 per cent of its shareholders voted against a 20 per cent pay rise for its chief executive.

- Drugs maker, Shire plc, where 49 per cent of investors voted against a 25 per cent pay increase for its chief executive.

- Bookmakers, Ladbrokes plc, where 42 per cent voted against the remuneration report.

- Mining company, Anglo American plc, where more than two-fifths of investors voted against a remuneration deal that included £3.4m for its chief executive.

The *UK Corporate Governance Code* advises that the total potentially available rewards should not be excessive, but what is excessive or not is, of course, indefinable. One method of measuring this is by comparison with other companies, and the Code says this should be used with caution, as it is a means of merely ratcheting up general levels of remuneration. Which public company would wish to say it is paying less than the average to its top executives?

Another subcommittee of the board of directors, the remuneration committee, made up of at least three independent non-executive directors, has responsibility for setting remuneration for the executive directors and the chairman. They also advise on, and monitor, senior management's remuneration. There has been recent debate as to the composition of this subcommittee, with some calling for employee representation, as is the case in other European countries. One issue is that many non-executive directors are or have been executive directors of other companies, and thus are likely to advise on remuneration policies and schemes which maintain the status quo. Many committees engage the use of external consultants to advise; however, research demonstrates that many of these may have independence issues as they carry out other work for the companies concerned.

The *UK Corporate Governance Code* stresses transparency in the area of directors' remuneration, and this is strengthened by companies legislation, with the Companies Act 2006 requiring an extensive directors' remuneration report, some of which is audited and reported on. Changes were made to this in 2013 following a Department of BIS review of issues concerning executive remuneration. The report is designed to be transparent and to promote engagement by shareholders. A summary of the disclosures is as follows:

- A forward-looking policy report to disclose a description of each element of pay and how it links to the company strategy; performance scenarios showing fixed pay, total remuneration when performing in line with expectations and maximum total remuneration.

- A retrospective implementation report disclosing details of each director's remuneration for the previous year, and which should include a single figure for total remuneration received in the year.

Despite the *UK Corporate Governance Code* and companies legislation disclosure requirements, there is a general consensus that directors' remuneration levels continue to be at extraordinarily high levels. In the past few years, some specific changes have been made by the Department of BIS as indicated earlier, and the 2014 Code was amended to include various recommendations concerning the recovery or withholding of variable pay when appropriate to do so, the setting of appropriate vesting and holding periods for deferred remuneration and the use of clawback provisions for poor performance. The FRC has indicated it will continue to review how market practice develops.

3.3.10 Relations with shareholders

Satisfactory engagement between company boards and investors is crucial to the UK's corporate governance regime. Institutional investors' ownership of UK listed companies is continuing to reduce as international ownership increases, and accounted for approximately 27 per cent of listed company ownership at the end of 2014. International ownership stood at 54 per cent at this date. The focus on institutional investors in the days of Cadbury's report could be considered less critical today, although their ownership still constitutes a sizeable minority:

> Given the weight of their votes, the way in which institutional shareholders use their power to influence the standards of corporate governance is of fundamental importance. Their readiness to do this turns on the degree to which they see it as their responsibility as owners, and in the interest of those whose money they are investing, to bring about changes in companies when necessary, rather than selling their shares.

(Cadbury Report, 1992, 50)

Various reviews have considered institutional investors' relationships with their investee companies and have concluded that the engagement is less than satisfactory, with their actions sometimes in opposition to corporate governance principles. Pension funds are a significant category of institutional investor:

> It is often said that [pension fund] trustees put fund managers under undue pressure to maximise short-term investment returns, or to maximise dividend income at the expense of retained earnings; and that the fund manager will be reluctant to support board proposals which do not immediately enhance the share price or the dividend rate ... We urge trustees to encourage investment managers to take a long view.

(Hampel Report, 1998, 41)

Lord Myners also conducted a review in 2001 into pension fund trustees' roles and responsibilities, and found that many pension fund trustees lacked the necessary investment expertise to act as strong and discerning customers of the investment consultants and fund managers who sold them services. There was insufficient focus on the potential for adding value through active shareholder engagement.

Effective engagement was a key theme of the Walker Review in 2009 and, at the same time, the FRC commissioned a study into this area. Both resulting reports concluded that a more proactive approach to engagement was required, otherwise there was the danger of legislation, which was contrary to the principles based approach to corporate governance. The engagement needed to be two-way, transparent and with constructive dialogue conducted not just at set-piece meetings, such as the annual general meeting (AGM) and results announcements, but at other times with the chairman and non-executive directors.

As a result of these reviews, section F of the *UK Corporate Governance Code* has been updated and the FRC produced a *UK Stewardship Code*, first issued in 2010, and then updated in 2012. The relationship between these Codes is illustrated in Figure 3.3.

The principles of the *UK Corporate Governance Code* relating to relations with shareholders are as follows:

- There should be a dialogue with shareholders based on the mutual understanding of objectives. The board as a whole has responsibility for ensuring that a satisfactory dialogue with shareholders takes place.
- The board should use general meetings to communicate with investors and to encourage their participation.

(FRC, 2014a)

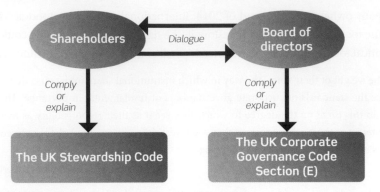

Figure 3.3 Shareholder engagement and the relevant Codes

Whilst in practice most contact is between shareholders and the chief executive and finance directors, the chairman has responsibility for communication and ensuring all directors are aware of the views of the shareholders.

The *UK Stewardship Code* sets out the role of institutional shareholders. They should recognise their stewardship responsibilities, with transparency on how they have achieved this. Internally, they need to ensure that those involved in fund management and corporate governance liaise effectively. They should be active in giving feedback on governance and other issues to their investee companies, using suitably qualified personnel to conduct this dialogue, to ensure governance issues do not build up. The level of pre-1990s voting by institutional shareholders at AGMs was fairly low and although it has been increasing since, this Code stipulates that they should use their votes at AGM 'thoughtfully' and disclose their level of voting. They should use channels of communication with the investee companies to address any issues rather than the blunt tool of selling shares.

3.4 Reporting of corporate governance

The reporting of corporate governance issues is governed by the FCA's *Disclosure and Transparency Rules* and *Listing Rules* together with the *UK Corporate Governance Code*. These require a listed company to include a corporate governance statement in its directors' report. This statement must contain a reference to:

1 the corporate governance code to which the issuer is subject;

2 the corporate governance code which the issuer may have voluntarily decided to apply; and

3 all relevant information about the corporate governance practices applied over and above the requirements under national law.

(FCA Handbook, 2016: Corporate governance statements, DTR 7.2.2)

The *Listing Rules* (LR 9.8.6) require a statement of how the company has applied the main principles in the *UK Corporate Governance Code,* together with confirmation that the company has complied with all relevant provisions. To the extent that a company departs from that corporate governance code, it must explain which parts of the code it departs from and the reasons for doing so—the 'comply or explain' approach—this is also required by the *Disclosure and Transparency Rules* (DTR 7.2.3(1)(b)).

In addition to these requirements the disclosure rules specify that the corporate governance statement should include a description of:

- the body that monitors the financial reporting process, the effectiveness of the internal control, internal audit and risk management systems, and the statutory audit (DTR 7.1.5)—this is the audit committee

- the main features of the issuer's internal control and risk management systems in relation to the financial reporting process (DTR 7.2.5)

- the composition and operation of the issuer's administrative, management, and supervisory bodies and their committees (DTR 7.2.7).

The *UK Corporate Governance Code* itself includes many specific requirements of disclosure.

In practice therefore, corporate governance statements in companies' annual reports add significantly to the length of the narrative information, as they usually include mini-biographies of the directors, explanations of how the board of directors functions, which subcommittees exist and how they have operated, how the company has managed risk and internal controls, the relationship it has with its auditors and shareholders, and an extensive directors' remuneration report. The information focuses often on systems and procedures.

The growth of narrative reporting and how corporate governance matters are reported have been recognised as concerns by many. Surveys have indicated that it is increasingly difficult for shareholders to distil the pertinent information they need, often about company strategy, from the wealth of information provided. There have been various initiatives for improvement. Part of the purpose of the recent legislative change requiring companies to produce a strategic report, which was discussed in section 3.3.4, was to separate out from the remainder of the published company data the strategic, headline information that all investors would wish to see in a concise report. The annual directors' statement would contain the remainder of the information and by default would be online.

The FRC's 2010 report, *Effective Company Stewardship,* suggests a number of improvements based on the principle that the directors should take full responsibility for ensuring that, viewed as a whole, the annual report should provide a fair and balanced report on their stewardship. This encourages companies to report on a bespoke basis, with boilerplate disclosures considered of little use, and with more description of the steps the directors have taken to ensure:

- the reliability of all information included

- transparency about the activities of the company and any associated risks.

The FRC has more recently produced another report, *Cutting Clutter*, setting out three key areas for action which would ensure reports ultimately clearly convey information of a company's business and the issues it faces, and that important information is not obscured. These are:

1   To encourage debate on materiality. This also impacts financial information, and the IASB's current actions in relation to this are discussed in Chapter 4.

2   To tackle what explanatory (narrative) information is provided and how it is presented.

3   To engage with other stakeholders regarding their information requests.

Unfortunately, it appears that however well intentioned these initiatives are, the many changes to financial reporting and disclosures over the past couple of decades have resulted in a continuing increase in the length of annual reports.

3.5 Corporate sustainability

The purpose of the corporate governance issues discussed so far are 'to facilitate effective, entrepreneurial and prudent management that can deliver the long-term success of the company' (FRC, 2014a: 1). Although much of the focus of corporate governance is on the relationship between the company, its directors and shareholders, it is accepted that directors have a responsibility to all stakeholders:

> The greatest shareholder today is ... the individual via his or her financial institution and pension fund. The same individual is also the employee of the company; the customer who chooses between the products of company A or B; the voter for the government of the day and for the trustee of the pension fund. In addition, the individual is a citizen of a country who expects his or her neighbour to act as a decent citizen, and as a consequence today, the individual citizen expects the corporate citizen to act as a decent citizen.

(Mervyn King, Chairman, King Committee on Corporate Governance; Chairman, International Integrated Reporting Committee)

Long-term success undoubtedly means companies have to find means of increasing profits and company value; ways this can be achieved include brand enhancement, the use of more efficient processes and effective management of risk. All of these have been cited by companies as reasons for the adoption of sustainability practices, which continue to move up the corporate agenda. The roots of corporate sustainability are in environmental reporting, and initially it was a niche activity for companies, such as IBM, which established a corporate environmental policy in 1971. Although environmental concerns remain a significant part of the sustainability agenda today, this has developed to include social and ethical issues, such as how human capital is valued in an entity, how intellectual capital is managed, the impact of an entity's operations on society as a whole, and the effect of climate change or resource scarcities on the entity's business operations. Some of these issues are also referred to under the heading of corporate social responsibility, but the terms corporate sustainability or the mnemonic ESG (environmental, social and governance) indicate a broader approach to environmental and social business practices.

It is difficult to define corporate sustainability concisely as it involves many different issues, but it should be seen as part of a continuing process of building long-term value. Everything a business does should help improve the business's reputation, and encourage customers and other stakeholders to stay involved with it. It also encompasses the continuing commitment by businesses to behave ethically and responsibly, and to contribute to economic development, while improving the quality of life of its workforce and their families, as well as of the local community and society at large. Corporate sustainability emphasises the need for companies to adopt a coherent approach to a range of stakeholders, including investors, employees, suppliers, customers and society, and to be accountable to them for their actions.

 Examples of how corporate sustainability can be practised

1 *Choice of suppliers*

   Companies should deal with suppliers who practise corporate sustainability themselves. Trading with suppliers who pollute the environment could be as irresponsible as doing so yourself. Customers may perceive companies which favour suppliers who demonstrate responsible policies more favourably. Using local suppliers as much as possible helps companies support their community and this action also reduces energy and carbon emissions from deliveries. Companies should examine their suppliers' employment, health and safety and environmental practices. Companies should also treat its suppliers fairly, particularly smaller businesses that rely on them. For example, being paid on time can make a big difference to a small business.

2 *How customers are treated*

   Companies should have effective communication with customers, telling them openly and honestly about their products and services. Customers are increasingly concerned about the wider impact of supply chains, e.g. on local workforces and environments.

3 *How employees are treated*

   For the responsible business, this means doing more than simply complying with legal requirements. In the UK, some companies pay their employees the living wage which is higher than the statutory minimum wage. A company's reputation can be damaged by being associated with businesses that abuse the rights of their own workers.

4 *The effect of the business on the local community*

   Local customers are an important source of sales. By improving their reputation, companies may find it easier to recruit employees locally. A good relationship with local authorities can also make companies' lives easier, e.g. some local authorities prefer to award contracts to businesses with a record of community involvement. There are many ways companies can get involved, e.g. by supporting a local charity or by sponsoring a local event.

5 *The effect of the business on the environment*

   Companies should use resources more efficiently and reduce pollution and waste. A company's reputation can be damaged by being associated with businesses that abuse their local environment.

3.5.1 What is driving corporate sustainability?

A 2010 global survey of companies' attitudes towards, and practices and processes in the area of, corporate sustainability carried out by KPMG, one of the big four accountancy firms, in cooperation with The Economist Intelligence Unit, revealed that a majority of the companies surveyed had a corporate sustainability strategy. The key factors driving this were regulation, brand enhancement, risk management and also a means of cost reduction. This latter factor had been seen as a barrier to progress on sustainability only a few years previously. However, there are a number of ways in which corporate sustainability can now be seen to help cut costs. For example:

- compliance with regulatory requirements ensures reduced litigation costs. Also it is often cheaper to change processes in advance of regulation that requires the changes

- reducing resource use, waste and emissions helps the environment and cuts utility bills and waste disposal costs

- a good reputation makes it easier to recruit employees. Employees may stay longer, reducing the costs and disruption of recruitment and retraining. Employees are better motivated and more productive

- understanding the wider impact of the business can help in the development of new products and services. Waste implications can be built into the design of new products and production processes.

In 2014, the Smith School of Enterprise and the Environment, part of the University of Oxford, produced a paper that reviewed more than 190 studies into whether sustainable practices were good for business. Their conclusions were that 90 per cent of the studies reviewed showed that a company's cost of capital is lower for companies with higher standards of sustainability practice; 88 per cent found that solid ESG practices have a positive impact on operational performance; and 80 per cent found a positive correlation between sustainability practice and share price performance.

This evidence shows that good sustainability practices therefore can improve business performance and financial metrics, and result in stronger customer loyalty and motivated employees. A reputation as a responsible business that behaves ethically to its suppliers, customers, employees, local community and society will also boost the corporate image. Sustainability is also seen by some companies as a source of innovation and new business opportunity, and can be a means of company or product differentiation, which, in turn, can lead to an improved share price. Many investors are now actively seeking environmentally and socially responsible companies, evidenced by the growth in international SRI (sustainable and responsible investment) markets.

Although corporate sustainability is undoubtedly increasing in importance for many companies, others continue to have poor knowledge about the issues. For many companies other, more pressing matters arising from the economic environment—for example, financial pressures and lack of credit from banks—or a focus on short-term performance head their concerns.

3.5.2 Environmental and social responsibility

Corporate sustainability grew out of environmental responsibility, and this issue still tops the sustainability agenda and is likely to continue to do so in the coming years. For example, a majority of companies report that they have improved their energy efficiency, reduced packaging and waste or taken other steps to reduce the environmental footprint of their products. Environmental legislation, for example, to cut greenhouse gases or other pollutants, has also affected business practices.

However, the social aspect of corporate sustainability is also important, and includes companies ensuring that human rights and workers' rights are not abused, that companies have ethical supply chains and that they do not carry out irresponsible marketing of their products and services. Many abuses of workers' rights in large global retailers' supply chains have been reported over the years, for example workers being forced to work more than 60 hours a week, receiving low wages, working in poor conditions, the use of child labour, cases of harassment or companies ignoring health and safety legislation, which can result in tragic disasters such as the collapse of the Rana Plaza garment manufacturing building in Dhaka, Bangladesh in 2013 due to the lack of building safety compliance. Such retailers, among them Nike, Gap, Marks and Spencer, Next, Tesco and Sainsbury, have attempted to improve ethical standards within their supply chains through codes of conduct policed by regular visits from ethical auditors. Despite such efforts, poor working conditions, low wages and abuse of those attempting to join workers' groups or unions often continues.

Some companies will demonstrate their commitment to ethical supply chains by retailing Fairtrade products. Fairtrade is an organised social movement that aims to help producers in developing countries make better trading conditions and promote sustainability. The movement advocates better prices and fair terms of trade for producers, as well as higher social and environmental standards. It focuses, in particular, on exports from developing countries to developed countries, most notably handicrafts, beauty products, coffee, cocoa, sugar, tea, bananas, cotton, flowers and gold.

3.5.3 Corporate sustainability today

The Global Reporting Initiative (GRI) is an international independent organisation that helps businesses, governments and other organisations understand and communicate the impact of business on critical sustainability issues such as climate change, human rights, corruption and many others. Its aims are to create a future where sustainability is integral to every organisation's decision-making process and to empower decision makers everywhere to take action towards a more sustainable economy and world. GRI pioneered sustainability reporting in the late 1990s, through promotion of a number of standards, and has transformed reporting from a niche practice to one now adopted by a growing majority of organisations. GRI's standards on sustainability reporting and disclosure are widely used across the world, and enable businesses, governments, civil society and citizens to make better decisions based on information that matters.

GRI believes that businesses have an important role to play in the sustainability agenda. As they create new opportunities to generate prosperity through global trade, knowledge-sharing and access to technology, they should recognise that these opportunities are not available for an ever-increasing human population, where millions face poverty and hunger. Sustainable development for businesses is therefore about developing new and innovative ways in which their operations, products and services impact the earth, people and economies to ensure that it is achieved.

Thus sustainability issues critical for businesses today have moved beyond environmental and social responsibilities and include the following:

Global issues	World population increase, climate change, data technology development
Society's development	Food and water security, wealth inequality, human rights protection, promotion of peace, conflict management and security
The environment	Global and regional management of natural resources, ecosystem protection, waste and contamination management
Efficiency	Efficiency in the production and distribution of goods and services, new models and new technology for energy production and distribution
Society's governance and economic models	Loss of trust and legitimacy in institutions, lack of creativity of political leaders, resulting in a new role for business leaders, a need to further develop governance structures, development of a new generation of economic growth and development models

Many of these issues are ones which could be described as the business risks and uncertainties which are increasingly reported on in companies' annual reports.

3.5.4 Reporting of corporate sustainability

The reporting of corporate sustainability is part of a company's accountability to its stakeholders. Companies increasingly acknowledge that effective communication of their strategies and performance on sustainability is important to gain the benefits from enhanced reputation and image. However, there is no overriding and comprehensive requirement for sustainability reporting. Although there is an increase in corporate responsibility reporting, this has been driven mainly by additional regulation, rather than voluntary disclosures. The regulation is varied, and mainly national.

Financial reporting standards require some related disclosures. For example, IAS 37 *Provisions, Contingent Liabilities and Contingent Assets* requires disclosures of provisions for future costs of rectifying environmental damage or the decommissioning of certain assets used, say, in the extraction of oil (see Chapter 13 for a full discussion of this accounting standard). IAS 1 *Presentation of Financial Statements* also encourages companies to disclose abnormally large items (which may be environmental fines and penalties) separately, otherwise their results would appear distorted. (Chapter 4 discusses this further.)

The UK Companies Act strategic report requires information about

(i)   environmental matters (including the impact of the company's business on the environment);

(ii) the company's employees; and

(iii) social and community and human rights issues, including information about any policies of the company in relation to those matters and the effectiveness of those policies.

These requirements, on their own, may be considered rather vague, however, the FRC does provide guidance and examples to assist companies on the sorts of issues that would be relevant under these headings.

Various countries have statutory requirements for certain sustainability or corporate responsibility information. For example:

- In the UK the Companies Act 2006 now requires quoted companies to report on greenhouse gas (GHG) emissions for which they are responsible.

- In Norway, boards of all public limited and listed companies must explain how they integrate corporate responsibility (CR) into their business strategy.

- Since 2013, it has been mandatory for large Indian companies to report on CR projects undertaken and to disclose details including spending on these projects in their annual report.

- In 2014, the Taiwan Stock Exchange required the largest chemical, food, finance and insurance companies to publish an annual CR report.

As a result of the EU's 2014 directive on corporate disclosure of non-financial and diversity information, for financial years beginning in 2017, all EU companies that have over 500 employees and which are classed as 'public interest' (in other words, all those listed on an EU stock exchange, credit institutions and insurance companies) will have to include in their management report a statement incorporating details of:

- environmental matters
- social and employee-related aspects
- respect for human rights
- anti-corruption and bribery issues.

The statement will have to include:

(a)   a brief description of the undertaking's business model

(b)   a description of policies, including due diligence processes implemented

(c)   outcomes of these policies

(d)   the risks relating to those areas and how the company manages those risks

(e)   non-financial key performance indicators relevant to the particular business.

Large listed undertakings will also have to disclose their diversity policies, including information on the age, gender and educational and professional backgrounds of their employees.

3.5.5 Problems with corporate sustainability reporting

One of the inherent problems of reporting in this area is that of what measures can be reported to show a company's performance and whether improvement has been made. For example, how does a business measure their impact on the environment? Basic facts like greenhouse gas emissions, and energy and water consumption can be measured, and there are methods by which a carbon footprint can be calculated, but many other sustainability issues cannot be reduced to figures; thus, measurement of progress proves difficult. The lack of consistent definitions is also challenging for companies doing business in several countries and across different business sectors.

Another issue is the verifiability of information included in the reports. Although progress has been made in this area, with third party assurance of corporate sustainability information being standard practice amongst the world's largest companies, there is inconsistency in how the reports are audited and verified, and a variety of assurance providers used.

As discussed in section 3.5.3, the GRI has pioneered the world's most widely used sustainability reporting framework by setting out principles and performance indicators that companies and other organisations can use to report their economic, environmental and social performance. The latest (fourth) version of their *Sustainability Reporting Guidelines*, known as the *G4 Guidelines*, was published in 2013 and is designed to be used by organisations of any size, sector or location. It contains general and sector-specific content that has been agreed by a wide range of stakeholders around the world. It is applicable mainly for stand-alone sustainability reports, rather than the sustainability information included in annual financial reports. Although there is an array of sustainability reporting standards issued by a number of different global organisations, a majority of companies globally use the GRI guidelines.

The *G4 Guidelines* are based on principles which include stakeholder inclusiveness, sustainability context, materiality, balance, comparability, accuracy, timeliness, reliability and clarity. Some of these are similar to the principles (qualitative characteristics) that make financial information useful. The principle of materiality is stressed in the latest G4 Guidelines, with an emphasis on the reporting focusing on topics that are significant to the business and its key stakeholders. It is intended that this should make reports relevant, more credible and more user-friendly. However, the guidelines are non-mandatory, thus there is the danger that companies may cherry-pick the guidelines to paint the organisation in as favourable a light as possible. Various high-profile companies do follow the guidelines, including Nestlé and Shell.

Companies are also encouraged to report properly in this area through a variety of national and international recognised reporting awards.

| Financial reporting in practice **3.5** | Sainsbury plc, 2015 |

Sainsbury plc has a sub-board Corporate Responsibility and Sustainability Committee, which reports on its responsibilities and activities in the company's corporate governance report. Included in here is the statutory greenhouse gas emissions information. The company has a corporate responsibility section on its website, and it is here that the company publishes full reports relating to its sustainability initiatives including its 20x20 Sustainability Plan.

Sainsbury's goal, as indicated in its 2015 annual report, is to make its customers' lives easier every day by offering great quality and service at fair prices. It aims to do this by setting five values—all of which are connected to corporate sustainability. These values are referred to throughout the strategic report, which includes the following information.

Our values make us different

Our values are part of our long-term strategy for growth and make good business sense. As we approach the half-way point in our 20x20 Sustainability Plan, we are working to review our commitments to ensure we remain focused on delivering value and values for customers, suppliers, colleagues and shareholders. We anticipate that we will change our corporate responsibility commitments and key delivery goals, to further align with our new strategy.

Best for food and health

We are committed to producing healthier baskets and set tough salt reduction targets for our own-brand products over 15 years ago. Historically, around ten per cent of our products missed the Government's 2012 salt targets. We are addressing products such as bacon where, as signatories to the Government's Responsibility Deal 2017 pledge on salt, the targets present the greatest challenge in terms of customer perception. During the last year, we have also worked with our suppliers to reformulate our own-brand soft drinks and have removed 2,256 tonnes of sugar annually from our customers' baskets, equating to 8.9 billion calories per year.

Sourcing with integrity

British dairy farmers have come under pressure this year due to price volatility. Our dedicated Dairy Development Group protects members through a cost of production model that ensures they are paid a fair price and rewarded for environmental standards and animal welfare. We have nine other Agricultural Development Groups that contribute to our range of over 1,900 British own-brand products.

We continue to work with our suppliers to address the sustainability of our products. In 2007, we set a stretching commitment to use only sustainable palm oil by 2014, a target we did not reach. As of December 2014, 95 per cent of the palm oil we use to make own-brand products is certified sustainable. We continue to work with our suppliers to bring the remaining sustainable alternatives to market. We have also improved our seafood offer with the launch of the first Marine Stewardship Council ('MSC') certified tuna sandwich and our exclusive Freedom Food British rainbow trout. We have received external recognition for having the best own-brand seafood policy, coming joint top of the Marine Conservation Society's 2014 survey.

Respect for our environment

We delivered industry leading environmental initiatives, including our Cannock store becoming the first retail outlet in the UK to be powered by food waste alone. Our Portishead store became our first

(continued)

(continued)

to run fridges powered by 'green' gas created using waste from sugar beet suppliers. We operate the UK's largest dual fuel lorry fleet and are working to increase this to beyond 12 per cent of our core fleet. We have also launched a unique lorry with a range of features designed to improve safety for cyclists and pedestrians.

Our pace of innovation for energy efficiency initiatives has slowed so we are searching for new ideas. Our existing efficiency programmes continue to deliver through award-winning initiatives such as the installation of over 100,000 LED lights. Our energy usage and associated emissions are discussed in more detail on page 52.

Making a positive difference to our community

This year, with help from our customers, colleagues and suppliers, we raised £52 million for charitable causes, including around £7 million in support of The Royal British Legion and over £11.5 million for Red Nose Day 2015. Through our Active Kids scheme, we have now donated over £150 million worth of equipment and experiences to schools and clubs since 2005, and the scheme was recognised in March 2015 by the Prime Minister, David Cameron, with a Big Society Award. We have 384 stores with a local food donation partner, 59 more stores than last year. However, 71 per cent of our stores are without a partner so we are focused on increasing this number.

A great place to work

Recognising that our colleagues make the difference, we have continued to provide training for a range of skills, introducing a new Level 2 Apprenticeship for Craft Skills for our fishmongers and bakers. We have also opened a new college for our Team Leaders and Store Managers, purely dedicated to leadership training.

Our business is changing, and as part of our strategic review we announced restructuring plans as well as a reduction in our store opening programme, which has disappointingly resulted in fewer job opportunities. We are, however, committed to being a good employer and work hard to promote the opportunities available. In the last year, over 450 colleagues pledged their time to mentor young people about careers in retail and since 2008, we have helped over 24,000 people who have faced barriers into work through our You Can scheme.

We are also proud to pay our fair share of tax. Whilst we are obliged to pay tax in accordance with the law, we also ensure that our taxation policy is aligned with our corporate values. We maintain good corporate practice and strict controls in order to protect our shareholders' funds. Further information about our values and our 20x20 Sustainability Plan can be found at www.j-sainsbury.co.uk/responsibility.

3.6 Ethics

A couple of words have been referred to a number of times in the preceding discussions of corporate governance and corporate sustainability, which are at the heart of the two issues and without which a company cannot hope to achieve success in the areas. The words are 'ethical behaviour'.

3.6.1 Ethics in business

Public interest in ethical behaviour by businesses is growing, whether it be in the amounts of corporate tax paid by multinational companies in the countries in which they operate, or the levels of remuneration directors receive compared to their workforce, or retailers' treatment of their suppliers (for example, farmers by supermarket retailers, or overseas manufacturers by the fashion retailers), or employees being able to speak out about company wrongdoing. It is considered by some to be of critical importance in maintaining confidence in capital markets as it is fundamental to an organisation's reputation, trustworthiness and long-term performance, and underpins high quality information that is fit for purpose. Structures, systems and procedures can be, and have been, established to ensure good corporate governance and good corporate sustainability within organisations, but without ethical and moral integrity these are meaningless. If the two case studies of Maxwell and Enron detailed earlier in the chapter are returned to, it can be seen that despite established structures, reporting systems and procedures (admittedly some of them flawed), a common thread was the lack of honesty, principally from the man at the top of both empires. If leaders do not demonstrate ethical behaviour, it is difficult for it to be truly embedded in an organisation. Integrity should be instilled at all levels in a business, from leadership tone, through strategy, policies, information and culture:

> Corporate governance is about what the board does and how it sets the values of the company...
>
> *(FRC, 2014a)*

Surveys on ethics in business conducted by various organisations indicate that since the financial crisis, corporate leadership is taking business integrity more seriously. Business organisations have placed greater emphasis on putting formalised structures for ethics in place, rather than relying on an ad hoc approach to such important issues. There has also been an increase in investment in the ethics function, which could include developing a code of ethics, formal procedures for whistleblowing and ethics training, However, it is seen that many issues persist, including the treatment of whistleblowers, the day-to-day pressures on management which (possibly unintentionally) conflict with the need to live up to ethical standards, and the level of training provided for employees. In addition, fuelled by the many stories in the media, public trust in companies and their behaviour is fairly low.

One problem is that there are wide variations in perceptions of what integrity in business actually means and how it can be put into practice. It goes beyond the legal requirements for a company and is, therefore, about discretionary decisions and behaviour guided by values. Integrity is essentially a personal quality, and to play its part in corporate ethical behaviour requires a joint endeavour of individuals, organisations and professions.

Many theories and frameworks have been proposed to guide companies in ethical decision making. One of these is the ICAEW's 2007 paper, *Reporting with Integrity*, based on literature of modern moral philosophy, which put forward five key aspects of integrity in an individual:

- moral values
- motives
- commitments

- qualities
- achievements.

The report suggests that an individual of integrity is guided by moral values and motives, which are translated into commitments. In turning these commitments into achievements, an individual draws on qualities such as rationality, open-mindedness and perseverance. The individual's integrity is demonstrated by certain behavioural characteristics, for example being honest and truthful, being fair and complying with laws.

The question is how these traits of an individual can be promoted through an organisation. In a company, as part of their strategy, oversight and risk-management responsibilities, the directors need to assess their company's approach and commitment to integrity. To be a truly ethical company, integral behaviour needs to be instilled, no matter what the other competing goals are. The company values, standards of behaviour and support mechanisms need to reinforce and encourage integrity at all levels. So a company needs a robust framework that links the individuals that work for it to a common view of the company's moral values, motives, commitments, qualities and achievements.

Reporting with Integrity suggests that there are five interconnected drivers of organisational integrity: leadership, strategy, policies, information and culture, and provides examples of how these may be put into practice, as given in Table 3.2.

Table 3.2 Drivers and practical examples of organisational integrity

Driver	Methods by which these may be put into practice
Leadership	Setting the right tone at the top Practising what is preached Signalling that integrity is important to performance and reputation
Strategy	Promoting integrity as integral to the company's strategy Devoting resources and management time Discussing integrity issues at board meetings and acting on the discussions Instilling integrity as part of risk management Ensuring business strategy does not conflict with integrity
Policies	Having a Code of Conduct that incorporates integrity and outlines expected behaviour Providing effective training and support Including discussion of behaviour in appraisals Linking rewards to integral behaviour Providing guidance on conflicts of interest
Information	Monitoring performance Ensuring a proper process for gathering information on the company's commitment to integrity Discussing and acting on this information
Culture	Encouraging employees to voice any concerns without fear of reprimand Encouraging employees to make decisions that are aligned with the company's values Monitoring and disciplining employees who behave without integrity

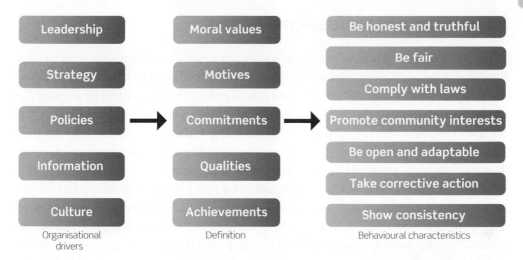

Figure 3.4 Framework for promoting organisational integrity. This article was first published in Reporting with Integrity: Abstract 2007. Reproduced with permission of ICAEW.

Thus, a framework for promoting integrity in a complex organisation can be represented as shown in Figure 3.4.

3.6.2 Do business ethics pay?

Ethics, if considered as a fundamental underpinning to corporate governance and long-term sustainability, will be of benefit to businesses for the reasons discussed in this chapter. A key question is whether it pays in terms of profitability. The Institute of Business Ethics (IBE) conducted research into whether companies exhibiting commitment to business ethics improved their financial performance. A sample of FTSE 350 companies were divided into those that demonstrated a commitment to ethical behaviour by providing training programmes to reinforce their code of ethics to their employees and those that merely disclosed that they had a code of ethics. The research concluded that in the five years from 2001 to 2005, the first group of companies, who were committed to embedding ethical values into business practice, demonstrated a better financial performance than the second group of companies. (Financial performance was measured by some common ratios—return on capital employed, return on assets (see Chapter 5)—and total return and market value added.) The study also found that accounting-based measures were more influenced by business ethics than market-based indicators.

The results of this research are thus consistent with assertions that companies with demonstrable ethics programmes do benefit financially. Confidence is instilled in their stakeholders, which facilitates reputation building, enhances relations with bankers and investors, helps attract better employees, increases **goodwill**, better prepares the companies for external changes and, generally, results in better-run companies.

3.6.3 Ethics in professional bodies

As part of the chain of ethical reporting, a company's own accountants, the directors and members of the audit committee and the external auditor all need to exhibit ethical behaviour. The FRC issues ethical standards for external auditors which contain basic principles and essential procedures together with related guidance in the form of explanatory and other material. They cover the integrity, objectivity and independence of auditors. External auditors, plus many of the individuals mentioned above, will be professionally qualified accountants, who, through membership of a professional accountancy body, are also required to abide by their body's Code of Ethics. Although not a new phenomenon, ethics has become an increasingly important aspect of professional accountancy bodies' standards in recent years, particularly post-Enron, as the public spotlight turned on the professions. Thus, all the major UK bodies have their own Codes of Ethics. As the ICAEW states, its code applies to all members, students, affiliates, employees of member firms and, where applicable, member firms in all of their professional and business activities, whether remunerated or voluntary.

These codes are based on the **International Ethics Standards Board of Accountants** (IESBA's) *Handbook of the Code of Ethics for Professional Accountants*. IESBA is an independent standard-setting board that develops and issues high quality ethical standards and other pronouncements for professional accountants worldwide. It is one of the **International Federation of Accountants'** (IFAC) standard-setting bodies. IFAC is a New York-based global organisation for the accountancy profession whose mission is to serve the public interest by contributing to the development, adoption and implementation of high quality international standards and guidance; contributing to the development of strong professional accountancy organisations and accounting firms, and to high quality practices by professional accountants; promoting the value of professional accountants worldwide; and speaking out on public interest issues where the accountancy profession's expertise is most relevant. The organisation has as members national accountancy organisations, such as the UK's ICAEW and CIMA.

IESBA's *Code of Ethics* is principles based rather than rules based, which brings all the advantages of such an approach, as discussed in Chapter 2, in relation to financial reporting standards. Examples and guidance are provided for many practical situations. The five key principles guiding the code are as follows:

1 *Integrity*
   To be straightforward and honest in all professional and business relationships

2 *Objectivity*
   To not allow bias, conflict of interest or undue influence of others to override professional or business judgements

3 *Professional competence and due care*
   To maintain professional knowledge and skill at the level required to ensure that a client or employer receives competent professional service based on current developments in practice, legislation and techniques
   To act diligently in accordance with applicable technical and professional standards

4 *Confidentiality*

To respect the confidentiality of information acquired as a result of professional and business relationships and, therefore, not disclose any such information to third parties, unless there is a legal or professional right or duty to disclose, nor use the information for the personal advantage of the professional accountant or third parties

5 *Professional behaviour*

To comply with relevant laws and regulations and avoid any action that discredits the profession

(IESBA, 2015)

The Code discusses threats facing professional accountants, such as those arising from financial or other interests, lack of evaluation of the results of judgements made or services performed, compromises to objectivity, having too long or close a relationship with a client or employer, and intimidation from others which would affect the work performed. Safeguards that can be put in place are either created by the profession, legislation or regulation, for example educational, training and experience requirements for entry into the profession, continuing professional development requirements, corporate governance regulations, disciplinary procedures and external reviews, or may exist in the work environment.

Ethical requirements for professional accountants in practice and those in business are then set out in more detail. For the accountant in practice, these cover the following areas:

- professional appointment
- conflicts of interest
- second opinions
- fees and other types of remuneration
- marketing professional services
- gifts and hospitality
- custody of client assets
- objectivity—all services
- independence—audit and review engagements
- independence—other assurance engagements.

 Example of principles based codes relating to auditor independence

The provision of non-assurance services to audit clients:

290.154   Firms have traditionally provided to their audit clients a range of non-assurance services that are consistent with their skills and expertise. Providing non-assurance services may, however, create threats to the independence of the firm or members of the audit team. The threats created are most often self-review, self-interest and advocacy threats.

290.155   New developments in business, the evolution of financial markets and changes in information technology make it impossible to draw up an all-inclusive list of non-assurance services that might be provided to an audit client. When specific guidance on a particular non-assurance service is not included in this section, the conceptual framework shall be applied when evaluating the particular circumstances.

290.156   Before the firm accepts an engagement to provide a non-assurance service to an audit client, a determination shall be made as to whether providing such a service would create a threat to independence. In evaluating the significance of any threat created by a particular non-assurance service, consideration shall be given to any threat that the audit team has reason to believe is created by providing other related non-assurance services. If a threat is created that cannot be reduced to an acceptable level by the application of safeguards, the non-assurance service shall not be provided.

(IESBA, 2015)

The ethical requirements for the accountant in business are briefer and encompass:

● conflicts of interest

● preparation and reporting of information

● acting with sufficient expertise

● financial interests

● inducements.

IFAC has also produced a good practice guide, *Defining and Developing an Effective Code of Conduct for Organisations* (2007), which defines key principles for organisations on which to base their ethics policies and internal codes.

Although ethics is now incorporated into professional accountancy bodies' professional qualifications, and it is included within continuing professional development (CPD) requirements, some research has indicated that the various codes have had little practical effect. It suggests that most professional accountants will gain experience of ethics from on-the-job situations and will not necessarily consult their professional body's theoretical code. Other research suggests that rather than serving public interest, the various ethical codes tend to serve the interests of the profession, so that it can hide behind them if a financial scandal involving poor ethical behaviour occurs.

 ## Summary of key points

A financial reporting system needs to provide high quality and transparent information to all stakeholders, who are interested in a wide range of corporate issues other than the financial results and position. It has been demonstrated many times through high-profile corporate collapses and scandals, and latterly the global financial crisis and subsequent public mistrust in 'big business', how important the question of how a company has achieved its results is, and how crucial an effective system of control and regulation over the financial reporting chain is. Ethical behaviour and honest accountability from all involved are at the heart of this. The ultimate goal of companies is that of wealth creation and protection, with the focus on long-term success and sustainability.

Many aspects of what a company must and may not do, what the duties of its directors and auditors are and what must be reported are governed by statutory legislation in the form of Companies Act 2006. However, regulation over how a company runs its affairs, in other words corporate governance, has developed in the UK through principles based regulation, issued by the FRC, largely as a result of high-profile corporate collapses or public disquiet. This has culminated in the publication of the *UK Corporate Governance Code*, which addresses key areas relating to 'how a company is directed and controlled'—the leadership and effectiveness of the board of directors, their accountability and remuneration, and relations with shareholders. The section dealing with accountability discusses the relationship with the external auditors. The audit is governed by its own statutory legislation, and professional and other regulations, including ethics, and is a key link in the financial reporting chain.

The requirements of the *UK Corporate Governance Code* are based on the stewardship principle of directors of companies being accountable to shareholders; however, other stakeholders are increasingly interested in these issues, together with information about the long-term sustainability of companies. Corporate sustainability encompasses issues of ethical environmental and social behaviour, and the number of companies embracing corporate sustainability practices as a means to long-term success is increasing globally.

The reporting of the corporate governance principles of the *UK Corporate Governance Code* is based on the principle of 'comply or explain', although the FSA's Disclosure Rules and Transparency Rules do require listed companies to provide information about their corporate governance practices. As yet, regulation governing the reporting of corporate sustainability matters is patchy, and different in different countries, and so there is wide variation in the quantity and quality of reporting practices here; however, this may well change as additional legislation is introduced.

 ## Further reading

FRC (Financial Reporting Council) (2010) *The UK Approach to Corporate Governance*. London: FRC.

FRC (Financial Reporting Council) (2014) *UK Corporate Governance Code*. London: FRC.

ICAEW (Institute of Chartered Accountants in England and Wales) (2007) *Reporting with Integrity: Abstract*. Available at: http://www.icaew.com/en/technical/financial-reporting/information-for-better-markets/ifbm-reports/reporting-with-integrity (accessed 3 October 2012). Why read? The ICAEW's thoughts on what integrity is and why it is important in reporting on businesses' activities.

KPMG (2015) *Currents of Change: The KPMG Survey of Corporate Responsibility Reporting* 2015. Switzerland: KPMG. Why read? Evidence of the growing significance of corporate sustainability issues to businesses from a global survey conducted by one of the leading accountancy firms.

 ## Bibliography

Anderson, G. E. and Varney, R. M. (2015) *Sustainability Reporting: Demonstrating Commitment and Adding Value*. National Association of Corporate Directors January/February 2015. Washington DC: NACD.

BIS (Department of Business, Innovation and Skills) (2012a) *Executive Remuneration Discussion Paper: Summary of Responses*. London: BIS.

BIS (Department of Business, Innovation and Skills) (2012b) *The Future of Narrative Reporting: The Government Response*. London: Department of BIS.

BIS (Department of Business, Innovation and Skills) (2015) *Improving the Gender Balance on British Boards*. London: Department of BIS.

BIS (Department of Business, Innovation and Skills) (2016) *The Non-Financial Reporting Directive: A Call for Views on Effective Reporting Alongside Proposals to Implement UE Requirements*. London: Department of BIS.

Butler, S. (2010) Workers can fight for their own rights, *Drapers Magazine*, March.

Cable, V. (2012) *Executive Remuneration*. Speech to Social Market Foundation. London, 24 January 2012.

Cadbury, A. (1992) *The Report of the Committee on the Financial Aspects of Corporate Governance*. Available at: http://www.ecgi.org/codes/documents/cadbury.pdf (accessed 3 October 2012).

Davies, E.M. (2012) *Women on Boards*. Available from https://www.gov.uk/government/uploads/system/uploads/attachment_data/file/31714/12-p135-women-on-boards-2012.pdf (accessed 9 April 2016).

Equality and Human Rights Commission (2016) *An Inquiry into Fairness, Transparency and Diversity in FTSE 350 Board Appointments: Executive Summary*. Manchester: EHRC.

Fairtrade Foundation. [website] http://www.fairtrade.org.uk/ (accessed 8 April 2016).

Fédération des Experts Comptables Européens (FEE) (2003) *A Conceptual Approach to Safeguarding Integrity, Objectivity and Independence throughout the Financial Reporting Chain*. Brussels: FEE.

Fédération des Experts Comptables Européens (FEE) (2009) *Integrity in Professional Ethics: A Discussion Paper*. Brussels: FEE.

FCA (Financial Conduct Authority) (2016) *Disclosure Rules and Transparency Rules*. Available from https://www.handbook.fca.org.uk/handbook/DTR.pdf (accessed 7 April 2016).

FRC (Financial Reporting Council) (2010) *The UK Approach to Corporate Governance*. London: FRC.

FRC (Financial Reporting Council) (2011) *Effective Company Stewardship: Enhancing Corporate Reporting and Audit*. London: FRC.

FRC (Financial Reporting Council) (2012) *The UK Stewardship Code*. London: FRC.

FRC (Financial Reporting Council) (2014a) *The UK Corporate Governance Code*. London: FRC.

FRC (Financial Reporting Council) (2014b) *Guidance on the Strategic Report*. London: FRC.

FRC (Financial Reporting Council) (2014c) *Guidance on Risk Management, Internal Control and Related Financial and Business Reporting*. London: FRC.

FRC (Financial Reporting Council) (2014d) Bulletin 4: *Recent Developments in Company Law, The Listing Rules and Auditing Standards that affect United Kingdom Auditor's Reports*. London: FRC.

FRC (Financial Reporting Council) (2014e) International Standard on Auditing (UK and Ireland) 700: *The Independent Auditor's Report on Financial Statements*. London: FRC.

FRC (Financial Reporting Council) (2014f) *Cutting Clutter. Combating Clutter in Annual Reports*. London: FRC.

FRC (Financial Reporting Council) (2014g) Lab Insight Report: *Towards Clear & Concise Reporting*. London: FRC.

FRC (Financial Reporting Council) (2015a) *Extended Auditor's Reports: A Review of Experience in the First Year*. London: FRC.

FRC (Financial Reporting Council) (2015b) *Audit Quality: Practice Aid for Audit Committees*. London: FRC.

FRC (Financial Reporting Council) (2015c) *Enhancing Confidence in Audit: Proposed Revisions to the Ethical Standard, Auditing Standards, UK Corporate Governance Code and Guidance on Audit Committees*. London: FRC.

FRC (Financial Reporting Council) (2016) *Developments in Corporate Governance and Stewardship 2015*. London: FRC.

Gardner, M. and Lienin, S. (2015) *Impact of the EU Directive on Non-Financial Reporting*. Available at http://www.environmentalleader.com/2015/08/06/impact-of-the-eu-directive-on-non-financial-reporting/ (accessed 7 April 2016).

GRI (Global Reporting Initiative) (2013) *G4 Sustainability Reporting Guidelines*. Amsterdam: GRI.

GRI (Global Reporting Initiative) (2016) *The Next Era of Corporate Disclosure: Digital, Responsible, interactive*. Amsterdam: GRI.

The Hampel Committee on Corporate Governance (1998) *The Final Report*. Available at: http://www.ecgi.org/documents/hampel_index.htm (accessed 7 October 2012).

IBE (Institute of Business Ethics) (2007) *Does Business Ethics Pay?—Revisited*. Executive summary. Available at: http://www.ibe.org.uk/userassets/pubsummaries/dbep_revisited.pdf (accessed 15 April 2016).

IBE (Institute of Business Ethics) (2016) Business Ethics Briefing *Surveys on Business Ethics 2015*. London: IBE.

ICAEW (Institute of Chartered Accountants in England and Wales) (2004) *Sustainability: The Role of Accountants*. London: ICAEW.

ICAEW (Institute of Chartered Accountants in England and Wales) (2007a) *Reporting with Integrity*. London: ICAEW.

ICAEW (Institute of Chartered Accountants in England and Wales) (2007b) *Dialogue in Corporate Governance: Beyond the Myth of Anglo-American Corporate Governance. Emerging Issues*. London: ICAEW.

ICAEW (Institute of Chartered Accountants in England and Wales) (2007c) *Instilling Integrity in Organisations*. London: ICAEW.

ICAEW (Institute of Chartered Accountants in England and Wales) (2011) *Code of Ethics*. Available at: http://www.icaew.com/ (accessed 15 April 2016).

IDS (Incomes Data Services) on behalf of the High Pay Centre (2014) *Executive Remuneration in the FTSE 350—A Focus on Performance-Related Pay*. London: IDS.

IESBA (International Ethics Standards Board for Accountants) [website] http://www.ethicsboard.org (accessed 16 November 2016).

IESBA (International Ethics Standards Board for Accountants) (2015) *Handbook of the Code of Ethics for Professional Accountants*. New York: IESBA.

IFAC (International Federation of Accountants) (2007) *Defining and Developing an Effective Code of Conduct for Organizations*. New York: IFAC.

J Sainsbury plc. (2015). *Annual Report and Financial Statements, 2015*. London: Sainsbury.

JD Wetherspoon plc (2015) *Annual Report and Financial Statements 2015*. Watford: JDWetherspoon.

Jensen, M. C. (1993) The modern industrial revolution, exit, and the failure of internal control systems, *Journal of Finance*, 48, 831–880.

KPMG (2015) *Currents of Change: The KPMG Survey of Corporate Responsibility Reporting* 2015. Switzerland: KPMG.

McPhail, K. and Walters, D. (2009) *Accounting and Business Ethics*. Abingdon: Routledge.

Marks and Spencer Group plc (2015) *Annual Report, 2015*. London: Marks and Spencer Group plc.

Mazars (2015) *Audit Reform for UK Listed Companies*. London: Mazars.

ONS (Office for National Statistics) Statistical bulletin: *Ownership of UK Quoted Shares: 2014*. Available from http://www.ons.gov.uk/economy/investmentspensionsandtrusts/bulletins/ownershipofukquotedshares/2015-09-02 (accessed 6 April 2016).

Solomon, J. (2010) *Corporate Governance and Accountability*, 3rd edn. Chichester: Wiley.

Spira, L. (2006) Black boxes, red herrings and white powder, UK audit committees in the 21st century, *Journal of International Banking Regulation*, 7(1): 180–188.

UK Companies Act 2006. [website] http://www.legislation.gov.uk/ (accessed 5 April 2016).

UK House of Lords Economic Affairs Committee (2011) *Auditors: Market Concentration and their Role*. Available at: http://www.publications.parliament.uk/pa/ld201011/ldselect/ldeconaf/119/119.pdf (accessed 15 April 2016).

Walker, D. (2009) *A Review of Corporate Governance in UK Banks and Other Financial Industry Entities: Final Recommendations*. Available at: http://webarchive.nationalarchives.gov.uk//www.hm-treasury.gov.uk/d/walker_review_261109.pdf (accessed 3 October 2012).

World Business Council for Sustainable Development (WBCSD) and UNEP Finance Initiative (2010) *Translating ESG into Sustainable Business Value*. Geneva: UNEP Finance Initiative and WBCSD.

 Questions

● Quick test

1   Comment on why corporate governance information is discussed in companies' annual reports.

2   Discuss the view that sustainability reporting recognises all corporate stakeholders.

●● Develop your understanding

3   Discuss how current developments in the project to update the IASB's *Conceptual Framework* relate to issues of accountability.

4   What role do ethics play in corporate governance?

5   Sustainability reporting is one issue in corporate governance. Some companies establish a subcommittee of the board to deal with sustainability issues. The audit function can also play a role in sustainability reporting. Outline the arguments for and against a greater role for a dedicated subcommittee and the audit function in corporate sustainability reporting.

6   Accounting should contribute to the protection of the environment. Discuss whether this is a proper role for accounting and outline ways in which it could.

7   Identify some common barriers to the successful adoption of ethical standards in business practice.

●●● Take it further

8   Obtain the GRI's 2013 *Sustainability Reporting Guidelines* from the GRI website at www.globalreporting.org. Discuss to what extent Sainsbury in its 2015 annual corporate responsibility report (available from www.j-sainsbury.co.uk/investor-centre/reports/2015/closer-to-customers-report/) has met the GRI's three principal performance indicators in its sustainability reporting.

9   In the 2015 annual report and financial statements of JD Wetherspoon plc the chairman makes the following statement in relation to corporate governance.

Financial reporting in practice 3.6   JD Wetherspoon plc, 2015

In last year's statement, the view was advanced that many aspects of current corporate governance advice, as laid out in the Combined Code, were 'deeply flawed'. The statement pointed out that 'compliant pub companies had often fared disastrously in comparison with non-compliant ones. In particular, pub companies in which the CEO became chairman and which had a majority of executives ... usually with previous experience of the pub trade, avoided making catastrophic errors to which compliant companies seem prone'. It was also pointed out that setting targets for bonuses had also often backfired, encouraging companies to take reckless decisions in order to enhance earnings.

Last year's statement was particularly critical of the Code itself, which placed a huge emphasis on meetings between directors and shareholders and placed almost no emphasis on directors taking account of the views of customers and employees which are far more important, in practice, to the future well-being of any company.

It was pointed out that the average institutional shareholder turns over his portfolio twice annually, so it would be absurd for directors to take account of the views of 'Mr Market' (in the words of Benjamin Graham), certainly in regard to short-term shareholders.

Having presented our views in previous annual reports and press articles, without receiving any dissent from any shareholders or their representatives, I believe the following propositions represent the views of sensible shareholders:

- Modern annual reports are far too long and are often almost unreadable. They are full of semiliterate business jargon, including accounting jargon, and are cluttered with badly written and incomprehensible governance reports.

- The limitations of corporate governance systems should be recognised. Common sense, management skills and business savvy are more important to commercial success than board structures. All the major banks and many supermarket and pub companies have recently suffered colossal business and financial problems, in spite of, or perhaps because of, their adherence to governance guidelines.

- There should be an approximately equal balance between executives and non-executives. A majority of executives is not necessarily harmful, provided non-executives are able to make their voices heard.

- It is often better if a chairman has previously been the chief executive of the company. This encourages chief executives, who may wish to become chairmen in the future, to take a long-term view, avoiding problems of profit-maximisation policies in the years running up to the departure of a chief executive.

- A maximum tenure of 9 years for non-executive directors is not advisable, since inexperienced boards, unfamiliar with the effects of the 'last recession' on their companies, are likely to reduce financial stability.

- An excessive focus on achieving financial or other targets for executives can be counter-productive. There's no evidence that the type of targets preferred by corporate governance guidelines actually work and there is considerable evidence that attempting to reach ambitious financial targets is harmful.

(continued)

(continued)

- It is far more important for directors to take account of the views of employees and customers than of the views of institutional shareholders. Shareholders should be listened to with respect, but caution should be exercised in implementing the views of short-term shareholders. It should also be understood that modern institutional shareholders may have a serious conflict of interest, as they are often concerned with their own quarterly portfolio performance, whereas corporate health often requires objectives which lie 5, 10 or 20 years in the future.

Comment on this statement in the light of the UK's approach to corporate governance.

 Visit the Online Resource Centre for solutions to all these end of chapter questions plus visual walkthrough solutions. You can test your understanding with extra questions and answers, explore additional case studies based on real companies, take a guided tour through a company report and much more. Go to the Online Resource Centre at **www.oxfordtextbooks.co.uk/orc/maynard2e/**

4

Published financial statements of companies

➤ Introduction

The usefulness of financial statements to users will be enhanced if they are comparable and understandable. There therefore needs to be some consistency in the presentation of the financial statements between different years of one company and between different companies. IAS 1 *Presentation of Financial Statements* sets out overall requirements for the presentation of the statements of financial position, comprehensive income and changes in equity, guidelines for their structure, and requirements for their content. IAS 7 *Statement of Cash Flows* sets out the same requirements for the statement of cash flows. Valid comparisons also require users to have knowledge of companies' accounting methods, and so IAS 8 *Accounting Policies, Changes in Accounting Estimates and Errors* specifies further details of how companies should select and disclose the accounting policies that underpin their financial numbers.

This chapter examines the requirements of these three financial reporting standards, including various related initiatives in progress, and illustrates how the financial statements are drawn up and presented through the use of examples and company annual reports.

★ Learning objectives

After studying this chapter you will be able to:

- draw up the four main financial statements in accordance with the requirements of IASs 1 and 7, including alternative presentations where permitted
- explain the underpinning principles relating to presentation contained in IAS 1
- understand the purpose and nature of notes to the financial statements
- understand the significance of accounting policies, when changes to these and accounting estimates can be made, and how this is presented.

✔ Key issues checklist

- ❑ Underpinning aim and principles of financial statement presentation.
- ❑ The going concern principle
- ❑ Materiality
- ❑ Presentation of the statement of financial position (IAS 1)
  - ❑ Required disclosures.
  - ❑ The distinction between current and non-current assets and liabilities.
- ❑ Presentation of the statement of comprehensive income (IAS 1)
  - ❑ The distinction between profit and loss, and other comprehensive income.
  - ❑ The two alternative methods of presenting the statement of comprehensive income— as one statement or as two.
  - ❑ Required disclosures.
  - ❑ The alternative methods for presenting the statement of profit or loss—analysing expenses by nature or function.
- ❑ Presentation of the statement of changes in equity (IAS 1)
- ❑ The statement of cash flows (IAS 7)
  - ❑ Aim and presentation.
  - ❑ Cash flows from operating, investing and financing activities.
  - ❑ The two alternatives of deriving cash flows from operating activities—the direct and indirect methods.
  - ❑ The net debt reconciliation to cash flows
- ❑ The purpose and types of notes to the financial statements.
- ❑ Accounting policies—the need for them and the areas requiring them.
- ❑ Accounting estimates and judgements.
- ❑ Changes in accounting policies.
- ❑ Changes in accounting estimates.
- ❑ Dealing with errors.
- ❑ Potential changes to the presentation of financial statements.

4.1 Key financial statements

As discussed in Chapter 1, the users of financial statements require information relating to the financial position, financial performance and cash flows of an entity in order to assist them in predicting the entity's future cash flows and, in particular, their timing and uncertainty. Companies produce four key financial statements at least annually to satisfy the information needs of their investors and lenders—the statement of financial position, the statement of comprehensive income (which incorporates the statement of profit or loss and **other comprehensive income**), the statement of cash flows and the statement of changes in equity, which analyses the changes that have occurred over the financial year to the equity balances, which may not be easily discernible from the other financial statements.

One of the underpinning enhancing characteristics of financial information is that it should be comparable, both within an entity from year to year and from entity to entity. Thus, the financial statements need to be structured and presented in a similar manner from year to year and entity to entity, and contain the same type of information.

The international financial reporting standard that addresses these issues is IAS 1 *Presentation of Financial Statements*. This standard sets out the components of financial statements and minimum requirements for disclosure in the statements of financial position, comprehensive income and changes in equity. These requirements for the statement of cash flows are specified in a different financial reporting standard, IAS 7 *Statement of Cash Flows*.

4.2 IAS 1 *Presentation of Financial Statements*

4.2.1 Present fairly

IAS 1 repeats some of the details relating to the purpose of financial statements contained in the IASB's *Conceptual Framework* (see discussion in Chapter 2). In addition it states that:

> Financial statements shall present fairly the financial position, financial performance and cash flows of an entity.

> *(IASB, 2007, para. 15)*

The key words here are 'present fairly'. Remember, for UK companies the statutory overriding requirement of financial statements is that they should show a 'true and fair' view, which is specified in Companies Act 2006. Thus, the IASB is including a similar requirement for all companies worldwide that use international financial reporting standards (IFRS). It is accepted that the phrases 'true and fair view' and 'present fairly' have the same meaning.

Fair presentation requires the faithful representation of the effects of transactions, other events and conditions in accordance with the definitions and recognition criteria for assets, liabilities, income and expenses set out in the *Conceptual Framework*. In virtually all circumstances a company achieves a fair presentation by complying with all applicable IFRS. UK legislation allows what is termed the 'true and fair override', which means that departure from the application of a standard is permitted if the alternative accounting treatment or disclosures ensure that the financial statements show a true and fair view. This is also permitted by IAS 1, where compliance with a requirement of an IFRS can be ignored if it would be so misleading that it would conflict with the objective of financial statements as set out in the *Conceptual Framework*. However, such departures are extremely rare, and the IASB provides no examples of such instances.

4.2.2 Underpinning principles

IAS 1 specifies that, apart from cash flow information, the basis of accounting is accruals; and here this means that the elements of financial accounting are recognised when they satisfy the definitions and recognition criteria set out in the *Conceptual Framework*.

Reminder *The elements are assets, liabilities, equity, income and expenses.*

The standard confirms that financial statements should be prepared on a going concern basis, unless management intends to liquidate the entity or to cease trading, or has no realistic alternative but to do so. There is minimal guidance about going concern in IAS 1 for the preparers, with an explanation that management must make an assessment of the company's ability to continue as a going concern and, in doing so, should take into account all available information about the future which is at least, but not limited to, 12 months from the end of the reporting period. The extent of the review period is a matter of judgement based on facts and circumstances. If there are material uncertainties that cast significant doubt upon a company's ability to continue as a going concern, these should be disclosed. If the company is not considered a going concern, this should be disclosed together with the basis of accounting that has been used. If there are no uncertainties identified, then going concern is presumed in the preparation of the financial statements.

The financial crisis of 2008 turned a spotlight on the assessment and reporting of issues relating to going concern. The auditors of financial institutions which collapsed during the financial crisis, such as Northern Rock in the UK, were criticised during the House of Lords Economic Affairs Committee 2010 investigation into 'Auditors: Market concentration and their role' for making little mention of issues to do with going concern. The Financial Reporting Council (FRC) commissioned an inquiry by Lord Sharman into going concern and **liquidity risk** which reported in 2012. Lord Sharman's conclusions set out that the going concern assessment process should be integrated with the directors' business planning and risk management processes, and not be seen as a separate exercise. The assessment process should always be transparent and not just carried out or reported on when there are heightened risks. Going concern should have an appropriate definition, and there should be clarity as to the thresholds to be used and the purposes of the required disclosures, which are all

Table 4.1 Assessment of going concern and relevant disclosures

Conclusion	Resulting disclosures
The going concern basis of accounting is appropriate and there are no material uncertainties.	A statement is made that the adoption of the going concern basis of accounting is considered appropriate. Disclosure will need to be made about liquidity risk, other uncertainties and key assumptions concerning going concern to give a true and fair view. Disclosure of principal risks and uncertainties is required.
The going concern basis of accounting is appropriate, but there are material uncertainties.	Disclosures explaining the specific nature of the material uncertainties that may cast significant doubt and explaining why the going concern basis has still been adopted. Other disclosures will have to be made to give a true and fair view.
The going concern basis is not appropriate (likely to be rare).	Disclosures explaining the basis of accounting adopted and providing any other information necessary to give a true and fair view.

consistently understood in an international arena. The recommendations of the inquiry have been incorporated into the *UK Corporate Governance Code 2014* (see Chapter 3 for details of this). In addition, further details of requirements are included in the FRC's *Guidance on Risk Management, Internal Control and Related Financial and Business Reporting*, which was published in 2014. This provides more guidance on how the assessment of material uncertainties could be performed, for example by considering how the company would react to a significant future catastrophe, and what mitigating controls were in place to minimise the impact. The minimum period of this assessment is extended beyond that required by IAS 1 and clarified as 12 months from the date of approval of the financial statements.

The reporting of the assessment of going concern is now more explicit with three alternative reporting scenarios as shown in Table 4.1.

In addition to an assessment of whether the going concern basis of accounting is appropriate, companies are also required to provide a longer term viability statement. This should explain how the directors have assessed the prospects of the company, over what period they have done so and why they consider that period to be appropriate. They should also state whether they have a reasonable expectation that the company will be able to continue in operation and meet its liabilities as they fall due over the period of their assessment, drawing attention to any qualifications or assumptions as necessary.

Financial reporting in practice 4.1 | Next 2015

This fairly brief statement on going concern is included in Next's 2015 corporate governance report. Note that it refers to other places in the annual report where the issues of risk are discussed. Typically this results in information about how companies have assessed going concern being scattered in various parts of their report, making it difficult for users to obtain a coherent picture.

(continued)

(continued)

Going concern

The Group's business activities, together with the factors likely to affect its future development, performance and position are set out in the Strategic Report. The Strategic Report also describes the Group's financial position, cash flows and borrowing facilities, further information on which is detailed in the financial statements. Information on the Group's financial management objectives, and how derivative instruments are used to hedge its capital, credit and liquidity risks, is provided in Note 27 to the financial statements.

The Directors report that, having reviewed current performance and forecasts, they have a reasonable expectation that the Group has adequate resources to continue its operations for the foreseeable future. For this reason, they have continued to adopt the going concern basis in preparing the financial statements.

4.2.3 Aggregation and materiality

Companies have to account for large numbers of transactions and other events every day, and determine how their accounting systems are to record these. This requires aggregation of the transactions and items into classes according to their nature or function, and a condensing of this data into the line items that make up the financial statements. IAS 1 requires companies to present separately each material class of similar items; this may be on the face of the financial statements or, if considered not sufficiently material for this, the item is, or items are, disclosed in the notes to the financial statements.

 Examples of aggregation

1   Companies have numerous tangible non-current assets which they use to generate their revenues and profits. These assets are aggregated into different classes, such as property, machinery, fixtures and fittings, and motor vehicles, as users of the financial statements do not need to know the values of all the individual assets. Information about the total values of each class is useful for the users and thus needs to be disclosed, but probably not on the face of the statement of financial position, where the key information is the value of the tangible non-current assets in aggregate. Thus, the breakdown of non-current assets showing the totals of the different classes will be in a note to the financial statements.

2   A company will have hundreds of overhead expense categories. Details of all of these would not be useful to users of financial information as this would be superfluous information. They are therefore aggregated on the face of the statement of comprehensive income, either according to the function of the expense (is it a cost of sale expense, or a distribution cost or an administrative expense?), or according to the nature of the expense (what type of expense is it, e.g. raw material used, employee cost, depreciation?).

Although IAS 1 specifies the minimum requirements for which line items are required to be shown on the face of the financial statements, it does not specify the recognition, measurement and disclosure requirements for specific transactions and other events. These are dealt with by other IFRS and are discussed in later chapters. IAS 1 does not prevent companies from presenting other line items if they choose to do so, but companies have to consider the qualitative characteristic of understandability, and ensure that the overall message needing to be conveyed about the financial results or position is not lost in extra information. This may mean that users find IAS 1 financial statements are less comparable from company-to-company; and this is a criticism of the standard.

Materiality is defined in the *Conceptual Framework* by reference to the underpinning characteristic of relevance, and is discussed in Chapter 1 (see section 1.3.1).

⚠ **Reminder** *Information is material if omitting it or misstating it could influence decisions that the users of financial statements make.*

Materiality therefore acts as a filter through which companies sift information, and is a matter of judgement for each company individually. Critics of international financial reporting suggest that the concept is often misapplied, leading to financial statements being both overloaded with immaterial detail and missing important information. Criticisms that are commonly cited include the use of disclosure requirements as a checklist, and **accounting policies** using words unnecessarily verbatim from the particular IFRS. Some companies and auditors appear to place too much focus on the quantitative aspect of materiality, including overreliance on numerical thresholds in making materiality judgements. It may be considered easier, particularly when under time pressure to produce and sign off financial statements, to include information instead of forming an opinion as to whether it is strictly necessary.

The IASB has responded to calls for improvements in disclosures, where materiality plays a large part, by undertaking a broad-based initiative to explore how disclosures in financial reporting can be improved. At the time of writing, various sub-projects under this initiative are continuing. As a first step, the initiative has resulted in some expansion of the advice on materiality being incorporated into IAS 1 to emphasise that materiality does not just relate to the main financial statements, but should be considered in relation to all the notes. Material information should not be obscured by immaterial detail, even if this is a disclosure requirement of an IFRS.

The IASB has also gone further, and in October 2015 issued an Exposure Draft of a Practice Statement (i.e. non-mandatory guidance) on the application of materiality to financial statements. The aim is for the statement to be a tool to help the management of companies exercise their judgement about what information is material and to facilitate discussions with auditors and regulators about those judgements. It provides guidance in the following three main areas:

(a) the characteristics of materiality

(b) how to apply the concept of materiality when making decisions about presenting and disclosing information in the financial statements

(c) how to assess whether omissions and misstatements of information are material to the financial statements.

Specifically it provides help to companies in determining whether information should be included or not, whether it should be presented on the face of the main financial statements or in the notes and whether it should be summarised or aggregated with other information.

4.2.4 Offsetting

In order for users to understand the substance of a transaction or other event, sufficient information about it needs to be presented. If a transaction gives rise to both an asset and a liability, which are material, these should be shown separately, and not netted off. The term used in IAS 1 for this is 'offsetting'. The same applies to transactions which give rise to both income and expenses; offsetting of these items is not allowed by IAS 1.

 Example of where offsetting is not permitted

A company acquires a non-current asset under a lease. The substance of this transaction is that the company has a resource, an asset and a liability for the amounts due under the lease agreement. Even though they are associated, the asset and the liability are shown separately and not netted off on the statement of financial position as both have separate cash flow implications.

   (Note: accounting for leases is discussed in full in Chapter 15.)

 Example of where offsetting is permitted

A retailer sells a motor vehicle, which has a net book value of £2,000, for £1,500. This transaction is incidental to the main revenue-generating activities of the company and the substance of the transaction is the net result of the disposal of the asset. The company therefore does not have to disclose the revenue received from the sale of £1,500 separately from the value of the asset that has been sold; the amounts can be netted off and the resulting loss on sale of £500 accounted for as a single item.

4.2.5 Comparative information and consistency

When a user examines a set of financial statements, probably one of the first things they wish to do is to compare key figures to the previous year to see what changes have occurred. This will also assist in assessment of trends for predictive purposes. (Methods of interpretation are discussed in more depth in Chapters 5 and 19.) It is important that these financial statements are readily available and so IAS 1 requires comparative quantitative information in respect of the previous period for all amounts reported on in the current year's financial statements. Comparative narrative and descriptive information should be provided if it is relevant to understanding the current period's financial statements.

Clearly, the information needs to be comparable, and so the presentation and classification of items should be retained from one reporting period to the next. If there is a significant change in the company's operations and the directors believe that a different presentation and classification would be more appropriate, a change in classification or presentation can be made. The reasons for this change and its impact on the financial statements must be explained fully in the notes to the financial statements so that the user can clearly understand the change made. The issue of a new or revised IFRS may also require a change in presentation. If there are changes, then the comparative information has to be reclassified unless it is impracticable to do so.

4.3 Structure and content of financial statements

IAS 1 defines a complete set of financial statements as comprising:

(a) a statement of financial position as at the end of the period;

(b) a statement of profit or loss and other comprehensive income for the period;

(c) a statement of changes in equity for the period;

(d) a statement of cash flows for the period;

(e) notes, comprising significant accounting policies and other explanatory information;

(f) comparative information in respect of the preceding period; and

(g) a statement of financial position as at the beginning of the preceding period when an entity applies an accounting policy retrospectively or makes a retrospective restatement of items in its financial statements, or when it reclassifies items in its financial statements.

(IASB, 2007, para. 10)

In revisions of IAS 1 in 2007 and 2011, the names of the financial statements were amended to those given in the list above; however, companies are still permitted to use the names balance sheet, income statement, statement of comprehensive income and cash flow statement, and, indeed, many UK companies still do. Throughout this textbook the titles 'statement of profit or loss', 'statement of comprehensive income' and 'statement of financial position' will be used, except in the financial reporting in practice examples which reproduce the terminology included in companies' actual financial statements.

For clarification, all financial statements and the notes must:

● be clearly identified with the name of the reporting company

- state whether the financial statements are for a single company or a group of companies
- show the date of the end of the reporting period
- show the currency in which the financial statements are presented
- state whether the amounts are in single units, thousands or millions.

Information to be presented for the statements of financial position, comprehensive income and changes in equity are discussed in the following sections.

4.4 Statement of financial position

! Reminder *The statement of financial position (or balance sheet) represents the fundamental accounting equation:*

$$Assets = Equity + Liabilities \quad or \quad Assets - Liabilities = Equity$$

An IAS 1 statement of financial position does not specify in which form the statement of financial position should be drawn up; it merely lists the line items which should be disclosed on the face of the statement:

(a) property, plant and equipment;

(b) investment property;

(c) **intangible assets**;

(d) financial assets (excluding amounts shown under (e), (h) and (i));

(e) investments accounted for using the **equity method**;

(f) biological assets;

(g) inventories;

(h) trade and other receivables;

(i) cash and cash equivalents;

(j) the total of assets classified as held for sale and assets included in **disposal groups** classified as held for sale in accordance with IFRS 5 *Non-current Assets Held for Sale and Discontinued Operations*;

(k) trade and other payables;

(l) **provisions**;

(m) financial liabilities (excluding amounts shown under (k) and (l));

(n) liabilities and assets for **current tax**, as defined in IAS 12 *Income Taxes*;

(o) **deferred tax** liabilities and deferred tax assets, as defined in IAS 12;

(p) liabilities included in disposal groups classified as held for sale in accordance with IFRS 5;

(q) **non-controlling interests**, presented within equity; and

(r) issued capital and reserves attributable to owners of the parent.

(IASB, 2007, para. 54)

4.4.1 Current and non-current classifications

IAS 1 also requires that both assets and liabilities are classified as current or non-current unless the company chooses a presentation based on liquidity, where all assets and liabilities are presented in order of liquidity. The distinction between non-current and current is important as it provides information about net assets that are circulating continuously as working capital as opposed to those used in the company's long-term operations, and assists in an assessment of the liquidity and solvency of the company (see Chapter 5 for further details of interpretation). The liquidity presentation, however, is relevant for financial institutions as such organisations do not supply goods or services within a clearly identifiable operating cycle.

Broadly, a current asset is one that a business holds primarily for trading purposes and expects to realise, sell or consume in its normal operating cycle (see Figure 4.1), for example inventory and trade receivables. A current liability is also one held primarily for trading purposes and which the business expects to settle within its normal operating cycle, for example trade payables. The usual period for the realisation of a current asset or the settlement of a current liability is 12 months after the end of the reporting period, but if these are items held primarily for trading purposes and it is expected that realisation or settlement will be after the 12-month period, they are still classified as current. All other assets and liabilities not meeting these criteria are defined as non-current.

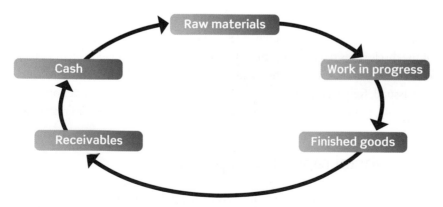

Figure 4.1 The operating cycle for a manufacturer

4.4.2 Presentation

The actual presentation of the statement of financial position, in other words the order of items, and where subtotals and totals are drawn, is not prescribed by IAS 1. Many UK companies, used to rigid Companies Act requirements prior to the 2005 change to IFRS, still present their statements of financial position vertically according to the second form of the balance sheet equation shown at the start of this section, thus arriving at a 'total' of net assets which equates to total equity; continental European companies tend to use the first form and may show a horizontal presentation with assets listed on the left-hand side, and liabilities and equity on the right.

Further line items may be included on the face of the statement of financial position if the judgement is that the items are relevant to an understanding of the company's financial position. In addition, sub-classifications of the line items presented should be disclosed in the notes to disaggregate the figures on the face of the statement. These disclosures are determined largely by the relevant IFRS, but also by the size, nature and function of the amounts involved.

 Examples of sub-classifications

1   Different classes of property, plant and equipment are disaggregated in accordance with IAS 16 *Property, Plant and Equipment*

2   Inventories are disaggregated into sub-classifications, such as goods for sale, production supplies, materials, and work in progress, in accordance with IAS 2 *Inventories*.

3   Financial assets are disaggregated into those measured at fair value through profit and loss, at fair value through other comprehensive income and at **amortised cost**, with further sub-classifications as required by IFRS 9 *Financial Instruments*.

4.4.3 Share capital

As share capital does not have its own international accounting standard, IAS 1 provides details of the disclosures required for this line item so that users will have an understanding of the different classes of share capital the company has and, for each class, the numbers of shares authorised, issued, fully paid or not fully paid, shares reserved for issue under options or other contracts for sale, their par value, and details of any rights, preferences and restrictions.

4.4.4 Financial reporting in practice

The following company example demonstrates the application of the IAS 1 requirements for a statement of financial position for the Spanish airline operator, International Airlines Group, which includes British Airways, Iberia and Vueling.

Financial reporting in practice 4.2   International Airlines Group, 2014

Consolidated Balance Sheet

	Note	December 31, 2014 €m	December 31, 2013 €m
Non-current assets			
Property, plant and equipment	13	**11,784**	10,228
Intangible assets	16	**2,438**	2,196
Investments in associates	17	**27**	25
Available-for-sale financial assets	18	**84**	1,092
Employee benefit assets	32	**855**	485
Derivative financial instruments	27	**80**	35
Deferred tax assets	10	**769**	501
Other non-current assets	19	**188**	197
		16,225	14,759
Current assets			
Non-current assets held for sale	15	**18**	12
Inventories		**424**	411
Trade receivables	19	**1,252**	1,196
Other current assets	19	**611**	631
Derivative financial instruments	27	**178**	135
Other current interest-bearing deposits	20	**3,416**	2,092
Cash and cash equivalents	20	**1,528**	1,541
		7,427	6,018
Total assets		**23,652**	20,777
Shareholders' equity			
Issued share capital	28	**1,020**	1,020
Share premium	28	**5,867**	5,867
Treasury shares	29	**(6)**	(42)
Other reserves	31	**(3,396)**	(2,936)
Total shareholders' equity		**3,485**	3,909
Non-controlling interest	31	**308**	307
Total equity		**3,793**	4,216

(continued)

(continued)

Non-current liabilities			
Interest-bearing long-term borrowings	23	**5,904**	4,535
Employee benefit obligations	32	**1,324**	738
Deferred tax liability	10	**278**	884
Provisions for liabilities and charges	25	**1,967**	1,796
Derivative financial instruments	27	**359**	66
Other long-term liabilities	22	**226**	225
		10,058	8,244
Current liabilities			
Current portion of long-term borrowings	23	**713**	587
Trade and other payables	21	**3,281**	3,297
Deferred revenue on ticket sales		**3,933**	3,496
Derivative financial instruments	27	**1,313**	528
Current tax payable		**57**	11
Provisions for liabilities and charges	25	**504**	398
		9,801	8,317
Total liabilities		**19,859**	16,561
Total equity and liabilities		**23,652**	20,777

Financial reporting in practice 4.3 illustrates the disclosures for share capital.

Financial reporting in practice 4.3   International Airlines Group, 2014

28 Share capital and share premium

Allotted, called up and fully paid	Number of shares 000s	Ordinary share Capital € million	Share premium € million
1 January 2014: Ordinary shares of €0.50 each	2,040,079	1,020	5,867
31 December 2014	2,040,079	1,020	5,867

4.5 Statement of profit or loss and other comprehensive income

As indicated in section 4.3, the name of this key performance statement was changed to 'statement of profit or loss and other comprehensive income' by the IASB in its project on the presentation of other comprehensive income, which concluded in June 2011. IAS 1 now uses the new name.

4.5.1 Presentation

The statement of comprehensive income effectively comprises two statements and a company may present it in one of two ways:

1   As a single statement that includes the items making up profit or loss (the statement of profit or loss) followed by items of other comprehensive income

2   As two separate statements—the statement of profit or loss and a second statement which starts with net profit or loss for the period, and includes the items of other comprehensive income.

If the financial statements are for a group of companies, both net profit or loss and net other comprehensive income must be allocated between that attributable to:

(a) non-controlling interests

(b) owners of the parent company.

This is discussed in more detail in Chapter 17.

As for the statement of financial position, IAS 1 specifies the line items that are to be presented on the face of the profit or loss section of the statement of comprehensive income. These are fairly minimal:

   (a)   Revenue;

   (b)   Gains and losses arising from the derecognition of financial assets measured at amortised cost;

   (c)   Finance costs;

   (d)   Impairment losses determined in accordance with IFRS 9;

   (e)   Share of the profit or loss of **associates** and **joint ventures** accounted for using the equity method;

   (f)   If a financial asset is reclassified from the amortised cost measurement category to fair value through profit or loss, any gain or loss arising from a difference between the previous amortised cost of the financial asset and its fair value at the reclassification date (as defined in IFRS 9);

(g) If a financial asset is reclassified out of the fair value through other comprehensive income measurement category to fair value through profit or loss, any cumulative gain or loss previously recognised in other comprehensive income that is reclassified to profit or loss;

(h) Tax expense; and

(i) A single amount comprising the total of **discontinued operations**.

(IASB, 2007, para. 82)

Many companies will elect to include other line items to show an analysis of the figures making up the totals and subtotals in the statement, and this is required when they are material and relevant to an understanding of the company's financial performance. These may include one-off items that are outside normal trading or business activities, or items that are material owing to their size in a particular period. These items are often referred to as **exceptional items**, although IAS 1 does not use this term. IAS 1 provides the following examples of circumstances which would give rise to separate disclosure of items of income and expense:

(a) Write-downs of inventories to **net realisable value** or of property, plant and equipment to **recoverable amount**, as well as reversals of such write-downs;

(b) **Restructurings** of the activities of an entity and reversals of any provisions for the costs of restructuring;

(c) Disposals of items of property, plant and equipment;

(d) Disposals of investments;

(e) Discontinued operations;

(f) Litigation settlements; and

(g) Other reversals of provisions.

(IASB, 2007, para. 98)

However, it is apparent from Financial reporting in practice 4.4 that companies will choose such disclosures according to their circumstances.

Financial reporting in practice 4.4 | J Sainsbury plc, 2015 |

J Sainsbury plc's financial statements provide an analysis of its loss before tax of £(72) million on the face of its income statement, analysing its loss before tax into what the company describes as 'underlying profit before tax', i.e. profit from its core supermarket activities, and other items of profit and loss. This will assist users in understanding how the company achieved its profits or losses in a particular year and provide more comparable information from one year to the next.

Group income statement for the 52 weeks to 14 March 2015

	Note	2015 £m	2014 £m
Revenue	4	**23,775**	23,949
Cost of sales		**(22,567)**	(22,562)
Gross profit		**1,208**	1,387
Administrative expenses		**(1,132)**	(444)
Other income		**5**	66
Operating profit	5	**81**	1,009
Finance income	6	**19**	20
Finance costs	6	**(180)**	(159)
Share of post-tax profit from joint ventures and associates	14	**8**	28
(Loss)/profit before taxation		**(72)**	898
Analysed as:			
Underlying profit before tax		**681**	798
Profit on disposal of properties	3	**7**	52
Investment property fair value movements	3	**7**	–
Retail financing fair value movements	3	**(30)**	(8)
IAS 19 pension financing charge	3	**(31)**	(23)
Defined benefit pension scheme expenses	3	**(6)**	(7)
Acquisition adjustments	3	**13**	18
One-off items	3	**(713)**	68
		(72)	898
Income tax expense	8	**(94)**	(182)
(Loss)/profit for the financial year		**(166)**	716

4.5.2 Statement of profit or loss analysis of expenses

The statement of profit or loss, whether presented as a separate statement or as part of the statement of comprehensive income, includes items of income and expense recognised in a period according to the accruals principle. A company can choose one of two methods for analysing its expenses according to which provides information that is reliable and more relevant—an analysis either by their nature or by their function within the company.

4.5.3 Nature of expense method

This can be thought of as analysing an expense by its type and may be simple to apply because the expenses do not have to be allocated to different functions across the business. An example of this form of statement of profit or loss is as follows.

 Example statement

Business XXX		
Statement of profit or loss for accounting period (expenses analysed by nature)		
	£	£
Revenue		XX
Other income		XX
Changes in inventories of finished goods and work in progress	XX	
Raw materials and consumables used	XX	
Employee benefits expense	XX	
Depreciation and **amortisation** expense	XX	
Other expenses	XX	
Total expenses		(XX)
Profit before tax		XX

The choice of this method will depend on a company's history and industry, but typically some engineering and manufacturing companies use this presentational format. One key figure which is not disclosed by this analysis is gross profit, which such companies may not wish their competitors to see.

Financial reporting in practice **4.5**	GKN plc, 2014

GKN plc is a global engineering company providing technology and engineering for automotive, aerospace, and off-highway manufacturers. It analyses expenses by their nature in its 2014 financial statements.

Consolidated Income Statement for the year ended 31 December 2014

	Notes	2014 £m	2013 £m
Sales	2	6,982	7,136
Trading profit		612	597

Change in value of derivative and other financial instruments		(209)	26
Amortisation of non-operating intangible assets arising on business combinations		(69)	(75)
Gains and losses on changes in Group structure		24	12
Impairment charges	11	(69)	–
Operating profit		289	560
Share of post-tax earnings of joint ventures	13	61	52
Interest payable		(75)	(76)
Interest receivable		2	3
Other net financing charges		(56)	(55)
Net financing costs	5	(129)	(128)
Profit before taxation		221	484
Taxation	6	(47)	(77)
Profit after taxation for the year		174	407

Note 4 to the income statement provides the analysis of expenses.

4 Operating profit

The analysis of the additional components of operating profit is shown below:

(a) Trading profit

	2014 £m	2013 £m
Sales by subsidiaries	6,982	7,136
Operating costs		
Change in stocks of finished goods and work in progress	44	46
Raw materials and consumables	(3,127)	(3,233)
Staff costs (note 9)	(1,809)	(1,847)
Reorganisation costs (ii):		
Redundancy and other employee related amounts	(3)	(24)
Depreciation of property, plant and equipment (iii)	(216)	(235)
Impairment of property, plant and equipment	(4)	(2)
Amortisation of operating intangible assets	(32)	(32)
Operating **lease rentals** payable:		
Plant and equipment	(17)	(16)

(continued)

(continued)		
Property	(29)	(30)
Impairment of trade receivables	(5)	(3)
Amortisation of government capital grants	2	3
Net exchange differences on foreign currency transactions	8	(11)
Acquisition restructuring accrual release	–	4
Other costs	(1,182)	(1,159)
	(6,370)	(6,539)
Trading profit	612	597

4.5.4 Function of expense method

Referred to also as the 'cost of sales' method, this is the more common method seen in companies as it is considered to provide more relevant information to the users than the nature of expense method. However, the allocation of expenses to different functions (for example, to cost of sales and administration) may be considered arbitrary and involve considerable judgement. An example of this form of statement of profit or loss is as follows.

 Example statement

Business XXX

Statement of profit or loss for accounting period (expenses analysed by function)

	£
Revenue	XX
Cost of sales	(XX)
Gross profit	XX
Other income	XX
Distribution costs	(XX)
Administrative expenses	(XX)
Other expenses	(XX)
Profit before tax	XX

IAS 1 requires companies that choose this method to provide additional information on the nature of some expenses in the notes to the financial statements, for example depreciation, and amortisation expenses and employee benefits costs.

Worked example 4.1: to show different methods of drawing up the statement of profit or loss

Oakthorpe plc is a manufacturing company and its trial balance at 31 March 20X6 includes the following balances:

		Debit £	Credit £
Sales			175,335
Inventories at 1 April 20X5			
Raw materials		1,675	
Finished goods (FG)		1,005	
Purchases of raw materials		92,895	
Wages and salaries:	production staff	18,600	
	other staff	15,315	
Insurance		3,400	
Telecommunications costs		2,820	
Hire of plant and machinery		1,550	
Depreciation expense:	buildings	1,000	
	plant and machinery	2,400	
	motor vehicles	520	
Other expenses:	distribution	6,250	
	administrative	8,520	

Inventories of raw materials and finished goods at 31 March 20X6 are valued at £2,200 and £960 respectively. There is no work in progress (WIP).

Required:

In so far as the information permits, draw up the statement of profit or loss for Oakthorpe plc for the year ended 31 March 20X6 showing expenses analysed (i) by nature and (ii) by function.

(i) Analysis of expenses by nature

	Changes in inventories of WIP & FG £	Employee benefits £	Raw materials & consumables £	Other expenses £
Opening inventories	1,005		1,675	
Purchases of raw materials				92,895
Wages and salaries:				
Production staff		18,600		
Other staff				15,315

Insurance				3,400
Telecommunications costs				2,820
Hire of plant and machinery				1,550
Other expenses:				
Distribution				6,250
Administrative				8,520
Closing inventories	(960)		(2,200)	
	45	18,600	92,370	37,855

Oakthorpe plc
Statement of profit or loss for the year ended 31 March 20X6

	£
Revenue	175,335
Changes in inventories of finished goods and work in progress	(45)
Raw materials and consumables used	(92,370)
Employee benefits expense	(18,600)
Depreciation and amortisation expense (1,000 + 2,400 + 520)	(3,920)
Other expenses	(37,855)
Profit before tax	22,545

(ii) Analysis of expenses by function

	Cost of sales	Distribution costs	Admin expenses
	£	£	£
Opening inventories (1,675 + 1,005)	2,680		
Purchases of raw materials	92,895		
Wages and salaries:			
Production staff	18,600		
Other staff			15,315
Insurance			3,400
Telecommunications costs			2,820
Hire of plant and machinery			1,550
Depreciation	2,400	520	1,000
Other expenses		6,250	8,520
Closing inventories (960 + 2,200)	(3,160)		
	113,415	6,770	32,605

Oakthorpe plc
Statement of profit or loss for the year ended 31 March 20X6

	£
Revenue	175,335
Cost of sales	(113,415)
Gross profit	61,920
Distribution costs	(6,770)
Administrative expenses	(32,605)
Profit before tax	22,545

4.5.5 Comprehensive income

Total comprehensive income is the change in equity that has arisen from all transactions other than with the owners in their capacity as owners. It includes both profits or losses and other comprehensive income. The rebuttable presumption is that items of income and expense will be included in profit or loss. Only where required or permitted by financial reporting standards are some items of income or expense classified in other comprehensive income.

 Example of other comprehensive income items

In the year 20X7 a company makes a profit after tax of £500,000. During the year the company issued new shares for £2 million and paid dividends of £200,000.

This will result in the following changes to the company's equity over 20X7:

1   An increase of £500,000 from the profits made

2   An increase of £2 million from the issue of new shares

3   A decrease of £200,000 from the payment of dividends.

Items 2 and 3 are transactions with the shareholders in their capacity as owners of the business. The statement of comprehensive income will therefore include only the transactions making up the profits after tax of £500,000.

However, suppose the company holds some financial assets which are valued at fair value (market value), and these increase in value over the course of 20X7 by £100,000.

The asset values on the statement of financial position have increased by £100,000 and, in order for the balance sheet equation to hold, equity will also increase by £100,000. Thus, the statement of comprehensive income needs to include this amount as this is not a transaction with the shareholders. Depending on the type of financial asset, the increase will be included either as part of profit or loss, or as other comprehensive income. (IFRS 9 Financial Instruments specifies which—see Chapter 14 for further details.)

IAS 1 provides the following examples of items which are classified as other comprehensive income:

- revaluation gains and losses
- **remeasurements** of defined benefit plans
- gains and losses arising from translating the financial statements of a foreign operation (not covered by this textbook)
- gains and losses from investments in equity instruments designated at fair value through other comprehensive income
- gains and losses on financial assets measured at fair value through other comprehensive income
- for particular liabilities designated as at fair value through profit or loss, the amount of the change in fair value that is attributable to changes in the liability's credit risk
- items relating to hedging instruments (which are beyond the scope of this textbook).

Some items included in other comprehensive income can have a considerable effect on the overall financial performance of an entity. The other comprehensive income items are therefore classified by nature and grouped into those that, in accordance with other IFRS:

(a) will not be reclassified subsequently to profit or loss; and

(b) will be reclassified subsequently to profit or loss when specific conditions are met.

The groupings are to make clear the effects these items may have on profit or loss in the future. Reclassifications arise when an item or transaction has been accounted for initially through other comprehensive income, and is subsequently required to be accounted for in profit or loss according to the relevant financial reporting standard. This is often referred to as 'recycling'. Examples of such reclassifications arise from the disposal of a foreign operation, or from cash flow hedges, and are largely outside the scope of this textbook.

4.5.6 Statement of comprehensive income pro forma

A full statement of comprehensive income with profit and loss expenses analysed by function is shown in the following example statement.

Example statement

XXX plc

Statement of comprehensive income for the year ended 31 December 20X7

	20X7
	£000
Revenue	390,000
Cost of sales	(245,000)
Gross profit	145,000
Other income	20,667
Distribution costs	(9,000)
Administrative expenses	(20,000)
Other expenses	(2,100)
Finance costs	(8,000)
Share of profit of associates[1]	35,100
Profit before tax	161,667
Income tax expense	(40,417)
Profit for the year from continuing operations	121,250
Loss for the year from discontinued operations[2]	–
Profit for the year	121,250
Other comprehensive income:	
Not subsequently reclassified to profit or loss	
Gains on property revaluation	933
Share of other comprehensive income of associates[1]	400
Income tax relating to components of other comprehensive income	(267)
Other comprehensive income for the year, net of tax	1,066
Total comprehensive income for the year	122,316
Profit attributable to:	
Owners of the parent	97,000
Non-controlling interests[1]	24,250
	121,250
Total comprehensive income attributable to:	
Owners of the parent	97,659
Non-controlling interests[1]	24,657
	122,316

[1] Associates and non-controlling interests, and their accounting treatment are explained in Chapters 17 and 18.
[2] Discontinued operations and their accounting treatment are explained in Chapter 6.

4.5.7 Why have a statement of comprehensive income?

The net income of simple entities that deal with day-to-day trading transactions related to the selling of a product or service is measured by net profit according to the accruals basis. For these entities the only changes to equity, apart from transactions with the owners, arise from the net profit or loss, and a statement of profit or loss is sufficient to show this. However, once changes in asset valuations from the end of one year to the next need to be accounted for as a result of some assets and liabilities being permitted to be measured using bases other than historic cost (such as when non-current assets are measured at fair value), the presentation of the effect of these changes on equity has had to be addressed. These changes are sometimes referred to as *unrealised* gains or losses (as opposed to *realised* gains and losses, which are profit and loss items) although these terms are not used in IFRS:

Prior to the current version of IAS 1, these changes were accounted for purely as a change in equity and were included only in the statement of changes in equity (see section 4.6). However, the definitions of income and expenses as given in the IASB's *Conceptual Framework* (see Chapter 1) mean that the IASB consider there are no clear principles that can be used to separate income and expenses into two statements, and therefore they should all be included in one statement of comprehensive income. There is recognition, though, that the economic events that underpin income and expense items are different, and so a distinction is made between profit and loss items, and other comprehensive income. Although the overarching purpose of the statement of comprehensive income is to provide information about the overall financial performance of an entity, the notion of profit or loss is fundamental to users, and it is also important in determining the key earnings per share ratio (discussed in detail in Chapter 8). Chapter 5 also discusses on which line items users may focus in their interpretation of performance.

! **Reminder** *The IASB's revised Conceptual Framework's ED defines income as increases in assets or decreases in liabilities that result in increases in equity other than those relating to contributions from holders of equity claims.*

Expenses are decreases in assets or increases in liabilities that result in decreases in equity, other than those relating to distributions to holders of equity claims.

As discussed in Chapter 2, the *Conceptual Framework* ED includes a chapter on presentation and disclosure which sets out underpinning principles for the distinction between items included in profit and loss and items included in other comprehensive income.

4.6 Statement of changes in equity

Shareholders are the principal users of financial statements and their investment in the net assets of a company is represented by the equity balances. Changes in net assets result in, or are caused by, changes in equity. The statement of changes in equity analyses all these changes so that the shareholders can more readily discern what has caused the change in their investment from the end of one accounting period to the end of the next.

The statement reconciles the opening and closing equity balances shown in the statement of financial position by including net comprehensive income from the statement of comprehensive income together with all transactions with the owners in their capacity as owners. IAS 1 expands on this by specifying that the following information should be shown in the statement of changes in equity:

(a) total comprehensive income for the period, showing separately the total amounts attributable to owners of the parent and to non-controlling interests;

(b) for each component of equity, the effects of retrospective application or retrospective restatement recognised in accordance with IAS 8 (see section 4.8.3); and

(c) for each component of equity, a reconciliation between the carrying amount at the beginning and the end of the period, separately disclosing changes resulting from:

(i) profit or loss;

(ii) other comprehensive income; and

(iii) transactions with owners in their capacity as owners, showing separately contributions by and distributions (i.e. dividends) to owners and changes in ownership interests in subsidiaries that do not result in a loss of control.

(IASB, 2007, para. 106)

The amount of dividends paid to the owners during the period and the related amount of dividends per share should be disclosed either in the statement or in a disclosure note.

An example of a statement in changes of equity is given in the following statement. This uses the figures from the statement of comprehensive income given in the previous example statement, and includes a change in accounting policy (which is discussed in more detail in section 4.8.3), an issue of shares, and payments of dividends.

 Example statement

XXX plc

Statement of changes in equity for the year ended 31 December 20X7

	Ordinary share capital	Preference share capital (irredeemable)	Share premium	Retained earnings	Revaluation surplus	Total	Non-controlling interest[1]	Total equity
	£000	£000	£000	£000	£000	£000	£000	£000
At 1 January 20X7	550,000	30,000	10,000	161,300	1,600	752,900	48,600	801,500
Changes in accounting policy	–	–	–	400	–	400	100	500

Restated balance	550,000	30,000	10,000	161,700	1,600	753,300	48,700	802,000
Issue of share capital	50,000	–	10,000	–	–	60,000	–	60,000
Final dividends on ordinary shares	–	–	–	(12,000)	–	(12,000)	–	(12,000)
Final dividends on irredeemable shares	–	–	–	(3,000)	–	(3,000)	–	(3,000)
Total comprehensive income for the year	–	–	–	97,000	659	97,659	24,657	122,316
Transfer to retained earnings	–	–	–	200	(200)	–	–	–
At 31 December 20X7	600,000	30,000	20,000	243,900	2,059	895,959	73,357	969,316

These closing balances are the figures that will be shown on the statement of financial position at 31 December 20X7.

[1] Non-controlling interests and their accounting treatment are explained in Chapter 17.

4.7 Statement of cash flows

Cash is said to be the life blood of any organisation. Cash is needed to conduct operations, pay obligations and provide a return to investors. Users make decisions about whether to provide resources to a business and, as stated in the IASB's *Conceptual Framework* (discussed in Chapter 2), this is based on an assessment of an entity's prospects for future net cash inflows. Information about how a business generates and uses cash is therefore of prime importance to users of financial information.

A statement of cash flows on its own will not provide sufficient financial information for users. However, used in conjunction with the rest of the entity's financial statements, it will provide information that should enable the users to evaluate the changes in the business's net assets, its financial structure, including its liquidity and solvency, and its ability to adjust its cash flows in order to adapt to changing circumstances and opportunities. Any financial statement reports historic information and historical cash flow information is often used as an indicator of the amount, timing and certainty of future cash flows.

Cash is also much more 'real' than profits, which are reported on the basis of accruals, and require estimates and judgements. The difference between profits and cash flow was shown in Worked example 1.1 in chapter 1, reproduced in section 4.7.1, and illustrates how different profits and cash flows are from the same set of transactions. Many corporate collapses of seemingly profitable businesses have occurred because the businesses have simply run out of cash. It was as a result of some high-profile company failures in the early 1990s, such as the Bank of Credit and Commerce International, that standard-setters introduced the requirement for companies to include a statement of cash flows in their financial statements. In 1994 IAS 7 *Cash Flow Statements* was issued by the IASC, which was retitled *Statement of Cash Flows* by the IASB in 2007.

4.7.1 Example of a simple statement of cash flows

A statement of cash flows essentially details all cash flowing into a business net of all cash flowing out of a business, with the net cash flow reconciling opening cash balances with closing cash balances. It should be noted that cash is taken to mean cash-in-hand and bank balances, although this is defined more precisely by IAS 7 (see section 4.7.2).

 Worked example 4.2: to show the difference between profit and cash flows (taken from Chapter 1)

On 1 January 20X7 Giles starts his own business by investing £8,000 of his own money and getting a business contact to lend the business £2,000 for 5 years, on which interest will be paid at 5% p.a. Giles rents office space and pays £1,000 for furniture and equipment. During the first year the business purchases goods for resale for £6,000, of which £5,500 had been paid by 31 December 20X7. The business makes sales of £5,000 on credit and £1,500 for cash, and Giles's credit customers have paid £4,000 by 31 December 20X7. Office running costs paid during the year total £2,200, and Giles takes £1,000 out of the business for personal expenses. At the year end goods which had cost £2,000 are still on hand.

Required:

Draw up a financial performance statement on a cash basis for Giles' business for the year ended 31 December 20X7.

Giles' business statement of cash flows for the year ended 31 December 20X7

		£	£
Cash inflows (receipts)			
Owner investment			8,000
Loan			2,000
From sales	(1,500 + 4,000)		5,500
			15,500

Cash outflows (payments)

Furniture and equipment	1,000
Goods for resale	5,500
Office running costs	2,200
Owner's personal expenses	1,000
	(9,700)
Net cash flow	5,800
Cash balance at 1 January 20X7 *	–
Cash balance at 31 December 20X7	5,800

* This is zero in this example as the business started on 1 January. The resulting net cash flow is therefore equivalent to the cash balance at 31 December 20X7.

4.7.2 IAS 7 *Statement of Cash Flows*

A statement of cash flows in this form is not particularly useful; users need to know from which business activities the cash flows have arisen. The format of the IAS 7 statement of cash flows groups net cash flows under three activities (see Table 4.2).

Table 4.2 Format of IAS 7 statement of cash flows

Activity	Definition	Examples
Operating	Principal revenue-producing activities of the entity and other activities that are not investing or financing activities. They generally result from transactions that determine profit or loss	• Receipts from the sale of goods • Payments to suppliers for goods and services • Payments to employees • Income tax payments and refunds
Investing	The acquisition and disposal of long-term assets and other investments not included in cash equivalents. Essentially, this is expenditure on resources intended to generate future income and cash flows	• Payments for, and receipts from the sale of, long-term tangible and intangible assets • Payments for, and receipts from the sale of, equity or debt instruments in other companies
Financing	Activities that result in changes in the size and composition of the equity and borrowings of the entity. This cash flow information assists in predicting future cash outflows to the providers of capital	• Receipts from the issue of shares, debentures, loans, bonds and other short and long-term borrowings • Repayments of amounts borrowed • Repayments under leases

Interest and dividends received and paid should be disclosed separately, and there is choice of the activity under which they can be presented.

Interest paid	Usually operating, but may be financing
Interest received	Usually investing, but may be operating
Dividends received	Usually investing, but may be operating
Dividends paid	Usually financing, but may be operating.

The choice for interest payments and receipts and dividend receipts arises because finance charges and investment income are included in the determination of profit or loss, and yet they are associated with investment or financing activities. Dividend payments are cost of obtaining financial resources for a company and are therefore usually shown a financing activity cash flow. However it may be considered useful to show dividend payments as an operating activity in order to assist users to determine the ability of an entity to pay dividends out of operating cash flows.

Cash is termed 'cash and cash equivalents', and these terms are defined as follows:

| Cash | Cash on hand and demand deposits |
| Cash equivalents | Short-term, highly liquid investments that are readily convertible to known amounts of cash and which are subject to an insignificant risk of changes in value. |

Cash equivalents are held for the purpose of meeting short-term cash requirements rather than for investment purposes. For example, a deposit account with a maturity of three months or less. Bank overdrafts that are repayable on demand are classified as cash and cash equivalents, as they usually form an integral part of a business's cash management. A characteristic of such banking arrangements is that the bank balance often fluctuates from being positive to overdrawn. However bank borrowings are generally considered to be financing activities. There is clearly some discretion here and so IAS 7 requires companies to disclose how it defines its cash and cash equivalents, and to provide a reconciliation of these balances in the statement of cash flows to those in the statement of financial position.

Financial reporting in practice 4.6   Vodaphone, 2015

Vodafone's financial statements for the year ended 31 March 2015 include the following disclosure note relating to how it defines cash and cash equivalents.

20. Cash and cash equivalents

The majority of the Group's cash is held in bank deposits, money market funds or in repurchase agreements which have a maturity of three months or less to enable us to meet our short-term liquidity requirements.

(continued)

(continued)

Accounting policies

Cash and cash equivalents comprise cash in hand and call deposits, and other short-term highly liquid investments that are readily convertible to a known amount of cash and are subject to an insignificant risk of changes in value.

	2015 £m	2014 £m
Cash at bank and in hand	2,379	1,498
Money market funds	2,402	3,648
Repurchase agreements	2,000	4,799
Commercial paper	101	–
Short-term securitised investments	–	189
Cash and cash equivalents as presented in the statement of financial position	**6,882**	**10,134**
Bank overdrafts	(21)	(22)
Cash and cash equivalents as presented in the statement of cash flows	**6,861**	**10,112**

Cash and cash equivalents are held by the Group on a short-term basis with all having an original maturity of three months or less. The carrying amount approximates their fair value.

4.7.3 Direct and indirect methods of reporting cash flows from operating activities

Operating activities are the principal revenue-generating activities of a company and cash flows from operating activities will include:

(a) cash receipts from the sale of goods and the rendering of services;

(b) cash receipts from royalties, fees, commissions and other revenue;

(c) cash payments to suppliers for goods and services;

(d) cash payments to and on behalf of employees;

(e) cash payments or refunds of income taxes unless they can be specifically identified with financing and investing activities; and

(f) cash receipts and payments from contracts held for dealing or trading purposes.

(IASB 2004a, para. 14)

ℹ Reminder: *Profit from operations in the statement of profit or loss is the profit from such activities.*

IAS 7 permits companies a choice as to how they present cash generated from operating activities:

Direct method   Major classes of gross cash receipts and gross payments are disclosed.

Indirect method   Adjusts the company's profit or loss before tax for finance costs and investment income, the effects of non-cash transactions, and deferrals or accruals of past or future operating receipts and payments (i.e. the changes in inventories and operating receivables and payables).

The amount of cash flows arising from operating activities is a key indicator of the extent to which the operations of a company have generated sufficient cash flows to repay loans, maintain the operating capability of the entity, pay dividends and make new investments without having to take out external sources of financing. Information about the specific components of historical operating cash flows is useful, in conjunction with other information, in forecasting future operating cash flows. IAS 7 therefore recommends the direct method of presentation, although the indirect method is the usual method chosen by UK companies. This latter method is also easier to produce from financial accounting records.

The reconciliation of profit before tax to cash generated from operating activities also provides very useful information to users of the financial statements about the cash management of the company; this will be explored in more detail in the Chapters 5 and 19 on financial statement analysis. The reconciliation is shown as a disclosure note to the statement of cash flows. A full pro-forma for this is as follows.

 Example statement

Company XXX plc

Reconciliation of profit/loss before tax to cash generated from operations for the year ended 31 December 20XX

	£
Profit/(loss) before tax	X
Finance costs	X
Investment income	(X)
Depreciation charge	X
Amortisation charge	X
Loss/(profit) on disposal of non-current assets	X/(X)
(Increase)/decrease in inventories	(X)/X

(continued)

(continued)

(Increase)/decrease in trade and other receivables	(X)/X
(Increase)/decrease in prepayments	(X)/X
Increase/(decrease) in trade and other payables	X/(X)
Increase/(decrease) in accruals	X/(X)
Increase/(decrease) in provisions	X/(X)
Cash generated from operations	X

Note carefully which way round the brackets are shown in relation to whether the items of working capital have increased or decreased.

 Worked example 4.3: to show the calculation of cash generated from operating activities using both the direct and indirect methods

Extracts from the financial statements for Dewberry plc for the year ended 30 June 20X6 are as follows:

Statement of profit or loss for the year ended 30 June 20X6

	£000	£000
Revenue		21,000
Opening inventory	500	
Purchases	16,400	
	16,900	
Closing inventory	1,500	
Cost of sales		(15,400)
Gross profit		5,600
Expenses		(3,405)
Interest		(165)
Profit before tax		2,030
Corporation tax		(520)
Profit for the year		1,510

Expenses includes depreciation of £460,000 and a loss on the disposal of non-current assets of £20,000.

Balances from the statement of financial position at 30 June 20X6

	20X6	20X5
	£000	£000
Current assets		
Inventory	1,500	500
Trade receivables	2,680	890
Current liabilities		
Trade payables	1,100	680

Required:

Calculate the cash generated from operating activities using:

(i) the direct method

(ii) the indirect method.

(i) Cash generated from operating activities using the direct method

	£000	£000
Cash received from customers:		
Sales	21,000	
– Closing receivables	(2,680)	
+ Opening receivables	890	
		19,210
Cash paid to suppliers of goods:		
Purchases	16,400	
– Closing payables	(1,100)	
+ Opening payables	680	
		(15,980)
Cash paid to employees and other suppliers:		
Expenses from statement of profit or loss	3,405	
– Non-cash expenses: depreciation	(460)	
loss on disposal of non-current assets	(20)	
		(2,925)
Cash generated from operating activities		305

Note: if a breakdown of cost of sales was not provided, cash paid to suppliers of goods would have to be calculated as follows:

	£000
Cost of sales	15,400
+ Closing inventories	1,500
− Opening inventories	(500)
− Closing payables	(1,100)
+ Opening payables	680
Payments to suppliers	15,980

(ii) Cash generated from operating activities using the indirect method

	£000
Profit before tax	2,030
Add back interest expense	165
Add back non-cash expenses: depreciation	460
loss on disposal of non-current assets	20
Change in inventory: increase (1,500 − 500)	(1,000)
Change in trade receivables: increase (2,680 − 890)	(1,790)
Change in trade payables: increase (1,100 − 680)	420
Cash generated from operating activities	305

4.7.4 Cash flows from investing and financing activities

Investing activities are the acquisition and disposal of long-term assets and other investments not included in cash equivalents. The separate disclosure of cash flows arising from such activities is important because they represent the extent to which expenditures have been made for resources intended to generate future income and cash flows. Only expenditure that results in a recognised asset in the statement of financial position is able to be classified as an investing activity. Examples of cash flows arising from investing activities include:

(a) cash payments to acquire property, plant and equipment, intangibles and other long-term assets;

(b) cash receipts from sales of property, plant and equipment, intangibles and other long-term assets;

(c) cash payments to acquire equity or debt instruments of other entities and interests in joint ventures;

(d) cash receipts from sales of equity or debt instruments of other entities and interests in joint ventures;

(e) cash advances and loans made to other parties;

(f) cash receipts from the repayment of advances and loans made to other parties.

(IASB, 2004a, para. 16)

Financing activities of a company are activities that result in changes in the size and composition of its equity and borrowings. The separate disclosure of cash flows arising from financing activities assists users in predicting claims on future cash flows by providers of capital to the entity. Examples include:

(a) cash proceeds from issuing shares or other equity instruments;

(b) cash payments to owners to acquire or redeem the entity's shares;

(c) cash proceeds from issuing debentures, loans, notes, bonds, mortgages and other short-term or long-term borrowings;

(d) cash repayments of amounts borrowed; and

(e) cash payments by a lessee for the reduction of the outstanding liability relating to a lease.

(IASB, 2004a, para. 17)

4.7.5 Full statement of cash flows

A complete pro-forma statement of cash flows follows; this has been adapted from the example given in IAS 7.

 ### Example statement

Company XXX plc

Statement of cash flows for the year ended 31 December 20XX

	£m	£m
Cash flows from operating activities		
Cash generated from operations	2,730	
Interest paid	(270)	
Income taxes paid	(900)	
Net cash from operating activities		1,560
Cash flows from investing activities		
Purchase of property, plant and equipment	(900)	
Proceeds from sale of property, plant and equipment	20	
Interest received	200	
Dividends received	200	
Net cash used in investing activities		(480)
Cash flows from financing activities		
Proceeds from issue of share capital	250	

(continued)

(continued)

Proceeds from issue of long-term borrowings	550	
Repayment of long-term borrowings	(300)	
Dividends paid	(1,290)	
Net cash used in financing activities		(790)
Net increase in cash and cash equivalents		290
Cash and cash equivalents at beginning of period		120
Cash and cash equivalents at end of period		£410

Note that cash inflows are shown as positive figures, and cash outflows are shown as negative figures in brackets. It is important that this convention is followed for users' understanding, as some cash flows could be either positive or negative.

An example of the preparation of a full statement of cash flows from the statement of profit or loss and opening and closing statements of financial position is now demonstrated by continuing the example for company Dewberry plc used in Worked example 4.3.

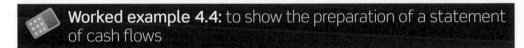

Worked example 4.4: to show the preparation of a statement of cash flows

The statement of comprehensive income can be taken to be the statement of profit or loss given in Worked example 4.3 (i.e. there is no other comprehensive income).

The statement of changes in equity and full statements of financial position are given.

Statement of changes in equity for the year ended 30 June 20X6

	Ordinary Share Capital £000	Share Premium £000	Retained Earnings £000	Total £000
Balance at 1/7/X5	400	–	600	1,000
Issue of share capital	200	15		215
Profit for year			1,510	1,510
Dividends paid			(500)	(500)
Balance at 30/6/X6	600	15	1,610	2,225

Statements of financial position at 30 June 20X6 and 20X5

	20X6 £000	20X5 £000
Property, plant and equipment		
Cost	2,190	1,310
Accumulated depreciation	895	500
	1,295	810
Current assets		
Inventories	1,500	500
Trade receivables	2,680	890
Bank	–	75
	4,180	1,465
Total assets	5,475	2,275
Equity		
Share capital	600	400
Share premium	15	
Retained earnings	1,610	600
	2,225	1,000
Current liabilities		
Bank overdraft	1,785	
Trade payables	1,100	680
Interest payable	25	15
Taxation	280	320
	3,190	1,015
Non-current liabilities		
Long-term loan	60	260
Total liabilities	3,250	1,275
Total equity and liabilities	5,475	2,275

Non-current assets were disposed of during the year ended 30 June 20X6. These had originally cost £100,000 and had accumulated depreciation at the date of disposal of £65,000.

Required:

Prepare the statement of cash flows for Dewberry plc for the year ended 30 June 20X6.

Step 1

Calculate the net cash flow during the year from the opening and closing cash and cash equivalent balances.

In this example cash and cash equivalents comprises an opening bank asset balance and a closing bank overdraft.

		£000
Balance at 1 July 20X5		75
Net cash outflow	(balancing figure)	(1,860)
Balance at 30 June 20X6		(1,785)

Step 2

Unless specified otherwise, calculate cash generated from operations by using the indirect method, i.e. by reconciling profit before tax to cash generated from operations.

This has already been done in Worked example 4.3.

Step 3

Set out the pro-forma statement of cash flows, identifying or calculating figures for each line item as necessary.

In this example the following calculations are required:

(a) Interest paid

Check whether there are accruals for interest payable in the opening and closing statements of financial position. In the absence of these, the interest paid figure will be the interest expense or finance charges figure from the statement of profit or loss. In this example interest paid is calculated as follows:

	£000
Interest expense from statement of profit or loss	165
Add: Accrual at 30 June 20X5	15
Less: Accrual at 30 June 20X6	(25)
Interest paid during the year	155

(b) Income taxes paid (note: in the UK, this means corporation tax paid)

Under UK pay-and-file systems, large companies pay corporation tax on account and settle the final amount owing for a financial year once this has been agreed with HM Revenue and Customs after the end of the year.

Corporation tax paid in the year ended 30 June 20X6 will therefore be the final 20X5 tax liability plus that part of the 20X6 tax paid on account. The amount paid for 20X6 will be the difference between the amount charged to profit and loss (given in Worked example 4.3) and the amount still owing at 30 June 20X6.

	£000
Final 20X5 tax liability	320
20X6 tax paid on account (520 – 280)	240
	560

(c) Purchase of property, plant and equipment

In the absence of any disposals of property, plant and equipment the purchases will be the difference between the opening and closing cost balances. However, in this example non-current assets were disposed of during the year ended 30 June 20X6. The original cost of these will have been deducted from the cost account during the year. The cost of items purchased during the year is found as follows:

	£000
Cost at 30 June 20X5	1,310
Less: Cost of disposals	(100)
Cost of additions (balancing figure)	980
Cost at 30 June 20X6	2,190

(d) Proceeds from the sale of property, plant and equipment

This is derived from:

Profit / (loss) on disposal = Proceeds – NBV of PPE disposed of
(Note: the loss on disposal was given in worked example 4.3)

Proceeds = (Loss) on disposal + NBV

$$= -20,000 + (100,000 - 65,000)$$

$$= 15,000$$

(e) Long-term borrowings

Look to see whether the balance has increased or decreased over the year. An increase represents the issue of further long-term debt, whereas a decrease represents a repayment of the debt.

	£000
Balance at 30 June 20X5	260
Balance at 30 June 20X6	60
Repayment of loan	200

(f) Any issue of shares and dividends paid will be shown in the statement of changes in equity. In the absence of this statement, the cash flow amounts can be calculated from a reconciliation of the opening and closing balances on the share capital and premium accounts for cash received from the issue of shares, and from a reconciliation of the opening and closing balances on the retained earnings account for dividends paid.

The complete statement of cash flows can now be drawn up.

Dewberry plc

Statement of cash flows for the year ended 30 June 20X6

	£000	£000
Cash flows generated from operating activities	305	
Interest paid	(155)	
Income taxes paid	(560)	
Net cash from operating activities		(410)
Cash flows from investing activities		
Purchase of property, plant and equipment	(980)	
Proceeds from sale of property, plant and equipment	15	
Net cash used in investing activities		(965)
Cash flows from financing activities		
Proceeds from issue of share capital	215	
Repayment of long-term borrowings	(200)	
Dividends paid	(500)	
Net cash used in financing activities		(485)
Net decrease in cash and cash equivalents		(1,860)
Cash and cash equivalents at beginning of period		75
Cash and cash equivalents at end of period		(1,785)

4.7.6 Other disclosures

Companies should disclose, together with a commentary by management, any other information likely to be of significance to users. This may include the following:

- restrictions on the use of or access to any part of cash equivalents
- the amount of borrowing facilities which are not drawn but are available
- cash flows which increased operating capacity compared with cash flows which merely maintained operating capacity.

Companies may also have investing and financing activities which do not have a direct impact on current cash flows although they do affect the capital and asset structure of an entity. If these 'non-cash transactions' are material, they should also be disclosed. Examples include:

- the acquisition of assets either by assuming directly related liabilities or by means of a lease
- the acquisition of an entity by means of an issue of equity shares
- the conversion of debt to equity.

4.7.7 Reconciliation of net cash flows to net debt

UK financial reporting standards used to require companies to provide information about net debt. Net debt and its changes over an accounting period are an important financial indicator for investors, and a reconciliation of net cash flows to net debt was also required to be given. This showed the change in total net debt, splitting out the cash and non-cash movements in greater detail and relating the cash movements to the statement of cash flows. Although not defined in IFRS, net debt is essentially:

Short-term debt + long-term debt – cash and cash equivalents

It is a measure of a company's ability to repay all debt if it were called in immediately, and gives investors an idea of a company's financial health and its level of gearing compared to liquid assets. This is discussed further in Chapter 5 which considers interpretation of all the financial statements, including the statement of cash flows.

Since adopting IFRS in 2005, some UK companies removed the reconciliations that were previously presented. Other companies retained them or now provide similar disclosures, as part of the financial statements, narrative reporting, preliminary announcements, investor presentations or a combination of these.

Financial reporting in practice 4.7 | J D Wetherspoon plc, 2015 |

An illustration of a statement of cash flows and the reconciliation of cash flows to changes in net debt is that of JD Wetherspoon plc in its 2015 financial statements.

Statement of cash flows for the 52 weeks ended 26 July 2015

		52 weeks ended 26 July 2015 £000	52 weeks ended 27 July 2014 £000
Cash flows from operating activities			
Cash generated from operations	9	**210,181**	212,505
Interest received		**180**	78
Interest paid		**(31,931)**	(33,996)
Corporation tax paid		**(13,293)**	(18,070)
Gaming machine settlement		**–**	(16,696)
Net cash inflow from operating activities		**165,137**	143,821

(continued)

(continued)

Cash flows from investing activities			
Purchase of property, plant and equipment		**(37,577)**	(46,300)
Purchase of intangible assets		**(7,176)**	(9,926)
Proceeds on sale of property, plant and equipment		**723**	505
Investment in new pubs and pub extensions		**(106,339)**	(97,694)
Freehold reversions		**(21,612)**	(14,823)
Investment properties		**–**	(8,754)
Lease premiums paid		**(635)**	(10)
Net cash outflow from investing activities		**(172,616)**	(177,002)
Cash flows from financing activities			
Equity dividends paid	11	**(14,591)**	(14,949)
Purchase of own shares for cancellation	28	**(12,714)**	(24,550)
Purchase of own shares for share-based payments		**(6,831)**	(7,338)
Advances under bank loans	10	**47,898**	92,151
Loan issue costs	10	**(3,775)**	(4,103)
Finance lease principal payments	10	**(2,648)**	(5,552)
Net cash inflow from financing activities		**7,339**	35,659
Net (decrease)/increase in cash and cash equivalents	10	**(140)**	2,478
Opening cash and cash equivalents	19	**32,315**	29,837
Closing cash and cash equivalents	19	**32,175**	32,315

10 Analysis of changes in net debt

	At 27 July 2014 £000	Cash flows £000	Non-cash movement £000	At 26 July 2015 £000
Borrowings				
Cash in hand	32,315	(140)	–	**32,175**
Finance lease creditor—due in one year	(2,636)	2,648	(2,063)	**(2,051)**
Current net borrowings	29,679	2,508	(2,063)	**30,124**
Bank loans—due after one year	(584,167)	(44,123)	(2,942)	**(631,232)**
Finance lease creditor—due after one year	(2,063)	–	2,063	–
Non-current net borrowings	(586,230)	(44,123)	(879)	**(631,232)**
Net borrowings	(556,551)	(41,615)	(2,942)	**(601,108)**
Derivatives				
Interest-rate swaps—due before one year	(3,149)	–	3,149	–

Current derivatives	(3,149)	–	3,149	–
Interest-rate swap asset—due after one year (note 23)	1,723	–	(1,723)	–
Interest-rate swap liability—due after one year (note 23)	(28,740)	–	(11,233)	**(39,973)**
Non-current derivatives	(27,017)	–	(12,956)	**(39,973)**
Total derivatives	(30,166)	–	(9,807)	**(39,973)**
Net debt	(586,717)	(41,615)	(12,749)	**(641,081)**

Non-cash movements

The non-cash movement in bank loans due after one year relates to the amortisation of bank loan issue costs.

The movement in interest-rate swaps of £9.8m relates to the change in the 'mark to market' valuations for the year.

The variability in the provision of this information has prompted many users to state that this information was of great importance to them in understanding a company's cash flows, and its relationship to the changes in the company's debt balances. It provides information about how sources of finance have been used over time, and helps them understand the company's exposure to risks associated with financing. Under its disclosure initiative, the IASB published an amendment to IAS 7 in January 2016, requiring companies to disclose a reconciliation between the amounts in the opening and closing statements of financial position for liabilities for which cash flows were, or future cash flows will be, classified as financing activities in the statement of cash flows. The IASB acknowledged that net debt was not defined anywhere in IFRS, but considered that the above reconciliation would provide the information that users were calling for.

4.8 Notes to the financial statements

The four key financial statements occupy, at most, five or six pages in an annual report. The notes may run to 50 pages or more! The purpose of them is to amplify the information given in the financial statements and to disaggregate figures so that users have a full understanding of what each line item represents, its measurement basis and, in some cases, how it has been derived.

IAS 1 specifies that the notes' aims are to:

(a) present information about the basis of preparation of the financial statements and the specific accounting policies used;

(b) disclose the information required by IFRS that is not presented elsewhere in the financial statements; and

(c) provide information that is not presented elsewhere in the financial statements, but is relevant to an understanding of any of them.

(IASB, 2007, para. 112)

As can be seen in the financial reporting in practice illustrations used throughout this textbook, notes are cross-referenced from the related line item in the particular financial statement, and they should be presented in a systematic manner to aid understanding and ease of use. The recommended order in which they are presented is as follows:

(a) A statement of compliance with IFRSs;

(b) A summary of significant accounting policies applied (see section 4.8.1);

(c) Supporting information for items presented in the statements of financial position and of comprehensive income, in the separate statement of profit or loss (if presented), and in the statements of changes in equity and of cash flows, in the order in which each statement and each line item is presented; and

(d) Other disclosures, including:

(i)   contingent liabilities (see Chapter 13) and unrecognised contractual commitments, and

(ii) non-financial disclosures, for example, the entity's financial risk management objectives and policies.

(IASB, 2007, para. 114(c))

Financial reporting in practice 4.8   International Airlines Group, 2014

A typical statement by a company of compliance with IFRSs is provided by International Airlines Group in the notes to its 2014 financial statements.

Basis of preparation

The consolidated financial statements of the Group have been prepared in accordance with the International Financial Reporting Standards as endorsed by the European Union (IFRSs as endorsed by the EU). The consolidated financial statements are presented in euros, rounded to the nearest million unless otherwise stated. These financial statements have been prepared on a historical cost convention except for certain financial assets and liabilities, including derivative financial instruments and available-for-sale financial assets that are measured at fair value. The carrying value of recognised assets and liabilities that are subject to fair value hedges are adjusted to record changes in the fair values attributable to the risks that are being hedged. The financial statements for the prior year include reclassifications that were made to conform to the current year presentation. The amendments have no material impact on the financial statements.

The Group's financial statements for the year to December 31, 2014 were authorised for issue, and approved by the Board of Directors on February 26, 2015.

The Directors have considered the business activities as set out on pages 8 to 15, the Group's principal risks and uncertainties as set out on pages 87 to 93, and the Group's financial position, including cash flows, liquidity position and available committed facilities. The Directors consider that the Group has adequate resources to remain in operation for the foreseeable future and have therefore continued to adopt the going concern basis in preparing the financial statements.

As indicated, the notes to financial statements add greatly to their length. Much information in the notes is provided because a particular IFRS specifies that it should be, and the increasing emphasis on disclosures of risk and uncertainty (discussed in section 4.8.2) has added to the requirements. As part of its disclosure initiative, the IASB is looking for ways in which disclosures can be improved. This part of the disclosure initiative is currently in a research phase. The IASB, in conjunction with other authoritative bodies such as the Financial Reporting Council, who have also done work in the area of disclosure, is aiming to produce overriding principles for disclosures, plus a guide for use when developing disclosure requirements in new and amended standards.

4.8.1 Accounting policies

Accounting policies are defined in IAS 8 *Accounting Policies, Changes in Accounting Estimates and Errors* as the specific principles, bases, conventions, rules and practices applied by an entity in preparing and presenting financial statements. The fundamental principle of accruals is accepted as being inherent in financial accounting and does not have to be explained, but if there are conditions which determine when certain items can be recognised and, in particular, which measurement bases have been used for items, users need to be informed of these matters because it will affect their interpretation. Some IFRS specify the relevant accounting policy that should be used; others allow alternative accounting methods, in which case disclosure of the method chosen is required. In the absence of an IFRS that applies specifically to a transaction or event, management may be required to develop and apply a policy. The guiding principle is that accounting policies need to be formulated and disclosed if they assist users in understanding how a transaction or other event and condition is reflected in the financial statements. Accounting policies should ensure that the resulting financial information exhibits the fundamental characteristics of relevance and faithful representation, as discussed in Chapter 1. IAS 1 requires disclosure of all accounting policies; however, as with disclosures in notes, this often leads to lengthy policies covering all areas of the financial statements, not just the significant ones, and standard wording taken straight from the particular financial reporting standard being used. This is also being reviewed by the IASB as part of its disclosure initiative.

 Examples of transactions and events requiring an accounting policy

These items will be discussed in more detail in later chapters; they are given here to illustrate the type of issue that would give rise to an accounting policy.

1 For property, plant and equipment, which measurement basis has been used for which class of asset—historic cost or fair value—could be used.

2 How inventory has been valued.

3   For companies such as those in the telecommunications industry, how and when revenue is recognised from the many different types of contracts they sell.

4   For business combinations, what method of accounting has been used for different investments in the consolidated financial statements.

4.8.2 Estimates, judgements and risks

It should be noted that in applying accounting policies, estimates are often used—the terms 'policies' and 'estimates' should not be confused, although it may be difficult to distinguish them. For example, for property, plant and equipment, the accounting policy would be the measurement basis, which could be depreciated historic cost. In applying this policy, estimates of expected useful life, residual value and pattern of usage have to be made to determine depreciation.

Many accounting policies produced by companies in their annual reports tend to regurgitate standard wording used in the related IFRS and appear similar from company to company. What is of more interest and, following the financial crisis, the focus of more attention, is the discussion of the areas where significant management judgement has had to be exercised in the process of applying the company's accounting policies that could significantly affect the amounts recognised in the financial statements. IAS 1 requires these judgements to be disclosed in the accounting policies.

 Examples of transactions and events where judgement has to be exercised

Again, these items will be discussed in more detail in later chapters, but they are given here for illustration.

1   Whether a sale of goods is a financing arrangement and does not give rise to revenue.

2   Whether there is sufficient evidence to permit the capitalisation of development expenditure.

3   Whether a company controls another company and should account for its investment as a **subsidiary**.

Management also has to exercise subjective judgement where the determination of the carrying amount of some assets and liabilities requires estimates to be made of the effects of uncertain future events. As the number of variables and assumptions affecting the future outcome of the uncertainty increases, these judgements become more subjective and complex, and the potential for material adjustments to the carrying amounts usually increases.

Examples of items where estimates about the uncertainty of future events have to be made

1   In determining whether an item of property, plant and equipment is impaired, an estimate of future cash flows which would result from using the asset is needed.
2   The impact of advances in technology on inventory obsolescence.
3   The future outcome of litigation.
4   Future pension benefits accruing to existing employees in a defined benefit plan.

IAS 1 requires disclosure of information about the assumptions it makes about the future and other major uncertainties that have a significant risk of resulting in material adjustments to the carrying amounts of assets and liabilities within the next financial year. (One exception to this is where the determination of fair value uses recently observed market prices as the measurement basis, for example for share prices. In this instance any material change in the market price would not arise from assumptions made about uncertainties at the financial reporting period end.) These disclosures may require sensitivity analyses using ranges of possible outcomes with associated probabilities and may be fairly lengthy. However, the objective is that users should understand where and how judgement has been exercised, where uncertainties exist and the impact of both on the financial statements.

This is an area of financial reporting that is of particular concern as it links to a company's financial exposure to risk. The discussion on corporate governance in Chapter 3 suggested that the perceived lack of management in this area and inadequate reporting of risk were major issues in the 2008 financial crisis. Further guidance has been issued by the FRC on the reporting of the principal areas of risk for a company and how the company manages this. The audit committee report is required to indicate the areas within the financial statements on which it specifically focussed its attention.

Financial reporting in practice 4.9 | Next plc, 2015

Next plc describes only a few areas of estimation and judgement in the accounting policies in its 2015 financial statements (however, further detail and discussions are contained in the cross-referenced notes).

Significant areas of estimation and judgement

The preparation of the financial statements requires judgements, estimations and assumptions to be made that affect the reported values of assets, liabilities, revenues and expenses. The nature of es-

(continued)

(continued)

timation and judgement means that actual outcomes could differ from expectation. Significant areas of estimation and judgement for the Group include:

→   Expected future cash flows applied in measuring impairment of Directory customer receivables (Note 14). Bad debt provisions are calculated using a combination of internally and externally sourced information, including historical collection rates and other credit data.

→   Estimated selling prices applied in determining the net realisable values of inventories. Historical sales patterns and post year-end trading performance are used to determine these.

→   The assumptions applied in determining the defined benefit pension obligation (Note 21), which is particularly sensitive to small changes in assumptions. Advice is taken from a qualified actuary to determine appropriate assumptions at each balance sheet date.

Other areas of estimation and judgement include sales returns rates, onerous lease provisions, gift card redemption rates, taxation and share schemes.

Financial reporting in practice 4.10   Nokia, 2015

Nokia has a much more extensive note about the principal areas where it has used estimates and judgement in its 2015 financial statements. Not all the detail has been reproduced in this extract.

Use of estimates and critical accounting judgments

The preparation of consolidated financial statements in accordance with IFRS requires the application of management judgment in selecting appropriate assumptions for calculating financial estimates. Management bases its estimates on historical experience, expected outcomes and various other assumptions that are believed to be reasonable under the circumstances. These estimates form the basis for the reported carrying values of assets and liabilities and recognized revenues and expenses that may not be readily apparent from other sources. Material estimates are revised if changes in circumstances occur or as a result of new information or more experience. As estimates inherently contain a varying degree of uncertainty, actual outcomes may differ, resulting in additional charges or credits to the consolidated income statement.

   Management considers that the estimates, assumptions and judgments about the following accounting policies represent the most significant areas of estimation uncertainty and critical judgment that may have an impact on the Group's financial information.

●   Business combinations: fair values, cash flow forecasts, discount rates, market risk premiums.

●   Revenue recognition: fair values, allocation to separately identifiable components.

●   Pension benefit obligations and expenses: discount rate, future mortality rate, annual rate of increase in future compensation levels, actuarial estimates.

●   Income taxes: forecasted future taxable income and tax planning strategies, future financial performance, amount and likelihood of outflow of economic resources and the timing of payments outcome of tax investigations in multiple jurisdictions.

- Carrying value of cash-generating units: fair values, recoverable amounts, discount rate, the terminal growth rate, estimated revenue growth rates, profit margins, costs of disposal and the cost level of operational and capital investment.
- Allowances for doubtful accounts: customers' inability to meet payment obligations.
- Allowances for excess and obsolete inventory: future demand for products.
- Fair value of derivatives and other financial instruments: valuation techniques used for derivatives and other financial instruments that are not traded in an active market.
- Provisions: the amount and likelihood of outflow of economic resources, and the timing of payment.
- Legal contingencies: outcome of pending litigation.

International auditing standards now require auditors to include details of the specific areas which they assess carry risks of material misstatement, and their approach to the audit of these areas. This information should complement the description of the significant issues contained in the report of the audit committee.

Financial reporting in practice 4.11 | Next plc, 2015 |

The auditor's report on the financial statements of Next plc for the year ended 24 January 2015 indicates that the following areas were assessed as being at risk of material misstatement. Some of these, but not all, are the areas disclosed by the directors in the accounting policies as being of significant estimation and judgement—see Financial reporting in practice 4.9.

- Adequacy of the directory debt provisions.
- Inventory provisions required in respect of unsold stock.
- Valuation of financial instruments which hedge foreign exchange and interest rate fluctuations.
- Management override of internal controls with regard to estimates and other provisions relevant to the retail environment (mainly relating to related party provisions).

4.8.3 Changes in accounting policies

One of the qualitative characteristics which enhances financial information is comparability; this also encompasses the idea of consistency. Companies are required to select internally consistent accounting policies and are, generally, not permitted to change their accounting policies from one year to the next. There are only two circumstances where this is allowed:

1   where the change is required by an IFRS
2   if it results in the financial statement providing reliable and more relevant information, which is a voluntary decision by a company.

If there is a change in an accounting policy, IAS 8 specifies that this be applied **retrospectively**. In other words, the financial statements are drawn up as if this policy had always been applied. This means that the opening balance of each affected component of equity has to be adjusted, and all affected comparative figures are restated.

IAS 8 does recognise that there may be circumstances where it is impracticable to determine the effect in a specific period or on a cumulative basis. Where this is the case the policy should be applied retrospectively to the earliest period for which it is practicable to do so.

In the rare circumstance where it is impracticable to restate retrospectively any financial results the new policy should be applied **prospectively**. This means that the effect of the change is recognised only from the date of the change and no restatement of previous years' results is required.

If a new financial reporting standard is issued, or one is revised, it will usually specify transitional provisions for the initial application. In the absence of this, the requirements mentioned previously should be followed.

Full disclosure of the effect of the change in accounting policy is required. Specifically the following should be included:

- nature of the change
- reasons for the change (e.g. why it results in more reliable and relevant information)
- amount of the adjustment for the current period and for each prior period presented for each line item
- amount of the adjustment relating to periods prior to those included in the comparative information
- the fact that comparative information has been restated or that it is impracticable to do so.

4.8.4 Changes in accounting estimates

Although management should exercise its best professional judgement in making accounting estimates, there will always be circumstances where estimates are revised as more relevant or reliable information becomes available. The fact that this happens does not undermine the reliability of financial information provided that relevant details of significant estimates are disclosed, as has been discussed previously.

By its nature, the revision of an estimate does not relate to previous accounting periods (nor is it correcting an error—see section 4.8.5). The effect of a change in an accounting estimate is therefore recognised prospectively and is included from the date of the change.

Typical examples where changes in accounting estimates occur include provisions for irrecoverable debts, inventory obsolescence, fair values of financial instruments, variable consideration in revenue contracts, the useful lives of depreciable assets and warranty provisions.

IAS 8 requires disclosures of the nature and amount of a change in an accounting estimate on the current accounting period and future accounting periods, unless the effect on the future is impracticable to estimate.

Example of a change in the estimate of useful life

A machine originally cost £200,000. At the date of acquisition the machine's useful life was estimated at ten years and the residual value as zero. The annual straight-line depreciation charge will be £20,000 and the carrying amount after three years will be £140,000.

If in the fourth year it is decided that as a result of changes in technology the remaining useful life is only three years (implying a total life of six years), then the depreciation charge in that year (and in the next two years) will be calculated by writing off the current carrying amount over the remaining useful life.

Annual depreciation will become $\dfrac{£140,000}{3} = £46,667$

The depreciation charge for the first three years is not restated.

The effect of the change is an increase in the annual depreciation charge from £20,000 to £46,667; this must be disclosed if considered material.

It is sometimes difficult to determine whether an accounting change represents a change in accounting policy, or a change in accounting estimate, and there are divergent practices in this area. The IASB has a current project to examine this issue, the aim of which is to amend the existing definitions of a change in accounting policy and a change in accounting estimate in order to clarify that:

- changes in the measurement bases that are specified in relevant financial reporting standards are changes in accounting policies;

- changes in the measurement bases include changes in cost measures and, therefore, changes in the methods used to determine different cost measures are changes in accounting policies; and

- changes in inputs, assumptions and methods that are used to make an accounting estimate are changes in accounting estimates.

(IASB, 2016b)

It is expected that an Exposure Draft to make amendments to IAS 8 will be issued in due course.

4.8.5 Errors

Even with good internal controls systems and external audits of financial statements, errors do occur from time to time. Irrespective of whether the error was intentional or fraudulent, or merely careless, IAS 8 deals with how to account for an error when it has been discovered. Obviously, if it is discovered in the same accounting period as when it happened, it should be corrected before the financial statements are issued to shareholders, but it may be discovered in a subsequent period.

If this is the case and it is considered material, then it is corrected retrospectively, as for a change in an accounting policy. In other words, comparative amounts for the prior period(s) presented in which the error occurred are restated and opening balances of the affected equity accounts are restated. If it is impracticable to determine either the period-specific effects or the cumulative effect of the error, the company should restate the comparative information to correct the error prospectively from the earliest date practicable. Full disclosure of the nature of the error and how the financial statements have been corrected is required.

Whenever there is a retrospective restatement of financial statements, or when a company reclassifies items in its financial statements from one period to the next, IAS 1 requires presentation of a statement of financial position as of the beginning of the earliest comparative period.

Worked example 4.5: to show the retrospective correction of an error

Alpha plc reported a profit in its statement of profit or loss for the year ended 31 December 20X3 as follows:

	£
Sales	14,700
Cost of sales	(8,900)
Gross profit	5,800
Distribution and administrative expenses	(1,800)
Profit before tax	4,000
Tax	(1,200)
Profit after tax	2,800

In 20X4 the company discovered that some products sold during 20X3 had been included incorrectly in inventory at 31 December 20X3 at £1,100. In 20X4, the company's records show sales of £20,800, cost of goods of £13,600 (including £1,100 for the error in opening inventory), and distribution and administrative expenses of £3,700. The company's corporation tax rate was 30% for both 20X3 and 20X4.

Alpha's retained earnings at 1 January and 31 December 20X3 were £4,000 and £6,800 respectively. The company had £5,000 of share capital and no other equity balances in 20X3 and 20X4.

Required:

In so far as the information permits, draw up Alpha plc's statement of profit or loss for the year ended 31 December 20X4, showing the 20X3 comparative statement, and the statement of changes in equity for the two years. Show any other disclosures.

Alpha plc

Extract from the statement of profit or loss for the year ended 31 December 20X4

	20X4	20X3 (restated)
	£	£
Sales	20,800	14,700
Cost of sales	(12,500)	(10,000)
Gross profit	8,300	4,700
Distribution and administrative expenses	(3,700)	(1,800)
Profit before tax	4,600	2,900
Tax	(1,380)	(870)
Profit after tax	3,220	2,030

Alpha plc

Statement of changes in equity

	Share capital	Retained earnings	Total
	£	£	£
Balance at 1 January 20X3	5,000	4,000	9,000
Profit for the year ended 31 December 20X3 as restated	–	2,030	2,030
Balance at 31 December 20X3	5,000	6,030	11,030
Profit for the year ended 31 December 20X4	–	3,220	3,220
Balance at 31 December 20X4	5,000	9,250	14,250

Extract from notes

Some products that had been sold in 20X3 were incorrectly included in inventory at 31 December 20X3 at £1,100. The financial statements of 20X3 have been restated to correct this error. The effect of the restatement on those financial statements is summarised as follows. There is no effect in 20X4.

	Effect on 20X3
	£
(Increase) in cost of goods sold	(1,100)
Decrease in tax expense	330
(Decrease) in profit and equity	(770)

4.9 Proposed changes to the presentation of financial statements

4.9.1 IASB/FASB convergence project

During the IASB/US FASB convergence period, one of the projects started was to develop a new standard for financial statement presentation. The objective of the project was to establish a global standard to guide the organisation and presentation of information in the financial statements to improve the usefulness of the information provided in an entity's financial statements to help users in their decision-making. Some of the disclosure projects referred to in previous sections have arisen out of this. However there was another phase to the project to address other users' concerns that:

1. existing requirements permit too many alternative forms of presentation

2. information in financial statements is highly aggregated and inconsistently presented, making it difficult to understand fully the relationship between an entity's financial statements and its financial results.

For example, the structure of the statements of comprehensive income and cash flows are very different, with the former differentiating expense elements of performance either by nature or function, and the latter classifying cash flow financial performance under different types of activity. This means users have to reclassify and reconcile items and subtotals in the different statements to gain a full understanding of performance. There are also key differences in presentation between IFRS and US generally accepted accounting principles (GAAP), leading to difficulties of comparison.

To address these concerns the project's main proposals were for:

- cohesive financial statements that share a common structure, separately presenting operating, investing, and financing activities, as well as income tax and discontinued operations

- disaggregation in each financial statement, considering the function, nature, and measurement bases of items, with some disaggregation included in the notes

- more disaggregation of operating cash receipts and payments, and reconciliation of profit or loss from operating activities to cash flows from operating activities

- analyses of changes in asset and liability line items

- and disclosure of remeasurement information.

The aim of the proposals was to improve the comparability and understandability of information presented in financial statements by imposing some degree of standardisation in the way that information is presented in the financial statements, particularly regarding how information is classified and the degree to which it is disaggregated.

4.9.2 Changes to the presentation of the key financial statements

This phase of the project aimed to produce a standard to replace both IAS 1 and IAS 7.

A staff draft which reflected tentative decisions made was published in July 2010. These were based on the core principles of cohesiveness and disaggregation, which are defined as follows:

Cohesiveness   The relationship between items in the financial statements is clear. The financial statements complement each other as much as possible.

Disaggregation Resources are separated by the activity in which they are used and by their economic characteristics.

A common structure for the statements of financial position, comprehensive income and cash flows would be established in the form of required sections, categories, subcategories and related subtotals. All three financial statements would display related information in the same sections, categories and subcategories so that the information is more easily associated. The proposals are summarised in Table 4.3.

Table 4.3 Proposed structures of key financial statements

Statement of financial position	Statement of comprehensive income	Statement of cash flows
Business section	Business section	Business section
Operating category	Operating category	Operating category
Operating finance subcategory	Operating finance subcategory	
Investing category	Investing category	Investing category
Financing section	Financing section	Financing section
Debt category	Debt category	
Equity category		
	Multicategory transaction section	Multicategory transaction section
Income tax section	Income tax section	Income tax section
Discontinued operation section	Discontinued operation section, net of tax	Discontinued operation section
	Other comprehensive income, net of tax	

The statement of changes in equity would not include the sections and categories used in the other statement because this presents information solely about changes in items classified in the equity category in the statement of financial position.

The business section would include items that are part of an entity's day-to-day and other income-generating activities, and segregate them into operating and investing categories. The financing section would include items that are part of an entity's activities to obtain or repay capital, and segregate them into debt and equity categories. This structure, which separates the functional activities of a business, would assist users of financial statements who commonly analyse a business's performance independently of its capital structure. (See Chapter 5 for discussion of analytical methods.)

The proposals are based clearly on the principles behind the current presentation of the statement of cash flows and would change the presentation of the statement of financial position the most. Here, assets and liabilities would either be grouped under each section, category or subcategory according to whether they were short or long term, or be presented in order of liquidity, depending on which provided the most relevant information. They would be disaggregated by measurement basis and/or by reference to the economic characteristics that distinguish them (i.e. their nature). In the statement of comprehensive income, an entity would disaggregate its income and expenses by function (i.e. the primary activities in which it is engaged, such as selling goods, providing services, manufacturing, advertising, marketing, business development or administration). The direct method for the presentation of cash flows for all sections and categories would be used in the statement of cash flows, but the reconciliation of operating income to operating cash flows would still be required.

Overall, more line items and subtotals would be presented enabling easier comparison of effects across the financial statements. For example, users would be able to assess how operating assets and liabilities generate operating income and cash flows.

Although the IASB had an original target date for the publication of a new accounting standard of late 2011, the board chose to concentrate on producing other, more pressing standards by mid-2011. This phase is currently suspended and the IASB is considering whether it will be continued.

Summary of key points

What constitutes the financial statements of a company and their presentation are set out in IAS 1 *Presentation of Financial Statements*. This accounting standard defines financial statements as:

- a statement of financial position
- a statement of comprehensive income
- a statement of changes in equity
- a statement of cash flows
- notes, comprising a summary of significant accounting policies and other explanatory information.

The line items that should be disclosed for the statements of financial position, comprehensive income and changes in equity are specified by the standard, which permits two alternative methods for drawing up the statement of comprehensive income. The format of the statement of cash flows is governed by IAS 7 *Statement of Cash Flows*; this also allows two alternative methods for companies to present cash flows from operating activities, and is not prescriptive about where dividend and interest cash flows are included. This flexibility and ensuing lack of comparability between companies is criticised by some users and may result in a new IFRS to replace both IAS 1 and IAS 7. Proposals which have been put forward significantly change the format of the statements to align related information across the statements under the same section and category headings. The IASB currently has not decided whether to continue with this project.

The current IAS 1 also explains the underpinning principles on which financial statements are based, namely accruals and going concern, materiality and aggregation, and that items should not be offset.

Notes to the financial statements are extensive, much of which information is specified by individual financial reporting standards. The underpinning principle of notes, as explained in IAS 1, is to disaggregate the aggregated figures on the face of the main financial statements so that users have a full understanding of what each line item represents and the measurement bases used. The notes should include a comprehensive set of accounting policies, and details of the criteria for selecting and changing these, together with the accounting treatment and disclosure of changes in accounting policies, changes in accounting estimates and corrections of errors, are set out in IAS 8 *Accounting Policies, Changes in Accounting Estimates and Errors*.

IAS 1 also describes the disclosures that should be made for areas which have required significant use of estimates and judgement, so that users have information about the principal areas of uncertainty in the financial statements.

All of these disclosures have led to increase in the length of financial statements and a wealth of information, some of which is considered standard, boilerplate detail, or immaterial. In conjunction with other authoritative bodies, the IASB has launched a disclosure initiative, various themes of which have resulted in some minor amendments to standards. Other themes are currently being explored, including the concept of how materiality should be applied in practice, and proposals for principles of disclosure. These link with the work on the revised *Conceptual Framework* which is discussed in Chapter 2.

 ## Further reading

Bruce, R. (2007) *Let's talk. Why a project on Financial Statement Presentation?* IASB's INSIGHT. London: IASB. Why read? This article expands upon some of the ideas discussed in this chapter relating to the important proposed changes to financial statement presentation.

IASB (International Accounting Standards Board) (2007) IAS 1 *Presentation of Financial Statements*. London: IASB.

IASB (International Accounting Standards Board) (2004a) IAS 7 *Statement of Cash Flows*. London: IASB.

IASB (International Accounting Standards Board) (2004b) IAS 8 *Accounting Policies, Changes in Accounting Estimates and Errors*. London: IASB.

 ## Bibliography

Bruce, R. (2007) *Let's talk. Why a project on Financial Statement Presentation?* IASB's INSIGHT. London: IASB.

FRC (Financial Reporting Council) (2011) *The Sharman Inquiry: Going Concern and Liquidity Risks: Lessons for Companies and Auditors, Preliminary Report and Recommendations of the Panel of Inquiry*. London: FRC.

FRC (Financial Reporting Council) (2012a) *The Sharman Inquiry: Going Concern and Liquidity Risks: Lessons for Companies and Auditors, Final Report and Recommendations of the Panel of Inquiry.* London: FRC.

FRC (Financial Reporting Council) (2012b) *Lab Project Report: Net Debt Reconciliations.* London: FRC.

FRC (Financial Reporting Council) (2013) *Illustrative Example of a UK Auditor's Report Reflecting the Requirements of ISA (UK and Ireland) 700.* London: FRC.

FRC (Financial Reporting Council) (2014) *Guidance on Risk Management, Internal Control and Related Financial and Business Reporting.* London: FRC.

GKN plc (2015) *Annual Report and Accounts, 2014.* Redditch: GKN.

IASB (International Accounting Standards Board) (2004a) IAS 7 *Statement of Cash Flows.* London: IASB.

IASB (International Accounting Standards Board) (2004b) IAS 8 *Accounting Policies, Changes in Accounting Estimates and Errors.* London: IASB.

IASB (International Accounting Standards Board) (2007) IAS 1 *Presentation of Financial Statements.* London: IASB.

IASB (International Accounting Standards Board) (2010) *Financial Statement Presentation: Staff draft of an exposure draft.* London: IASB.

IASB (International Accounting Standards Board) (2011) *Presentation of Items of Other Comprehensive Income (Amendments to IAS 1).* Project summary and feedback statement. London: IASB.

IASB (International Accounting Standards Board) (2013) *Discussion Forum—Financial Reporting Disclosure: Feedback Statement.* London: IASB.

IASB (International Accounting Standards Board) (2014) *Disclosure Initiative Amendments to IAS 1.* London: IASB.

IASB (International Accounting Standards Board) (2015a) Exposure Draft ED/2015/8 IFRS Practice Statement *Application of Materiality to Financial Statements.* London: IASB.

IASB (International Accounting Standards Board) (2015b) Snapshot: IFRS Practice Statement *Application of Materiality to Financial Statements.* London: IASB.

IASB (International Accounting Standards Board) (2016a) *Disclosure Initiative: Amendments to IAS 7.* London: IASB.

IASB (International Accounting Standards Board) (2016b) Staff Paper *Review of IAS 8 Accounting Policies, Changes in Accounting Estimates and Errors.* London: IASB.

ICAEW (Institute of Chartered Accountants in England and Wales) (2010) *IAS 1 Revised.* IFRS Factsheet. London: ICAEW.

International Airlines Group (2015) *2014 Annual Report and Accounts.* Madrid: IAG.

J Sainsbury plc (2015) *Annual Report and Financial Statements 2015.* London: Sainsbury.

J D Wetherspoon plc (2015) *Annual Report and Financial Statements 2015.* Watford: Wetherspoon.

Next plc (2015) *Annual Report and Accounts, 2015.* Enderby: Next.

Nokia (2015) *Annual Report 2014.* Nokia

Robinson, K. (2015) *Financial Statement Disclosures: Towards Effective Communication.* London: ICAEW By All Accounts.

Vodafone Group plc (2015) *Annual Report, 2015.* Newbury: Vodafone.

? Questions

● Quick test

1   A company's credit sales are £45,678 during 20X8. Accounts receivable at 1 January 20X8 are £4,602 and at 31 December 20X8 are £5,709. What cash has the company received from its credit customers during 20X8?

2   A company's cost of sales in its statement of profit or loss for the year ended 31 October 20X5 is £105,066. Inventory at 31 October 20X4 is £6,430 and at 31 October 20X5 is £5,757. Accounts payable at 31 October 20X4 are £9,204 and at 31 October 20X5 are £8,580.

(a) What are the purchases for the year?

(b) Assuming all purchases are made on credit, what cash has the company paid to suppliers during the year?

3   A company's rent expense in its statement of profit or loss is £35,100. Opening and closing prepayments are £8,460 and £9,000 respectively. What cash has the company paid for rent in the year?

4   A company's corporation tax charge in its statement of profit or loss is £75,267. The liabilities for corporation tax at the end of the previous year and at the end of the current year are £34,609 and £41,957 respectively. What cash has the company paid for corporation tax during the year?

5   Information about a company's fixtures and fittings at 30 September in two successive years is as follows:

	20X1	20X0
	£	£
Cost	143,201	126,587
Accumulated depreciation	76,613	64,293

(a) If the company did not sell any fixtures and fittings during the year ended 30 September 20X1:

(i)   What is the depreciation expense for the year?

(ii)   What cash did the company spend on fixtures and fittings during the year?

(b) During the year ended 30 September 20X1 the company sold some shelving for £3,500. This shelving had originally cost £24,500 and at the time of sale had accumulated depreciation of £14,700.

(i)   What is the depreciation expense for the year?

(ii)   What cash did the company spend on fixtures and fittings during the year?

(iii) What is the profit or loss on the sale of the shelving?

6   At 30 June 20X3 a company has issued £100,000 7% debentures. On 1 April 20X4 the company issues a further £50,000 of the same debentures.

(a) What is the interest expense for the year ended 30 June 20X4?

(b) (i) Assuming the company pays interest quarterly in arrears on the last day of each quarter (31 March, 30 June, 30 September, and 31 December) and the company pays all interest when it is due, what is the cash paid for interest in the year ended 30 June 20X4?

(ii) If there is an accrual for interest at 30 June 20X3 and 20X4 of £1,750 and £2,625, respectively, what is the cash paid for interest in the year ended 30 June 20X4?

●● Develop your understanding

7   The following information relates to the activities of Pilot plc:

Statements of financial position at 31 March

	20X8		20X7	
	£000	£000	£000	£000
Non-current assets				
Freehold land at cost		780		700
Plant and equipment—cost	660		560	
Less: accumulated depreciation	296		230	
		364		330
		1,144		1,030
Current assets				
Inventory	498		356	
Receivables	304		330	
Bank	–		30	
		802		716
Total assets		£1,946		£1,746
Equity				
Equity £1 shares	550		400	
Share premium	210		160	
Retained earnings	490		376	
		1,250		936
Current liabilities				
Trade payables	230		240	
Corporation tax	90		120	
Bank overdraft	126		–	
	446		360	
Non-current liabilities				
6% debentures	250		450	
Total liabilities		696		810
Total equity and liabilities		£1,946		£1,746

Statement of comprehensive income for the year ended 31 March 20X8

	£000
Revenue	4,520
Cost of sales	(3,420)
Gross profit	1,100
Expenses	(766)
Profit before tax	334
Corporation tax	(150)
Profit after tax	£184

Statement of changes in equity for the year ended 31 March 20X8

	Share Capital	Share Premium	Retained Earnings	Total
	£000	£000	£000	£000
Balance at 1 April 20X7	400	160	376	936
Issue of share capital	150	50		200
Profit for the year			184	184
Dividends paid			(70)	(70)
Balance at 31 March 20X8	550	210	490	1,250

You are informed that:

(a) Plant which originally cost £80,000 was sold for cash of £14,000. The profit/loss on disposal is included in expenses. Accumulated depreciation relating to the plant sold amounted to £58,000.

(b) The debentures were repaid on 30 September 20X7. Interest of £21 for the year was fully paid by 31 March 20X8 and is included in expenses.

Required:

(i) Calculate the net increase/decrease in cash for the year ended 31 March 20X8.

(ii) Calculate the cash flow from operating activities using the indirect method (i.e. reconciling profit before tax to cash flow from operating activities).

(iii) Prepare the complete statement of cash flows for Pilot plc for the year ended 31 March 20X8 in accordance with IAS 7 *Statement of Cash Flows*.

(iv) Comment on the information provided by the statement of cash flows.

8   (Question 6 from Chapter 1 with the addition of property, plant and equipment revaluation) Falmouth plc has an authorised share capital of £2,000,000 divided into 3,000,000 equity shares of 50p and 500,000 12% redeemable preference shares of £1.

The following trial balance has been extracted from the accounting records at 30 June 20X1:

	Debit £000	Credit £000
50p equity shares (fully paid)		500
12% £1 preference shares (fully paid)		200
8% debentures		400
Retained earnings 1 July 20X0		368
Freehold land and buildings (cost)	860	
Plant and machinery (cost)	1,460	
Motor vehicles (cost)	440	
Accumulated depreciation at 1 July 20X0:		
Freehold buildings		40
Plant and machinery		444
Motor vehicles		230
Inventory at 1 July 20X0	380	
Sales		6,590
Purchases	4,304	
Final dividends for year end 30 June 20X0:		
Equity	40	
Interim dividends for year end 30 June 20X1:		
Preference	12	
Equity	16	
Debenture interest	16	
Wages and salaries	508	
Light and heat	62	
Irrecoverable debt expense	30	
Other administration expenses	196	
Receivables	578	
Payables		390
Allowance for doubtful debts		20
Corporation tax paid	112	
Bank	168	
	£9,182	£9,182

The following information needs to be dealt with before the financial statements can be completed:

(a) Inventories at 30 June 20X1 were valued at £440,000 (cost).

(b) Other administration expenses include £18,000 paid in respect of a machinery maintenance contract for the 12 months ending 30 November 20X1. Light and heat does not include an invoice of £12,000 for electricity for the quarter ending 3 July 20X1, which was paid in August 20X1.

(c) The directors wish to provide for:

    (i)   any debenture interest due

    (ii)   directors' bonuses of £24,000

    (iii) the year's depreciation.

(d) The allowance for doubtful debts required at 30 June 20X1 is £24,000.

(e) During the year ended 30 June 20X1, a customer whose receivables balance of £8,000 had been written off in previous years paid the full amount owing. The company credited this to receivables.

(f) The debentures have been in issue for some years.

(g) Corporation tax of £256,000 is to be charged on the profits.

(h) During the year a piece of machinery, which had originally cost £320,000 and had been owned by the company for six years, was scrapped. Proceeds received were £40,000. These have been credited incorrectly to the plant and machinery cost account.

(i) The buildings element of the freehold land and buildings cost is £400,000. Depreciation methods and rates are as follows:

Buildings	Straight-line over 50 years
Plant and machinery	10% straight-line
Motor vehicles	33% reducing balance

(j) At 30 June 20X1 the freehold land and buildings are revalued at £1,200,000, and this revaluation is to be incorporated into the financial statements.

Required:

Prepare the statements of comprehensive income and changes in equity of Falmouth plc for the year ended 30 June 20X1, and a statement of financial position at that date in accordance with IAS 1 *Presentation of Financial Statements*. Expenses are to be analysed by function.

●●● Take it further

9   Birch plc manufactures alarm systems. Its trial balance at 31 March 20X9 showed the following balances:

	£	£
Freehold land and buildings		
Cost (land: £400,000)	1,120,000	
Accumulated depreciation at 31 March 20X8		691,200
Plant and equipment		
Cost	182,860	
Accumulated depreciation at 31 March 20X8		74,100
Retained earnings at 31 March 20X8		119,704

(continued)

(continued)

Equity share capital (£1 shares)		200,000
5% Preference share capital (50p irredeemable shares)		100,000
Share premium		130,000
Cash in hand	124	
Bank overdraft		2,820
Trade and other receivables	172,800	
Trade and other payables		111,580
Sales		660,340
Manufacturing costs		
Direct costs	269,120	
Overheads	107,340	
Wages and salaries	63,150	
Administrative expenses	138,010	
Distribution costs	7,020	
Costs of Product Y (see note (iv))	25,200	
Inventory at 31 March 20X8	9,120	
Allowance for doubtful debts at 31 March 20X8		5,000
	2,094,744	2,094,744

The following additional information is available:

(i)   Inventory at 31 March 20X9 was valued at £7,570.

(ii) The finance director has estimated that the allowance for doubtful debts at 31 March 20X9 should be £7,000.

(iii) Wages and salaries should be apportioned 60% to administrative expenses and the remainder to distribution costs.

(iv) Costs of Product Y relate to the materials and labour costs incurred over the period 1 April 20X8 to 31 December 20X8 relating to the development of a new type of alarm system which Birch plc had started in the year ended 31 March 20X8. In this year the company had spent a total of £5,340, which was written off against the year's profits as part of cost of sales. On 30 September 20X8 the project was judged commercially viable and sales of the system commenced on 1 January 20X9. The marketing director estimates that it will take three years before a competitor launches a superior product. The materials and labour costs accrued evenly over the period from 1 April 20X8 to 31 December 20X8. (See Chapter 11 for accounting treatment.)

(v) On 30 September 20X8 the directors decided to sell a machine which had cost Birch plc £30,000 on 1 October 20X6. At 30 September 20X8 the machine met the criteria of IFRS 5 *Non-current Assets Held for Sale and Discontinued Operations* to be classified as 'held for sale', but no adjustments were made to the accounting records in respect of the machine at this date. The machine was expected to sell for £16,000, with selling costs of £60. A buyer was found on 6 March 20X9 at this price, although the sale was not completed until after the year end. (See Chapter 6 for accounting treatment.)

(vi) Depreciation on property, plant and equipment has yet to be charged. Birch plc charges depreciation as follows:

Type	Depreciation policy	Depreciation presented in
Freehold buildings	Straight-line basis over 50 years	20% in administrative expenses, 80% in cost of sales
Plant and equipment	Straight-line basis over 5 years	Cost of sales

(vii) At 31 March 20X9 the directors of Birch decided to incorporate a revaluation of freehold land and buildings into the financial statements. At this date the land and buildings were valued at £800,000.

(viii) The 5% preference share dividend for the year was declared on 31 March 20X9. No equity dividend is to be paid.

(ix) The income tax charge for the year has been estimated at £6,100.

Required:

Prepare the statements of comprehensive income and changes in equity for Birch plc for the year ended 31 March 20X9, and a statement of financial position as at that date in a form suitable for publication.

Note: (i) notes to the financial statements are not required and (ii) expenses should be analysed by function.

10 The statements of financial position of Hemmingway plc at 30 June 20X4 and 20X3, and a summary of the statement of profit or loss for the year ended 30 June 20X4, are given as follows.

Statements of financial position at 30 June

	20X4		20X3	
	£	£	£	£
Non-current assets				
Land and buildings				
Cost	47,000		47,000	
Accumulated depreciation	(12,000)		(10,000)	
Plant and machinery				
Cost	36,000		29,100	
Accumulated depreciation	(17,000)		(12,600)	
		54,000		53,500
Investments at cost		7,500		6,000
		61,500		59,500

(continued)

(continued)

Current assets

Inventory	12,631		11,412
Receivables and prepayments	10,987		12,784
Cash at bank	–		4,713
		23,618	28,909
Total assets		£85,118	£88,409

Equity

£1 equity shares	33,000		33,000
Retained earnings	34,115		28,597
		67,115	61,597

Current liabilities

Bank overdraft	1,490		-
Trade payables and accruals	10,713		9,812
Corporation tax	3,000		4,000
	15,203		13,812

Non-current liabilities

10% debentures	2,800		13,000
Total liabilities		18,003	26,812
Total equity and liabilities		£85,118	£88,409

Summarised statement of profit or loss for the year ended 30 June 20X4

	£
Profit before tax	10,518
Tax	(2,000)
Profit after tax	£8,518

You are given the following additional information:

(a) During the year certain items of machinery were disposed of for proceeds of £1,200. The machines had originally cost £4,000 and had a net book value at disposal of £500.

(b) The debentures were repaid on 30 September 20X3. All interest due has been paid.

Required:

Prepare a statement of cash flows for the year ended 30 June 20X4 in accordance with IAS 7.

11 Vodafone plc includes the following information in its 2015 annual report:

| Financial reporting in practice 4.12 | Vodaphone, 2015 |

Basis of preparation

The consolidated financial statements are prepared in accordance with IFRS as issued by the International Accounting Standards Board (IASB) and are also prepared in accordance with IFRS adopted by the European Union (EU), the Companies Act 2006 and Article 4 of the EU IAS Regulations. The consolidated financial statements are prepared on a going concern basis.

The preparation of financial statements in conformity with IFRS requires management to make estimates and assumptions that affect the reported amounts of assets and liabilities and disclosure of contingent assets and liabilities at the date of the financial statements and the reported amounts of revenue and expenses during the reporting period. A discussion on the Group's critical accounting judgements and key sources of estimation uncertainty is detailed below. Actual results could differ from those estimates. The estimates and underlying assumptions are reviewed on an ongoing basis. Revisions to accounting estimates are recognised in the period in which the estimate is revised if the revision affects only that period; they are recognised in the period of the revision and future periods if the revision affects both current and future periods.

IFRS requires the Directors to adopt accounting policies that are the most appropriate to the Group's circumstances. In determining and applying accounting policies, Directors and management are required to make judgements in respect of items where the choice of specific policy, accounting estimate or assumption to be followed could materially affect the Group's reported financial position, results or cash flows; it may later be determined that a different choice may have been more appropriate.

Management has identified accounting estimates and assumptions relating to revenue recognition, taxation, business combinations and goodwill, joint arrangements, finite lived intangible assets, property, plant and equipment, post employment benefits, provisions and contingent liabilities and impairment that it considers to be critical due to their impact on the Group's financial statements. These critical accounting judgements, assumptions and related disclosures have been discussed with the Company's Audit and Risk Committee (see page 64).

Discuss this statement in the context of the underpinning characteristics of financial information.

 Visit the Online Resource Centre for solutions to all these end of chapter questions plus visual walkthrough solutions. You can test your understanding with extra questions and answers, explore additional case studies based on real companies, take a guided tour through a company report and much more. Go to the Online Resource Centre at **www.oxfordtextbooks.co.uk/orc/maynard2e/**

5

Techniques for the interpretation of financial statements

➤ Introduction

Investors, lenders and other creditors require information to help them make decisions about providing resources to a company. Other users will also use financial information to assist them in the decisions they make in relation to their interactions with a company. Many decisions are determined by the returns that the users gain from their investment, for example from dividends, by principal and interest payments or from market price increases.

But how is this information ascertained from a complex set of financial statements that contains a wealth of information? How is return measured and evaluated? How are the returns of one company compared with another? How can it be evaluated whether a loan to a company will be repaid in the future?

This chapter provides details of a range of standard analytical techniques that can be applied in financial statement interpretation to help answer these sorts of questions. These techniques are used in all subsequent chapters to explain the implication of accounting methods specified by financial reporting standards for users' interpretation of the financial information provided.

The methods demonstrated in this chapter are just part of interpretation. At this stage it is about providing some tools that can be used. Full interpretation of financial statements requires an understanding of far more than some line-by-line comparisons and ratio calculations. For example, the bases for the recognition and measurement of different figures need to be understood, and, crucially, to be meaningful, any interpretation must be set in the context of the company's internal and external environments.

Interpretation of financial statements is returned to at the end of the textbook. At this point readers will have knowledge of the accounting and measurement methods used for many items and a greater understanding of the relationships between figures in the financial statements.

★ Learning objectives

After studying this chapter you will be able to:

- interpret a set of simple financial statements using horizontal, vertical and ratio analytical techniques for a variety of users
- understand key limitations of the analysis performed
- understand that an interpretation of a set of financial statements requires more than the use of the analytical techniques included in this chapter.

✔ Key issues checklist

- ❑ Different users and their needs.
- ❑ The key question—'why?'
- ❑ Obtaining an overview of financial statements through horizontal and vertical analyses.
- ❑ Calculations and interpretation of the main ratios in order to analyse profitability, liquidity, efficiency, gearing and investor returns.
- ❑ The interrelationships of ratios.
- ❑ Interpretation of the statement of cash flows.
- ❑ Limitations of ratio analysis.

5.1 Where does an interpretation begin?

5.1.1 Purpose of the analysis

Before any financial figures are considered, the purpose of the analysis must be established. Different users of financial statements will have different reasons for examining and analysing the financial statements, and will therefore focus on different aspects.

 Examples of different purposes of analysis

1 If a shareholder wishes to assess the ongoing returns they receive from their investment, they will focus on dividend payments and the quality of the profits the company is making to estimate what any future level of dividend may be.

2 Alternatively, a shareholder may be holding shares for growth in market value. This shareholder will be more interested in predicting future earnings or the quality of the asset base of the business.

3 A venture capital provider will be more concerned that profit levels and liquidity are sufficient to meet the servicing costs of their investment.

4 A bank lender will have the same concerns as the venture capital provider and may have set the company requirements for sufficient liquidity levels measured by financial ratios (referred to as covenants).

5 One company interested in purchasing another may be doing so for reasons of growth to expand its customer base, to acquire part of the production chain or to acquire a brand name. The reasons will determine on which aspects of the financial performance and position the interpretation is particularly focused.

Thus, any analysis needs to be directed to the specific requirements of the user.

However, for the purposes of the example used in this chapter, a full financial analysis will be provided covering all aspects from different users' perspectives.

5.1.2 Business information

The type of business must always be noted before any analysis is performed and any particular internal information provided or known about the company. External information, such as how the industry is performing, the markets in which the company operates, competitive forces, general economic conditions or exchange rates (if applicable), will all need to be taken into account in order to provide the context for the analysis.

How this is used will be discussed in more detail in Chapter 19.

5.1.3 The question 'why?'

Before any analytical techniques are explained, it must be emphasised that the most important question that can be asked by the analyst is 'why?' The analytical techniques applied to a set of published financial statements by an external user should be seen as a series of steps. If the question 'why?' is asked after each technique or calculation performed, this will lead to further analytical stages.

However, these techniques will not necessarily provide all the answers. Chapter 4, which discussed the information provided by published financial statements, explained that many figures are aggregated, with a detailed breakdown of the amounts that make up the disclosed balance not necessarily being available. Disclosures in the notes to the financial statements, where provided, will usually have to be used to enhance the analysis, but, even then, without internal management information, some questions will still go unanswered and educated guesses may have to be part of the analytical process.

5.1.4 Financial statements to be used for analysis

The following financial statements are to be used throughout this chapter in the application of the analytical techniques:

Worked example 5.1: to show the financial statements of a company

Sharples plc is a company that wholesales non-electrical office equipment, from pens and stationery to filing cabinets. The company has just one warehouse and, during 20X7, replaced much of its shelving, as well as investing in new computer equipment to maintain its inventory and other records.

In October 20X7 the company tendered for, and won, a contract to supply some goods to the local high street office supplies and stationery shop.

The financial statements for both 20X7 and the previous year are given as follows.

Sharples plc

Statements of comprehensive income for the years ended 31 December 20X7 and 20X6

	20X7 £000	20X6 £000
Revenue	3,000	2,500
Cost of sales	(1,800)	(1,425)
Gross profit	1,200	1,075
Administration expenses	(544)	(453)
Distribution costs	(250)	(245)
Profit from operations	406	377
Finance costs	(66)	(60)
Profit before tax	340	317
Tax	(180)	(122)
Profit for the year	£160	£195

Statements of changes in equity for the years ended 31 December 20X7 and 20X6

	Equity share capital £000	Preference share capital £000	Retained earnings £000	Total £000
Balance at 1 January 20X6	1,000	200	640	1,840
Profit for the year			195	195
Dividends paid			(95)	(95)
Balance at 31 December 20X6	1,000	200	740	1,940
Profit for the year			160	160
Dividends paid			(100)	(100)
Balance at 31 December 20X7	1,000	200	800	£2,000

Statements of financial position at 31 December 20X7 and 20X6

	20X7 £000	20X6 £000
Non-current assets	2,320	2,080
Current assets		
Inventory	400	290
Receivables	450	350
Cash at bank	50	200
	900	840
Total assets	£3,220	£2,920
Equity		
Equity share capital (£1 shares)	1,000	1,000
10% irredeemable preference share capital (£1 shares)	200	200
Retained earnings	800	740
Total equity	2,000	1,940
Non-current liabilities		
10% debentures (20X9)	720	600
Current liabilities		
Payables	400	300
Tax	100	80
	500	380
Total equity and liabilities	£3,220	£2,920

Statements of cash flow for the years ended 31 December 20X7 and 20X6

	20X7 £000	20X6 £000
Cash flow from operating activities		
Cash generated from operations	636	580
Interest paid	(66)	(60)
Taxation paid	(160)	(115)
Net cash from operating activities	410	405
Cash flow from investing activities		
Purchase of non-current assets	(600)	(180)
Proceeds from sale of non-current assets	20	10
Net cash used in investing activities	(580)	(170)

Cash flow from financing activities

Issue of debentures	120	–
Preference dividends paid	(20)	(20)
Equity dividends paid	(80)	(75)
Net cash from/(used in) financing activities	20	(95)
Net (decrease)/increase in cash	(150)	140
Cash and cash equivalents at beginning of year	200	60
Cash and cash equivalents at end of year	£50	£200

Reconciliation of profit before tax to cash generated from operations

	20X7 £000	20X6 £000
Profit before tax	340	317
Add back: finance costs	66	60
depreciation	330	250
loss/(profit) on sale of non-current assets	10	(17)
(Increase)/decrease in inventory	(110)	20
(Increase) in receivables	(100)	(40)
Increase/(decrease) in payables	100	(10)
Cash generated from operations	£636	£580

5.2 Overview of financial statements

5.2.1 Horizontal analysis

As given in Worked example 5.1, a published set of financial statements will include comparative figures. A good initial analytical technique is to compare key figures in the two sets of accounts, selecting those which are of particular interest for the purposes of the analysis. The aim of this, sometimes referred to as **horizontal analysis**, is to gain a 'feel' for the financial performance and position of the company at least for the later year compared with the previous year, and to start directing attention to areas which require additional investigation.

If figures are keyed or copied into a spreadsheet, changes in all figures can be easily calculated. Identification of which are the key figures and which are significant changes can then be made.

Absolute differences in figures are of little use unless they are put in the context of the actual figures themselves, so expressing the changes in percentage terms provides the necessary analytical information.

Worked example 5.2: to show horizontal analysis

Key figures and changes have been highlighted.

Statements of comprehensive income

	20X7 £000	20X6 £000	Change
Revenue	3,000	2,500	20%
Cost of sales	(1,800)	(1,425)	26%
Gross profit	1,200	1,075	12%
Administration expenses	(544)	(453)	20%
Distribution costs	(250)	(245)	2%
Profit from operations	406	377	8%
Finance costs	(66)	(60)	10%
Profit before tax	340	317	7%
Tax	(180)	(122)	**48%**
Profit for the year	£160	£195	−18%

Statements of financial position

	20X7 £000	20X6 £000	
Non-current assets	2,320	2,080	**12%**
Current assets			
Inventory	400	290	**38%**
Receivables	450	350	**29%**
Cash at bank	50	200	**−75%**
	900	840	7%
Total assets	£3,220	£2,920	10%
Equity			
Equity share capital	1,000	1,000	**0%**
10% preference share capital	200	200	**0%**
Retained earnings	800	740	8%
Total equity	2,000	1,940	3%
Non-current liabilities			
10% debentures	720	600	20%

Current liabilities			
Payables	400	300	33%
Tax	100	80	25%
	500	380	32%
Total liabilities	1,220	980	24%
Total equity and liabilities	£3,220	£2,920	10%

Statements of cash flow

	20X7 £000	20X6 £000	
Cash flow from operating activities			
Cash generated from operations	636	580	10%
Interest paid	(66)	(60)	10%
Taxation paid	(160)	(115)	39%
Net cash from operating activities	410	405	1%
Cash flow from investing activities			
Purchase of non-current assets	(600)	(180)	233%
Proceeds from sale of non-current assets	20	10	100%
Net cash used in investing activities	(580)	(170)	**241%**
Cash flow from financing activities			
Issue of debentures	120	–	–
Preference dividends paid	(20)	(20)	0%
Equity dividends paid	(80)	(75)	7%
Net cash from/(used in) financing activities	20	(95)	**121%**
Net (decrease)/increase in cash and cash equivalents	£(150)	£140	**−207%**

Key points revealed by this overview and further questions raised are as follows:

Statements of comprehensive income

- Revenue shows an increase of 20%.
  - How much of this is from the new contact obtained?
  - Are there any other significant changes in customers or products sold?
- However, gross profit has increased by only 12% and profit from operations by only 8%.
- Conclusion—costs are proportionately much higher. Which costs and why?
- Profit after tax has fallen—the tax charge has disproportionately increased. Why?

Statements of financial position

- All assets and liabilities have increased except cash and net current assets.
- Increased business would lead to increases in net assets.
- Why has cash decreased?
- There has been no new equity funding, but additional debentures have been issued.

Statements of cash flow

- Large cash decrease in 20X7—this was an increase in 20X6.
- Main cause—investment in non-current assets.
- The reconciliation of profit before tax to operating cash flow reveals working capital increases.

5.2.2 Common size statements

Another way of providing an overview of the financial statements and the comparative figures is to produce common size statements, a technique referred to as **vertical analysis**. For each financial statement a key figure is identified, such as revenue for the statement of comprehensive income and total assets for the statement of financial position, and all other figures are expressed as a percentage of this figure. For the statement of comprehensive income, comparison of the two years provides information about how the levels of different costs and profits have varied, and, for the statement of financial position, details of changes in the capital structure of the business are revealed.

 Worked example 5.3: to show vertical analysis

Key figures have been highlighted.

Statements of comprehensive income

	20X7	20X6
Revenue	100%	100%
Cost of sales	60%	57%
Gross profit	**40%**	**43%**
Administration expenses	18%	18%
Distribution costs	8%	10%
Profit from operations	**13%**	**15%**
Finance costs	2%	2%
Profit before tax	**11%**	**13%**
Tax	6%	5%
Profit for the year	**5%**	**8%**

Statements of financial position

	20X7	20X6
Non-current assets	72%	71%
Current assets		
Inventory	12%	10%
Receivables	14%	12%
Cash at bank	2%	7%
	28%	29%
Total assets	100%	100%
Equity		
Equity share capital	31%	34%
10% preference share capital	6%	7%
Retained earnings	25%	25%
Total equity	62%	66%
Non-current liabilities		
10% debentures	22%	21%
Current liabilities		
Payables	12%	10%
Tax	3%	3%
	16%	13%
Total liabilities	38%	34%
Total equity and liabilities	100%	100%

Key points revealed by this review are as follows.

Statements of comprehensive income

- Confirmation of the fall in all profits in relation to revenues.

Statements of financial position

- Not many significant differences in relative sizes of asset and liability balances, and financial structure over the two years except for confirmation of the fall in cash balances by the end of 20X7.

Note: the analysis has not been performed for the statements of cash flows, as there is no meaningful key figure in relation to which all other figures could be expressed.

Common size statements are particularly useful in the comparison of cost and profit levels, and financial structures of companies in different industry sectors.

Worked example 5.4: to show different companies' common size statements of financial position

The common size statements of financial position given as follows are of the following companies:

Company:	Incorporated in:	Industry:
Severn Trent	UK	Water services
Deutsche Bank	Germany	Financial institution
Nestlé	Switzerland	Food and household goods manufacturer
Tesco	UK	Supermarket

	A %	B %	C %	D %
Land and buildings	2	15	25	64
Plant equipment and infrastructure assets	1	22	62	18
Intangible assets	–	11	–	5
Inventories	–	14	2	7
Receivables	78	22	5	2
Cash and securities	19	16	6	4
Total assets	100	100	100	100
Equity	5	41	35	47
Long-term loans	3	18	46	10
Short-term loans	–	17	8	8
Trade payables	91	16	1	28
Other liabilities	1	8	10	7
Total equity and liabilities	100	100	100	100

Required:
Identify which common size statement relates to which company.

	Company	Main reasons
A	Deutsche Bank	Low equity; very high receivables and payables; no inventories; low plant and buildings.
B	Nestlé	Medium inventories; high receivables; medium payables; medium land, buildings and plant.

C	Severn Trent	High plant, equipment and infrastructure assets; low inventories, receivables and payables.
D	Tesco	High land and buildings; medium plant and inventories; high payables; low receivables.

5.2.3 Five-year data

An analysis is usually performed by users to help them make decisions about their interaction with the company. This will usually entail some prediction of what may happen in the future. Clearly, two years of figures does not provide sufficient information to predict the future, especially if there are one-off anomalies within either, or both, of the years. Listed companies do, though, provide five-year summaries (sometimes ten-year summaries) of key financial figures towards the back of their published annual report; thus, the techniques mentioned earlier can be extended to this data to establish a longer trend from which more reliable predictions of the future may be able to be made.

Two main methods to describe changes in figures over time can be used in analysis.

1 A year-on-year change in percentage terms.

2 A percentage change from a base year—index numbers can be used here.

 Worked example 5.5: to show trend analysis

Revenue and profit before tax figures for Sharples plc for the five years 20X3–20X7 are as follows.

	20X7 £000	20X6 £000	20X5 £000	20X4 £000	20X3 £000
Revenue	3,000	2,500	2,100	1,700	1,300
Profit before tax	340	317	250	186	165

Required:

Describe the changes in the figures over the five years.

1 *Year-on-year percentage change*

	20X7	20X6	20X5	20X4	20X3
Revenue	20%	19%	24%	31%	–
Profit before tax	7%	27%	34%	13%	–

2 *Change from base year*—expressing each figure as an index number with 20X3 as the base year

	20X7	20X6	20X5	20X4	20X3
Revenue	231	192	162	131	100
Profit before tax	206	192	152	113	100

Method 1 shows that revenue has increased over the years, but the rate of increase has fallen. Profit before tax has also increased over the years, but the increase year-on-year is more erratic.

Method 2 establishes that both revenue and profit before tax have grown steadily over the five-year period and have more than doubled over the years.

5.3 Ratio analysis

In addition to reviewing and comparing individual line items, the relationships of different figures within a single set of financial statements are of importance and can provide much useful information to a user. A ratio can be calculated using any two or more figures, but, for the ratio to be useful, it must have meaning. For example, receivables and credit sales are related, and a ratio of one to the other will have some meaning, but a ratio of distribution costs to non-current assets will not make any sense.

Thus, there are some standard ratios that are used in financial analysis. Remember that different users require different information from financial statements, so will use different groups of ratios. Appropriate ratios should, therefore, be selected for the purposes of the particular analysis.

A ratio, once calculated, may have some meaning on its own, for example if year-end receivables are 15% of the year's credit sales this gives some indication of the ability of the business to convert its sales into cash. However, to be really useful, a ratio should be put in context and related to some sort of reference point or standard. These points of reference might include:

- ratios from past years, to provide a standard of comparison
- ratios of other businesses in the same industry
- standards required by an interested organisation, e.g. a bank.

To properly interpret ratios, the make-up of the figures used in the ratios has to be considered. For example, is an aggregate of different figures being used and is this the same in the two ratios being compared? What are the valuation bases of the figures included in the ratio, and has this changed or is it different? It is also important to understand the relationship between ratios, as one ratio may give one interpretation of the state of the business, but this needs to be supported by other ratios.

Ratio analysis, used with the overview techniques explained, provides a useful tool in the interpretation of financial statements, but it is not the final answer to understanding what the accounts mean. It is emphasised again that ratios should always be put in the context of the business itself: What is the business's trade? How does it operate? Where is it located? Does it own property? What relationships does it have with customers, suppliers, competitors and banks? Is it a company and, if so, is it private or public? What deals have been entered into or are about to be entered into?, etc. Only if all these facts are considered can a full understanding of the financial statements be achieved. However, it can provide pointers to areas of financial control and decision-making which need investigation—the key question 'why?' needs to be asked at every stage until it cannot be answered any more from the information the user has.

5.3.1 Categories of ratios

Ratios calculated commonly are divided into the different categories shown in Table 5.1 depending on their purpose or for whom they are likely to be used.

Different ratios falling within each category are now explained and calculated for the example company, Sharples plc. An analysis of these ratios is also included. A summary of all ratio formulae and the calculations is included at the end of the sections on the different categories.

It is important to note that for some ratios there is no definitive formula and one definition can be considered as valid as another. Also, in any analysis using real data, there are many choices to be made about which figures to use in the selected ratio. In carrying out a ratio analysis it is vitally important to explain how the ratios have been defined and calculated with an explanation of why they have been calculated in that way. In addition, when comparisons are to be made, consistency in how the ratios have been calculated is necessary. (This is discussed in more detail in Chapter 19 where an interpretation of a 'real' company is performed.)

Table 5.1 Ratio categories and their principal users

Ratio category	Category definition	Principal user groups
Profitability	Effectiveness in generating profits	Investors, lenders, employees, suppliers, customers, government, and their agencies
Liquidity	Ability to meet liabilities when they fall due	Lenders, suppliers, investors, customers
Efficiency/activity	Effectiveness of use of business assets	Investors, suppliers
Gearing	Financial structure	Investors, lenders
Investor/stock market	Returns to investors	Investors

5.4 Profitability ratios

Ratios included in this category are:

- return on capital employed
- asset turnover
- net profit margin
- gross profit margin
- expenses as a percentage of sales.

Asset turnover is strictly an efficiency ratio; however, it is considered here because it is used in the interpretation of return on capital employed (ROCE).

5.4.1 Return on capital employed (ROCE)

$$\frac{\text{Net profit}}{\text{Capital employed}}$$

ROCE expresses the net profit generated by the business from the capital employed by the business and is given as a percentage.

An existing, or potential, investor wishes to know what return is being generated from the use of the capital in the business. The percentage return could then be compared to returns which could be gained elsewhere simply, for example, from a bank deposit or building society. However, note that the risks in running a business are considerably greater than depositing money with a bank or building society, and an additional return to compensate for this is needed.

It is impossible to state categorically what represents a 'good' or 'bad' return, but comparison with previous years or the industry as a whole will reveal differences which require investigation and explanation. In a well-established business this ratio may be fairly constant or show a slight increase from year to year. It is influenced by the level of profitability in a particular year and whether there are any significant changes in the capital structure of the business.

There are variations in the calculation of this ratio which stem from how profit and capital employed are defined.

A basic definition is that capital employed is all long-term capital in a business—in a company this includes equity (the shareholders' funds) and long-term debt, including the current portion of long-term debt. The ratio then takes a profit figure generated by the business from the use of this capital before the actual return (interest and dividends) to these providers of capital. It is also a profit figure before tax is deducted, as the business has no control over tax rates which are set by the government, and limited control over taxable profits. The profit figure used is therefore profit before interest and tax (PBIT), also called operating profit. So ROCE becomes:

$$\frac{\text{PBIT}}{\text{Equity + long-term debt}}$$

Other definitions of capital employed often seen are:

1 Equity + non-current liabilities (also equivalent to: Total assets—current liabilities)   Similar to the earlier definition, but includes other non-current liabilities, which are arguably not part of the long-term financing of the business, such as deferred tax or provisions

The resulting ratio can also be called return on net assets (RONA)

2 Total assets   The interpretation of the ratio is slightly different as it considers the returns generated from the use of the assets, the business's resources, only

Capital employed at the start or the end of the year, or an average, can be used as long as a consistent approach is taken to all calculations.

Net profit can also be taken to exclude depreciation and amortisation in addition to interest—the result is referred to as EBITDA (earnings before interest, tax, depreciation and amortisation). The reason why depreciation and amortisation are excluded is because, firstly, they depend on a business's chosen accounting policies, which can vary from company to company, and, secondly, they are non-cash expenses and so the resulting 'profit' numerator is closer to a 'real' profit figure based on cash flows.

Net profit may also exclude unusual or one-off items, or fair value changes that have passed through the statement of comprehensive income, as demonstrated by the following company example.

Financial reporting in practice 5.1   J Sainsbury plc, 2015

Sainsbury, in its 2015 annual report, includes 'pre-tax return on capital employed' as one of its key financial performance indicators, and defines this as:

> Underlying profit before interest and tax, divided by the average of opening and closing capital employed (net assets before net debt).

where underlying profit is defined as:

> Profit before tax before any profit or loss on the disposal of properties, investment property fair value movements, retail financing fair value movements, impairment of goodwill, IAS 19 pension financing element, defined benefit pension scheme expenses, acquisition adjustments and one-off items that are material and infrequent in nature.

Taken simply as Net profit/Capital employed, ROCE can be subdivided into two further ratios, the results of each of which will influence the return achieved. These two ratios are asset turnover and net profit margin, and their product gives ROCE.

5.4.2 Asset turnover

$$\frac{\text{Revenue}}{\text{Capital employed}}$$

If capital employed is defined as equity plus long-term debt, and there are no other significant non-current liabilities, capital employed is equivalent to total assets net of current liabilities. For the purposes of this textbook, this will be referred to as net assets. However, note that the term 'net assets' is sometimes taken as total assets minus total liabilities (in other words, equity). So care must be taken in defining and interpreting ratios that use this term.

The asset turnover ratio shows the value of revenue generated per £1 of net assets employed in the year and is used to assess the efficiency of the use of net assets during the year. It is strictly an efficiency ratio; however, it is explained here because it is used in the interpretation of ROCE. Generally, a larger figure for this ratio indicates that higher volume of sales have been generated with more efficient use of assets.

Some businesses, particularly those in the retail trade, may break down this ratio further and consider revenues generated from only non-current assets:

$$\frac{\text{Revenue}}{\text{Non-current assets}}$$

This indicates the efficiency of their stores in generating revenues. However, this would be influenced particularly by valuation methods and depreciation policies for non-current assets.

5.4.3 Net profit margin

$$\frac{\text{Net profit}}{\text{Revenue}}$$

This expresses the profit the business has earned on its sales and is given as a percentage. The net profit should be defined in the same way as for ROCE, the best measure being PBIT, or it may exclude certain items as discussed earlier.

Ideally, this percentage should be similar from year to year and comparable with other businesses in the same industry. There are two main influences over this ratio—the gross profit earned and the overheads incurred.

5.4.4 Gross profit margin

$$\frac{\text{Gross profit}}{\text{Revenue}}$$

This measures the profit earned from the trading activities of the business—the buying or manufacturing and selling of goods or services—and is expressed as a percentage. For example, a gross profit of 30% means that for every £100 of sales a gross profit of £30 is earned.

Businesses monitor their gross profit margin extremely closely. Ideally, it should be the same from year to year, but many things will influence it including:

- fluctuations in purchase prices and manufacturing costs
- bad purchasing policy resulting in inventories being sold at a reduced profit or even a loss
- changes in the selling prices (e.g. cutting the selling margin)
- changes in the mix of sales
- inventory losses through theft or reduction in value.

Different types of businesses will have very different gross profit margins, for example a supermarket will have a much lower gross profit margin compared with a jewellery business. Even within a business, different products will have very different gross profits, for example the supermarket's green grocery products' gross profit margin will be much lower than pre-packed meals or luxury items. Hence, the product mix's influence over the gross profit is important.

Whatever the type of business, gross profit needs to be sufficient to cover the expenses and to provide an acceptable level of net profit.

5.4.5 Expenses as a percentage of sales

$$\frac{\text{Expense item}}{\text{Revenue}}$$

This can be calculated for any expense individually or in total, and gives some idea as to whether the business has been controlling expenses in relation to the level of revenue achieved. It is expressed as a percentage.

Facts about the business—the type of property, whether it is a labour-intensive business or a highly computerised one, whether costs are fixed in nature or variable, whether they are directly related to revenues or not, etc.—will have much influence over these ratios; this should be considered when comparing different businesses, in particular. Within the same business these ratios should, ideally, stay the same from year to year or, as the business grows, the ratios may be expected to decrease as economies of scale are seen.

5.4.6 Relationship between profitability ratios

Figure 5.1 indicates the relationship between the profitability ratios. If, for example, the gross profit falls from one year to the next, this will cause a fall in net profit margin (everything else remaining the same). As an analysis is being conducted, the relationship between these ratios may be used to explain the cause of changes in ratios higher up the relationship tree. For example, if there is a decrease in net profit margin from one year to the next, the question

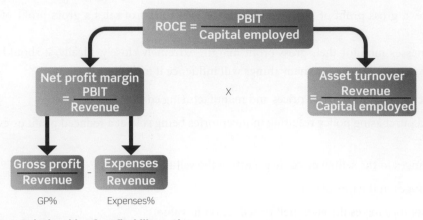

Figure 5.1 Relationship of profitability ratios

that should be asked is: *why* has it decreased? If the gross profit margin is found to have fallen, this would go some way to explaining the decrease in the net profit margin. Likewise, the question 'why has ROCE increased?' can be analysed further by examining the changes in the two ratios net profit margin and asset turnover.

Worked example 5.6: to show the calculation and interpretation of the profitability ratios

The profitability ratios are calculated for Sharples plc.

		20X7		20X6	
ROCE	$\dfrac{\text{PBIT}}{\text{Equity + long-term debt}}$	$\dfrac{406}{2,000 + 720}$	14.9%	$\dfrac{377}{1,940 + 600}$	14.8%
Asset turnover	$\dfrac{\text{Revenue}}{\text{Capital employed}}$	$\dfrac{3,000}{2,720}$	1.10	$\dfrac{2,500}{2,540}$	0.98
Net profit margin	$\dfrac{\text{PBIT}}{\text{Revenue}}$	$\dfrac{406}{3,000}$	13.5%	$\dfrac{377}{2,500}$	15.1%
Gross profit margin	$\dfrac{\text{Gross profit}}{\text{Revenue}}$	$\dfrac{1,200}{3,000}$	40.0%	$\dfrac{1,075}{2,500}$	43.0%
Administration expenses %	$\dfrac{\text{Administration expenses}}{\text{Revenue}}$	$\dfrac{544}{3,000}$	18.1%	$\dfrac{453}{2,500}$	18.1%
Distribution costs %	$\dfrac{\text{Distribution costs}}{\text{Revenue}}$	$\dfrac{250}{3,000}$	8.3%	$\dfrac{245}{2,500}$	9.8%

ROCE

● ROCE is fairly constant over the two years. Both PBIT and capital employed have increased in 20X7, but proportionately by the same rate. Both equity and long-term debt have increased.

- Is this a reasonable return for this type of business?
- A similar ROCE in each year masks other changes that have occurred.

	ROCE	=	Asset turnover	×	Net profit margin
20X7	14.9%	=	1.10	×	13.5%
20X6	14.8%	=	0.98	×	15.1%

- This breakdown shows that more sales have been generated from the use of assets (has the company been more efficient in 20X7?), but profitability as shown by the net profit margin has fallen.
- Overall capital (and net assets) have only increased marginally; revenue shows a large growth.

Net profit margin

An analysis of what has caused the fall in the net profit margin is as shown:

	20X7 %	20X6 %
Gross profit margin	40.0	43.0
Administrative expenses %	(18.1)	(18.1)
Distribution costs %	(8.4)	(9.8)
Net profit margin	13.5	15.1

- This shows it has been caused by a fall in gross profit margin from 43% to 40%, slightly mitigated by distribution costs being a smaller percentage of sales.
- The fall in gross profit margin could be as a result of any, or all, of the following:
  - increase in the cost of purchases (e.g. different suppliers, delivery charges, exchange rates) not passed on to customers
  - a reduction in sales prices (possibly unlikely)
  - special deals with the new high street customer in order to gain the contract
  - changes in the sales mix from higher margin goods to lower margin goods
  - inventory damage, theft or other losses.
- Has the company tried consciously to control distribution costs or have economies of scale had an impact as the company has grown?

5.5 Liquidity ratios

Ratios included in this category are:

- current ratio
- liquid ratio.

Liquidity is the ability of a business to meet its short-term liabilities as they fall due. Clearly, a business needs sufficient cash in order to be able to achieve this, but other assets, which will turn into cash in the short term as trading activities continue, are also considered in the measure of liquidity. An analysis of the liquidity of a business therefore involves an assessment of what makes up working capital. Working capital is defined as net current assets (i.e. current assets – current liabilities) and is needed by all businesses in order to finance day-to-day trading activities. Many UK companies still present their statements of financial position in a format to show the key figure of working capital, although this is not specified by IAS 1 formats (see Chapter 4 for details of these).

Sufficient working capital enables a business to hold adequate inventories, allow a measure of credit to its customers, and to pay its suppliers as payments fall due. The amount of working capital required by a business will vary from business to business depending on:

- the nature of the business, e.g. a shop is likely to need less working capital than an engineering business because a shop has few, if any, trade receivables
- the size of the business, e.g. a small corner shop will need less working capital than a large department store.

5.5.1 Current ratio

$$\frac{\text{Current assets}}{\text{Current liabilities}}$$

This measures the balance of current assets and current liabilities, and is a measure of how easily a business can meet its current liabilities as they fall due; in other words, for every £1 of current liabilities, how much there is in the form of current assets?

Although there is no ideal current ratio, an often quoted ratio is 2:1. However, the nature of the business will greatly influence the size of this ratio; these days many businesses work with a much lower ratio, even less than 1:1. Traditionally, retailers will have low current ratios because they deal mainly in sales for cash and so do not have large figures for receivables. A current ratio can be too high. If it is above, say, 3:1 the business may have too much cash tied up in inventories, or too many receivables, or too much cash sitting in a current bank account, or it is not benefitting from having enough trade payables.

5.5.2 Liquid ratio

$$\frac{\text{Current assets} - \text{Inventories}}{\text{Current liabilities}}$$

Also called the acid test or quick ratio, this is a more pertinent measure of the ability of a business to meet its liabilities as they fall due because it omits the least liquid current asset—inventories—from the numerator. Inventory has to be sold to customers who then have to pay before the asset converts to cash; some inventories may never be sold. Again, an often quoted minimum is 1:1, at which a business could pay the current liabilities on the statement of financial position from its receivables, if they were collected, and its cash balances. A figure below this might indicate that the business would have difficulty in meeting its liabilities. However, many businesses survive with a ratio well below this and, again, the level of the ratio is influenced by the nature of the business.

Financial reporting in practice 5.2 | Current and liquid ratios

The following are the current and liquid ratios for a selection of companies in different industries:

Company:	Industry:	Current:	Liquid:
Tesco plc, 2015	Supermarket	0.60	0.45
Marks and Spencer plc, 2015	High street retailer	0.69	0.31
Vodafone plc, 2015	Telecommunications	0.69	0.67
Rolls-Royce plc, 2014	Manufacturing	1.46	1.10
Balfour Beatty plc, 2015	Construction	0.88	0.66

The statement of cash flows should also be used in the interpretation of liquidity, and this is discussed further in section 5.9.

 Worked example 5.7: to show the calculation and interpretation of the liquidity ratios

The liquidity ratios are calculated for Sharples plc.

		20X7		20X6	
Current ratio	$\dfrac{\text{Current assets}}{\text{Current liabilities}}$	$\dfrac{900}{500}$	1.8	$\dfrac{840}{380}$	2.2
Liquid ratio	$\dfrac{\text{Current assets} - \text{Inventories}}{\text{Current liabilities}}$	$\dfrac{900 - 400}{500}$	1.0	$\dfrac{840 - 290}{380}$	1.4

- No apparent liquidity problems are indicated by these ratios with the company able to pay its liabilities as they fall due.
- Cash balances and the two liquidity ratios have fallen, but the company is still able to cover its current liabilities from its liquid assets (receivables and cash).
- The key question is why have cash balances fallen? An analysis of the statement of cash flows will assist in this (see Worked example 5.12).

5.6 Efficiency ratios

Ratios included in this category are:

- asset turnover (discussed in section 5.4.2)
- inventory turnover
- receivables collection period
- payables payment period.

One important issue arising from the earlier discussion on liquidity is the ability of a business to convert its current assets to cash to pay its liabilities. An understanding of the liquidity of a business must, therefore, include a study of the management of these conversion times, for example how long it takes to sell its inventories and collect the cash from its credit customers. The efficiency ratios provide figures which can help in this analysis.

5.6.1 Inventory turnover

$$\frac{\text{Inventories}}{\text{Cost of sales}} \times 365$$

This ratio shows the number of days inventories are held on average. Average inventory levels held over the year are the best measure to use in the calculation, but these will not be available from a set of financial statements. The average of opening and closing inventories can used as a substitute or, if opening inventories are not available, then inventories at the end of the year is the best figure available. The ratio can, alternatively, be stated as the number of times inventories are turned over, on average, each year by inverting the previous formula:

$$\frac{\text{Cost of sales}}{\text{Inventories}}$$

The nature of the inventories is crucial in interpreting this ratio, for example a greengrocer will have an inventory turnover of a few days, while a furniture shop's ratio may be 60–90 days. Nevertheless, inventory turnover should not be too long and review of the trend from year to year is important. Inventories sitting on a shelf unnecessarily tie up working capital which could be put to better uses. The business's inventory holding policies, for example just-in-time, make-to-order and make-to-stock also have much influence over the ratio.

5.6.2 Receivables collection period

$$\frac{\text{Trade receivables}}{\text{Credit sales}} \times 365$$

This ratio shows, on average, how long credit customers take to pay for the goods sold to them. The denominator of the ratio should be credit sales only, but usually this is not available from the accounts, so revenue from sales or total revenue will have to be used instead. An average of opening and closing receivables may be used, but the year-end receivables is often the figure included in the calculation.

The ratio calculated can be compared with the credit period the business allows to its customers—often 30 days, although 60 or 90 days is not uncommon—to see whether the business is efficient in its debt collection. Certainly, businesses do not wish to see this ratio increase from period to period; however, certain factors could influence it such as export sales or a very large sale just before the year end.

5.6.3 Payables payment period

$$\frac{\text{Trade payables}}{\text{Credit purchases}} \times 365$$

Similar in concept to the previous ratio, this shows how long, on average, it takes for a business to pay its credit suppliers. Often, the figure for credit purchases is not available from the financial statements, in which case it could be approximated by total purchases or cost of sales. Another issue with the ratio is that payables will include amounts owing to suppliers of services, for example electricity and telephone, so the numerator and denominator are internally inconsistent.

However, the ratio provides a useful indicator of the length of credit period taken from suppliers. While payables can be a useful source of short-term finance, delaying payment too long may cause problems with suppliers' relationships, or deter new suppliers from entering into business arrangements, so a business does not necessarily want this ratio to be as large as possible.

5.6.4 Working capital cycle

Figure 5.2 shows a simplified working capital cycle. This uses the earlier efficiency ratios and estimates the time taken to convert cash back into cash through the operating cycle, in other words the time from the payment of goods to the receipt of cash from the sale of these goods. The shorter this time, the lower the value of working capital required to be financed by the business.

The length of the working capital cycle can be calculated as follows:

Inventory turnover + Receivables collection period – Payables payment period

Like all accounting ratios, a comparison needs to be made with previous years or another similar business. Businesses can reduce this time by:

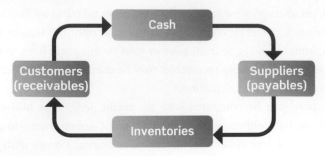

Figure 5.2 The working capital cycle

- reducing inventories
- speeding up the receivables collection period
- slowing the rate at which suppliers are paid.

However these steps may have other consequences:

- reducing inventories may mean a poorer service is offered to customers, who may take their business elsewhere
- giving customers less time to pay may cause them to seek alternative suppliers who are offering better terms
- taking extra credit from suppliers may cause them to decline to supply goods.

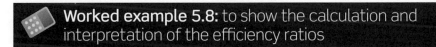

Worked example 5.8: to show the calculation and interpretation of the efficiency ratios

The efficiency ratios are calculated for Sharples plc.

		20X7	Days	20X6	Days
Inventory turnover	$\frac{\text{Inventories}}{\text{Cost of sales}} \times 365$	$\frac{400}{1,800} \times 365$	81	$\frac{290}{1,425} \times 365$	74
Receivables collection period	$\frac{\text{Receivables}}{\text{Revenue}} \times 365$	$\frac{450}{3,000} \times 365$	55	$\frac{350}{2,500} \times 365$	51
Payables payment period	$\frac{\text{Payables}}{\text{Cost of sales}} \times 365$	$\frac{400}{1,800} \times 365$	81	$\frac{300}{1,425} \times 365$	77
Working capital cycle		81 + 55 − 81	55	74 + 51 − 77	48

- The efficiency or working capital management ratios have all increased, indicating that the company is holding onto inventories longer, is taking longer to collect its receivables, and is taking longer to pay its payables.

- Why? Possible reasons may be:

  - the company is building up inventories to supply the new customer

  - other large orders are about to go out in early January 20X8

  - there is a large debt uncollected at the 20X7 year end

  - the company has negotiated longer payment terms with the new customer to gain business.

- The extension of the payables payment period has been negated by less efficient collection of receivables—the company must not risk upsetting its suppliers.

- Overall, the working capital cycle indicates less efficient cash management and may have contributed to the reduction in the liquidity of the company.

5.7 Gearing

Ratios included in this category are:

- gearing
- financial leverage
- interest cover.

Gearing (or leverage) is a measure of the balance between the two main types of long-term capital or funding in a business—that provided by equity (i.e. ordinary share capital and reserves) and that provided by debt (i.e. long-term loans, such as debentures).

As for many other ratios there are alternative ways of calculating a gearing ratio. Two basic gearing ratios are:

$$\frac{\text{Debt finance}}{\text{Equity}} \quad \text{or} \quad \frac{\text{Debt finance}}{\text{Debt finance} + \text{equity}}$$

Debt finance may be replaced by net debt, which reduces debt balances by positive cash and cash equivalent balances. The reason for this is that net debt is the figure that represents the outcome of treasury management policies.

Financial reporting in practice 5.3	J Sainsbury plc, 2015

Sainsbury, in its 2015 annual report, shows net debt as total borrowings (including accrued interest) plus bank overdrafts plus finance lease liabilities plus financial derivative liabilities net of interest bearing available-for-sale financial assets, other derivative financial assets, and cash and cash equivalents.

ity**

An alternative way of viewing gearing is to consider how net assets are financed. If net assets are considered equivalent to capital employed, as discussed in section 5.4.2, this can be given by the financial leverage ratio:

$$\frac{\text{Capital employed}}{\text{Equity}}$$

and measures the proportion of assets that are financed by equity as opposed to debt.

Whichever way gearing is calculated, a company that has a high proportion of debt finance is considered highly geared, while a company that has mainly equity financing is considered a low-geared company.

A business that is highly geared is perceived as a riskier investment for the equity investor. This is because there is a greater chance that dividends to the ordinary shareholders will be reduced as profits are used to pay the fixed returns to the loan providers and preference shareholders first. In a highly geared company the earnings per equity share (see section 5.8.2) can fluctuate enormously as profits fluctuate; investors are often wary of companies with large variations in key ratios from one year to the next. However, if the cost of borrowed capital is lower than the profits which can be earned on it, the earnings available to ordinary shareholders will rise as a consequence of additional borrowing.

5.7.1 Interest cover

$$\frac{\text{PBIT}}{\text{Finance costs}}$$

This ratio is of particular interest to lenders as it indicates the ability of the business to meet its debt-servicing costs from its profits. A low ratio may indicate the business will have difficulties meeting these requirements, which could, potentially, have serious consequences.

 Worked example 5.9: to show the calculation and interpretation of the gearing ratios

The gearing ratios are calculated for Sharples plc.

		20X7		20X6	
Gearing	$\frac{\text{Net debt}}{\text{Equity}}$	$\frac{720-50}{2,000}$	33.5%	$\frac{600-200}{1,940}$	20.6%
Interest cover	$\frac{\text{PBIT}}{\text{Finance costs}}$	$\frac{406}{66}$	6.2	$\frac{377}{60}$	6.3

- Although gearing has increased, the company is not very highly geared.

- Both long-term borrowings (additional debentures issued) and equity have increased, but cash balances have fallen significantly—all contributing to the increase in gearing.

- Although the company issued more debentures, the company can comfortably meet its interest payments. As the company has fairly low gearing, the equity shareholders face little risk in their investment.

5.8 Investor ratios

Ratios included in this category are:

- return on equity (ROE)
- earnings per share (EPS)
- price/earnings ratio (P/E ratio)
- dividend per share
- dividend cover
- dividend yield
- total shareholder returns.

These are a group of ratios which apply to companies only, and in which a potential or existing equity investor will be particularly interested and may use to assess the success or failure of the investment.

5.8.1 Return on equity

$$\frac{\text{Profit attributable to equity shareholders}}{\text{Shareholders' funds (equity)}}$$

Profit attributable to equity shareholders is profit after tax and after preference dividends. Care must be taken if a company publishes a full statement of comprehensive income, as the profit figure used here excludes other comprehensive income.

This ratio, expressed as a percentage, measures the return to the equity shareholders on their investment. Profits are after the servicing costs of other forms of finance—this is what is left for the equity shareholder—but before the actual returns to them. Returns to shareholders can be either in the form of dividend distributions or through the growth of share price; the latter may result from companies reinvesting their profits. Thus, this ratio is assessing total return to the shareholders.

5.8.2 Earnings per share

$$\frac{\text{Profit attributable to equity shareholders}}{\text{No. of equity shares}}$$

This is a key ratio for equity investors. Companies are required to calculate and disclose EPS on the face of the statement of comprehensive income; the ratio has its own accounting standard, IAS 33 *Earnings per share*, which is examined in detail in Chapter 8. The ratio measures earnings available to the equity shareholder per share and is usually expressed as an amount in pence. Companies and investors like to see this value rising from year to year.

 Worked example 5.10: to show the effect of gearing on EPS

Companies Alpha and Beta have the same total capital as follows:

	Alpha £	Beta £
Equity share capital (£1 shares)	1,000	4,000
Retained earnings	1,000	1,000
Long-term loans	4,000	1,000
	6,000	6,000

Assume the long-term loans have a fixed interest rate of 10% and a corporation tax rate of 30% on accounting profits.

Required:

Calculate and comment on the gearing ratio and earnings per share for each company for the three years when profits before interest and tax in each company were:

20X1	£400
20X2	£600
20X3	£1,000

	Company Alpha	Company Beta
Gearing $\dfrac{\text{Debt}}{\text{Equity}}$	$\dfrac{4,000}{2,000} = 200\%$	$\dfrac{1,000}{5,000} = 20\%$

	Company Alpha			Company Beta		
	20X1	20X2	20X3	20X1	20X2	20X3
	£	£	£	£	£	£
PBIT	400	600	1,000	400	600	1,000
Interest	400	400	400	100	100	100
Profit before tax	–	200	600	300	500	900
Tax	–	60	180	90	150	270
Profit after tax	–	140	420	210	350	630
No. of ordinary shares	1,000	1,000	1,000	4,000	4,000	4,000
EPS	–	140	420	210	350	630
		1,000	1,000	4,000	4,000	4,000
	–	14p	42p	5.25p	8.75p	15.75p

Alpha is a highly geared company, while Beta's gearing is fairly low. In a year of low profits, such as 20X1, Alpha's profits are wiped out by the interest it has to pay on its debt, leaving nothing for its equity investors. However, in more profitable years, Alpha's EPS is much higher than company Beta.

Note the large increases in company Alpha's EPS as profits increase over the years compared with Beta's more modest increases. As profit levels vary, Alpha's EPS will fluctuate more widely—an aspect that may deter equity investors.

5.8.3 Price/earnings ratio (P/E)

$$\frac{\text{Market price per share}}{\text{Earnings per share}}$$

Note: the market price of a share will only be available for listed companies and may not be disclosed in the annual report.

Quoted daily in the financial press, this ratio is a measure of market confidence in a company. It shows the number of times the market value of a share exceeds the earnings per share and indicates the number of years an investor would have to wait to recover his/her investment sum. For example, a P/E ratio of 10 implies 10 years until cumulative future EPS reaches the level of the current share price.

It might, therefore, be considered that a lower P/E ratio is better for the potential equity investor because they would have to wait fewer years to recoup their investment from earnings. However, a high P/E ratio implies investors are willing to pay a high multiple for expected earnings because of underlying strength and growth opportunities.

Any increase in the P/E ratio tends to indicate that either the market price of the share is rising more quickly than earnings or the earnings are falling in relation to the market price. The reasons for the change are important, but a number of factors might affect the market price unconnected to the performance of the business. For example, the ratio will rise if there is a general increase in share prices in the markets.

P/E ratios may also be calculated using analysts' forecasts of earnings rather than annual reported earnings.

5.8.4 Dividend per share

$$\frac{\text{Total equity dividends}}{\text{No. of equity shares}}$$

This is also required to be stated in the financial statements of a company—usually in a note. Care should be taken to ensure consistency in its calculation. Dividends accounted for in the statement of changes in equity are dividends paid, and comprise the previous year's final dividend and the current year's interim dividend (if one is paid). Total dividends for the current financial year (interim which has been paid and final which has been proposed) is the figure more usually used in the ratio. The final dividend for the current year will have to be identified from the notes to the financial statements.

Obviously, investors would wish to see the ratio rise year on year, however companies have to balance this with retaining profits for future growth.

5.8.5 Dividend cover

$$\frac{\text{Profit after tax and preference dividends}}{\text{Total equity dividends}}$$

The above comments relating to dividends also apply to this ratio.

The ratio shows the number of times the funds available from a year's profits exceed the size of the equity dividend and is an indicator of the riskiness of the dividend. The greater the cover the more secure the dividend, while leaving substantial funds to be retained in the business for expansion or consolidation.

5.8.6 Dividend yield

$$\frac{\text{Dividend per share}}{\text{Market price per share}}$$

Expressed as a percentage, this ratio gives the actual dividend return for an investment in equity shares made at the latest market price.

5.8.7 Total shareholder returns

$$\frac{\text{Change in market share price} + \text{Dividend per share}}{\text{Opening market price per share}}$$

This ratio combines the two forms of return to an equity shareholder:

- the dividend
- capital growth (in the form of share price increases).

It expresses this as a percentage of the opening share price.

 Worked example 5.11: to show the calculation and interpretation of the investor ratios

The investor ratios are calculated for Sharples plc.

Assume that the market prices per share at 31 December 20X7, 20X6 and 20X5 are £1.80, £1.64 and £1.45 respectively.

		20X7		20X6	
Return on equity	$\dfrac{\text{Profit after tax and preference dividends}}{\text{Equity}}$	$\dfrac{160-20}{2,000}$	9.0%	$\dfrac{195-20}{1,940}$	9.0%
Earnings per share	$\dfrac{\text{Profit after tax and preference dividends}}{\text{No. of equity shares}}$	$\dfrac{160-20}{1,000}$	£0.14	$\dfrac{195-20}{1,000}$	£0.175
P/E ratio	$\dfrac{\text{Market price per share}}{\text{Earnings per share}}$	$\dfrac{1.80}{0.14}$	12.9	$\dfrac{1.65}{0.175}$	9.4
Dividend per share	$\dfrac{\text{Total equity dividends}}{\text{No. of equity shares}}$	$\dfrac{80}{1,000}$	£0.08	$\dfrac{75}{10,000}$	£0.075
Dividend cover	$\dfrac{\text{Profit after tax and preference dividends}}{\text{Total equity dividends}}$	$\dfrac{160-20}{80}$	1.75	$\dfrac{195-20}{75}$	2.33
Dividend yield	$\dfrac{\text{Dividend per share}}{\text{Market price per share}}$	$\dfrac{0.08}{1.80}$	4.4%	$\dfrac{0.075}{1.65}$	4.5%
Total shareholder returns	$\dfrac{\text{Change in share price} + \text{dividend per share}}{\text{Opening share price}}$	$\dfrac{(1.80-1.65+0.08)}{1.65}$	13.9%	$\dfrac{(1.65-1.45+0.075)}{1.45}$	19.0%

- Return on equity and earnings per share have both fallen owing to the fall in profit for the year, which, in turn, is a result of the abnormally looking large tax charge. Reasons for this are not evident from the financial statements.

- Despite this, the company has marginally increased the dividend per share, with the result that the dividend cover has fallen. However, dividends are still covered nearly twice by available profits. This ratio should be monitored closely, as shareholders looking for growth in the company and share price may be concerned that the ratio has fallen because of proportionately more of profits being paid out through dividends, possibly to maintain a stable dividend yield.

- The P/E ratio has increased significantly because the share price has risen, while EPS has fallen. This does indicate that the markets have confidence in the company, possibly because it has shown good growth in 20X7, and profitability and liquidity show no causes for concern.

- The increase in share price in 20X7 has not been as large as that in 20X6. This has resulted in the total shareholder returns being lower. Reasons for this are not apparent and would require details of the interpretation of the financial results for 20X6 in comparison to 20X5.

5.9 Statements of cash flows and their interpretation

The statement of cash flows should also be used to assist in the interpretation of business performance and liquidity. The statement's importance lies in the fact that many businesses fail through lack of cash rather than lack of profits. For example a profitable and expanding business may find its inventories and trade receivables rise more quickly than its trade payables, which provide interest-free short-term credit. Without adequate financing for its working capital, this sort of business may find itself unable to pay its debts as they fall due.

The statement shows why cash and cash equivalent balances have increased or decreased over the year, and the different business activities in which cash has been used or which have raised cash. This information, when used in conjunction with the rest of the financial statements, assists in the assessment of changes in net assets, the financial structure and the ability of a company to generate cash inflows in the future. Significant cash receipts or payments figures should be identified, which together with the liquidity ratios, can provide some answers as to why liquidity may have increased or decreased, or why the liquidity position of one company differs from another. It should also be remembered that cash flow information is absolute, in other words it is not influenced by accounting policies or accruals-based accounting methods.

5.9.1 Analysis of operating activities

Operating cash flows should be compared with profit from operations. The extent to which profits are matched by strong cash flows is an indication of the *quality* of profit from operations, in that while profit from operations represents the earnings surplus available for dividend distribution, operating cash flows represent the cash surplus generated from trading, which a company can then use for other purposes.

However, caution is required where there are significant non-current assets, because depreciation will cause a significant part of the difference between operating profits and cash flows. Depreciation could therefore be added back to operating profit before the comparison with cash flows, as the cash flows for non-current asset replacement are presented under investing, not operating, activities.

If operating cash flows are significantly lower than profit from operations, this may indicate that the company is in danger of running out of cash and encountering liquidity problems. In such cases, particular attention needs to be paid to the liquidity and efficiency ratios.

Significant operating cash outflows are unsustainable in the long run. If operating cash flow is negative, this needs to be investigated. Possible reasons include:

- building up inventory levels due to expansion of the business, which tends to increase cash paid to suppliers but does not produce profit from operations because costs are included in inventories
- declining revenue or reduced margins.

Rapid expansion of a business is often associated with operating cash outflows. In the short term, this may not be a problem provided that sufficient finance is available.

The ability of the business to cover its interest payments with its operating cash flows is important. Terms of loan agreements usually require the payments to be made, even if the business is not profitable. If there are insufficient operating cash flows, the company is likely to be in serious financial trouble, unless there is an identifiable non-recurring cause for the shortfall or new equity finance is forthcoming, for example to reduce interest-bearing debts.

Taxation cash flows are also non-discretionary. They tend to lag behind tax charges recognised in the statement of profit or loss and other comprehensive income. In growing businesses, tax cash outflows will often be smaller than tax charges.

5.9.2 Analysis of investing activities

This heading in the statement of cash flows includes cash flows relating to property, plant and equipment. In the short-term, these cash flows are at the discretion of a business, since the business will normally survive even if property, plant and equipment expenditure is delayed for some months, or even years.

Significant cash outflows indicate property, plant and equipment additions, which should lead to the maintenance or enhancement of operating cash flows in the long term. However, such investment must be financed, either from operating cash flows or from new financing.

Net outflows on property, plant and equipment replacement can also be compared with the depreciation expense in the statement of comprehensive income. A significant shortfall of capital spend compared to depreciation may indicate that the company is not replacing its property, plant and equipment as they wear out, or might suggest that depreciation rates are wrongly estimated.

5.9.3 Analysis of financing activities

Financing cash flows show how the company is raising finance (by debt or shares) and what finance it is repaying.

There are many reasons underlying financing cash flows need to be analysed. For example, inflows may be to finance additions to property, plant and equipment to expand the business or renew assets. The issue of new share capital may be used to repay debt, thus reducing future interest costs. Alternatively, new financing may be necessary to keep the company afloat if it is suffering significant operating and interest cash outflows. This last situation is unsustainable in the long term, as the company will eventually become insolvent.

Equity dividends paid are, in theory, a discretionary cash flow. However, companies are often under significant investor pressure to maintain dividends even where their profits and cash flows are falling. Equity dividends paid should be compared to the cash flows available to pay them. If a company is paying out a significant amount of the available cash as dividends, it may not be retaining sufficient funds to finance future investment or the repayment of debt.

It is common policy amongst private equity companies, who own a number of well-known companies, both in the UK and overseas, to not pay dividends and focus instead on debt minimisation.

5.9.4 Cash flow ratios

Traditional ratios as described in sections 5.4 to 5.8 are based on information in the statements of comprehensive income and financial position. Some of these can be adapted to produce equivalent ratios based on cash flow.

Cash return on capital employed

$$\frac{\text{Cash return} \times 100}{\text{Capital employed}}$$

Cash return is defined as:

$$\text{Cash generated from operations} + \text{Interest received (from investing activities)} + \text{Dividends received (from investing activities)}$$

Capital employed is the same as that used in ROCE.

The cash return is an approximate cash flow equivalent to profit before interest payable. As capital expenditure is excluded from the cash return, care is needed in comparing cash ROCE to traditional ROCE which takes account of depreciation of non-current assets.

Cash from operations/profit from operations

$$\frac{\text{Cash generated from operations} \times 100}{\text{Profit from operations}}$$

This measures the quality of the profit from operations. If a profitable company has to allocate a large proportion of the cash it generates from operations to finance investment in additional working capital, the profit from operations can be regarded as of poor quality, since it is not realised in a form which can be used either to finance the acquisition of non-current assets or to pay back borrowings and/or pay dividends. So the higher the resulting percentage, the higher the quality of the profits from operations.

Liquidity

$$\frac{\text{Cash generated from operations}}{\text{Current liabilities}}$$

An alternative liquidity ratio—this ratio gives an indication of the ability to meet current obligations from cash that has been generated over the accounting period.

Cash interest cover

$$\frac{\text{Cash return (as defined previously)}}{\text{Interest paid}}$$

This is the equivalent of interest cover calculated from the statement of comprehensive income. Capital expenditure is normally excluded on the basis that management has some discretion over its timing and amount. Caution is therefore needed in comparing cash interest cover with traditional interest cover, as profit from operations is reduced by depreciation. Cash interest cover will therefore tend to be slightly higher.

Cash flow per share

$$\frac{\text{Cash flow for equity shareholders}}{\text{Number of equity shares}}$$

Cash flow for equity shareholders is defined as:

$$\text{Cash return (as previously) – Interest paid – Tax paid.}$$

This is the cash flow equivalent of earnings per share. Capital expenditure is excluded from this measure, because of the discretion over the timing of such expenditure.

Cash dividend cover

$$\frac{\text{Cash flow for equity shareholders (as defined previously)}}{\text{Equity dividends paid}}$$

This is the cash flow equivalent of dividend cover based on earnings. Similar comments apply regarding exclusion of capital expenditure as are noted under cash flow per share.

5.9.5 Free cash flow

One measure relating to cash flow that investors use is termed free cash flow. There are alternative ways of defining this, but a common one is:

Cash flows from operating activities (after tax and interest payments) – Capital expenditure

Ideally capital expenditure here should be replacement expenditure, although this is not distinguished from new capital expenditure in a statement of cash flows. If this is the case, free cash flow is a measure of the cash available to grow a business and pay dividends to shareholders.

 Worked example 5.12: to show the interpretation of the statement of cash flows

Sharples plc has an overall outflow of cash and cash equivalents over the year ended 31 December 20X7, compared to an inflow in the previous year. In itself, this is not necessarily of concern, as cash flows, particularly from investing and financing activities, can fluctuate from year to year. This is due to the non-recurring nature of significant items under these headings. There has been a reduction in the bank balance at the end of 20X7, however the liquidity ratios, although reduced, did not show any immediate concern for the company.

The cash inflow from operating activities was insufficient to cover the cash outflow from investing activities, which was principally caused by the acquisition of non-current assets—the new shelving and computer equipment. Although debentures were issued during 20X7, the amount raised after dividend payments did not contribute significantly to this acquisition. It should be noted that the cost of the new assets (£600,000) was significantly larger than the annual depreciation charge of £330,000, indicating that this was new equipment, rather than merely replacement. If this is therefore a one-off investment, then the company appears to be able to afford it.

A further analysis of cash flow from operations should be made to assess the quality of the operating profits.

	Operating profit £000	Operating profit with depreciation added back £000	Cash generated from operations £000	Cash generated from operations/Profit from operations £000
20X7	406	736	636	1.57
20X6	377	627	580	1.54

In both years the cash generated from operations was approximately 50% higher than operating profit, indicating healthy cash generation from operating activities. Since depreciation is a significant expense, this has also been added back to operating profit, and this shows cash generated being lower than this adjusted profit in both years, with a larger difference in 20X7. The reconciliation of profit before tax to cash generated from operations shows the reasons for this. In 20X7 there are large increases in inventories and receivables, mitigated to some extent by the increase in payables.

Possible reasons for this were identified in the analysis of the working capital ratios (see section 5.6). There are indications here of a growing company investing in working capital, and although not critical in 20X7, Sharples needs to ensure that sufficient finance is available if this growth continues in the future. The company also needs to ensure that profit margins do not fall further (it was identified in previous analysis that profitability as measured by the net profit and gross profit margins had fallen).

The other cash flow ratios described above are also calculated for completeness:

		20X7		20X6	
Cash return on capital employed	$\dfrac{\text{Cash return}}{\text{Capital employed}}$	$\dfrac{636}{2,720}$	23.4%	$\dfrac{580}{2,540}$	22.8%
Cash interest cover	$\dfrac{\text{Cash return}}{\text{Interest paid}}$	$\dfrac{636}{66}$	9.6	$\dfrac{580}{60}$	9.7
Cash flow per share	$\dfrac{\text{Cash flow for equity shareholders}}{\text{No. of equity shares}}$	$\dfrac{(636-66-160)}{1,000}$	41p	$\dfrac{(580-60-115)}{1,000}$	40.5p
Cash dividend cover	$\dfrac{\text{Cash flow for equity shareholders}}{\text{Equity dividends paid}}$	$\dfrac{410}{80}$	5.13	$\dfrac{405}{75}$	5.4

None of these ratios show any cause for concern for cash availability to meet interest and dividend payments.

5.10 Limitations in ratio analysis

As demonstrated by the analysis of Sharples plc's financial statements, ratio analysis does not provide all the answers to why a business's financial performance and position has changed from one year to the next, or why it may differ from another business. Chapter 19, on interpretation of financial statements, demonstrates how a more detailed understanding of the recognition and measurement policies of figures in the financial statements will enhance the analysis. Consideration of external and internal factors, and the use of the additional narrative information provided in the financial statements are also included here. So, at this point in the textbook, interpretation is at a half-way stage.

However, there are some fundamental limitations of the ratio analysis techniques discussed so far, which will apply in most cases.

1   **Retrospective nature**

As they are often calculated from the financial statements of a business, ratios are based on historical information, and conditions which affected their result may now not be relevant, or other significant events may have happened. For example, a large customer with a large outstanding balance may become insolvent, which would threaten the business with a large bad debt and also reduce sales in the future.

2   **Inflation**

Inflation may also prove an issue as the basis for many figures in the financial statements is historical cost. As a result, comparison of figures from one year to the next may be impacted.

 Example of the inflationary effect over a number of years

Even if inflation is only 2% per annum, over a 5-year period prices will have risen by over 8%. Add in inflation in one of these years at 4%, and the 5-year increase becomes greater than 10%.

---

3   **Statement of financial position data**

Figures on the statement of financial position data may not represent the business's 'normal' position. For example, many businesses deliberately run down inventory levels at the year end in order to make its verification easier. Also, businesses with seasonal trade will have varying levels of working capital balances throughout the year, and a different interpretation will be gained depending on when the financial year end falls.

4   **Business-to-business comparisons**

The comparison of companies needs to be on a 'like with like' basis. Different businesses' financial statements will not, necessarily, be drawn up on the same basis owing to different accounting policies, for example in the area of depreciation.

Differences, such as the ownership of assets versus non-ownership, for example, owning property versus renting, or owning vehicles versus leasing, will affect profitability and the statement of financial position structure. Likewise, the balance between equity and debt financing will vary from company to company, and have implications for the analysis.

As discussed in Chapter 4, the aggregation of figures which appear in the financial statements may vary from business to business. For example, the interpretation of profitability will be affected by whether a business classifies expense items, such as motor expenses as a distribution cost or an administrative expense, or which overhead expenses it includes within cost of sales as opposed to administrative expenses.

5   **Combined operations**

For large organisations or groups of companies the key financial statements will aggregate financial figures from operations which differ radically in nature, for example manufacturing and retailing. This means it will be impossible to draw sensible conclusions from an analysis that uses these figures. (See Chapter 6 for details of analytical techniques applied to **operating segments**.)

6   **Reliance on 'norms'**

Any interpretation should not rely too heavily on suggested norms for certain ratios or industry standards. For example, as discussed earlier, the current and liquid ratio norms will vary significantly depending on the nature of the business. There may be perfectly acceptable reasons why businesses are operating with different ratios.

 ## Summary of key points

This chapter has discussed some key analytical techniques used in the interpretation of financial statements. Different users are interested in different aspects of financial information, and therefore the analysis performed will vary according to its purpose. However any user performing an interpretation will be carrying out some form of comparison:

● within the same business from one year to the next, or over a number of years

● of one business to another

● of a business to industry norms.

The main analytical techniques are:

● horizontal analysis, which provides an overview of the financial performance and position

● ratio analysis, which takes two or more related figures within a set of financial statements to calculate a ratio, which is then used in comparisons.

Some ratios can be calculated in equally valid, but different ways, and care needs to be taken that, in interpretation, the basis of calculation is the same. This may not always be possible, particularly for business-to-business comparisons, where the aggregation of figures may differ.

In the interpretation of ratios, details of what makes up their component parts needs to be taken into account, as well as their interrelationships—no ratio can ever be interpreted in isolation. The most important question to be asked in any interpretation is 'why?' but this may never be fully answered, as it will require internal or detailed information, which is not available to external users. There are also certain inherent limitations to the analysis.

Analysis of the statement of cash flows including various ratios taken from this is necessary to enhance the interpretation of a company's liquidity and financial performance.

The techniques demonstrated are only part of a more complete analysis applied to a full set of financial statements. An enhanced interpretation will include consideration of external factors and other internal information about the business, which may be available from narrative reports contained in the published financial statements. Details of the recognition and measurement policies are also needed to fully interpret differences in financial items. These aspects will be incorporated in Chapter 19, which will also draw on the techniques demonstrated in this chapter.

 ## Bibliography

Balfour Beatty plc (2016) *Annual Report and Accounts, 2015*. London: Balfour Beatty.

J Sainsbury plc (2015) *Annual Report and Financial Statements, 2015*. London: J Sainsbury.

Marks and Spencer plc (2015) *Annual Report and Financial Statements, 2015*. London: Marks and Spencer.

Rolls-Royce plc (2015) *Annual Report, 2014*. London: Rolls-Royce.

Tesco plc (2015) *Annual Report and Financial Statements, 2015*. Cheshunt: Tesco.

Vodafone Group plc (2015) *Annual Report, 2015*. Newbury: Vodafone.

? Questions

● Quick test

1   Snappy Ltd is a manufacturer and retailer of handbags. The following are extracts from the company's draft financial statements.

Statements of profit or loss for the years ended 31 December

	20X7 £000	20X6 £000
Revenue	3,900	4,300
Cost of sales	(2,652)	(2,795)
Gross profit	1,248	1,505
Distribution costs	(302)	(430)
Administrative expenses	(91)	(210)
Profit from operations	855	865
Finance costs	(4)	(15)
Profit before tax	851	850
Tax	(290)	(285)
Profit for the year	561	565

Statements of financial position at 31 December

	20X7 £000	20X6 £000
ASSETS		
Non-current assets	770	810
Current assets		
Inventories	470	340
Trade and other receivables	470	360
Cash and cash equivalents	20	40
	960	740
Total assets	1,730	1,550
EQUITY AND LIABILITIES		
Equity		
Equity share capital	350	350
Retained earnings	790	325
Total equity	1,140	675
Non-current liabilities		
Borrowings	50	150

Current liabilities		
Trade and other payables	270	455
Taxation	240	270
Borrowings	30	–
	540	725
Total equity and liabilities	1,730	1,550

Required:

(a) Perform horizontal and vertical analyses on these financial statements.

(b) Comment on what this shows and identify the areas requiring particular investigation.

2 The statements of profit or loss for the years ended 31 December 20X9 and 20X8, and the statements of financial position at these dates for Squirt Ltd are shown as follows.

Statements of profit or loss for the years ended

	20X9 £000	20X8 £000
Revenue	1,200	900
Cost of sales	(600)	(525)
Gross profit	600	375
Operating expenses	(300)	(225)
Operating profit	300	150
Interest	(60)	(15)
Profit before tax	240	135
Taxation	(90)	(45)
Profit for the year	150	90

Statements of financial position at 31 December

	20X9 £000	20X9 £000	20X8 £000	20X8 £000
Non-current assets		1,800		1,320
Current assets				
Inventory	300		360	
Trade receivables	96		66	
Cash	–		18	
		396		444
Total assets		2,196		1,764
Equity		1,653		1,592

Non-current liabilities			
Loan		300	75
Current liabilities			
Trade payables	180		97
Bank	63		–
		243	97
Total equity and liabilities		2,196	1,764

(a) Calculate the following ratios for the company for each of the two years:
  (i) Return on capital employed
  (ii) Asset turnover
  (iii) Net profit margin
  (iv) Gross profit percentage
  (v) Current ratio
  (vi) Liquid ratio
  (vii) Inventory turnover
  (viii) Receivables collection period
  (ix) Payables payment period.
(b) Comment on the financial performance and financial position of Squirt Ltd based on these ratios.

●● Develop your understanding

3   Smokey plc, an engineering company, has approached its bank for a £5 million long-term secured loan to finance the rebuilding of part of its plant to comply with new regulations to control emissions.

You are a financial advisor in the bank and you have extracted the following information from the latest financial statements of the company.

Year ended 31 March	20X4	20X5
Return on capital employed	27%	30%
Gross profit margin	45%	47%
Net profit margin	18%	25%
Asset turnover	1.5	1.2
Inventory turnover	4.7 times	5.8 times
Receivables collection period	46 days	35 days
Payables payment period	26 days	34 days
Current ratio	0.9	1.2
Acid test (liquid) ratio	0.6	0.9

Required:

Write a report to your manager which:

(a) analyses the financial performance and position of the company based on these ratios

(b) recommends whether the bank should be willing to lend.

4 The statements of financial position and statements of profit or loss for the year ended 30 June 20X6 of Gold Ltd and Silver Ltd, two companies in the same industry, are given as follows.

Statements of financial position at 30 June 20X6

	Gold Ltd		Silver Ltd	
	£	£	£	£
Non-current assets: cost		90,000		30,000
Accumulated depreciation		30,000		10,000
		60,000		20,000
Current assets				
Inventories	85,500		30,000	
Receivables	33,000		20,000	
Cash	16,500		10,000	
		135,000		60,000
Total assets		£195,000		£80,000
Equity				
Equity share capital	142,500		45,000	
Retained earnings	7,500		5,000	
		150,000		50,000
Current liabilities		45,000		30,000
Total equity and liabilities		£195,000		£80,000

Statements of profit or loss for the year ended 30 June 20X6

	Gold Ltd		Silver Ltd	
	£	£	£	£
Revenue		240,000		120,000
Opening inventory	58,500		20,000	
Purchases	171,000		85,000	
	229,500		105,000	
Closing inventory	(85,500)		(30,000)	
Cost of sales		(144,000)		(75,000)
Gross profit		96,000		45,000
General expenses		(84,000)		(39,000)
Profit before tax		12,000		6,000

Taxation	(3,000)	(1,000)
Profit for the year	£9,000	£5,000
Dividends paid	£6,000	£1,500

You may assume that inventories have increased evenly throughout the year.

Required:

(a) Calculate the following ratios for each company:

    (i)   Return on capital employed

    (ii)   Asset turnover

    (iii) Net profit margin

    (iv) Gross profit margin

    (v)   Current ratio

    (vi) Liquid (acid test) ratio

    (vii) Inventory turnover

    (viii) Receivables collection period

    (ix) Payables payment period.

(b) Discuss the main conclusions drawn from a comparison of the ratios calculated for each company.

5   Micawber & Sons, an unincorporated business founded approximately 20 years ago, is in the retail trade. Since then, the business has shown increasing profits. Summarised financial statements for the last two completed financial years are as follows.

Statements of profit or loss for the years ended 31 December

	20X6 £000	20X5 £000
Revenue	940	800
Cost of sales	(583)	(480)
Gross profit	357	320
Expenses	(259)	(222)
Interest	(20)	(6)
Profit for the year	78	92

Statements of financial position at 31 December

	20X6 £000	20X6 £000	20X5 £000	20X5 £000
Non-current assets				
Cost		1,227		807
Accumulated depreciation		546		404
		681		403

Current assets

Inventory	240		150	
Accounts receivable	33		23	
Bank and cash	28		97	
		301		270
Total assets		£982		£673
Capital		543		501
Non-current liabilities				
Long-term bank loan		280		60
Current liabilities		159		112
Total capital and liabilities		£982		£673

Required:

(a) Calculate the following ratios for Micawber & Sons for the financial year ended 31 December 20X6 (the ratios for year ended 31 December 20X5 have already been calculated):

		Year ended 31 December 20X5
(i)	Return on capital employed	17.5%
(ii)	Net profit percentage	12.3%
(iii)	Gross profit percentage	40.0%
(iv)	Expenses as a percentage of revenue	27.8%
(v)	Asset turnover	1.4
(vi)	Current ratio	2.4
(vii)	Liquid ratio	1.1
(viii)	Inventory turnover	114 days
(ix)	Payables payment period	85 days

(b) Using the financial statements, together with the ratios in part (a), comment on the financial performance and position of Micawber & Sons for the year ended 31 December 20X6 in comparison with the previous year.

●●● Take it further

6   Deepa & Co. is an unincorporated family business and wholesaler, importing silk fabric from Far Eastern countries, and selling on to specialist curtain and upholstery retailers. During the year ended 31 December 20X1 the business entered into a new contract with the local branches of a national retail chain. The business also expanded its warehouse and automated its office processes in the year.

Summarised financial statements for 20X1 and 20X0 for the business are as follows.

Statements of profit or loss for the years ended 31 December

	20X1 £	20X1 £	20X0 £	20X0 £
Revenue		382,100		289,800
Cost of sales		(275,150)		(194,170)
Gross profit		106,950		95,630
Administrative expenses	45,235		44,240	
Distribution costs	16,430		14,680	
Interest	1,875		–	
		(63,540)		(58,920)
Profit for the year		43,410		36,710

Statements of financial position at 31 December

	20X1 £000	20X1 £000	20X0 £000	20X0 £000
Non-current assets		130,000		78,750
Current assets				
Inventory	24,650		15,600	
Accounts receivable	22,850		11,275	
Bank and cash	3,750		11,700	
		51,250		38,575
Total assets		181,250		117,325
Capital		77,760		73,350
Non-current liabilities				
5% bank loan, repayable 20X5		50,000		–
Current liabilities				
Accounts payable		53,490		43,975
Total capital and liabilities		181,250		117,325

Required:

(a) Calculate the following ratios for Deepa & Co. for the financial years ended 31 December 20X1 and 20X0:

    (i) Return on capital employed

    (ii) Net profit percentage

    (iii) Gross profit percentage

    (iv) Administrative expenses as a percentage of revenue

    (v) Distribution costs as a percentage of revenue

    (vi) Asset turnover.

(b) Using both the summarised financial statements and the ratios from part (a) produce a report that provides an analysis of the financial performance of Deepa & Co. for the year ended 31 December 20X1 in comparison with the previous year.

(c) Give details of any other information you would require to improve your analysis of the financial performance of the business, providing reasons for the requirement.

7   The following financial data is available for Ash plc:

Extracts from statements of financial position at 31 March

	20X5 £000	20X4 £000	20X3 £000
Equity			
Equity share capital (20p shares)	6,000	5,000	5,000
6% irredeemable preference share capital (£1 shares)	1,000	1,000	1,000
Share premium	5,500	1,200	1,200
Retained earnings	2,610	1,890	2,270
Total equity	15,110	9,090	9,470
Non-current liabilities			
7% debentures (20X8)	5,000	5,000	3,000
Current liabilities	7,140	7,530	6,180
Total equity and liabilities	27,250	21,620	18,650

Retained earnings columns from statements of changes in equity for the years ended 31 March

	20X5 £000	20X4 £000	20X3 £000
At start of year	1,890	2,270	1,700
Profit for the year	4,230	2,180	2,880
Dividends paid	(3,510)	(2,560)	(2,310)
At end of year	2,610	1,890	2,270

Extracts from the statements of profit or loss for the years ended 31 March

	20X5 £000	20X4 £000	20X3 £000
Profit before tax	6,040	3,200	3,960
Tax	(1,810)	(1,020)	(1,080)
Profit after tax	4,230	2,180	2,880
	20X5	20X4	20X3
Market price per equity share	72p	58p	60p

Ash plc issued the additional debentures on 1 September 20X3 and the new equity shares on 1 April 20X4.

Required:

(a) Calculate the following ratios for Ash plc for the years ended 31 March 20X5, 20X4 and 20X3:

    (i)   Return on equity

    (ii)   Earnings per share

    (iii) Price earnings

    (iv) Dividend per share

    (v)   Dividend cover

    (vi) Dividend yield

    (vii) Gearing.

(b) On the basis of the ratios calculated in part (a), produce a report for a potential equity investor, advising whether to invest in the company or not.

8   The financial statements of Mono plc for 20X7 and 20X6 are as follows.

Statements of financial position at 31 December

	20X7 £000	20X6 £000
Non-current assets		
Freehold premises	3,875	4,025
Plant and equipment	2,607	2,167
	6,482	6,192
Current assets		
Inventories	1,435	2,625
Receivables	3,900	2,277
Cash	13	198
	5,348	5,100
Total assets	11,830	11,292
Equity		
Equity share capital (50p ordinary shares)	1,000	1,000
Share premium	350	350
Retained earnings	5,979	5,864
	7,329	7,214
Non-current liabilities		
9% Redeemable debenture stock 20X7–20Y1	2,000	2,500
Current liabilities		
Payables	2,501	1,578
Total equity and liabilities	11,830	11,292

Statements of profit or loss for the years ended 31 December

	20X7 £000	20X6 £000
Revenue	11,450	10,874
Profit before tax	434	721
Taxation	(119)	(178)
Profit after tax	315	543
Dividends proposed and paid	200	200
Year end share price	£3.15	£4.20

Notes to the accounts

1 Analysis of operating profit

	20X7 £000	20X6 £000
Revenue	11,450	10,874
Cost of sales	(6,764)	(6,351)
Gross profit	4,686	4,523
Administrative expenses	(4,072)	(3,577)
Operating profit	614	946

2 Operating profit is stated after charging:

	20X7 £000	20X6 £000
Depreciation	890	750
Auditor's remuneration	55	50
Leasing charges	95	115
Director's emoluments	135	120

3 Interest paid

	20X7 £000	20X6 £000
Payable on debenture stock	180	225

Required:

Analyse the financial performance of Mono plc as an investment prospect during the two years of 20X6 and 20X7.

9   Jewelax Ltd is a long-established chain of provincial fashion boutiques, offering mid-price clothing to a target customer base of late teens/early twenties. However, over the past eighteen months, the company appears to have lost its knack of spotting which trends from the catwalk shows will succeed on the high street. As a result, the company has had to close a number of its stores just before its year end of 31 December 20X2.

You have been provided with the following information for the years ended 31 December 20X1 and 20X2.

Statement of cash flows for the year ended 31 December

	20X2 £000	20X1 £000
Cash flows from operating activities		
Cash generated from operations	869	882
Interest paid	(165)	(102)
Tax paid	(13)	(49)
Net cash from operating activities	691	731
Cash flows from investing activities		
Dividends received	–	55
Proceeds from sales of investments	32	–
Proceeds from sale of property, plant and equipment	1,609	12
Net cash generated from investing activities	1,641	67
Cash flows from financing activities		
Dividends paid	–	(110)
Borrowings taken out	500	100
Net cash generated from/(used in) financing activities	500	(10)
Net change in cash and cash equivalents	2,832	788
Cash and cash equivalents brought forward	910	122
Cash and cash equivalents carried forward	3,742	910

Reconciliation of profit before tax to cash generated from operations

	20X2 £000	20X1 £000
Profit before tax	2,293	162
Investment income	–	(55)
Finance cost	165	102
Depreciation charge	262	369

Loss on disposal of investments	101	–
Profit on disposal of property, plant and equipment	(1,502)	(2)
(Increase) in inventories	(709)	(201)
(Increase)/decrease in trade and other receivables	(468)	256
Increase in trade and other payables	727	251
Cash generated from operations	869	882

Extracts from the statement of comprehensive income and statement of financial position for the same period were as follows.

	20X2 £000	20X1 £000
Revenue	2,201	3,102
Equity and liabilities		
Equity		
Equity share capital	100	100
Retained earnings	7,052	4,772
	7,152	4,872
Long-term liabilities		
Borrowings	1,500	1,000
Current liabilities		
Trade and other payables	1,056	329
	9,708	6,201

Required:

(a) Comment on the above information, calculating three cash flow ratios to assist you in your analysis.

(b) You have now learnt that the financial controller of Jewelax Ltd has been put under severe pressure by his operational directors to improve the figures for the current year. Discuss how this pressure might have influenced both the above information and other areas of the financial statements.

Visit the Online Resource Centre for solutions to all these end of chapter questions plus visual walkthrough solutions. You can test your understanding with extra questions and answers, explore additional case studies based on real companies, take a guided tour through a company report and much more. Go to the Online Resource Centre at **www.oxfordtextbooks.co.uk/orc/maynard2e/**

Part 3

Statement of profit or loss reporting issues

6

Reporting performance

➤ Introduction

This chapter discusses how financial performance is presented by, and may be evaluated from, the statement of profit or loss and other comprehensive income. (Note: throughout the chapter this is referred to as the statement of comprehensive income.) It builds on the discussion of the statement which was included in Chapter 4. A published statement of comprehensive income for large multinational corporations contains aggregated figures for the many different segments of the business. For a complete evaluation of the performance of the business, details of the performance of the individual segments are needed. The financial performance shown in the statement is also only for one year, and one-off or less regularly occurring events can have an enormous impact on the figures. These events may be within the control of the business, such as decisions to close or curtail parts of the business, or outside its control. If material, the financial effect of these events should be disclosed, and companies use a variety of ways to do this. Any analysis performed will have to take account of such events.

The interpretation of performance is therefore not straightforward, and users also need to bear in mind that any profit or loss figure shown in the statement of comprehensive income is not exact, and is influenced by estimates and judgements made by the company's management and the accounting policies selected. These may not necessarily be related directly to income and expense figures, but could still affect them.

Disclosures are required by certain financial reporting standards to assist users in understanding the performance of a company; this chapter will discuss how this information can help in this assessment.

★ Learning objectives

After studying this chapter you will be able to:

- understand how the evaluation of the performance of a company, as given by the statement of comprehensive income, has to take into account the effect of underpinning financial accounting principles, management's judgements and estimates, and other significant items and transactions that have occurred during the financial reporting period
- account for non-current assets held for sale and discontinued operations
- produce disclosures required for operating segments and understand how the information may be used in an analysis of performance
- understand the significance of the disclosures required for **related party transactions**.

✔ Key issues checklist

- ❑ The accruals concept.
- ❑ Management's influence over reported profit and loss through estimations, judgements and choice of accounting policies.
- ❑ Exceptional, one-off or significant items, how they may be reported and their impact on performance.
- ❑ Accounting for non-current assets classified as held for sale—International Financial Reporting Standard (IFRS) 5.
- ❑ Accounting for discontinued operations—IFRS 5.
- ❑ Issues with accounting for discontinued operations.
- ❑ Disclosures required for operating segments—IFRS 8.
- ❑ Issues raised by the management approach taken by IFRS 8.
- ❑ Disclosures required for **related parties** and related party transactions—International Accounting Standard (IAS) 24.
- ❑ How and why these issues affect an analysis of financial performance, as given by the statement of comprehensive income.

6.1 Underpinning principles of performance

As seen in Chapter 5, the analysis of performance is based frequently on measures of profit taken from the statement of comprehensive income. All existing and potential investors will use profit or earnings figures in their assessment of the performance of a business and for future predictions so that they can more readily understand the returns that have been, or will be, generated by the business. It is therefore important that these figures are reliable and that sufficient, relevant information is provided about their make-up.

6.1.1 Accruals concept

🛈 **Reminder** *The statement of comprehensive income consists of a statement of profit or loss, which shows a break-down of net profit made during the financial year, and a statement of other comprehensive income. This second part of the statement includes items such as surpluses arising from the revaluation of properties and may be presented as a separate statement. Full discussion of the statement of comprehensive income is included in Chapter 4.*

The statement of comprehensive income is based on the accruals concept. At a basic level this means items are accounted for in the period in which the underpinning transaction occurred and not when the related cash flow occurs. Financial performance measured on the accruals basis provides a better basis for assessing a business's past and future performance than information about cash receipts and payments, which can be determined by other factors and may not be directly comparable from one year to the next.

IAS 1 *Presentation of Financial Statements* explains the accruals concept by specifying that when it is used 'an entity recognises items as assets, liabilities, equity, income and expenses (the elements of financial statements) when they satisfy the definitions and recognition criteria for those elements in the [*Conceptual*] *Framework*' (para. 28). In other words, net comprehensive income, which is the difference between income and expenses, is determined by the definitions of these items and the criteria for their recognition. The definitions of income and expenses are given in the Exposure Draft (ED) of the revised *Conceptual Framework* (see Chapter 2 for further details of this) as follows:

● Income is increases in assets or decreases in liabilities that result in increases in equity other than those relating to contributions from holders of equity claims

● Expenses are decreases in assets or increases in liabilities that result in decreases in equity, other than those relating to distributions to holders of equity claims

The ED specifies, rather broadly, that all elements should be recognised if they provide relevant and faithfully representative information.

Revenues and expenses that result directly and jointly from the same transactions or other events should be recognised simultaneously. This is commonly referred to as 'matching'. However, the application of the matching concept does not allow the recognition of items in the statement of financial position that do not meet the definition of assets or liabilities.

6.1.2 Balance sheet approach to profit recognition

These definitions and recognition criteria for income and expenses mean that their net result, i.e. profit, is determined largely by the definitions of and recognition and measurement criteria for assets and liabilities. This is why the International Accounting Standards Board's (IASB) decision-usefulness approach to financial reporting has acquired the label of a 'balance sheet approach'. As discussed further in Chapter 2, the IASB has, however, confirmed that it is not designating information about financial position as the primary focus.

The recognition in profit of simple day-to-day transactions and items, such as sales and purchases on credit, and accounting for usual overhead expenses and depreciation, does not change with these definitions. However, there is much critical debate about the effect of other transactions on profit that results from this approach. Such transactions include the change in the value of financial assets and liabilities, which are measured at fair or market value, being included as either income or expense, or the recognition of revenue from more complex arrangements.

Although some of these items may be disclosed separately in other comprehensive income and can be identified easily, others are included in profit or loss. The interpretation of performance, as given by a net profit figure, will, therefore, be affected. The actual accounting for those items which are within the scope of this textbook are discussed in later, relevant chapters.

6.1.3 Estimates, judgement and choices of accounting policies

As is evident from discussion in previous chapters, financial accounting is not an exact science. Many, if not most, figures included in the statements of comprehensive income and financial position are based on management's judgement. Examples include:

● depreciation—estimates of useful lives and residual values

● estimates of accrued expenses

● allowances for irrecoverable debts

● fair values of assets and liabilities requiring this valuation base, particularly where market values are unavailable

● inventory obsolescence

● capitalisation of internal development costs—the point at which certain criteria have been met, such as whether a market exists for the product or service being developed

● the financial impact of ongoing legal cases or industrial tribunals.

Estimates of figures required for the statement of financial position, for example an allowance for irrecoverable debts, affect profit and loss directly.

Is there a problem with this? International financial reporting standards are principles based and inherent in this is the necessity for professional judgement. It is assumed that users will be able to understand the implication of this, provided sufficient information is given about where these judgements have been made, and that this is clear and concise. Remember, understandability is an enhancing characteristic of financial information and implies that, although users do not have to be financial experts, they should have a reasonable knowledge of business and economic matters, and also know when to seek the help of a financial expert.

The section on accounting policies in Chapter 4 discusses the disclosures that companies are required to make regarding estimates and judgements, and provides some company examples. Detailed disclosures of the recognition and measurement methods and policies are also required by many financial reporting standards to aid users' understanding, and these will be examined in the relevant chapters.

The more sceptical user may consider that companies produce the financial results and performance that they want, and hide behind the use of estimates and professional judgement as a justification. Undoubtedly, financial directors can, and do, 'tweak' their judgements to produce the financial figures they require for a variety of reasons (to meet bank covenants, to ensure the company credit rating is not affected adversely, to ensure earnings per share is in line with market expectations, etc.). However, there are other ways of 'massaging' earnings, including asking suppliers to delay delivery of goods and shipping large orders out just prior to the year end. The auditors will take their own professional view on whether the financial statements can still be said to be 'fairly stated'. No financial reporting system can eliminate this.

The even more sceptical user will also cite major corporate collapses, such as Enron and WorldCom, to suggest that earnings figures of companies are completely fictional. The evolution of financial reporting systems, particularly over the past 30 years, has included the development and acceptance of international financial reporting standards and corporate governance mechanisms. These attempt to ensure that financial statements do represent faithfully companies' financial performance and position, and that these sorts of events do not happen again. As discussed throughout this textbook, this development is an ongoing process.

6.2 One-off, unusual items

One-off or unusual items are sometimes referred to as exceptional items. Although this term is not one that is used by the IASB, it used to be included in UK generally accepted accounting principles (GAAP), which allowed companies to classify one-off or non-recurring material items which had affected the year's performance (not necessarily adversely) as exceptional, and disclose them separately on the face of the statement of comprehensive income. The argument for separate disclosure of items, such as the costs of restructuring activities, or large changes in asset valuations, or the results of litigation, is to aid the user of financial statements to understand the performance of the regular underlying business without these items and to ensure a 'true and fair' view is presented.

IAS 1 *Presentation of Financial Statements* specifies the minimum disclosures that have to be made on the face of the main financial statements; it does not prevent a company from including other items it considers will make the information provided by the financial statements more relevant to the user. Indeed, the standard requires that such items should be disclosed if they are material and relevant to an understanding of the company's financial performance, and provides examples of items which may be included. However, in presenting additional line items, companies should be neutral about whether they are gains and losses, and the items should be clearly disclosed and applied consistently from one year to the next. Users need to be able to understand and rely on the trends in and quality of companies' profitability.

Some UK companies, in particular, have various presentations of their statements of profit or loss, as shown by the following examples. The first has already been used in Chapter 4, but it is worth repeating here.

Financial reporting in practice 6.1 — J Sainsury plc, 2015

J Sainsbury plc's financial statements provide an analysis of its loss before tax of £(72) million on the face of its income statement, analysing its loss before tax into what the company describes as 'underlying profit before tax', i.e. profit from its core supermarket activities, and other items of profit and loss. This will assist users in understanding how the company achieved its profits or losses in a particular year and provide more comparable information from one year to the next.

Group income statement for the 52 weeks to 14 March 2015

	Note	2015 £m	2014 £m
Revenue	4	23,775	23,949
Cost of sales		(22,567)	(22,562)
Gross profit		1,208	1,387
Administrative expenses		(1,132)	(444)
Other income		5	66
Operating profit	5	81	1,009
Finance income	6	19	20
Finance costs	6	(180)	(159)
Share of post-tax profit from joint ventures and associates	14	8	28
(Loss)/profit before taxation		(72)	898
Analysed as:			
Underlying profit before tax		681	798
Profit on disposal of properties	3	7	52
Investment property fair value movements	3	7	–
Retail financing fair value movements	3	(30)	(8)
IAS 19 pension financing charge	3	(31)	(23)
Defined benefit pension scheme expenses	3	(6)	(7)

Acquisition adjustments	3	**13**	18
One-off items	3	**(713)**	68
		(72)	898
Income tax expense	8	**(94)**	(182)
(Loss)/profit for the financial year		**(166)**	716

Financial reporting in practice 6.2 — Arsenal Holdings plc, 2015

Arsenal Holdings' view of relevance and understandability results in it separating out the results of player trading from its other activities. These other activities comprise the football-related business and results from property development. The company defines player trading as primarily loan fees receivable, the amortisation of the costs of acquiring player registrations, any impairment charges and profit on disposal of player registrations. Financial results from player trading could vary significantly from one year to the next as they arise, in part, from the transfers of players that occur in a particular year.

Consolidated profit and loss account: for the year ended 31 May 2015

	Note	Operations excluding player trading £000	Player trading £000	Total £000
Turnover of the group including its share of joint ventures		346,498	805	347,303
Share of turnover of joint venture		(2,779)	–	(2,779)
Group turnover	3	343,719	805	344,524
Operating expenses		(281,400)	(55,365)	(336,765)
Operating profit/(loss)		62,319	(54,560)	7,759
Share of joint venture operating result		762	–	762
Profit on disposal of player registrations		–	28,944	28,944
Profit/(loss) on ordinary activities before net finance charges		63,081	(25,616)	37,465
Net finance charges				(12,751)
Profit on ordinary activities before taxation				24,714
Taxation				(4,670)
Profit after taxation retained for the financial year				20,044

Other, predominantly UK, companies use the columnar format for separating exceptional items from all other operations, as shown by JD Wetherspoon's income statement.

Financial reporting in practice 6.3 | JD Weatherspoon plc, 2015

This income statement shows that exceptional items have caused a reduction of overall profit. Profits from normal operating activities therefore appear higher. The related note indicates the nature of the items which have been classified as exceptional and which are considered to be outside the normal operating activities of the pub chain. The question remains whether companies would choose this explicit voluntary disclosure if exceptional items had increased profits.

Income statement for the 52 weeks ended 26 July 2015

	52 weeks ended 26 July 2015 Before exceptional items £000	52 weeks ended 26 July 2015 Exceptional items (note 4) £000	52 weeks ended 26 July 2015 After exceptional items £000	52 weeks ended 27 July 2014 Before exceptional items £000	52 weeks ended 27 July 2014 Exceptional items (note 4) £000	52 weeks ended 27 July 2014 After exceptional items £000
Revenue 1	1,513,923	–	1,513,923	1,409,333	–	1,409,333
Operating costs	(1,401,415)	(6,013)	(1,407,428)	(1,292,329)	–	(1,292,329)
Operating profit 2	112,508	(6,013)	106,495	117,004	–	117,004
Property gains/(losses) 3	(694)	(13,053)	(13,747)	(1,429)	–	(1,429)
Finance income 6	180	–	180	67	–	67
Finance costs 6	(34,196)	–	(34,196)	(36,280)	997	(36,280)
Profit/(loss) before taxation	77,798	(19,066)	58,732	79,362	(997)	78,365
Income tax expense 7	(20,343)	6,435	(13,908)	(20,499)	(16,744)	(37,243)
Profit/(loss) for the year	57,455	(12,631)	44,824	58,863	(17,741)	41,122

Note 4 discloses the nature of the exceptional items.

4 Exceptional items

	52 weeks ended 26 July 2015 £000	52 weeks ended 27 July 2014 £000
Operating exceptional items		
Inventory valuation	5,231	–
Restructuring costs	782	–
	6,013	–

Exceptional property losses		
Onerous lease provision	**1,858**	–
Property impairment	**11,195**	–
	13,053	–
Other exceptional items		
Interest payable on gaming machine VAT repayment	–	997
Income tax expense—current tax	–	(4,375)
Exceptional tax items—deferred tax	**(4,809)**	21,119
Tax effect on operating exceptional items	**(1,626)**	–
	(6,435)	17,741
Total exceptional items	**12,631**	17,741

During the year, the company changed the method used for calculating the consumption of non-consumable inventories. Non-consumable inventories comprise items like glassware, plates, cutlery and cleaning products used in the pubs and hotels. The company has taken a more prudent view on recognition of non-consumable inventories as expenses. The change in the accounting policy for the expected life of those inventories resulted in an exceptional charge of £5,231,000 (2014: £Nil). The effect of this change was not presented as a prior-year adjustment, as management did not believe that previously reported results were materially affected and the treatment adopted provides full information.

In the table above, property impairment relates to the situation in which, owing to poor trading performance, pubs are unlikely to generate sufficient cash in the future to justify their current book value.

The onerous lease provision relates to pubs for which future trading profits, or income from sub-leases, are not expected to cover the rent. The provision takes several factors into account, including the expected future profitability of the pub, but also the amount estimated as payable on surrender of the lease, where this is a possible outcome. In the year, £1,858,000 (2014: £Nil) was charged in respect of onerous leases.

In the year, an exceptional charge of £11,195,000 (2014: £Nil) was incurred in respect of the impairment of property, plant and equipment, as required under IAS 36. This comprises an impairment charge of £12,383,000 (2014: £Nil), offset by impairment reversals of £1,188,000 (2014: £Nil).

A reduction in the deferred tax liability on rolled-over gains for differences between the tax-deductible cost and the residual value of the reinvestment assets has resulted in a credit of £4,809,000. Owing to the magnitude of the reduction and the fact that it relates to prior periods, it was considered exceptional.

6.3 Discontinued operations and non-current assets held for sale

Users will use historic trends in profit or loss to make predictions about future performance. In order for the forecasting techniques to be as good as possible, the earnings that are sustainable (in other words, are likely to continue in future years) need to be identifiable. Information about items which may affect future results is therefore important. One of these is whether a company has discontinued a part of its business and how much of its current earnings relate to this and will, therefore, not be present in the future. Businesses may also dispose of the assets of discontinued operations and users also need to be able to evaluate the financial effect of such disposals on the results for the year. The assets of a discontinued operation may not have been disposed of by the end of the financial period. In this case they will be classified as held for sale, and different measurement principles for such assets apply.

The financial reporting standard that addresses these issues is IFRS 5 *Non-current Assets Held for Sale and Discontinued Operations*, which was issued in 2004 as part of the IASB/ Financial Accounting Standards Board (FASB) convergence project. The IFRS firstly explains what an asset held for sale is and how this is accounted for, and this approach will be followed in this chapter. Assets held for sale may not arise exclusively from a discontinued operation, although in many instances they do.

Note that Chapter 10 deals with accounting for non-current assets. Although the main accounting treatment for assets held for sale will be discussed in this chapter, complete understanding of some of this material may only be achieved when Chapter 10 has been read.

6.3.1 What is a non-current asset held for sale?

A non-current asset or a group of non-current assets to be disposed of in a single transaction (termed a **'disposal group'**) are classified as held for sale if their carrying amounts (in other words, the amount at which they are included in the financial statements) will be recovered principally through a sale transaction rather than through continuing use. This requires the following criteria to be met:

- management is committed to a plan to sell
- the asset or disposal group is available for immediate sale in its present condition
- an active programme to locate a buyer has been initiated
- the asset or disposal group is being actively marketed for sale at a price that is reasonable in relation to its current fair value
- the sale is highly probable and is expected to be completed within a year from the date of classification
- it is unlikely that significant changes will be made to the plan or it will be withdrawn.

There must, therefore, be formal commitment to disposal with evidence of positive steps taken towards this before the year end. It is possible that the sale may not be completed within one year, but the delay must be due to circumstances outside the company's control. In this case, the classification as held for sale will still be applicable.

Example of criteria for classification as held for sale

The directors of a company have agreed, in a board meeting, to sell a building and have instructed the chief administrative officer to start looking for a buyer. They wish to sell the building for £3 million, even though the current market prices indicate a value of £2.5 million. The company will continue to use the building until other, suitable property has been found and no staff will be relocated until this is the case.

The building will not be classified as held for sale because the situation fails to meet the criterion of being available for immediate sale—staff will remain in the building until new premises have been found. In addition, it does not appear that an active programme to locate a buyer has been initiated yet—only internal instructions to an officer to 'start looking for a buyer'. In addition, the sale price would, at present, not be considered reasonable in relation to its fair value (market price).

The same criteria apply to an asset or disposal group that is held for distribution to the owners.

Any non-current assets or disposal groups that are to be 'abandoned', for example because the assets have reached the end of their useful lives or as a result of a company winding up certain operations, are not classified as held for sale as their carrying amount will be recovered through use (and not a sale). Hence, the accounting for these assets just continues as normal under the relevant financial reporting standard (see Chapter 10).

Non-current assets that become idle because they are taken out of use temporarily because, for example, current market conditions cause businesses to reduce their operating capacity, are not classified as abandoned. They may be classified as part of a discontinued operation if the relevant criteria for this are met.

Some non-current assets are acquired exclusively with the intention of re-selling them. These are classified as held for sale at the acquisition date only if it is anticipated that the sale will occur within one year and that it is highly likely that any of the other criteria not met at acquisition will be within a short time period—usually taken as three months.

Certain non-current assets are also outside the scope of IFRS 5 and their accounting treatment is according to the relevant financial reporting standard, as detailed as follows:

(a) deferred tax assets (IAS 12 *Income Taxes*)

(b) assets arising from employee benefits (IAS 19 *Employee Benefits*)

(c) financial assets within the scope of IFRS 9 *Financial Instruments*

(d) non-current assets that are accounted for in accordance with the fair value model in IAS 40 *Investment Property*

(e) non-current assets that are measured at fair value less costs to sell in accordance with IAS 41 *Agriculture*

(f) contractual rights under insurance contracts as defined in IFRS 4 *Insurance Contracts*.

6.3.2 Accounting for a non-current asset classified as held for sale

Immediately prior to the classification of a non-current asset or disposal group as held for sale, they are measured in accordance with the applicable IFRS (usually IAS 16 *Property, Plant and Equipment*, as detailed in Chapter 10). On classification, the asset or disposal group is measured at the lower of carrying amount and fair value less costs to sell.

Reminder *Fair value is defined in IFRS 13 as 'the price that would be received to sell an asset in an orderly transaction between market participants at the measurement date' and assumes that the market is the principal, or most advantageous, market available, and the sale is under current market conditions. Further details are provided in Chapter 2.*

The accounting treatment means that if the expected net selling price is lower than the carrying amount, the asset is written down to this value—the expected amount to be realised from the asset. On this first classification of an asset as held for sale, if the expected net selling price is higher than the carrying amount, no adjustment is made.

If the sale is expected to occur in more than one year's time, the costs to sell are discounted to present value. Any increase in the present value of these costs as time passes (owing to the **unwinding of the discount rate**) is included as a finance cost in profit and loss.

If the fair value less costs to sell is less than the carrying amount, an **impairment loss** is recognised, and charged to profit and loss.

 Worked example 6.1: to show the accounting for an asset classified as held for sale

Brea plc, which has a financial year end of 31 December, has an item of plant which meets the criteria to be classified as held for sale at 1 July 20X9. The original cost of the asset was £120,000 with an estimated useful life of 10 years and, at 1 January 20X9, had accumulated depreciation of £36,000. At 1 July 20X9 the fair value of the plant is £50,000 with costs to sell estimated at £4,000.

Required:

Show how this asset would be accounted for in the 20X9 financial statements.

Depreciation would be charged for the first 6 months of 20X9, i.e. $6/12 \times £120,000/10 = £6,000$.
At 1 July 20X9 the plant has a carrying amount (net book value) of $£120,000 - (£36,000 + £6,000) = £78,000$.
Fair value less costs to sell = $£50,000 - £4000 = £46,000$.
The asset would be written down to £46,000 and an impairment loss of $£78,000 - £46,000 = £32,000$ would be charged to profit and loss.

Once an asset or disposal group is classified as held for sale and remeasured, no further depreciation is charged, even if the asset is still being used in the business.

If the asset or disposal group is still held at the subsequent financial year end, the fair value less costs to sell must be estimated again and compared to the carrying amount. A further impairment loss may be recognised; however, if the fair value less costs to sell have increased, a gain may be recognised in profit and loss, but only up to the amount of any previous impairment losses that have been recognised.

Worked example 6.2: to show the accounting for subsequent estimation of fair value less costs to sell

Using the same details as Worked example 6.1, suppose that the plant is still held for sale at 31 December 20X9, and, at this date, the fair value and estimated costs to sell are respectively:

(a) £45,000 and £4,000
(b) £55,000 and £5,000.

Required:
For (a) and (b) show how the changes in fair value less costs to sell would be accounted for.

	(a)	(b)
	£	£
At 31 December 20X9		
Fair value	45,000	55,000
Costs to sell	(4,000)	(5,000)
	41,000	50,000
Carrying amount (from above example)	46,000	46,000
Impairment (loss)/gain	(5,000)	4,000

Under (a) and (b) the plant would be revalued to £41,000 and £50,000 respectively. A further impairment loss of £5,000 would be recognised under scenario (a) and a gain of £4,000 would be able to be recognised under scenario (b), as this is less than the original impairment loss of £32,000.

6.3.3 Change of plans

If the criteria for an asset or disposal group to be classified as held for sale are no longer met, then the asset or disposal group ceases to be held for sale. In this case the asset must be remeasured at the lower of:

- the carrying amount immediately prior to its classification as held for sale, adjusted for any depreciation, amortisation or revaluations that would have been recognised if it had not been classified as held for sale (in other words, on its original measurement basis as if the classification as held for sale and subsequent reclassification had never happened)

- its recoverable amount (this is the higher of fair value less costs to sell and recoverable amount, and is discussed in more detail in the section dealing with impairment in Chapter 10).

6.3.4 Disclosures

To enable the user to understand which non-current assets will be in use in the future to generate operating profits, assets which are classified as held for sale are disclosed separately on the face of the statement of financial position, usually below current assets. Further information is provided in the notes to the financial statements explaining what assets are held for sale, and the facts and circumstances of the anticipated sale.

The impairment losses and any gains do not have to be disclosed separately, but companies may choose to if they consider they are material.

Financial reporting in practice 6.4　　　　BG Group plc, 2014

BG group plc has a broad portfolio of business interests focused on gas and oil exploration and production, and on liquefied natural gas. Its 2014 financial statements contain the following disclosures relating to assets classified as held for sale.

Balance sheets

These include the following line items:

	Note	31 Dec 2014 $m
Assets		
Assets classified as held for sale	7	2,088
Liabilities		
Liabilities associated with assets classified as held for sale	7	(63)

Note 7 Discontinued operations and assets held for sale
Assets held for sale

	31 Dec 2014 $m
Property, plant and equipment	2,078
Trade and other receivables	10
Assets classified as held for sale	2,088
Trade and other payables	(27)
Provisions for other liabilities and charges	(36)
Liabilities associated with assets classified as held for sale	(63)
Net assets classified as held for sale	2,025

Assets held for sale as at 31 December 2014 comprised QCLNG Pipeline Pty Limited in the Upstream segment and two LNG vessels in the LNG Shipping & Marketing segment, the disposals of which are expected to complete in the first half of 2015.

6.3.5 What is a discontinued operation?

The accounting for discontinued operations uses some of the issues and accounting methods relating to assets held for sale, but before this is explained the question that must be asked is: what is a discontinued operation? How significant a part of a business does it have to be? A separate subsidiary company? A factory? A department? What is the distinction between a discontinued operation and the merger or reorganisation of parts of the business? Is it part of the business that has already been closed down in the year? Or is it one where there are plans to close it?

IFRS 5 defines a discontinued operation as:

A **component of an entity** that either has been disposed of or is classified as held for sale and:

(a) represents a separate major line of business or geographical area of operations,

(b) is part of a single co-ordinated plan to dispose of a separate major line of business or geo-graphical area of operations, or

(c) is a subsidiary acquired exclusively with a view to resale.

(IASB, 2004: Appendix A)

A component of an entity comprises operations and cash flows that can be clearly distinguished, operationally, and for financial reporting purposes from the rest of the entity. The IFRS also terms this a cash-generating unit, which, in turn, is defined as 'the smallest identifiable group of assets that generates cash inflows that are largely independent of the cash inflows from other assets or groups of assets'. A cash-generating unit may also have some directly associated liabilities, for example if property is part of the unit there may be a related mortgage.

The business operation would therefore have to be seen as separate from other parts of the business and separate reporting of it would have to be possible. Examples would include a major product line, a factory, a retail outlet or a development division.

The disposal of the business operation does not need to have actually happened in the financial period to be treated as a discontinued operation, but the criteria for being classified as held for sale, as given in section 6.3.1, need to be fulfilled.

6.3.6 Accounting for discontinued operations

The essential requirement is that anything to do with a discontinued operation is disclosed separately on the face of the statement of comprehensive income. This includes:

1   the profits or losses from the actual operation of the component during the year, plus

2   any gains or losses arising from the disposal of the component, or from any remeasurement of its assets to fair value less costs to sell.

A single figure of the overall profit or loss from these two items must be shown separately on the face of the statement of comprehensive income (in the statement of profit or loss section)

and, under the IAS 1 presentation, it is be included after tax, but before profit or loss for the year.

An analysis of this single figure into:

(i) the revenue, expenses and pre-tax profit or loss of discontinued operations;

(ii) the related income tax expense;

(iii) the gain or loss recognised on the measurement to fair value less costs to sell or on the disposal of the assets or disposal group(s) constituting the discontinued operation; and

(iv) the related income tax expense

(IASB 2004, para. 33(b))

must be disclosed either on the face of the statement of comprehensive income or, more usually, in a note.

In addition, the net cash flows relating to the operating, investing and financing activities of discontinued operations must be disclosed, either on the face of the statement of cash flows or as part of the disclosure note. All comparative figures are also adjusted to separate out results from these business components in the previous years, even though, at the time, they were not classified as discontinued operations. This is to ensure the impact on performance of the discontinuance is clear, and users can identify separately the trends in the results for the continuing operations.

Worked example 6.3: to show the accounting for a discontinued operation

The statement of profit or loss for Blacker plc for the year ended 31 March 20X6 is as follows:

	£000
Revenue	1,650
Cost of sales	(1,230)
Gross profit	420
Distribution costs	(150)
Administrative expenses	(210)
Profit before tax	60
Income tax expense	(20)
Profit for the year	40

As a result of the company deciding to outsource its manufacturing overseas, the manufacturing division was classified as held for sale and, on 1 February 20X6, the criteria for being classified as a discontinued operation were judged to have been met.

The results of the division for the year were as follows (note: these are included in the preceding figures):

	£000
Revenue	380
Cost of sales	(290)
Distribution costs	(60)
Administrative expenses	(70)
Income tax effect	10

Required:

Ignoring the effect of remeasuring the assets of the division at fair value less costs to sell, redraw the statement of profit or loss of Blacker plc for the year ended 31 March 20X6 in accordance with IFRS 5.

		£000
Revenue	(1,650 – 380)	1,270
Cost of sales	(1,230 – 290)	(940)
Gross profit		330
Distribution costs	(150 – 60)	(90)
Administrative expenses	(210 – 70)	(140)
Profit before tax		100
Income tax expense	(20 – (–10))	(30)
Profit for the year from continuing operations		70
Loss for the year from discontinued operations		(30)
Profit for the year		40

A disclosure note would show the detail of the discontinued operation:

	£000
Revenue	380
Cost of sales	(290)
Distribution costs	(60)
Administrative expenses	(70)
Income tax effect	10
Loss after tax	(30)

Financial reporting in practice 6.5   Tesco plc, 2014

Between 2012 and 2014 Tesco plc sold all or part of its operations in Japan, the US and China. All disposals met the criteria to be defined as discontinued operations, and so the company's financial statements for a number of years showed disclosures relating to these. The following extracts are from Tesco's 2014 financial statements.

Group income statement

	Notes	52 weeks 2014 £m	52 weeks 2013 (restated) £m
Continuing operations			
Revenue	2	**63,557**	63,406
Cost of sales		**(59,547)**	(59,252)
Gross profit		**4,010**	4,154
Administrative expenses		**(1,657)**	(1,482)
Profits/losses arising on property-related items		**278**	(290)
Operating profit		**2,631**	2,382
Share of post-tax profits of joint ventures and associates	13	**60**	72
Finance income	5	**132**	120
Finance costs	5	**(564)**	(517)
Profit before tax	3	**2,259**	2,057
Taxation	6	**(347)**	(529)
Profit for the year from continuing operations		**1,912**	1,528
Discontinued operations			
Loss for the year from discontinued operations	7	**(942)**	(1,504)
Profit for the year		**970**	24
Attributable to:			
Owners of the parent		**974**	28
Non-controlling interests		**(4)**	(4)
		970	24

Note 7 Discontinued operations and non-current assets classified as held for sale

Discontinued operations

During the period, the Group entered into definitive agreements, subject to the usual regulatory approvals, with China Resources Enterprise, Limited ('CRE') to combine respective Chinese retail operations. The definitive agreements allow for the exchange of the Group's Chinese retail and property interests plus cash of HK$4,325m for a 20% interest in the combined businesses.

In the second half of the financial year, independent valuations were completed, for accounting purposes, of both businesses separately to determine the fair value of the consideration for the disposal. As a result of these valuations, the Group has concluded a charge of £540m is required to remeasure the assets and liabilities of the disposal group to the fair value less costs to sell. The valuation was completed by considering a number of different commercial valuation methodologies rather than relying on any single method. The different methodologies included discounted cash flows, enterprise value ('EV')/revenue multiples and income approach for Tesco and CRE businesses as appropriate. Observable and unobservable inputs have been used in the models and therefore the fair value is classified as level 3 within the fair value hierarchy. The key unobservable inputs used included discount rates (from 7.5% to 10.5%), long term growth rates (from 3.0% to 4.0%) and EV/revenue multiples (from 0.6x to 1.0x).

IFRS 13 'Fair value measurement' requires these valuations to be produced on a standalone existing basis for each business and consequently they do not incorporate the significant long term synergies and strategic value that the Directors believe exist in the new enlarged business.

On 27 November 2013 the Group completed a sale of the substantive part of its US operations to YFE Holdings, Inc. The remaining assets of the US operation are in the process of being disposed of as part of an orderly restructuring process. In addition, the exit of the Japanese operations was successfully completed on 1 January 2013.

The above operations have been classified as disposal groups classified as held for sale in accordance with IFRS 5 *Non-current assets held for sale and discontinued operations*.

The tables below show the results of the discontinued operations which are included in the Group Income Statement, Group Balance Sheet and Group Cash Flow Statement respectively. At 23 February 2013, the Group's Chinese operations had not yet been classified as held for sale; assets and liabilities of the disposal group at this date comprise only those of the US.

Income statement

	US		China		Total	
	2014 £m	2013 £m	2014 £m	2013 £m	2014 £m	2013 £m
Revenue	496	697	1,489	1,420	1,985	2,117
Cost of sales	(532)	(1,567)	(2,060)	(1,485)	(2,592)	(3,052)
Administrative expenses	(104)	(50)	(89)	(80)	(193)	(130)
Loss arising on property-related items	(125)	(286)	-	(49)	(125)	(335)
Share of post-tax losses on joint ventures and associates	-	–	(17)	(18)	(17)	(18)
Finance costs	(1)	(4)	3	(10)	2	(14)
Loss before tax of discontinued operations	(266)	(1,210)	(674)	(222)	(940)	(1,432)
Taxation	6	(5)	(8)	(16)	(2)	(21)
Loss after tax of discontinued operations	(260)	(1,215)	(682)	(238)	(942)	(1,453)
Loss after tax of discontinued operations in Japan					-	(51)
Total loss after tax of discontinued operations					(942)	(1,504)

6.3.7 Judgement in classification

Although the classification of what constitutes a discontinued operation seems precisely set out in IFRS 5, in practice it is not necessarily straightforward. It requires the exercise of management's judgement, often of future events, which may not be entirely within their control.

 Examples of where the classification as a discontinued operation may not be straightforward

1　A manufacturer ceases production of a number of its product lines which are not selling in current economic conditions. What is meant by a 'major line of business'? How many product lines have to be ceased? What happens if economic conditions improve, which, in turn, may mean the product lines are reinstated?

2　A company merges a subsidiary company's operations into its own because its business is similar and then sells the subsidiary. The operations and cash flows of the subsidiary would be clearly distinguishable, but would this be a separate line of business?

Management may be tempted to classify continuing, but underperforming, operations as discontinued so that the performance of the continuing operations to be used in future forecasts appears 'better'. Some research indicates that this does happen.

6.3.8 Possible changes to accounting for discontinued operations

Although IFRS 5 was issued by the IASB as part of its short-term convergence project with the US FASB, the boards' definitions of discontinued operations remained different. In their joint project on financial statement presentation, the boards decided to develop common definitions of, and require, common disclosures about components of an entity that have been disposed of or are classified as held for sale. An exposure draft (ED) was issued in 2008 which, among other matters, aligned the definition of a discontinued operation to that of an operating segment, as defined in IFRS 8 *Operating Segments* (see section 6.4.1). However, respondents to the ED raised concerns, as some felt the definition would include operations that were too small and thus provide information of limited usefulness.

The IASB has listened to these comments, with the result that the definition of a discontinued operation will now probably not change much from the one currently in IFRS 5. A staff draft of a new exposure draft was published in July 2010; however, further progress towards a revised IFRS is currently paused.

6.4 Operating segment reporting

One of the main difficulties with interpreting the performance of a large company is that the figures on the face of the main financial statements are aggregated. Many listed companies are multinational, operating in several different economic environments and providing a range of different products and services. Each product, service or economic environment is subject to:

- different rates of profitability and growth
- different future prospects and opportunities
- different risks.

To fully understand the performance of a company as a whole, the information needs to be disaggregated into the different operations conducted, so that the effect of the performance of the different operations on the company can be determined. This will enable users to take appropriate actions if those parts of the business which are performing poorly can be identified from the financial statements. IFRS 8 *Operating Segments* was issued by the IASB in 2006 as part of its convergence programme with the US FASB, and replaced IAS 14 *Segment Reporting*. When issued, the standard was criticised widely, and this is discussed in section 6.4.5. The core principle of IFRS 8 is to:

> ... disclose information to enable users of its financial statements to evaluate the nature and financial effects of the business activities in which it engages and the economic environments in which it operates.

(IASB, 2006, para. 1)

This standard is therefore not about how to account for an item or transaction; it is about additional disclosures that companies are required to make in the notes to their financial statements to aid the interpretation of financial performance.

6.4.1 What is an operating segment?

The key issue to note is that management determines what an operating segment is for their company, but based on guidance set out in IFRS 8. This specifies that an operating segment is a component of a business:

(a) that engages in business activities from which it may earn revenues and incur expenses,

(b) whose operating results are regularly reviewed by the entity's chief operating decision maker to make decisions about resources to be allocated to the segment and assess its performance, and

(c) for which discrete financial information is available.

The business component may be a group of similar products or services, or a geographical location of production, or a geographical location of where sales are made, or be defined on an entirely different basis.

Start-up operations may also be classified as operating segments before they start earning revenues. However, other parts of a company may not be operating segments if they do not earn revenue, or they earn revenues that are only incidental to the activities of the company, for example a corporate headquarters. In particular, IFRS 8 excludes a company's pension schemes from being operating segments.

The chief operating decision-maker is used in the standard as a description of the role; a company does not have to have an individual employee with that title. In practice, the chief operating decision maker is a company's chief executive officer (CEO), but it may be the whole board of directors. To help companies determine what may be an operating segment, IFRS 8 suggests that an operating segment usually has an individual in charge, the segment 'manager'; again, the title is not important, it is the role that is. However, the standard acknowledges that companies will have different operational and management structures, and that some companies will have to determine their operating segments by reference to the core principle as given earlier.

6.4.2 Reportable operating segments

Disaggregated information about an operating segment is only required to be disclosed if certain size thresholds are reached. Only one of the following thresholds has to be reached:

1   Reported revenue, including both sales to external customers and intersegment sales or transfers, is 10% or more of the combined revenue, internal and external, of all operating segments.

2   The absolute amount of its reported profit or loss is 10% or more of the greater, in absolute amount, of (i) the combined reported profit of all operating segments that did not report a loss and (ii) the combined reported loss of all operating segments that reported a loss.

3   The assets are 10% or more of the combined assets of all operating segments.

(Note: internal revenue would be that earned from transactions with other segments within the company or group.)

Operating segments that do not meet any of these thresholds should be combined with other operating segments if they have similar economic characteristics and their products, services and operations are similar, and the aggregated figures tested for reportability. Management may also classify an operating segment as reportable, even if the thresholds are not reached, if it believes this information would be useful to users.

To ensure that sufficient detailed information is disclosed about the company's business activities, particularly where the activities are dispersed across many segments, the standard requires that if the total external revenue of the reportable segments constitutes less than 75% of the company's revenue, additional operating segments have to be identified as reportable, even if they do not meet the criteria detailed earlier. However, so that information does not become too detailed and at risk of losing its usefulness and understandability, IFRS 8 suggests that the maximum number of reportable segments should be ten. Reconciliations to total figures shown on the face of the main financial statements of all segmental information have to be provided.

A company has to ensure that all comparative information is adjusted to disclose the details of all segments which are classed as reportable in the current year. This works the other way as well, in that if a segment was reportable in the previous year and management still considers it significant in the current year, it will continue to be reportable even if it does not meet the criteria.

Worked example 6.4: to show the identification of reportable segments

Financial data relating to the operating segments of Drax plc is as follows:

Segment	External revenue £000	Profit/(loss) £000	Assets £000
A	2,000	250	1,500
B	400	(70)	1,100
C	3,000	300	1,900
D	1,500	(20)	600
E	50	(120)	400
	6,950	340	5,500

Required:

Identify the reportable segments of Drax plc. (Assume all revenue earned is external.)

Revenue threshold	10% × combined revenue	= 10% × 6,950	= £695
Profit/(loss) threshold	10% × combined profits	= 10% × 550	= £55
	10% × combined losses	= 10% × 210	= £21
	Profit threshold of £55 is greater		
Asset threshold	10% × combined assets	= 10% × 5,500	= £550

Do the segments meet the thresholds?

Segment	External revenue	Profit/(loss)	Assets
A	✓	✓	✓
B	✗	✓*	✓
C	✓	✓	✓
D	✓	✗*	✓
E	✗	✓*	✗

*Ignore the loss in these segments and take the absolute figure for the threshold test.

All segments meet at least one of the threshold criteria, and therefore all segments are reportable.

6.4.3 Disclosures for reportable segments

The disclosure requirements are to enable users of the financial statements to evaluate the nature and financial effects of the business activities in which a company engages and the economic environments in which it operates. They are, therefore, fairly extensive.

Given that the approach taken in the determination of operating segments is based on management's decision, the factors that have been used to identify these are to be disclosed. This will include some information about how management has organised the business, for example whether this is around different products or services, or geographically, or based on different regulatory environments.

For each reportable segment the following information is then required to be disclosed:

- The types of products and services from which revenues are earned
- A measure of profit or loss
- The following items, if they are included, in the measure of profit or loss that is reported to the chief operating decision-maker:
  - External revenues
  - Internal revenues
  - Interest revenue
  - Interest expense
  - Depreciation and amortisation
  - Other material items of income and expense
  - The company's interest in the profit or loss of associates, and joint ventures
  - Income tax expense
- A measure of total assets and liabilities if these are provided regularly to the chief operating decision-maker.

Further disclosures include:

- The basis for accounting for transactions between segments
- Explanations of the measurement of the reportable segments' profits or losses, and assets and liabilities, as provided to the chief operating decision-maker, including any changes
- Explanations of the differences between these measurement bases and those used for financial reporting purposes
- Any asymmetrical allocations, for example if depreciation is allocated to a segment without the related asset to that segment
- Reconciliations of revenues, measures of profit or loss, assets, and liabilities to the figures included in the financial statements.

Financial reporting in practice 6.6 | Greene King plc, 2015

Greene King plc, a UK pub retailer and brewer, lists its main businesses as:

- Retail, which includes managed pubs and restaurants
- Pub partners, which includes the operation of tenanted and leased pubs
- Brewing and brands, which encompasses brewing, marketing and selling beer

The company states that they are largely organised and managed separately according to the nature of the products and services provided, their distribution channels and the profile of customers. They are therefore the three reportable segments. The following segment information note is included in the 2015 financial statements. This also shows the reconciliation of the segments' operating profits (the measure of profit) to net profit as reported in the company's statement of profit or loss. (Details for 2015 only are shown.)

2 Segment information

The group has determined the following three reportable segments that are largely organised and managed separately according to the nature of products and services provided, distribution channels and profile of customers:

Retail: Managed pubs and restaurants

Pub Partners: Tenanted and leased pubs

Brewing and Brands: Brewing, marketing and selling beer

These are also considered to be the group's operating segments and are based on the information presented to the chief executive who is considered to be the chief operating decision maker.

Transfer prices between operating segments are set on an arm's length basis.

2015

	Retail £m	Pub Partners £m	Brewing & Brands £m	Corporate £m	Total Operations £m
Revenue	1,000.7	121.9	192.7	–	1,315.3
Operating costs	(809.9)	(37.9)	(162.9)	(18.4)	(1,059.1)
Segment operating profit	**190.8**	**54.0**	**29.8**	**(18.4)**	**256.2**
Exceptional items					(43.9)
Net finance costs					(94.1)
Income tax expense					(28.9)
					89.3
Balance sheet					
Segment assets	2,058.2	608.7	358.7	51.0	3,076.6
Unallocated assets[1]					272.3
	2,058.2	608.7	358.7	51.0	3,348.9

(continued)

(continued)

Segment liabilities	(110.0)	(14.1)	(73.7)	(103.9)	(301.7)
Unallocated liabilities[1]					(2,018.3)
	(110.0)	(14.1)	(73.7)	(103.9)	(2,320.0)
Net assets	**1,948.2**	**594.6**	**285.0**	**(52.9)**	**1,028.9**
Other segment information					
Capital expenditure—tangible assets	139.4	18.9	4.7	2.6	168.6
Goodwill disposed	(0.8)	(2.1)	–	–	(2.9)
Impairment of property, plant and equipment	(21.1)	(6.3)	–	–	(27.4)
Depreciation	(49.0)	(7.6)	(5.1)	(1.1)	(62.8)
EBITDA[2]	239.8	61.6	34.9	(17.3)	319.0

[1] Unallocated assets/liabilities comprise cash, borrowings, pensions, net deferred tax, net current tax, and derivatives.
[2] EBITDA represents earnings before interest, tax, depreciation and exceptional items and is calculated as operating profit before exceptionals adjusted for the depreciation charge for the period.

Management reporting and controlling systems

Management monitors the operating results of its strategic business units separately for the purpose of making decisions about allocating resources and assessing performance. Segment performance is measured based on segment operating profit or loss referred to as trading profit in our management and reporting systems. Included within the corporate column in the table above are functions managed by a central division.

No information about geographical regions has been provided as the group's activities are predominantly domestic.

6.4.4 Entity-wide disclosures

Owing to the many different ways of companies organising their businesses and determining their operating segments, there are some catch-all disclosures to ensure certain information is provided to users to meet the overriding aim of the standard. Some of these may already be met by the disclosures for the reportable segments, but, if not, the following additional information needs to be shown:

- External revenue for each product and service group
- Geographical information
  - External revenues
  - Non-current assets
- Reliance on major customers—revenue from each major customer, if it constitutes more than 10% of the company's revenues (the actual customer does not have to be identified).

Financial reporting in practice 6.7 | Rolls-Royce plc, 2014

Rolls-Royce plc, in applying IFRS 8, has determined its operating segments along product groups (civil aerospace, defence aerospace, power systems, marine, nuclear and energy), and, given its customers are global, provides the following information in its segmental analysis note.

Geographical segments

The Group's revenue by destination from continuing operations is shown below:

	2014 £m	2013 £m
United Kingdom	1,599	1,677
Norway	322	520
Germany	734	972
Switzerland	670	868
Spain	113	174
Italy	201	233
France	292	259
Russia	86	111
Rest of Europe	575	637
USA	3,751	3,910
Canada	472	474
South America	407	302
Saudi Arabia	327	544
Rest of Middle East	418	339
India	161	230
China	1,290	1,038
South Korea	485	452
Japan	272	235
Malaysia	280	235
Singapore	396	544
Rest of Asia	493	596
Africa	115	87
Australasia	207	143
Other	70	62
	13,736	14,642

No single customer represented 10% or more of the Group's revenue.

(continued)

(continued)

The carrying amounts of the Group's non-current assets, excluding financial instruments, deferred tax assets and post retirement benefit surpluses, by the geographical area in which the assets are located, are as follows:

	2014 £m	2013 £m
United Kingdom	3,864	3,649
United States of America	827	872
Nordic countries	724	823
Germany	2,493	2,739
Other	912	924
	8,820	9,007

6.4.5 Evaluation of IFRS 8

At the time it was issued IFRS 8 received much criticism and has continued to do so in the IASB's post-implementation review conducted in 2013. Some of this may have been because it was largely based on the US standard dealing with operating segments, Statement of Financial Accounting Standard (SFAS) 131, rather than the then existing international standard, IAS 14. UK and European critics saw this as a political solution between the IASB and FASB, rather than the IASB selecting the best accounting methods for users.

The main criticisms concern the management approach to the determination of defining an operating segment, the fact that detailed requirements for geographical disclosures have gone (IAS 14 required these) and that different accounting methods can be applied to segment information from that used in the remainder of the financial statements. At the time of the issue of IFRS 8, the matter even reached the UK parliament, where a group of members of parliament called the standard 'totally unacceptable' by giving company directors too much choice about what they disclose and how they do it.

One issue is that the approach taken by IFRS 8 means that comparability of key segment information from one company to another is now difficult (remember, comparability is an enhancing characteristic of financial information). Another doubt is whether publication of figures based on internal management accounting bases generates great benefit for investors if the figures differ from those based on IFRS. Others criticise the fact that only a minimum 75% of trading activity has to be analysed into segmental disclosures. Another issue (which was also present under IAS 14) is whether common costs should be allocated across segments, for example general building costs if a number of segments are based in the same property, or directors' remuneration costs. Some critics have suggested that management could mislead the users of their financial statements or at least hide some of their activities, possibly those which are loss-making, or those conducted overseas.

On the other hand, the use of the management approach has been reported to have had an overall positive effect on the quality of the segment information, whose usefulness and relevance has increased, outweighing any concerns expressed about the comparability of financial reports. Some interested parties have stated that the management approach ensures that the usefulness of information is improved because the results of business activities are presented 'through the eyes of management', which uses this information to make key decisions, allocate resources and monitor performance. The information prepared using the management approach can also provide a better linkage between the financial statements and information reported in the operating and financial review, and other management commentaries, including assessments of risk.

The information has been able to be produced in a timelier manner and at a reduced cost as it is based on that already produced internally by the company. Although the geographical information of revenue by customer country is considered useful, some respondents to the IASB's review thought that information based on economic characteristics might be of more use.

The UK's Financial Reporting Review Panel (FRRP) in 2010 issuing a warning to some UK companies about how they were applying IFRS 8. Specific complaints included:

- some companies with different divisions and significant operations in different countries reporting only one segment

- the operating analysis in the narrative reports differing from the operating segments included in the financial statements

- the measurement bases used in narrative reports and in the segmental information being different.

From its review, the IASB concluded that overall IFRS 8 achieved its objectives and has improved financial reporting. The board does consider that some improvements could be made, and are currently investigating these. The areas that may be addressed include:

- How and what segmental information should be disclosed when the basis of segmentation changes in the event of a reorganisation

- Guidance on the nature of 'similar economic characteristics'

- The presentation of reconciliations to IFRS-based figures.

6.4.6 How can segmental information be used?

If disclosures are within the spirit of the standard, the information supplied provides the user with a breakdown of the different business activities of a company. They can then analyse which activities have the greatest effect upon the performance of the company as a whole. The relative size of each segment can be ascertained and, together with intersegment comparisons, including horizontal and some ratio analysis, this can provide some detailed understanding of the different segments' performance.

Worked example 6.5: to show how operating segment disclosures may be used in analysis

Goodman plc has determined three reportable operating segments based upon three different product groups, A, B and C. Details of revenues (which are all external), profits and assets of each of the segments are shown as follows:

	Product Group A £m	Product Group B £m	Product Group C £m
Revenue			
UK sales	37	41	66
Export sales—Europe	123	15	43
Export sales—USA	76	3	91
	236	59	200
Profit before interest	38	23	42
Total assets	128	35	101

Required:

Apply analytical techniques to this information to enhance an interpretation of the financial performance of Goodman plc. Comment on the results of this analysis.

1   Establish the relative sizes of each segment:

	Product Group A	Product Group B	Product Group C	Total
Revenue				
UK sales	26%	28%	46%	100%
Export sales—Europe	68%	8%	24%	100%
Export sales—USA	45%	2%	53%	100%
Total revenue	48%	12%	40%	100%
Profit before interest	37%	22%	41%	100%
Total assets	48%	13%	38%	100%

2   The relative sizes of sales to different markets can also be established:

	Product Group A	Product Group B	Product Group C	Total
Revenue				
UK sales	16%	70%	33%	29%
Export sales—Europe	52%	25%	21%	37%
Export sales—USA	32%	5%	46%	34%
	100%	100%	100%	100%

Analysis of this information includes the following:

- Although product group A produces the highest revenues, and has the highest related assets, it does not produce the highest profits, which are from product group C.
- Total sales to the three different markets are not significantly different, with European sales being the largest, followed by the USA and then the UK. The different economic environments of these geographical areas may have a bearing on these figures.
- The majority of export sales to Europe are of product group A, the majority of UK sales are of product group C, and product groups A and C have similar proportions of sales to the USA.
- Product group B sells mainly to the domestic market.
- Product group B yields far less revenue than the other product groups at only 12% of total revenue, yet relative to this it contributes 22% of profit.

3 Some ratios which have meaning can be calculated and compared segment-to-segment:

	Product Group A	Product Group B	Product Group C	Total
Return on total assets				
(PBIT/total assets)	30%	66%	42%	39%
Net profit margin				
(PBIT/total revenue)	16%	39%	21%	21%
Asset turnover (Total revenue/total assets)	1.8	1.7	2.0	1.9

Analysis of, and questions raised by, this information include the following:

- Although product group B is the smallest, it is the most profitable by far by both measures of return on total assets and net profit margin. Should the company try to increase its business in these products? Or, given that the majority of this group's sales are to the UK market, are there conditions in the home market economic environment which lead to this result?
- Despite its greater profitability, product group B has generated less revenue per £ of assets allocated to the group compared with the other products. Information about the nature of the product group is needed to assess this ratio.
- Product group A, despite having the largest revenues, is the least profitable. Can the company influence this or is it connected to the fact that the majority of the sales of this product group are to overseas customers?

6.5 Related party disclosures

6.5.1 The need for information

Discussion of IFRS 8 *Operating Segments* touched upon one issue which may affect the users' interpretation of the performance of a company—that of reliance on one or more significant customers. Disclosure of this is required by this standard. However, the performance of a company may also be influenced by the existence of transactions with individuals or other businesses which are related in some way to the company and where the transactions may not be (or not perceived to be) at arm's length or under normal commercial arrangements. The monetary value of such transactions may be different to other 'normal' ones. The company's financial position may also be influenced by the existence of outstanding balances with such related parties, for example, preferential payment arrangements may be present.

A transaction with a related party may not even have happened for the financial statements to have been affected. Where a relationship exists, one company may be able to influence another company not to act, for example, a subsidiary company may be instructed not to carry out research and development, or to produce a product (such as the instruction from NewsCorp to the News of the World to cease production of its Sunday newspaper in 2011).

There is nothing inherently wrong about such transactions—they are a normal feature of business. For example, companies frequently conduct their activities through subsidiary or associate companies where the parent company has the ability to control, or significantly influence, decisions being made.

However, what is important is that the financial statements faithfully represent all transactions and that users have knowledge of all relevant information to enable them to evaluate whether the performance has been distorted by any transactions not on an arm's length basis. The users also need to be able to compare companies' performance and financial position, including assessments of the risks and opportunities facing the companies.

 Examples of transactions which are not on normal commercial terms

1 Company B controls company A. Company A sells goods to company B at cost.
2 A company makes a loan to another company in which it has a significant investment at a preferential rate of interest.
3 A director of a company persuades the board of directors to award a contract to a company owned by her brother.

The IASB has had a financial reporting standard relating to related parties for some years. The current revised version of IAS 24 *Related Party Disclosures* was issued in 2009 and sets out the information that companies are required to disclose about related parties and transactions with such parties. Note, like IFRS 8, it does not specify any accounting methods—it is a disclosure standard only—thus companies will have a note, or notes, relating to these matters in their financial statements.

6.5.2 What is a related party?

A related party can be a person or another business entity that is related to the company that is reporting its financial statements. Although IAS 24 provides what may appear to be clear-cut definitions of a related party, the emphasis of determining whether there is a related party relationship is very much on the substance of the relationship and not merely the legal form.

A person is related to the reporting company if any of the following apply:

(i)   The person has control or **joint control** over the reporting company

(ii) The person has significant influence over the reporting company

(iii) The person is a member of the key management personnel of the reporting company or of a parent of the reporting company.

A **close family member** of the person concerned is also considered a related party. A close family member is defined as those family members who may be expected to influence, or be influenced by, the person in their dealings with the company and include:

(a) the person's children and spouse or domestic partner

(b) children of the person's spouse or domestic partner

(c) dependants of the person or the person's spouse or domestic partner.

A business entity is considered to be related to the reporting entity if any of the following apply:

(i)   The entity and the reporting entity are members of the same group (which means that each parent, subsidiary and fellow subsidiary is related to the others).

(ii)   One entity is an associate or joint venture of the other entity (or an associate or joint venture of a member of a group of which the other entity is a member).

(iii) Both companies are joint ventures of the same third party.

(iv)   One entity is a joint venture of a third entity and the other entity is an associate of the third entity.

(v)   The entity is a **post-employment benefit** plan for the benefit of employees of either the reporting entity or an entity related to the reporting entity. If the reporting entity is itself such a plan, the sponsoring employers are also related to the reporting entity.

(vi)   The entity is controlled or jointly controlled by a person identified as a related party.

(vii) A person identified as a related party has significant influence over the entity or is a member of the key management personnel of the entity (or of a parent of the entity).

These criteria relate to the key question of what constitutes a group of companies – the relationships between different companies and how much control or influence one company exerts over another. At a basic level, a group comprises a parent company which controls one or more subsidiary companies, through holding, directly or indirectly, more than 50% of the voting (equity) shares of the subsidiary. An associate company is one in which the reporting company can exert significant influence, and the rebuttable presumption is that this relationship is evidenced by the holding of between 20% and 50% of the voting shares of the associate. A joint venture is a company which is controlled jointly by two or more other companies. Do note that there are other indicators which may provide evidence of control or significant influence, and, indeed, exactly what is meant by control or significant influence needs to be defined and discussed. These matters are not necessarily straightforward, and they are discussed in Chapters 17 and 18, which deal with group financial statements.

Note, some relationships may appear to be close, but they are actually specified as not being related parties. They are as follows:

(a) Two entities simply because they have a director or other member of key management personnel in common or because a member of key management personnel of one entity has significant influence over the other entity.

(b) Two venturers simply because they share joint control over a joint venture.

(c) (i) Providers of finance,
    (ii) trade unions,
    (iii) public utilities, and
    (iv) departments and agencies of a government that does not control, jointly control or significantly influence the reporting entity, simply by virtue of their normal dealings with an entity (even though they may affect the freedom of action of an entity or participate in its decision-making process).

(d) A customer, supplier, franchisor, distributor or general agent with whom an entity transacts a significant volume of business, simply by virtue of the resulting economic dependence.

 Worked example 6.6: to illustrate related parties

1 Xavier plc owns 75% of the equity shares of Yoyo plc and 18% of the equity shares of Zed plc.

2 Christie owns 25% of the equity share capital of Xavier plc and Bill is her husband.

3 Clive is a director of Xavier plc. He owns 60% of the equity shares of Alpen Ltd Muriel is his partner who owns 10% of the equity shares of Bixit Ltd.

4 James works for Xavier plc as a manager, but he is not a director. Clare is his daughter.

5 Xavier plc has a pension scheme for its employees.

6 Xavier plc obtains approximately 30% of its main product from one overseas supplier.

Required:
Establish the related parties under each of the circumstances for company Xavier plc:

1 Xavier plc controls Yoyo plc, so Yoyo is a related party. However, Xavier plc does not control Zed plc and prima facie does not exert significant influence over the company as the shareholding is less than 20%. So, Zed plc is not a related party.

2 Christie is a related party unless it can be demonstrated that her shareholding does not give her significant influence over Xavier plc. If Christie is a related party then Bill, her husband, will also be.

3 Clive is a member of the key management personnel of Xavier plc and is therefore a related party. Clive controls Alpen Ltd, so Alpen is a related party. Muriel, Clive's partner, is considered a close family member of Clive and so is also a related party. Muriel does not control Bixit Ltd and

is unlikely to exert significant influence with a shareholding of only 10%, so Bixit is not a related party.

4   James may or may not be a member of key management personnel of Xavier plc. If he is a related party, then so is Clare, his daughter.

5   The pension scheme is a related party.

6   The overseas supplier is not a related party.

___

6.5.3 What is a related party transaction?

A related party transaction is any transfer of resources, services or obligations between the reporting company and a related party, irrespective of whether a price is charged.

6.5.4 Disclosures

These are fairly extensive and include the following:

1   Irrespective of whether there have been any transactions between them, all relationships between the company and its subsidiary companies must be disclosed. The company also needs to disclose the name of its parent, if any, and, if different, the ultimate controlling company.

2   Key management personnel compensation, which includes all employee benefits as defined in IAS 19 *Employee Benefits* and to which IFRS 2 *Share-based Payment* applies. In other words all forms of consideration paid or provided in return for services rendered to the company by the employee should be disclosed. IAS 24 requires this information to be categorised as:

 (a) Short-term benefits (for example, wages, salaries, bonuses, holiday pay, National Insurance and benefits-in-kind)

 (b) Post-employment benefits (for example, pensions and post-employment insurance)

 (c) Other long-term benefits (for example, long-service leave, long-term disability benefits and deferred benefits)

 (d) **Termination benefits**

 (e) **Share-based payment**.

Key management personnel are those who have authority and responsibility for planning, directing and controlling the activities of the entity, directly or indirectly, and includes any director (both executive and non-executive) of that entity.

 ! **Reminder** *As discussed in Chapter 3 in relation to corporate governance, extensive disclosures of directors' remuneration is already required by Companies Act 2006 for UK companies. The IAS 24 disclosures are covered mainly by these requirements and, if not, are usually added to the information provided in the narrative report.*

3   For all transactions with a related party separate disclosure of:

(a)   The nature of the relationship

(b)   Information about the transaction and any outstanding balances, including any provisions made if a debt is considered doubtful.

 Examples of the types of transactions that are disclosed if they are with a related party

1   Purchases or sales of goods (finished or unfinished).
2   Purchases or sales of property and other assets.
3   Rendering or receiving of services.
4   Leases.
5   Transfers of research and development.
6   Transfers under licence agreements.
7   Transfers under finance arrangements (including loans and equity contributions in cash or in kind).
8   Provision of guarantees or collateral.
9   Commitments to do something if a particular event occurs or does not occur in the future.
10   Settlement of liabilities on behalf of the entity or by the entity on behalf of that related party.

Financial reporting in practice 6.8   Kingfisher plc, 2015

Included in the note relating to investments of the parent company, Kingfisher plc lists its principal subsidiary companies. It is interesting to note that it does not list them all on the grounds of excessive information, which may detract from relevance and understandability. Other related party transactions are detailed in a later note.

Notes to the company financial statements 2014/2015

5 Investments

The Directors consider that to give the full particulars of all subsidiary undertakings would lead to a statement of excessive length. In accordance with Section 410(2)(a) of the Companies Act 2006, the information below relates to those Group undertakings at the financial year end whose results or financial position, in the opinion of the Directors, principally affect the figures of the consolidated financial statements of Kingfisher plc. Details of all subsidiary undertakings will be annexed to the next Annual Return of Kingfisher plc to be filed at Companies House.

	Country of incorporation and operation	% interest held and voting rights	Class of share owned	Main activity
B&Q plc	Great Britain	100%	Ordinary & special[1]	Retailing
B&Q Properties Limited	Great Britain	100%	Ordinary	Property investment

CMW (UK) Limited[2]	Great Britain	100%	Ordinary	Holding company
Halcyon Finance Ltd	Great Britain	100%	Ordinary	Finance
Kingfisher Information Technology Services (UK) Limited	Great Britain	100%	Ordinary	IT services
Kingfisher UK Investments Limited[3]	Great Britain	100%	Ordinary	Holding company
Screwfix Direct Limited	Great Britain	100%	Ordinary	Retailing
Sheldon Holdings Limited	Great Britain	100%	Ordinary	Holding company
Zeus Land Investments Limited	Great Britain	100%	Ordinary	Holding company
B&Q Ireland Limited	Ireland	100%	Ordinary	Retailing
Brico Dépôt S.A.S.U0.[4]	France	100%	Ordinary	Retailing
Castorama Dubois Investissements S.C.A0.[4]	France	100%	Ordinary	Holding company
Castorama France S.A.S.U0.[4]	France	100%	Ordinary	Retailing
Euro Dépôt S.A.S.U0.[4]	France	100%	Ordinary	Property investment
L'Immobilière Castorama S.A.S.U0.[4]	France	100%	Ordinary	Property investment
Kingfisher France S.A.S.U0.[4]	France	100%	Ordinary	Holding company
Kingfisher Asia Limited	Hong Kong	100%	Ordinary	Sourcing
Castim Sp.z.o.o0.[4]	Poland	100%	Ordinary	Property investment
Castorama Polska Sp.z.o.o0.[4]	Poland	100%	Ordinary	Retailing
Brico Dépôt Portugal S.A0.[4]	Portugal	100%	Ordinary	Retailing
Castorama RUS LLC[5]	Russia	100%	Ordinary	Retailing
Bricostore Romania S.A0.[5]	Romania	100%	Ordinary	Retailing
Euro Depot España S.A.U0.[4]	Spain	100%	Ordinary	Retailing

[1] The special shares in B&Q plc are owned 100% by Kingfisher plc and are non-voting.
[2] Holding company for the Group's Chinese retailing operations, which have a December year end.
[3] Held directly by Kingfisher plc.
[4] Owing to local conditions, these companies prepare their financial statements to 31 January.
[5] Owing to local conditions, these companies prepare their financial statements to 31 December.

The following notes are taken from the Kingfisher's consolidated financial statements.

(continued)

(continued)

Notes to the consolidated financial statements 2014/2015

16 Investments in joint ventures and associates

Some detail is provided about the Kingfisher Group reclassifying an investment in an associate as an asset held for sale.

Details of the remaining significant joint ventures and associates are shown below:

	Country of incorporation and operation	% interest held and voting rights	Class of share owned	Main activity
Principal joint ventures				
Koçtas‚ Yapi Marketleri Ticaret A.S.[1]	Turkey	50%	Ordinary	Retailing
Principal associates				
Crealfi S.A.[1]	France	49%	Ordinary	Finance

[1] This company prepares its financial statements to 31 December.

37 Related party transactions

During the year, the Company and its subsidiaries carried out a number of transactions with related parties in the normal course of business and on an arm's length basis. The names of the related parties, the nature of these transactions and their total value are shown below:

	2014/15		2013/14	
£ millions	Income/ (expense)	Receivable/ (payable)	Income/ (expense)	Receivable/ (payable)
Transactions with Koctas Yapi Marketleri Ticaret A.S. in which the Group holds a 50% interest				
Provision of employee services	(0.1)	(0.1)	(0.1)	–
Commission and other income	1.2	0.2	1.2	0.6
Transactions with Hornbach Holding A.G. in which the Group holds a 21% interest				
Commission and other income	n/a	n/a	0.3	–
Transactions with Crealfi S.A. in which the Group holds a 49% interest				
Provision of employee services	0.1	–	0.1	–
Commission and other income	6.6	1.5	7.1	0.4

Transactions with Kingfisher Pension Scheme				
Provision of administrative services	1.3	0.4	0.8	0.1

Services are usually negotiated with related parties on a cost-plus basis. Goods are sold or bought on the basis of the price lists in force with non-related parties.

The remuneration of key management personnel is given in note 8.

Other transactions with the Kingfisher Pension Scheme are detailed in note 27.

 ## Summary of key points

As the discussion in this chapter has shown, a company's performance, as shown by the statement of comprehensive income, is influenced by many factors:

- by the changes in the measurement of certain assets and liabilities which pass through the statement
- by the judgements and estimates made by management, which can arise from both simple and complex transactions and items
- by the accounting policies selected by management
- by any unusual material, exceptional or one-off items that occur during an accounting period
- by the potential write-down of non-current asset values when they are classified as held for sale
- by discontinued operations
- by the fact that the performances of individual business segments are aggregated
- by the existence of related party relationships.

Various international financial reporting standards have been issued in order to specify how the accounting should be carried out or the additional disclosures required for many of these factors. The aim of these standards is to ensure that the financial statements provide relevant information about the transactions undertaken by companies and that users understand the effect these have had, or may have, on the performance. Users are often assessing past performance in order to predict what may happen in the future and therefore need knowledge of any material items which will influence future results.

Some of these factors, and the application of the detailed provisions in the standards, rely upon management's interpretation and judgement; thus, there is always scope for some 'massaging' of results and how performance might be portrayed, however minor this may be. Remember, though, details of significant estimates and judgements that have been made also need to be disclosed. Users should therefore be provided with sufficient information to analyse the performance and assess what may have influenced the results.

 ## Further reading

IASB (International Accounting Standards Board) (2004) IFRS 5 *Non-current Assets Held for Sale and Discontinued Operations*. London: IASB.

IASB (International Accounting Standards Board) (2006) IFRS 8 *Operating Segments*. London: IASB.

IASB (International Accounting Standards Board) (2009) IAS 24 *Related Party Disclosures*. London: IASB.

Bibliography

Arsenal Holdings plc (2015) *Statement of Accounts and Annual Report* 2014/15. London: Arsenal Holdings.

BG Group plc (2015) *Annual Report and Accounts, 2014*. Reading: BG Group.

Bush, T. (2007) *IFRS 8: What is it Good For?* Available at: http://www.accountancyage.com (accessed 10 October 2012).

GAAPweb (2007) *MPs Criticise IFRS 8*. Available at: http://www.gaapweb.com/ (accessed 10 October 2012).

Greene King plc (2015) *Annual Report, 2015*. Bury St Edmonds: Greene King.

IASB (International Accounting Standards Board) (2004) IFRS 5 *Non-current Assets Held for Sale and Discontinued Operations*. London: IASB.

IASB (International Accounting Standards Board) (2006) IFRS 8 *Operating Segments*. London: IASB.

IASB (International Accounting Standards Board) (2007) IAS 1 *Presentation of Financial Statements*. London: IASB.

IASB (International Accounting Standards Board) (2009) IAS 24 *Related Party Disclosures*. London: IASB.

IASB (International Accounting Standards Board) (2013) *Post-implementation Review: IFRS 8 Operating Segments*. London: IASB.

IASB (International Accounting Standards Board) (2015) Exposure Draft *Conceptual Framework for Financial Reporting*. London: IASB.

ICAEW (Institute of Chartered Accountants in England and Wales) (2013) *IFRS Factsheet: IFRS 8 Operating Segments*. London: ICAEW.

J Sainsbury plc (2015) *Annual Report and Financial Statements, 2015*. London: J Sainsbury.

JD Wetherspoon plc (2015) *Annual Report and Accounts, 2015*. Watford: JD Wetherspoon.

Kingfisher plc (2015) *Annual Report and Accounts, 2014/15*. London: Kingfisher.

Murphy, R. (2010) *IFRS in Trouble—Country-by-Country Reporting is the Answer*. Available at: http://www.taxresearch.org.uk/ (accessed 10 October 2012).

Next plc (2015) *Annual Report and Accounts, 2015*. Enderby: Next.

Robins, P. (2007) *IFRS 8 Operating Segments*. Available at: http://www2.accaglobal.com (accessed 10 October 2012).

Rolls-Royce plc (2015) *Annual Report, 2014*. London: Rolls-Royce.

Stockdyk, J. (2010) *FRRP Unhappy with IFRS 8 Dodgers*. Available at: http://www.accountingweb.co.uk (accessed 10 October 2012).

Tesco plc (2014) *Annual Report and Financial Statements 2014*. London: Tesco.

Whitbread plc (2015) *Annual Report and Accounts 2014/15*. Dunstable: Whitbread.

 Questions

● Quick test

1   A company which prepares financial statements to 31 December classifies a non-current asset as held for sale on 1 September 20X2. The asset's carrying amount at that date is £20,000 and

its fair value is £15,600, with estimated costs to sell of £600. The asset is sold in June 20X3 for £16,000 (net of costs). Calculate any impairment losses or gains that should be recognised in the company's statement of profit or loss for the year ended 31 December 20X2 if the asset's fair value less costs to sell at 31 December 20X2 is:

(a) 14,000

(b) 17,000

(c) 22,000.

In each case, also calculate the profit or loss that should be recognised on the disposal of the asset in 20X3 and comment on the results shown.

2 Dewy plc is a company with six operating segments and no other activities except those of the six operating segments. It reports in accordance with the minimum requirements of IFRS 8.

Operating segment	Internal revenue £m	External revenue £m	Total revenue £m	Profit (loss) £m	Assets £m
Sparrow	50	940	990	310	80
Hawk	30	80	110	(50)	70
Eagle	–	400	400	130	570
Owl	240	220	460	80	120
Robin	50	160	210	(100)	80
Thrush	30	200	230	30	80
TOTAL	400	2,000	2,400	400	1,000

Required:

Explain whether each of the operating segments is a reportable segment.

3 Discuss whether the following relationships of Alpha plc constitute a related party relationship as defined by IAS 24:

(a) Beta is a separate entity in which one of Alpha's junior managers owns 10% of the share capital

(b) The daughter of a director of Alpha

(c) A director of Alpha owns 60% of the share capital of another entity called Gamma Ltd

(d) Miss Delta owns 25% of the share capital of Alpha

(e) A director of Alpha is also a director of Epsilon plc (which is independent of Alpha), but is not a shareholder in either entity

(f) Zeta Ltd is an entity owned by the niece of the finance director of Alpha.

4 Discuss the disclosures that would be required by IAS 24 in the financial statements of Black plc in respect of each of the following transactions:

(a) Black sells goods on credit to White Ltd, which is a company owned by the son of one of the directors of Black. At the year end there was a receivable of £100,000 owing from White to Black. The £100,000 was expensed to the statement of profit or loss as it was considered as being non-recoverable. Debt collection costs incurred by Black were £4,000.

(b) Black purchased goods from Blue plc for £600,000, which was deemed to be an arm's length price. Black owns 40% of the ordinary share capital of Blue.

(c) An amount of £90,000 is due to one of Black's distributors, Red Ltd.

(d) A house owned by Black, with a carrying amount of £200,000 and a market value of £450,000, was sold to one of its directors for £400,000. Black guaranteed the loan taken out by the director to purchase the property.

●● Develop your understanding

5 During the year to 30 September 20X6 Price plc carried out a major reorganisation of its activities as follows:

(a) The only remaining manufacturing division of the company was closed down on 1 June 20X6. As a result of the closure Price's only activity will be in retail.

(b) Owing to fierce competition, on 31 August 20X6 it was decided to sell the only division that operated in Europe. The company was confident of a sale within the year. The sale actually took place on 20 January 20X7.

(c) The activities carried on by the research division were terminated during the period. This division was one of a number of smaller ones which operated from the same location as the main headquarters of Price. All these divisions use the same central accounting system and operating costs are allocated between them for the purpose of the management accounts.

The accounts for the year ended 30 September 20X6 were approved on 5 January 20X7.

Required:

Discuss how these events should be accounted for in the financial statements of Price plc for the year ended 30 September 20X6 in relation to IFRS 5 *Non-current Assets Held for Sale and Discontinued Operations*.

6 Bullfinch plc is an international hotel group whose sole business is that of operating hotels. The group reports to management on the basis of regions, these being Europe, South East Asia, and the Americas. The hotels are located in capital cities in these regions and the company sets individual performance indicators for each hotel based on its city location. The results of these regional segments for the year ended 30 June 20X9 are as follows:

| | Revenue | | Segment | Segment | Segment |
| | External | Internal | Profit / (loss) | Assets | Liabilities |
Region	£m	£m	£m	£m	£m
Europe	200	3	(10)	300	200
South East Asia	300	2	60	800	300
Americas	500	5	105	2,000	1,400

There were no significant intersegment balances in the asset and liability figures.

Required:

(a) For an international company such as Bullfinch plc, discuss the purpose behind the requirements of IFRS 8 *Operating Segments*.

(b) Explain the principles in IFRS 8 for the determination of a company's reportable segments, and how these principles would be applied for Bullfinch plc, using the information given.

(c) Demonstrate how an analyst might use the segmental information and outline any conclusions that may be reached.

(d) Evaluate the usefulness of the segmental information, including in your answer details of other information that is required to be disclosed by IFRS 8 or would be considered useful for analytical purposes.

7   Whitbread plc is a UK hospitality company, which has built some successful brands such as Premier Inn (hotel chain), Costa (coffee shop), Beefeater (restaurant), Brewers Fayre (pub chain), and Taybarns (family restaurant).

The following information has been extracted from the financial statements of Whitbread plc for the year ended 26 February 2015:

Income statement

Year to 26 February 2015	Notes	£m
Revenue	3, 4	2,608.1
Operating costs	5	(2,110.6)
Operating profit		497.5
Share of profit from joint ventures	16	2.6
Share of profit from associate	17	0.8
Operating profit of the Group, joint ventures and associate		500.9
Finance costs	8	(39.4)
Finance revenue	8	2.3
Profit before tax	4	463.8
Tax expense		(97.7)
Profit for the year		366.1

Note 4—Segment information

Year ended 26 February 2015	Hotels & Restaurants £m	Costa £m	Unallocated & elimination £m	Total £m
Revenue				
Underlying revenue from external customers	1,659.2	948.9	–	2,608.1
Inter–segment revenue	–	3.0	(3.0)	–
Total revenue	1,659.2	951.9	(3.0)	2,608.1
Underlying operating profit	401.4	132.5	(29.5)	504.4
Underlying interest	–	–	(16.3)	(16.3)
Underlying profit before tax	401.4	132.5	(45.8)	488.1

(continued)

(continued)

Exceptional items and various adjustments:

....

Profit before tax	405.0	125.4	(66.6)	463.8
Tax expense				(97.7)
Profit for the year				366.1

Assets and liabilities

Segment assets	3,293.0	395.8	–	3,688.8
Unallocated assets	–	–	45.0	45.0
Total assets	3,293.0	395.8	45.0	3,733.8
Segment liabilities	(308.7)	(109.7)	–	(418.4)
Unallocated liabilities	–	–	(1,337.5)	(1,337.5)
Total liabilities	(308.7)	(109.7)	(1,337.5)	(1,337.5)
Net assets	2,984.3	286.1	(1,292.5)	1,977.9

Required:

Using the segment information provided, comment on the statement in Whitbread plc's annual report that growth of Costa in the UK and internationally is a key strategy.

● ● ● Take it further

8 The following list of balances was extracted from the books of Crompton plc on 31 December 20X7:

	£	£
Sales		2,640,300
Administration expenses	220,280	
Selling and distribution costs	216,320	
Interest paid on loan stock	10,000	
Dividends received		2,100
Profit on sale of premises (see note 6)		40,000
Purchases	2,089,600	
Inventories at 1 January 20X7	318,500	
Bank		11,860
Trade receivables	415,800	
Allowance for doubtful debts at 1 January 20X7		10,074
Loss on sale of business operation (see note 6)	8,800	

Trade payables		428,250
Corporation tax paid	32,500	
10% loan stock		200,000
Investments in other listed companies	20,000	
Office equipment	110,060	
Vehicles	235,000	
Equity share capital (£1 shares)		200,000
Retained earnings at 1 January 20X7		144,276
	£3,676,860	£3,676,860

The following information needs to be dealt with before the financial statements can be finalised:

1   Provide for the loan stock interest which is due for payment on 1 January 20X8

2   Provide for administration expenses paid in advance at 31 December 20X7 of £12,200 and distribution costs of £21,300 owing at this date

3   The provision for doubtful debts is to be maintained at 3% of receivables

4   Inventories are valued at 31 December 20X7 at £340,600

5   The total corporation tax payable on the company's profits for 20X7 is estimated at £45,700

6   During the year, the company sold a material business operation with all activities ceasing on 28 February 20X8. The premises were sold separately, and gave a profit on sale of £40,000. The loss on sale of the remainder of the operation amounted to £8,800.

The operating results of the business segment were as follows (these figures are *included* in the relevant trial balance figures):

	£
Sales	180,634
Cost of sales	153,539
Administration expenses	20,240
Distribution costs	22,823
Corporation tax effect	3,500 reduction

7   In addition, the company is negotiating the sale of another business sector, which should be completed by 30 April 20X8. Relevant values of the assets of this sector at 31 December 20X7 are as follows:

	Book value £	Fair value less costs to sell £
Vehicles	43,554	20,000
Office equipment	16,566	5,000
Inventories	66,000	68,000

Required:

Prepare a statement of comprehensive income for the year ended 31 December 20X7 and a statement of financial position at that date, which comply, as far as the information allows, with relevant international financial reporting standards.

9   Next is a UK based retailer offering exciting, beautifully designed, excellent quality clothing, footwear, accessories and home products. NEXT is one of the largest clothing and home products retailers in the UK by sales, and a member of the FTSE-100 index. The Group is primarily comprised of:

- NEXT Retail, a chain of more than 500 stores in the UK and Eire. The majority of our stores sell clothing, footwear, accessories and home products; we also operate over 60 large Home Standalone and department style stores. The predominantly leased store portfolio is actively managed, with openings and closures based on store profitability and cash payback.

- NEXT Directory, an online and catalogue shopping business with over 4 million active customers and international websites serving approximately 70 countries. By embracing the internet, providing exceptional customer service and developing overseas opportunities, over the last ten years NEXT Directory's sales have grown by more than 150%.

- There are strong synergies between NEXT Retail and NEXT Directory: through efficient stock management and customer service opportunities (such as handling Directory collections and returns in-store) the Group has been able to successfully develop both parts of the business.

- NEXT International Retail, with around 200 mainly franchised stores across the world. NEXT's franchise partners operate over 180 stores in 37 countries; there are also a small number of stores which NEXT operates directly.

- NEXT Sourcing, which designs, sources and buys NEXT branded products. Last year, around 40% of the Group's products were procured or produced by NEXT Sourcing.

- Lipsy, which designs and sells Lipsy branded younger women's fashion products.

Next's consolidated income statement for the financial year ended 24 January 2015 and the comparative 2014 statement are shown as follows. An extract from the company's balance sheet at 24 January 2015, plus the segmental analysis as disclosed in the 2015 financial statements, are also shown.

Financial reporting in practice 6.9   Next plc, 2015

Consolidated income statement for the year ended 24 January 2015

	Notes	2015 £m	2014 £m
Revenue	1, 2	**3,999.8**	3,740.0
Cost of sales		**(2,656.4)**	(2,499.9)
Gross profit		**1,343.4**	1,240.1
Distribution costs		**(322.9)**	(296.2)

	Notes		
Administrative expenses		**(218.2)**	(217.7)
Unrealised foreign exchange gains/(losses)	3	**8.9**	(5.9)
Trading profit		**811.2**	720.3
Share of results of associates		**0.9**	2.5
Operating profit	3	**812.1**	722.8
Finance income	5	**0.8**	0.7
Finance costs	5	**(30.7)**	(28.3)
Profit before taxation and exceptional items		**782.2**	695.2
Exceptional gains	6	**12.6**	-
Profit before taxation		**794.8**	695.2
Taxation	7	**(159.9)**	(142.0)
Profit for the year attributable to equity holders of the parent company		**634.9**	553.2

Extract from consolidated balance sheet at 24 January 2015

	Notes	2015 £m	2014 £m
ASSETS AND LIABILITIES			
Non-current assets			
Property, plant and equipment	10	**503.3**	509.2
Intangible assets	11	**44.0**	44.4
Interests in associates and other investments	12	**2.1**	7.9
Defined benefit pension surplus	21	**37.9**	70.3
Other financial assets	15	**65.7**	17.7
Deferred tax assets	7	**13.3**	27.0
		666.3	676.5
Current assets			
Inventories		**416.8**	385.6
Assets under construction	13	**12.7**	-
Customer and other receivables	14	**844.3**	808.0
Other financial assets	15	**66.7**	1.2
Cash and short term deposits	16	**275.5**	273.3
		1,616.0	1,468.1
Total assets		**2,282.3**	2,144.6

Note 1. Segmental analysis

The Group's operating segments under IFRS 8 have been determined based on management accounts reviewed by the Board. The performance of operating segments is assessed on profits before interest and tax, excluding equity settled share option charges recognised under IFRS 2 *Share-Based Payment* and unrealised foreign exchange gains or losses on derivatives which do not qualify for hedge accounting. The activities, products and services of the operating segments are detailed in the Strategic Report on page 22. The Property Management segment holds properties and property leases which are sub-let to other segments and external parties.

Segment sales and revenue

Year to January 2015	Total sales excluding VAT £m	Commission sales adjustment £m	External Revenue £m	Internal Revenue £m	Total Segment Revenue £m
NEXT Retail*	2,348.2	(6.7)	2,341.5	7.2	2,348.7
NEXT Directory*	1,540.6	(20.8)	1,519.8	–	1,519.8
NEXT International Retail	86.2	–	86.2	–	86.2
NEXT Sourcing	7.5	–	7.5	593.1	600.6
	3,982.5	(27.5)	3,955.0	600.3	4,555.3
Lipsy*	36.8	(0.5)	36.3	24.5	60.8
Property Management	5.6	–	5.6	196.6	202.2
Total segment sales/ revenues	4,024.9	(28.0)	3,996.9	821.4	4,818.3
Third party distribution	2.9	–	2.9	–	2.9
Eliminations	–	–	–	(821.4)	(821.4)
Total	4,027.8	(28.0)	3,999.8	–	3,999.8

Year to January 2014	Total sales excluding VAT £m	Commission sales adjustment £m	External Revenue £m	Internal Revenue £m	Total Segment Revenue £m
NEXT Retail*	2,240.5	(0.8)	2,239.7	6.1	2,245.8
NEXT Directory*	1,373.9	(17.4)	1,356.5	–	1,356.5
NEXT International Retail	85.6	–	85.6	–	85.6
NEXT Sourcing	11.0	–	11.0	560.2	571.2
	3,711.0	(18.2)	3,692.8	566.3	4,259.1
Lipsy*	35.3	–	35.3	20.5	55.8

Property Management	4.8	–	4.8	192.9	197.7
Total segment sales/ revenues	(18.2)	3,732.9	779.7	4,512.6	
Third party distribution	7.1	–	7.1	–	7.1
Eliminations	–	–	–	(779.7)	(779.7)
Total	3,758.2	(18.2)	3,740.0	–	3,740.0

Lipsy sales made through NEXT Retail and Directory are now reported in those divisions. For comparability, prior year figures have been restated resulting in £12.1m of Lipsy sales being re-allocated to NEXT Retail and £15.5m to Directory.

Where third party branded goods are sold on a commission basis, only the commission receivable is included in statutory revenue. Total sales represents the amount paid by the customer, excluding VAT.

Segment profit

	2015 £m	2014 £m
NEXT Retail	**383.8**	347.7
NEXT Directory	**376.8**	358.5
NEXT International Retail	**11.7**	12.1
NEXT Sourcing	**41.4**	34.1
	813.7	752.4
Lipsy	**5.1**	2.7
Property Management	**6.9**	1.8
Total segment profit	**825.7**	756.9
Central costs and other	**(10.0)**	(14.9)
Share option charge	**(13.4)**	(15.8)
Unrealised foreign exchange gains/(losses)	**8.9**	(5.9)
Trading profit	**811.2**	720.3
Share of results of associates	**0.9**	2.5
Finance income	**0.8**	0.7
Finance costs	**(30.7)**	(28.3)
Profit before tax and exceptional items	**782.2**	695.2
Exceptional gains	**12.6**	–
Profit before tax	**794.8**	695.2

Transactions between operating segments are made on an arm's length basis in a manner similar to those with third parties. Segment revenue and segment profit include transactions between business segments which are eliminated on consolidation. The substantial majority of NEXT Sourcing's revenues and profits are derived from sales to NEXT Retail and NEXT Directory.

Segment assets, capital expenditure and depreciation

	Property, plant and equipment		Capital expenditure		Depreciation	
	2015 £m	2014 £m	2015 £m	2014 £m	2015 £m	2014 £m
NEXT Retail	342.1	347.8	91.4	88.0	96.2	101.8
NEXT Directory	81.3	80.7	13.5	8.4	13.0	11.8
NEXT International Retail	1.1	0.9	0.6	0.4	0.3	0.4
NEXT Sourcing	2.3	2.4	0.6	0.8	0.8	0.9
Lipsy	2.3	4.7	-	0.9	1.5	1.9
Property Management	74.1	72.5	4.1	6.6	0.1	0.1
Other	0.1	0.2	-	0.2	0.1	0.1
Total	503.3	509.2	110.2	105.3	112.0	117.0

Analyses of the Group's external revenues (by customer location) and non-current assets (excluding investments, the defined benefit pension surplus, other financial assets and deferred tax assets) by geographical location are detailed below:

	External revenue by geographical location		Non-current assets by geographical location	
	2015 £m	2014 £m	2015 £m	2014 £m
United Kingdom	3,648.0	3,447.0	508.3	514.1
Rest of Europe	225.6	197.7	7.3	7.5
Middle East	60.4	46.5	4.7	4.3
Asia	37.5	19.6	27.0	27.6
Rest of World	28.3	29.2	-	0.1
	3,999.8	3,740.0	547.3	553.6

Required:

Produce an analysis of the performance of NEXT plc for the year ended 24 January 2015 in comparison with 2014 using the segmental information as far as possible in this analysis.

 Visit the Online Resource Centre for solutions to all these end of chapter questions plus visual walkthrough solutions. You can test your understanding with extra questions and answers, explore additional case studies based on real companies, take a guided tour through a company report and much more. Go to the Online Resource Centre at **www.oxfordtextbooks.co.uk/orc/maynard2e/**

7

Revenue from contracts with customers

Revenue is a key figure in any business's financial statements, widely used as a measure of the size of a business and in any assessment of its performance and prospects. Any misstatement of revenue has a significant impact on profit or loss. US studies have shown that over half of all financial statement frauds and restatements of previously published financial information have involved revenue manipulation. It is therefore important that the principles behind the recognition and measurement of revenue are applied consistently if financial statements are to present fairly the true economic activity of a business. This is particularly so given the complexities of modern business transactions which give rise to revenue.

In July 2014, the International Accounting Standards Board (IASB)'s lengthy convergence project with the US Financial Accounting Standards Board (FASB) to improve the accounting standards relevant to revenue finally resulted in the issue of International Financial Reporting Standard (IFRS) 15 *Revenue from Contracts with Customers*. This replaces International Accounting Standard (IAS) 18 *Revenue* and IAS 11 *Construction Contracts*. For many years, these were the relevant accounting standards to be applied when determining how and when revenue should be recognised, and how revenue arising from long-term construction contracts should be determined.

IFRS 15 provides a different set of principles to be applied in the recognition of revenue from IAS 18 and will apply to all contracts with customers, whether for goods or services or whether short- or long-term. The implementation date is for accounting periods beginning on or after 1 January 2018 to enable companies and users sufficient transition time.

This chapter discusses the accounting requirements of IFRS 15.

★ Learning objectives

After studying this chapter you will be able to:

- understand the significance of revenue reporting to businesses and their users and the issues with this
- understand and apply the accounting methods for revenue recognition and measurement set out in financial reporting standard IFRS 15 *Revenue from Contracts with Customers*

✔ Key issues checklist

- ❑ Definition of revenue.
- ❑ Key issues with revenue recognition.
- ❑ Inadequacies of accounting for revenue under IASs 18 and 11.
- ❑ Accounting for revenue from contracts with customers under IFRS 15:
    - ❑ Principles and five-step approach.
    - ❑ Identification of the contract.
    - ❑ Principal versus agent.
    - ❑ Identification of the **performance obligations**.
    - ❑ Recognition of revenue from the satisfaction of the performance obligations.
    - ❑ Transfer of control.
    - ❑ Performance obligations satisfied over time—**input** and **output methods**.
    - ❑ Performance obligations satisfied at a point in time.
    - ❑ Determination of the **transaction price**.
    - ❑ Variable consideration.
    - ❑ Contracts with a significant financing element.
    - ❑ Allocation of the transaction price to the performance obligations—use of stand-alone selling prices.
    - ❑ Accounting for contract costs.
    - ❑ Contract assets and liabilities.
    - ❑ Contracts with warranties.
    - ❑ Contracts with options to buy additional goods or services.
    - ❑ Accounting for contracts with a repurchase of goods.
    - ❑ Disclosures.
    - ❑ The impact of IFRS 15.

7.1 Issues with revenue

Revenue is a topic of relevance to virtually all companies. A headline figure, it is one of the most crucial numbers used to assess a company's financial performance. A company's growth or contraction is often framed in terms of changes in revenue; and numerous ratios employed in the interpretation of financial statements, for example net profit margin, gross margin and asset turnover, use revenue in their calculation. Any interpretation of profit is affected by the reported revenue figures.

 Example of when revenue recognition goes wrong: the case of Tesco

In September 2014 Tesco, the supermarket giant, announced it had overstated its first half-year profits by £250 million. The company later revised the error upwards to £263 million. The disclosure of the error wiped over £2 billion from the value of Tesco's shares, and the matter was soon referred to the UK's Serious Fraud Office (SFO) to investigate whether fraud or other illegal practices had been perpetrated. Although the SFO has yet to report at the time of writing, it appears that Tesco accelerated the recognition of revenue relating to suppliers' rebates together with delaying the recognition of some costs. As with all large supermarkets, Tesco has a large number of individual arrangements with its suppliers for rebates, discounts and other promotional support, which add complexity to its accounting. The vagueness of the current accounting standard, IAS 18 *Revenue*, may have contributed to the accounting error.

The issues relating to revenue recognition are explored in the following sections, but, first, revenue needs to be defined clearly.

7.1.1 Definition of revenue

Revenue is a subset of income. Income is defined in the IASB's 2015 *Conceptual Framework* Exposure Draft (ED) as:

> ... increases in assets or decreases in liabilities that result in increases in equity, other than those relating to contributions from holders of equity claims.

In bookkeeping terms, an increase in an asset is a debit entry to the asset account; a decrease in a liability is a debit to the liability account. The other side of the double-entry must be a credit entry which results in an increase in equity. This cannot be from the shareholders, such as a share issue, so the credit to equity must arise from an increase in retained earnings (and therefore from net income) or some other reserve, such as a **revaluation reserve**. (Note: revaluation reserves are discussed in detail in Chapter 10.)

Revenue is income that arises in the course of the ordinary activities of a business and includes sales, fees, royalties, rent, interest and dividends. It excludes gains, which is the other subset of income and which includes gains from the sale of non-current assets, impairment gains or gains from the revaluation of net assets to fair value at each statement of financial position date.

 Examples of revenue

Determine which of the following transactions gives rise to revenue and how much the revenue is in these cases:

1   A company sells goods for £1,200, including sales tax of £200.

   Revenue = £1,000. Sales tax is collected by the company on behalf of the tax authorities (HM Revenue & Customs in the UK) and does not increase equity.

2   A company sells goods for £500 with a trade discount of £25. The customer is offered a further discount of £19 if payment is made within 30 days.

   Revenue = £475. Trade discounts are netted off with selling price. Cash discounts are treated as an expense.

3   A company issues 100,000 £1 equity shares at £2 each.

   Revenue = 0. This is a contribution from shareholders.

4   A manufacturing company, which is moving to a new factory, sells its old factory for £450,000.

   Revenue = 0. Any profit on sale is treated as a gain in accordance with IAS 16.

7.1.2 Revenue recognition issues

As discussed in Chapter 2, the IASB's *Conceptual Framework* ED includes generic recognition criteria for the elements. Essentially assets and liabilities, and any related income, expense or changes in equity, should be recognised if this provides users of financial statements with relevant and faithfully representative information.

However, one of the key issues relating to revenue is the timing of when it should be recognised, since under a single contract goods and services may be provided in the current and in future periods. The *Conceptual Framework* ED confirms that an important method of assessing financial performance and profit is by accrual accounting. This therefore means that revenue should be recognised in the period in which the transaction giving rise to the revenue occurs; in other words, the revenue must have been earned.

Consider the operating cycle for a manufacturing company as represented by Figure 7.1. The main question is at what point in this cycle revenue should be recognised?

Assuming that this figure does not relate to a long-term contract, such as a **construction contract** which spreads over a number of accounting periods, the usual point at which revenue is recognised is when the goods are delivered to the customer. It is at this point that a transaction has occurred with the customer, which gives rise to an expected inflow of cash (an asset), and when relevant and faithfully representative information about the transaction will be provided.

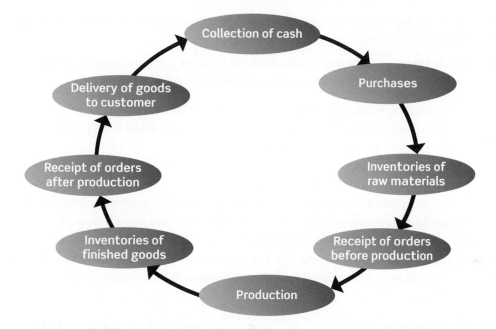

Figure 7.1 The operating cycle for a manufacturing company

One way in which a company can increase its reported revenue is to make the recognition point earlier in the cycle.

This is an example of creative accounting, or aggressive earnings management.

 Examples of aggressive earnings management

There have been many real-life examples of companies pursuing aggressive earnings management, for example dot.com companies and Enron. In these companies revenue was recognised essentially on the promise of goods or services being delivered rather than when the goods were delivered or the services performed.

Enron also pursued other aggressive policies which related to how it measured its revenue from wholesale trading and risk management in the supply of energy. It inflated its revenues by recording them at wholesale prices rather than just at service fee levels. For example, when it acted as a middleman between a seller and buyer of an energy contract, it would record the gross revenue in the contract rather than just the commission or fee for the delivery of the contract. The result of this was that between 1996 and 2000 Enron's revenues increased from $13.3 billion to $100.8 billion—an unprecedented rise of over 750% or 66% per year. At the time, the energy industry considered annual growth of 2–3% to be respectable.

Revenues can also be manipulated by companies which sell goods as follows:

● keeping 'the quarter open' to improve sales figures

● recording phoney sales and shipping products to, perhaps, an employee's premises where they are kept until requested by legitimate customers

- asking customers to accept additional products sooner than needed—often allowing them to delay payment beyond their usual credit period

- reducing production quality standards to meet volume goals and shipping products of poor quality knowing that they will be returned during the next quarter.

Not all companies engage in these practices, but internal control departments and auditors need to be alert to them, and design their testing accordingly to detect them and, if necessary, to advise on adjustments required to financial statements.

The arrangements businesses enter into to sell their products and services to customers have become ever more complex. One only has to consider a typical sale a telecommunications company makes, which will include any, or all, of the following elements: a handset; a subscription to a particular network; calls and texts for a certain period, some of which will be 'free' to the customer and some of which, if unused, can be carried forward to another period; and various downloads, etc. The key question arising in this situation is how and when revenue should be recognised for the various elements of this transaction.

7.2 IFRS 15 *Revenue from Contracts with Customers*

7.2.1 The need for a revised standard dealing with revenue

IAS 18 *Revenue*, the latest version of which was issued in 2004, set out broad principles for the recognition of revenue from the sale of goods, the rendering of services and from interest, royalties and dividends. IAS 11 *Construction Contracts*, the latest version also issued in 2004, addressed the allocation of revenue and costs to accounting periods for long-term contracts, which included construction and service contracts. Even from the early 2000s both standards were considered as providing limited guidance for the increasingly complex transactions into which companies were entering, such as multiple element arrangements, whereby more than one good or service was delivered under one arrangement. Some companies were turning to US generally accepted accounting principles (GAAP) to provide the accounting solutions. US GAAP contains numerous industry-specific requirements, but these can result in economically similar transactions being accounted for differently. Thus, much diversity in the recognition of revenue existed which was not helpful for users in understanding this all-important figure in their interpretation of financial statements.

Some users also criticised the disclosure requirements as being inadequate for them to fully understand the estimates and judgements made by companies in recognising their revenues. In particular, they were concerned that the information disclosed was often of a 'boilerplate' nature, in other words formulaic and not specific to the particular company's transactions.

In 2002 the IASB and US FASB started work on a convergence project on revenue recognition. The aim was to produce a principles-based approach which would make it easier to account for and analyse all situations giving rise to revenue. After a couple of Exposure Drafts and much feedback and discussion, the IASB finally issued IFRS 15 *Revenue from Contracts with Customers* in 2014. It is considered such an important financial reporting standard that its implementation is not required until after 1 January 2018 to enable companies and users to fully assess and prepare for its requirements, although earlier adoption is permitted. In order to preserve trend information, IFRS 15 is required to be applied retrospectively, meaning that existing contracts which are not yet complete, and possibly all contracts (companies have a choice of how they apply the transition process) would have to be restated in accordance with the standard.

7.2.2 The revenue recognition model

The objective of IFRS 15 demonstrates how challenging the project was. It is to provide a robust and comprehensive framework for the recognition, measurement and disclosure of revenue and some contract costs which will be applicable to, and therefore comparable across, all industries. Revenue is affected particularly by new commercial practices, which has given rise in the past to the development of case-by-case guidance and the standard seeks to reduce this need. It also aims to provide more useful information to users of financial statements through improved disclosures.

The definition of revenue is not altered by IFRS 15. Also, the basic principle of revenue recognition is the same as in IASs 18 and 11, in that revenue should be recognised as an entity delivers goods and services to a customer. However, the standard removes the distinction between goods and services and whether the contract is short- or long-term. The standard also clarifies that the goods and services are transferred when the customer has control of them, rather than the IAS 18 basis of when the risks and rewards of ownership have passed. The measurement of revenue should reflect the consideration to which the seller expects to be entitled from the customer.

In order to achieve these principles a five-step approach should be applied to all contracts with customers, as shown in Figure 7.2.

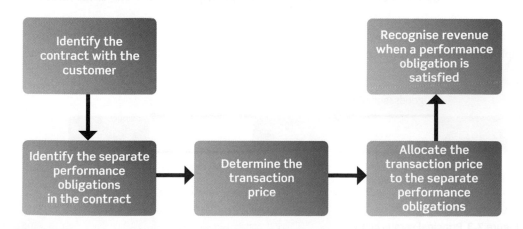

Figure 7.2 Five-step approach to the recognition of revenue

The first, second and fifth steps deal with recognition, and the third and fourth steps are concerned with measurement. Discussion of these steps takes recognition first, followed by measurement matters.

7.3 Recognition steps

7.3.1 Identification of the contract with the customer

IFRS 15 applies to all contracts with customers except those dealt with by other standards, such as leases, insurance contracts and those within the scope of financial instruments. Essentially, a contract is an agreement between two parties that creates enforceable rights and obligations, with enforceability being determined by law. The contract may be written, oral or implied by the business's customary practices. For IFRS 15 to apply, the contract must have commercial substance (i.e. the risk, timing or amount of the company's cash flows is expected to change) and a collectability threshold, which means that it must be probable, in other words, more likely than not, that the company will collect consideration from the customer. Note the consideration may be a fixed amount which is stated in the contract. However, consideration can be variable, or it may alter at a later date because the company offers the customer a price concession once the customer's ability and intention to pay are fully evaluated.

IFRS 15 defines a customer as:

> a party that has contracted with an entity to obtain goods and services that are an output of the entity's ordinary activities in exchange for consideration.

> *(IASB, IFRS 15, 2014)*

In many transactions, a customer is easily identifiable. However, in transactions involving multiple parties, it is less clear which party is the customer and judgement needs to be exercised. The standard makes the distinction between a principal and an agent, as the measurement of revenue for each is different.

Figure 7.3 shows the flow of goods or services that may exist in an arrangement with multiple parties whereby a company engages another party such as a subcontractor (the agent) to

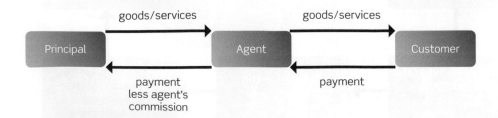

Figure 7.3 Principal versus agent

carry out all or part of the contract. The principal is defined as a party that controls the goods or services before it transfers them to the customer. The principal recognises revenue at the gross amount of consideration it expects to receive in exchange for the goods or services. An agent is the party that arranges for the provision of the goods or services. The agent recognises revenue as the fee or commission it expects to receive for arranging the sale. This will typically be the net amount of consideration that it retains from the customer after paying the principal (the supplier) for the goods or services passed to it.

 Example of principal versus agent

A company operates a website that enables customers to purchase goods from a range of suppliers who deliver goods directly to the customers. When a good is purchased via the website, the company is entitled to a commission of 10% of the sales price. The company's website facilitates payment between the customer and supplier at prices that are set by the supplier. The company requires payment from the customers before orders are processed and all orders are non-refundable. The company has no further obligations to the customer after arranging for the goods to be provided to the customer.

The company needs to determine whether it is a principal or agent. The following factors are taken into account:

1. The supplier is primarily responsible for fulfilling the contract, i.e. shipping the goods to the customer
2. The company does not assume risk for the inventory at any point during the transaction
3. The company's consideration is in the form of a commission
4. The company does not have discretion in establishing prices for the supplier's goods, therefore the benefits it can receive from the goods is limited
5. Neither the company nor the supplier assumes **credit risk**.

The conclusion is that the company is an agent and its performance obligation is to arrange for the provision of goods from the supplier to the customer. It will recognise revenue as the commission to which it is entitled.

Contract terms may include various options, and the determination of the enforceable rights and obligations may need to be considered carefully.

 Example of enforceable rights and obligations

A company enters into a contract with a customer for the sale of a product and a service that will be provided over two years. The customer can elect whether to renew the service for a third year at market rates. The product cannot be used without the associated service. The company does sell the service separately from the product to other customers, and other businesses also sell the service separately.

The contract that is enforceable is for the product and two years' worth of service.

Contracts should be accounted for individually unless they are clearly commercially related or dependent upon one another, in which case contracts should be combined and accounted for as a single contract. IFRS 15 provides guidance for the case of the modification of an existing contract to determine whether this constitutes a new contract. Essentially a contract modification is accounted for as a separate contract if:

(a) The scope of the contact increases because of the addition of distinct additional goods or services; and

(b) The price increases by an amount that reflects the company's stand-alone selling prices of the additional goods or services.

(IASB, IFRS 15, para. 20)

Otherwise a contract modification is accounted for as:

1. the termination of the existing contract and the creation of a new contract if the remaining goods or services are distinct, or

2. part of the existing contract if the remaining goods or services are not distinct, and the adjustment to revenue is made on a cumulative catch-up basis.

7.3.2 Identification of the separate performance obligations in the contract

Many contracts with customers have multiple elements, with their delivery at different times and under different conditions. IAS 18 did not sufficiently address how revenue from these contracts should be accounted for, giving rise to variations between companies. IFRS 15 specifies that a separate element in a contract, which it terms a performance obligation, is a promise to transfer a good or a service to the customer. It is an important issue because revenue is recognised when a performance obligation is satisfied. If the relevant goods or services are distinct, in other words if they are regularly sold separately or the customer benefits from their separate delivery, then the promised goods or services transfer is a separate performance obligation. If the promised goods or services are not distinct, they should be combined with other promised goods or services within the contract until a bundle of goods or services that is distinct can be identified. This bundle is then treated as a single performance obligation. Some contracts may have to be 'unbundled' to identify the separate performance obligations.

 Examples of separate or bundled performance obligations

1 A software developer enters into a contract with a customer to transfer a software licence, perform an installation service and provide unspecified software updates and technical support (online and telephone) for a two-year period. The company sells the licence, installation service

and technical support separately. The installation service includes changing the web screen for each type of user (for example, marketing, inventory management and information technology). The installation service is routinely performed by other entities and does not significantly modify the software. The software remains functional without the updates and the technical support.

The company would need to assess the goods and services promised to the customer to determine which goods and services are distinct. Given that the software is delivered before the other goods and services and remains functional without the updates and the technical support, the customer can benefit from each of the goods and services either on their own or together with the other goods and services. In addition, the promise to transfer each good and service to the customer is separately identifiable from each of the other promises. In particular, the installation service does not significantly modify or customise the software itself and, as such, the software and the installation service are separate outputs promised by the company rather than inputs used to produce a combined output.

Therefore, the company should identify four performance obligations in the contract for the following goods or services:

- the software licence
- an installation service
- software updates
- technical support.

2 A company enters into a contract to design and build a hospital. The company is responsible for the overall management of the project and identifies various goods and services to be provided, including engineering, site clearance, foundation, procurement, construction of the building, piping and wiring, installation of equipment, and finishing.

The company would account for the bundle of goods and services as a single performance obligation because the goods or services are highly interrelated. Providing them to the customer also requires the company to provide a significant service of integrating the goods or services into the combined item—the hospital—for which the customer has contracted. In addition, the goods or services are modified significantly and customised to fulfil the contract.

Some companies offer sales incentives or other items that they consider are otherwise incidental to the promised goods or services in the contract. The contract may include a promise to provide the incentive or incidental goods or services, or they may be implicit in the contract because historically the company has provided them. For example, it is common for motor car dealers to sell cars with incentives such as free maintenance for a number of years. Assuming that such sales incentives and incidental obligations are distinct goods and services, these will be considered separate performance obligations and the related revenue will need to be deferred until those goods and services are transferred to the customer.

The particular circumstances of the goods or services contracted for need to be considered. For example, a building company agrees to construct a brick wall for a customer. Even if the company supplies just bricks or just the labour separately in other circumstances, and the customer could benefit from their separate supply, these items would not be distinct in this case, since the promise in the contract is to construct a brick wall.

7.3.3 Satisfaction of a performance obligation

Revenue is to be recognised when a performance obligation is satisfied so this step, the fifth in the model, includes a number of important issues. The first issue dealt with is that the satisfaction is determined when the goods or services are transferred to the customer, and this is defined as when the customer obtains control of the goods or services. To help with the practical application of determining whether control has been transferred, the second important issue is that a distinction is made between a transfer either over time, which generally applies to services, or at a point in time, which generally applies to goods.

The transfer of control basis for the recognition of revenue has been generally accepted as being appropriate, and IFRS 15 contains guidance as to how this may be determined. The standard specifies that goods and services are assets, even if only momentarily, when they are received and used. Essentially, control is obtained if the buyer obtains the ability to use and obtain substantially all of the benefits from receiving the asset. It also includes the ability to prevent other entities from using or benefitting from the use of the asset. The benefits are potential cash flows that can be obtained directly or indirectly. For many straightforward sales of goods, transfer of control can be taken to mean transfer of the significant risks and rewards of ownership, which was the criterion used by IAS 18 for the recognition of revenue. Under IFRS 15 the point at which revenue will be recognised will therefore be the same in practice.

 Example of when control has transferred

A company enters into a contract to sell a product to a customer. The company uses a third-party carrier to deliver the product. The delivery terms of the contract are free on board shipping point, in other words legal title to the product passes to the customer when the product is handed over to the carrier. In accordance with the company's past business practices, it will provide the customer with a replacement product, at no additional cost, if a product is damaged or lost while in transit. The company has determined that its past business practice of replacing damaged products has implicitly created a performance obligation.

Here, the company has two performance obligations:

(i) to provide the customer with a product

(ii) to cover the risk of loss during transit.

The customer obtains control of the product at the point of shipment. Although it does not have physical possession of the product at that point, it has legal title and therefore can sell the product to or exchange it with another party. The company is also precluded from selling the product to another customer. The company would allocate a portion of the transaction price to the performance obligation to deliver the product and recognise this when the goods were handed over to the carrier.

The additional performance obligation for risk coverage does not affect when the customer obtains control of the product. However, it does result in the customer receiving a service from the entity while the product is in transit. Hence, the entity has not satisfied all of its performance obligations at the point of shipment. The remaining portion of the transaction price allocated to the performance obligation to provide risk coverage would be recognised as revenue as that performance obligation is satisfied, in other words when the shipping is complete.

Control may be transferred over time or at a point in time and therefore revenue is recognised over time or at a particular point. IFRS 15 provides provisions and guidance for control being transferred over time and companies need to determine whether these apply. If these are not fulfilled, then the performance obligation is deemed to be satisfied at a point in time.

7.3.4 Performance obligations satisfied over time

The transfer of control of goods or services over time will relate mainly to contracts for the construction of assets and the provision of services over time. There are three criteria, if any of which is satisfied, revenue is recognised over time:

(a) The customer simultaneously receives and consumes the benefits as the company performs, for example, from a cleaning contract

(b) The company's performance creates or enhances an asset (e.g. work in progress) that the customer controls, for example, the construction of a building on land owned by the customer

(c) The company's performance does not create an asset with an alternative use to the company, and the company has an enforceable right to payment for the performance completed to date.

The third criterion is the most complex. An asset has alternative use if, both practically and contractually, it could be supplied to another customer.

 Example of whether an asset has alternative use

A firm of consultants is carrying out services that will culminate in it issuing a professional opinion. The work carried out would relate to the facts and circumstances that were specific to the particular customer and would be unlikely to be able to be redirected to another customer. So the work would be unlikely to have alternative use, and therefore the revenue would be recognised over time, provided there was an enforceable right to payment.

The aim of recognising revenue over time is to depict the company's performance, and is particularly relevant for construction companies. The methods of accounting for the revenue are similar to those specified in IAS 11 *Construction Contracts*, which were based on a percentage of completion basis, and thus for companies that applied this previous standard, their method of revenue recognition may not change significantly. Revenue is recognised over time by the company selecting a method to measure the progress towards complete satisfaction of the relevant performance obligation. The method should be applied consistently to all similar circumstances and performance obligations. Specific methods are not described in IFRS 15, but the standard specifies that these could be what it terms output and input methods.

Output methods measure the progress towards the performance obligation on the basis of the value to the customer of the goods or services transferred, such as a survey of work completed to date, milestones reached, or units produced or delivered. These may provide the best method for measuring revenue, but, practically, may be difficult to achieve as relevant information may not be available.

Input methods measure the progress towards the performance obligation on the basis of the selling company's efforts, such as resources consumed, labour hours worked or costs incurred. These methods are easier to use, but may not relate directly to the transfer of control of goods or services to the customer.

When measuring progress, the company should exclude any goods or services for which control is not transferred to the customer. Also, as circumstances change over time, a company should update its measure of progress to reflect the company's performance completed to date. Any changes are accounted for as changes in estimates according to IAS 8 *Accounting Policies, Changes in Accounting Estimates and Errors* (see Chapter 4 for further details).

The measurement of progress must be reasonably reliable. If significant information is unavailable, then revenue may not be able to be recognised. If the reasonably reliable test is not met, but costs incurred are expected to be recoverable, for example, in the early stages of a contract, then revenue is recognised to the extent of these costs.

 Example of measuring the progress towards satisfaction of a performance obligation

A company enters into a contract with a customer to construct a building for £15 million over 2 years. The company estimates the total costs of the construction at £12 million. Assume, as discussed in the example in section 7.3.2, the contract is a single performance obligation because all of the promised goods and services in the contract are highly interrelated, and the construction company integrates these into the building for which the customer has contracted.

In order for the construction company to recognise revenue, as the contract progresses it has to select a method to measure the progress towards the satisfaction of the performance obligation, i.e. the completion of the building.

Surveyors may, at stages, certify the stage the construction has reached. If so, these certifications can be used as an output method. For example, at the end of the first financial year in which construction took place, suppose the surveyor certifies that the value of work completed is £5 million. This figure will be used as the revenue-recognised figure for this year's financial statements.

An alternative method may be based on inputs. For example, at the end of the first financial year in which construction took place, suppose costs of the construction project are £2.4 million. Progress towards satisfaction of the performance obligation could be measured on the basis of costs incurred relative to total costs expected to be incurred, i.e. £2.4 million/£12 million = 20%. Revenue recognised in this year would be 20% × £15 million = £3 million.

Note: the method chosen would have to be applied consistently to this contract.

How the related contract costs are accounted for is discussed in section 7.5.

7.3.5 Performance obligations satisfied at a point in time

If a performance obligation is not satisfied over time, a company satisfies the performance obligation at a point in time. This is when the transfer of control of a promised asset takes place. Indicators of the transfer of control include the following:

(a) the company has a present right to payment for the asset

(b) the customer has legal title to the asset

(c) the company has transferred physical possession of the asset

(d) the customer has the significant risks and rewards of ownership of the asset

(e) the customer has accepted the asset.

7.4 Measurement steps

7.4.1 Determination of the transaction price

The principle underpinning the determination of the transaction price is that it is the amount of consideration a company expects to be entitled to in exchange for transferring the promised goods or services. To determine this, the company should consider the terms of the contract and its customary business practices. In many cases there will be a fixed price specified in the contract. However, there are a number of situations where this may have to be adjusted.

7.4.2 Variable consideration

Variable consideration is one of the areas which was not addressed by the previous accounting standards and, for some industries, the application of IFRS 15 could represent a significant change from current practices. Variable consideration encompasses a range of items, such as discounts, rebates, refunds, credits, incentives, performance bonuses, penalties and price concessions. In these cases the company has to estimate the transaction price, by either:

(a) calculating the expected value, in other words the sum of probability-weighted amounts for a range of possible alternative consideration amounts; or

(b) using the most likely amount, in other words the amount of consideration for the single most likely outcome.

There is often uncertainty over variable consideration, so IFRS 15 specifies a hurdle that must be passed before any variable consideration can be included in the transaction price. Specifically, some or all of the variable consideration can be included only if it is highly probable that there will not be a significant reversal of cumulative revenue recognised when the uncertainties surrounding the variability of the revenue have been resolved.

 Worked example 7.1: to show the calculation of revenue with variable consideration arising from returned goods

Sexton plc enters into 100 contracts with 100 customers, each of which includes the sale of a product for £200 which cost £120. The company's customary business practice is to allow a customer to return any unused product within 30 days and receive a full refund. The company estimates that 3% of products will be returned.

Required:

Show how the above transactions would be accounted for in accordance with IFRS 15.

Sexton plc can treat the portfolio of 100 contracts as one contract because it can reasonably expect that the effect on the financial statements from applying the requirements of IFRS 15 to the portfolio would not be materially different from applying the requirements to each contract individually. Because the contract allows a customer to return the product, the consideration received from the customer is variable.

Upon transfer of control of the 100 products, Sexton plc only recognises revenue from the sale of goods which it expects *not* to be returned, i.e. from the sale of 97 products. So revenue = 97 × £200 = £19,400.

A refund liability of 3 × £200 = £600 is recognised.

An asset of £360 (3 × cost of £120) is recognised as the right to recover the products from the customers on settling the refund liability—in other words the cost of sales would match the cost of selling only 97 products with the revenues from 97 products.

The double-entry would be as follows:

			£	£
Debit	Receivable	(100 × £200)	20,000	
Credit	Revenue	(97 × £200)		19,400
Credit	Refund liability			600
Debit	Cost of sales	(97 × 120)	11,640	
Credit	Inventory			11,640

If Sexton plc's returns estimate turns out to be correct and three products are returned, after 30 days the double-entry is:

		£	£
Debit	Refund liability	600	
Credit	Receivables		600

If no goods are returned, after 30 days the double-entry is:

		£	£
Debit	Refund liability	600	
Credit	Revenue		600
Debit	Cost of sales	360	
Credit	Inventory / Right to recover products asset		360

At the end of each reporting period, any estimated variable consideration should be reassessed and changes accounted for as for any other change that may occur in a contract price. This requires the changes in the contract price to be allocated to the performance obligations on the same basis as at the start of the contract. New amounts allocated to a performance obligation which has already been satisfied (and therefore the revenue already recognised), should be recognised as revenue, or a reduction in revenue, in the period in which the change in price occurs—alterations are not made retrospectively.

Worked example 7.2: to show the accounting for an estimated volume discount and the effect of a change in the estimate

On 1 January 20X8 Robshaw plc enters into a contract with a customer to sell Product A for £100 per unit. If the customer purchases more than 1,000 units in the calendar year, the contract specifies that the price per unit is retrospectively reduced to £90 per unit.

During the first quarter ended 31 March 20X8, Robshaw sells 75 units of Product A to the customer and estimates that the customer's purchases will not exceed 1,000 units in 20X8.

In May 20X8, due to changes at the customer's business, Robshaw sells a further 500 units of Product A. In the light of this, Robshaw estimates that sales to the customer will exceed the 1,000-unit threshold for 20X8 for the price reduction to apply.

Required:

Show how Robshaw plc would account for the sales in the first and second quarters of 20X8.

This is an example of a contract with variable consideration, and Robshaw plc has to make a best estimate of the consideration it will receive from the customer in each quarter.

Quarter 1

Provided Robshaw plc concludes that it is highly probable that a significant reversal in the cumulative amount of revenue recognised at £100 per unit will not occur by the end of 20X8, the revenue recognised in the 1st quarter is $75 \times £100 = £7,500$.

Quarter 2

Robshaw plc has changed its estimate, and the change in the transaction price is accounted for fully in this quarter.

		£
2nd quarter's sales revenue	500 × £90	45,000
Change in transaction price for 1st quarter's sales	75 × £(10)	(750)
Revenue recognised		44,250

7.4.3 Significant financing component

The time value of money has to be taken into account where there is a significant financing component to a contract. This arises where goods or services are transferred to a customer with payment by the customer being at a time which provides either the company or the customer a significant benefit of financing. The objective is to recognise revenue at an amount that reflects what it would have been if the customer had paid at the time of transfer of the goods or services. The financing element is therefore presented separately as either interest income or interest expense in the statement of profit or loss.

The assessment of whether the financing component is significant is a matter of judgement. However, for practical purposes IFRS 15 has specified that an adjustment for the time value of money need not be done if the period between the transfer of the goods or services, and the expected receipt of all, or substantially all, of the consideration is one year or less. A contract is also considered not to have a significant financing component if:

(a) the customer paid for the goods or services in advance and the delivery of them is at their discretion

(b) a substantial amount of the consideration is variable, and it depends on the occurrence or non-occurrence of a future event that is not within the control of either the customer or the company, such as a sales-based royalty, or

(c) the difference in the timing of delivery of the goods or services and the payment arises for reasons other than financing.

The discount rate to be used in any time value calculation should reflect that which would be used in a separate financing transaction between the company and its customer at the inception of the contract. This could be determined by identifying the rate that discounts the nominal amount of the promised consideration to the price the customer would pay in cash for the goods or services on transfer.

 Worked example 7.3: to show the calculation of and accounting for a significant financing component: payment after delivery

DXS plc, a furniture retailer, sells goods to a customer for £2,500 on 1 January 20X5. Delivery will take place within 7 days, and the company has given the customer an interest-free credit period of 2 years. If the goods were sold for cash on this date, the retail price would be £2,066, implying an effective rate of interest of 10%.

Required:

Show how DXS plc would account for this transaction in 20X5, 20X6 and 20X7.

There is a significant financing component in this transaction being the difference between the cash price at 1 January 20X5 and the consideration required at 1 January 20X7, i.e. 2,500 – 2,066 = £434.

The revenue recorded as the performance obligation is satisfied (the delivery of the goods) is the cash price of £2,066:

		£	£
Debit	Receivable	2,066	
Credit	Revenue		2,066

The financing component is recognised as interest income over the 2 years 20X5 and 20X6 using the **effective interest method**:

		£
Receivable at 1 January 20X5		2,066
Interest income in 20X5	(10% × 2,066)	207
Receivable at 31 December 20X5		2,273
Interest income in 20X6	(10% × 2,273)	227
Receivable at 31 December 20X6		2,500

The accounting in each year is:

Debit	Receivable
Credit	Interest income

The cash received on 1 January 20X7 clears the receivable balance.

Worked example 7.4: to show the accounting for a significant financing component: payment in advance

A customer makes a down payment of £900 on 1 January 20X4 for goods which Zedex plc will deliver on 1 January 20X6. If the customer paid for the goods at the time of delivery the selling price would be £1,000.

Required:

Show how Zedex plc would account for this transaction in 20X4, 20X5 and 20X6.

There is a significant financing component in this transaction being the difference between the down payment at 1 January 20X4 and the selling price at 1 January 20X6, i.e. 1,000 – 900 = £100.

The interest rate implicit in this agreement is 5.4% ($900 \times 1.054^2 = 1,000$).

Revenue will not be recorded until satisfaction of the performance obligation—the delivery of the goods—which is on 1 January 20X6, and will be recorded at the cash price of £1,000. The advance payment will be recorded as a contract liability for the obligation to transfer the goods to the customer in the future. Interest expense will accrue on this balance.

The accounting will be as follows:

			£	£
On 1 January 20X4:				
Debit	Bank		900	
Credit	Contract liability			900
On 31 December 20X4:				
Debit	Interest expense	(5.4% x 900)	49	
Credit	Contract liability			49
On 31 December 20X5:				
Debit	Interest expense	(5.4% x 949)	51	
Credit	Contract liability			51
On 1 January 20X6:				
Debit	Contract liability		1,000	
Credit	Revenue			1,000

7.4.4 Other issues relating to the determination of the transaction price

If consideration is promised by the customer in a form other than cash, this is measured at the fair value of the non-cash consideration. If this cannot be reasonably estimated, the consideration is measured at the stand-alone selling price of the goods or services to be delivered.

❶ Reminder *Fair value is defined in IFRS 13 as 'the price that would be received to sell an asset or paid to transfer a liability in an orderly transaction between market participants at the measurement date'.*

If the company providing the goods or services pays any amounts to the customer in cash or any other non-cash form which the customer can apply against the amount it owes, then this amount reduces the transaction price and therefore the revenue recorded. The exception to this is if this consideration is for distinct goods or services that the customer transfers to the company, which would be accounted for as a normal purchase.

After some debate in the exposure drafts to the standard, IFRS 15 has determined that determination of the collectability of the consideration, in other words, whether the customer will pay or not, should not be taken into account when determining the transaction price. With the increasing emphasis on the transparency of disclosures relating to risk in financial statements and annual reports—in this case a customer's credit risk—the question was whether any allowance for non-collectability should be included, not as an administrative expense, but deducted from revenue to give some form of net revenue figure. The final version of IFRS 15 requires the transaction price of a contract to be based on the gross amount that a company expects ultimately to invoice, rather than on a net amount that reflects the efforts of collectability. Collectability is instead accounted for by applying the impairment requirements of IFRS 9 *Financial Instruments*, which essentially requires impairment losses—in other words allowances for non-collectability (or irrecoverable debts)—to be accounted for as an expense and disclosed appropriately. (See Chapter 14 for further details.)

7.4.5 Allocation of the transaction price to the separate performance obligations

Once the transaction price has been determined, the final step of the model to be discussed is the allocation of this to each separate performance obligation. The allocation should reflect the amount that the company would expect to be entitled to in exchange for satisfying each separate performance obligation. The method by which companies achieve this requires them to use, or estimate, the stand-alone selling price of the goods or services underlying each separate performance obligation at the time of the inception of the contract, and to divide the total transaction price between the performance obligations relative to their stand-alone prices.

The stand-alone selling price is the price at which a company would separately sell the goods or services relating to a particular performance obligation to other customers in similar circumstances. This may be a list price, but is not presumed to be so.

If a stand-alone selling price is not available, a number of approaches to its estimate are given in IFRS 15, which include an adjusted market-based assessment, a cost plus margin approach or a residual approach. The residual approach would estimate the stand-alone selling price of a particular performance obligation as the difference between the total contract price and the sum of the observable stand-alone selling prices of the other performance obligations' goods or services. This should only be used where any other estimate is highly variable or uncertain.

 Worked example 7.5: to show the allocation of a transaction price to separate performance obligations

A telecommunications company offers a 'free' phone handset to a customer who signs a 2-year contract paying £30 per month over the life of the contract for telecoms services. The handset has a stand-alone selling price of £200, and the stand-alone selling price of the telecoms services is estimated as £25 per month.

Required:

How should the telecommunications company recognise revenue from this contract?

This is a contract with two performance obligations:

(a) The sale of the handset

(b) The sale of the telecoms services.

The total consideration of the contract = 24 months x £30 = £720.

This needs to be allocated to the performance obligations in proportion to their relative stand-alone selling prices:

	Stand-alone selling price		Allocation of total consideration	
		£		£
Handset		200	200/800 x £720	180
Telecoms services	24 x £25	600	600/800 x £720	540
		800		720

£180 revenue would be recognised when control of the handset passes to the customer.

Revenue from the telecoms services would be recognised over time as the services are provided and consumed, on a monthly basis at £540/24 = £22.50 per month.

A company may offer a discount to a customer who buys a bundle of goods or services as opposed to buying the goods or services separately. The discount would be deducted from the total consideration before this is allocated in proportion to the relative stand-alone prices of the distinct goods and services, unless all the following criteria hold:

(a) The company regularly sells each distinct good or service on a stand-alone basis

(b) A discount is regularly offered on an individual (or a group of) goods or services

(c) This discount is substantially the same as the discount offered in the whole contract.

If these criteria are satisfied, the discount will be allocated just to the individual (or group of) goods or services that are identified in (b).

7.5 Contract costs

Although IFRS 15 is concerned mainly with revenue recognition and measurement, it does replace IAS 11 *Construction Contracts*, which specified the accounting methods for all aspects of construction contracts, including their costs. The proposed new standard therefore includes a section which deals with contract costs.

The principle underlying the treatment of costs is that the incremental costs of obtaining a contract plus the costs of fulfilling a contract are recognised as an asset (a contract cost asset) if a company expects to recover the costs.

Many costs associated with obtaining a contact will be expensed as incurred as they would have been incurred regardless of whether the contract was obtained. However, some costs will be incremental, in other words, costs which the company would not have incurred if the contract had not been obtained (for example, sales commission) or they are costs explicitly chargeable to the customer.

The costs incurred by a company to fulfil a contract are recognised as an asset if all of the following criteria are met:

(a) the costs relate directly to a contract (or a specific anticipated contract);

(b) the costs generate or enhance the resources of the company that will be used in satisfying performance obligations in the future; and

(c) the costs are expected to be recovered.

(IASB, IFRS 15, para. 95)

Some of these costs will be within the scope of another financial reporting standard (e.g. property, plant and equipment, or inventories). Other costs will include direct materials and labour, allocation of overhead costs that relate directly to the contract, such as management time, insurance, depreciation of tools and equipment, and payments to subcontractors. Costs which must be expensed when incurred include general administrative costs, costs of waste and any costs relating to performance obligations that have already been satisfied, in other words, costs relating to past performance.

 Example of contract costs

A construction company incurs £500,000 in annual rental expense for the office space occupied by a group of engineers and architects and their support staff. The company utilises this group to act as the quality assurance team that overlooks all contracts undertaken by the company. Annual costs of electricity, water and maintenance of the office space occupied by this group are £200,000.

These costs cannot be attributed to a specific contract. However they relate to the general contract activity of the company and should be allocated across all the company's contracts using a systematic and rational basis of allocation, for example:

- Labour hours utilised in each contract
- Contract revenue.

Costs that are recognised as an asset are expensed (IFRS 15 uses the term amortised) on a systematic basis consistent with the pattern of transfer of the goods or services to which the asset relates. So, costs are recognised in profit or loss either over time or at a point in time in accordance with the method used for recognising the related revenue.

7.6 Contract assets and liabilities

The method of accounting for contracts with customers will give rise to assets and liabilities at the end of an accounting period.

Revenue is essentially recognised on the delivery of the goods or services to the customer which will differ from when the customer makes payment. If the customer has paid, or been invoiced, before the transfer of goods or services, the company has an obligation to transfer the goods or services to the customer. The company therefore has a contract liability or, in other words, deferred revenue.

A contract asset is a company's right to payment in exchange for goods or services that it has transferred to a customer. Amounts presented as contract assets are reduced by amounts which are transferred to receivables. A receivable is presented separately from contract assets because it is an unconditional right to consideration, and this arises only when the passage of time is required before payment is due. Contract assets and receivables are accounted for in accordance with IFRS 9 *Financial Instruments*, and this requires the amounts to be assessed for impairment.

An impairment loss is recognised in profit or loss if:

Carrying amount of asset	>	Remaining amount of consideration expected to be received in exchange for the goods and services	less	Costs that have not yet been recognised

To summarise, the double-entry for accounting for contract costs and revenue is as follows.

As contract costs are incurred:

Debit	Contract cost account (a statement of financial position account)
Credit	Accounts payable / Bank

Revenue and costs to be recognised in the statement of profit or loss are accounted for as follows:

Debit	Contract cost account
Credit	Contract revenue (statement of profit or loss)
Debit	Contract costs (statement of profit or loss)
Credit	Contract cost account

The net result of these two entries is that the contract profit (or loss) is debited (credited for a loss) to the contract cost account.

As invoices are issued to the customer, the accounting for this is as follows:

Debit	Accounts receivable
Credit	Contract cost account

and as the customer pays, the normal accounting treatment is:

Debit	Bank
Credit	Accounts receivable

If the contract asset is impaired, the accounting for this is:

Debit	Impairment loss
Credit	Contract cost asset

Worked example 7.6: to show the accounting for contract revenue and costs

Bilbo Builders plc is involved in a construction contract which was started in 20X8. It is to be accounted for as a single performance obligation with revenue recognised over time. Bilbo Builders measures the progress towards the performance obligation using an input method. The following figures for the year ended 31 December 20X8 are relevant:

	20X8
	£
Total contract price	1,000,000
Costs incurred to 31 December	320,000
Estimated costs to completion	480,000
Invoices sent to customer	360,000
Value of work certified at 31 December *	390,000

* Value of work certified represents a valuer's assessment of the value of the contact completed by 31 December 20X8 at selling prices.

Assume all invoices have been paid by the customer.

Required:

Show how this contract would be accounted for in 20X8.

Step 1

Select the method of measuring progress towards the performance obligation for the contract.

An input method would imply Bilbo Builders will recognise revenues and costs on the proportion of costs incurred to date.

$$\text{Stage of completion} = \frac{320}{800} = 40\%$$

Step 2

Apply this percentage to total contract revenue and costs to calculate the cumulative revenue and costs that can be recognised in 20X8's statement of profit or loss.

		£000
Revenue	40% x £1,000,000	400
Cost of sales		320
Recognised profits less recognised losses		80

Step 3

Account for the statement of financial position balance.

The contract cost account will have had the following entries:

		£000	£000
Debit	Costs as incurred	320	
Debit	Contract revenue recognised in profit or loss	400	
Credit	Costs recognised in profit or loss		320
Credit	Invoices recorded as receivables		360

There is therefore a net debit balance of £40,000 on the account which represents Bilbo Builders' right to payment in exchange for goods or services that it has transferred to the customer.

Step 4

Check whether the asset is impaired.

The remaining amount of consideration expected to be received = Total contract price of £1,000,000 – Invoices sent to customer of £360,000 = £640,000

Costs not yet recognised = £480,000

The net of these two amounts is £160,000, which is greater than the contract asset. The contact asset is not impaired, and is therefore recognised at £40,000 on the statement of financial position.

7.7 Other aspects of contracts with customers

IFRS 15's aim to set out principles that will cover all types of revenue-raising contracts with customers is a challenging one. To assist preparers and users in its application, the standard is accompanied by extensive application guidance and many illustrative examples. Some of the more common issues covered by these are discussed and illustrated in the following sections.

7.7.1 Warranties

It is common for a company to provide a warranty in connection with the sale of a product. The nature of a warranty can vary significantly across industries and contracts. Some warranties provide a customer with assurance that the related product will function as the parties intended because it complies with agreed-upon specifications—in other words, that it is not faulty. Other warranties provide the customer with a service in addition to the assurance that the product complies with agreed-upon specifications. Some contracts give the customer the option to purchase a warranty separately.

If the warranty is a distinct service, because the company promises to provide the service to the customer in addition to the product that has the functionality described in the contract, the company should account for the promised warranty as a performance obligation and allocate a portion of the transaction price to that performance obligation. It may not be entirely clear whether a warranty is a separate performance obligation, and so the following factors should be considered in assessing whether a warranty provides a customer with a service in addition to the assurance that the product complies with agreed-upon specifications:

(a) Whether the warranty is required by law—if the entity is required by law to provide a warranty, the existence of that law indicates that the promised warranty is not a performance obligation because such requirements typically exist to protect customers from the risk of purchasing defective products.

(b) The length of the warranty coverage period—the longer the coverage period, the more likely it is that the promised warranty is a performance obligation because it is more likely to provide a service in addition to the assurance that the product complies with agreed-upon specifications.

(c) The nature of the tasks that the company promises to perform—if it is necessary for a company to perform specified tasks to provide the assurance that a product complies with agreed-upon specifications (for example, a return shipping service for a defective product), then those tasks do not give rise to a performance obligation.

When the warranty simply provides the customer with the assurance that the product will function as the parties intended, then there is no separate performance obligation, and the warranty will be accounted for as a provision (a type of liability) in accordance with IAS 37 *Provisions, Contingent Liabilities and Contingent Assets*. (See Chapter 15 for details of this.)

 Example of a warranty

As part of its sales prices, Dixit plc, which sells electrical equipment, includes, as standard, a year's warranty.

If this warranty is simply providing the customer with the assurance that the equipment will work as intended and is not faulty, then it is not a separate performance obligation. The revenue from the contract will be recognised at the sale price when control of the equipment purchased passes to the customer.

IAS 37 requires the company to account for the warranty as a provision. This will require Dixit plc to produce a reliable estimate of the costs of providing the warranty. Such costs will include replacements or repair work carried out under the warranty period. The company is likely to have past records which show the proportion of sales which result in warranty work and the costs of such work, so a reliable estimate could be made of the costs.

7.7.2 Options for the customer to buy additional goods or services

Where a contract gives the customer material rights to buy additional goods or services for free or at a discount, these rights are treated as a separate performance obligation. This is because the customer is in effect paying in advance for future goods or services. A typical example is a retailer granting its customer loyalty points on current purchases that can be redeemed against future purchases. The company would recognise the related revenue from the sale of the future goods and services at the point at which these goods or services were transferred to the customer, or when any option expired. Note that material rights means that the discount would have to be incremental (i.e. more than) the range of discounts typically given for these goods or services to that class of customer in that geographical area or market. If the future goods or services could be acquired at a price that reflects their stand-alone price, the option would not provide the customer with a material right. This situation would be viewed as merely a marketing offer, and accounted for at the time the customer exercised their option to purchase the additional goods and services.

If the contract is considered to give the customer material rights, then the company would set up a contract liability for that portion of the consideration which was allocated to the future sale performance obligation.

In some circumstances a customer may not exercise all of their contractual rights. IFRS 15 gives the term **breakage** to the unexercised rights. If a company expects a breakage amount, for example, because of the previous pattern of customer behaviour, this should be taken into account in calculating the revenue recognised and the contract liability.

 Worked example 7.7: to show how a contract with an option for future goods and breakage is accounted for

Priceright plc has entered into a contract with a customer whereby the customer pays £1,000 which gives it the right to acquire 100 units of a product which are priced at £10 each. Previous analysis of such contracts indicates that the customer will only claim 80 units before the expiry date of the offer. The customer initially acquires 30 units.

Required:

Show how this transaction would be accounted for by Priceright plc.

At the inception of the contract, the customer's payment of £1,000 is recorded as a contact liability (debit cash; credit contract liability)

The breakage amount (the rights unlikely to be exercised) is:

$20 \times £10 = £200$

When 30 units have been transferred to the customer, Priceright recognises revenue of:

$(30 \times £10) + (30/80 \times £200) = £375$ (Debit Contract liability; Credit Revenue)

(Alternatively, this can be calculated as $30/80 \times £1,000 = £375$)

The contract liability after the recognition of this revenue is:

$1,000 - 375 = £625$

7.7.3 Repurchase agreements

A **repurchase agreement** is a contract in which a company sells an asset and also promises or has the option to repurchase the asset. The repurchased asset may be the asset that was originally sold to the customer, an asset that is substantially the same as that asset, or another asset of which the asset that was originally sold is a component. There are three types of repurchase agreements:

(a) The company has an obligation to repurchase the asset (a forward contract);

(b) The company has a right to repurchase the asset (a **call option**); and

(c) The company has an obligation to repurchase the asset at the customer's request (a **put option**).

(IASB, IFRS 15 Application guidance, para. B65)

Forward contracts and call options mean that the company has not transferred control of the asset, because the customer is limited in its ability to direct the use of, and obtain substantially all of the remaining benefits from, the asset even though they may have physical possession. Therefore revenue cannot be recognised. The accounting treatment is as follows:

1. If the repurchase price is less than the original sales price, the transaction will be accounted for as a lease under IFRS 16 (see Chapter 15).

2. If the repurchase price is greater than the original sales price, the transaction is accounted for as a financing arrangement, and the liability created from the receipt of cash (debit cash; credit liability) is a financial liability (see Chapter 14).

A put option is treated as a lease if the customer has a significant economic incentive to exercise its right and the repurchase price is lower than the original selling price of the asset. If the customer does not have a significant economic incentive to exercise its right at a price that is lower than the original selling price of the asset, the company shall account for the agreement as if it were the sale of a product with a right of return. If the repurchase price exceeds the original sales price and is more than the expected market value of the asset, the option is accounted for as a financing arrangement.

IFRS 15 provides further application guidance and examples of other types of revenue-raising contracts with customers. For example, consignment arrangements (where a company delivers a product to another party such as a dealer or a distributor), bill and hold arrangements and licences of intellectual property. The main principle is that contracts involving goods will only result in the recognition of revenue when the other party has gained control of the product. For licences, revenue is recognised when the licence has been transferred to the customer, and it may be at a point in time or over time depending on the rights conveyed.

 Example of a sale and repurchase agreement

A whisky distiller holds inventories for long periods. It sells some of its inventories to a finance company, with a binding obligation to repurchase the inventories in the future at a price equal to the repayment of original amount plus interest.

How should the distiller account for this transaction?

This is a forward contract with the whisky distiller having an obligation to repurchase the inventories at a repurchase price which is greater than the sales price. (Effectively the company has a loan on which it will pay interest.) Thus, the accounting treatment is that no revenue is recognised on the transfer of goods and, instead, a financial liability is recorded and accounted for in accordance with IFRS 9:

Debit   Bank

Credit   Loan liability

The appropriate amount of interest is accrued over the period of the loan. The inventories held by the finance company remain in the whisky distiller's financial statements.

7.8 Disclosures

The disclosures required by IFRS 15 are more extensive and specific than the disclosures included in IASs 18 and 11. Although the feedback received by IASB from preparers and auditors of financial statements was that the requirements may result in voluminous disclosures and possibly useful information for a company's competitors, the users of financial statements were broadly supportive of the requirements. The aim of the disclosures is to help users understand the nature, timing, amount and uncertainty of revenue and cash flows arising from contracts with customers.

To achieve this, a company is required to disclose quantitative and qualitative information about the following:

(a) Revenue recognised from contracts with customers. This includes a breakdown of revenue into categories to show how revenue is affected by economic factors such as those arising from the type of good or service provided or the geographic region in which sales are made. The relationship between this disaggregation and revenue information provided for reportable segments in accordance with IFRS 8 *Operating Segments* would need to be made clear.

(b) Contract assets, liabilities and receivables balances. This includes reconciliations of opening and closing balances, explanations of significant changes in the balances, and impairment. From this information, users would be able to assess when the rights and obligations would convert to revenue.

(c) Performance obligations. This includes details of when the company typically satisfies its performance obligations, the amount of the transaction price that is allocated to the remaining performance obligations and when the remaining performance obligations are expected to be fulfilled.

(d) The significant estimates and judgements, and changes in judgements, made in applying the standard to those contracts. At a minimum this includes judgements relating to the timing of the satisfaction of performance obligations, and the transaction price and amounts allocated to performance obligations.

(e) Any assets recognised from the costs to obtain or fulfil a contract with a customer.

There are no practical company examples to illustrate the application of IFRS 15 yet available. However, given the long lead-time of its issue, revenue has received a significant focus in financial reporting, and companies, even when accounting for revenue under the previous standards, IASs 18 and 11, have provided reasonably extensive accounting policies. A couple of illustrations from companies in industries for which IFRS 15 will mean significant changes follow.

Financial reporting in practice 7.1 | Vodafone plc, 2015

Vodafone plc's revenue accounting policy in its 2015 financial statements is as follows:

Accounting policies: revenue

Revenue is recognised to the extent the Group has delivered goods or rendered services under an agreement, the amount of revenue can be measured reliably and it is probable that the economic benefits associated with the transaction will flow to the Group. Revenue is measured at the fair value of the consideration receivable, exclusive of sales taxes and discounts.

The Group principally obtains revenue from providing the following telecommunication services: access charges, airtime usage, messaging, interconnect fees, data services and information provision, connection fees and equipment sales. Products and services may be sold separately or in bundled packages.

Revenue for access charges, airtime usage and messaging by contract customers is recognised as services are performed, with unbilled revenue resulting from services already provided accrued at the end of each period and unearned revenue from services to be provided in future periods deferred. Revenue from the sale of prepaid credit is deferred until such time as the customer uses the airtime, or the credit expires.

Revenue from interconnect fees is recognised at the time the services are performed.

Revenue from data services and information provision is recognised when the Group has performed the related service and, depending on the nature of the service, is recognised either at the gross amount billed to the customer or the amount receivable by the Group as commission for facilitating the service.

Customer connection revenue is recognised together with the related equipment revenue to the extent that the aggregate equipment and connection revenue does not exceed the fair value of the equipment delivered to the customer. Any customer connection revenue not recognised together

(continued)

(continued)

with related equipment revenue is deferred and recognised over the period in which services are expected to be provided to the customer.

Revenue for device sales is recognised when the device is delivered to the end customer and the significant risks and rewards of ownership have transferred. For device sales made to intermediaries, revenue is recognised if the significant risks associated with the device are transferred to the intermediary and the intermediary has no general right to return the device to receive a refund. If the significant risks are not transferred, revenue recognition is deferred until sale of the device to an end customer by the intermediary or the expiry of any right of return.

In revenue arrangements including more than one deliverable, the arrangements are divided into separate units of accounting. Deliverables are considered separate units of accounting if the following two conditions are met: (i) the deliverable has value to the customer on a stand-alone basis; and (ii) there is evidence of the fair value of the item. The arrangement consideration is allocated to each separate unit of accounting based on its relative fair value. Revenue allocated to deliverables is restricted to the amount that is receivable without the delivery of additional goods or services. This restriction typically applies to revenue recognised for devices provided to customers, including handsets.

Commissions

Intermediaries are given cash incentives by the Group to connect new customers and upgrade existing customers.

For intermediaries who do not purchase products and services from the Group, such cash incentives are accounted for as an expense. Such cash incentives to other intermediaries are also accounted for as an expense if:

- the Group receives an identifiable benefit in exchange for the cash incentive that is separable from sales transactions to that intermediary; and
- the Group can reliably estimate the fair value of that benefit.

Cash incentives that do not meet these criteria are recognised as a reduction of the related revenue.

With the increased focus on areas where estimates and judgements have particularly been applied, Vodafone includes some revenue issues in these:

Revenue recognition

Arrangements with multiple deliverables

In revenue arrangements where more than one good or service is provided to the customer, customer consideration is allocated between the goods and services using relative fair value principles. The fair values determined for deliverables may impact the timing of the recognition of revenue. Determining the fair value of each deliverable can require complex estimates. The Group generally determines the fair value of individual elements based on prices at which the deliverable is regularly sold on a stand-alone basis after considering volume discounts where appropriate.

Gross versus net presentation

When the Group sells goods or services as a principal, income and payments to suppliers are reported on a gross basis in revenue and operating costs. If the Group sells goods or services as an agent, revenue and payments to suppliers are recorded in revenue on a net basis, representing the margin earned.

Whether the Group is considered to be the principal or an agent in the transaction depends on analysis by management of both the legal form and substance of the agreement between the Group and its business partners; such judgements impact the amount of reported revenue and operating expenses but do not impact reported assets, liabilities or cash flows.

Financial reporting in practice 7.2 | Carillion plc, 2014

The construction company, Carillion plc, includes accounting policies for both revenue and its construction contracts:

Revenue recognition

Revenue represents the fair value of consideration receivable, excluding sales-related taxation, for services supplied to external customers. It also includes the Group's proportion of work carried out under joint operations during the year. Revenue from the Group's principal business streams is recognised on the following basis:

- Revenue from service contracts is recognised by reference to services performed to date as a percentage of total services to be performed.
- Revenue from construction contracts is recognised in accordance with the Group's accounting policy on construction contracts.
- Revenue from the delivery of carbon-saving measures to utility companies and other related activities is recognised at the date of sale, except if services are to be provided over future periods, where the income is deferred and recognised over the relevant service period.
- Revenue from the installation of energy-efficiency measures such as central heating and other renewable technologies is recognised by reference to the number of energy efficiency measures installed.
- Revenue from the sale of a licence is recognised immediately where an agreement is, in substance, an outright sale. For an outright sale to have occurred, the Group must have signed a non-cancellable contract, have provided the licensee with the rights to freely exploit its contractual rights, have no significant ongoing delivery obligations to perform and have received a fee which is not expected to be subject to a material adjustment based on future activity. Where there is an element of contingent revenue to such an agreement, an assessment of the estimated fair value of this future revenue is considered. If this fair value is minimal then the risks and rewards of the agreement are considered to have been transferred in full and therefore the determinable sale income is recognised as revenue immediately, with any contingent revenue recognised as it is earned. Should the contingent revenue be assessed as significant, the sale income is recognised as revenue over a period consistent with the life of the technology or other appropriate measure.

Construction contracts

When the outcome of a construction contract can be estimated reliably, contract revenue and costs are recognised by reference to the degree of completion of each contract, as measured

(continued)

(continued)

by the proportion of total costs at the balance sheet date to the estimated total cost of the contract.

Insurance claims, incentive payments and variations arising from construction contracts are included in revenue where it is probable that they will be recovered and are capable of being reliably measured.

When the outcome of a construction contract cannot be estimated reliably, contract revenue is recognised to the extent of contract costs incurred where it is probable those costs will be recoverable.

The principal estimation technique used by the Group in attributing profit on contracts to a particular period is the preparation of forecasts on a contract by contract basis. These focus on revenues and costs to complete and enable an assessment to be made of the final out-turn of each contract. Consistent contract review procedures are in place in respect of contract forecasting.

When it is probable that total contract costs will exceed total contract revenue, the expected loss is recognised immediately. Contract costs are recognised as expenses in the period in which they are incurred.

Where costs incurred plus recognised profits less recognised losses exceed progress billings, the balance is shown as due from customers on construction contracts within trade and other receivables. Where progress billings exceed costs incurred plus recognised profits less recognised losses, the balance is shown as due to customers on construction contracts within trade and other payables.

Financial reporting in practice 7.3 — Sainsbury plc, 2015

In relation to its supplier rebate arrangements, Sainsbury plc includes the following accounting policy in its 2015 financial statements:

Supplier income

Supplier incentives, rebates and discounts, collectively known as 'supplier income', are recognised within cost of sales on an accruals basis as they are earned for each relevant supplier contract. The accrued value at the reporting date is included in trade receivables or trade payables, depending on the right of offset.

The most common types of supplier income, in order of magnitude, which Sainsbury's receives, are:

- Discounts and supplier incentives, representing the majority of all supplier income, linked to individual unit sales. The incentive is typically based on an agreed sum per item sold on promotion for a period.

- Fixed amounts agreed with suppliers primarily to support in-store activity including promotions, such as utilising specific space.

- Supplier rebates are the smallest proportion of supplier income. These are typically agreed on an annual basis, aligned with the financial year and are earned based on pre-agreed targets, mainly linked to sales.

7.9 Impact of IFRS 15 *Revenue from Contracts with Customers*

The issue of IFRS 15 was a landmark for the IASB. Years of work with the FASB had finally culminated in a financial reporting standard which aims to provide a robust and comprehensive approach to the recognition and measurement of revenue comparable for all reporting entities. It is difficult to be precise about how the standard will affect different companies and industries, but 'the devil is in the detail' and there is a lot of detail in this standard.

Many companies will probably find that the provisions contained in IFRS 15 will not fundamentally change how they currently recognise revenue. For instance, for the sale of goods under straightforward contracts, revenue recognition under IAS 18 depends on the transfer to the customer of the significant risks and rewards of ownership. IFRS 15 bases revenue recognition on the transfer of control, using the transfer of the risks and rewards as one indicator of this. In practice, the effect may be the same. Under IAS 18, revenue recognition from the provision of a service depended on the stage of completion of the contract. IFRS 15 uses the transfer of control model with revenue recognised over time. In practice, the effect may be similar, although there could be some major differences, for example relating to set-up activities. For construction contracts, under IAS 11 revenue recognition depended on the stage of completion of the contract activity. IFRS 15 bases revenue recognition on the transfer of control to the customer with revenue probably recognised over time. In practice, the effect may be the same, which is likely to please companies in the construction industry:

> The new standard allows complex projects with interdependent elements to continue to be accounted for under the stage of completion method. We therefore think it unlikely that it will have a significant effect on the recognition and measurement of revenue for most companies in the sector.
>
> (Stuart Leadhill, former financial controller of Balfour Beatty plc, (2015), cited in ICAEW, *By all Accounts*, January 2015)

Some companies, however, will find that the timing of the recognition of revenue and profits is very significantly affected. The recognition of revenue may be accelerated or deferred; it may now have to be recognised over time or at a point in time, which is different from past accounting practices. Industries which are likely to be particularly affected are telecommunications, aerospace and defence, and high-tech.

The standard contains much more detailed guidance than IASs 18 and 11, so most companies are likely to find that there is some aspect of their contracts which will have to be accounted for differently. For example, those companies offering warranties will have to review these carefully and consider whether the warranty represents a separate performance obligation, which will have the effect of deferring some revenue. Companies will have to consider whether changes to their accounting systems and processes are required to comply with the changed requirements. For all companies there will be increased disclosures, so this information will have to be available.

Changes to revenue recognition and measurement will also have a broader impact on other areas of companies' business. For example, companies' compensation and bonus plans, the availability of profits for distribution, compliance with loan covenants, the profile of tax payments and even marketing strategies may all be affected. The changes also bring associated costs.

It is not just the preparers, though, who are having to get ready for the implementation of IFRS 15. Given the importance of revenue as a key performance indicator (KPI) and its use in other key metrics, analysts and other users will all have to be educated in the changes it will bring. It will be necessary for companies to explain to their major investors the impact of implementing the standard so that there are no unforeseen surprises, and this will actually have to be disclosed in their financial statements prior to adoption. Auditors will also be working with their client companies.

With such a significant new financial reporting standard, the IASB is anticipating some teething problems. It is almost inevitable that as companies start to apply IFRS 15 in practice, ambiguities and possibly some flaws will emerge. The IASB together with the US's FASB has set up a Joint Transition Resource Group to support companies in implementing the standard and to examine any problems as and when they arise. The Group has already caused the issue of an Exposure Draft issued in July 2015 which provides some clarifications relating to how performance obligations in a contract should be identified, how to identify the principal and agent in a contract and how to determine whether a licence provides the customer with a right to access or a right to use a company's intellectual property.

Financial reporting in practice 7.4	Vodafone plc, 2015

Vodafone has included the following information in its 2015 financial statements to explain the likely impact of the Group implementing IFRS 15.

New accounting pronouncements to be adopted on or after 1 April 2016

IFRS 15 'Revenue from Contracts with Customers' was issued in May 2015; although it is effective for accounting periods beginning on or before 1 January 2017, the IASB has proposed to defer the mandatory adoption date by one year. IFRS 15 has not yet been adopted by the EU. IFRS 15 will have a material impact on the Group's reporting of revenue and costs as follows:

● IFRS 15 will require the Group to identify deliverables in contracts with customers that qualify as 'performance obligations'. The transaction price receivable from customers must be allocated between the Group's performance obligations under the contracts on a relative stand-alone selling price basis. Currently revenue allocated to deliverables is restricted to the amount that is receivable without the delivery of additional goods or services; this restriction will no longer be applied under IFRS 15. The primary impact on revenue reporting will be that when the Group sells subsidised devices together with airtime service agreements to customers, revenue allocated to equipment and recognised when control of the device passes to the customer will increase and revenue recognised as services are delivered will reduce.

- Under IFRS 15, certain incremental costs incurred in acquiring a contract with a customer will be deferred on the balance sheet and amortised as revenue is recognised under the related contract; this will generally lead to the later recognition of charges for some commissions payable to third party dealers and employees.

- Certain costs incurred in fulfilling customer contracts will be deferred on the balance sheet under IFRS 15 and recognised as related revenue is recognised under the contract. Such deferred costs are likely to relate to the provision of deliverables to customers that do not qualify as performance obligations and for which revenue is not recognised; currently such costs are generally expensed as incurred.

The Group is currently assessing the impact of these and other accounting changes that will arise under IFRS 15; however, the changes highlighted above are expected to have a material impact on the consolidated income statement and consolidated statement of financial position. It is expected that the Group will adopt IFRS 15 on 1 April 2018.

Summary of key points

Revenue is income which arises in the course of the ordinary activities of a business. It is a key headline figure for the majority of businesses, and used widely in users' interpretation and assessment of the business. The main issue in accounting for revenue is determining when it should be recognised.

In 2014 the IASB published a new, long-awaited financial reporting standard, IFRS 15 *Revenue from Contracts with Customers*, which was the result of a convergence project with the US FASB. This replaces both IAS 18 *Revenue* and IAS 11 *Construction Contracts*, which were increasingly considered inadequate for the multitude of revenue contracts and arrangements that exist in today's complex global business environment, and which had resulted in diverse and inconsistent revenue recognition practices existing. IFRS 15's implementation is not required until after 1 January 2018. IFRS 15 provides a comprehensive approach to revenue recognition and measurement for all companies across all industries. Inevitably for a standard with such ambitious aims, the application guidance and examples also provided are extensive.

IFRS 15 takes a five-step approach to revenue recognition and measurement. A contract with a customer firstly has to be identified. This must have commercial substance and it must be probable that consideration will be received from the customer. The second step is that the contract is broken down into performance obligations, which are separately identifiable transfers of goods and services. Careful judgement may be needed to determine how and the extent to which a contract should be 'unbundled'.

The third step is to determine the transaction (contract) price which is the total amount the seller expects to be entitled to as consideration. It may include non-cash consideration, and it may need to be adjusted for the time value of money if the customer is paying significantly in advance or in arrears of performance. Some contracts include variable consideration such as bonuses, penalties, variable discounts and contingent fees. The variable consideration should only be included in the estimated transaction price to the extent that it is highly probable there will not be a significant revenue reversal when the associated uncertainty is resolved.

The fourth step is to allocate the transaction price to the performance obligations. Typically the amount is allocated in proportion to the stand-alone selling prices of the goods or services underlying each performance obligation. There are special rules, which can be quite complex, relating to discounts and to variable consideration. Step four is potentially the most logistically challenging step as stand-alone selling prices will have to be determined or estimated for all performance obligations for all contracts a business has.

Step five requires revenue to be recognised when a performance obligation has been satisfied. IFRS 15 does not have separate rules for goods and services. Instead it includes guidance on whether the satisfaction is over time, when a suitable method for determining how revenue can be measured to reflect the performance of the selling company needs to be determined, or whether it is at a point in time.

IFRS 15 includes detailed guidance on a number of other topics, such as when and how contract costs are recognised, contract modifications, warranties and licences. The standard also specifies increased quantitative and narrative disclosures of the nature, timing, amount and uncertainty of revenue and cash flows arising from contracts with customers, with an emphasis on the risks associated with future revenues. These disclosure proposals have been broadly welcomed by users of financial statements.

Although companies have not yet adopted IFRS 15, many are in the process of analysing its impact, which for some may be substantial. For other companies it will not change their revenue recognition a great deal. However, relatively small differences between otherwise similar contracts can have a significant impact on the overall timing of the recognition of revenue, with the detail in contracts mattering. The standard's impact in practice is yet to be fully seen, but preparers and users all need to be aware of the changes that are expected.

 ## Further reading

IASB (International Accounting Standards Board) (2014a) IFRS 15 *Revenue from Contracts with Customers*. London: IASB.

 ## Bibliography

Barden, P. (2012) *Revenue Recognition: One Step Further Towards a Converged Standard*. London: ICAEW By All Accounts.

Barden, P. (2014) *Hot off the Press—the IASB's New Revenue Recognition Standard*. London: ICAEW By All Accounts.

Barden, P. (2015) *Five Steps to Danger*. London: ICAEW By All Accounts.

Carillion plc (2015) *Annual Report and Accounts 2014*. Wolverhampton: Carillion.

IASB (International Accounting Standards Board) (2004a) IAS 18 *Revenue*. London: IASB.

IASB (International Accounting Standards Board) (2004b) IAS 11 *Construction Contracts*. London: IASB.

IASB (International Accounting Standards Board) (2014a) IFRS 15 *Revenue from Contracts with Customers*. London: IASB.

IASB (International Accounting Standards Board) (2014b) IFRS 15 *Revenue from Contracts with Customers*. Illustrative examples. London: IASB.

IASB (International Accounting Standards Board) (2014c) IFRS 15 *Revenue from Contracts with Customers*. Basis for conclusions. London: IASB.

IASB (International Accounting Standards Board) (2014d) Project Summary and Feedback Statement: *Revenue from Contracts with Customers*. London: IASB.

IASB (International Accounting Standards Board) (2014e) IFRS 15 *Revenue from Contracts with Customers*. Application guidance. London: IASB.

IASB (International Accounting Standards Board) (2015) Exposure Draft ED/2015/6 *Clarifications to IFRS 15*. London: IASB.

ICAEW (Institute of Chartered Accountants in England and Wales) (2015a) *Revenue from Contracts with Customers IFRS Factsheet*. London: ICAEW.

ICAEW (Institute of Chartered Accountants in England and Wales) (2015b) *IFRS 15 Revenue from Contracts with Customers Webinar*. London: ICAEW. (Listened to 9 September 2014.)

J Sainsbury plc (2015) *Annual Report and Financial Statements 2015*. London: Sainsbury.

KPMG (2014) *IFRS and U.S. GAAP Issues in Depth: Revenue from Contracts with Customers*. London: KPMG.

McConnell, P. (2014) *Revenue Recognition: Finally, a Standard Approach for All*. London: IFRS Investor Perspectives.

O'Donovan, B. (2011) *Recognise the Impact of Revenue Changes*. Available at: http://www.accountancyage.com (accessed 10 October 2012).

PWC (PricewaterhouseCoopers) and FERF (Financial Executives Research Foundation) (2015) *The New Revenue Recognition Standard: Assessing Impact and Implementation*. London: PWC.

Vodafone Group plc (2015) *Annual Report, 2015*. Newbury: Vodafone.

 Questions

● **Quick test**

1   On 1 January 20X3 Precision Manufacturing plc enters into a contact with a customer to provide a product which it will deliver on 31 December 20X4. The customer makes a down payment of £25,000 on 1 January 20X3, and will be required to pay a further £50,000 on delivery. The customer would be required to pay £80,000 on 31 December 20X4 if it did not make the down payment.

In accordance with IFRS 15 *Revenue from Contracts with Customers,* how would this transaction be accounted for in the financial statements of Precision Manufacturing plc for the years ended 31 December 20X3 and 20X4?

2   Grier plc sells computer software to Amos Ltd on 1 April 20X7 for £180,000, a price which includes the provision of a support service for 2 years. Grier plc sells this software to other customers without the support service for £150,000 and has other service contracts providing similar support at a price of £25,000 per annum.

How should this transaction be accounted for in the statement of profit or loss of Grier plc for the year ended 31 December 20X7 and the statement of financial position at that date according to IFRS 15 *Revenue from Contracts with Customers*?

3   A company in the automotive sector builds:

(a) a standard vehicle, and

(b) a highly customised car for a specific customer.

Discuss how the revenue from the sale of these cars should be recognised in accordance with IFRS 15.

4   On 1 July 20X6 Pentose Construction plc entered into a contract to construct a bridge over a river. The agreed price of the bridge is £5 million and construction is expected to be completed on 30 June 20X8. Pentose incurred the following costs in relation to this contract by 31 December 20X6:

	£000
Materials, labour and overheads	1,200
Specialist plant acquired 1 July 20X6	800

The value of the work certified at 31 December 20X6 has been agreed at £2.2 million and the estimated costs to complete (excluding plant depreciation) are £1 million. The specialist plant will have no residual value at the end of the contract and should be depreciated on a monthly basis.

Progress billings to the customer by 31 December 20X6 total £570,000. Pentose recognises revenues on such contracts using an input method.

Required:

Discuss the accounting treatment of this contract in accordance with IFRS 15 *Revenue from Contracts with Customers*, and show the resulting figures which would appear in the statement of profit or loss for the financial year ended 31 December 20X6 and statement of financial position at this date.

●● Develop your understanding

5   Explain whether, in the following situations, the company is acting as a principal or an agent.

(a) Company A negotiates with major airlines to purchase tickets at reduced rates compared with the price of tickets sold directly by the airlines to the public. The company agrees to buy a specific number of tickets and must pay for those tickets regardless of whether it is able to resell them. The reduced rate paid by the company for each ticket purchased is negotiated and agreed in advance.

Company A determines the prices at which the airline tickets will be sold to its customers. It sells the tickets and collects the consideration from customers when the tickets are purchased.

The company also assists the customers in resolving complaints with the service provided by airlines. However, each airline is responsible for fulfilling obligations associated with the ticket, including remedies to a customer for dissatisfaction with the service.

(b) Company B sells vouchers that entitle customers to future meals at specified restaurants. These vouchers are sold by the company and the sales price of the voucher provides the customer with a significant discount when compared with the normal selling prices of the meals (for example, a customer pays £50 for a voucher that entitles the customer to a meal at a restaurant that would otherwise cost £100). Company B does not purchase vouchers in advance; instead, it purchases vouchers only as they are requested by the customers. It sells the vouchers through its website and the vouchers are non-refundable.

Company B and the restaurants jointly determine the prices at which the vouchers will be sold to customers. Company B is entitled to 30% of the voucher price when it sells the voucher.

Company B also assists the customers in resolving complaints about the meals and has a buyer satisfaction programme. However, the restaurant is responsible for fulfilling obligations associated with the voucher, including remedies to a customer for dissatisfaction with the service.

6 A software developer enters into a contract with a customer to transfer a software licence, perform an installation service and provide unspecified software updates and technical support (online and telephone) for a 2-year period. The company sells the licence, installation service and technical support separately. As part of the installation service, the software is to be substantially customised to enable it to interface with other customised software applications used by the customer. The customised installation service can be provided by other companies.

Required:

Explain what performance obligations would be identified in this contract according to IFRS 15 *Revenue from Contracts with Customers*.

7 Triad plc has a 31 December year end. The company sells goods to a customer on 1 January 20X7 on the understanding that the customer will pay £5,000 immediately and will then pay two further instalments of £5,000 each on 1 January 20X8 and 1 January 20X9.

Required:

Applying the provisions of IFRS 15 *Revenue from Contracts with Customers*, and assuming an effective interest rate of 10% p.a., calculate the amount of revenue that should be recognised in the years 20X7, 20X8 and 20X9, and the resulting accounting treatment of this transaction for the years ended 31 December 20X7, 20X8 and 20X9.

8 Hafford plc, a manufacturer, sells a product to a customer together with a warranty. The warranty provides assurance that the product complies with agreed-upon specifications and will operate as promised for one year from the date of purchase. The contract also provides the customer with the right to receive up to 20 hours of training services on how to operate the product at no additional cost.

Required:

Discuss how Hafford plc should account for this transaction according to IFRS 15 *Revenue from Contracts with Customers*.

9 On 1 July 20X5, Morse plc sells goods worth £800,000 to Lewis plc for £500,000. The sales agreement states that Morse plc is entitled to repurchase the goods on 30 June 20X8 for £500,000 plus compound interest calculated at 10% per annum and it is expected that repurchase will, in fact, occur.

Required:

Discuss how Morse plc should account for this transaction on 1 July 20X5 according to IFRS 15 *Revenue from Contracts with Customers*.

10   On 1 January 20X1 Cleaner Solutions plc enters into a 3-year contract to clean a customer's offices on a weekly basis. The customer promises to pay £100,000 per year. The stand-alone selling price of the services at 1 January 20X1 is £100,000 per year. At 31 December 20X2, the contract is modified and the fee for the third year is reduced to £80,000. In addition, the customer agrees to extend the contract for three additional years for £200,000 payable in three equal annual instalments of £66,667 on 1 January 20X4, 20X5 and 20X6. Assume the stand-alone selling price of the services at 1 January 20X3 is £80,000 per year.

Required:

In accordance with IFRS 15 *Revenue from Contracts with Customers*, calculate and explain how much revenue would be recognised in the statement of profit or loss of Cleaner Solutions plc for the years 20X1–20X6.

11   In November 20X2, Crow plc, a company with a December year end, contracts with a customer to refurbish a three-storey building and install new elevators for total price of £5 million. The promised refurbishment service, including the installation of elevators, is considered a single performance obligation satisfied over time. Total expected costs are £4 million, including £1.5 million for the elevators.

Crow plc uses an input method based on costs incurred to measure its progress towards complete satisfaction of the performance obligation. The elevators are delivered to the site in December 20X2, although they will not be installed until June 20X3. At 31 December 20X2 other costs incurred, excluding the elevators, are £500,000.

Required:

In accordance with IFRS 15, show how this contract would be accounted for in the statement of profit or loss of Crow plc for the year ended 31 December 20X2.

12   Xian plc enters into a service contract to manage a customer's information technology data centre for five years. The contract is renewable for subsequent one-year periods. The average customer term is seven years. Xian pays an employee a £10,000 sales commission upon the customer signing the contract. Before providing the services, Xian plc designs and builds a technology platform for its own internal use that interfaces with the customer's systems. That platform is not transferred to the customer, but will be used to deliver services to the customer.

The initial costs incurred to set up the technology platform are as follows:

	£
Design services	40,000
Hardware	120,000
Software	90,000
Migration and testing of data centre	100,000
Total costs	350,000

In addition to the initial costs to set up the technology platform, Xian plc also assigns two employees who are primarily responsible for providing the service to the customer. Their combined annual salaries amount to £38,000.

Required:

Discuss how the above costs would be accounted for in accordance with international financial reporting standards.

13 Priestly Bakers plc operates its retail outlets on a franchise basis. On 1 January 20X0 a new outlet was opened with a six-year franchise arrangement. The franchisee paid a fee of £600,000 for the equipment necessary to operate a franchise store. In addition, the contract requires the franchisee to pay a fee of 5% of its monthly sales commencing on 1 January 20X0 to cover marketing, managerial and other support services provided by Priestly Bakers during the franchise period.

Required:

Discuss how this transaction would be accounted for in Priestly Baker plc's financial statements for the year ended 31 December 20X0 in accordance with IFRS 15 *Revenue from Contracts with Customers*.

14 Rightstore plc is a retailer that operates a customer loyalty programme. For every pound that a customer spends in any of the company's stores, they receive one point. Once a customer has accrued 1,000 points they are entitled to buy a free product to the value of £100 from any of Rightstore's department stores.

During August 20X8, the total sales price of items sold to loyalty card holders is £6,500. Prior experience has shown that 10% of customers do not redeem their points before they expire.

Required:

Show how Rightstore plc should account for the cash received of £6,500 in the month of August 20X8 according to IFRS 15 *Revenue from Contracts with Customers*.

●●● Take it further

15 Triangle plc is in the process of preparing its draft financial statements for the year to 31 March 20X2.

On 1 April 20X1 Triangle sold maturing inventory that had a carrying value of £3 million (at cost) to Factorall, a finance house, for £5 million. Its estimated market value at this date was in excess of £5 million. The inventory will not be ready for sale until March 20X3 and will remain on Triangle's premises until this date.

The sale contract includes a clause allowing Triangle to repurchase the inventory at any time up to 31 March 20X5 at a price of £5 million plus interest of 10% p.a. compounded from 1 April 20X1. The inventory will incur storage costs until maturity. The cost of storage for the current year of £300,000 has been included in trade receivables (in the name of Factorall). If Triangle chooses not to repurchase the inventory, Factorall will pay the accumulated storage costs on 31 March 20X5.

The proceeds of the sale have been debited to the bank and the sale has been included in Triangle's sales revenue.

Required:

Discuss how this item should be treated in Triangle's financial statements for the year ended 31 March 20X2 in accordance with IFRS 15 *Revenue from Contracts with Customers*. Your answer should quantify amounts where possible.

16 On 1 April 20X3, Bright Solutions plc, a company which provides industrial cleaning services, entered into an 18-month contract with a new customer. The contract price was agreed at £525,000 and total contract costs were estimated to be £400,000.

At 31 December 20X3 amounts relating to the contract were as follows.

	£
Certified sales value of work completed	367,500
Contract costs incurred	300,000
Invoices raised to customer	325,000
Progress payments received	287,500
Estimate of additional costs to complete contract	150,000

Required:

(a) Explain, with calculations where appropriate, how the amounts in respect of this contract should be presented in the statement of profit or loss and statement of financial position of Bright Solutions plc for the year to 31 December 20X3 if the stage of completion of the contract is calculated using:

(i)   An input method

(ii) An output method.

(b) Explain briefly why the two accounting policies result in different amounts in the 20X3 financial statements.

17 Wickhams plc specialises in bridge construction and has two contracts in progress at its year end, 31 March 20X8. Contract details extracted from the company's costing records at 31 March 20X8 were as follows:

	Stour Bridge £000	Avon Bridge £000
Total contract selling price	7,000	4,000
Work certified to date	4,200	300
Costs to date	3,500	600
Estimated costs to completion	1,500	3,150
Progress billings	5,000	200

Construction on the Stour Bridge started in April 20X6. Work certified to date at 31 March 20X7 was £2,800,000 and revenue and costs were recognised for the year ended 31 March 20X7. No changes to the total estimated contract selling price or costs occurred between the start of the construction and 31 March 20X8.

However, on 11 April 20X8, the customer's surveyor notified Wickhams plc of a fault in one of the bridge supports constructed during a severe frost in January 20X8. This will require remedial work in May 20X8 at an estimated additional cost of £400,000.

Construction on the Avon Bridge started in January 20X8.

Wickhams plc uses an output method based on the value of work certified at each year end to measure the progress towards satisfaction of the performance obligation.

Required:

For both contracts calculate the amounts to be included in the statement of profit or loss and statement of financial position of Wickhams plc for the year ended 31 March 20X8 in accordance with IFRS 15 *Revenue from Contracts with Customers.*

18 Just before the end of the financial year, a customer requested Murray plc to delay the delivery of 500,000 units of products until early the following year because, at the time, the customer did not have enough space to store the goods. The customer, however, indicated to Murray that it could still issue the invoice as if the goods had been delivered at the date specified in the purchase order and he agreed to settle the amount within 90 days of the invoice date under the usual credit terms granted to him. Murray plc invoiced the customer before the year ended 31 December 20X8.

Pinkerton plc operates a logistics company. Customers place their orders with the company for airfreight or surface transportation services required. Pinkerton, in turn, places its order with the necessary carriers. Pinkerton can cancel its order with the carrier if its customers cancel their orders with the company. Pinkerton does not bear the risk of loss or other responsibility during the transportation process. Pinkerton can normally earn a margin of 10% on airfreight and 5% on surface transportation. The company's customers usually pay the gross amount to Pinkerton directly, while it pays the gross amount to the carriers.

Required:

Determine how the transactions of Murray plc and Pinkerton plc should be accounted for in accordance with IFRS 15 *Revenue from Contracts with Customers* in terms of the timing of recognition and the amounts to be included in their statements of profit or loss.

 Visit the Online Resource Centre for solutions to all these end of chapter questions plus visual walkthrough solutions. You can test your understanding with extra questions and answers, explore additional case studies based on real companies, take a guided tour through a company report and much more. Go to the Online Resource Centre at **www.oxfordtextbooks.co.uk/orc/maynard2e/**

8

Earnings per share

> **Introduction**

Earnings per share (EPS) has been introduced in Chapter 5 as one of the key ratios that equity investors will use to assess the performance of a company and the return to them. As a component of the price earnings ratio, EPS is considered so important that it is required to be disclosed on the face of the statement of comprehensive income. For these reasons it is crucial that there is consistency in its calculation from company to company; it therefore, has its own international accounting standard (IAS), IAS 33 *Earnings per Share*.

The main focus of this standard is the denominator of the EPS ratio, the number of shares used in its calculation, particularly where there are changes in equity share capital during the accounting period. Diluted EPS, which takes into account the future reduction or dilution of EPS from potential equity shares which are outstanding, is also dealt with by IAS 33, to ensure consistency in its calculation and related disclosures.

After studying this chapter you will be able to:

- explain the significance of basic and diluted EPS as a measure of financial performance
- calculate basic and diluted EPS for a variety of situations, including changes in share capital, and where share options and convertible financial instruments exist
- understand the presentation and disclosure requirements for EPS.

- ❑ Definition of basic EPS.
- ❑ The importance of EPS and its significance in relation to the price earnings ratio.
- ❑ The need for, and aims of, IAS 33 *Earnings per Share*.
- ❑ Definition and criticisms of earnings used in EPS.
- ❑ Alternative earnings figures.
- ❑ Different types of preference shares.
- ❑ The calculation of basic EPS where there are changes in share capital from issues and repurchases of shares at market price, bonus issues and rights issues.
- ❑ What diluted EPS is.
- ❑ The calculation of diluted EPS where share options and warrants, convertible financial instruments, and contingently issuable shares exist.
- ❑ Dilutive and anti-dilutive potential shares and the effect on the calculation of diluted EPS.
- ❑ Presentation of EPS on the face of the statement of profit or loss.
- ❑ Disclosures required.
- ❑ Proposed changes to IAS 33 *Earnings per Share*.

8.1 Earnings per share (EPS)

8.1.1 Definition

EPS is one of a number of measures that equity investors use to assess the performance of a company. It provides a measure of the earnings that are attributable (or available) to the equity (ordinary) shareholders on a per share basis. **Basic EPS** is given by the ratio:

$$\frac{\text{Profit/(Loss) attributable to ordinary equity holders}}{\text{Number of equity shares outstanding during the period}}$$

The profit or loss attributable to equity holders includes *all* items of income and expense recognised in an accounting period, and is after tax and after any preference dividends. It can be viewed as what is left for the equity shareholders after all other investors have had what is due to them. If there is a profit remaining, a company can use this to pay a dividend to its equity shareholders or retain for reinvestment. Thus, EPS is a measure of the wealth-creating abilities of a company.

8.1.2 Why is EPS important?

 Example of importance of EPS

Often, investors will use underlying sales growth as an indicator of future share price performance. But a group of analysts at RBC Capital Markets have thrown the robustness of this measure into doubt. Instead, the best correlation they can find is that between earnings per share (EPS) growth and share price performance.

Investors should look at cash conversion and growth in free cash flow, but ultimately EPS growth and share price performance have the closest historical correlation, says RBC.

'Investors aren't stupid. Surely the reason that EPS has survived so long as arguably the main measure of company performance and basis of shares' valuation (by way of P/E ratios) is because in a lot of cases it does a pretty good job despite its manifest imperfections. It doesn't seem a bad rule of thumb to assume that EPS upgrades and downgrades are likely to have corresponding effects on share price performance.'

Extract from Mann, H., Investing: It's as Easy as EPS
Interactive Investor (II) article, 31 July 2015

EPS is the denominator in the price earnings (PE) ratio:

$$\frac{\text{Market price per share}}{\text{Earnings per share}}$$

which, for listed companies, is published daily in the financial press. As discussed in Chapter 5, the PE ratio is a measure of the market's confidence in a company as it compares the price investors are required to pay to acquire an equity share in the company to the current earnings per share. Confidence can arise for a variety of reasons; examples include a company's past successes, or the fact that it has launched a new product or service, or has entered into new markets, or has completed a successful takeover. Confidence is not measurable from merely looking at the current market price of shares or even from EPS on its own.

 Example of the use of the PE ratio

The following information is available for companies A and B, which both have £1 equity share capital:

	Company A	Company B
EPS	13.5p	9.2p
Market price per share	£1.14	£1.05

Both EPS and the market price per share are higher for company A, which may lead to a conclusion that company A has performed better and whose shares are more in demand compared to company B. However, a calculation of the PE ratio for both companies reveals:

	Company A	Company B
PE ratio	$\dfrac{114}{13.5} = 8.4$	$\dfrac{105}{9.2} = 11.4$

The PE ratio for company B is considerably higher, which means that investors are willing to pay 11.4 times the current earnings in this company compared with only 8.4 times to invest in company A. This indicates that the markets, in general, consider that company B's future prospects and earnings potential are better than company A—possibly for the sorts of reasons given earlier.

Of course, the PE ratio is not necessarily a true or accurate measure as market confidence, which affects share prices, can be misplaced.

Financial reporting in practice 8.1 — The dot.com boom

In the late 1990s a new group of Internet-based companies were founded, which were commonly referred to as dot.com companies. Initially, these companies provided their services for free and therefore had little revenue as their focus was on growing market share. The promise was that they could build enough brand awareness to charge profitable rates for their services later. It was all about 'getting big fast'.

A combination of a variety of factors at that time, including apparently realistic plans that the companies would eventually be profitable, low interest rates, the wide availability of capital from venture capitalists and the pure novelty of such companies in the developing internet age, created an environment in which many investors were willing to overlook traditional financial measures to assess companies, such as the PE ratio, in favour of confidence in technological advancements. Share prices in the dot.com companies rose and rose.

However, by 1999–2000 Western economies' growth began to slow down, interest rates began to rise and share prices on stock markets started to fall. The investors in the dot.com companies soon realised that it was a speculative bubble. The dot.com boom was over, and many of the companies ceased trading as they had no profits and they ran out of capital.

8.1.3 The need for an accounting standard

A reliable and consistent calculation of EPS for companies is vital to ensure that there is some degree of reliability and comparability between companies' PE ratios. IAS 33 *Earnings per Share* was therefore issued with the aims of:

- prescribing the principles for the calculation and presentation of EPS
- improving comparisons of performance between different companies in the same reporting period and between different reporting periods for the same company.

The standard recognises that EPS has limitations because of the different accounting policies that may be used for determining 'earnings'. Its focus is therefore on the determination of the denominator of the ratio to ensure consistency in this. Thus, it sets out how this should be calculated where there are changes in share capital in an accounting period.

Potential future issues of shares through, for example, share option schemes or convertible financial instruments, can have a significant effect on EPS. The standard addresses how the impact of such issues should be shown, as it sets out how **diluted EPS** should be calculated. This is discussed and illustrated in section 8.4.

The significance of the EPS ratio is emphasised by the requirement for the disclosure of basic and diluted EPS on the face of the statement of profit or loss. IAS 33 prescribes the disclosures required to enable users to fully understand the calculations of the ratios.

8.2 Earnings

8.2.1 Definition

The numerator of the EPS ratio is defined as profit or loss attributable to equity holders. It includes all income and expenses recognised in the financial year and is after tax. For a single company that produces a separate statement of profit or loss, it will be the bottom line of this statement (profit or loss for the year) less any preference dividends, and will therefore include all items which may be labelled as exceptional and results from discontinued operations (see Chapter 6 for further details of these items), but will exclude any items included in other comprehensive income in the statement of comprehensive income.

For a group producing consolidated financial statements earnings excludes the non-controlling interests' share of the profit or loss.

> ❶ **Reminder** *A consolidated statement of profit or loss combines the profit and loss items of a parent company and its subsidiary companies, irrespective of whether the parent holds all the equity shares. If there are other investors in a subsidiary company who hold (usually) less than 50% of the equity share capital, they are termed the non-controlling interest. Their share of the profits or losses of the subsidiary is shown on the face of the consolidated statement of profit or loss.*

Note: this is explained further in Chapter 17 dealing with consolidated financial statements.

 Example of earnings

An extract from Beta Holdings plc's statement of profit or loss is given as follows. The company has both equity share capital and irredeemable cumulative preference share capital.

Extract from consolidated statement of profit or loss

	£m
Profit from operations	65
Finance costs	(18)
Profit before taxation	47
Tax expense	(14)
Profit for the year	33
Attributable to:	
Shareholders of the parent	29
Non-controlling interests	4
	33

The statement of changes in equity includes:

		£m
Dividends:	Irredeemable preference	2
	Equity	6
		8

Earnings for the EPS calculation = £29m − £2m = £27 million.

8.2.2 Other definitions of earnings

As noted in section 8.1.3, earnings as a comparative performance measure is limited owing to different accounting policies being used in different companies. Thus, the question remains whether EPS is truly comparable from company to company. In addition, and as discussed in Chapter 6, earnings can be subject to some manipulation by companies, and there may be pressure for companies to maintain a steady upward trend in their EPS ratio or to avoid large fluctuations from year to year. However, the days are gone when earnings in the EPS calculation could exclude one-off or unusual items (which may have been referred to as extraordinary items). Basic EPS has to include all items recognised in profit and loss. Changes in fair value measurements from one year end to the next, and unexpected losses or write-offs, can lead to volatility in profits and losses and these will be included in this ratio.

Many companies therefore include in their financial statements additional EPS figures using alternative measures of profit. For example, some companies will present an additional EPS figure based on continuing operations only.

Financial reporting in practice 8.2 — Tesco plc, 2014

Tesco plc, the UK's largest supermarket group, disclosed discontinued operations in its 2014 financial statements, as discussed in Chapter 6, and the company disclosed an additional EPS from its continuing operations as shown.

Income statement (extract)

	Note	2014 £m	2013 £m
Profit for the year from continuing operations		1,912	1,528
Discontinued operations			
Loss for the year from discontinued operations	7	(942)	(1,504)
Profit for the year		970	24
Attributable to:			
Owners of the parent		974	28
Non-controlling interests		(4)	(4)
		970	24
Earnings per share from continuing and discontinued operations			
Basic	9	12.07p	0.35p
Earnings per share from continuing operations			
Basic	9	23.75p	19.07p

Other companies choose to show an additional EPS figure using a different definition of earnings.

Financial reporting in practice 8.3 — J Sainsbury plc, 2014

The following extract from Sainsbury's income statement for the 52 weeks ended 15 March 2014 shows the company analysing its profit before tax into underlying profit from its core supermarket activities and other, less comparable (year-to-year), items. The company has shown basic EPS based on the final profit for the financial year of £716 million (2013: £602 million) and a further basic EPS based on this underlying profit figure as a measure of earnings.

It can be seen that basic EPS has increased by 18% from 2013 to 2014 as the profit for the financial year has; however, this has been significantly affected by the increase in the one-off items. The underlying basic EPS is much more comparable over these two years and a better measure of the company's core business performance.

	Note	£m	£m
Profit before taxation		**898**	772
Analysed as:			
Underlying profit before tax		**798**	758
Profit on sale of properties	3	**52**	66
Investment property fair value movements	3	**–**	(10)
Retailing financing fair value movements	3	**(8)**	(10)
IAS 19 Revised pension financing charge	3	**(23)**	(16)
Defined benefit pension scheme expenses	3	**(7)**	(7)
Acquisition adjustments	3	**18**	–
One-off items	3	**68**	(9)
		898	772
Income tax expense	8	**(182)**	(170)
Profit for the financial year		**716**	602
Earnings per share	9	**pence**	pence
Basic		**37.7**	32.0
Underlying basic		**32.8**	30.8

In its five-year data, Sainsbury's includes its underlying profit and underlying basic EPS, rather than profit and EPS, including all items of income and expense.

Five year financial record	2014	2013	2012	2011	2010
Underlying profit before tax	**798**	758	712	665	610
Increase on previous year (%)	**5.3**	6.5	7.1	9.0	17.5
Earnings per share					
Underlying basic (pence)	**32.8**	30.8	28.1	26.5	23.9
Increase on previous year (%)	**6.5**	9.6	6.0	10.9	12.7

8.2.3 Preference dividends

It is necessary to include a word of caution about preference dividends. There are different types of preference shares and different conditions under which they are issued, and it may not be a question of merely deducting a dividend that has been paid and included in the statement of changes in equity in order to calculate earnings for EPS. IAS 33 specifies that the amounts deducted in relation to preference dividends should be 'the after-tax amounts of preference dividends, differences arising on the settlement of preference shares, and other similar effects of preference shares classified as equity'. The treatments of these differences on the earnings figure to be used in EPS are shown in Table 8.1.

Note also that some redeemable preference shares under *IAS 32 Financial Instruments: Presentation* are treated either in full or in part as a liability. Any dividend on these shares is treated in full, or in part, as a finance charge, and will already be deducted from profit before tax. (This is discussed in more detail in Chapter 14.)

Table 8.1 Treatment of different types of preference share or issue conditions on earnings

Type of preference share/ issue condition	Treatment in earnings for EPS
Non-cumulative	Dividends declared in respect of the period
Cumulative	Dividend required for the period irrespective of whether they have been declared. Deduction does not include dividends paid or declared in respect of previous periods
Increasing rate*	Original issue discount or premium is amortised to retained earnings—this is treated as a dividend for EPS
Repurchased by company	Excess of fair value of consideration over carrying amount deducted
Repurchased by company	Excess of carrying amount over fair value of consideration is added to earnings
Convertible—early conversion	Excess of fair value of equity shares issued or other consideration over fair value of equity shares under original conversion terms deducted

* Dividend is not fixed because either it is initially lower to compensate the company for shares issued at a discount or it is higher later to compensate the investor for shares issued at a premium.

8.3 Changes in shares

8.3.1 Definition of EPS denominator

Basic EPS requires earnings to be divided by the weighted average number of equity shares outstanding during the period. This is to take account of changes in equity share capital during the period arising from shares issued and bought back. A time-weighting factor is applied, and although IAS 33 specifies that this should be measured in days, a reasonable approximation, such as months, can be used.

8.3.2 Issue and repurchase of shares at fair value

If the number of shares increases through some form of issue, the immediate effect on the EPS ratio will be a decrease. However, for an issue of shares at fair (market) value, the resources of the company are increased, and thus it would be expected that profits (earnings) will also increase over time. So for this form of share issue at fair value, a straightforward weighted average number of equity shares is calculated and used as the denominator in EPS as it is considered the EPS will not be reduced unfairly.

The same argument applies, but in reverse, for a company that repurchases its shares at fair value.

 Worked example 8.1: to calculate EPS where there is an issue and repurchase at market price

Cox plc has post-tax profits for the calendar years as follows:

20X1	£510,000
20X2	£650,000

The company's share capital of £1,000,000 consists of 2,000,000 50p equity shares in issue at 1 January 20X1. The company makes the following share transactions in 20X2:

31 May 20X2	Issues 800,000 further shares at market value
1 December 20X2	Purchases 250,000 of its own shares at market value

Required:

Calculate the EPS for disclosure in Cox plc's 20X1 and 20X2 financial statements.

$$20X1 \; EPS = \frac{Profit \; after \; tax}{No \; of \; shares \; in \; issue}$$
$$= \frac{£510,000}{2,000,000}$$
$$= 25.5p$$

20X2 weighted average no. of shares

	Shares in issue	Time factor	
1 Jan–31 May	2,000,000	5/12	833,333
1 Jun–30 Nov	2,800,000	6/12	1,400,000
1 Dec–31 Dec	2,550,000	1/12	212,500
Weighted average			2,445,833

$$20X2 \; EPS = \frac{£650,000}{2,445,833}$$
$$= 26.6p$$

8.3.3 Bonus issue of shares

When a company makes a bonus issue of shares (sometimes called a capitalisation issue), there is no change to the resources of a company. In this case the company is giving away shares to its shareholders perhaps in lieu of a dividend, or to increase an undercapitalised company, or to widen the number of potential shareholders. The impact on EPS will be an automatic reduction, which seems inappropriate given that bonus issues are often made by successful companies.

IAS 33 addresses this by requiring that the weighted average number of equity shares outstanding before the issue be adjusted for the proportionate change in the number of shares outstanding, as if the bonus issue had happened at the beginning of the earliest period presented. In other words, EPS is calculated for the both the financial year in which the bonus issue was made and all other comparative periods presented in the financial statements using the increased number of shares.

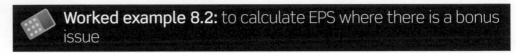

Worked example 8.2: to calculate EPS where there is a bonus issue

Pippin plc has post-tax profits for the calendar year as follows:

20X1	£180,000
20X2	£225,000

There are 600,000 equity shares outstanding at 1 January 20X1. On 1 October 20X2 the company makes a 2 for 1 bonus issue.

Required:

Calculate the EPS for disclosure in Pippin plc's 20X1 and 20X2 financial statements.

20X1 financial statements

$$20\text{X1 EPS} = \frac{£180,000}{600,000}$$
$$= 30\text{p}$$

20X2 financial statements

For 20X2 EPS, there is no weighted average calculation. The number of shares outstanding is adjusted to assume that the bonus issue had occurred at beginning of the year. As 20X1 is presented as a comparative in the 20X2 financial statements, it is also assumed that the bonus issue had occurred at the start of this year.

A 2 for 1 bonus issue (2 shares are issued for every 1 share held) means that 1,200,000 shares will be issued.

$$20\text{X2 EPS} = \frac{£225,000}{600,000 + 1,200,000}$$
$$= 12.5\text{p}$$

20X1 comparative EPS adjusted to:

$$\frac{£180,000}{1,800,000} \quad \text{OR} \quad \frac{£180,000}{600,000 \times 3^*}$$
$$= 10\text{p}$$

*The number of shares has increased by a factor of $3 = [(2 + 1)/1]$.

Without the adjustment of the 20X1 comparative EPS it would have appeared there had been a large drop in EPS from 30p in 20X1 to 12.5p in 20X2. With the adjustment the comparison makes more sense (EPS is more fairly stated): 10p in 20X1 compared with 12.5p in 20X2.

8.3.4 Rights issue of shares

A rights issue of shares is an offer of shares to existing shareholders in some proportion to their holding at a reduced price. It is the most common method by which companies raise capital from a share issue. It can be thought of as combining the two elements—an issue of shares at full market price plus a bonus issue.

 Example of a rights issue

A company has 300,000 equity shares in issue. It makes a 2 for 3 rights issue to its existing shareholders, which is fully subscribed. The current market price per share is £4 and the shares are offered at £2.50 under the rights issue.

The company will issue 200,000 shares and (ignoring issue costs) will raise 200,000 × £2.50 = £500,000. This may be considered equivalent to an issue of £500,000/£4 = 125,000 shares at full market price, plus a bonus issue of 200,000 − 125,000 = 75,000 shares.

The calculation of the weighted average number of shares outstanding therefore contains elements of the previous two EPS calculations—a time-weighting factor and an adjustment to the number of shares outstanding before the rights issue for the bonus element. This latter adjustment is achieved through the calculation and use of a 'bonus fraction', which is defined in IAS 33 as:

$$\frac{\text{Fair value per share immediately before the exercise of rights}}{\text{Theoretical ex-rights fair value per share}}$$

The theoretical ex-rights fair value per share is a weighted combined price of the shares immediately after the rights issues has happened. (Note: ex-rights means after the rights issue.) It is calculated by adding the aggregate market value of the shares immediately before the exercise of the rights to the proceeds from the rights issue and dividing by the number of shares outstanding after the exercise of the rights.

 Worked example 8.3: to calculate EPS where there is a rights issue

Braeburn plc has post-tax profits for the calendar years as follows:

20X1	£30,000
20X2	£38,000
20X3	£45,000

The company has 500,000 shares outstanding before it makes a 1 for 4 rights issue. The exercise price is £5 and the last date to exercise rights is 1 March 20X2. The fair value of one equity share immediately before exercise is £11.

Required:

Calculate the EPS for disclosure in the company's 20X1, 20X2 and 20X3 financial statements.

20X1 EPS

$$= \frac{£30,000}{500,000}$$
$$= 6p$$

20X2 EPS

Theoretical ex-rights fair value per share $= \frac{4 \times £11 + 1 \times £5}{4+1} = £9.80$

Bonus fraction = 11/9.8 (better not to round at this stage)

No. of shares issued in 1 for 4 rights issue =125,000

Weighted average number of shares including effects of 'bonus' element of rights issue:

	Shares in issue		Bonus fraction *	Time factor	
1 Jan–28 Feb	500,000	×	11/9.8	2/12	93,537
1 Mar–31 Dec	625,000			10/12	520,833
Weighted average					614,370

* Note that it is only the period prior to the rights issue that is multiplied by the bonus fraction.

$$20X2 \text{ EPS} = \frac{£38,000}{614,370}$$
$$= 6.2p$$

The 20X1 EPS requires restating as there is a bonus element involved. This is achieved by multiplying the weighted average number of shares used in the 20X1 EPS calculation by the bonus fraction:

$$\text{Restated 20X1 EPS} = \frac{\text{Earnings}}{\text{Restated no. of shares}}$$
$$= \frac{£30,000}{500,000 \times 11/9.8}$$
$$= 5.3p$$

$$20X3 \text{ EPS} = \frac{£45,000}{625,000}$$
$$= 7.2p$$

Summary

Disclosed in financial statements of year	EPS	Comparative
20X1	6p	Not available
20X2	6.2p	5.3p
20X3	7.2p	6.2p

8.4 Diluted earnings per share

8.4.1 What is diluted EPS?

Most listed companies will have a variety of financial instruments funding them, including convertible preference shares and convertible debentures and bonds. In addition, many employee remuneration packages (particularly those of directors and senior employees) will offer share options and warrants. All of these arrangements mean that at some date in the future additional equity shares may be issued either in lieu of paying off a debt or at a price which is fixed under the particular arrangement and which will be different from the market price at this date. (Note: the incentive for employee share options is for the option price to be lower than market at the date they are exercised.)

For existing equity shareholders reviewing EPS, this may not be good news, as the impact will be a reduction in or a dilution of EPS. However, this information is considered important for the investors and so diluted EPS is calculated and disclosed. It may be thought of as a 'worst-case' scenario EPS which assumes all convertible instruments are converted, and all options and warrants exercised to give the maximum dilution of EPS. Unlike basic EPS, diluted EPS is not an exact figure based on actual events. It is a theoretical figure that accounts for future events which may or may not happen, or only partially happen.

Its calculation takes the numerator and denominator of the current basic EPS as the starting point and makes adjustments as follows.

Earnings	Adjustments made for the effect, including the tax effect, of any conversion of preference shares, debentures and bonds into shares. Preference dividends and interest will no longer be payable, so should be added back to earnings.
Number of shares	Incorporates an assumed number of shares from the conversions of dilutive potential equity shares from debt instruments, and the exercise of options and warrants.

8.4.2 Share options and warrants

Share options and warrants are financial instruments that give the holder the entitlement to purchase shares at some point in the future at a predetermined price. Some resource will flow to the company when they are exercised, but the dilutive effect of these arrangements on EPS is where the exercise price is lower than the market price (fair value). A notional calculation of the number of shares issued at no consideration needs to be made. The market price is taken as the average market price during the year. For share options and other share-based payment arrangements to which IFRS 2 *Share-based Payment* applies, the actual issue price should include the fair value of any goods or services to be supplied to the company in the future by the employee under the option arrangement. (See Chapter 16 for further details of share-based payment arrangements.)

Worked example 8.4: to show the calculation of basic and diluted EPS where there are share options

Seville plc made post-tax profits of £1,200,000 in 20X1. The number of equity shares in issue during the year was 5 million, with the average market value per share being £4.00.

The company has share option schemes in existence, with 1 million equity shares issuable in 20X2 at an exercise price of £3.00 per share. There are no other goods or services to be supplied to the company under the option schemes.

Required:

Calculate the basic and fully diluted EPS figures for disclosure in Seville plc's 20X1 financial statements.

	Earnings £	Shares (million)	Per share
Post-tax profit	1,200,000		
Weighted average shares in issue		5	
Basic EPS (£1.2m/5m)			24p
No. of shares under option *		1	
No. of shares issued at fair value (1m × £3.00/£4.00)*		(0.75)	
	1,200,000	5.25	
Diluted EPS (£1.2m/5.25m)			22.9p

* In other words, 1m – 0.75m = 0.25m shares are treated as if they are to be issued for no consideration. These are added to the number of shares already issued for the diluted EPS calculation.

Where more than one basis of conversion exists, for example where share options are offered with their exercise at different dates and prices, the calculation assumes the most advantageous conversion rate or exercise price from the standpoint of the holder of the potential equity shares.

8.4.3 Convertible instruments

As discussed in Chapter 14, where convertible debt is issued, IAS 32 *Financial Instruments: Presentation* requires that the proceeds received are accounted for in part as a liability and in part as equity. Remember also that whatever the interest rate of the actual debt instrument is, an effective interest rate is used for the recognition of interest payable in the statement of profit or loss.

Both earnings and the number of shares are adjusted in the diluted EPS calculation.

Worked example 8.5: to show the calculation of basic and diluted EPS where there are convertible bonds

Gala plc has 10,000 equity shares in issue and has made post-tax profits of £1,000. The company has convertible 6% bonds of £1,000, with each block of £10 bonds convertible into 15 equity shares.

When the convertible bonds were issued originally, the proceeds were split between the equity component and the debt component, as required by IAS 32 *Financial Instruments: Presentation*. The liability component carried in the statement of financial position at the start of the period is £800 and the effective interest rate is 8%.

Required:

Assuming a corporation tax rate of 25%, calculate the basic and fully diluted EPS figures for disclosure in Gala plc's financial statements.

$$\text{Basic EPS} = \frac{£1,000}{10,000}$$
$$= 10p$$

For diluted EPS adjust both earnings and the number of shares:

	£
Earnings	1,000
Add back interest saved on conversion (net of tax) 8% × £800 × (100 − 25)%	48
	1,048

No. of equity shares resulting from conversion: 1,500.

$$\text{Diluted EPS} = \frac{£1,048}{10,000+1,500}$$
$$= 9.1p$$

8.4.4 Contingently issuable shares

Contingently issuable equity shares are shares issuable for little, or no, cash or other consideration upon the satisfaction of specified conditions given in a contingent share agreement. There may be one condition, or a combination of conditions, that have to be fulfilled and these may include a certain level of profit that has to be reached, or a certain level for the future market price of shares or some other event, for example the opening of a specific number of retail stores.

If the conditions are satisfied then the shares will be issued and included in both the basic and diluted EPS calculations. For diluted EPS, the shares are treated as if they had been issued from the beginning of the accounting period (or the date of the contingent share agreement, if later). If the conditions are not met, the number of contingently issuable shares included in the diluted EPS calculation is based on the number of shares that would be issuable if the end of the accounting period were the end of the contingency period.

Worked example 8.6: to show the calculation of basic and diluted EPS where there are contingently issuable shares

Discovery plc has 1 million equity shares outstanding at 1 January 20X1. There were no options, warrants or convertible instruments outstanding during the period. An agreement relating to a recent business combination provides for the issue of additional equity shares based on the following conditions:

- 5,000 additional equity shares for each new retail site opened during 20X1
- 1,000 additional equity shares for each £1,000 of consolidated profit in excess of £2 million for the year ended 31 December 20X1.

During the year Discovery opened two new retail sites on 1 May 20X1 and 1 September 20X1. The consolidated profit attributable to equity holders of the parent company for the year ended 31 December 20X1 was £2.9 million.

Required:

Calculate basic and diluted EPS for disclosure in Discovery plc's 20X1 financial statements.

5,000 shares will be issued on both 1 May and 1 September for the new retail stores opened.

Although the year's profit exceeds £2 million, it is not certain that this will be achieved until the very end of the year. These contingent shares cannot, therefore, be issued before the end of the year.

Basic EPS

The weighted average calculation for the number of shares outstanding during the year is as follows:

	Shares outstanding	Time period	
1 January–30 April	1,000,000	4/12	333,333
1 May–31 August	1,005,000	4/12	335,000
1 September–31 December	1,010,000	4/12	336,667
Weighted average			1,005,000

$$\text{Basic EPS} = \frac{£2,900,000}{1,005,000} = £2.89$$

Diluted EPS

The number of shares added to the initial 1 million assumes that the end of the financial year is the end of the contingency period. A weighted average calculation for the number of shares is therefore not required.

No. of shares issued for opening of the two retail stores = 2 × 5,000 = 10,000

No. of shares issued for achieving profit target = (900,000/1000) × 1,000 = 900,000

No. of shares to include in diluted EPS = 1,000,000 + 10,000 + 900,000 = 1,910,000

$$\text{Diluted EPS} = \frac{£2,900,000}{1,910,000} = £1.52$$

8.4.5 Dilutive and antidilutive potential equity shares

Diluted EPS must always be lower than basic EPS (or, if the company has made a loss, the diluted loss per share will be higher) as it includes the effects of all dilutive potential equity shares. However, a conversion of a financial instrument or exercise of an option may not automatically dilute EPS, in which case this future event will not be included in the calculation. The potential equity shares in this situation are referred to as antidilutive. In order to determine whether potential equity shares are dilutive or antidilutive a company should use profit or loss from continuing operations attributable to the shareholders of the parent company as a control number. In other words, this is used as the earnings to determine whether the shares are dilutive or antidilutive.

 Example of reason for the control number

A company's statement of profit or loss shows the following (all figures are net of tax):

	£000
Profit from continuing operations	4,800
Loss from discontinued operations	(7,200)
Loss for the year	(2,400)

The company has 2,000,000 equity shares in issue and 400,000 potential equity shares outstanding.

$$\text{Basic loss per share} = \frac{£(2,400)}{2,000} = (120)p$$

Assuming the 400,000 potential shares outstanding have no effect on profit and loss, a calculation for whether these are dilutive or antidilutive using the total loss for the year would show:

$$\text{Diluted loss per share} = \frac{£(2,400)}{2,400} = (100)p$$

As the loss per share has been reduced, it appears that the potential shares outstanding are antidilutive and it would follow that no diluted EPS would be disclosed.

However, the control number is profit from continuing operations, and so the correct calculations and comparison should be as follows:

$$\text{EPS (based on profit from continuing operations)} = \frac{£4,800}{2,000} = 240p$$

$$\text{Diluted EPS (based on profit from continuing operations)} = \frac{£4,800}{2,400} = 200p$$

On these calculations EPS has been reduced by the inclusion of the potential shares outstanding, thus they are dilutive and a diluted EPS would be disclosed.

Companies may have any number of arrangements, including share options and convertible instruments. In determining whether the potential equity shares are dilutive or antidilutive, each arrangement that gives rise to potential shares must be considered separately rather than taking them all together. The order in which the arrangements are considered may affect whether they are dilutive. As the objective is to maximise the dilution of basic EPS, the order will take the most dilutive to the least dilutive. This is achieved by calculating the 'earnings per incremental share' and then taking the lowest 'earnings per incremental share', and continuing in size order to the highest 'earnings per incremental share'.

Worked example 8.7: to show the order in which to include dilutive arrangements

Delaware plc has the following financial data for 20X3:

	£
Profit from continuing operations	16,400,000
Loss from discontinued operations	(4,000,000)
Profit for the year	12,400,000
Preference dividends	6,400,000
No. of equity shares outstanding	2,000,000
Average market price of one equity share during the year	£75

The company has outstanding share options and convertible instruments as follows:

Share options	100,000 with exercise price of £60.
Convertible preference shares	800,000 shares with a par value of £100 entitled to a cumulative dividend of £8 per share. Each preference share is convertible to two equity shares.
5% convertible bonds	Nominal amount £100 million. Each £1,000 bond is convertible to 20 equity shares. There is no amortisation of premium or discount affecting the determination of the interest expense.

Assume the tax rate is 40%.

Required:

Calculate basic and diluted EPS for disclosure in Delaware plc's 20X3 financial statements.

Increase in earnings attributable to equity holders on conversion of potential equity shares

	Increase in earnings	Increase in number of equity shares	Earnings per incremental share
	£		£
Share options			
Increase in earnings	Nil		

Incremental shares issued for no consideration 100,000 × (£75 − £60)/£75		20,000	Nil

Convertible preference shares

Increase in earnings

800,000 × £8	6,400,000		

Incremental shares

2 × 800,000		1,600,000	4.00

5% convertible bonds

Increase in earnings

£100,000,000 × 5% × (1−0.4)	3,000,000		

Incremental shares

100,000 × 20		2,000,000	1.50

The order in which to include the dilutive instruments is therefore:

1 Share options

2 5% convertible bonds

3 Convertible preference shares.

Calculation of diluted EPS

Note: this is based on profit from continuing operations as shown in the previous example.

	Profit £	No. of equity shares	Per share £
Profit from continuing operations	16,400,000		
Preference dividends	(6,400,000)		
Profit attributable to equity shareholders	10,000,000	2,000,000	5.00
Share options	–	20,000	
	10,000,000	2,020,000	4.95 Dilutive
5% convertible bonds	3,000,000	2,000,000	
	13,000,000	4,020,000	3.23 Dilutive
Convertible preference shares	6,400,000	1,600,000	
	19,400,000	5,620,000	3.45 Anti-dilutive

Because diluted EPS is increased when taking the convertible preference shares into account, these shares are antidilutive and are ignored in the calculation of diluted EPS.

EPS figures disclosed are as follows (see section 8.5 for full requirements of disclosures):

	Basic EPS £	Diluted EPS £
Profit from continuing operations attributable to equity holders	5.00	3.23
Loss from discontinued operations attributable to equity holders	(2.00)[1]	(0.99)[1]
Profit attributable to equity holders	3.00[2]	2.24[2]
[1] Calculated as: $\dfrac{\text{Loss from discontinued operations}}{\text{No. of shares}}$	$\dfrac{£(4,000,000)}{2,000,000}$	$\dfrac{£(4,000,000)}{4,020,000}$
[2] Calculated as: $\dfrac{\text{Profit}}{\text{No. of shares}}$	$\dfrac{£(6,000,000)}{2,000,000}$	$\dfrac{£(9,000,000)}{4,020,000}$

8.5 Disclosure of EPS

Various EPS figures must be presented on the face of the statement of comprehensive income (or the statement of profit or loss, if presented separately) for each class of equity shares that has a different right to share in the profit or loss for the accounting period. If the earnings figure is negative, a loss per share is disclosed. The disclosures are:

1 Basic and diluted EPS for profit or loss from continuing operations and for profit and loss for the period attributable to the equity holders of the parent company. Basic and diluted EPS must be presented with equal prominence.

2 Basic and diluted amounts per share for any discontinued operations—these may be presented in the notes.

Companies may choose to present EPS figures using alternative definitions of earnings, as seen in the earlier Sainsbury example. These figures must be calculated using the weighted average number of equity shares, as specified by IAS 33, and must include the related diluted EPS.

In the notes to the financial statements, the following disclosures are required:

(a) The amounts used as the numerators in calculating basic and diluted earnings per share, and a reconciliation of those amounts to profit or loss attributable to the parent company for the period. The reconciliation shall include the individual effect of each class of instruments that affects earnings per share.

(b) The weighted average number of equity shares used as the denominator in calculating basic and diluted earnings per share, and a reconciliation of these denominators to each other. The reconciliation shall include the individual effect of each class of instruments that affects earnings per share.

(c) Instruments (including contingently issuable shares) that could potentially dilute basic earnings per share in the future, but were not included in the calculation of diluted earnings per share because they are antidilutive for the periods presented.

(d) A description of equity share transactions or potential equity share transactions that occur after the reporting period and that would have changed significantly the number of equity shares or potential equity shares outstanding at the end of the period if those transactions had occurred before the end of the reporting period. For example, issues of shares for cash, or the conversion or exercise of potential equity shares into equity shares.

If a company has presented alternative EPS figures on the face of the statement of comprehensive income (or statement of profit or loss), additional disclosures are required to indicate the basis on which the numerator(s) is (are) determined, including whether amounts per share are before tax or after tax. If an earnings figure is used that is not reported as a line item in the statement of comprehensive income, the company is required to show a reconciliation between the figure used and a line item that is reported in the statement of comprehensive income.

Financial reporting in practice 8.4 — Marks and Spencer plc, 2014

Like Sainsbury's, in its 2014 financial statements Marks and Spencer plc presents alternative EPS figures based on what it defines as its underlying profit. It therefore shows four EPS figures on its income statement—basic EPS, diluted EPS, underlying basic EPS and underlying diluted EPS. The disclosure note showing the various reconciliations is as follows.

8 Earnings per share

The calculation of earnings per ordinary share is based on earnings after tax and the weighted average number of ordinary shares in issue during the year.

The underlying earnings per share figures have also been calculated based on earnings before items that are one-off in nature, significant and are not considered normal operating costs of the underlying business (see note 5). These have been calculated to allow the shareholders to gain an understanding of the underlying trading performance of the Group.

For diluted earnings per share, the weighted average number of ordinary shares in issue is adjusted to assume conversion of all dilutive potential ordinary shares. The Group has only one class of dilutive potential ordinary shares being those share options granted to employees where the exercise price is less than the average market price of the Company's ordinary shares during the year.

Details of the underlying earnings per share are set out below:

	2014 £m	2013 £m
Profit attributable to owners of the parent	**524.8**	453.5
Add/(less) (net of tax):		
Profit on property disposals	(76.3)	–
UK and Ireland one-off pension credit	(23.3)	–

(continued)

(continued)

Interest income on tax repayment net of fees	**(2.5)**	–
Restructuring costs	**62.5**	7.1
International store review	**17.3**	–
IAS 39 Fair value movement of embedded derivative	**2.8**	(4.7)
Strategic programme costs	**1.6**	5.0
Fair value movement of the Puttable Callable Reset medium-term notes	**-**	57.3
Reduction in M&S Bank income for the impact of the mis-selling provision	**39.1**	11.8
Non-underlying adjustment to tax charge in respect of prior periods	**(26.0)**	(20.4)
Underlying profit attributable to owners of the parent	**520.0**	509.6

	Million	Million
Weighted average number of ordinary shares in issue	**1,615.0**	1,599.7
Potentially dilutive share options under Group's share option schemes	**14.1**	10.6
Weighted average number of diluted ordinary shares	**1,629.1**	1,610.3

	Pence	Pence
Basic earnings per share	**32.5**	28.3
Diluted earnings per share	**32.2**	28.2
Underlying basic earnings per share	**32.2**	31.9
Underlying diluted earnings per share	**31.9**	31.6

Financial reporting in practice 8.5   Ahold, 2014

This illustration shows the disclosures where there are discontinued operations.

Ahold is an international retailing group based in the Netherlands which operates mainly supermarket businesses in Europe and the USA. Its 2014 income statement showed discontinued operations which comprised the sale of some business operations and provisions for litigation in relation to previous disposals. The company disclosed basic and diluted EPS based on total net profit and continuing operations, and showed amounts per share from discontinued operations in the disclosure note.

Extracts from the company's income statement and the EPS disclosure note are as follows.

Consolidated income statement

€ million	Note	2014	2013
Income before income taxes		**1,015**	948
Income taxes	10	**(248)**	(153)
Share in income of joint ventures	14	**24**	10

		2014	2013
Income from continuing operations		**791**	805
Income (loss) from discontinued operations	5	**(197)**	1,732
Net income		**594**	2,537

Earnings per share	29		
Net income per share attributable to common shareholders			
Basic		**0.68**	2.48
Diluted		**0.67**	2.39
Income from continuing operations per share attributable to common shareholders			
Basic		**0.90**	0.79
Diluted		**0.88**	0.77
Weighted average number of common shares outstanding (in millions)			
Basic		**879**	1,021
Diluted		**924**	1,072

29 Earnings per share

	2014	2013
Earnings (€ million)		
Net income attributable to common shareholders for the purposes of basic earnings per share	**594**	2,537
Effect of dilutive potential common shares—reversal of preferred dividends from earnings	**22**	25
Net income attributable to common shareholders for the purposes of diluted earnings per share	**616**	2,562
Number of shares (in millions)		
Weighted average number of common shares for the purposes of basic earnings per share	**879**	1,021
Effect of dilutive potential common shares:		
Share options and conditional shares	**11**	13
Cumulative preferred financing shares	**34**	38
Weighted average number of common shares for the purposes of diluted earnings per share	**924**	1,072

€ million	2014	2013
Income from continuing operations, attributable to common shareholders for the purposes of basic earnings per share	**791**	805

(continued)

(continued)

Effect of dilutive potential common shares—reversal of preferred dividends from earnings	**22**	25
Income from continuing operations, attributable to common shareholders for the purposes of diluted earnings per share	**813**	830

Basic and diluted income per share from discontinued operations attributable to common shareholders amounted to negative €0.22 and negative €0.21 respectively (2013: €1.69 basic and €1.62 diluted). They are based on the loss from discontinued operations attributable to common shareholders of €197 million (2013: income €1,732 million) and the denominators detailed above.

8.6 Future changes to IAS 33

As part of the convergence project between the International Accounting Standards Board (IASB) and the Financial Accounting Standards Board (FASB), an exposure draft of proposed amendments to IAS 33 was published by the IASB in August 2008 in order to achieve convergence of the denominator in the EPS calculation, and to clarify and simplify the calculation of EPS where more complex financial instruments were involved. The key proposals were:

To achieve convergence:

1   A principle should be established to determine which instruments are included in the calculation of basic EPS. The weighted average number of equity shares should include only those instruments that give (or are deemed to give) their holder the right to share currently in profit or loss of the period, and if equity shares issuable for little, or no, cash or other consideration or convertible instruments do not meet this condition, they will not be included in basic EPS.

2   Contracts where a company is purchasing its own equity shares for cash or other financial assets through, for example, gross physically settled written put options, forward purchase contracts and mandatorily redeemable equity shares, should be treated as if the entity had already repurchased the shares.

3   The calculation of diluted EPS for participating instruments and two-class equity shares should include a test to determine whether a convertible financial instrument would have a more dilutive effect if conversion is assumed. The diluted EPS calculation should assume the more dilutive treatment.

Clarification and simplification of the calculation of EPS:

1   Profits or losses from changes in fair value for financial instruments measured at fair value through profit or loss should remain in the numerator of diluted EPS, as changes in fair value reflect the economic effect of such instruments on current equity holders for the period.

2   The calculation of the dilutive effect of options, warrants and their equivalents should use the year-end share price, rather than the average for the period.

3   For the calculation of diluted EPS an entity should assume that equity shares relating to forward contracts to sell an entity's own shares are sold and the effect is dilutive.

4   No adjustments should be required in calculating diluted EPS where there are contracts to repurchase an entity's own shares and contracts that may be settled in equity shares or cash owing to classification requirements of these items as financial instruments.

Responses to the exposure draft have been received by the IASB, but more urgent projects have taken precedence and currently the IASB states that this project will resume at some future date.

Summary of key points

Earnings per share is a key ratio used by equity investors as a measure of the performance and, to some extent, the wealth-creating abilities of a company. It calculates the profit or loss available to the equity shareholders on a per share basis. Its significance is emphasised by the requirement for companies to disclose basic and diluted EPS on the face of their statements of comprehensive income.

Consistency in its calculation from company to company is particularly important, as EPS is used in the price earnings ratio, which is published daily in the financial press and which provides some indication of markets' confidence in a company. Although published profit or loss available to the equity shareholders may be questioned as a truly comparable performance measure, IAS 33 *Earnings per Share* was issued to ensure the calculation of EPS has some degree of consistency. The accounting standard concentrates mainly on how the denominator is to be calculated where there are changes in the number of shares outstanding during the financial year from different types of share issue and repurchases of shares.

Companies also have many different types of arrangements involving share options and warrants, and convertible financial instruments, all of which mean that at some point in the future the number of equity shares will increase and thus dilute EPS. Given that investors are using EPS trends to help in forecasting, the impact of these arrangements on EPS is important, and thus diluted EPS, a theoretical figure, is required to be calculated and disclosed. IAS 33 gives guidance on the calculation of diluted EPS for many different types of these arrangements, and this chapter has provided examples of those that are within the scope of the textbook.

Further reading

IASB (International Accounting Standards Board) (2005) IAS 33 *Earnings per Share*. London: IASB.

Bibliography

Ahold (2015) *Annual Report, 2014*. Amsterdam: Ahold.

IASB (International Accounting Standards Board) (2005) IAS 33 *Earnings per Share*. London: IASB.

J Sainsbury plc (2014) *Annual Report and Financial Statements, 2014*. London: J Sainsbury.

Mann, H. (2015) Investing: It's as Easy as EPS. Available from http://www.iii.co.uk/articles/258511/investing%3A-its-easy-eps (accessed 5 August 2016)

Marks and Spencer plc (2014) *Annual Report and Financial Statements, 2014*. London: Marks and Spencer.

Tesco plc (2014) *Annual Report and Financial Statements, 2014*. London: Tesco

 Questions

● Quick test

1   On 1 January 20X8 a company with no subsidiaries had 3 million equity shares of £1 each in issue. On 1 May 20X8 the company made an issue of 1 million shares at full market price of £2 per share. On 30 September 20X9 the company made a 2 for 5 bonus issue.

The post-tax earnings of the company for the years ended 31 December 20X8 and 2009 were £750,000 and £1,200,000 respectively.

Calculate the EPS for the years ended 31 December 20X8 and 20X9, showing (where possible) comparatives for reporting purposes.

2   You are given the following information relating to Santos plc:

	£000	£000
Profit before tax		4,131
Tax		(1,629)
Profit after tax		2,502
Non-controlling interests		(90)
		2,412
Retained profits at 1 January 20X3		5,268
		7,680
Dividends: preference	45	
equity	669	(714)
Retained profits at 31 December 20X3		6,966

(i) From 1 January 20X2 until 31 March 20X3 the issued share capital of Santos plc was as follows:

Equity 25p shares	£3,000,000
5% irredeemable preference shares of £1 each	£900,000

(ii) On 1 April 20X3 Santos made a 1 for 4 rights issue of equity shares at £1. The market price of an equity share of Santos on the last day of quotation cum rights was £1.50.

(iii) The earnings per share for the year ended 31 December 20X2 had been calculated at 15.0 pence.

In accordance with the requirements of IAS 33, you are required to:

(a) Calculate the basic EPS of Santos plc for the year ended 31 December 20X3

(b) Calculate the adjusted basic EPS of Santos plc for the year ended 31 December 20X2

(c) Show how the results of your calculations, together with any necessary notes, would be disclosed in the financial statements of Santos plc.

●● Develop your understanding

3   Discuss why earnings per share, as a measure of financial performance, is required to be disclosed on the face of the statement of profit or loss and whether it is possible to distil the performance of a complex organisation into a single measure, such as earnings per share.

4   At 1 January 20X7 and 20X8 the issued share capital of Coombe plc comprised:

Equity share capital (20p shares)	£1,500,000
4% irredeemable preference share capital (£1 shares)	£600,000

On 1 September 20X8 Coombe made a rights issue of three new equity shares at a price of 90p per share for every two shares held. The offer was fully subscribed. The market price of Coombe's equity shares immediately prior to the offer was £1.65 each.

At the start of 20X9 the company offered a 1 for 3 bonus issues of shares to its equity shareholders in lieu of the 20X8 final equity dividend; 40% of shareholders accepted this offer on 31 March 20X9.

Coombe's profits after tax for the years ended 31 December were as follows:

20X7: £3,460,000

20X8: £2,300,000

20X9: £3,970,000.

Preference dividends were paid at the end of each quarter.

Required:

Calculate Coombe plc's earnings per share for disclosure in its financial statements for the years ended 31 December 20X8 and 20X9, including comparative figures.

5   Extracts from the statements of profit or loss of Longstone plc for the years ended 31 December 20X4 and 20X5 are set out as follows:

	20X4	20X5
	£000	£000
Profit from operations	4,030	4,890
Finance charges	(730)	(760)
Profit before tax	3,300	4,130
Taxation	(1,150)	(1,360)
Profit after tax	2,150	2,770

On 1 January 20X4 the issued share capital of the company was £4,600,000 in 6% irredeemable preference shares of £1 each and £4,140,000 in equity shares of 50p each.

On 1 October 20X4 the company made a rights issue of 50p equity shares in the proportion of 1 for every 5 shares held, at a price of £0.60. The market price for the shares on the last day of quotation cum rights was £0.90 per share.

On 1 May 20X5 the company raised £2,750,000 from an issue of equity shares at full market value of £1.10 per share.

The company has paid the full preference dividend each year.

Basic earnings per share for 20X3 was 20.5p.

Required:

Calculate the earnings per share figures for disclosure in Longstone plc's financial statements for the years ended 31 December 20X4 and 20X5, including comparative figures.

6   On 1 January 20X1 a company had in issue 6 million £1 equity shares and £7.5 million of 7% convertible redeemable loan stock, on which the conversion terms were:

On 31 December 20X4	40 equity shares for each £125 of loan stock
On 31 December 20X5	40 equity shares for each £130 of loan stock
On 31 December 20X6	40 equity shares for each £135 of loan stock

The liability component of the convertible redeemable loan stock was carried in the statement of financial position on 1 January 20X1 at £7.2 million and the effective interest rate 8.5%. The company pays tax at the rate of 20%.

The profit attributable to the equity holders for the year ended 31 December 20X1 was £1.5 million.

Required:

Calculate the basic and diluted EPS for the year ended 31 December 20X1.

●●● Take it further

7   EPS is generally regarded as a key accounting ratio for use by investors and others. Like all accounting ratios, however, it has its limitations.

Critically examine why EPS is regarded as so important and discuss its limitations for investors who are comparing the performance of different companies.

8   Berkeley plc, a company with no subsidiaries, has issued share capital at 31 December 20X6 of £2.4 million made up of £1.8 million in equity share capital and £0.6 million in 6% £1 irredeemable preference shares. The nominal value of its equity shares is 20p. The company's profit after tax for the year ended 31 December 20X6 was £846,000. There were no changes in share capital during 20X6.

From 20X5, the company has had an executive share option scheme which gives the company's directors the option to purchase a total of 500,000 equity shares for £1.50 each. These options are exercisable in 20Y0.

On 1 March 20X7 Berkeley raised £1.11 million from an issue of equity shares at full market value of £1.85 per share. During 20X7 the average market price of the equity shares was £2.10 per share. No further shares were issued in accordance with the executive share option scheme. The post-tax profit for 20X7 was £960,000.

On 1 May 20X8 Berkeley made a rights issue of one new equity share for every four equity shares held at £1.80 per share. The cum rights price on the last day of quotation cum rights was £2.50 per share.

The average market price per equity share in 20X8 was £2.60 per share and the post-tax profit was £1.25 million.

Required:

Calculate Berkeley plc's basic and diluted earnings per share figures for the years ended 31 December 20X7 and 20X8, including the comparative figures for both years.

9   The following financial statement extracts relate to Silver plc for the year ended 31 December 20X6.

Share capital at 31 December 20X6:

Issued and fully paid equity shares of £1 each	12,500,000
7% convertible cumulative preference shares of £1 each	1,000,000

The net profit after tax for the year 20X6 was £4,820,000.

The 7% convertible cumulative preference shares were issued on 1 January 20X4. There were no preference dividends in arrears in 20X5; however, preference dividends were not declared in the year 20X6. The cumulative preference shares are convertible into equity shares in the ratio of 20 cumulative preference shares to 3 equity shares. No shares have been converted in 20X6.

On 1 August 20X6, 3.6 million equity shares were issued at £4.50 each.

The company has a share option scheme whereby certain employees can subscribe for company shares. Options outstanding on 1 January 20X6 were as follows:

1.2 million equity shares at £2 each

2 million equity shares at £3 each

1 million equity shares at £4 each.

The options relative to the 1.2 million equity shares at £2 were exercised on 1 October 20X6. The average fair value of one equity share during the year was £5.

Silver issued £6 million of 6% convertible bonds on 1 January 20X5, and each £1,000 bond is convertible into 200 equity shares. The corporation tax rate applicable is 35%.

Required:

(i)   Calculate the number of shares in issue at 1 January 20X6.

(ii) Calculate the basic and diluted earnings per share for the year ended 31 December 20X6.

10 On 1 January 20X3, Juno plc had the following capital and debt structure:

● 800,000 equity shares of £10 each

● 1,200,000 6% cumulative convertible preference shares of £1 each (1 year of dividends in arrears)

● £1,300,000 8% convertible bonds.

Each preference share is convertible to one equity share in 20X3 and every £10 nominal value of the bonds carries a right to convert into one equity share before 1 April 20X6.

Juno also issued two share options during 20X3. Option A was granted to directors to subscribe for 700,000 equity shares at £3.00 per share on 1 July, whereas option B was granted to key management personnel to subscribe for 500,000 equity shares at £6.00 per share on 1 August. Both options would be exercisable from 1 January 20X6.

On 1 May 20X3 Juno issued 300,000 additional equity shares at full market price. On 1 July 20X3, Juno declared and issued a bonus issue of 2 bonus shares for every 10 existing shares. On 1 October 20X3, an additional 400,000 shares were issued at full market price.

Net income (assuming no discontinuing operations) for the year ended 31 December 20X3 was £1,172,000. No dividends were declared during the year. The average market price of Juno's equity shares for 20X3 was £5.00 and the corporate tax rate in 20X3 was 15%.

Required:

(a) Compute the weighted average number of equity shares outstanding during 20X3.

(b) Compute the earnings per incremental share for each arrangement giving rise to potential equity shares (namely, options A and B, convertible preference shares, and convertible bonds), identifying whether they are dilutive or antidilutive.

(c) Using your answer to parts (a) and (b), compute basic earnings per share and diluted earnings per share for the year ended 31 December 20X3.

(d) Using the two options (A and B) in the question to illustrate your answer, discuss whether options are always included in calculating diluted earnings per share.

Visit the Online Resource Centre for solutions to all these end of chapter questions plus visual walkthrough solutions. You can test your understanding with extra questions and answers, explore additional case studies based on real companies, take a guided tour through a company report and much more. Go to the Online Resource Centre at **www.oxfordtextbooks.co.uk/orc/maynard2e/**

9

Taxation

➤ Introduction

This chapter focuses on the tax relating to the profits or losses a company makes, the assets and liabilities a company has, and how this is accounted for. In the UK this is generally referred to as corporation tax, but, from an international accounting perspective, it is called income tax. It includes both current tax and deferred tax.

Every transaction a company undertakes has a tax consequence. As a result, income tax may become payable or the amount due may be reduced; the effect may be on current tax payable or recoverable, or it may relate to tax amounts payable or recoverable in the future. This chapter will not cover in detail how such taxes are calculated as this will be different in every tax jurisdiction. It will, however, discuss the principles behind, and the accounting treatment of, the tax consequences of both transactions and other events which are recognised in a company's financial statements, and the future recovery and the settlement of assets and liabilities recognised in the statement of financial position.

International Accounting Standard (IAS) 12 *Income Taxes* is the accounting standard that explains and specifies the accounting treatment of current and deferred taxes, and sets out the presentation and disclosure requirements.

★ Learning objectives

After studying this chapter you will be able to:

● understand why accounting profits and **taxable profits** are not the same

● explain the components of companies' **income tax**—current and deferred tax

● understand why deferred tax balances are accounted for and the issues with this

● account for current tax and deferred tax in accordance with IAS 12 *Income Taxes*.

✔ Key issues checklist

❏ Tax on companies' profits.

❏ Definitions of current tax and deferred tax.

❏ Differences between accounting profit and taxable profit—permanent and temporary differences.

❏ Accounting for current tax.

❏ The tax base of assets and liabilities.

❏ Taxable and deductible temporary differences.

❏ Recognition of deferred tax liabilities and deferred tax assets.

❏ Tax rate to be used.

❏ Accounting for changes in deferred tax balances.

❏ Concepts underpinning the accounting for deferred tax.

❏ Alternative views.

❏ Disclosures.

9.1 Taxation on companies' profits

9.1.1 Introduction

Governments have an influence on the economic activity of a country by withdrawing money through taxes, which it then injects through public sector spending. Different countries will raise taxes in different ways, and have different rules and regulations which determine the amounts they collect. Within a particular country these will vary, as they depend on the stance of a particular government on social justice and the amounts of revenues it determines need to be raised. Governments will change taxes periodically to encourage or discourage certain types of individual and corporate activity, or to respond to issues in society. In the UK, tax legislation is set by Parliament each year in the Finance Act.

Businesses' actions give rise to many different types of taxation. A business will deduct taxes from its employees' wages and salaries, and pay these to the government. In the UK these taxes are called pay-as-you-earn (or **PAYE**) and employees' **National Insurance** (NI).

A business, in addition, has to pay a further amount of employers' National Insurance to the government. Businesses that are large enough are required to include tax on the selling price of their goods and services (although this does not apply to all goods and services) and then pay this tax to the government. In the European Union (EU) this is termed value added tax (or **VAT**). The VAT a business has been charged on goods and services it has acquired is deducted from the amount payable.

Companies have a separate legal identity from their owners (shareholders). Because of this, companies are liable for taxes charged on the profits and gains they make. In the UK this is referred to as corporation tax. Although not the largest revenue raiser for governments, this is still a significant tax, and has recently been a topic of great public interest as a result of the amounts multinational corporations such as Google and Starbucks are reported to have paid in various jurisdictions. Statistics show that between 5% and 15% of total government revenue in developed countries is raised from taxes on corporate profits.

This chapter deals with the accounting for taxes on a company's profits or losses. This tax is called income tax in international financial reporting and refers to all domestic and foreign taxes on corporate profits. (However, note that in the UK the term income tax is usually taken to refer to tax on an individual's earnings.)

For all companies there are tax consequences of the transactions recognised in profit or loss. There are also tax consequences of transactions which are recognised outside profit and loss, for example property revaluations and other items recognised as other comprehensive income or items recognised directly in equity. These can be immediate, for example tax is payable or recoverable once the profit or loss has been recognised, but can also affect future tax payments. Accounting standard-setters have debated and changed methods of accounting for these tax consequences for many years, and IAS 12 *Income Taxes*, which was issued in 1996 by the International Accounting Standards Board's (IASB) predecessor body, the International Accounting Standards Committee (IASC), sets out the accounting treatment of these to ensure consistency of treatment. It does not specify how tax amounts are calculated, as these will be different according to each country's tax legislation, but takes the principle of the tax consequence, and specifies how and when the tax should be accounted for and the disclosures needed for the users to understand this.

Income tax includes both current tax and deferred tax, which are defined as follows:

Current tax   The amount of income taxes payable (or recoverable) in respect of the taxable profit (tax loss) for a period.

Deferred tax   An accounting measure representing income taxes payable or recoverable in the future relating to transactions that have already taken place.

9.1.2 Taxable profit or loss

The taxable profit (or loss) for a period will seldom be the same as profit for accounting purposes. Taxable profit will be determined in accordance with the rules established by the government or taxation authorities, and upon which taxes are payable (or recoverable). The differences between taxable and accounting profits are of two types.

1   **Temporary differences**—where income or expenses are recognised for both accounting and tax purposes, but in different time periods. For example, accounting requires the accruals basis for the recognition of expenses, such as pension contributions, but the expense is only deductible as a tax expense on a cash basis.

   Another major temporary difference is depreciation. Depreciation for accounting purposes is an accounting mechanism to spread the cost of an asset on a systematic basis over the accounting periods expected to benefit from the use of the asset. It is judgemental, requiring estimates of the useful life, any residual value and patterns of usage. For tax purposes depreciation is replaced by deductions allowed by taxation authorities (sometimes referred to as capital allowances or writing down allowances). These are often varied to encourage investment by companies in certain types of asset.

2   **Permanent differences**—where expenses are included for accounting purposes, but are never allowed to be deducted for tax purposes. For example, entertainment expenses, and donations to political parties and national charities.

9.2 Current tax

As detailed in section 9.1.1, current tax is the income tax payable or recoverable once the profit or loss has been recognised. It is based on taxable profit. To determine taxable profit, companies produce a reconciliation of accounting profit (or loss) to taxable profit (or loss), which takes into account both temporary and permanent differences (see Worked example 9.1). Current tax is then calculated by applying the relevant corporation tax rate to the taxable profit. If tax is payable, this is recognised as an expense and a liability:

Debit	Income tax expense (statement of profit or loss)
Credit	Current tax liability

Current tax may be recoverable for the following reasons:

(a) Amounts may already have been paid to the tax authorities in respect of current and prior periods which exceed the amounts due for these periods

(b) Tax losses may be able to be carried back to recover current tax of a previous period.

These give rise to a benefit, which can be recognised as a current tax asset, as the definition of an asset as given in the 2015 Exposure Draft of the IASB's *Conceptual Framework* is met.

● **Reminder** *An asset is a present economic resource controlled by the entity as a result of past events.*

In this case the accounting is:

Debit	Current tax asset
Credit	Income tax expense (statement of profit or loss)

Worked example 9.1: to show the reconciliation of accounting profit to taxable profit

Lilliput plc's summarised statement of profit or loss for the year ended 31 March 20X6 is as follows:

	£
Revenue	346,140
Cost of sales	(235,380)
Gross profit	110,760
Distribution and administrative expenses	(97,470)
Other income	12,000
Profit before tax	25,290

Included in the distribution and administrative expenses are the following items:

- depreciation of £36,500
- donations to a political party of £500
- contribution to company pension scheme accrued £5,000.

Other income represents dividends receivable from an overseas investment, which are taxable on receipt.

The capital allowances have been calculated as £27,300.

Required:

Produce the reconciliation of accounting profit to taxable profit for Lilliput for the year ended 31 March 20X6.

		£
Profit before tax		25,290
Add back:	Depreciation	36,500
	Donations to political party	500
	Accrued pension scheme contribution	5,000
		67,290
Deduct:	Dividends receivable	(12,000)
	Capital allowances	(27,300)
Taxable profit		27,990

The current tax liability or asset is measured using rates 'that have been enacted or substantively enacted by the end of the reporting period', and companies have to be aware of the time between the passing of tax legislation and when it is actually applicable. In the UK, corporation tax rates have been reducing for many years and are currently (in 2016) 20% for all companies, with a target rate of 18% by 2020.

From a practical point of view, listed companies will usually publish their financial statements before they have agreed the final tax liability with the tax authorities. (In many cases, agreement of the amount payable or recoverable may take many months or years!) Thus, the tax liability or asset will be an estimate, the value of which requires management's and the auditor's expertise and judgement to be exercised. The amount actually settled will therefore differ from this estimate. As with other accounting estimates, and in accordance with IAS 8 *Accounting Policies, Changes in Accounting Estimates and Errors*, any over-/under-estimates of tax are included in the tax expense in the period in which the final settlement or agreement is reached.

In the UK, large companies have to make quarterly payments based on their estimate of the corporation tax payable for the year. Thus, any total liability will be reduced by these amounts. Other companies are required to pay their corporation tax within nine months and one day of the end of the accounting period.

 Worked example 9.2: to show the calculation of current tax

Verne plc estimates that current tax for the year ended 30 June 20X4 is £750,000. This figure takes into account new tax rates which were announced in March 20X4 and which are confidently expected to be enacted in August 20X4. If the new tax rates were to be disregarded the amount due would be £810,000. Verne has made payments on account totalling £390,000 during the year to 30 June 20X4 in relation to the current tax for the year.

Current tax for the year ended 30 June 20X3 was estimated at £620,000, but the final settlement was £590,000, which was paid on 29 March 20X5.

Required:

Calculate the current tax amounts which should be shown in the financial statements for the year ended 30 June 20X4 and show the resulting accounting entries.

Statement of profit or loss expense	£
Current tax for y/e 30 June 20X4	750,000
Overestimate of current tax for y/e 30 June 20X3	
(590,000–620,000)	(30,000)
	720,000

Statement of financial position current liability	£
Current tax for y/e 30 June 20X4	750,000
Less: payments on account	(390,000)
	360,000

This can also be achieved through double-entry and T accounts.

At 1 July 20X3 there will be an opening credit balance on the tax liability account of £620,000 – £590,000 = £30,000 being the overestimate of tax for the year ended 30 June 20X3. This will be cleared to the tax expense account by:

		£	£
Dr	Tax liability	30,000	
Cr	Tax expense		30,000

The estimate of tax for the current year ended 30 June 20X4 will be based on the tax rates that are confidently expected to be enacted in August 20X4 and so will be £750,000. The double-entry for this is:

		£	£
Dr	Tax expense	750,000	
Cr	Tax liability		750,000

Payments on account will be posted as follows:

		£	£
Dr	Tax liability	390,000	
Cr	Bank		390,000

T accounts will give the final balances for the statement of profit or loss (SoPL) and statement of financial position (SoFP):

Tax expense (SoPL)			
Tax liability	750,000	Tax liability	30,000
		I/S expense	720,000
	750,000		750,000

Tax liability (SoFP)			
Tax expense	30,000	Balance b/f	30,000
Bank	390,000	Tax expense	750,000
Balance c/f	360,000		
	780,000		780,000

9.3 Deferred tax

9.3.1 What is deferred tax?

Deferred tax is tax attributable to temporary differences. Temporary differences have been explained in the previous sections in terms of the timing difference between the accounting and tax recognition of income and expense. However, IAS 12 takes a statement of financial position approach to deferred tax and defines temporary differences as differences between the carrying amount of an asset or liability in the statement of financial position and its **tax base**. However, these different approaches do not give a different result. If a statement of financial position was drawn up with assets and liabilities using tax bases, and this was compared with the statement of financial position drawn up according to accounting rules, the difference in net assets value would be the same as the difference between taxable profit and accounting profit.

The tax base of an asset or liability is defined as the amount attributed to that asset or liability for tax purposes, and is explained further in section 9.3.3.

The tax attributable to temporary differences may give rise to a deferred tax liability or asset depending on whether the temporary differences are:

(a) *Taxable temporary differences*, which are temporary differences that will result in taxable amounts in determining taxable profit (tax loss) of future periods when the carrying amount of the asset or liability is recovered or settled.

Taxable temporary differences give rise to deferred tax liabilities.

(b) *Deductible temporary differences*, which are temporary differences that will result in amounts that are deductible in determining taxable profit (tax loss) of future periods when the carrying amount of the asset or liability is recovered or settled.

Deductible temporary differences give rise to deferred tax assets.

9.3.2 Approach to the recognition of deferred tax

The IAS 12 approach to the recognition and measurement of deferred tax requires the following steps to be taken which will be explained and illustrated in the following sections:

1   Determine the tax base of an asset or liability, and compare this to the carrying (accounting) amount.

2   If they are not the same, calculate the temporary difference, and determine whether this is a taxable or deductible difference.

3   Identify if there are any exceptions to the recognition of a deferred tax asset or liability.

4   Consider the recoverability of any deferred tax asset.

5   Establish the tax rate to be used in the measurement of deferred tax.

6   Account for the deferred tax, and present and disclose according to IAS 12.

9.3.3 Tax base of an asset or liability

The definitions of the tax base of an asset or liability given in IAS 12 are not straightforward. These definitions are given in Table 9.1.

Table 9.1 Defining the tax base as an asset or liability

Tax base	Definition
Asset	The amount that will be deductible for tax purposes against any taxable economic benefits that will flow to an entity when it recovers the carrying amount of the asset. If those economic benefits will not be taxable, the tax base of the asset is equal to its carrying amount.
Liability	The carrying amount, less any amount that will be deductible for tax purposes in respect of that liability in future periods. In the case of revenue which is received in advance, the tax base of the resulting liability is its carrying amount, less any amount of the revenue that will not be taxable in future periods.

Essentially, the tax base reflects the tax consequences that will occur when the carrying amount of the asset or liability is recovered or settled, in other words how much will be deducted for tax purposes when the asset is sold or the liability is paid. If there are no future tax consequences, the tax base is the same as the carrying amount.

 Examples of tax bases

1   A machine whose original cost was £100,000 is depreciated in accordance with normal accounting rules and has a net book value of £40,000. For tax purposes, writing down allowances (tax depreciation) of £30,000 have been allowed.

  Use of the machine will generate future economic benefits (revenues), which will be taxable. As the machine is used the remaining cost not already deducted for tax purposes will be deductible in the future either through tax depreciation or as a deduction on disposal. Hence, the tax base is the cost not already deducted of £100,000 – £30,000 = £70,000.

2   Income receivable of £40,000 included in current assets. This income is taxed on a cash basis.

  The tax statement of financial position will not include an asset for income receivable as the income is taxed when received. The tax base is therefore nil.

3   Trade receivables of £50,000.

  The related revenue has already been included in taxable profit so there will be no further taxable economic benefits. The tax base is equal to the carrying amount of £50,000.

4   Accrued overhead expenses of £15,000.

  The overhead expenses have already been deducted in arriving at taxable profit so there are no further future deductions. The tax base is equal to the carrying amount of £15,000.

5   An expense payable of £20,000 included in current liabilities. This expense is allowable for tax on a cash basis.

  The tax statement of financial position will not include a liability for interest payable as interest is taxed when paid. The tax base is therefore nil. Alternatively, applying the definition in IAS 12, there will be future deductions for the interest to be paid, so the tax base is £20,000 – £20,000 = nil.

6   A loan of £200,000 included in non-current liabilities.

  The repayment of the loan will have no tax consequences so the tax base is the carrying amount of £200,000.

9.3.4 Taxable and deductible temporary differences

Once the tax base of assets and liabilities have been established these are compared to the carrying amounts, and the differences are determined as either taxable or deductible, as given in Figure 9.1.

Typical examples of items giving rise to taxable and deductible temporary differences are provided in Table 9.2.

Under certain financial reporting standards assets may be revalued to fair value. This will not adjust the tax base of the asset, and so the difference between carrying amount and tax base will change and give rise to a temporary difference, and, hence, to a deferred tax asset or liability.

Figure 9.1 Taxable and deductible temporary differences

Table 9.2 Examples of taxable and deductible temporary differences

Taxable temporary differences	Deductible temporary differences
1 Royalty revenue—included in accounting profit on the accruals basis, but included in taxable profit on a cash basis.	1 Retirement benefit costs—deducted from accounting profit as service is provided by the employee, but deducted from taxable profits either when contributions are paid to the retirement fund or when the retirement benefits are paid.
2 Depreciation—deducted from accounting profit according to matching and estimates of expected life, residual value and pattern of usage. Deducted from taxable profit according to tax rules.	2 Research costs—recognised as an expense in accounting profit, but may not be permitted as a deduction for taxable profits until a later period.
3 Development costs—may be capitalised and amortised for accounting profit purposes, but deducted in full for taxable profit.	3 A liability recognised in a business combination—the related costs may be deducted from taxable profits in a later period.

Examples of taxable and deductible temporary differences

Using the tax base examples given in the previous example.

1   A machine whose original cost was £100,000 is depreciated in accordance with normal accounting rules and has a net book value of £40,000. For tax purposes, writing down allowances (tax depreciation) of £30,000 have been allowed.

Carrying amount = £40,000. Tax base = £70,000.

- Deductible temporary difference.
- Deferred tax asset.

2   Income receivable of £40,000 included in current assets. This income is taxed on a cash basis.

Carrying amount = £40,000; Tax base = nil.

- Taxable temporary difference.
- Deferred tax liability.

3   Trade receivables of £50,000.

Carrying amount = Tax base = £50,000.

- No deferred tax implications.

4   Accrued overhead expenses of £15,000.

Carrying amount = Tax base = £15,000.

- No deferred tax implications.

5   Expense payable of £20,000 included in current liabilities. This expense is allowable for tax on a cash basis.

Carrying amount = £ (20,000); Tax base = nil.

Be careful with liabilities where there are differences between the carrying amount and the tax base. Treat the liability as a negative number. Here, the carrying amount is less than the tax base.

- Deductible temporary difference.
- Deferred tax asset.

6   A loan of £200,000 included in non-current liabilities.

Carrying amount = Tax base = £200,000.

- No deferred tax implications.

9.3.5 Exceptions to the recognition of deferred tax assets and liabilities

IAS 12 requires the recognition of deferred tax liabilities and assets for all taxable and deductible temporary differences, except for the following:

1   The initial recognition of goodwill in a business combination

2   The initial recognition of an asset or liability outside a business combination and in a transaction that does not affect accounting profit or taxable profit

3   Investments in subsidiaries and associates where the investor is able to control the timing of the reversal of any temporary differences and it is probable that the temporary difference will not arise in the foreseeable future.

As discussed in Chapter 17, which deals with consolidated financial statements, goodwill arising on the acquisition of a business is essentially the difference between the consideration and the investor's share of the fair value of the net assets acquired. In other words, it is a residual amount. Many tax authorities do not allow reductions in goodwill (through impairment) as a deductible expense for tax purposes, nor do they permit deductions for goodwill when the business, to which goodwill relates, is disposed of. The tax base of goodwill in these jurisdictions is therefore nil. It could be argued that there would, therefore, be a taxable temporary difference. However, because goodwill is a residual amount, the recognition of a deferred tax liability in the goodwill computation would increase the carrying amount of goodwill (because the fair value of the net assets would reduce). The deferred tax liability is therefore not recognised.

If a business acquired an asset through a transaction which was not a business combination, and which affected neither accounting nor taxable profits, a difference between the carrying amount and the tax base of the asset could still exist. It could be argued that a deferred tax liability (or asset) should be accounted for. However, this recognition would mean the carrying amount of the asset would have to be adjusted by the same amount, which would gross up the value of the asset. This would lead to less transparency in the financial statements. Therefore, in these circumstances, the deferred tax liability or asset is not permitted to be recognised.

9.3.6 Recoverability of a deferred tax asset

Subject to the exceptions detailed previously, deferred tax liabilities are recognised in full. This is because deferred tax liabilities arise when the carrying amount of an asset exceeds its tax base. In other words, the amount of taxable economic benefits will exceed the amount that will be allowed as a deduction for tax purposes in the future. The company will, therefore, have future taxable profits, which will give rise to an outflow of economic benefits in the form of tax payments. Thus, the definition of a liability, as given in the exposure draft (ED) of the IASB's *Conceptual Framework*, is satisfied.

🛈 **Reminder** *A liability is a present obligation of the entity to transfer an economic resource as a result of past events. The liability will be recognised if it provides relevant and faithfully representative information.*

Also, subject to the exceptions detailed previously, a deferred tax asset arises when there are deductible temporary differences which result from the tax base exceeding the carrying amount of an asset or liability. Alternatively, this can be viewed as future taxable profits being reduced as tax deductions are allowed, thus giving rise to future economic benefits. However, these economic benefits will only flow to a company if there are sufficient future taxable profits. Therefore, a deferred tax asset is only recognised when it is probable that taxable profits will be available. Companies need to consider this and exercise judgement.

In order to do this, companies will need to identify how future taxable profits arise. Broadly, there are three main sources:

1   *The reversal of existing taxable temporary differences*

    Taxable profits will increase when taxable temporary differences reverse. If they are expected to reverse in the same period as the deductible temporary differences and relate to the same taxation authority, the related deferred tax asset should be recognised.

2   *Future trading profits*

    A company needs to consider whether its future operations will generate sufficient taxable profits. It also has to take into account whether there are unused tax losses which can be set against future taxable profits. This clearly requires use of budgets and forecasts, and includes making estimates and applying judgement.

3   *Tax planning opportunities*

    Tax planning opportunities are actions which a company would take to realise a deferred tax asset. For example, a company may accelerate taxable income to an earlier period to ensure a tax loss does not expire, or make certain elections, if allowed by the tax jurisdiction, as to whether income is to be taxed on a receivable basis rather than received basis.

In addition, a company will need to consider whether the tax law in the jurisdiction in which it operates restricts the sources of taxable profits against which it may make deductions on the reversal of the deductible temporary differences. This may restrict the amount of the deferred tax asset which can be recognised.

The IASB published an amendment to IAS 12 in January 2016 to clarify the treatment of deferred tax assets for unrealised losses on debt instruments measured at fair value. (Note— Chapter 14 discusses the accounting for financial instruments.)

 Example of deferred tax implications for a debt instrument measured at fair value

A company purchases a debt instrument with a nominal value of £1,000 on 1 January 20X1 for £1,000. The instrument has an interest rate of 2% payable at the end of each year, and £1,000 is payable on maturity in 5 years. The debt instrument is measured at fair value.

Any gains or losses on the instrument are taxable (deductible) only when realised. The gains (losses) arising on the sale or maturity of the debt instrument are calculated for tax purposes as the difference between the amount collected and the original cost of the instrument. Accordingly the tax base of the debt instrument is its original cost of £1,000.

Suppose, at 31 December 20X2, the fair value of the debt instrument has decreased to £918 as a result of an increase in market interest rates to 5%. The difference between the carrying amount of the instrument of £918 and its tax base of £1,000 gives rise to a deductible temporary difference of £82 at this date. This is irrespective of whether the company expects to recover the carrying amount by sale or use, i.e. by holding it and collecting the interest, or a combination of both.

The company still has to assess whether sufficient future taxable profits will be available to determine whether the related deferred asset can be recognised.

A company may have unused tax losses or credits which it can offset against future taxable profits. IAS 12 states that a deferred tax asset may be recognised in such circumstances to the extent that it is probable future taxable profit will be available against which unused tax losses can be utilised, as for other deductible temporary differences. Note that the existence of unused tax losses may well indicate a limit on future taxable profits, so the company has to have convincing evidence that they will materialise.

9.3.7 Tax rate to be used in measuring deferred tax

The recovery of a deferred tax asset or the settlement of a deferred tax liability may not occur for many years. However, as for current tax, the tax rates to be used in measuring deferred tax assets and liabilities are those expected to apply when the asset is realised or the liability is settled. This should be based upon tax rates and laws that have been enacted, or substantively enacted, at the statement of financial position date.

In some jurisdictions the tax rate may vary according to the manner in which the asset is recovered or the liability is settled. A company has to apply the appropriate rate according to its plans.

 Example of tax rate to use in the calculation of deferred tax

An item of property, plant and equipment has a carrying amount of £10,000 and a tax base of £6,000. A tax rate of 20% would apply if the item were sold and a tax rate of 30% would apply to other income.

The entity recognises a deferred tax liability of £800 ((£10,000 − £6,000) at 20%) if it expects to sell the item without further use, and a deferred tax liability of £1,200 (£4,000 at 30%) if it expects to retain the item and recover its carrying amount through use.

(From IAS 12)

9.3.8 Recognition of deferred tax

One of the underpinning principles of IAS 12 is that the tax effects of a transaction or other event should be consistent with the accounting for the transaction or event itself. Therefore, deferred tax is recognised as either income or expense, and included in profit or loss for the period:

Debit	Income tax expense	OR	Debit	Deferred tax asset
Credit	Deferred tax liability		Credit	Income tax income

Once a deferred tax liability or asset is created, the change in the required liability or asset is debited or credited to profit and loss in subsequent reporting periods.

Examples of the accounting for deferred tax

Using the relevant tax base examples given in sections 9.3.3 and 9.3.4 and assuming a tax rate of 25%:

1 A machine whose original cost was £100,000 is depreciated in accordance with normal accounting rules and has a net book value of £40,000. For tax purposes, writing down allowances (tax depreciation) of £30,000 have been allowed.

   Carrying amount = £40,000. Tax base = £70,000.

   ● Deductible temporary difference.
   ● Deferred tax asset of 25% × (£70,000 – £40,000) = £7,500.

		£	£
Dr	Deferred tax asset	7,500	
Cr	Income tax expense		7,500

2 Income receivable of £40,000 included in current assets. This income is taxed on a cash basis.

   Carrying amount = £40,000; Tax base = nil.

   ● Taxable temporary difference.
   ● Deferred tax liability of 25% × (£40,000 – nil) = £10,000.

		£	£
Dr	Income tax expense	10,000	
Cr	Deferred tax liability		10,000

3 No deferred tax implications.

4 No deferred tax implications.

5 Expense payable of £20,000 included in current liabilities. This expense is allowable for tax on a cash basis.

   Carrying amount = £ (20,000); Tax base = nil.

   ● Deductible temporary difference.
   ● Deferred tax asset of 25% × (£20,000 – nil) = £5,000.

		£	£
Dr	Deferred tax asset	5,000	
Cr	Income tax expense		5,000

6 No deferred tax implications.

An exception to this accounting treatment is where the underpinning transaction or event is recognised outside profit or loss. If this is the case, then the related deferred tax is also to be recognised outside profit or loss. Examples include the surplus arising on the revaluation of a non-current asset, which is recognised in other comprehensive income (see Chapter 10 for further details), and adjustments to opening retained earnings from a change in accounting policy or error applied retrospectively, which are recognised directly in equity. Any deferred tax asset or liability arising from these items would be also included in other comprehensive income and equity respectively.

9.3.9 Right of offset

As companies may have both deferred tax liabilities and deferred tax assets, the question arises whether these can be netted off on the statement of financial position. One of the underpinning principles of presentation outlined in IAS 1 *Presentation of Financial Statements* (discussed in Chapter 4) is that companies should not offset assets and liabilities, as this leads to lack of transparency. However, it is permitted where another IFRS does allow it—deferred tax is one such area. There are restrictions on this though and IAS 12 states that the offset is only allowed if:

(a) the entity has a legally enforceable right to set off current tax assets against current tax liabilities; and

(b) the deferred tax assets and the deferred tax liabilities relate to income taxes levied by the same taxation authority on either:

(i) the same taxable entity; or

(ii) different taxable entities which intend to either settle or current tax liabilities and assets on a net basis, or to realise the assets and settle the liabilities simultaneously, in each future period in which significant amounts of deferred tax liabilities or assets are expected to be settled or recovered.

(IASB, IAS 12, para. 74)

Deferred tax balances are never offset against current tax balances, as they relate to different issues.

Worked example 9.3: to show the calculation and recognition of deferred tax

Warrington plc commenced operations on 1 January 20X8. Its book and tax financial statements are consistent except for two items.

1 Warrington purchased a piece of equipment in 1 January 20X8 for £2,000. The equipment has a useful life of four years and is depreciated on a straight-line basis for accounting purposes. The tax authority allows the company to claim tax allowances for the cost of the asset over two years, also on a straight-line basis.

2 Warrington sells products that have a warranty attached. The warranty essentially guarantees that the products are not defective. Accordingly the company records a warranty provision in its financial statements when the revenue is recognised (Dr Warranty expense; Cr Warranty provision). The tax authority does not allow a deduction for the warranty expense until cash is paid to settle a warranty claim. The warranty provision at 31 December 20X8 is estimated at £1,200.

Warrington recorded a net profit of £10,000 for its first year of trading before accounting for these two items. The tax rate in Warrington's jurisdiction is 40%.

Required:

Calculate and show the accounting for the current tax and deferred tax for Warrington plc for 20X8.

Before dealing with deferred tax, the *current tax* should be calculated.

	Accounting profit £	Tax profit £
Net profit	10,000	10,000
Depreciation	(500)	(1,000)
Warranty provision	(1,200)	–
Profit before tax/taxable profit	8,300	9,000
Current tax 40% × £9,000	3,600	

		£	£
Debit	Income tax (SoPL)	3,600	
Credit	Tax liability (SoFP)		3,600

Deferred tax

1 Determine the tax base of an asset or liability and compare this to the carrying amount.

2 If they are not the same, the temporary difference is calculated and whether this is a taxable or deductible difference is determined.

	Equipment £	Warranty £
Carrying amount	1,500	(1,200)
Tax base	1,000	Nil
Taxable temporary difference	500	–
Deductible temporary difference	–	1,200
Deferred tax	Liability	Asset

3 Identify if there are any exceptions to the recognition of a deferred tax asset or liability.

The exceptions are not relevant in this example.

4 Consider the recoverability of any deferred tax asset.

Warrington is able to recognise at least £500 of the £1,200 deductible temporary difference related to the warranty provision because of the £500 taxable temporary difference related to the equipment. The recognition of the remaining deductible temporary difference depends on whether future taxable profits will be available. For the purposes of this example, assume the company does expect to make sufficient profits in the future from ongoing operations and is therefore able to recognise the entire deferred tax asset.

5 Establish the tax rate to be used in the measurement of deferred tax.

Assuming there have been no laws enacted that will change future tax rates, the present rate of 40% is used as the best estimate of the tax rate in force when the deferred tax liability will be settled and the asset realised.

		£
Deferred tax liability	40% × 500	(200)
Deferred tax asset	40% × 1,200	480

6 Account for the deferred tax and present and disclose according to IAS 12.

Given the deferred tax liability and asset arise for a single company, Warrington can offset these two balances on its statement of financial position. The accounting will therefore be:

		£	£
Debit	Deferred tax asset (SoFP)	280	
Credit	Income tax (SoPL)		280

The full statement of profit or loss for Warrington for the year ended 31 December 20X8 will appear as follows:

	£
Net profit	10,000
Depreciation	(500)
Warranty provision	(1,200)
Profit before tax	8,300
Income tax (3,600 – 280)	(3,320)
Profit for the year	4,980

On the statement of financial position at 31 December 20X8, the current tax liability of £3,600 will be included in current liabilities and a non-current deferred tax asset of £280 will be presented.

Note that the Warrington's effective tax rate (i.e. income tax expense divided by profit before tax) is now 40% (3,320/8,300), which is consistent with the tax rate in the company's jurisdiction. If only current tax had been included in the statement of profit or loss, the effective tax rate would have been 3,600/8,300 = 43%. The deferred tax has had the effect of 'normalising' the effective tax rate; this issue is discussed further in section 9.4.

9.4 The effect of accounting for deferred tax

As shown by the Worked example 9.3, one effect of accounting for deferred tax is to 'normalise' the effective tax rate, so that a user looking at the statement of profit or loss sees the income tax charge as approximating to the tax rate multiplied by profit before tax. (Note: they will never be exactly the same because of permanent differences, among other matters.) It could be argued that this makes the income tax figure in the statement of profit or loss more relevant and understandable.

If this idea is extended, the 'income smoothing' effect of accounting for deferred tax can be seen. Worked example 9.4 shows this by considering a company's profits for more than one year.

 Worked example 9.4: to show the income smoothing effect of deferred tax

Belay plc has issued share capital of 2 million £1 equity shares. The company has exactly the same profit before tax for the three years to 31 December 20X4:

	20X2	20X3	20X4
	£000	£000	£000
Profit before tax (PBT)	2,000	2,000	2,000
Depreciation (included in above PBT)	600	600	600
Tax allowances on non-current assets	800	500	200

The depreciation and tax allowances relate to an asset which was acquired for £2,400 on 1 January 20X2. Assume that there are no other permanent or temporary differences, and that the rate of tax is 25% throughout the full period.

Required:

(a) Accounting only for current tax, calculate Belay's profit after tax and earnings per share (EPS) for the three years, and comment on these results.

(b) Repeat the calculations required in (a), but include accounting for deferred tax. Comment on the results.

(a) Current tax charge

	20X2	20X3	20X4
	£000	£000	£000
Profit before depreciation	2,600	2,600	2,600
Tax allowances on non-current asset	800	500	200
Taxable profits	1,800	2,100	2,400
Current tax (25% × taxable profits)	450	525	600

If only current tax is accounted for, the statements of profit or loss would show:

	20X2 £000	20X3 £000	20X4 £000
Profit before tax	2,000	2,000	2,000
Income tax	450	525	600
Profit after tax	1,550	1,475	1,400
EPS	78p	74p	70p

For a company with identical profits before tax for three years and no change in taxation rates, falling profits after tax and EPS certainly look strange, and, to users, would certainly lack transparency. Remember, tax allowances are not shown in the financial statements—these figures are used in the company's tax returns.

(b) Deferred tax

	20X2 £000	20X3 £000	20X4 £000
Carrying amount of asset	1,800	1,200	600
Tax base	1,600	1,100	900
Taxable/(deductible) temporary difference	200	100	(300)
Deferred tax (liability)/asset (@ 25%)	(50)	(25)	75

In 20X2 the deferred tax liability would be set up:

		£000	£000
Debit	Income tax (SoPL)	50	
Credit	Deferred tax liability		50

In 20X3 and 20X4 this balance is adjusted, with the change being accounted for in the statement of profit or loss; so, for 20X3:

		£000	£000
Debit	Deferred tax liability	25	
Credit	Income tax (SoPL)		25

For 20X4:

		£000	£000
Debit	Deferred tax liability	100	
Credit	Income tax (SoPL)		100

The effect of including changes in deferred tax balances in the income tax charge is as follows:

	20X2 £000	20X3 £000	20X4 £000
Current tax	450	525	600
Change in deferred tax	50	(25)	(100)
Income tax charge	500	500	500

The statements of profit or loss and EPS are thus 'smoothed':

	20X2 £000	20X3 £000	20X4 £000
Profit before tax	2,000	2,000	2,000
Income tax	500	500	500
Profit after tax	1,500	1,500	1,500
EPS	75p	75p	75p

9.5 Is the approach of IAS 12 *Income Taxes* to accounting for deferred tax relevant?

As mentioned previously, methods of accounting for deferred tax have been changed over the years by different countries' accounting standard-setters. In the UK, accounting profit and taxable profit are determined relatively independently of each other. Deferred tax has always, therefore, been a significant accounting issue and there have been many changes, such as the question of whether deferred tax should be recognised in full or only partially. However, in countries where accounting and tax systems are closer, for example Germany, deferred tax has been less of an issue and deferred tax balances will be much smaller.

The IASB's approach to deferred tax is based on the principles behind the recognition of assets and liabilities. It is inherent in the recognition of assets or liabilities that a company expects to recover or settle the carrying amount of that asset or liability. If it is probable that recovery and settlement of the carrying amount will make future tax payments larger or smaller, then, with certain limited exceptions, the company should recognise a related deferred tax liability or asset. The IASB's discussion of an asset given in the ED of its *Conceptual Framework* explains that:

> ...the economic benefits produced by an economic resource (the asset) could include receiving contractual cash flows or receiving another economic resource ...

> *(IASB, 2015: para. 4.14)*

Given this, it would be difficult to argue for the tax consequences of the economic benefits of an asset being ignored in its measurement.

This can also be considered as the application of accruals or matching, one of the core underpinning concepts of financial reporting. On one hand, the IASB's approach requires the tax consequences of transactions and other events to be accounted for in the same way, and in the same accounting period that the transactions and other events are accounted for themselves.

On the other hand, the *Conceptual Framework*'s definition of a liability includes the requirement that there is a present obligation. A present obligation means that the event or transaction giving rise to the obligation has happened before the date of the statement of financial position. Critics of the IASB's approach to deferred tax argue that the reversal of taxable temporary differences may not result in future tax payments because of events that occur in the future, for example because of rolling capital investment programmes. A further argument is that tax is only payable when tax legislation requires it to be paid. However, this latter argument is contrary to the 'substance over form' principle that underpins much of the IASB's standard-setting.

Critics raise further objections to accounting for deferred tax by claiming it is difficult to understand. The IASB, in explaining its enhancing qualitative characteristic of understandability, states that the complexity of an event or a transaction should not be a barrier to any accounting treatment. Clear and comparable disclosures relating to how and where deferred tax has been accounted for, and its effect on the financial statements, are therefore very important to provide this understanding to users.

Research into the financial reporting of income tax, undertaken by the Financial Reporting Council (FRC) and the European Financial Reporting Advisory Group (EFRAG) in 2012, indicated that users of IAS 12 felt the standard is not fundamentally flawed and is generally well-understood by preparers and users of financial statements. Changes to the existing model for the accounting for income tax may therefore add further complexity and may not satisfy user needs. The IASB has made certain limited improvements to the standard since it was adopted in 2001, but has also launched a research project which aims to better understand the needs of financial statement stakeholders regarding income taxes.

Although all companies will have to consider and calculate deferred tax, the financial impact on their statements of financial position may not be particularly significant. Industries that are particularly affected by large deferred tax balances are those which include assets on a fair value basis, as the difference between the accounting and tax bases is likely to be substantial.

9.6 Disclosures

Transparency in accounting for tax is critical and the disclosures required by IAS 12 are there to ensure this as far as possible. Companies will generally include a brief accounting policy relating to taxation.

The major components of the statement of profit or loss tax charge should be disclosed, which will include:

- the current tax expense or income for the period
- adjustments relating to under- or overestimates of current tax from previous periods
- the amount of deferred tax expense or income relating to temporary differences
- the amount of deferred tax expense or income relating to changes in tax rates or legislation.

If income tax is recognised outside profit and loss, for example in other comprehensive income, the amount of tax relating to each component of other comprehensive income is disclosed separately.

An explanation of the relationship between the tax expense and accounting profit is also required, and a company can present this in two alternative ways:

1 A reconciliation between the tax expense and the figure obtained by multiplying accounting profit by the tax rate used

2 A reconciliation between the effective tax rate and the tax rate used.

This is often a key requirement of users who, as research shows, often ask why there is such a large difference between the statutory rate of tax of income tax and the amount companies actually pay to the tax authorities.

Financial reporting in practice 9.1 — Nestlé, 2014

Nestlé's 2014 detailed tax note shows this information. The company's profit before tax and share of profits from associates and joint ventures was CHF 10,268 million (2013: CHF 12,437 million). (Note: CHF denotes Swiss francs.)

Note 14—Taxes

14.1 Taxes recognised in the income statement

In millions of CHF	2014	2013
Components of taxes		
Current taxes (a)	(3,148)	(2,970)
Deferred taxes	132	(846)
Taxes reclassified to other comprehensive income	(357)	558
Taxes reclassified to equity	6	2
Total taxes	(3,367)	(3,256)
Reconciliation of taxes		
Expected tax expense at weighted average applicable tax rate	(2,245)	(2,812)
Tax effect of non-deductible or non-taxable items	(527)	(8)
Prior years' taxes	92	243
Transfers to unrecognised deferred tax assets	(136)	(59)
Transfers from unrecognised deferred tax assets	12	6
Changes in tax rates	9	(15)
Withholding taxes levied on transfers of income	(357)	(381)
Other	(215)	(230)
Taxes from continuing operations	(3,367)	(3,256)

(continued)

(continued)

(a) Current taxes related to prior years represent a tax income of CHF 133 million (2009: tax income of CHF 172 million).

The expected tax expense at weighted average applicable tax rate is the result from applying the domestic statutory tax rates to profits before taxes of each entity in the country it operates. For the Group, the weighted average applicable tax rate varies from one year to the other depending on the relative weight of the profit of each individual entity in the Group's profit as well as the changes in the statutory tax rates.

14.2 Taxes recognised in other comprehensive income

In millions of CHF	2014	2013
Tax effects relating to		
Currency retranslations	39	317
Fair value adjustments on available-for-sale financial instruments	(48)	64
Fair value adjustments on cash flow hedges	14	(91)
Remeasurement of defined benefit schemes	352	(848)
	357	(558)

A company shall also disclose for each type of temporary difference the amount of deferred tax liability or asset, and the amount of deferred tax expense or income recognised in the statement of profit or loss.

Financial reporting in practice 9.2 — Marston's plc, 2015

Marston's has a policy of revaluation of its properties to fair value (see Chapter 10). The company therefore has a relatively large deferred tax liability (nearly 10% of its non-current liabilities) and clearly shows the different types of temporary difference. The company does not offset its deferred tax asset against its deferred tax liabilities as it explains in its deferred tax disclosure note.

Note 22 Deferred tax

Net deferred tax liability

Deferred tax is calculated on temporary differences between tax bases of assets and liabilities and their carrying amounts under the liability method using a tax rate of 20% (2014: 20%). The movement on the deferred tax accounts is shown below:

	2015 £m	2014 £m
At beginning of the period	82.2	88.2
Credited to the income statement	(4.4)	(9.0)
Charged/(credited) to equity		
Impairment and revaluation of properties	18.5	2.0
Hedging reserve	(8.7)	0.5
Retirement benefits	1.4	0.5
At end of the period	89.0	82.2

The movements in deferred tax assets and liabilities (prior to the offsetting of balances within the same jurisdiction as permitted by IAS 12 'Income Taxes') during the period are shown below. Deferred tax assets and liabilities are only offset where there is a legally enforceable right of offset and there is an intention to settle the balances net.

Deferred tax liabilities

	Pensions £m	Accelerated capital allowances £m	Revaluation of properties £m	Rolled over capital gains £m	Other £m	Total £m
At 5 October 2014	1.6	29.8	95.6	1.3	3.0	131.3
Charged to the income statement	–	0.5	1.3	2.0	1.8	5.6
Charged to equity	1.4	–	18.5	–	–	19.9
At 3 October 2015	**3.0**	**30.3**	**115.4**	**3.3**	**4.8**	**156.8**

Deferred tax assets

	Tax losses £m	Hedging reserve £m	Other £m	Total £m
At 5 October 2014	(24.1)	(23.3)	(1.7)	(49.1)
Credited to the income statement	(6.3)	–	(3.7)	(10.0)
Credited to equity	–	(8.7)	–	(8.7)
At 3 October 2015	**(30.4)**	**(32.0)**	**(5.4)**	**(67.8)**

Net deferred tax liability	
At 4 October 2014	82.2
At 3 October 2015	**89.0**

Deferred tax assets have been recognised in respect of all tax losses and other temporary differences where it is probable that these assets will be recovered.

Disclosures relating to deferred tax assets and liabilities that have not been recognised are also important to emphasise transparency. In particular, where a deferred tax asset has not been recognised because it is unlikely that there will be future taxable profits available as the company has unused tax losses which it is carrying forward, the amount of the losses and their expiry date should be disclosed.

Financial reporting in practice 9.3 — Nestlé, 2014

To illustrate this, see the note Nestlé includes in its 2014 financial statements.

Note 14—Taxes

14.4 Unrecognised deferred taxes

The deductible temporary differences as well as the unused tax losses and tax credits for which no deferred tax assets are recognised expire as follows:

In millions of CHF	2014	2013
Within one year	35	18
Between one and five years	331	365
More than five years	2,375	1,642
	2,741	2,025

At 31 December 2014, the unrecognised deferred tax assets amount to CHF 629 million (2013: CHF 512 million).

In addition, the Group has not recognised deferred tax liabilities in respect of unremitted earnings that are considered indefinitely reinvested in foreign subsidiaries. At 31 December 2014, these earnings amount to CHF 20.0 billion (2013: CHF 17.1 billion). They could be subject to withholding and other taxes on remittance.

Accounting for income taxes requires many estimates and management judgements, and has to look forward. Although companies will include a brief accounting policy in relation to the recognition of current and deferred tax, many will also include income taxes in their disclosures of critical estimates and judgements.

Financial reporting in practice 9.4 — Next plc, 2015

Next plc's 2015 accounting policy relating to the recognition of taxes largely uses words from IAS 12.

Taxation

Taxation, comprised of current and deferred tax, is charged or credited to the income statement unless it relates to items in other comprehensive income or directly in equity. In such cases, the related tax is also recognised in other comprehensive income or directly in equity.

Current tax liabilities are measured at the amount expected to be paid, based on tax rates and laws that are enacted or substantively enacted at the balance sheet date.

Deferred tax is accounted for using the balance sheet liability method and is calculated using rates of taxation enacted or substantively enacted at the balance sheet date which are expected to apply when the asset or liability is settled.

Deferred tax liabilities are generally recognised for all taxable temporary differences. Deferred tax assets are only recognised to the extent that it is probable that taxable profits will be available against which deductible temporary differences can be utilised. Deferred tax is not recognised in respect of investments in subsidiaries and associates where the reversal of any taxable temporary differences can be controlled and are unlikely to reverse in the foreseeable future.

Financial reporting in practice 9.5 | J Sainsbury plc, 2011

J Sainsbury plc does detail deferred tax as a particular area where significant judgements and estimates have been made, despite its deferred tax liability balance on the statement of financial position neither being particularly significant (approx. 5% of total non-current liabilities) nor if the movement in deferred is measured as a proportion of the company's statement of profit or loss tax charge (4%).

Income taxes

The Group recognises expected liabilities for tax based on an estimation of the likely taxes due, which requires significant judgement as to the ultimate tax determination of certain items. Where the actual liability arising from these issues differs from these estimates, such differences will have an impact on income tax and deferred tax provisions in the period when such determination is made. Details of the tax charge and deferred tax are set out in notes 8 and 21 respectively.

9.7 Users' interpretation of tax

Care needs to be taken by users when interpreting financial statements by using ratio analysis as to whether tax balances are included or not in the figures used for the ratios. Most performance ratios will use earnings or profit figures before tax, as it is argued that companies have little control over the tax that is charged on profits or tax that can be recovered if losses are made. This is true up to a point—companies do not set tax rates or determine tax legislation. However, companies can, for example, decide when they invest in non-current assets which will affect tax allowances given, and, through other tax planning means, minimise tax to be paid or influence when it will be due. International companies can also 'move profits' around from one country to another through, for example, internal determination of where sales have arisen, transfer pricing used and the location of buying departments, in order to 'generate' their profits in jurisdictions with lower tax rates.

For ratios that use net assets figures (e.g. return on net assets) questions usually arise as to whether deferred tax balances should be included or excluded. Given that deferred tax balances arise from the difference between the carrying amount and the tax base of assets and liabilities, it may be appropriate to include these related tax balances, which are the tax consequence of having these balances. However, as mentioned previously, they could be excluded as the issue of whether the company has control over these tax consequences is applicable.

For ratios that use long-term financing, such as return on capital employed and gearing, there are issues over the definition of 'debt', as discussed in Chapter 5. Deferred tax liabilities, although disclosed in non-current liabilities, are not a long-term source of finance and should be not be included in such figures.

 ## Summary of key points

Tax on a company's profit is referred to as income tax for international accounting purposes and comprises current tax and deferred tax. Current tax is tax payable or recoverable in respect of the taxable profit for a period, and its accounting is relatively straightforward. The amounts included in a company's financial statements are usually estimates and, once final agreement has been reached with the tax authorities, any changes in these estimates are accounted for in accordance with IAS 8.

Deferred tax is income tax either payable or recoverable in future periods in respect of temporary differences, and may also arise due to the carry forward of unused tax or unused tax credits. Temporary differences arise because some items or transactions are accounted for in a different period to the period in which the tax effect occurs. A key example of this is depreciation versus tax allowances for non-current assets. Temporary differences may be taxable or deductible, and result in deferred tax liabilities or deferred tax assets respectively. The IASB's approach, as specified in IAS 12 *Income Taxes*, is that all deferred tax liabilities are fully recognised, but that deferred tax assets are recognised only if it is probable that there are sufficient future taxable profits. This approach stems from the IASB's definitions of assets and liabilities, as set out in its *Conceptual Framework*. There are alternative views to this and alternative accounting treatments have been used in the past. The impact of accounting for deferred tax is that it makes the income tax figure in the statement of profit or loss appear to relate more closely to the actual profit before tax and has a smoothing effect.

IAS 12 was revised in readiness for the 2005 EU requirement for the use of IFRS, and there has only been one specific amendment since. The standard sets out fairly extensive disclosure requirements to ensure transparency in how the statement of profit or loss tax figure and deferred tax balances have been arrived at. Deferred tax, in particular, is dependent on future plans and estimates, with judgement inherent in this. Users may have less understanding of tax than they do of accounting issues so the disclosures will be particularly important for them.

 ## Further reading

IASB (International Accounting Standards Board) (2004) IAS 12 *Income Taxes*. London: IASB.

 ## Bibliography

Abdela, M., Davids, K. and Jehle, N. (2009) Hidden Gems or Pure Fiction? *Accountancy Magazine*, 143(1387): 63–64.

EFRAG (European Financial Reporting Advisory Group) (2013) *Improving the Financial Reporting of Income Tax: Feedback Statement*. Brussels: EFRAG.

IASB (International Accounting Standards Board) (2004) IAS 12 *Income Taxes*. London: IASB.

IASB (International Accounting Standards Board) (2015) Exposure Draft *Conceptual Framework for Financial Reporting*. London: IASB.

IASB (International Accounting Standards Board) (2016) *Recognition of Deferred Tax Assets for Unrealised Losses (Amendments to IAS 12)*. London: IASB.

J Sainsbury plc (2015) *Annual Report and Financial Statements, 2015*. London: J Sainsbury.

Kingfisher plc (2015) *Annual Report and Accounts 2014/15*. London: Kingfisher.

Maloney, B. (2009) *IFRS News—Beginners' Guide: Nine Steps to Income Tax Accounting*. London: PricewaterhouseCoopers.

Marston's plc (2015) *Annual Report, 2015*. Wolverhampton: Marston's.

Nestlé S.A. (2015) *2014 Financial Statements*. Vevey: Nestlé.

Next plc (2015) *Annual Report and Accounts, 2015*. Enderby: Next.

 ## Questions

● Quick test

1   The following assets and liabilities appear in a company's statement of financial position at 31 March 20X6:

    (a) A motor lorry which cost £200,000 is shown at its carrying amount of £40,000. For tax purposes, its written down value is £60,000

    (b) A loan payable is shown at £120,000. The repayment of the loan will have no tax consequences

    (c) A provision of £10,000 for product warranty costs made in the year. For tax purposes, the product warranty costs will not be deductible until the company pays claims

    (d) An account receivable is shown at £90,000. Of this amount, £50,000 has already been taxed, but the remaining £40,000 will be taxed in the accounting period in which it is received. The whole £90,000 has been included in accounting profit

    (e) An account payable is shown at £6,000. This relates to an expense which has already been deducted when computing accounting profit, but which will not be deducted for tax purposes until it is paid.

    Compute the tax base of each of these assets and liabilities, and identify any taxable or deductible temporary differences.

2   Markham plc acquires a machine for £200,000 on 1 January 20X2. The company estimates the useful life to be eight years with zero residual value, and adopts the straight-line basis of depreciation. The writing down allowance for tax purposes for this asset is 20% per annum on a reducing balance basis.

    Required:

    In relation to this machine, calculate the deferred tax asset or liability balance at each of Markham plc's financial year ends 20X2–20X9, and show the accounting entries which would be made. You may assume a tax rate of 25%.

●● Develop your understanding

3   The draft statement of profit or loss of Hedley plc for the year ended 31 March 20X3 shows an income tax expense of £55,000. The draft statement of financial position shows a non-current liability of £280,000 for deferred tax, but does not show a current tax liability.

Tax on the profit for the year ended 31 March 20X3 is estimated at £260,000. The figure in the draft statement of profit or loss is the under-provision for the year ended 31 March 20X2. The carrying amount of Harrington's net assets at 31 March 20X3 is £1.4 million more than their tax base on that date. Assume a tax rate of 25%.

Required:

Restate the figures which should appear in relation to taxation in the company's statement of profit or loss for the year ended 31 March 20X3 and in the statement of financial position at that date.

4   A company purchases an item of equipment on 1 January 20X1 for £48,000 which it estimates will have a seven-year useful life, at the end of which it is estimated it will be sold for £6,000. The company pays tax at 30% and the tax allowances for the equipment are as follows:

	£
20X1	12,000
20X2	9,000
20X3	7,000
20X4	5,000
20X5	4,000
20X6	3,000
20X7	2,000

The company had the same accounting profit before tax for each year of £80,000.

Assume that there are no other non-current assets, and that there are no differences between taxable profit and accounting profit other than those relating to depreciation.

Required:

For each year determine the company's income tax figure that would be shown in the company's statement of profit or loss and the deferred tax balance that would be disclosed on the company's statement of financial position.

5   The accounting policies of Kingfisher plc, in its 2015 financial statements, include the following:

Deferred tax is the tax expected to be recoverable or recoverable on differences between the carrying amounts of assets and liabilities in the financial statements and the corresponding tax bases used in the computation of taxable profit and is accounted for using the balance sheet liability method.

You are required to explain this policy.

6   Deferred tax may be seen as an income-smoothing device which distorts the true and fair view. Explain the impact of deferred tax on reported income and justify its continued use.

●●● Take it further

7   Garrick plc's statement of financial position at 30 June 20X6 is as follows:

	£000
Assets	
Non-current assets	
Property, plant and equipment	10,000
Other intangible assets	5,000
Investments	10,500
	25,500
Current assets	
Trade receivables	7,000
Other receivables	4,600
Cash and cash equivalents	6,700
	18,300
Total assets	43,800
Equity and liabilities	
Equity	
Equity share capital	9,000
Revaluation surplus	1,500
Retained earnings	7,510
	18,010
Non-current liabilities	
8% Long-term borrowings	9,600
Deferred tax liability	3,600
Pension liabilities	4,520
	17,720
Current liabilities	
Current tax liability	3,070
Trade and other payables	5,000
	8,070
Total equity and liabilities	43,800

The following information is relevant to the above statement of financial position.

(i) The investments are shown at their fair value at 30 June 20X6. The original cost of the investments was £9 million. The difference between cost and fair value has been accounted for through the revaluation surplus. Taxation is payable on the sale of the investments.

(ii) Other intangible assets are development costs which were all allowed for tax purposes when the cost was incurred in 20X5.

(iii) Trade and other payables include an accrual for compensation to be paid to employees. This amounts to £1 million and is allowed for taxation when paid.

(iv) The tax bases of the other assets and liabilities are the same as their carrying amounts in the statement of financial position at 30 June 20X6 except for the following:

	£000
Property, plant and equipment	2,400
Trade receivables	7,500
Other receivables	5,000
Pension liabilities	5,000
8% long term borrowings	10,000

(v) Assume taxation is payable at 30%.

Required:

Calculate Garrick plc's deferred tax liability or asset at 30 June 20X6. Show how this would be dealt with in the financial statements at this date. (Assume that any adjustments do not affect current tax.)

8   Sapper plc has reported profit before tax for the two years ended 31 December 20X5 and 20X6 of £8,775,000 and £8,740,000 respectively. In 20X5 the enacted income tax rate was 40% of taxable profit. In 20X6 the enacted income tax rate was 35% of taxable profit.

The company made charitable donations of £500,000 and £350,000 in 20X5 and 20X6 respectively. Charitable donations are recognised as an expense when they are paid and are not deductible for tax purposes.

In 20X5, the company was notified by the relevant authorities that they intend to pursue an action against the company with respect to sulphur emissions. Although at December 20X6 the action had not yet come to court, the company recognised a liability of £700,000 in 20X5 being its best estimate of the fine arising from the action. Fines are not deductible for tax purposes.

In 20X2, the company incurred £1,250,000 of costs in relation to the development of a new product. These costs were deducted for tax purposes in 20X2. For accounting purposes, the company capitalised this expenditure and amortised it on the straight-line basis over five years. At 31 December 20X4, the unamortised balance of these product development costs was £500,000.

In 20X5, the company entered into an agreement with its existing employees to provide health-care benefits to retirees. The company recognises as an expense the cost of this plan as employees provide service and recognised £2,000,000 and £1,000,000 as expenses in 20X5 and 20X6 respectively. No payments to retirees were made for such benefits in 20X5 or 20X6. Healthcare costs are deductible for tax purposes when payments are made to retirees. The company has determined that it is probable that taxable profit will be available against which any resulting deferred tax asset can be utilised.

Details of the company's building and motor vehicles cost, and accumulated depreciation for the years 20X5 and 20X6 are as follows:

	Building £000	Motor vehicles £000	Total £000
Cost			
Balance at 31/12/X4	50,000	10,000	60,000
Additions 20X5	6,000	–	6,000
Balance at 31/12/X5	56,000	10,000	66,000

Elimination of accumulated depreciation on revaluation at 1/1/X6	(22,800)	–	(22,800)
Revaluation at 1/1/X6	31,800	–	31,800
Balance at 1/1/X6	65,000	10,000	75,000
Additions 20X6	–	15,000	15,000
Balance at 31/12/X6	65,000	25,000	90,000
Accumulated depreciation			
Balance at 31/12/X4	20,000	4,000	24,000
Depreciation 20X5	2,800	2,000	4,800
Balance at 31/12/X5	22,800	6,000	28,800
Revaluation at 1/1/X6	(22,800)	–	(22,800)
Balance at 1/1/X6	–	6,000	6,000
Depreciation 20X6	3,250	5,000	8,250
Balance at 31/12/X6	3,250	11,000	14,250
Carrying amount			
31/12/X4	30,000	6,000	36,000
31/12/X5	33,200	4,000	37,200
31/12/X6	61,750	14,000	75,750

Buildings are depreciated for accounting purposes at 5% a year on a straight-line basis and at 10% a year on a straight-line basis for tax purposes. Motor vehicles are depreciated for accounting purposes at 20% a year on a straight-line basis and at 25% a year on a straight-line basis for tax purposes. A full year's depreciation is charged for accounting purposes in the year that an asset is acquired.

At 1 January 20X6, the building was revalued to £65,000,000 and the company estimated that the remaining useful life of the building was 20 years from the date of the revaluation. The revaluation did not affect taxable profit in 20X6 and the taxation authorities did not adjust the tax base of the building to reflect the revaluation.

Required:

For the years 20X5 and 20X6 calculate the income tax figures that would be shown in Sapper plc's statement of comprehensive income and the deferred tax balances that would be disclosed on the company's statement of financial position.

Visit the Online Resource Centre for solutions to all these end of chapter questions plus visual walkthrough solutions. You can test your understanding with extra questions and answers, explore additional case studies based on real companies, take a guided tour through a company report and much more. Go to the Online Resource Centre at **www.oxfordtextbooks.co.uk/orc/maynard2e/**

Part 4

Statement of financial position reporting issues

10

Property, plant and equipment, and impairment

➤ Introduction

Property, plant and equipment are tangible non-current assets, such as land and buildings, plant and machinery, office equipment, and motor vehicles. It is often the largest item in monetary terms on the face of the statement of financial position, affects other figures in the financial statements and underpins many accounting ratios. It is therefore important that financial statements communicate relevant and faithfully representational information about property, plant and equipment.

There are also inherent issues relating to the future when businesses acquire property, plant and equipment. This means that estimates and judgements are an integral part of accounting for property, plant and equipment.

The key accounting standard, which provides the framework for the accounting methods, is International Accounting Standard (IAS) 16 *Property, Plant and Equipment*. There are, however, a number of related issues dealt with by other accounting standards. These address how additional elements of the cost of an asset are determined, for example related interest costs and government grants. Additionally, IAS 36 *Impairment of Assets* deals with the crucial question of whether the carrying amount of an asset reflects the value to the business, and whether an asset is consequently deemed to be impaired or not.

Property held for investment purposes and other non-currents which are held for sale purposes are different categories of non-current asset requiring different accounting treatment and separate disclosure. How these are accounted for is addressed by two further accounting standards, IAS 40 *Investment Property* and International Financial Reporting Standard (IFRS) 5 *Non-current Assets Held for Sale and Discontinued Operations*.

★ Learning objectives

After studying this chapter you will be able to:

- understand the issues relating to accounting for property, plant and equipment, and why and where judgements are required
- account for the acquisition, subsequent use of and derecognition of property, plant and equipment, including the determination of cost and depreciation, and how to deal with revaluations
- understand what impairment of non-current assets is and account for this issue
- define and account for investment properties and assets held for sale.

✔ Key issues checklist

- ❏ Significance of property, plant and equipment.
- ❏ Definition of an asset and property, plant and equipment.
- ❏ Relationship to underpinning principles.
- ❏ Initial measurement—what is cost?
- ❏ Borrowing costs.
- ❏ Government grants.
- ❏ Subsequent costs.
- ❏ Depreciation—estimates, methods and accounting.
- ❏ The two measurement models—historic cost and valuation.
- ❏ Impairment—what it is, why it is accounted for and accounting treatments.
- ❏ Cash-generating units.
- ❏ Investment properties—definition of and accounting alternatives: the cost and fair value models.
- ❏ Assets held for sale—definition of and accounting for.
- ❏ Disclosures in published financial statements—what and why.
- ❏ Interpretation and the effect of alternative measurement models and estimates on financial information.

10.1 Significance of property, plant and equipment

Many industries, such as manufacturing and retailing, are described as capital intensive and therefore property, plant and equipment is often the largest group of assets on the businesses' statements of financial position. In these industries the cost and associated cash flows of items of property, plant and equipment will be monitored closely by users of the financial statements. Relevant and faithfully representational information about property, plant and equipment is therefore essential for users, as this will have significant implications for funding and future cash flows.

There may be pressures on businesses to enhance the figures for property, plant and equipment to improve the presentation of their statements of financial position. However, overstating the carrying amount of non-current assets, either intentionally or unintentionally, leads to the inflation of earnings. Inflated earnings have consequential effects on key performance indicators, such as earnings per share, return on capital employed and gearing. The accounting standards relating to property, plant and equipment set out provisions to counter any such pressures.

10.2 Definition of property, plant and equipment

Expenditure in a business is generally either of a capital nature or related to ongoing expenses (revenue expenditure). The classification of expenditure as an asset or an expense often has to be based on judgement and will have a significant impact on the financial statements. The key question is where the 'debit' of the double-entry goes: either in the statement of financial position as an asset or in the statement of profit or loss as an expense and reduction of profit. One of the main issues in the WorldCom scandal revolved around the inappropriate capitalisation of expenses.

Financial reporting in practice 10.1   WorldCom

At its peak, WorldCom was the second largest long distance telephone company in the USA. WorldCom grew largely by aggressively acquiring other telecommunications companies, most notably MCI Communications in 1998, and had ambitions to become the largest company in the industry. In 2000 the telecommunications industry suffered a downturn and the market prices for WorldCom's shares started to fall. Pressures from his business empires meant that the Chief Executive Officer (CEO), Bernard Ebbers, wanted WorldCom's share price to remain high. From 1999 to 2002 the company, under the direction of Ebbers and other company officers, used fraudulent accounting methods to mask its declining earnings by painting a false picture of financial growth and profitability to prop up the price of the company's shares.

The $3.8 billion fraud involved inflating profits by inappropriately capitalising expenses and inflating revenues with bogus accounting entries. The costs that were erroneously capitalised related to fees that WorldCom paid to other telecom companies for the right to access their networks.

The fraud was discovered by a small team of internal auditors which informed the audit committee and board of directors. The company filed for Chapter 11 bankruptcy protection in 2002.

Note: the auditors of WorldCom were Arthur Andersen.

The definition of an asset in the IASB's proposed Exposure Draft of its revised *Conceptual Framework* is:

> ... a present economic resource controlled by the entity as a result of past events ...
>
> *(IASB, 2015)*

and is discussed in detail in Chapter 2 together with the recognition and measurement principles that apply to assets. What this means is that for an item to be classified and recognised as an asset, it has to have the potential to contribute, directly or indirectly, to the flow of cash and cash equivalents to the company. The current IAS 16 *Property, Plant and Equipment* is based on the 2010 *Conceptual Framework*, however it is unlikely that significant changes to IAS 16 will be necessary following any revised definitions of the elements and recognition and measurement principles in the new *Conceptual Framework*.

IAS 16 defines property, plant and equipment as tangible resources that are:

- held for use in the production or supply of goods or services, for rental to others, or for administrative purposes; and
- expected to be used during more than one financial year.

(IASB, 2003a, para. 6)

Property, plant and equipment are, therefore, non-current assets, and have physical form and are often owned, but the legal right of ownership does not have to be present for control to be present. (Note: the accounting for property, plant and equipment which are leased is dealt with in Chapter 15.) Assets may be donated or provided by the government, for example as part of a programme to encourage economic growth in an area. However, property, plant and equipment are often purchased and the acquisition transaction must have occurred before the end of the financial year. The intention to purchase an asset, even if agreed and documented, does not give rise to an asset.

10.3 Recognition of property, plant and equipment

10.3.1 Initial recognition

The recognition criteria for property, plant and equipment in the financial statements as detailed in IAS 16 are the same as the requirements for the recognition of any of the elements of financial statements as set out in the 2010 *Conceptual Framework*:

- it is probable that any the future economic benefits associated with the asset will flow to the entity
- the cost of the asset can be measured reliably.

These criteria no doubt will be updated once the revised *Conceptual Framework* is issued, with relevance, faithful representation and the cost benefit constraint being required for recognition.

For many items classified as property, plant and equipment the related future economic benefits are clear to see. For example, a manufacturing business's machines are producing the products that will be sold to customers and the business will receive cash once the customers pay; the delivery vehicles are being used to transport the goods to the customers. Other items of property, plant and equipment may not directly increase future economic benefits. However, the property, furniture and computer systems of the business and the motor vehicle driven by the chief financial officer are considered necessary for the business to obtain future economic benefits from its other assets and can, therefore, be recognised as property, plant and equipment.

10.3.2 Recognition of subsequent expenditure

The acquisition of an item of property, plant and equipment may result in other transactions which could occur at a later time. These include:

- the acquisition of spare parts
- future improvements or expansion of the capacity of the asset
- replacement of part of or the servicing of the asset.

A key question is whether the expenditure arising from such transactions is capitalised as property, plant and equipment, or whether the expenditure should be written off to the statement of profit or loss as an expense. Rather than creating a set of additional criteria, IAS 16 specifies that if the main recognition criteria are met, as discussed earlier, this subsequent expenditure will be recognised as property, plant and equipment.

Recognition of subsequent expenditure as property, plant and equipment may lead to the different parts of a larger asset being treated as separate components, with separate lives and depreciation being applied.

 Examples of recognition

Discuss whether the following items are property, plant and equipment, and, if so, whether they are able to be recognised in the financial statements.

1 A chemical manufacturer installs new chemical handling processes which are necessary to comply with environmental requirements for the production and storage of dangerous chemicals.

 Although these plant enhancements do not directly increase the future economic benefits of the manufacturer, they are able to be recognised as an asset because without them the business is unable to manufacture and sell chemicals.

2 On acquisition of a specialised item of machinery a manufacturer purchases spare parts for the motor that drives the machine. The motor is expected to run without needing replacement parts for 18 months.

 The spare parts are to be used only in connection with this particular machine, and the business expects to use them during more than one accounting year. It is assumed the cost is known. They can therefore be recognised as property, plant and equipment.

3 A business fits interior partitions into its general office space.

A business does this often as part of a restructuring programme or to enable its employees to work more efficiently. Thus, the business will derive future economic benefits from this building work. It is likely the partitions will be in place for more than one year and the cost can be established. They can therefore be recognised as property, plant and equipment.

4 A business repaints its warehouse.

The repainting expenditure only maintains the future economic benefits flowing from the use of the warehouse; there is no increase in the benefits originally identified when the warehouse was first acquired. This expenditure is therefore treated as repairs and maintenance, and is written off to profit and loss when incurred.

10.4 Initial measurement of property, plant and equipment

10.4.1 Cost

An item of property, plant and equipment is measured (*remember this means valued*) on its recognition at its cost. This comprises all costs directly attributable to bringing the asset to the location and condition necessary for it to be capable of operating in the manner intended by the business, and will include:

(a) The purchase price net of trade discounts

(b) Import duties and taxes

(c) Costs of site preparation

(d) Delivery and handling costs

(e) Construction, installation and assembly costs

(f) Wages and salaries, and other employee benefits relating to the acquisition, construction and installation of the asset

(g) Costs of testing whether the asset is working properly

(h) Professional fees.

If, as a result of having acquired the asset, a business has an obligation to dismantle and remove the item and restore the site on which it is located at the end of its use, an estimate of these costs will be included in the cost of the property, plant and equipment. This applies, for example, to oil exploration or drilling companies, where they are required to remove all drilling rigs and restore the land or sea bed to its original state. This obligation means that a provision, which is a liability, has to be accounted for:

Debit   Property, plant and equipment

  Credit   Non-current liability

and the measurement of this liability, and hence the amount added to the asset cost, will be on a discounted cash flow basis if the discounting is considered material. This is discussed further in Chapter 13 which deals with accounting for provisions.

Once an asset is capable of operating as the business intended, any further costs relating to the asset are not capitalised as property, plant and equipment, even if the asset is not yet being operated or it is being operated, but not at full capacity. So, for example, losses incurred while the demand for the asset's output builds up and costs of reorganising the business's operations during this time are written off to profit and loss.

If an asset is constructed internally by a business, the same principles apply in determining its cost. However, any abnormal costs, for example related to wasted material, labour or other resources, are not included. In practice this may be difficult to ascertain.

If an item of property, plant and equipment is acquired by an exchange of non-monetary assets, the cost of the asset is measured at fair value. There are two exceptions to this:

1 Where the exchange transaction lacks commercial substance, for example where two similar assets are exchanged

2 Where the fair value of neither asset exchanged can be measured reliably.

In these cases the cost of the acquired asset is measured at the carrying amount of the asset transferred.

10.4.2 Borrowing costs

Some items of property, plant and equipment take a substantial period of time to get ready for their intended use. The acquisition itself may take some time, if, for example, planning permission has to be obtained to enable the development of a plot of land, and then the asset may have to be constructed. A business in this position may fund the acquisition or construction itself, and take out some form of loan and incur finance and other charges in relation to this. Alternatively, a business may acquire a complete asset immediately ready for use. The cost of this asset would include financing costs incurred by the third party during the development phase.

To enhance comparability of these two situations, the asset in the former case described previously is called a **qualifying asset** and the borrowing costs incurred by the business that are directly attributable to the acquisition or construction of this qualifying asset form part of the cost of the asset. IAS 23 *Borrowing Costs* sets out the accounting treatment and requirements.

If a business borrows funds specifically for the purpose of obtaining a qualifying asset, it is straightforward to identify the borrowing costs. However, it may be difficult to identify a direct relationship between particular borrowings and a qualifying asset. For example, many businesses will coordinate their financing activities centrally, or a parent company in a group obtains the borrowing and lends out funds on various bases to the other group companies. In this case the amount of borrowing costs that should be capitalised is calculated by reference to the weighted average cost of the general borrowings. This calculation excludes borrowings directly related to another qualifying asset.

Borrowing costs are capitalised from the commencement date until the date when substantially all the activities necessary to prepare the asset for its intended use are complete. The commencement date is the first date when all three of the following conditions are met:

(a) The company incurs expenditure on the asset

(b) The company incurs borrowing costs

(c) The company undertakes activities that are necessary to prepare the asset for its intended use.

Cessation of the capitalisation of the borrowing costs is when the asset is substantially available for use and not when the asset is actually used. So, if, for example, the move of the business to the property that has been constructed is delayed but the property is complete, the interest incurred during the period of the delay cannot be added to the cost of the property.

10.4.3 Government grants

Businesses may receive financial assistance from the government or government agencies for a variety of reasons and in various forms. For example:

● monetary assistance may be provided to stimulate employment or investment in particular geographical areas or for specific industries

● business start-up grants may be awarded

● governments may actually invest in the business (as the UK government has in financial institutions as a result of the financial crisis)

● tax breaks may be given or reductions in certain taxes allowed.

IAS 20 *Accounting for Government Grants and Disclosure of Government Assistance* was issued to ensure that companies which received government assistance and those which had not could be compared fairly, and that the companies' performances could be interpreted properly.

Government grants are a particular form of government assistance and are awarded 'in return for past or future compliance with certain conditions relating to the operating activities of the entity' (IASB, IAS 20 *Accounting for Government Grants and Disclosure of Government Assistance*, para. 3). They may include the actual transfer of an asset, such as a plot of land, or be in the form of cash to assist companies in the acquisition of non-current assets.

Government grants can be recognised when there is reasonable assurance that:

1   The company will comply with any conditions attached to the grant

2   The company will actually receive the grant.

The recognition of the grants follows the accruals or matching principle (called the 'income approach' in IAS 20), and should be included in profit and loss over the periods in which the company recognises the costs for which the grants are intended to compensate. In relation to grants received for depreciating non-current assets the grants are recognised over the periods in which the asset is depreciated and on the same systematic basis as the depreciation is charged.

Table 10.1 shows the two alternative accounting methods by which this may be achieved.

On one hand, the net effect of the two accounting methods on profit is the same; however, the statement of financial position of a company choosing the netting-off method will be less comparable to companies who have not received grants. On the other hand, impairment (see section 10.7 below) may be less of an issue as the carrying amount of the asset is lower.

Table 10.1 Alternative methods for accounting for government grants

	Approach	Accounting
1	**Deferred income approach**	Dr Bank/cash
	Set up grant as deferred income (a liability on the statement of financial position)	Cr Deferred income
	The income is recognised in profit and loss over the useful life of the asset corresponding to the method of depreciation used	Dr Deferred income Cr Income
2	**Netting-off method**	Dr Bank/cash
	Deduct the grant from the cost of the asset	Cr Asset
	The grant is recognised in profit and loss through the reduced depreciation	

10.5 Subsequent measurement— depreciation

The matching concept requires revenues and costs that result directly from the same transactions or other events to be recognised in the same period. The cost of an item of property, plant and equipment therefore needs to be matched against the benefits the resource brings in and the accounting mechanism for this is depreciation. Depreciation is therefore a measure of the consumption of an item of property, plant and equipment and should be calculated on a systematic basis over the asset's useful life. Subsequent expenditure on an item of property, plant and equipment may mean the cost of the asset comprises different parts. In this case, each part of the asset may have to be depreciated separately. For example, for an aircraft it may be appropriate to depreciate the airframe and the engines separately. This splitting of an asset into component parts is a key feature of IAS 16 and may provide specific challenges where property, plant and equipment, and intangible assets are linked closely, for example where a machine is preloaded with application software.

The following terms are used in connection with depreciation.

Depreciation	The systematic allocation of the depreciable amount over its *useful life*.
Depreciable amount	Cost of asset (or other amount substituted for cost) less its *residual value*.
Residual value	Estimated amount that the entity would currently obtain from the disposal of the asset, net of costs of disposal, if the asset were already in the condition expected at the end of its *useful life*.
Useful life	The period over which an asset is expected to be available for use.
	Or:
	The number of production units expected to be obtained from the asset.

10.5.1 Accounting for depreciation

Depreciation is an expense charged to profit or loss. The effect is to write down the cost (or other amount substituted for cost) for each accounting period. The resulting value of the asset is termed net book value or carrying amount. Businesses need to keep the depreciation that accumulates on an asset in a separate account from the cost, as they are required to disclose both amounts (see section 10.11 for disclosure requirements). So the basic bookkeeping for depreciation is:

Debit	Depreciation expense
Credit	Accumulated depreciation

Instead of being expensed depreciation may be capitalised as part of the cost of another asset. For example, suppose a crane owned by a business is used in the construction of a new building which the business will own and occupy. The depreciation expense of the crane is a directly attributable cost incurred in the construction of another asset, the building. Hence, the bookkeeping will be:

Debit	Building cost
Credit	Crane accumulated depreciation

Depreciation should commence once an asset is available for its intended use, which may be different from when it is actually used, and ceases:

1 Either when the asset is classified as 'held for sale' (see section 10.10)

2 Or when the asset is derecognised, i.e. it is disposed of, or no future economic benefits are expected from its use or disposal.

A few further points about depreciation should be made. All assets classified as property, plant and equipment should be depreciated, except land as this has an unlimited useful life. Exceptions to this land exception are quarries and mines, which are depreciated as the land is consumed.

Depreciation is required even if the fair value of the asset exceeds its carrying amount. Arguably, companies such as breweries, which own chains of pubs, and hotel and leisure complexes, which maintain their assets in a good state of repair by carrying out frequent refurbishments, should not have to depreciate these assets. However, IAS 16 makes clear that it is only if the residual value exceeds the carrying amount that depreciation would not be required.

The future economic benefits of an asset are consumed mainly through its use. However, other factors may result in the reduction of the economic benefits and should, therefore, be taken into account when estimating the useful life. These factors could include:

- expected physical wear and tear
- level of maintenance
- technical or commercial obsolescence
- change in demand for the products produced by the asset.

10.5.2 Method of depreciation

The depreciation method chosen by the company should reflect the pattern in which the asset's future economic benefits are expected to be consumed by the company and be reviewed at least at each financial year end. Three alternative methods are mentioned in IAS 16:

- the straight-line method
- the diminishing (or reducing) balance method (which can be approximated by the sum of digits method)
- the units of production method.

Note that the standard does not specify that a company has to select one of these methods. Many companies choose the straight-line method as they estimate the pattern of consumption of an asset to be similar from year to year.

 Worked example 10.1: to show the different depreciation methods

Details relating to a machine acquired by Quin plc are as follows:

Cost of machine	£25,000 purchased at the start of year 1
Expected useful life	4 years
Residual value	£5,000

The machine is to be used in production and the forecast output of the units is as follows:

Year 1	15,000 units
Year 2	10,000 units
Year 3	20,000 units
Year 4	5,000 units
	50,000

Required:

For each of the four years the asset is used, calculate the annual depreciation and the resulting figures that will appear in the financial statements for each of the following methods of depreciation:

(a) Straight-line

(b) Diminishing (reducing) balance

(c) Sum of digits

(d) Units of production.

(a) Straight-line method

Annual depreciation expense = Depreciable amount/useful life
= (£25,000 – £5,000)/4
= £5,000

Year	SoPL expense £	Net book value £
1	5,000	25,000 – 5,000 = 20,000
2	5,000	20,000 – 5,000 = 15,000
3	5,000	15,000 – 5,000 = 10,000
4	5,000	10,000 – 5,000 = 5,000*

* Note the net book value at the end of year 4 is the expected residual value.

The depreciation expense is the same each year; thus, this method should be chosen if the pattern of consumption is similar each year.

(b) Diminishing (reducing) balance method

A constant proportion is written off the net book value each year. The appropriate proportion is obtained from the formula

$$1 - \sqrt[n]{(r/c)}$$

where c = cost, r = residual value, and n = useful life.

Substituting the appropriate values into the formula gives the proportion as $1 - \sqrt[4]{(5,000/25,000)} = 0.331$, which will be rounded to 0.35 or 35% for this example.

Annual depreciation expense = 35% × net book value

Year	SoPL expense £	Net book value £
1	35% × 25,000 = 8,750	25,000 – 8,750 = 16,250
2	35% × 16,250 = 5,688	16,250 – 5,688 = 10,562
3	35% × 10,562 = 3,697	10,562 – 3,697 = 6,865
4	35% × 6,865 = 2,403	6,865 – 2,403 = 4,462*

* The effect of rounding the answer given by the formula to 35% means that the net book value at the end of year 4 is £4,462 and not the expected residual value of £5,000.

The depreciation expense reduces each year, and thus this method should be used for assets whose use is greater in earlier years and then reduces.

(c) Sum of digits method

This is an approximation to the reducing balance method.

Annual depreciation expense = Depreciable amount × depreciation rate
Depreciable amount = 25,000 – 5,000 = £20,000
Depreciation rate = No. of years of useful life remaining/sum of digits
Sum of digits = [n(n + 1)]/2 (where n = estimated useful life)
= [4 × (4 + 1)]/2 = 10

Year	Depreciation rate	SoPL expense £	Net book value £
1	4/10	× 20,000 = 8,000	25,000 – 8,000 = 17,000
2	3/10	× 20,000 = 6,000	17,000 – 6,000 = 11,000
3	2/10	× 20,000 = 4,000	11,000 – 4,000 = 7,000
4	1/10	× 20,000 = 2,000	7,000 – 2,000 = 5,000

(d) Units of production method

Annual depreciation expense = Depreciable amount × depreciation rate
Depreciable amount = 25,000 – 5,000 = £20,000
Depreciation rate = $\dfrac{\text{Units of output produced in the period}}{\text{Total no. of units}}$

Year	Depreciation rate	SoPL expense £	Net book value £
1	15/50	× 20,000 = 6,000	25,000 – 6,000 = 19,000
2	10/50	× 20,000 = 4,000	19,000 – 4,000 = 15,000
3	20/50	× 20,000 = 8,000	15,000 – 8,000 = 7,000
4	5/50	× 20,000 = 2,000	7,000 – 2,000 = 5,000

This method matches exactly the consumption of the benefits of the machine to the expected production levels of the units and, given that these estimates have been made, is the best of the four methods to be chosen.

10.5.3 Changes in estimates

Although comparability in accounting from one year to the next is one of the enhancing characteristics of financial reporting, if the circumstances in a company change, then this should be reflected in the financial statements so that they faithfully represent these circumstances. Therefore, if a company decides that the original estimates of useful life or residual value or of how the asset was to be used need revising, it is permitted to do this. IAS 8 *Accounting Policies, Changes in Accounting Estimates and Errors* is then relevant (see discussion in Chapter 4). As these are changes in estimates (and not a change in accounting policy) the effect of the change is applied prospectively, i.e. from the date of change.

An example of a change in estimate of useful life is shown in Chapter 4, but here is another.

 Example of a change in residual value

A company purchases an item of machinery on 1 March 20X2 for £50,000 and estimates the useful life to be 10 years with zero residual value. The company applies a straight-line depreciation method to its plant and machinery.

Owing to an increase in the price of scrap metal, on 1 March 20X6 the company revises its estimate of the residual value to £3,000.

Annual depreciation charged for years ended 28 February 20X3 – 20X6 = 50,000/10 = £5,000

Carrying amount of the machine at 28 February 20X6 = 50,000 – (4 × 5,000) = £30,000.

There are six years of useful life remaining.

Annual depreciation to be charged from 1 March 20X6 = (30,000 – 3,000)/6 = £4,500.

10.6 Subsequent measurement—alternative models

There are two alternative measurement models for property, plant and equipment—the cost model or the revaluation model—and companies can decide which one they should choose as an accounting policy choice. Under the two models the carrying amount of an asset is defined as:

Cost model Cost *minus* accumulated depreciation *minus* accumulated impairment losses.

Revaluation model Fair value at date of revaluation *minus* accumulated depreciation *minus* accumulated impairment losses.

Note that impairment for both models is discussed in section 10.7. What constitutes cost has been discussed earlier, so the fair value model will now be dealt with.

10.6.1 Fair value

The fair value of an asset is defined in IFRS 13 *Fair Value Measurement* as:

> … the price that would be received to sell an asset in an orderly transaction between market participants at the measurement date.

(IASB, 2011, para. 9)

This standard sets out guidance in how the fair value for non-financial assets may be ascertained. Briefly, these are that when measuring fair value, the following must be considered:

- the condition, location and any restrictions on sale of the asset being measured
- the principal (or most advantageous) market in which an orderly transaction would take place for the asset

- the highest and best use of the asset, and whether the asset is used in combination with other assets or on a standalone basis
- the assumptions that market participants would use when pricing the asset.

Approaches to the determination of fair value include a market approach (based on market prices), a cost approach (based on the current cost of replacing the asset), and an income approach (using discounting techniques applied to the cash flows the asset is estimated to bring in). The approach taken should maximise the relevant observable inputs and minimise the use of unobservable inputs, in order to produce a more reliable value. Chapter 2 has discussed the hierarchy of methods.

! Reminder *The 'fair value hierarchy' specifies three levels, with Level 1 being the preferable (most reliable) method if available:*

- *level 1—unadjusted quoted prices for identical assets in active markets*
- *level 2—other observable inputs for the asset, such as quoted prices in active markets for similar assets or quoted prices for identical assets in markets which are not active*
- *level 3—unobservable inputs developed by an entity using the best information available where there is little, or no, market activity for the asset at the measurement date.*

In practice the fair value of land and buildings, and plant and equipment may be determined from market-based evidence, such as appraisals undertaken by professionally qualified valuers. If there is no market-based evidence of fair value, for example, because assets have been customised by the business, IFRS 13 suggests that fair value is estimated using a current replacement cost approach. This reflects the current amount that would be required to replace the asset in its current condition, taking into account all obsolescence factors.

 Example of current replacement cost

A company chooses the revaluation model for its land and buildings. Its headquarters building was acquired three years ago for £500,000 and the useful life at this time was estimated at 20 years. The company now wishes to revalue the building. The cost for a similar new building is £600,000.

Fair value estimated by the current replacement cost approach takes the cost of the new building and applies the company's depreciation policy for the length of time the asset has been held to reflect the comparable condition of the building now.

Hence, the cost of the new building is depreciated for three years and the resulting net book value is taken as the fair value of the asset:

$$\text{Fair value} = £600,000 - [3 \times (£600,000/20)] = £510,000$$

Note that other obsolescence factors, in addition to depreciation, should also be taken into account to estimate the current replacement cost.

In practice the process of estimating the fair value of an item of property, plant and equipment is difficult and requires extensive judgement. If professional valuers have been used this fact is disclosed together with extensive details of where and how fair value has been used in the financial statements. This information will assist users in assessing the reliability of the values stated.

10.6.2 Revaluation model

If a company selects the revaluation model, it cannot 'cherry-pick' which assets it chooses to revalue to increase asset values on the statement of financial position. IAS 16 requires that the whole class of property, plant and equipment to which the asset belongs is revalued. Typical classes would be:

- land
- land and buildings
- aircraft or ships
- machinery
- motor vehicles
- fixtures and fittings
- office equipment.

To ensure the financial information is relevant, revaluations need to be made with sufficient regularity to ensure the carrying amount does not differ from an up-to-date fair value. In practice this means the frequency of revaluations depends upon changes in fair values. If the markets related to the assets are particularly volatile, this may mean that annual revaluation is required, but, for other assets, revaluations may only be necessary every 3–5 years.

10.6.3 Accounting for the revaluation model

On revaluation the asset's fair value is compared to its carrying amount.

1   If the fair value is greater than the carrying amount, the difference is credited to a revaluation surplus account, which is an equity reserve:

Debit	Asset (carrying amount)
Credit	Revaluation surplus

The increase in revaluation is recognised in other comprehensive income in the statement of comprehensive income and it will also be shown in the statement of changes in equity.
 The increase is recognised in profit and loss (i.e. the statement of profit or loss) to the extent that it reverses any previous revaluation decrease which had been recognised in profit and loss.

2   If the fair value is less than the carrying amount, the difference is recognised as an expense in profit and loss:

Debit	Profit and loss
Credit	Asset (carrying amount)

If, however, a credit balance relating to the asset exists on the revaluation surplus account, the decrease in value is debited to the revaluation surplus to the extent this exists, recognised in other comprehensive income in the statement of comprehensive income, and is also shown in the statement of changes in equity:

Debit	Revaluation surplus
Credit	Asset (carrying amount)

The adjustment to the asset carrying amount can be achieved in two alternative ways:

(i) The accumulated depreciation on the asset is eliminated against the asset's cost (or revaluation) account and the resulting net book value in the cost account is then restated to the revalued amount. This method is often used for buildings

(ii) The asset's cost and accumulated depreciation accounts are both restated proportionately so that the resulting carrying amount (cost—accumulated depreciation) equals the revalued amount.

Following revaluation there are also two alternative subsequent accounting treatments for the revaluation surplus account:

(i) Its balance is transferred to retained earnings when the asset is derecognised

(ii) Its balance is transferred to retained earnings as the asset is used—the amount being transferred being the additional depreciation based on the revalued amount over the depreciation based on the cost (or previous revaluation).

The IASB recommends that alternative (ii) is followed. It also ensures that distributable profits (profits out of which dividends can legally be paid) are not reduced as a result of revaluations.

It should be noted that both alternatives constitute a transfer between reserves which does not pass through profit and loss.

 Worked example 10.2: to show the accounting for a revaluation

Squib plc, which has a 31 December year end, adopts the revaluation model for its plant and machinery. The company acquires one item of plant for £10,000 on 1 January 20X1. The plant is depreciated on a straight-line basis over its useful economic life, which is estimated to be five years. On 1 January 20X3 the company revalues the plant at its fair value of £9,600.

On 1 January 20X5 the plant is sold for £4,000. Any revaluation surplus is amortised to retained earnings as the plant is being depreciated.

Required:

Show the accounting entries for the transactions for the years 20X3 to 20X5.

The carrying amount of the asset at the date of revaluation of 1 January 20X3 needs to be established:

	£
Cost at 1 Jan 20X1	10,000
Depreciation expense for y/e 31 Dec 20X1	(2,000)
Depreciation expense for y/e 31 Dec 20X2	(2,000)
Net book value (NBV) at 1 Jan 20X3	6,000
Revalued amount	9,600
Surplus on revaluation	3,600

Method 1—elimination of accumulated depreciation account on revaluation

		£	£
Dr	Accumulated depreciation	4,000	
Cr	Asset cost		4,000
Dr	Asset cost	3,600	
Cr	Revaluation surplus		3,600

As a result of these entries the asset cost has a balance of £9,600—the revalued amount. This is depreciated over the remaining useful life of three years:

		£	£
Dr	Depreciation expense	3,200	
Cr	Accumulated depreciation		3,200

Each year the excess depreciation of £3,200 − £2,000 = £1,200 is transferred from Revaluation surplus to Retained earnings:

		£	£
Dr	Revaluation surplus	1,200	
Cr	Retained earnings		1,200

At the date of sale of 1 January 20X5 (two years later):
Asset revalued 'cost' account has a balance of £9,600 Dr
Accumulated depreciation has a balance of £6,400 Cr
Revaluation surplus has a balance of (£3,600 − £2,400) £1,200 Cr

The accounting for the sale of the asset is as follows:

		£	£
Dr	Bank	4,000	
Dr	Accumulated depreciation	6,400	
Cr	Asset revalued amount		9,600
Cr	Profit on sale (balancing figure)		800

The remaining balance on the Revaluation surplus is transferred to Retained earnings:

		£	£
Dr	Revaluation surplus	1,200	
Cr	Retained earnings		1,200

Method 2—'grossing up' of cost and accumulated depreciation accounts

The asset's net book value of £6,000 is effectively increased by a factor of 1.6 to fair value of £9,600 (£6,000 × 1.6 = £9,600).

The asset's cost and accumulated depreciation accounts are increased by the same factor:

		£	£
Dr	Asset cost (£10,000 × 1.6 – £10,000)	6,000	
Cr	Accumulated depreciation (£4,000 × 1.6 – £4,000)		2,400
Cr	Revaluation surplus		3,600

As a result:

Asset 'cost' account has a balance of	£16,000
Accumulated depreciation has a balance of	£6,400

The net book value of the asset = £9,600, which is the revalued amount.
The 'cost' continues to be depreciated over five years:

		£	£
Dr	Depreciation expense	3,200	
Cr	Accumulated depreciation		3,200

As for Method 1, each year the excess depreciation of £3,200 – £2,000 = £1,200 is transferred from the Revaluation surplus to Retained earnings:

		£	£
Dr	Revaluation surplus	1,200	
Cr	Retained earnings		1,200

At the date of sale 1 January 20X5 (2 years later):

Asset 'cost' account has a balance of	£16,000 Dr
Accumulated depreciation has a balance of	£12,800 Cr
Revaluation surplus has balance of (£3,600 – £2,400)	£1,200 Cr

The accounting for the sale of the asset is as follows:

		£	£
Dr	Bank	4,000	
Dr	Accumulated depreciation	12,800	
Cr	Asset 'cost'		16,000
Cr	Profit on sale (balancing figure)		800

The remaining balance on the Revaluation surplus is transferred to Retained earnings:

		£	£
Dr	Revaluation surplus	1,200	
Cr	Retained earnings		1,200

10.6.4 Choice of revaluation model

Market values of businesses are often significantly higher than their reported net asset values, reflecting significant differences in values which are not reflected in the financial statements. Many believe that the usefulness of financial statements is undermined unless the updated values for items of property are reflected in the financial statements. So one argument for a company choosing the revaluation model is that the method provides more up-to-date values of assets, and thus can be said to be more relevant than historic cost to investors in their decision making. (*Remember, relevance is one of the fundamental qualitative characteristics.*) For many years revaluations have resulted in higher asset values, particularly for property. This has been useful for companies wishing to enhance their statements of financial position, especially if they have net current liabilities or high gearing.

However, the resulting depreciation expense is higher, resulting in lower profits. Additional costs of having to keep revaluations current and employing expert valuers will also be incurred. In addition, a decline in the property market may mean that companies have to explain falls in their non-current asset values.

In the UK, surveys of companies have revealed that only a small proportion (less than 5%) actually use the revaluation model. Those that do tend to be in the brewing industry, with chains of pubs, or those with hotel and leisure complexes. These are the same industries that, prior to IAS 16, argued against the depreciation of property as they are constantly refurbishing and maintaining these assets to keep them in good order.

Financial reporting in practice 10.2	Marston's plc, 2014

Marston's plc is a brewery and pub retailer. In its 2014 financial statements it discloses the accounting policy for its properties:

Freehold and leasehold properties are initially stated at cost and subsequently at valuation. Plant and machinery and fixtures, fittings, tools and equipment are stated at cost.

Properties are revalued by qualified valuers on a sufficiently regular basis using open market value so that the carrying value of an asset does not differ significantly from its fair value at the balance sheet date. Substantially all of the Group's properties have been externally valued in accordance with the Royal Institution of Chartered Surveyors' Red Book. These valuations are performed directly by reference to observable prices in an active market or recent market transactions on arm's length terms. Internal valuations are performed on the same basis.

10.7 Impairment of assets

10.7.1 What is impairment?

In order to provide a fair view of a company's long-term resources, non-current assets should not be included in the statement of financial position at values in excess of what they are worth to the company, that is in excess of amounts the company can expect to recover through their use in the future. This recoverable amount is the amount the company could recover through either the use or the sale of the asset. Assets are therefore carried at the lower of their carrying amount and their recoverable amount. If the recoverable amount is less than the carrying amount, the asset is impaired, and an impairment loss is recognised:

Debit Impairment loss
   Credit   Asset (carrying amount)

IAS 36 *Impairment of Assets*, which was issued in 1998 and then revised in 2004 as a result of the IASB's business combinations project, addresses accounting for the impairment of assets. It applies to property, plant and equipment, investment properties accounted for under the cost model, intangible assets and subsidiaries, associates, and joint ventures. It does not apply to inventories, assets arising from construction contracts, deferred tax assets, assets arising from employee benefits, or assets classified as held for sale (or included in a disposal group that is classified as held for sale) because other IFRS are applicable to these assets.

10.7.2 When is an impairment test required?

An impairment test is the comparison of an asset's carrying amount with its recoverable amount. At each statement of financial position date a company is required to assess whether there are any indications that an impairment loss may have occurred. Only if there are such indications does the company need to perform the impairment test, in other words determine the recoverable amount of the asset and compare this to the carrying amount.

There are three exceptions to this—intangible assets with indefinite useful lives, intangible assets not yet available for use, and goodwill acquired in a business combination. These must be tested annually for impairment. These are discussed further in Chapter 11.

Indications of impairment arise from factors both external and internal to the business and include the following.

External indicators:

- a decline in the market value for specific assets
- significant adverse changes in the technological, market, economic or legal environment in which assets are used (e.g. in recessionary times or times of economic uncertainty)
- increases in market interest rates (because this affects value in use—see section 10.7.3)

- a decline in the company's market capitalisation, resulting in the company's net assets exceeding market capitalisation
- competitor actions.

Internal indicators:

- obsolescence or physical damage to an asset
- significant internal changes to the company's operations that may adversely affect an asset's remaining useful life or utility
- reorganisation of the business
- internal reporting data indicating that the economic performance of an asset is (or will become) worse than previously anticipated
- idle assets
- change of use of assets
- major loss of key employees
- poor asset performance or operating losses in the business where the assets are used.

When assessing internal factors a company should compare the cash flows associated with an asset, or group of assets, with those budgeted. For example, cash outflows may exceed budgeted figures due to higher than expected maintenance costs. Cash inflows may be lower than budgeted due to increased competition. Both would indicate potential impairment.

10.7.3 Impairment test

If an impairment test is required a company must determine the recoverable amount. The recoverable amount is defined as the higher of:

- the value in use of the asset
- the fair value less costs of disposal of the asset.

This assumes a rational approach to what a business would do with an asset given the two values—it would either keep it (value in use) or sell it (fair value less costs of disposal), i.e. it would choose whichever gives the higher amount.

The asset will be valued at the lower of its current carrying amount and the recoverable amount, as shown in Figure 10.1.

Fair value has been defined and discussed previously in this chapter (see section 10.6.1). Costs of disposal include legal costs, stamp duty, other transaction taxes, removal costs and other incremental costs of bringing the asset into a condition for sale, but exclude any reorganisation costs.

The value in use is the present value of the future cash flows expected to be derived from an asset. Estimates of future cash in- and outflows from the use and ultimate disposal of the asset need to be made, and an appropriate discount rate to be used has to be determined. Both

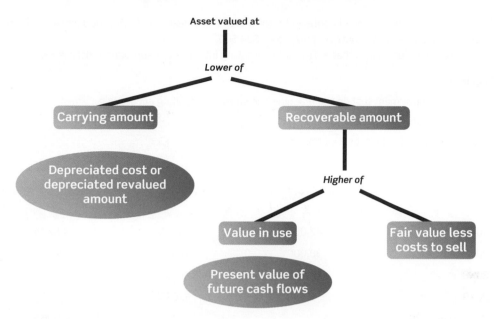

Figure 10.1 The impairment test

of these require a great deal of judgement to be exercised and IAS 36 provides much guidance in this area to help ensure a consistent approach. For example, the cash flows should be based on recent budgets or forecasts for a maximum of five years, and if the expected useful life of the asset extends beyond this, a steady growth/decline rate in cash flows should be applied. The cash flows should exclude the effects of future restructurings or improving and enhancing the asset's performance. The discount rate to be used should be a pre-tax rate reflecting current market assessments of the time value of money and risks specific to the asset.

 Worked example 10.3: to show an impairment test

Idaho plc owns a machine which produces a range of products and, at 31 December 20X5, this has a carrying amount of £123,000 (based on depreciated historic cost). In the past year Idaho's competitors have brought out similar, but more technologically advanced products and the company believes this indicates that there may be evidence of impairment. The company estimates future cash inflows and outflows, based on the diminishing productivity expected of the machinery as new products are produced, and also increasing costs as follows:

Year	£ Revenues	£ Costs (excluding depreciation)
20X6	75,000	28,000
20X7	80,000	42,000
20X8	65,000	55,000
20X9	20,000	15,000
	240,000	140,000

The fair value of the machine is obtained from a prominent dealer and, after deducting estimated disposal costs, the net amount is estimated as £84,500.

The company determines that a discount rate taking into account appropriate risks is 5%.

Required:

Carry out an impairment test on the machine and show the resulting accounting.

Carrying amount = £123,000

Fair value less costs of disposal = £84,500

Value in use:

Year	Net cash flow £	Discount factor	PV of cash flow £
20X6	47,000	0.952	44,744
20X7	38,000	0.907	34,466
20X8	10,000	0.864	8,640
20X9	5,000	0.823	4,115
Value in use			91,965

Value in use > FV less costs of disposal:

- Recoverable amount = £91,965.

Recoverable amount < Carrying amount.

- Impairment loss of £123,000 – £91,965 = £31,035 needs to be accounted for:

Dr   Impairment loss (profit or loss)
  Cr   Asset carrying amount

10.7.4 Accounting for the results of the impairment test

If the recoverable amount is greater than the current carrying amount, no adjustments are required.

If the recoverable amount is less than the carrying amount, the company accounts for this impairment loss as follows:

1   If the asset is valued under the cost model, the impairment loss is recognised in profit or loss:

Debit   Profit or loss
  Credit   Asset accumulated depreciation and impairment

2   If the asset is valued under the revaluation model, the impairment loss is written off directly against any revaluation surplus to the extent that it relates to the asset which is impaired, with any excess recognised in profit or loss:

Debit	Revaluation surplus
(Debit	Profit or loss)
Credit	Asset accumulated depreciation and impairment

The impaired value, less any residual value is depreciated over the asset's remaining useful life, which may need to be reassessed at the date of impairment.

Worked example 10.4: to show the accounting for an impairment loss

Stag plc, which has a 31 December year end, acquired an item of property, plant and equipment on 1 January 20X4 for £50,000 for which it applies the revaluation model. The asset is depreciated on a straight-line basis over its useful economic life of ten years (the assumed residual value is nil). On 1 January 20X5 it was revalued to £54,000. On 31 December 20X6, there are indications that the asset is impaired, an impairment test is carried out, and the recoverable amount at that date is estimated as £30,000.

Required:

Show the accounting entries for the transactions for the years 20X5 and 20X6.

Account for the revaluation on 1 January 20X5

	£
Original cost at 1 Jan 20X4	50,000
Accumulated depreciation (1 year 20X4)	(5,000)
Net book value at 31 December 20X4	45,000
Revalued amount	54,000
Revaluation surplus	9,000

		£	£
Dr	Asset cost	9,000	
Dr	Accumulated depreciation	5,000	
Cr	Asset cost		5,000
Cr	Revaluation surplus		9,000

Accounting entries in years 20X5 and 20X6

Each year:
Asset is depreciated at £54,000/9 = £6,000:

		£	£
Dr	Depreciation expense	6,000	
Cr	Accumulated depreciation		6,000

The additional depreciation of £1,000 is transferred from revaluation surplus to retained earnings each year:

		£	£
Dr	Revaluation surplus	1,000	
Cr	Retained earnings		1,000

At 31 December 20X6, balances on the relevant accounts are:

Asset cost		£54,000 Dr
Accumulated depreciation	(2 × £6,000)	£12,000 Cr
(NBV		£42,000)
Revaluation surplus	(£9,000 – 2 × £1,000)	£7,000 Cr

Account for the impairment at 31 December 20X6

Carrying amount	= £42,000
Recoverable amount	= £30,000
Impairment loss of	£12,000

This can be written off against the revaluation surplus to the extent it exists, with any balance to profit and loss:

		£	£
Dr	Revaluation surplus	7,000	
Dr	Statement of profit or loss	5,000	
Cr	Accumulated depreciation and impairment		12,000

10.7.5 Cash-generating units

In practice it may be difficult to estimate the recoverable amount for a single asset. In this case the impairment test must be performed for the cash-generating unit (CGU) to which the asset belongs. Any impairment loss is allocated on a pro rata basis to the individual assets in the CGU.

A CGU is defined as the smallest identifiable group of assets that generates cash inflows which are largely independent of cash inflows from other assets or groups of assets. The identification of CGUs within a company will depend on how management monitors the company's operations. This may be, for example, by product lines, businesses or individual locations, or by how management makes decisions about continuing or disposing of the company's assets and operations. This is extremely judgemental, but does require consistent treatment from year to year.

There are further complexities where assets are used by a number of different CGUs, for example a head or corporate office. An allocation of these assets' carrying amounts to the relevant CGUs should be made on a 'reasonable and consistent basis'.

10.7.6 Goodwill

As detailed in section 10.7.2, goodwill arising from a business combination and which is capitalised as an intangible asset is required to be tested annually for impairment. (See Chapter 17 for details of how goodwill arises and is valued.) It is meaningless to test this goodwill as a separate asset, so the carrying amount is allocated to the CGUs expected to benefit from the synergies of the combination, and these CGUs are tested for impairment. This is discussed and illustrated further in Chapter 11.

10.7.7 Reversal of impairment losses

There is no such thing as an impairment gain. However, companies are required to assess at the end of each financial year whether there are any indications that a previously recognised impairment loss has decreased or may no longer exist. Essentially, indications of this are the opposite of the indications for impairment, as given in section 10.7.2. An impairment loss should only be reversed if there has been an increase in the asset's service potential. This means it will only be reversed if there is a change in the estimates that were used to determine the asset's recoverable amount.

The reversal is recognised as:

Debit	Asset (carrying amount)
Credit	Profit or loss

but only to the extent that the increased carrying amount does not exceed the amount it would have been (after any subsequent depreciation) if no impairment loss had originally been recognised. Otherwise, this would amount to a revaluation. Note that impairment of goodwill is never reversed.

 Worked example 10.5: to show the reversal of an impairment loss

Jules plc has a CGU comprising two classes of asset. On 31 December 20X3 the CGU was found to be impaired, and an impairment loss of £35,000 was recognised and allocated pro rata to the assets. On 31 December 20X5 the assets' carrying values were:

	£000
Land and buildings	40
Plant and machinery	50
	90

At this date there are indications that the conditions giving rise to the original impairment have changed. The recoverable amount of the CGU is assessed as £120,000. Calculations indicate that if the original impairment had not occurred, the land and buildings would have a carrying amount of £52,000, and the plant and machinery £63,000.

Required:

Show the accounting for the reversal of the impairment loss at 31 December 20X5.

The difference between the carrying amount and the new recoverable amount is £30,000 (i.e. £120,000 – £90,000).

However, the total carrying amount of other assets if the original impairment had not occurred = £52,000 + £63,000 = £115,000.

This is the maximum carrying amount permitted for these assets, so the reversal of the original impairment loss is restricted to £115,000 – £90,000 = £25,000.

This would be allocated to the assets again on a pro rata basis.

Financial reporting in practice 10.3   J Sainsbury plc, 2015

J Sainsbury plc made a loss of £166 million for the 52 weeks ended 14 March 2015 for the first time for many years. In common with other supermarkets, which are having to react to strong competition from discount supermarkets and changing shopping patterns of its customers, the company carried out a reassessment of its store development programme and reviewed its unprofitable and marginally profitable stores. Sainsbury concluded that its properties were impaired and has included an impairment loss of £548 million in its income statement, which contributed to the overall loss. The impairment credit of £540 million to total PPE accumulated depreciation and impairment amounted to over 5% of the opening carrying amount of PPE.

Its accounting policy for impairment of non-financial assets in its 2015 financial statements is as follows. This uses language taken from the accounting standard.

Impairment of non-financial assets

At each reporting date, the Group reviews the carrying amounts of its property, plant and equipment and intangible assets to determine whether there is any indication that those assets have suffered an impairment loss. If any such indication exists, the recoverable amount of the asset, being the higher of its fair value less costs to dispose and its value in use, is estimated in order to determine the extent of the impairment loss. Where the asset does not generate cash flows that are independent from other assets, the Group estimates the recoverable amount of the cash-generating unit ('CGU') to which the asset belongs. For retail property, plant and equipment and intangible assets excluding goodwill, the CGU is deemed to be each trading store or store pipeline development site. For retail goodwill, the CGU is deemed to be each retail chain of stores acquired. Sainsbury's Bank is a separate CGU, and non-store assets, including depots and IT assets, are reviewed separately.

Any impairment loss is recognised in the income statement in the year in which it occurs. Where an impairment loss, other than an impairment loss on goodwill, subsequently reverses due to a change in the original estimate, the carrying amount of the asset is increased to the revised estimate of its recoverable amount, or its original carrying value less notional accumulated depreciation if lower.

10.8 Derecognition of property, plant and equipment

As discussed in Chapter 2, the IASB's revised *Conceptual Framework* is to incorporate underlying principles relating to derecognition of assets and liabilities, in other words, when assets and liabilities should be removed from the statement of financial position. The key principle is likely to be that an asset should be derecognised when the recognition criteria are no longer met, essentially when the asset is no longer controlled. The principles will also include approaches available and factors to be considered when an entity retains a component (part) of an asset.

IAS 16 currently specifies that property, plant and equipment is derecognised when an asset is disposed of, and also when there are no future economic benefits expected from its use or disposal. For example, an old piece of machinery in a corner of a factory that is no longer used and is going to be scrapped should be derecognised. If a company has recognised replacement parts as part of the cost of an asset, the older replaced parts must be derecognised when the replacement parts are brought into use.

The gain or loss arising from the derecognition of an item of property, plant and equipment is the difference between net disposal proceeds (if any) and the carrying amount of the item. This is accounted for as a gain, not revenue, and included in profit or loss.

The exception to this is if a business routinely sells items of property, plant and equipment, where the sale proceeds are classified as revenue, and the requirements of IFRS 15 *Revenue from Contracts with Customers* or its predecessor standard, IAS 18 *Revenue*, apply.

10.9 Investment properties

Businesses may hold property for reasons other than the production or supply of goods and services, or for administrative purposes. These investment reasons are:

- to earn rentals
- for capital appreciation
- or both.

Examples of investment property include:

- land held for long-term capital appreciation
- land held for an undetermined future use
- buildings owned by the company and leased out under one or more operating leases*
- vacant buildings held by an entity to be leased out under one or more operating leases*
- property being constructed or developed for future use as investment property.

   * Operating leases are discussed in detail in Chapter 15.

Table 10.2 Applicable accounting standards for different types of property

Type of property	Applicable IAS
Property intended for sale in the ordinary course of business	IAS 2 *Inventories*
Owner-occupied property or property held for future use as owner-occupied property	IAS 16 *Property, Plant and Equipment*
Property leased to another entity under a finance lease	IAS 17 *Leases* which is to be replaced by IFRS 16 *Leases*

In some cases it may be possible to treat a part of a property as an investment property. For example, a company may use a number of floors of a building as its head office and let out the rest. If these different parts can be separated, the relevant components should be treated as investment property.

Judgement may be required to determine if property is to be classified as investment property. If a company holds property and provides some services to the occupants, it will need to determine how significant these services are to the overall arrangement. For example, if a company owns and manages a hotel, then the services provided to the guests are significant and the hotel property would be classified as owner-occupied property and not investment property. If, however, a company merely provides security and maintenance services to the occupiers, then these services would be viewed as insignificant to the agreement, and the property would be classified as investment property.

IAS 40 *Investment Property* deals with the accounting for this class of asset. It specifically excludes certain types of property which are dealt with by other standards, as given in Table 10.2.

10.9.1 Accounting for investment property

The holding of property as an investment will generate cash flows that are independent of the other assets held by the business, and therefore distinguishes investment property from owner-occupied property. The commercial purpose of holding such property being capital appreciation suggests that measuring investment property at a depreciated historical cost will not provide meaningful information for the users of the financial statements. Instead, it is widely accepted that market values would be more appropriate so that users can evaluate the success of property managers in creating this capital appreciation. However, the IASB has recognised that in some countries property markets are less developed than in others, and reliable market values may be difficult to obtain. Subsequent to initial acquisition, IAS 40 therefore permits investment properties to be accounted for under two alternative models:

● the cost model
● the fair value model.

The policy chosen should be applied consistently to all of the company's investment property.

Although it does not recommend the fair value model, there are indicators that the IASB would prefer this model to be used. These include the requirement for disclosure of fair values for investment properties accounted for under the cost model. Also, it is highly unlikely that a company using the fair value model would change its accounting policy to the cost model.

The cost model is the same as under IAS 16 *Property, Plant and Equipment*, in that the investment property is measured at:

Cost *minus* Accumulated depreciation *minus* Accumulated impairment losses

Similar definitions of cost apply as in IAS 16.

The fair value model requires the investment property to be measured at fair value and this should be assessed at each statement of financial position date. Note this is not the same as the revaluation model available for property, plant and equipment. No revaluation equity reserve is created; instead, changes in fair value are accounted for through profit or loss. An implication of this is that no depreciation is charged.

Adoption of this model may cause volatility in reported profits for investment property-owning companies in addition to significant changes in return and gearing ratios. However, it is considered that the information provided about the capital appreciation is of key importance to users.

10.10 Non-current assets held for sale

Users will wish to assess the resources a company has not only now, but also in the future. This will require information about significant resources that are not going to be available for use in the future. Companies therefore need to provide details of assets where it is known that they are going to be disposed of and sold, in other words non-current assets held for sale.

This issue was discussed fully in Chapter 6 which dealt with reporting performance, as non-current assets are often classified as held for sale because they are part of a discontinued operation. IFRS 5 *Non-current Assets Held for Sale and Discontinued Operations* specifies the accounting treatment for these connected situations.

For the statement of financial position, non-current assets held for sale are disclosed separately from other non-current assets, and they are measured at the lower of carrying amount and fair value less costs to sell, with fair value as defined in IFRS 13 *Fair Value Measurement*.

🔴 **Reminder** *IFRS 5 sets out criteria for the recognition of non-current assets as held for sale, including the requirements that management must have taken steps towards the sale of the assets, the assets must be available for immediate sale, and the sale must be expected within a year.*

If the fair value less costs to sell is less than the carrying amount, an impairment loss is recognised, and charged to profit or loss.

Once an asset or disposal group is classified as held for sale and remeasured, no further depreciation is charged.

10.11 Disclosures

Accounting for property, plant and equipment deals with many different issues, and it is not surprising, therefore, that extensive disclosures are required. Given the many choices available to companies, it is crucial that accounting policies explain the measurement models selected by a company for its property, plant and equipment and investment properties so that there is a basis for comparability. Details of depreciation methods and useful lives or depreciation rates are required; the basis on which interest has been capitalised as part of the cost of assets and how government grants have been treated should also be provided. As seen earlier, companies also explain when and how they account for impairment, and, importantly, the related assumptions.

Financial reporting in practice 10.4	JD Wetherspoon plc, 2014

JD Wetherspoon has the following accounting policies relating to property, plant and equipment in its 2014 financial statements.

Property, plant and equipment

Property, plant and equipment is stated at cost or deemed cost, less accumulated depreciation and any impairment in value.

Cost of assets includes acquisition costs, as well as other directly attributable costs in bringing the asset into use.

Depreciation is charged on a straight-line basis, over the estimated useful life of the asset as follows:

Freehold land is not depreciated.
Freehold and long-leasehold buildings are depreciated to their estimated residual values over 50 years.
Short-leasehold buildings are depreciated over the lease period.
Equipment, fixtures and fittings are depreciated over three to 10 years.
Unopened properties are not depreciated until such time as economic benefits are derived.
Residual values and useful economic lives are reviewed and adjusted, if appropriate, at each balance sheet date.
Profits and losses on disposal of property, plant and equipment reflect the difference between the net selling price and the carrying amount at the date of disposal and are recognised in the income statement.
Impairment losses are recognised in the income statement in those expense categories consistent with the function of the impaired asset.

Investment property

Freehold properties which are held primarily to derive a rental income and for which there is no immediate intention to develop into Wetherspoon pubs, are classified as investment properties.

These properties are stated at cost less accumulated depreciation and any impairment in value and are depreciated in line with the accounting policy for freehold land and buildings.

Assets held for sale

Where the value of an asset will be recovered through a sale transaction, rather than continuing use, the asset is classified as held for sale. Assets held for sale are valued at the lower of book value and fair value, less any costs of disposal, and are no longer depreciated.

Borrowing costs

Borrowing costs are recognised as an expense in the period in which they are incurred, unless the requirements by the adopted accounting standards for the capitalisation of borrowing costs relating to assets are met.

The main disclosure note relating to property, plant and equipment is of a standard format showing for each class of property, plant and equipment a reconciliation of the opening and closing cost (or revalued amount) and accumulated depreciation balances. This will detail all changes that have occurred in the year arising from:

- additions
- disposals
- acquisitions through business combinations
- revaluations
- depreciation charged
- impairments
- classification as held for sale.

Financial reporting in practice 10.5   IMI plc, 2013

A typical disclosure note for property, plant and equipment is provided by IMI plc in its 2013 financial statements.

Note 3.3 Property, plant and equipment

	Land and buildings £m	Plant and equipment £m	Assets in the course of construction £m	Total £m
Cost				
As at 1 January 2013	197.2	662.1	12.0	871.3
Exchange adjustments	(1.0)	(1.7)	(0.3)	(3.0)
Acquisitions	0.2	0.2	–	0.4
Additions	2.1	20.2	19.7	42.0
				(continued)

(continued)

	£m	£m	£m	£m
Transfers to assets held for sale	(22.0)	(99.4)	(3.2)	(124.6)
Transfers from assets in the course of construction	0.5	10.4	(10.9)	–
Disposals	(3.4)	(22.9)	(0.1)	(26.4)
As at 31 December 2013	**173.6**	**568.9**	**17.2**	**759.7**
Accumulated depreciation				
As at 1 January 2013	**93.1**	**532.9**	**–**	**626.0**
Exchange adjustments	(0.2)	(0.5)	–	(0.7)
Disposals	(2.1)	(22.6)	–	(24.7)
Transfers to assets held for sale	(14.4)	(86.7)	–	(101.1)
Impairment reversal	–	(0.5)	–	(0.5)
Depreciation	4.3	33.6	–	37.9
As at 31 December 2013	**80.7**	**456.2**	**–**	**536.9**
NBV as at 31 December 2013	**92.9**	**112.7**	**17.2**	**222.8**

Where a company has adopted the revaluation method, additional disclosures are required:

● the date of the revaluation

● whether an independent valuer was involved

● for each revalued class of property, plant and equipment, the carrying amount that would have been recognised had the assets been carried under the cost model

● the revaluation surplus, indicating the change for the period and any restrictions on the distribution of the balance to shareholders.

Financial reporting in practice 10.6 — Marston's plc, 2014

Marston's accounting policy for property, plant and equipment shown in Financial reporting in practice 10.2 states that the company adopts the revaluation method for its freehold and leasehold properties. The revaluation amounts are included in the property, plant and equipment note.

Additional information about the revalued properties and bases of fair value are provided.

Cost or valuation of land and buildings comprises:

	2014 £m	2013 £m
Valuation	1,647.2	1,770.2
At cost	179.7	119.4
	1,826.9	1,889.6

If the freehold and leasehold properties had not been revalued, the historical cost net book amount would be £1,325.9 million (2013: £1,372.5 million).

Fair value of land and buildings

IFRS 13 requires fair value measurement to be recognised using a fair value hierarchy that reflects the significance of the inputs used in the measurements, according to the following levels:

Level 1—unadjusted quoted prices in active markets for identical assets or liabilities.
Level 2—inputs other than quoted prices included within Level 1 that are observable for the asset or liability, either directly or indirectly.
Level 3—inputs for the asset or liability that are not based on observable market data.

The table below shows the level in the fair value hierarchy into which the fair value measurements of land and buildings have been categorised:

| | 2014 | | | | 2013 | | | |
	Level 1 £m	Level 2 £m	Level 3 £m	Total £m	Level 1 £m	Level 2 £m	Level 3 £m	Total £m
Recurring fair value measurements								
Land and buildings:								
Specialised brewery properties	–	–	**23.7**	**23.7**	–	–	23.7	23.7
Other land and buildings	–	**1,799.5**	–	**1,799.5**	–	1,864.0	–	1,864.0
	–	**1,799.5**	–	**1,823.2**	–	1,864.0	23.7	1,887.7

There were no transfers between Levels 1, 2 and 3 fair value measurements during the current or prior period.

The Level 2 fair values of land and buildings have been obtained using a market approach, primarily using earnings multiples derived from prices in observed transactions involving comparable businesses.

The Level 3 fair values of the specialised brewery properties have been obtained using a cost approach. These breweries represent properties that are rarely, if ever, sold in the market, except by way of a sale of the business of which they are part, due to the uniqueness arising from their specialised nature, design and configuration. As such the valuation of these properties has been performed using the depreciated replacement cost approach, which values the properties at the current cost of replacing them with their modern equivalents less deductions for physical deterioration and all relevant forms of obsolescence and optimisation.

The significant unobservable inputs to the Level 3 fair value measurements are:

	Sensitivity of fair value to unobservable inputs
Current cost of modern equivalent asset	The higher the cost the higher the fair value
Amount of adjustment for physical deterioration/obsolescence	The higher the adjustment the lower the fair value

(continued)

(continued)

Level 3 recurring fair value measurements	2014 £m	2013 £m
At beginning of period	23.7	23.4
Additions	0.3	0.6
Depreciation charge for the period	(0.3)	(0.3)
At end of period	23.7	23.7

The Group's properties are revalued by external independent qualified valuers at least once in each rolling three year period. The last external valuation of the Group's freehold and leasehold properties was performed as at 1 July 2012. The Group has an internal team of qualified valuers and at each reporting date the estate is reviewed for any indication of significant changes in value. Where this is the case internal valuations are performed on a basis consistent with those performed externally.

Extensive disclosures are required relating to impairment, including:

- amounts of impairments or reversals of impairment recognised in profit or loss and other comprehensive income
- details of the circumstances giving rise to the impairments
- details of the assets or CGUs impaired
- whether the recoverable amount is value in use or fair value less costs of disposal
- the bases of how these amounts have been estimated.

If a CGU includes goodwill or intangible assets with indefinite useful lives, further details are required to explain the key assumptions used in estimating recoverable amount. Companies are also encouraged to provide sensitivity information about the level of changes required in assumptions before impairment would arise.

10.12 Understanding property, plant and equipment information

Once depreciation is understood, the figures relating to property, plant and equipment in the financial statements may, initially, seem straightforward to derive and inherently reliable. However, as seen in this chapter, the level of judgement required in recognition and measurement, and the choices available to companies for different accounting policies and methods, means that there is a high level of complexity behind the figures presented. A full understanding of this requires a diligent approach by the user. Where intercompany comparisons are to be performed, users need to be very careful that they are comparing like with like, and they may need to make various adjustments in their calculations. As detailed in section 10.11, there are extensive disclosures so that the information to enable a user to do this is available.

10.12.1 Judgements

Companies are required to disclose areas where significant judgement has been exercised; impairment is frequently mentioned here. However, it is unlikely that all issues requiring judgement that relate to property, plant and equipment will be highlighted. The distinction between capital and revenue expenditure is not always clear-cut, and it will probably not be indicated in the financial statements where this has been considered. This distinction can have a significant impact on both profit and statement of financial position figures and many performance ratios. (Consider, for example, the inappropriate capitalisation of £10 million of repairs and maintenance expenditure on an asset with, say, an estimated useful life of 10 years.) The determination of the cost of an asset, or a part of an asset, may require judgement. The capitalisation of the appropriate amount of interest relating to qualifying assets where the borrowings are not related directly provides another example of where judgement is necessary.

Judgement is required in estimating the useful lives of property, plant and equipment. While property, plant and equipment manufacturers will often give guidance as to the maximum operating life of assets, the useful life is more likely to be determined by reference to the threat of new technology and changing patterns of demand for the assets' outputs. Businesses have to consider when new property, plant and equipment will make their existing assets an uneconomic way of producing goods. In addition, estimates of how long customers will buy the goods, before they move on to something new, will have to be made.

Residual values are often estimated as zero as it may be seen as prudent in the light of ever-changing technology. However, scrapping or decommissioning costs at the end of the assets' lives have to be considered and estimated; these judgements will affect the amounts charged for depreciation.

If a company adopts the revaluation method for a class of property, plant and equipment, fair values are required. While experts may be employed to provide these, there will be a great deal of judgement exercised for very individual, possibly custom-built, items of property, plant and equipment. Although it is argued that a revalued basis for property, plant and equipment provides more relevant information for users, the verifiability is lessened, which is a key enhancing qualitative characteristic.

Impairment is about ensuring that assets are not stated at more than they are worth to the business and that the reported values are generating positive returns. This assurance for the users is, of course, important, especially in adverse market and trading conditions, but accounting for impairment has led to volatility of earnings, of which users are wary. The determination of the recoverable amount of an asset requires extensive judgement to be exercised. Although users will see much information of how the estimates and judgements have been arrived at, including sensitivity analysis, again, the verifiability of the measurements is an issue. In recent years interest rates in most developed economies have been at low levels; however, even relatively modest increases in general interest rates could have a significant impact on the present value of projected cash flows. The combination of lower income streams, resulting from the economic downturn, and higher discount rates can have significant implications for asset measurement.

Finally, the classification of an asset as being held for sale is based entirely on management's intentions, which is highly judgemental. Interpretations of the guidance set out in IFRS 5 can also vary from company to company, and situation to situation. For example, what is really meant by management being committed to a plan to sell the asset; how verifiable should the evidence to support this be? Can a company be sure that an asset or disposal group will be sold within a year—particularly in a difficult economic environment?

 ## Summary of key points

The definition of an asset in the IASB's *Conceptual Framework* as a resource which is controlled and which has the potential to contribute to inflows of benefits underpins which items are accounted for as property, plant and equipment. Costs which can be capitalised are various; they may be incurred to get the asset into a condition ready for use; they may arise subsequent to the initial acquisition of the asset; they may include interest on borrowings taken out in order to fund the acquisition. Essentially, they are costs which would not be incurred unless the asset was being acquired. Government grants may be deducted from the cost or, alternatively, accounted for as deferred income.

Although few in the UK, some companies decide to subsequently value certain classes of property, plant and equipment (mainly property) using the revaluation model rather than basing measurement on the historic cost. The revaluation model uses fair value as the measurement basis, which is considered to provide more relevant information for users. The accounting for revaluations adds a reserve, the revaluation surplus, to equity and there are alternative ways of carrying out the bookkeeping. Once the revaluation model is adopted, assets must be revalued continually and revaluations may decrease, as well as increase. How fair value is determined depends on whether observable or only unobservable inputs are available, and this may affect the perceived reliability of the values attributed. Companies have to weigh up carefully whether this is the best model for their business and users need to understand the financial implications. Additional disclosures are made to assist in comparisons with other companies. Whichever model is used, depreciation is the method by which the cost or revalued amount of the asset is systematically matched against the recognised benefits the asset brings.

Users need to be sure that the carrying amount of assets on the statement of financial position does not exceed a fair representation of their worth to a business. Companies are therefore required to be aware of any internal or external factors which may have reduced their value. If such factors are present, a test for the impairment of an asset, or a group of assets which collectively generate cash flows, is required. The comparison of carrying amount and recoverable amount may result in impairment losses being recognised in profit and loss. If the asset is valued using the revaluation model, the impairment loss is set against any revaluation surplus.

Some property, plant and equipment may be acquired for investment purposes. In this instance, users require information about capital appreciation or depreciation, and so different accounting rules are recommended so that these assets are included at up-to-date fair values.

Other property, plant and equipment may no longer be being used in the business, but be held for sale purposes. The future economic benefits will therefore be from sale proceeds; thus, different valuation methods are used for these assets.

Given the number of areas where estimates and judgements have to be applied, and alternative accounting methods that are available, there are extensive accounting policies and other disclosures to assist the user in understanding and interpreting property, plant and equipment figures.

Further reading

IASB (International Accounting Standards Board) (2003a) IAS 16 *Property, Plant and Equipment.* London: IASB.

IASB (International Accounting Standards Board) (2003b) IAS 40 *Investment Property.* London: IASB.

IASB (International Accounting Standards Board) (2004a) IAS 36 *Impairment of Assets.* London: IASB.

IASB (International Accounting Standards Board) (2004b) IFRS 5 *Non-current Assets Held for Sale and Discontinued Operations.* London: IASB.

Bibliography

Elstrom, P. (2002) How to hide $3.8 billion in expenses. *Business Week* (8 July 2002).

IASB (International Accounting Standards Board) (2001) IAS 20 *Accounting for Government Grants and Disclosure of Government Assistance.* London: IASB.

IASB (International Accounting Standards Board) (2003a) IAS 16 *Property, Plant and Equipment.* London: IASB.

IASB (International Accounting Standards Board) (2003b) IAS 40 *Investment Property.* London: IASB.

IASB (International Accounting Standards Board) (2004a) IAS 36 *Impairment of Assets.* London: IASB.

IASB (International Accounting Standards Board) (2004b) IFRS 5 *Non-current Assets Held for Sale and Discontinued Operations.* London: IASB.

IASB (International Accounting Standards Board) (2007) IAS 23 *Borrowing Costs.* London: IASB.

IASB (International Accounting Standards Board) (2010) *Conceptual Framework for Financial Reporting 2010.* London: IASB.

IASB (International Accounting Standards Board) (2011) IFRS 13 *Fair Value Measurement.* London: IASB.

IASB (International Accounting Standards Board) (2013) Discussion Paper DP/2013/1 *A Review of the Conceptual Framework for Financial Reporting.* London: IASB.

IASB (International Accounting Standards Board) (2015) IASB Staff Paper: Effect of Board Deliberations on DP *A Review of the Conceptual Framework for Financial Reporting.* London: IASB.

ICAEW (Institute of Chartered Accountants in England and Wales) (2008) IFRS Factsheet, *Impairment: applying IAS 36.* London: ICAEW.

IMI plc (2014) *Annual Report and Accounts, 2013.* Birmingham: IMI.

J Sainsbury plc (2014) *Annual Report and Financial Statements, 2014.* London: J Sainsbury.

JD Wetherspoon plc (2014) *Annual Report and Financial Statements, 2014.* Watford: JD Wetherspoon.

Marston's plc (2014) *Annual Report, 2014.* Wolverhampton: Marston's.

? Questions

● Quick test

1 Discuss whether the following items are property, plant and equipment, and, if so, whether they are able to be recognised in the financial statements:

(a) A machine has broken down unexpectedly and the company spends £2,000 on its repair, including £800 for spare parts. Not all the parts are used and £100 worth is available for use by the company in the future.

(b) The costs of relining a furnace after 8,000 hours of use amount to £20,000.

(c) A company which owns an aircraft spends £60,000 on the major airworthiness inspection required by the Civil Aviation Authority after the mandatory number of hours flying.

(d) A company has installed a new machine in a new factory and incurs costs of £3,000 relocating the production team to these premises.

2 Georgi plc sold a non-current asset on 7 July 20X5 for £200,000. The asset had been bought for £100,000 three years before, on 1 July 20X2, when it was estimated to have a life of 10 years. The company uses the revaluation model for this class of asset and, on 1 July 20X4, undertook a revaluation. At that date the fair value of this individual asset was deemed to be £150,000. The company uses the straight-line method of depreciation.

Required:

Show how this asset would be accounted for in the statements of comprehensive income and financial position for the years ended 30 June 20X3, 20X4, 20X5 and 20X6, indicating clearly the profit or loss on disposal.

3 Explain the difference between depreciation charges and charges for impairment of non-current assets.

4 An item of property, plant and equipment was acquired on 1 January 20X2 at a cost of £150,000. The useful life and residual value were estimated at 10 years and £15,000 respectively.

On 1 January 20X5 the asset was classified as held for sale. Its fair value was estimated at £60,000 and the costs of disposal at £3,000.

The asset was sold on 30 June 20X5 for £57,000.

Required:

(a) Show the accounting treatment for this asset at 1 January and 30 June 20X5, identifying clearly all entries in the statement of profit or loss for the year ended 31 December 20X5.

(b) How would your answers change if the sale proceeds on 30 June 20X5 were £48,000?

(c) Rework the question with the fair value on classification as held for sale being estimated at £120,000, the costs of disposal at £4,500 and the asset being sold for £115,000.

●● Develop your understanding

5 Sephco plc has recently purchased an item of plant, the details of which are:

	£
Basic list price of plant	240,000
Trade discount applicable to Sephco	12.5% on list price
Ancillary costs:	
Shipping and handling costs	2,750
Estimated preproduction testing	12,500
Maintenance contract for three years	24,000
Site preparation costs:	
Electrical cable installation	14,000
Concrete reinforcement	4,500
Own labour costs	7,500

Sephco paid for the plant (excluding the ancillary costs) within 4 weeks of order, thereby obtaining an early settlement discount of 3%.

Sephco had incorrectly specified the power loading of the original electrical cable to be installed by the contractor. The cost of correcting this error of £6,000 is included in the figure of £14,000.

The plant is expected to last for 10 years. At the end of this period there will be compulsory costs of £15,000 to dismantle the plant and £3,000 to restore the site to its original use condition. Assume a discount rate of 6%.

Required:

Calculate the amount at which the initial cost of the plant should be measured.

6 On 1 January 20X0 a company acquires a building for £336,000 and estimates its useful life as 12 years with a nil residual value. The company adopts the revaluation model for its property and on 1 January 20X2 and 1 January 20X7 undertakes two revaluations.

Required:

Show how the revaluation gain on 1 January 20X7 should be recognised in the financial statements if the revalued amounts were:

(a) On 1 January 20X2 £120,000 and on 1 January 20X7 £144,000

(b) On 1 January 20X2 £400,000 and on 1 January 20X7 £144,000.

7 Draytex plc has the following non-current assets at 1 January 20X7:

	Cost £000	Accumulated depreciation £000
Freehold factory	2,880	288
Plant and equipment	3,936	514
Office fixtures and fittings	1,776	1,166
Motor vehicles	898	388
	9,490	2,356

You are given the following information for the year ended 31 December 20X7.

(a) The company's depreciation policies are as follows.

Factory (acquired on 1 January 20X2)	straight-line over 50 years
Plant and equipment	straight-line at 10%
Fixtures and fittings	straight-line at 20%
Motor vehicles	straight-line at 25%

(b) On 1 January 20X7 the factory was revalued to an open market value of £4.4 million and an extension costing £1 million became available for use. The directors have decided to adopt the revaluation model for buildings.

(c) Two cars costing £35,000 each were bought on 1 January 20X7. On this date plant and fittings for the factory extension were also acquired, costing £150,000 and £44,000 respectively.

(d) On 1 January 20X7 the directors decided to change the method of depreciating motor vehicles to 30% reducing balance to give a more relevant presentation of the results and of the financial position.

(e) When reviewing the expected lives of its non-current assets, the directors felt that it was necessary to reduce the remaining life of a 2-year-old grinding machine to 4 years when it is expected to be sold for £16,000 as scrap. The machine originally cost £596,000 and, at 1 January 20X7, had related accumulated depreciation of £116,000.

Required:

Prepare the disclosure notes for property, plant and equipment for the year ended 31 December 20X7 in accordance with relevant IFRS.

●●● Take it further

8 The financial statements for the year ended 31 January 20X8 of Sacramento plc, an engineering company, included the following balances in respect of property, plant and equipment:

	Cost/valuation £	Accumulated depreciation £
Land and buildings	1,800,000	378,000
Plant and machinery	1,531,800	1,055,160
Office equipment	427,680	252,480

Sacramento has adopted the cost model for all of the assets with the exception of land and buildings in respect of which it has adopted the revaluation model.

Additional information:

1   Land is included in the figures at a valuation of £1,020,000.

   All other items of property, plant and equipment are depreciated on a straight-line basis as follows:

Buildings	over 50 years
Plant and machinery	at a rate of 25% per annum on cost
Office equipment	at a rate of 20% per annum on cost

   Sacramento charges depreciation on a monthly basis.

2   During January 20X9 Sacramento's structural engineer noticed some cracks appearing at one of the company's outlying workshops and, as a result, a full structural survey was carried out. It was discovered that the foundations of the workshop were insufficient to support some of the machinery which had been housed there. This workshop had cost £180,000 on 1 February 20X4 and had been revalued to £252,000 on 31 January 20X6. It is now estimated that its fair value is only £120,000 and that costs of disposal would be £6,000. Its value in use has been estimated at £108,000.

3   On 1 December 20X8 the directors decided to sell a major piece of machinery. At that date a buyer had been identified and contracts were on the point of being exchanged, at an agreed price of £13,200. Selling costs were expected to be £1,800. The machine had not actually been sold by 31 January 20X9. This machine had cost £60,000 on 1 June 20X6.

Required:

(a) In respect of property, plant and equipment, show all the figures which would appear in Sacramento plc's statement of comprehensive income for the year ended 31 January 20X9 and in non-current assets on the statement of financial position at that date. (Show all workings.)

(b) Discuss how the accounting treatments of the property, plant and equipment of Sacramento plc apply the IASB's qualitative characteristics as set out in the *Conceptual Framework* (2010).

9   Perth plc was formed on 1 January 20X3 to provide delivery services for packages to be taken between the city and the airport. Details of Perth's non-current assets at 31 December 20X5 were as follows:

Tangible Assets			Intangible Assets	
	£	£		£
	Vehicles	Buildings		Software
Cost			Cost	
At 01.01.20X5	990,000	600,000	At 01.01.20X5	–
Additions	–	–	Additions	250,000
Disposals	–	–	Disposals	–
Revaluation	–	–	Revaluation	–
At 31.12.20X5	990,000	600,000	At 31.12.20X5	250,000

Accumulated depreciation			Accumulated amortisation	
At 01.01.20X5	132,000	–	At 01.01.20X5	–
Provided during the year	66,000	60,000	Provided during the year	25,000
Disposals	–	–	Disposals	–
Revaluation/impairment	–	–	Revaluation/impairment	–
At 31.12.20X5	198,000	60,000	At 31.12.20X5	25,000
NBV 01.01.20X5	858,000	600,000	NBV 01.01.20X5	–
NBV 31.12.20X5	792,000	540,000	NBV 31.12.20X5	225,000

The following information is also available:

1   The vehicles were acquired upon formation of Perth plc and are being depreciated on a straight-line basis over their useful economic life of 15 years (a zero residual value is estimated). As part of an expansion programme, Perth plc paid a cash price of £30,000 to acquire two new vehicles on 1 July 20X6. The vehicles needed some repairs for the elimination of rust (cost £2,300), major servicing to the engine (cost £480) and the replacement of all tyres (cost £690). Perth plc incorrectly specified the requirements of the tyres to be installed and the cost of £140 for correcting this error was included in the figure. As part of the expansion programme, Perth plc also decided to spend £15,000 on a marketing campaign to advertise and promote its services.

2   The buildings were acquired on 1 January 20X5 and are being depreciated on a straight-line basis over their useful economic life of 10 years. On 1 January 20X6 the buildings were revalued. No fair value was available, but, instead, their gross replacement cost was established to be £700,000. Perth plc has a policy of amortising any revaluation surplus arising on the revaluation of non-current assets into retained earnings. On 31 December 20X7 there were indications that the buildings might be impaired so an impairment test was conducted. The value in use of the buildings was estimated to be £410,000, whereas their estimated net selling price was £380,000.

3   On 1 July 20X5 Perth plc acquired a logistics software package for £250,000 to allow customers to place and track their orders online. Owing to rapidly changing technology, management estimated a useful life of only five years and decided that straight-line amortisation was to be used. At 1 January 20X6 management was uncertain about the economic feasibility of the logistics process. Therefore, it decided to write down the software to an estimated market value of £75,000 and to re-estimate its useful economic life at only 3 years.

Required:

Using the non-current assets schedule for the year ended 31 December 20X5 as a guide, prepare Perth plc's non-current assets schedule for the year ended 31 December 20X7. For each asset category show clearly your workings in all intermediate years and state any assumptions you make. All accounting adjustments should comply with the requirements of IAS 16 *Property, Plant and Equipment*, IAS 38 *Intangible Assets* and IAS 36 *Impairment of Assets*.

10   Alpha plc and Beta plc are manufacturing companies, and Gamma plc is a property investment company. All three companies have recently acquired and disposed of freehold properties which were identical in every respect. Details of the properties are as follows:

1 January 20X3	Each company bought its property for £300,000. The buildings element in the cost of each property was estimated at £120,000 with an estimated useful life of 40 years.
30 June 20X4	The fair value of each property was estimated at £380,000 (including buildings element £160,000). The estimated remaining useful life at this date was revised to 50 years.
30 June 20X5	Following an impairment review each property was revalued at £290,000 (including buildings element £100,000).
30 Nov 20X5	Each property was sold for £320,000.

Alpha plc and Beta plc both use their properties for their business operations, and both provided a full year's depreciation (straight-line) in the year of acquisition and none in the year of disposal. Alpha plc uses the revaluation model for its properties, whereas Beta plc uses the cost model.

Gamma plc leased its property to produce a rental income negotiated at arm's length.

All three companies have accounting periods ending on 30 June.

Required:

Show how the properties would be dealt with in the accounts for years ended 30 June 20X3 – 20X6 of each company separately. (The rental income of Gamma plc should be ignored.) You should answer in accordance with all relevant IFRS.

11 Hybrid plc has two operating divisions, X and Y, which it has determined are CGUs. The carrying amounts of the assets within each CGU at 31 December 20X1 are as follows:

	Division X £000	Division Y £000
Goodwill	8,000	1,000
Property, plant and equipment	36,000	10,000
Inventories and receivables	9,000	8,000

When carrying out the annual impairment test, Hybrid has estimated that the fair value less costs of disposal of Division X is £28 million and of Division Y is £20 million.

The divisions' net cash flow forecasts for the next six years are as follows:

	Division X £000	Division Y £000
20X2	8,000	3,200
20X3	9,000	2,400
20X4	7,200	3,600
20X5	9,600	4,000
20X6	6,000	4,500
20X7	12,000	4,800

Appropriate discount rates for activities in Divisions X and Y are 12% and 10% respectively.

Required:

(a) Determine whether the divisions are impaired at 31 December 20X1.

(b) If the divisions are impaired, show the accounting for the impairment losses.

Visit the Online Resource Centre for solutions to all these end of chapter questions plus visual walkthrough solutions. You can test your understanding with extra questions and answers, explore additional case studies based on real companies, take a guided tour through a company report and much more. Go to the Online Resource Centre at **www.oxfordtextbooks.co.uk/orc/maynard2e/**

11

Intangible assets

➤ Introduction

An intangible asset is an identifiable non-monetary asset without physical substance. Examples include goodwill, patents, trademarks, licences, brands, intellectual property rights, customer relationships and computer software. Businesses expend vast resources on intangible assets, and debates have raged for many years as to whether they should be recognised in the financial statements and, if so, how they should be valued. Although the accounting methods specified for intangible assets have been established and consistently applied for some years, an understanding of these is key to understanding which resources of a business are included in financial statements and why, and how the values attributed to them have been determined. This aids a fuller understanding of the financial statements. This chapter discusses intangible assets' importance, and explains and illustrates when they should be recognised and how they should be valued in the businesses' financial statements.

After studying this chapter you will be able to:

- understand the main accounting issues relating to intangible assets
- define what an intangible asset is, and distinguish between those purchased externally, acquired as part of a business combination and internally generated
- explain how intangible assets are accounted for in accordance with International Accounting Standard (IAS) 38 *Intangible Assets* at the point of recognition and subsequently
- understand how the accounting treatments affect a user's interpretation of the financial statements
- discuss alternative methods which may be used in the reporting of intangible assets.

- ❑ Why is accounting for intangibles important?
- ❑ Recognition and measurement of assets from the International Accounting Standards Board's (IASB) *Conceptual Framework*.
- ❑ Recognition issues—control, identifiable, separable, future economic benefits, reliable measurement.
- ❑ Initial measurement at cost.
- ❑ Intangible assets and goodwill acquired in a business combination (International Financial Reporting Standard (IFRS) 3 *Business Combinations*).
- ❑ Internally generated intangible assets—**research** and **development** phases, subsequent capitalisation of development costs if six criteria met.
- ❑ Cost or revaluation models.
- ❑ Amortisation and impairment—finite or indefinite lives.
- ❑ Disclosures in financial statements.
- ❑ What do the accounting treatment and disclosures mean to the user?
- ❑ Other measures to provide information to users.
- ❑ The current IASB position.

11.1 Why is accounting for intangibles important?

In the latter part of the twentieth and in the twenty-first centuries more of the economic growth of companies is being driven by investments not in physical assets such as property, plant and equipment, but in non-physical or intangible items, such as intellectual capital, organisational and institutional assets, and reputation. The dot.com boom of the 1990s saw enormous growth in internet and telecommunications companies, which has continued into the twenty-first century with large technology companies such as Microsoft, Google, Samsung and Nokia playing an increasingly important role in the world's economy. Today's 'products' are increasingly intangible and the assets used to produce them are increasingly intangible. Even traditional companies are more reliant now on knowledge-based assets as a source of competitive advantage and to generate their wealth.

One indicator of the growing significance of intangible assets is the difference between the value of companies' net assets, as included in their statements of financial position (book value), and their stock market values. Over the 1990s, surveys of companies in Europe and the USA demonstrated large increases in these **market-to-book ratios**, which may be partly attributable to the growth in investment in intangibles and the values placed on them, which were not appearing on statements of financial position. Despite recent fluctuations in stock markets, market-to-book ratios of greater than 5 are still prevalent.

The ability to identify, measure and account for these intangible assets and, ultimately, provide sound information about them is of great importance to users of financial reports. It is argued that the lack of good reporting of intangibles could lead to systematic undervaluation by investors of the shares of companies, particularly intangibles-intensive enterprises, and higher costs of capital as the raising of finance for such companies is more difficult. It also adds to the question about the decision-usefulness of financial reporting.

11.2 Issues in accounting for intangible assets

An intangible asset in its broadest sense can be taken to include:

> ... any resource that is both intangible (lacking physical substance) and of economic value to the firm. This includes all types of intellectual capital, including those items associated with the firm's human capital (the value of employee training, morale, loyalty, knowledge, etc.), process-related capital (the value of intangibles associated with information technology, production processes, etc.), and external relations (customer satisfaction, customer loyalty, business relationships, other components of brand values, etc.).
>
> *(Skinner, 2008)*

11.2.1 Recognition issues

The question of how to account for intangible assets has exercised accounting standard setters for a long time, particularly during the last 30 years. Businesses spend much money acquiring or developing the sorts of resources referred to in the previous section to improve their competitiveness and to grow, and one key question arises: is this type of expenditure an investment for the future or a general business cost? What this means in financial accounting terms is whether the expenditure is on an asset to be included in the statement of financial position (in other words the expenditure is capitalised) or whether the expenditure is written off as an expense in the statement of profit or loss. Comparability is one of the qualitative characteristics of financial reporting, and the consistency of treatment of this expenditure between businesses, the consistency of the accounting treatment of expenditure on intangibles acquired in external transactions and those that are internally developed, are key issues.

 Example of capitalisation versus write-off of expenditure

A company's draft financial statements for the year ended 31 December 20X5 show net profit before tax of £300,000 and net assets (defined here as total assets minus total liabilities) of £2.5 million. The company has not yet accounted for expenditure on intangible items of £100,000.

If this expenditure is capitalised, the accounting entries will be:

		£	£
Debit	Intangible asset	100,000	
Credit	Bank		100,000

If this expenditure is written off, the accounting entries will be:

		£	£
Debit	Profit or loss	100,000	
Credit	Bank		100,000

The resultant effect on the financial statements will be:

	Capitalisation	Write-off	Difference
	£	£	£
Net profit before tax	300,000	200,000	100,000 (33%)
Net assets	2,500,000	2,400,000	100,000 (4%)
Equity	2,500,000	2,400,000	100,000 (4%)

It can be seen from this example that if there is no proper guidance for the accounting treatment of this expenditure, there is scope for significantly different financial results and position to be reported. The impact on accounting ratios is examined in Worked example 11.6.

11.2.2 Measurement issues

Further to the question of whether intangible assets can be recognised in the financial statements is the question of measurement or valuation. Given the nature of these assets and their uniqueness, regular trade in many of them is difficult; thus, there is a lack of reliable market values. The inclusion of intangible assets with poor or incomparable valuations will not assist the users of financial information.

11.3 IAS 38 *Intangible Assets*

The current IAS 38 *Intangible Assets* was issued by the IASB in March 2004 following various reissues over the years as the nature of which intangible assets are significant to businesses has changed. From a historical perspective the focus was initially on the accounting treatment of research and development expenditure. With decision-usefulness of financial statements becoming a key principle of financial reporting, the standard had to address issues such as whether brands should be accounted for. More recent changes in the current version of the standard were concerned primarily with the accounting for goodwill and intangible assets acquired in business combinations.

IAS 38 deals with most intangible assets except for financial assets, assets that are the particular subject of another standard and assets that are broadly associated with the exploration for and extraction of minerals, oil and gas. Note that IFRS 3 *Business Combinations* addresses the recognition and measurement requirements of goodwill acquired in a business combination.

As discussed in Chapter 10 in relation to tangible assets, the definition and recognition criteria for intangible assets in IAS 38 are based on the definition and recognition criteria of an asset given in the 2010 *Conceptual Framework*. That part of the definition of an asset which requires 'future economic benefits to be expected to flow to the entity', which are in the 2010 *Framework* and the current IAS 38, is likely to be removed. However this and the other changes to the recognition and measurement criteria proposed in the revised *Conceptual Framework* exposure draft are unlikely to significantly change which intangible assets are recognised and how they are valued.

The current IAS 38 definition of an asset is:

> a resource controlled by the entity as a result of past events and from which future economic benefits are expected to flow to the entity.

> *(IASB, 2004, para. 8)*

IAS 38 also defines an intangible asset as:

> ... an identifiable non-monetary asset without physical substance.

> *(IASB, 2004, para. 8)*

11.3.1 Identifiable

The word 'identifiable', included in the IAS 38 definition of an intangible asset, has two meanings:

1 Either the asset is able to be separated from the business and sold, transferred, licensed, rented or exchanged either on its own or with other assets and liabilities, or

2 The asset arises from contractual or other legal rights, regardless of whether these rights are separable.

If an intangible asset, such as a customer list, a patent, a broadcasting licence or software is purchased by an entity, then it is separable and, therefore, identifiable. However, many intangible assets are not separate or saleable items. Examples of such items include employee loyalty, customer satisfaction and certain brand names. These resources all interact to add value to a business and they cannot be identified uniquely. They cannot, therefore, be regarded as intangible assets in the financial statements of the entity.

11.3.2 Control

An intangible asset, like any other asset, also needs to be controlled by a business. This means that the business should have the power to obtain future economic benefits from the asset and restrict these benefits from other third parties. Control is usually evidenced by legal rights, which are enforceable in a court of law; however, this is not actually necessary for control to be evident.

 Examples of control

1   Specific technical knowledge that will give rise to a future product or service has been developed by a business and has been patented. Future economic benefits will arise from the products or services that are protected by the legal right of the patent. The business is restricting the benefits of the knowledge to itself and therefore has control.

2   A business considers it has built up a loyal customer base over many years through quality and good customer relations, and expects the customers will continue to buy from the business. If there are no legal rights to protect this relationship, then the business has insufficient control over the expected economic benefits as the customers can decide to buy the products or services elsewhere. Therefore, the business lacks control.

11.3.3 Recognition

IAS 38 *Intangible Assets* follows the 2010 *Conceptual Framework* almost word-for-word in respect of recognition:

An intangible asset shall be recognised if, and only if:

(a)   it is probable that the expected future economic benefits that are attributable to the asset will flow to the entity; and

(b)   the cost of the asset can be measured reliably.

(IASB, 2004, para. 21)

As for property, plant and equipment, once the revised *Conceptual Framework* is issued, these criteria may change, and all intangible assets that provide information that is relevant and faithfully representative will be required to be recognised. Currently for internally generated intangible assets the management of a business is required to use its best judgement to assess the degree of certainty of the flow of future economic benefits. The reasonableness and reliability of any assumptions will have to be considered.

 Example of uncertainty in future economic benefits

A defence contractor has developed a new radar system for use in fighter aircraft which uses wide-angle microwaves. Initial experiments have been promising, but there is little immediate prospect of a saleable product because the transmitter is too large and heavy to install in an aeroplane.

In the absence of any sales contacts, and the identification of design problems, the likelihood of any future economic benefits is considered fairly remote, and so the criterion for the probable inflow of future economic benefits is not met and no intangible asset can be recognised.

 Reminder *When determining whether the cost of an intangible asset can be measured reliably, the attributes of reliability given in the* Conceptual Framework *(faithful representation, freedom from bias, prudent estimation, if applicable, and completeness) must be considered.*

11.4 Initial measurement

If an intangible asset can be recognised, it will initially be recorded at cost.

If the asset is acquired for cash or in a normal credit transaction, then the purchase price can clearly be measured reliably and, as for tangible assets, the cost of the asset will include:

(a) Purchase price

(b) Import duties

(c) Non-refundable purchase taxes

(d) Deductions for trade discounts and rebates

(e) Directly attributable costs of preparing the asset for its intended use (e.g. labour costs, professional fees, and testing costs)

and exclude:

(a) Costs of introducing a new product or service (such as advertising costs)

(b) Costs of conducting business in a new location or with a new customer

(c) Administration and other general overheads

(d) Costs incurred while the asset which is ready for use has not yet been brought into use

(e) Initial operating losses incurred while the asset is being prepared for use.

Worked example 11.1: to show initial costs

Bream plc purchases an online sales order control computer package for £150,000 from Xentov plc. Included in the purchase price is a maintenance agreement for 2 years, which is listed at £20,000. Bream plc employs the services of an external computer consultant to install and test the package; this costs £1,000. Costs incurred to train the staff in the use of the new package are £4,000 and costs relating to advertising the new system to customers are £2,500. There are a few delays during the switchover to the new system, caused by technical problems, and the company estimates that the costs of unproductive sales staff in this time amounted to £1,200 and potential lost orders would have yielded profits of £3,000.

Required:

Identify which of the items will be included in the cost of the intangible asset.

Initial cost of intangible asset computer software:

	£	
Purchase price	150,000	
Less: maintenance agreement	(20,000)	This item would be expensed over the subsequent two years.
Installation and testing	1,000	
	£131,000	

Staff training costs and the costs of advertising the new system to customers are specifically excluded from the cost of the asset by IAS 38, and costs and losses relating to the delays in implementation are not costs of bringing the asset to the condition necessary for it to be capable of operation, and so would be excluded from the initial cost.

11.5 Intangible assets and goodwill acquired in a business combination

One business may acquire an intangible asset or a group of assets which includes intangible assets from another business. This is not a business combination, and the total cost of the acquisition is allocated to the assets on the basis of their relative fair values.

If, however, one business acquires **control** of another business, with the acquired business continuing in some form, then this is classed as a business combination. A key accounting issue in a business combination is how the intangible assets and any goodwill acquired in a business combination are accounted for.

The question of what goodwill in a business is needs to be determined first. This returns to the question of what gives rise to the difference between the market and book values of a business, as outlined in section 11.1. Goodwill is an asset 'unlike any other asset' as it represents that portion of the value of a business that is not identified by other recognised tangible and intangible assets. Examples of items within a business that may be considered part of goodwill include its reputation, the skills of the workforce, efficient processes, whether its location is close to good transportation networks and customer loyalty. These items are all resources capable of generating benefits for the business. However, they are built up by a business over its life and are not separable from the business. Thus this internally generated goodwill cannot be recognised in the business's individual financial statements (see section 11.7 for further discussion of internally generated intangible assets).

However, when one business acquires control of another in a business combination, it is acquiring these benefits. Through the purchase price, which provides a reliable measurement, the acquiring business is paying an amount, part of which relates to this goodwill. Goodwill acquired in a business combination satisfies the recognition criteria for an asset; a reliable measurement can be ascertained; and it is therefore recognised in the financial statements produced for the combined business. So on acquisition of the control of one business by another, the purchase price is allocated to the identifiable net assets acquired at their fair values. The difference between the purchase price and the fair value of the net assets is the value given to this goodwill. (Note that the measurement of goodwill acquired in a business combination where the controlled business is not 100% owned by the acquiring business is more precisely defined in IFRS 3 *Business Combinations*.)

The identification of the net assets should include all identifiable intangible items, some of which may already be recognised as intangible assets in the acquiree business's financial statements, but some of which may not. Prior to the current inclusion of the word 'identifiable' in the standard's definition of an intangible asset, acquiring companies would subsume the value of these non-recognised intangible assets in goodwill. Acquiring companies are required by IAS 38 and IFRS 3 to assess whether any of the intangible items acquired are identifiable, in other words whether they meet the separability or contractual-legal criteria. If so, they must be recognised as an identifiable intangible asset in the combined business financial statements and not form part of the overall goodwill figure. This additional information about the different resources acquired is considered to enhance the usefulness of the financial statements.

 Worked example 11.2: to show the accounting for intangible assets acquired in a business combination and the resulting goodwill

Alpha plc acquires 100% of the share capital of company Beta Ltd for cash of £400,000 and therefore acquires control. Immediately prior to the acquisition the statements of financial position of the two companies are as follows:

	Alpha £000	Beta £000
Non-current assets		
PPE	1,000	110
Intangible assets	–	30
Net current assets	1,050	90
	2,050	230
Non-current liabilities	450	40
	1,600	190
Equity		
Share capital	900	150
Share premium	300	–
Retained earnings	400	40
	1,600	190

IFRS 3 specifies that in accounting for the acquisition, all identifiable net assets of Beta are required to be valued at fair value. This may mean that some intangible assets not recognised in Beta's financial statements are now identified.

Suppose Beta Ltd has a 5-year agreement to supply goods to one of its customers, Gamma Ltd. Both Beta and Alpha believe that Gamma will renew the agreement, which is not separable, at the end of the current contract. The agreement, whether cancellable or not, meets the contractual-legal criterion for determining whether an intangible asset can be considered identifiable. Additionally, because Beta has established its relationship with Gamma through a contract, not only the agreement itself, but also Beta's customer relationship with Gamma meet this criterion. This agreement will now be recognised as an intangible asset and its fair value will therefore need to be estimated.

Assume that the revaluation to fair values and the identification of the supply agreement leads to valuations of Beta's net assets as follows:

	Beta £000
Non-current assets	
PPE	160
Intangible assets (including supply agreement)	50
Net current assets	80
	290
Non-current liabilities	40
	250

Required:

Show the final statement of financial position of Alpha plc after its acquisition of Beta Ltd.

The difference between the purchase price of £400,000 and the fair values of the separable net assets acquired of £250,000 represents future economic benefits arising from these assets that have not been individually identified and recognised separately. This is defined as goodwill arising on acquisition of £150,000, which is now recognised in the financial statements of the combined Alpha group:

		£000
Non-current assets		
PPE	(1,000 + 160)	1,160
Intangible assets	(50)	50
Goodwill		150
		1,360
Net current assets	(1,050 − 400* + 80)	730
		2,090
Non-current liabilities	(450 + 40)	490
		1,600
Capital and reserves	(Co. Alpha)	
Share capital		900
Share premium		300
Retained earnings		400
		1,600

* Cash paid for Beta reduces the net current assets.

(See Chapter 17 for further details of accounting for business combinations.)

IFRS 3 *Business Combinations* provides many examples of intangible assets regularly acquired in business combinations which are to be regarded as identifiable because they meet one of the two necessary criteria. Examples include:

- marketing-related intangible assets, such as trademarks, newspaper mastheads, and internet domain names

- customer-related intangible assets, such as customer lists and contacts, order backlogs and non-contractual arrangements

- artistic-related intangible assets, such as copyrights to plays, books, magazines, song lyrics, photographs and video and audio-visual material

- other contract-based intangible assets, such as licences, franchise agreements, construction permits and employment contracts

- technology-based intangible assets, such as software, trade secrets and databases.

Note that the terms 'brand' and 'brand name' are not included in these examples. This is because they are considered, from an accounting point of view, marketing terms, which encompass a group of complementary assets, such as a trademark and its related trade name, formulas, recipes and technological expertise. A single intangible asset called a 'brand', representing these sorts of complementary assets, may be recognised if its fair value can be measured reliably and the assets that make up the group have similar useful lives. Some companies will refer to this as a 'brand'; others use the terminology of 'trade mark' or 'trade name'.

Despite the IASB's intentions to provide more useful information through these requirements of IFRS 3 and IAS 38, debate has continued as to whether these aims have been achieved. Many financial analysts just ignore reported intangible assets and goodwill, and research conducted by the Financial Reporting Council (FRC) in 2014 found that more than half of the investors they contacted expressed a preference for different accounting treatments for different types of intangible assets. The nub of their argument was that intangible assets fall into two main categories: 'wasting' and 'organically replaced'. Wasting intangible assets, such as patents, are considered separable from the business, have finite useful lives and do lead to identifiable future revenue streams. They therefore should be capitalised, and separate information about them is useful. However the investors expressed doubt over whether organically replaced intangibles, such as customer lists and brands, are capable of being separated from the business, or have reliably determinable useful lives, or be a source of future economic benefits which can be distinguished from the business as a whole. Values attributed to these assets may be better subsumed within goodwill, and issues of subsequent accounting for goodwill then also addressed (see section 11.8.3).

11.5.1 Fair value

The cost of intangible assets acquired in a business combination, as for tangible assets, and in accordance with IFRS 3 *Business Combinations*, is the fair value at the date of acquisition. IAS 38 states that if an intangible asset is able to be recognised there will be sufficient information available to measure its fair value. This will be in accordance with the guidance given in IFRS 13 *Fair Value Measurement*.

🛈 **Reminder** *Fair value is defined as 'the price that would be received to sell an asset or paid to transfer a liability in an orderly transaction between market participants at the measurement date'. Ideally, fair value can be obtained from observable prices or data, but, in the absence of this, unobservable data or financial models may have to be used. This leads to increased subjectivity.*

The fair value of an intangible asset may be more difficult to ascertain than that for a tangible asset, as more estimates may have to be made. If there is a range of possible outcomes with different probabilities, this uncertainty enters into the measurement of the asset's fair value.

Some assets may be grouped together as a single asset if their fair value as individual items cannot be estimated, but the fair value for the group can be.

Example of assets grouped together for fair value

An acquiree company is a company bottling water from a single natural spring. The company has a registered trademark for the spring water.

The trademark and the actual spring cannot be sold separately, so the two intangible assets are grouped together as one asset in the group financial statements, for which the fair value is determined.

11.6 Financial reporting in practice

The following examples of the intangible assets in companies' financial statements demonstrate the diverse nature of what assets companies recognise and the uniqueness of such assets to individual businesses. As required by IAS 38, the companies disclose separately the additions to the categories of intangible assets from acquisitions of other companies and from external purchases.

Financial reporting in practice **11.1**

Examples of different intangible assets recognised by companies

Nokia Corporation

This Finnish telecommunication company's statement of financial position at 31 December 2014 includes intangible assets of €2,913 million out of total non-current assets of €7,339 million, comprising goodwill (€2,563 million), customer relationships (€177 million), developed technology (€99 million) and licences to use tradename and trademark (€10 million).

Vodafone Group plc

The UK mobile network operator's statement of financial position at 31 March 2015 includes £20,953 million of intangible assets, excluding goodwill, out of total non-current assets of £102,726 million. The principal categories of intangible assets are licence and spectrum fees, computer software and others, including brands and customer bases.

AstraZeneca plc

This is a global biopharmaceutical company. Its 31 December 2014 financial statements include intangible assets, excluding goodwill, of US$20,981 million out of total assets of US$41,898 million. These comprise product, marketing and distribution rights relating to product development, licensing and other rights to contractual income streams and software development costs.

(continued)

(continued)

Rolls-Royce plc

Rolls-Royce designs, develops, manufactures and services integrated power systems for civil and defence aircraft, marine and energy markets, and, in line with this, has intangible assets comprising goodwill, development costs, certification costs and participation fees, contractual aftermarket rights, customer relationships and software costs. Intangible assets at 31 December 2014 contribute £3,446 million of total assets of £11,036 million.

11.7 Internally generated intangible assets

So far, this chapter has concentrated on intangible assets that are acquired externally, either on their own or through a business combination. However, many intangible assets are ones which develop within a business as it operates and produces its goods or services. It is sometimes difficult to assess whether these internally generated intangible assets meet the recognition criteria because of problems in identifying whether they will generate future economic benefits and if their costs can be determined reliably. Specifically, questions that must be asked are:

1   Can an internally generated asset be separated and sold from the business?

2   Can the costs of generating an asset internally be distinguished from the cost of maintaining or enhancing the business's internally generated goodwill or of running day-to-day operations?

 Example of footballers as intangible assets

Consider a footballer, such as Wayne Rooney. Initially, he played for Everton FC after being trained through this club's youth training scheme. In 2004 Manchester United paid £25.6 million for him, and he has played for this club ever since. From both clubs' point-of-view, Rooney was/is a resource of (huge) economic value, and he does exactly the same 'job' for both companies. However, he was not recognised as an asset in Everton FC's financial statements, but was initially on Manchester United's statement of financial position.

Clearly, Rooney meets the separability (identifiable) criterion for an intangible asset. However, a reliable measurement of the cost of the intangible asset is required for recognition. The question for Everton FC was whether the development costs associated with this one particular star footballer could be identified reliably. Rooney would have been one of a number of players going through the youth training programme, so costs associated solely with him would be difficult to separate out. In addition, it would be difficult to identify what type of costs should be associated with his development—coaching costs: yes; promotion: possibly; training overheads: more difficult to identify; and so on. So the recognition criteria cannot be fulfilled and footballers who have come up through a club's ranks cannot be recognised as intangible assets.

However, once a footballer is sold to another club, all identifiable and recognition criteria are satisfied:

- the footballer is separable
- the purchase cost is established.

Hence, there is inconsistency in recognition of the same 'asset' on football clubs' statements of financial position, dependent upon whether the player has come up through the ranks or been bought from another club.

Financial reporting in practice 11.2   Arsenal plc, 2015

This issue is explained clearly in the accounting policies of the 31 May 2015 financial statements of Arsenal plc.

Player costs

The costs associated with acquiring players' registrations or extending their contracts, including agents' fees, are capitalised and amortised, in equal instalments, over the period of the respective players' contracts. Where a contract life is renegotiated, the unamortised costs, together with the new costs relating to the contract extension, are amortised over the term of the new contract. Where the acquisition of a player registration involves a non-cash consideration, such as an exchange for another player registration, the transaction is accounted for using an estimate of the market value for the non-cash consideration. Under the conditions of certain transfer agreements or contract renegotiations, further fees will be payable in the event of the players concerned making a number of first team appearances or on the occurrence of certain other specified future events. Liabilities in respect of these additional fees are accounted for, as provisions, when it becomes probable that the number of appearances will be achieved or the specified future events will occur. The additional costs are capitalised and amortised as set out earlier.

Profits or losses on the sale of players represent the transfer fee receivable, net of any transaction costs, less the unamortised cost of the applicable player's registration.

Remuneration of players is charged in accordance with the terms of the applicable contractual arrangements and any discretionary bonuses when there is a legal or constructive obligation.

The disclosure note relating to intangible assets also spells out:

The figures for cost of player registrations are historic cost figures for purchased players only. Accordingly, the net book amount of player registrations will not reflect, nor is it intended to, the current market value of these players, nor does it take any account of players developed through the Group's youth system. The directors consider the net realisable value of intangible fixed assets to be significantly greater than their book value.

The accounting treatment set out in IAS 38 attempts to provide a solution to one of the key accounting issues in relation to recognition of an internally generated asset, and which was outlined as one of the key issues in accounting for intangible assets at the start of the chapter: is the expenditure an asset or should it be written off?

In addition to complying with the requirements for the recognition and initial measurement of an intangible asset, IAS 38 adds further requirements for the recognition of internally generated intangible assets. Entities are required to divide the generation of such assets into two phases:

(a) a research phase

(b) a development phase.

11.7.1 Research

Research can be defined as the obtaining of new knowledge, the search for application of this knowledge and the search for, and design of, possible alternative materials, devices, products, processes, systems or services. A business undertaking these sorts of activities cannot demonstrate that any intangible asset which may result will generate probable future economic benefits and so all such expenditure is recognised as an expense when it is incurred.

11.7.2 Development

Development is the application of research towards specific new or alternative materials, devices, products, processes, systems or services. It can involve design, construction and testing of pre-production or pre-use plants, models and prototypes, involving new technology. For development costs to be recognised as an intangible asset six criteria have to be demonstrated by a business:

(a) the technical feasibility of completing the intangible asset so that it will be available for use or sale.

(b) its intention to complete the intangible asset and use or sell it.

(c) its ability to use or sell the intangible asset.

(d) how the intangible asset will generate probable future economic benefits. Among other things, the entity must demonstrate the existence of a market for the output of the intangible asset or the intangible asset itself or, if it is to be used internally, the usefulness of the intangible asset.

(e) the availability of adequate technical, financial and other resources to complete the development and to use or sell the intangible asset.

(f) its ability to measure reliably the expenditure attributable to the intangible asset during its development.

(IAS 38, 2004, para.57)

Note all six criteria have to be met, otherwise the expenditure is recognised as an expense when it is incurred, as for research costs. This may appear fairly clear-cut, but the terminology used (e.g. 'intention', 'ability' and 'technical feasibility') means that management's, and sometimes specialists', experience and judgement have to be relied upon in practical application. Some of the criteria are also forward-looking, so the recognition of development expenditure as an intangible asset is relying upon assessment of future plans. IAS 38 does provide some guidance as to how businesses may 'demonstrate' that these criteria are fulfilled, such as having prepared business plans which include the required resources or having lenders' indications of willingness to fund the plans.

 Worked example 11.3: to show the application of the criteria necessary for capitalisation of development costs

1   Hayley plc, a textile manufacturer, has incurred expenditure of £600,000 over the past 2 years on one project to develop unique bandaging to treat muscular injuries. Samples have been tested, appropriate clinical approval has been granted, and there have been strong expressions of interest from some hospitals and sports organisations. The company confidently expects that orders for the bandaging will start to be received in the following year, and sales and costs are included in the company's budgets.

Hayley has also purchased a machine to be used in its research laboratory for £2 million. The machine measures the tensile strength of different yarns the entity is developing and experimenting with, and is expected to be used for ten years. Hayley uses the straight-line method of depreciation for machinery.

Required:

Discuss the accounting treatment of the £600,000 development expenditure and the purchase of the machine according to IAS 38.

The £600,000 expenditure relates to a development project which appears to satisfy the six criteria stated in IAS 38:

(a) if clinical approval has been granted the project must be technically feasible

(b) and **(c)** the entity is clearly able to produce the bandaging and anticipates sales of the product

(d) a market exists, as evidenced by the interest shown by potential customers

(e) provided the budgets demonstrate that funding is available to support the project, resources are there to complete the development

(f) the entity appears to be able to identify the costs of development.

Costs of development can therefore be included in the statement of financial position as an intangible asset. The point at which this can be done is discussed in the following section.

The machine is a tangible asset and should be accounted for as property, plant and equipment, i.e. capitalised and depreciated in the normal way over its expected useful life. Depreciation of £200,000 per year will, therefore, need to be accounted for. As the machine has been acquired by the manufacturer to provide facilities for research and development, if it is used in development activities, the depreciation can be included as a development cost and capitalised if the aforementioned criteria for such projects are met. The depreciation of £200,000 will need to be allocated across the various projects; part of this expense may then be capitalised as development costs.

The depreciation arising from the use of the machine on any projects which are not identified as development projects will be written off to profit and loss in the usual way.

So, if 40% of the machine usage is on development projects where all six criteria have been fulfilled, the accounting for the depreciation will be:

		£	£
Debit	Development (intangible asset)	80,000	
	Depreciation expense	120,000	
Credit	Accumulated depreciation		200,000

2 Gordons, a bakery, has spent £150,000, £120,000 and £75,000 over the past three successive years creating and promoting a range of its products under the brand name 'Simply Yummy!', and is now successfully selling these in its high-street shops.

During the most recent year the bakery acquired the business and assets of a sole trader. As part of the total acquisition price of £1,300,000 the bakery valued the brand 'Crunchie Munchies' at a fair value of £200,000.

Required:

Discuss and contrast the accounting treatment of the costs of promoting Gordons' own-brand products and the costs associated with the acquisition.

IAS 38 does not permit internally generated brands, mastheads, publishing titles and customer lists to be recognised as intangible assets because expenditure on these items cannot be distinguished from the cost of developing the business as a whole (IAS 38, paras 63 and 64). The expenditure in developing the 'Simply Yummy!' range is, therefore, written off to profit and loss in its respective years.

However, a brand name acquired in a business combination can be recognised as an intangible asset provided its fair value can be measured reliably. The allocation of £200,000 of the purchase price for the brand name 'Crunchie Munchies' means the fair value has been identified and the bakery will include this as a separately identified intangible asset in its statement of financial position.

11.7.3 Cost of an internally generated intangible asset

A key point to note is that only new development expenditure is recognised as an intangible asset from the point of the fulfilment of the recognition criteria; there is no retrospective capitalisation of previously incurred costs.

Costs which can be capitalised typically include:

(i) costs of direct materials and services

(ii) wages and salaries and related costs

(iii) fees to register a patent or licence

(iv) amortisation of such patents or licences

but exclude general selling and administrative expenditure, and costs of training staff to operate the asset.

Worked example 11.4: to show the accounting for the capitalisation of development costs

Wigton Manufacturers plc, a company with a 31 December financial year end, is developing a new production process and, during 20X5, incurred expenditure of £1,000,000. Wigton Manufacturers is able to demonstrate that at 1 December 20X5 the production process met the criteria for recognition as an intangible asset. Of the total expenditure £900,000 was incurred before 1 December 20X5, and the remainder was incurred between 1 December and 31 December 20X5. In 20X6 the entity incurred further expenditure of £2,000,000 on development of the process.

Required:

Show how the development costs will be accounted for in 20X5 and 20X6.

At the end of 20X5 the production process is recognised as an intangible asset at a cost of £100,000 as this is the expenditure incurred since the date when the recognition criteria were met, i.e. 1 December 20X5. The £900,000 incurred prior to this is recognised as an expense in profit and loss:

		£	£
Debit	Intangible assets (cost)	100,000	
	Development expense	900,000	
Credit	Bank		1,000,000

During 20X6 all expenditure is capitalised:

		£	£
Debit	Intangible assets (cost)	2,000,000	
Credit	Bank		2,000,000

At the end of 20X6 the cost of production process recognised as an intangible asset is £2,100,000.

Financial reporting in practice 11.3   Rolls-Royce plc, 2014

Rolls-Royce plc states that it follows the requirements of IAS 38 in the research and development accounting policy in its 2014 financial statements

Research and development

In accordance with IAS 38 *Intangible Assets*, expenditure incurred on research and development is distinguished as relating either to a research phase or to a development phase.

All research phase expenditure is charged to the income statement. Development expenditure is capitalised as an internally generated intangible asset only if it meets strict criteria, relating in particular to technical feasibility and generation of future economic benefits. As described on page 103, the Group considers that it is not possible to distinguish reliably between research and development activities until relatively late in the programme.

11.8 Measurement of an intangible asset after recognition

The accounting methods applied to an intangible asset once it has been recognised are very similar to those applied to tangible non-current assets. This makes sense, as both are long-term resources being used by a business to generate future benefits. A business can choose either the cost model or the revaluation model, with all assets in the same class using the same model. Accumulated amortisation and accumulated impairment losses are deducted to give the carrying amount. (Note—for intangible assets, amortisation is the term used instead of depreciation.)

If the revaluation model is chosen, all the assets in the class should be revalued at the same date, with the revalued amount being the fair value at this date. However, the use of the revaluation model is less common for intangible assets, as the determination of fair value generally requires an active market for the assets to exist. An active market means that items traded in the market are uniform, willing buyers and sellers are readily available and prices are in the public domain. The very nature of many intangible assets leads them to be unique (e.g. brands, newspaper mastheads, patents and trademarks, and any internally generated asset) and any trading in them to be relatively infrequent. There may be an active market for some licences and quotas; nevertheless, most businesses use the cost model for intangible assets.

In the event that the revaluation model is used, there is no set time limit for when a new valuation has to be carried out or even a recommendation as to how long this should be. Again, it is because of the uniqueness of each intangible asset that businesses are required to revalue the assets only if their fair value differs materially from their carrying amount. This may result in annual revaluations for some asset classes; others will be far less frequently revalued.

🔵 **Reminder** *The accounting for revaluation surpluses or deficits is the same as for tangible non-current assets as discussed in Chapter 10:*

1   *If the asset's carrying amount is increased as a result of a revaluation, the increased amount is:*

   (a) recognised in other comprehensive income in the statement of comprehensive income

   (b) credited to a revaluation surplus account in equity.

   However, if the increase reverses a previous revaluation decrease which had been recognised in profit and loss, the increase is credited to profit and loss, limited to the amount of the previous decrease. Any excess in increase is treated as before.

2   *If the asset's carrying amount is decreased as a result of a revaluation, the decrease is recognised in profit and loss.*

   However, if there is a credit balance on a revaluation surplus account relating to the asset, the decrease, which is limited to the amount of this balance, is:

(a) *debited to the revaluation surplus account*

(b) *credited to the asset's carrying amount.*

Any excess in decrease is recognised in profit and loss.

3 *The balance on the revaluation reserve may be realised as the intangible asset is used by the entity by transferring the difference between the amortisation charged on the revalued amount and the amortisation which would have been charged on the historic cost from the revaluation reserve to retained earnings. Note: this does not pass through profit and loss—it is an inter-reserve transfer.*

11.8.1 Amortisation and useful life

As for tangible non-current assets, the question arises as to what happens to the intangible asset's value once it has been capitalised. For tangible assets this results in depreciation being accounted for—to spread the cost or value of the asset over the periods expected to benefit from the asset's use—and it would seem logical to apply the same approach to intangible assets.

So, if the useful life of an intangible asset can be reliably estimated or, in other words, it is finite, then the asset must be amortised from the point at which the asset is available for use. A similar accounting approach as that applied to tangible assets and depreciation is used. The actual estimation of the life of an intangible asset may be difficult and management will have to consider many factors, such as:

- technical or commercial obsolescence
- future changes in market demand for the products or services output from the asset
- the period of control over the asset
- typical product life cycles.

Financial reporting in practice 11.4 — Vodafone plc, 2015

In its 2015 financial statements Vodafone plc indicates the factors it takes into account when estimating the useful life of its intangible assets:

Finite lived intangible assets accounting policy

Other intangible assets include amounts spent by the Group acquiring licences and spectrum, customer bases and brands and the costs of purchasing and developing computer software.

Where intangible assets are acquired through business combinations and no active market for the assets exists, the fair value of these assets is determined by discounting estimated future net cash flows generated by the asset. Estimates relating to the future cash flows and discount rates used may have a material effect on the reported amounts of finite lived intangible assets.

(continued)

(continued)

Estimation of useful life

The useful life over which intangible assets are amortised depends on management's estimate of the period over which economic benefit will be derived from the asset. Reducing the useful life will increase the amortisation charge in the consolidated income statement. Useful lives are periodically reviewed to ensure that they remain appropriate. The basis for determining the useful life for the most significant categories of intangible assets is discussed below.

Licence and spectrum fees

The estimated useful life is generally the term of the licence unless there is a presumption of renewal at negligible cost; this is adjusted if necessary, for example taking into account the impact of any expected changes in technology.

Customer bases

The estimated useful life principally reflects management's view of the average economic life of the customer base and is assessed by reference to customer churn rates. An increase in churn rates may lead to a reduction in the estimated useful life and an increase in the amortisation charge.

Capitalised software

For computer software, the useful life is based on management's view, considering historical experience with similar products as well as anticipation of future events which may impact their life such as changes in technology. The useful life will not exceed the duration of a licence.

Management also has to consider whether the intangible asset has any residual value. This is presumed to be zero unless there is a commitment by a third party to purchase the asset at the end of its useful life, or a residual value can be determined by the presence of an active market in the type of asset.

The depreciable amount, established as the difference between the cost or value of the asset and any residual value, is then written off on a 'systematic basis' over its useful life, taking into account the pattern of how it is going to be used. In practice most companies will use a straight-line basis. All estimates used to determine amortisation require review at the end of each financial period and, if these change, then the amortisation method and amount will alter from that point.

11.8.2 Impairment

Because intangible assets, by their nature, arise in very different ways and are individual, it may be difficult to reliably assess their useful life. Any asset in this case is deemed to have an indefinite life and IAS 38 specifies that it shall not be amortised. However, the asset must be tested each year for impairment, and also whenever there are indications that the asset is impaired, in accordance with IAS 36 *Impairment of Assets*.

⚠ *Reminder As detailed previously in Chapter 10 for tangible non-current assets, a test for impairment means that the recoverable amount of the asset has to be determined (this is the higher of the asset's fair value less costs to sell and its value in use). The carrying amount of the asset is compared to the recoverable amount. If the recoverable amount is lower than the carrying amount, an impairment loss is recognised, either in profit and loss or, if the asset is using the revaluation model and there is a revaluation surplus in relation to the asset, the loss can be debited to the surplus to the extent that it exists, with any excess recognised in profit and loss.*

In addition to the test for impairment, other conditions need to be reviewed each year to determine whether the indefinite useful life assessment of the asset is still appropriate. If a finite life can be subsequently estimated, then the asset must start to be amortised, and this is treated as a change in accounting estimate in accordance with IAS 8 *Accounting Policies, Changes in Accounting Estimates and Errors*. This is usually accompanied by a test for impairment to determine the carrying amount, as the conditions which indicate the asset now has a finite life often indicate the asset is impaired.

 Examples of finite and indefinite lives

1 A direct-mail marketing company with a financial year end of 31 December purchases a customer list on 1 September 20X8 for £4,500. The company expects that it will be able to derive benefit from the information on the list for at least one year, but no more than three years. The first mail shot using the list is on 1 October 20X8.

   The customer list would be amortised over management's best estimate of its useful life, say 18 months. Although the direct-mail marketing company may intend to add customer names and other information to the list in the future, the expected benefits of the acquired customer list relate only to the customers on the list at the date it was acquired. Amortisation would commence from the point at which the asset is available for use, in other words from 1 September 20X8. Amortisation charged to the statement of profit or loss in 20X8 would amount to £1,000 (4/18 × £4,500). At the end of each reporting period the company would also assess whether there were any indications that the customer list may be impaired in accordance with IAS 36.

2 An airline company has acquired an airline route authority between two European cities. The route authority expires in three years and then may be renewed every five years. Route authority renewals are granted routinely at a minimal cost and, historically, have been renewed when the airline has complied with the applicable rules and regulations. The airline company intends to comply with these, and expects to provide service indefinitely between the two cities from its hub airports and expects that supporting infrastructure (airport gates, slots and terminal facility leases) will remain in place at those airports for as long as it has the route authority. An analysis of the company's demand and cash flows supports these assumptions.

   Because the facts and circumstances support the airline company's ability to continue providing air service indefinitely between the two cities, the intangible asset related to the route authority is treated as having an indefinite useful life. Therefore, the route authority would not be amortised until its useful life is determined to be finite. It would be tested for impairment in accordance with IAS 36 annually and whenever there is an indication that it may be impaired.

   (Based on IAS 38 *Illustrative examples*.)

11.8.3 Impairment of goodwill

The issue of whether and how goodwill acquired in a business combination should be amortised, and indeed whether this acquired goodwill should be recognised at all, is one which has caused much debate amongst accounting standard setters and many other stakeholders in financial reporting over many years. It has led to various accounting treatments being required by different versions of financial reporting standards. Ignoring the once permitted practice of writing off acquired goodwill against equity immediately on acquisition (the majority of users of financial statements would now agree that acquired goodwill is a recognisable asset), the two accounting treatments that have been used are:

1. systematic amortisation over a period

2. impairment.

IAS 36 currently requires that goodwill acquired in a business combination should not be amortised, but tested each year for impairment. The main argument for this is that it is not considered possible to reliably determine the useful life and the pattern of consumption, so that any amortisation expense would only ever be an arbitrary estimate.

For the purpose of its impairment testing, the goodwill is allocated to the cash-generating units (CGUs) expected to benefit from the combination, which are then tested for impairment. Any impairment loss is allocated first to goodwill and then to the net assets of the CGU.

 Worked example 11.5: to show the accounting for impairment of goodwill

Peter plc acquired the whole of company Saul Ltd in 20X5 and the goodwill arising on acquisition was calculated at £200,000. Peter identifies the net assets of Saul as a CGU. No impairment losses or gains have previously been accounted for in relation to Saul, but, at 31 December 20X7, the recoverable amount of Saul was assessed to be £750,000. At this date, the carrying amount of net assets of Saul, excluding goodwill, was £850,000.

Required:

Show how the goodwill impairment is accounted for in the 20X7 financial statements of Peter plc.

	£
Carrying amount of CGU	
Carrying amount of identifiable net assets	850,000
Goodwill	200,000
	1,050,000
Recoverable amount	750,000
Impairment loss	300,000

The loss is recognised as an expense in profit and loss, and allocated to the net assets as follows:

	Goodwill £	Net assets of CGU £	Total £
Carrying amount	200,000	850,000	1,050,000
Impairment loss	(200,000)	(100,000)	(300,000)
New carrying amount	Nil	750,000	750,000

The IASB's post implementation review on IFRS 3 *Business Combinations*, which reported in 2015, plus research conducted by the European Financial Reporting Advisory Group (EFRAG) and the standard setters of Italy (OIOC) and Japan (ASBJ) in 2014, have concluded that some users consider the impairment-only model does not provide the most appropriate method for subsequent measurement of the goodwill, and that amortisation should be reintroduced. In addition, for preparers of financial statements, impairment testing is complex, time-consuming, expensive and involves significant judgements.

Many of the respondents to these research projects indicated that they would prefer the subsequent measurement of goodwill to be the same as for other intangible assets; in other words amortised and tested for impairment when indications exist that it may be impaired. The reasons given for this include the following:

● goodwill acquired in a business combination is an asset that is consumed and replaced over time by internally generated goodwill, which is not recognised

● it is possible to estimate the useful life of goodwill, as this could be linked to business models developed at the time of the acquisition

● amortising goodwill would decrease volatility in profit or loss compared to impairment

● the amortisation of goodwill would reduce the requirement at the point of acquisition to identify intangible assets which were not recognised in the financial statement of the acquired company, since both would be amortised.

The IASB has indicated that it will carry out further research in this area.

11.8.4 Derecognition

As for a tangible non-current asset, an intangible asset is derecognised either when it is disposed of, or when no future economic benefits are expected from its use or disposal. The gain or loss on derecognition is calculated as the difference between the proceeds from disposal, if any, and the carrying amount at the date of derecognition.

11.9 Disclosures

These are extensive and are very similar to those required for property, plant and equipment. Generally, there will be information provided in the company's accounting policies for each class of intangible asset about:

- whether the lives are indefinite or finite, and, if indefinite, the reasons for this assessment
- for assets with finite lives, the estimated useful lives and amortisation methods used.

A disclosure note breaking down the total carrying amount of intangible assets will contain a full reconciliation, by class of asset, of the opening and closing carrying amounts, which will include:

- additions, showing separately those acquired externally, those from internal development, and those acquired in a business combination
- assets classified as held for sale
- disposals
- increases/decreases arising from revaluations
- impairment losses or reversals of impairment losses recognised previously
- amortisation recognised during the period
- any other changes in the carrying amounts
- the gross carrying amount and accumulated amortisation at the beginning and end of the accounting period.

If any class of intangible asset uses the revaluation model, there are additional disclosures:

- the date(s) of revaluation(s)
- the carrying amount of revalued intangible assets
- the carrying amount that would have been recognised if the cost model had been applied to the class of asset
- the amount of the revaluation surplus relating to intangible assets at the beginning and end of the accounting period.

Further disclosures include:

- the amount of research and development expenditure recognised as an expense during the accounting period
- the line item in the statement of comprehensive income in which amortisation of intangible assets is included.

Financial reporting in practice 11.5   Vodafone plc, 2015

Vodafone Group plc's 2015 financial statements contain extensive information about its intangible assets in its disclosure note. It highlights some key issues relating to intangible assets, followed by its accounting policies.

Note 10. Intangible assets

Our statement of financial position contains significant intangible assets, mainly in relation to goodwill and licences and spectrum. Goodwill, which arises when we acquire a business and pay a higher amount than the fair value of its net assets primarily due to the synergies we expect to create, is not amortised but is subject to annual impairment reviews. Licences and spectrum are amortised over the life of the licence. For further details see 'Critical accounting judgements' in note 1 'Basis of preparation' to the consolidated financial statements.

Accounting policies

Identifiable intangible assets are recognised when the Group controls the asset, it is probable that future economic benefits attributed to the asset will flow to the Group and the cost of the asset can be reliably measured.

Goodwill

Goodwill arising on the acquisition of an entity represents the excess of the cost of acquisition over the Group's interest in the net fair value of the identifiable assets, liabilities and contingent liabilities of the entity recognised at the date of acquisition.

Goodwill is initially recognised as an asset at cost and is subsequently measured at cost less any accumulated impairment losses. Goodwill is not subject to amortisation but is tested for impairment or whenever there is evidence that it may be required. Goodwill is denominated in the currency of the acquired entity and revalued to the closing exchange rate at each reporting period date.

Negative goodwill arising on an acquisition is recognised directly in the income statement.

On disposal of a subsidiary or a jointly controlled entity, the attributable amount of goodwill is included in the determination of the profit or loss recognised in the income statement on disposal.

Goodwill arising before the date of transition to IFRS, on 1 April 2004, has been retained at the previous UK GAAP amounts, subject to being tested for impairment at that date. Goodwill written off to reserves under UK GAAP prior to 1998 has not been reinstated and is not included in determining any subsequent profit or loss on disposal.

Finite lived intangible assets

Intangible assets with finite lives are stated at acquisition or development cost, less accumulated amortisation. The amortisation period and method is reviewed at least annually. Changes in the expected useful life or the expected pattern of consumption of future economic benefits embodied in the asset is accounted for by changing the amortisation period or method, as appropriate, and are treated as changes in accounting estimates.

Licence and spectrum fees

Amortisation periods for licence and spectrum fees are determined primarily by reference to the unexpired licence period, the conditions for licence renewal and whether licences are dependent on specific technologies. Amortisation is charged to the income statement on a straight-line basis over the estimated useful lives from the commencement of related network services.

Computer software

Computer software comprises computer software purchased from third parties as well as the cost of internally developed software. Computer software licences are capitalised on the basis of the costs incurred to acquire and bring into use the specific software. Costs that are directly associated with

(continued)

(continued)

the production of identifiable and unique software products controlled by the Group, and are probable of producing future economic benefits, are recognised as intangible assets. Direct costs include software development employee costs and directly attributable overheads.

Software integral to a related item of hardware equipment is classified as property, plant and equipment.

Costs associated with maintaining computer software programs are recognised as an expense when they are incurred.

Internally developed software is recognised only if all of the following conditions are met:

- an asset is created that can be separately identified;
- it is probable that the asset created will generate future economic benefits; and
- the development cost of the asset can be measured reliably.

Amortisation is charged to the income statement on a straight-line basis over the estimated useful lives from the date the software is available for use.

Other intangible assets

Other intangible assets including brands and customer bases, are recorded at fair value at the date of acquisition. Amortisation is charged to the income statement, over the estimated useful lives of intangible assets from the date they are available for use, on a straight-line basis, with the exception of customer relationships which are amortised on a sum of digits basis. The amortisation basis adopted for each class of intangible asset reflects the Group's consumption of the economic benefit from that asset.

Estimated useful lives

The estimated useful lives of finite lived intangible assets are as follows:

- Licence and spectrum fees 3–25 years
- Computer software 3–5 years
- Brands 1–10 years
- Customer bases 2–7 years

The reconciliation of opening and closing carrying amounts of intangible assets follows:

	Goodwill £m	Licences and spectrum £m	Computer software £m	Other £m	Total £m
Cost:					
1 April 2013	73,316	22,871	8,879	2,905	113,971
Exchange movements	(3,054)	(1,757)	(375)	(434)	(5,620)
Arising on acquisition	6,859	1,319	464	2,861	11,503
Additions	–	2,228	1,437	–	3,665

Disposals	–	(74)	(296)	–	(370)
Other	–	5	103	–	108
31 March 2014	**77,121**	**30,592**	**10,212**	**5,332**	**123,257**
Exchange movements	(8,756)	(1,235)	(1,036)	(542)	(11,569)
Arising on acquisition	1,634	–	48	905	2,587
Additions	–	467	1,844	17	2,328
Disposals	–	–	(464)	(12)	(476)
Other	–	(20)	11	–	(9)
31 March 2015	**69,999**	**29,804**	**10,615**	**5,700**	**116,118**
Accumulated impairment losses and amortisation:					
1 April 2013	48,926	12,534	6,112	2,260	69,832
Exchange movements	(1,720)	(732)	(261)	(338)	(3,051)
Amortisation charge for the year	–	1,683	1,282	557	3,522
Impairment losses	6,600	–	–	–	6,600
Disposals	–	(65)	(278)	–	(343)
Other	–	–	9	–	9
31 March 2014	**53,806**	**13,420**	**6,864**	**2,479**	**76,569**
Exchange movements	(6,344)	(717)	(707)	(234)	(8,002)
Amortisation charge for the year	–	1,751	1,491	1,277	4,519
Disposals	–	–	(454)	(12)	(466)
Other	–	–	8	–	8
31 March 2015	**47,462**	**14,454**	**7,202**	**3,510**	**72,628**
Net book value:					
31 March 2014	23,315	17,172	3,348	2,853	46,688
31 March 2015	22,537	15,350	3,413	2,190	43,490

For licences and spectrum and other intangible assets, amortisation is included within the cost of sales line within the consolidated income. Licences and spectrum with a net book value of £2,059 million (2014: £3,885 million) have been pledged as security against borrowings.

The net book value and expiry dates of the most significant licences are as follows:

	Expiry date	2015 £m	2014 £m
Germany	2016/2020/2025	2,843	3,743
Italy	2018/2021/2029	1,094	1,301

(continued)

(continued)			
UK	2033	3,050	3,425
India	2015–2034	3,994	3,885
Qatar	2028/2029	987	945
Netherlands	2016/2029/2030	940	1,188

The remaining amortisation period for each of the licences in the table above corresponds to the expiry date of the respective licence. A summary of the Group's most significant spectrum licences can be found on page 200.

11.10 What do the accounting treatment and disclosures of intangible assets mean to the user?

As seen in this chapter, only certain intangible assets which meet the definition and recognition criteria set out by IAS 38 are actually included on a company's statement of financial position. The same type of asset may be treated differently depending on whether it was internally generated or acquired externally, possibly through a business combination. Hence, a user of the financial statements could be said to get an incomplete picture of the resources that a company uses to generate its revenues and wealth. In addition, some businesses actively pursue strategies to develop their own intangible assets, which they see as the core success of their business, and which will never be capitalised. As Bill Gates of Microsoft highlighted:

> The law requires circa 40 pages of figures in the annual company report but these figures represent only 3% of the company's value and assets. The remaining 97% are the company's intangible assets.

Even if a company followed the requirements of IAS 38, the whole issue of accounting for intangible assets can be considered prone to 'earnings management', particularly if there is pressure on earnings. Management's judgement and estimations of future events, which may not be entirely in its control, are required to determine whether recognition criteria have been fulfilled. Alternative interpretations of these subjective criteria can be made, which may also lead to a different approach to capitalisation from one company to another, or even within the same company from one project to another.

As for tangible assets, two alternative measurement bases are available for intangible assets—the cost basis and the revaluation basis—which can lead to difficulties in comparability between companies. The revaluation model uses fair value, which, for intangible assets, can be particularly subjective.

The extensive disclosures will aid the comparability of different companies, but these show mainly what has been capitalised and subsequent treatment of these costs; there is less information on what has not been capitalised. Companies' financial statements generally quote the words of IAS 38 to explain accounting treatments, and will not explicitly show management's interpretations and decision-making processes. However in recent years, companies have been encouraged to provide more information on areas where significant estimates and judgements have been made. These will often include intangible assets' lives, the identification and valuation of intangible assets, including goodwill, in business combinations, and how figures relating to impairment have been determined.

So is this, therefore, a problem? Non-recognition of intangible assets will result in the understatement of net assets and capital employed, and variations in recognition methods will have an impact on these figures. Analysis of the financial performance of a company using ratios which include these items will clearly be affected.

 Worked example 11.6: to show the effect of capitalisation versus non-capitalisation of intangible assets on accounting ratios

Jenmark plc has its own internally generated brand, which it has spent years developing. Annual expenditure on maintaining the brand is £1 million and, as a result of this, the company's directors estimate that the brand has an indefinite useful life. Brand valuation experts have recently estimated the fair value of the brand at £15 million.

The financial statements of Jenmark properly excluding the brand as an intangible asset and also if the brand were recognised are shown as follows.

Note: if the brand were recognised, equity would be increased. As the brand has an indefinite life, there is no amortisation to be recognised. The annual expenditure on maintaining the brand remains an expense.

Statement of financial position	Excluding brand £m	Brand recognised £m
Intangible assets	–	15
Other assets	14	14
	14	29
Equity	5	20
Long-term borrowings	3	3
Current liabilities	6	6
	14	29
Statement of profit or loss		
Revenue	20	20
Profit before interest and tax	7	7

Required:

Calculate and comment on the following accounting ratios using the financial information including and excluding the recognition of the brand:

- return on capital employed
- return on assets
- net profit margin
- gearing.

		Excluding brand	Brand recognised
Return on capital employed	$\dfrac{\text{PBIT}}{\text{Capital employed}}$	88%	30%
Return on assets	$\dfrac{\text{PBIT}}{\text{Total assets}}$	50%	24%
Net profit margin	$\dfrac{\text{PBIT}}{\text{Revenue}}$	35%	35%
Gearing	$\dfrac{\text{Debt}}{\text{Debt + Equity}}$	38%	13%

The two performance ratios—return on capital employed and return on assets—are much higher without the brand, but these ratios could be considered meaningless as the capital employed or assets do not reflect the 'true' resources of the company. Inclusion of the brand gives more meaningful ratios.

The net profit margin is unaffected and is therefore a good ratio to use when comparing companies' performances. Even if the brand had a finite life and amortisation were included in the statement of profit or loss, profit before interest, tax and amortisation is often taken as the measure of profit.

Although the gearing ratio looks much improved when the intangible asset is recognised, companies' borrowings depend, in part, on their ability to provide security in the form of tangible assets. Lenders will usually discount any intangible assets.

One of the initial issues set out at the beginning of the chapter was that non-recognition of intangible assets could lead to undervaluation of the shares of companies. It must be remembered that the purpose of a statement of financial position is not to provide a market value for a business, and stock market analysts understand this. Market values are based largely on earnings reported in the statement of profit or loss and many stock market analysts will ignore intangible assets actually included in statements of financial position.

11.11 Does this mean the current accounting and reporting of intangible assets is acceptable?

It is important for users of financial statements to have information about all resources an entity has available, including intangibles which are not recognised on the statement of financial position. However, adding intangibles to this statement, where it is difficult or too early to assess whether they may bring future benefits to the entity, or where their value is dubious, will not assist the relevance or reliability of financial statements.

Proposals for the reform of accounting for intangibles have been put forward in the past by various international groups, including the chief executive officers (CEOs) of the world's six largest auditing firms, Meritum (a European Union-sponsored group of researchers), the Danish Ministry of Science Technology and Innovation, and Baruch Lev (an American accounting academic who has written widely on financial reporting for intangibles). None of these propose abandoning the accounting and reporting methods of current financial reporting standards; they all suggest that additional information should be disclosed. This information would require companies to identify and explain key intangibles which drive their business, and provide measures of these. For example, the ratio of the number of personal computers to the total number of employees could be used if information technology is critical to achieving the entity's objectives.

There are obvious problems with these voluntary disclosures—many would be industry or company-specific, and so would not be comparable; they would be subjective and their reliability would be called into question; and companies would probably not wish to disclose information which may be helpful to competitors and be costly to produce. However, to make these sorts of disclosures mandatory would also be problematic as some form of standardisation would be required, which would be impossible across all industries and, possibly, meaningless for some. The ability to audit the information would also be very difficult and the additional information would add to the length of company annual reports.

11.12 The current IASB position

The IASB was contemplating undertaking a project on the accounting for identifiable intangible assets (excluding goodwill) jointly with the Financial Accounting Standards Board (FASB). The project proposed addressing concerns that the current accounting requirements lead to inconsistent treatments for some types of intangible assets depending on how they arise.

However, the IASB decided not to add a project on intangible assets to its active agenda in December 2007 because of the large demand of such a project on its limited resources.

Following the post-implementation review of IFRS 3 *Business Combinations* in 2015, the IASB has added a research project to its agenda which will look at topics such as the identification and fair value measurement of intangible assets such as customer relationships and brand names in business combinations and the subsequent accounting for goodwill including impairment versus amortisation. Such research projects take a considerable amount of time and resources; consequently any amendments to current accounting methods are unlikely to take effect for some years.

Summary of key points

Intangible assets are key resources of businesses, and the question of whether, and how, they should be included in financial statements to enable users to have reliable and comparable information about the entity is an important one. Recognition and measurement are key issues for intangibles owing to the assets' nature, with subjective judgements often required.

IAS 38 defines an intangible asset as an identifiable non-monetary asset without physical substance; common examples are computer software, patents, copyrights, trademarks, customer lists, licences, quotas and franchises. An intangible asset must be separable, or arise from contractual or other legal rights, and, to be recognised, IAS 38 currently requires that future economic benefits will flow to the entity and the cost is capable of being measured reliably.

Intangible assets may be purchased from an external source when they are measured initially at cost; be acquired as part of a business combination when they are measured initially at fair value; or be internally generated. In the latter case only expenditure arising in the development phase can be recognised as an intangible asset and this only if certain criteria are met.

The accounting for recognised intangible assets is similar to that for property, plant and equipment, with the cost and valuation models being available, amortisation being required for intangible assets with finite lives, and annual impairment testing required for assets with indefinite lives and for goodwill. The accounting treatment for impairment losses is the same as for property, plant and equipment, although testing for impairment of goodwill requires the allocation of goodwill to related CGUs. Disclosures for the two types of non-current asset are also similar.

Current accounting methods lead to some inconsistencies and suggestions have been made by interested groups for additional disclosures. The IASB does not have any current plans to address these issues, although it has added a research project to its agenda to consider issues of accounting for intangibles, including goodwill, in business combinations.

Further reading

Anderson, N. (2004) Value judgments, *Accountancy*, November 2004: 86–87. Why read? The article illustrates the practical difficulties of valuing intangible assets acquired in a business combination.

IASB (International Accounting Standards Board) (2004) IAS 38 *Intangible Assets*. London: IASB.

ICAEW (Institute of Chartered Accountants in England and Wales) (2009) *Developments in New Reporting Models*, pp. 15–22. Available at: http://www.icaew.com (accessed 27 August 2015). Why read? The highlighted pages explore why the issue of accounting for intangibles has always prompted criticism in the context of financial reporting models.

Skinner, D. J. (2008) *Accounting for Intangibles—A Critical Review of Policy Recommendations*. Presented at ICAEW Information for Better Markets Conference, 17–18 December 2007. Why read? A critical evaluation of the arguments for reforming accounting methods applied to intangible assets.

Bibliography

Arsenal Holdings plc (2015) *Annual Report, 2015*. London: Arsenal Holdings.

AstraZeneca plc (2015) *Annual Report and Form 20-F Information 2014*. London: AstraZeneca.

EFRAG (European Financial Reporting Advisory Group) (2014) *Should Goodwill still not be Amortised? Accounting and Disclosure for Goodwill*, July 2014. Brussels: EFRAG.

FRC (Financial Reporting Council) (2014) *ARP Staff Research Report: Investor Views on Intangible Assets and their Amortisation*, March 2014. London: FRC.

IASB (International Accounting Standards Board) (2004a) IAS 38 *Intangible Assets*. London: IASB.

IASB (International Accounting Standards Board) (2004b) IFRS 3 *Business Combinations*. London: IASB.

IASB (International Accounting Standards Board) (2010) *Conceptual Framework for Financial Reporting 2010*. London: IASB.

IASB (International Accounting Standards Board) (2011) IFRS 13 *Fair Value Measurement*. London: IASB.

IASB (International Accounting Standards Board) (2015) *Post-implementation Review of IFRS 3 Business Combinations*. London: IASB.

ICAEW (Institute of Chartered Accountants in England and Wales) (2003) *New Reporting Models of Business—Proposals for Reform*, pp. 51–57. Available at: http://www.icaew.com (accessed 14 October 2012).

ICAEW (Institute of Chartered Accountants in England and Wales) (2009) *Developments in New Reporting Models*, pp. 15–22. Available at: http://www.icaew.com (accessed 27 August 2015).

Leadbetter, C. (2000) *New Measures for the New Economy*. Report produced by the Centre for Business Performance for the ICAEW. London: ICAEW.

Meritum (2001) *Guidelines for Managing and Reporting on Intangibles—Intellectual Capital Report*. Report produced by Meritum, a group of European researchers brought together under the auspices of the EU. Available at: http://www.pnbukh.com/ (accessed 27 August 2015).

Nobes, C. (2014) *Goodwill: The Never-ending Puzzle*. Available at http://ifrs.wiley.com/news/goodwill-the-never-ending-puzzle?elq_mid=2223&elq_cid=119332 (accessed 5 November 2014).

Nokia Corporation (2015) *Annual Report, 2014*. Espoo: Nokia.

PricewaterhouseCoopers (2009) *Making Sense of a Complex World—IAS 36 Impairment of Assets A Discussion Paper on the impact on the Telecoms Industry*. Paper produced for the PwC telecommunications industry accounting group (TIAG). London: PricewaterhouseCoopers.

Rolls-Royce plc (2015) *Annual Report, 2014*. London: Rolls-Royce.

Singleton-Green, B. (2013) *Capitalising intangibles: an update*. Available at http://www.icaew.com (accessed 16 May 2013).

Skinner, D. J. (2008) *Accounting for Intangibles—A Critical Review of Policy Recommendations*. Presented at ICAEW Information for Better Markets Conference, 17–18 December 2007.

Vodafone Group plc (2015) *Annual Report, 2015*. Newbury: Vodafone.

 ## Questions

● Quick test

1   A company is developing improved production processes and has recruited a manager to head up the team responsible for this. The manager is on an annual salary of £64,000. The company has also incurred costs of £50,000 in training the personnel and now has a highly skilled team.

 Discuss whether the company has any intangible assets, as defined by IAS 38 *Intangible assets*.

2   Warmington plc produces a range of children's toys, and markets and sells them under its internally developed brand, KidzToys. The brand is now highly respected and the products are regarded as 'must have' toys.

On 1 July 20X3 Fraser plc acquired the whole of Warmington plc for £50 million. At this date a brand valuation expert valued the KidzToys brand at £15 million on the basis of a useful life of 5 years. Other net assets were deemed to have a fair value of £25 million.

Required

Assuming that the goodwill arising on the acquisition of Warmington was not impaired at 30 June 20X4, what amounts for intangible assets should be recognised in Fraser plc's consolidated financial statements at 30 June 20X4 in respect of this transaction?

●● Develop your understanding

3   (a) Company Alpha acquires Company Beta in a business combination. Beta manufactures goods in two distinct lines of business: sporting goods and electronics. Gamma, a customer of Beta, purchases both sporting goods and electronics from Beta, which has a contract with Gamma to be its exclusive provider of sporting goods, but has no such contract for the supply of electronics. Both Beta and Alpha believe that only one overall customer relationship exists between Beta and Gamma.

(b) Company Delta acquires Company Epsilon in a business combination on 31 December 20X5. Epsilon does business with its customers solely through purchase and sales orders. At 31 December 20X5, Epsilon has a backlog of customer purchase orders from 60% of its customers, all of whom are recurring customers. The other 40% of Epsilon's customers are also recurring customers. However, as of 31 December 20X5, Epsilon has no open purchase orders or other contracts with those customers.

Required

For each scenario determine whether there are identifiable intangible assets in these business combinations.

4   On 1 January 20X2 a company acquires computer software specific to a project for £200,000. Although the project is in its early stages, and is not expected to make profits or positive cash flows for a number of years, the company will start to use the software straight away; it is estimated it has a useful life of 10 years. The company negotiated to defer the payment to the supplier until 1 January 20X4. The company currently pays interest on its borrowings at 6% per annum.

Required:

Show how this transaction would be accounted for at 1 January 20X2 and in the financial statements of the company for the year ended 31 December 20X2.

5   (a) On 1 January 20X1 a broadcasting company with a 31 December financial year end acquires a broadcasting licence for £360,000 that is renewable every 10 years if the holder provides at least an average level of service to its customers and complies with the relevant legislative requirements. The licence may be renewed indefinitely at little cost. At the date of acquisition, the licence has been renewed twice by the previous owner and it will require renewing again on 1 January 20X6. The acquiring company intends to renew the licence indefinitely and evidence supports its ability to do so. Historically, there has been no compelling challenge to the licence renewal. The technology used in broadcasting is not expected to be replaced by another technology at any time in the foreseeable future.

(b) On 1 January 20X3 the licensing authority decides that it will no longer renew broadcasting licences, but will auction the licences when the renewal is due. The broadcasting company expects to hold the licence until this date and will then decide whether it will bid for the licence.

Required:

Determine the useful life of the broadcasting licence, and discuss the subsequent accounting treatment at the two dates 1 January 20X1 and 20X3.

●●● Take it further

6   Airpro plc is a newly established company in the business of providing engineering and operational support services to aircraft manufacturers.

Airpro plc has received a confirmed order from a well-known aircraft manufacturer to develop new designs for ducting the air conditioning of their aircraft. For this project, Airpro needed funds totalling £1 million. It was able to obtain this funding from two venture capitalists at the start of 20X6.

During 20X6 Airpro incurred the following expenditures in respect of this research and development project:

January	Paid £175,000 toward salaries of the technicians (engineers and consultants).
March	Incurred £250,000 toward cost of developing the duct and producing the test model.
June	Paid an additional £300,000 for revising the ducting processes to ensure that product could be introduced in the market.
August	Developed, at a cost of £80,000, the first model (prototype) and tested it with the air conditioners to ensure its compatibility.
October	A focus group of other engineering providers was invited to a conference of the introduction of this new product. Cost of the conference aggregated to £50,000.
December	The development phase was completed and a cash flow budget was prepared. Net profit for the year was estimated to equal £900,000.

Required

Discuss the proper accounting treatment of the various costs incurred in the financial statements of Airpro plc for the year ended 31 December 20X6, in accordance with IAS 38 *Intangible Assets*.

7   On 31 December 20X6 Jolyon Pharmaceuticals plc acquired the whole of the share capital of Gillet Ltd for a total consideration of £10 million. Gillet Ltd had been involved in the research and development of a drug to help asthma sufferers. By 31 December 20X6 Gillet had written off to profit and loss total research and development costs of £500,000, as the criteria for recognition of any of the costs as an intangible asset had not yet been met. At the date of acquisition, Jolyon Pharmaceuticals estimated the fair value of the asthma drug project at £800,000 and agreed to provide funding to support its further development.

During 20X7 and 20X8 work on this project continued, and Gillet incurred further costs of £900,000 in 20X7 and £1 million in 20X8 up to 31 October—the costs being incurred evenly over the years. On 31 March 20X8 the drug was approved by the regulatory authorities, at which point Gillet considered that it was also commercially viable. On 1 November 20X8 the drug started being marketed and sold. Gillet estimates the product to have a useful life of 10 years.

Required:

Explain how the costs relating to this drug project should be accounted for in the consolidated financial statements of Jolyon Pharmaceuticals plc for the years ended 31 December 20X7 and 20X8. Justify your answer by reference to IAS 38 *Intangible Assets*.

 Visit the Online Resource Centre for solutions to all these end of chapter questions plus visual walkthrough solutions. You can test your understanding with extra questions and answers, explore additional case studies based on real companies, take a guided tour through a company report and much more. Go to the Online Resource Centre at **www.oxfordtextbooks.co.uk/orc/maynard2e/**

12

Inventories

➤ Introduction

Current assets are used to assess the liquidity and efficiency of working capital management of a business; thus, it is important that the items included in current assets are as accurate as possible and comparable. For many businesses, inventories are a significant current asset. There are two main issues with accounting for inventories—quantities and measurement. Many frauds involving the existence of inventories have been perpetrated, and companies should have proper controls in place to ensure that quantities of inventory are not misstated at their reporting period end.

International Accounting Standard (IAS) 2 *Inventories* deals with the issue of measurement, to ensure consistency of approach. It is this issue that is discussed in detail in this chapter.

★ Learning objectives

After studying this chapter you will be able to:

● understand the significance of inventories in companies' financial statements

● understand how inventory quantities may be manipulated

● understand the main valuation principles for inventories, and explain how cost and net realisable value are determined.

✔ Key issues checklist

❑ The definition of a current asset.

❑ Issues with validating the physical presence of inventories.

❑ The key valuation principle for inventories—lower of cost and net realisable value.

❑ Definition of cost—with a focus on the manufacturer.

❑ First-in, first-out versus other cost methods.

❑ Definition of net realisable value.

❑ Disclosures in financial statements.

12.1 Significance of inventories

Users of financial statements need to be able to distinguish between those assets which are long-term resources and those which are continuously circulating and changing as working capital. Businesses therefore separate non-current assets from current assets on their statements of financial position and thus highlight assets which are expected to be realised within their operating cycle (the time it takes between the acquisition of the asset and its ultimate conversion into cash or cash equivalents). This enables users to assess the liquidity of a business.

❶ **Reminder** *Liquidity is the ability of a business to meet its liabilities as they fall due. An analysis of the liquidity of a business involves an assessment of what makes up working capital or net current assets (i.e. current assets – current liabilities), which is needed by all businesses in order to finance day-to-day trading activities. The efficiency of the management of working capital is also important in an assessment of liquidity. Various financial ratios relevant to this assessment are discussed in Chapter 5.*

Current assets are defined in IAS 1 *Presentation of Financial Statements* as those which:

(a) a business expects to realise, or intends to sell or consume in its normal operating cycle;

(b) a business holds primarily for the purpose of trading;

(c) a business expects to realise within twelve months after the reporting period; or

(d) are cash or a cash equivalent (as defined in IAS 7 *Statement of Cash Flows*).

(IASB, IAS 1, para. 66)

Inventories are therefore a current asset, and in many cases a significant figure within this balance on the statements of financial position of most businesses which produce and/or sell goods. For example:

- M&S plc 2015 (retailer)—inventories (£798 million) 55% of total current assets (£1,455 million), by far the largest current asset

- Nestlé Group 2014 (food and consumables manufacturer)—inventories (CHF 9,172 million) 27% of total current assets (CHF 33,961 million)

- Rolls-Royce plc 2014 (manufacturer)—inventories (£2,768 million) 25% of total current assets (£11,188 million).

Inventories for retailers and distribution companies encompass goods purchased and held for resale, and, for manufacturers, inventories include finished goods produced, work in progress being produced, and also materials and supplies yet to be used in the production process. Costs incurred to fulfil a contract with a customer that do not give rise to inventories are accounted for in accordance with IFRS 15 *Revenue from Contracts with Customers* (and this is discussed in Chapter 7).

The under-/overvaluation of inventories can have a material impact on the calculation of profits: if inventories are undervalued, profits are reduced; if inventories are overvalued, profits are increased.

Financial reporting in practice 12.1 | Rolls-Royce plc 2014

Rolls-Royce plc 2014 results show the company made a net profit before tax of £67 million. Closing inventories are valued at £2,768 million.

Only a 2.5% error in inventory valuation (2.5%×£2,768 million = £69 million) would mean that Rolls-Royce's profit would be converted into a loss.

An error in inventory one year also has a knock-on effect on next year's profit, as one year's closing inventory becomes next year's opening inventory.

12.2 Issues with accounting for inventories

Key issues relating to the accounting for inventories are:

- the physical existence of inventories
- whether the business actually controls the asset
- measurement (or valuation), which is what IAS 2 *Inventories* addresses.

Many frauds or accounting scandals have concerned inventories, as illustrated by the following cases.

Examples of inventory-related accounting scandals

1 US case of McKesson & Robbins (1938)—fictitious inventories conveniently 'abroad' in Canada (note the auditors did not perform a physical check).

2 UK case of the GEC/AEI takeover (1967)—a forecast profit of £10 million turned into an actual loss of £4.5 million, where much of the difference related to the valuation of inventories.

3 UK case of Pergamon Press, a Maxwell company (1969)—significant differences in inventory valuation leading to a reduction in audited profits.

Companies may be tempted into 'managing' the physical presence of inventories in order to 'manage' earnings, and cases have been known of companies shipping goods to customers early or having goods in transit so that they are not physically present at any premises. This may be relatively easy if this occurs between companies in the same group. Consignment inventories (in other words, goods received from a supplier or sent to a customer on a sale or return basis) and the inclusion of obsolete inventories can also be used to manipulate recorded physical quantities. Auditors have to be alert to these issues and also be particularly careful that a company has accounted for the year end cut-off correctly. This means a check has to be made that purchases recorded before and after the year end match inventories on hand or goods not included in inventories, respectively, and that goods sold before the year end are not included in inventories.

12.3 **Measurement of inventories**

The key issue in the measurement of inventories is the amount of cost to be recognised as an asset and carried forward to be matched against the related revenues in future accounting periods. Thus, the underpinning principle of valuation is that of accruals, but, as an asset, inventories should not be carried at amounts in excess of their value to the business. So IAS 2 requires inventories:

> … to be measured at the lower of cost and net realisable value.

> *(IASB, 2003: para. 9)*

Inventories where this requirement does not apply are shown in Table 12.1.

Table 12.1 Businesses where the measurement requirement of IAS 2 does not apply

Type of business	Valuation method used
Producers of agriculture, forest products, agricultural produce after harvest, minerals and mineral products	Net realisable value
Commodity brokers and traders	Fair value less costs to sell

12.4 Cost of inventories

The criteria for determining whether a cost can be included in the measurement of inventories are similar to those set out in IAS 16 *Property, Plant and Equipment* for the cost of an item of property, plant and equipment:

> Cost shall comprise all costs of purchase, costs of conversion and other costs incurred in bringing the inventories to their present location and condition.

(IASB, 2003, para. 10)

In other words, all costs which have been incurred in getting the inventory to its particular state of completion wherever located are part of the cost. Costs of purchase and costs of conversion are defined in Figure 12.1.

Techniques such as absorption costing or activity-based costing, which are used to allocate fixed production overheads to the cost of products for management accounting purposes, are therefore incorporated into financial reporting measurement requirements. The allocation of these production overheads should be based on the normal capacity of the business, which is the level of production that the business expects to achieve under normal circumstances. If production is lower than usual, or machinery is not used, the amount of fixed overhead allocated to each unit of production is not increased; these unallocated overheads are recognised as an expense. However, if production is abnormally high, the amount of overhead allocated to each unit of production is lower and this is not increased to normal levels, otherwise inventories would be measured at greater than cost.

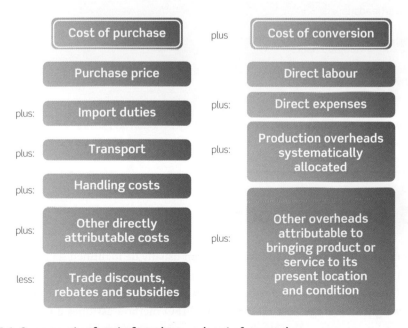

Figure 12.1 Components of cost of purchase and cost of conversion

> **Worked example 12.1:** to calculate the cost of inventory, including capacity considerations

The Staybright Company plc has inventories of finished goods at 31 December 20X5 and has gathered the following information in relation to these:

	£
Cost of materials	32,000
Labour	1,000 hours @ £8.00 per hour
Other variable overheads	1,400
Fixed production overheads incurred	
1 October 20X5 – 31 December 20X5	80,000
Selling and distribution expenses	20,000

The number of hours worked in the period 1 October 20X5 – 31 December 20X5 was 18,000. During December, 2,000 hours of work were lost because of an industrial dispute.

Required:

Calculate the cost of Staybright's finished goods at 31 December 20X5.

The cost of inventories at 31 December 20X5 is determined as follows:

	£
Cost of materials	32,000
Labour (1,000 X £8.00)	8,000
Variable overheads	1,400
Fixed overheads $\dfrac{£80,000}{20,000 \text{ hours}} \times 1,000$	4,000
Cost of inventories	45,400

Notes

Note 1: Selling and distribution costs are not a cost of production and so are not included.
Note 2: The allocation of the fixed production overheads to the costs of conversion is based on the normal capacity of the production facilities, in other words 20,000 hours.

12.5 Cost methods

The costs of specific or specialised inventories can usually be identified separately. However, where there are large numbers of inventories which cannot be distinguished from each other (e.g. a container of the same-sized bolts), the cost is determined by using the **first-in, first-out (FIFO)** or **weighted average cost methods**. The FIFO method assumes a rational approach to the use of inventories in that the items purchased or produced first are sold first, so that the inventories remaining at the end of the accounting period are those which were most recently purchased or produced. Under the weighted average cost method, the cost of each item is the weighted average of the cost of similar items at the beginning of a period and the cost of similar items purchased or produced during the period.

Other costing methods may be used by businesses for internal management accounting reasons, and include:

- last-in, first-out (LIFO)
- replacement cost
- current purchase price.

These are not permitted to be used for cost purposes under IAS 2. However, many businesses carry their inventories at **standard cost** and retailers will often use selling price minus gross margin. Provided these methods approximate to cost, they may be used to establish the measurement for financial reporting purposes.

 Worked example 12.2: to show the calculation of FIFO and average cost

Glazier plc has 100 units of raw material X on hand at 1 March 20X7, which had cost £10 per unit. The following transactions in material X occurred in the month of March:

3 March	Purchases	80 units at £12 per unit
8 March	Used in production	60 units
15 March	Purchases	70 units at £11 per unit
18 March	Used in production	110 units

Required:

Compute the cost of inventory of material X at 31 March 20X7 on the following bases:

(i) First-in, first-out

(ii) Weighted average.

(i) First-in, first-out

		Purchases		Used		Balance		
		No.	Cost	No.	Cost	No.		£
1 March	On hand	100	£10			100	£10	1,000
3 March	Purchases	80	£12			80	£12	960
						180		1,960
8 March	Used			60	£10	40	£10	400
						80	£12	960
						120		1,360

15 March	Purchases	70	£11		40	£10	400
					80	£12	960
					70	£11	770
					190		2,130
18 March	Used		40	£10			
			70	£12	10	£12	120
			110		70	£11	770
					80		890

Cost of inventory at 31 March 20X7 under FIFO method is £890.

(ii) _Weighted average_

		Purchases		Used		Balance		
		No.	Cost	No.	Cost	No.		£
1 March	On hand	100	£10			100	£10	1,000
3 March	Purchases	80	£12			80	£12	960
						180	£10.89	1,960
8 March	Used			60	£10.89	120	£10.89	1,307
15 March	Purchases	70	£11			120	£10.89	1,307
						70	£11	770
						190	£10.93	2,077
18 March	Used			110	£10.93	80	£10.93	874

Cost of inventory at 31 March 20X7 under weighted average method is £874.

12.6 Net realisable value

Net realisable value (NRV) is defined as:

> ... the estimated selling price in the ordinary course of business less the estimated costs of completion and the estimated costs necessary to make the sale.

> _(IASB, 2003, para. 6)_

A number of reasons may cause the NRV of inventories to fall below cost. For example, there may be a permanent fall in the market price of inventories, inventories may physically deteriorate or become obsolete, or the business may deliberately decide to sell below cost, perhaps to dispose of high inventory levels or seasonal items. In addition, costs of completing the inventory or estimated costs to make the sale may have increased. NRV is subjective as it is based on future estimates.

The effect of writing down inventory to NRV is to recognise a loss on inventory before any sale has actually occurred; this may appear to contradict the matching principle. However, it is consistent with the view that the carrying amount of assets should not be in excess of amounts expected to be realised from their sale or use.

The lower of cost and NRV basis is also an example of where asymmetric prudence is used in a financial reporting standard.

🛈 **Reminder:** *Asymmetric prudence is where an accounting method results in losses being recognised at an earlier stage than gains.*

As discussed in Chapter 2, in the redrafting of its *Conceptual Framework*, the IASB has taken the view that this does not conflict with neutrality provided the selection of a company's accounting policies is done in a neutral way.

 Example of the effect of writing inventory down to NRV

An inventory item was purchased by a retailer in December 20X0 for £150 and usually retails for £200. Before the 31 December financial year end the company slashes selling prices by 50%.

At 31 December the inventory item's NRV is £100, which is lower than the cost of £150. By writing down the inventory item to £100, the retailer has recognised a loss of £50 in 20X0.

If the inventory item is sold in 20X1, the value of £100 will be matched to the sale price of £100, and no profit or loss will be recognised.

The determination of the lower of cost and NRV is done inventory item by inventory item, unless, for example, it is impracticable to evaluate items of inventory from others produced from the same production process that have similar purposes or end uses.

Raw materials held for use in the production of inventories are not written down below cost if the finished products in which they will be incorporated are expected to be sold at a price at or above cost. However, if this is not the case, the NRV of the raw materials needs to be considered; the best estimate of this may be replacement cost.

 Worked example 12.3: to show cost versus NRV calculations

The Standard Mix Company plc has the following items in inventories at its year end:

Item	Cost (£)	Selling price (£)
A	7,000	10,000
B	8,400	10,200
C	9,200	10,400

Item A is ready for immediate resale.
Item B is also ready for sale, but, owing to falling demand, a 25% special discount will be offered.
Item C requires packaging before it can be sold; this cost is estimated at £1,800.

Required:

Calculate the value of inventories to be included in the company's year-end financial statements.

Item	Cost £	NRV	£	Lower of cost and NRV £
A	7,000		10,000	7,000
B	8,400	10,200 – (25%X10,200)	7,650	7,650
C	9,200	10,400 – 1,800	8,600	8,600
	24,600		26,250	23,250

The cost versus NRV comparison is performed for each item of inventory separately; therefore, the value of inventory for financial reporting purposes is £23,250.

12.7 Disclosures

Information about the carrying amount of different categories of inventories and the extent of the changes in these assets is useful to users of financial statements in their assessment of liquidity. Although companies can choose the categories that are appropriate to their business, common classifications are:

● merchandise

● production supplies

● materials

● work in progress

● finished goods.

The accounting policies adopted by the company, including the cost formula used, are also disclosed. This tends to be similar for most companies. The amount recognised as an expense during the period, in other words cost of sales, is required to be disclosed. Companies that choose to analyse expenses according to their nature for the format of their income statements (see Chapter 4 for details of this) do not actually include this figure. Details of amounts of inventory write-down to net realisable value or reversals of write-downs are also to be disclosed.

Financial reporting in practice 12.2 — Rolls-Royce plc, 2014

Rolls-Royce plc includes the following accounting policy in relation to the valuation of inventories. The note to the financial statements showing a breakdown of inventory categories and other disclosures is also included.

Accounting policy—Inventories

Inventories and work in progress are valued at the lower of cost and net realisable value on a first-in, first-out basis. Cost comprises direct materials and, where applicable, direct labour costs and those overheads, including depreciation of property, plant and equipment, that have been incurred in bringing the inventories to their present location and condition. Net realisable value represents the estimated selling prices less all estimated costs of completion and costs to be incurred in marketing, selling and distribution.

Note 12—Inventories

	2014	2013
	£m	£m
Raw materials	553	593
Work in progress	984	1,177
Long-term contracts work in progress	22	15
Finished goods	1,149	1,426
Payments on account	60	108
	2,768	3,319
Inventories stated at net realisable value	265	447
Amount of inventory write-down	62	89
Reversal of inventory write-down	1	5

 ## Summary of key points

An assessment of the liquidity of a company requires consistent information relating to the current assets that a company holds. Inventories vary so much in nature between companies that this is particularly important for this asset. Companies have to ensure they have controls in place to ensure that the quantities of inventories on hand are not mis-stated, and the accounting standard that addresses the measurement of inventories is IAS 2 *Inventories*.

The basis of the measurement of inventories is that they should be valued at the lower of cost and NRV. Cost for manufacturers includes all costs of converting the materials purchased into the final products and uses management accounting techniques to allocate manufacturing overheads to the products. NRV is the expected selling price less costs to complete the product and costs to be incurred in selling the goods. Lower of cost and NRV is consistent with the principle that the carrying amount of assets should not be in excess of amounts expected to be realised from their sale or use. Inventory valuation is based on the FIFO or standard cost approach, with most other bases of valuation not permitted, unless they approximate to FIFO.

 ## Further reading

IASB (International Accounting Standards Board) (2003) IAS 2 *Inventories*. London: IASB.

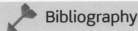

Bibliography

IASB (International Accounting Standards Board) (2003) IAS 2 *Inventories*. London: IASB.

IASB (International Accounting Standards Board) (2007) IAS 1 *Presentation of Financial Statements*. London: IASB.

IASB (International Accounting Standards Board) (2010) *Conceptual Framework for Financial Reporting 2010*. London: IASB.

IASB (International Accounting Standards Board) (2015) Exposure Draft *Conceptual Framework for Financial Reporting*. London: IASB.

M&S (2015) *Annual Report and Financial Statements 2015*. London: M&S.

Nestlé (2015) *Financial Statements, 2014*. Vevey: Nestlé.

Rolls-Royce Holdings plc (2015) *Annual Report, 2014*. London: Rolls-Royce.

Questions

● Quick test

1 Indicate which of the following costs would be included in the cost of inventory according to IAS 2 *Inventories*:

- discounts on purchase price
- interest charge for late payment
- import duties
- recoverable value added tax (VAT)
- irrecoverable tax
- quality certificates
- insurance during transit from supplier
- depreciation of factory
- costs of leasing machinery
- cost of factory canteen
- research on new products
- costs of extra scrap/waste
- sales department salaries
- purchase department salaries
- maintenance of factory
- rebuilding of factory
- audit fees
- costs of using patent.

2 Tomac Enterprises commenced the manufacture of lockable petrol caps on 1 July 20X5. By 31 December 20X5, when the half-yearly financial reports were prepared, 2,000 complete petrol caps and 200 half-finished (as regards materials, labour and factory overheads) petrol caps were produced. No orders from customers had yet been taken. Costs in the six-month period were as follows:

	£
Materials consumed	1,650
Labour	2,160
Production overheads	390
Administrative overheads	270
	4,470

At 31 December 20X5 it was estimated that the sale value of each completed petrol cap was £2.75.

At this date, the firm also held stocks of raw materials as follows:

	Cost	Net realisable value
	£	£
Material X	1,200	1,370
Material Y	300	240
Material Z	530	680

Required:

Acceptable valuations at 31 December 20X5 for financial reporting purposes for:

(i) materials to be consumed

(ii) assets in the process of production

(iii) assets held for sale.

3 Byson Ltd is an established company operating in the highly competitive business of manufacturing domestic appliances. Its best-selling product is a vacuum cleaner, the 'Byson Dust Buster 400'.

A standard dust buster has the following costs:

	£
Direct labour and materials	58
Bought-in components	25
Factory overhead costs	18
Royalty on sale payable to owner of a patent	12

For 1,000 dust busters the other overhead costs are £14,000 made up as follows:

	£
Salary and office costs of production director	4,000
General office administration	2,500
Selling and distribution costs	7,500

The selling and distribution costs include a fixed commission of £4 per vacuum cleaner payable to the salesmen.

The advertised selling price of this model has recently been reduced to £119 due to increased competition.

Required:

(a) Calculate the unit value of closing inventory for the Byson Dust Buster 400 on the basis of IAS 2 *Inventories*. State any assumptions you have made.

(b) IAS 2 *Inventories* states that the cost of inventory includes production overheads and other overheads. Explain the principle on which the inclusion of these costs is based and how these costs should be allocated to units of inventory.

●● Develop your understanding

4   Tintagel plc produces one product, sharp stones, which it manufactures from rocks bought from a company in Wales. Two tonnes of stones are produced from three tonnes of rocks. During the year Tintagel plc purchased rocks in loads of 4,000 tonnes, the purchase price being fixed at £210 per tonne, with delivery and handling charges per load of £10,000.

Direct production costs throughout the year were £40 per tonne of sharp stones produced. Production capacity exists to process 5,000 tonnes of the stones per week; fixed production costs were £45,000 per week. General management costs for the year were £2,500,000.

The sharp stones sell for £449 per tonne. Loading costs are £15 per tonne and delivery is subcontracted at an annual cost of £210,000. During the year Tintagel plc sold 70,000 tonnes of sharp stones.

At the year end Tintagel plc had the following inventories:

Rocks	12,000 tonnes
Sharp stones	2,000 tonnes

There were no inventories in the process of production.

Required:

Calculate the value of inventories at the year end in accordance with IAS 2.

●●● Take it further

5   Harness Technology plc designs, constructs and installs wind turbine systems. The company compiles its accounts on the basis of relevant international standards and its financial year end is 31 December. You are being asked to compile the inventory information and relevant contract revenue, expenditure and profit information for the statement of financial position and statement of profit or loss based on the following information.

(i) The company produces two types of engine cooling system, the ZX100 and the ZX150, which are generally sold to customers who experience system problems and need replacement parts. The ZX100 is a now outdated, but still usable, model, which has been superseded by the ZX150 model. The inventory count at 31 December 20X8 confirmed that there were 300 turbine blades (spare parts) in stock and 100 engine cooling systems in stock (20 ZX100s and 80 ZX150s). It is estimated that owing to the ZX100 being technically superseded by the ZX150, the 20 ZX100s are likely to sell for 60% of their usual selling price.

Twelve blades which were not included in the inventory count are in transit under an arrangement where the buyer pays transportation costs and legal ownership has already passed to the customer. It is anticipated that 50 of the blades will need very minor repairs costing £150 (per blade) to make them usable (due to damage through poor storage). The rest of this inventory is in good condition and likely to be sold at existing market prices in the future.

Standard information is provided in Table 12.2 to assist you in determining the total value for the inventory which should be included in the statement of financial position and income statement.

Table 12.2 Figures for Question 5 (i)

	Blades (per unit) £	ZX100 (per unit) £	ZX150 (per unit) £
Direct labour and materials	350	125	125
Bought-in components*	175	250	300
Factory overhead	200	110	110
Head office general administrative overhead	45	40	40
Selling price	1,000	600	750

* Each unit cost (blade, ZX100 and ZX150) includes £10 per unit transport cost incurred in transporting the components to Harness Technology's factory.

(ii) Harness Technology plc has recently begun work on a large wind turbine system, the MidGreen project, in the Midlands. The company is contracted to design, build and install the system. Work began in September 20X8 and is expected to be completed by January 20Y0. The agreed price of the contract was £55 million and the original estimated cost of the project was £38 million.

By November 20X8 the company had to revise its estimate of the total direct costs and now estimates this as £38.5 million. In addition, research costs not specified in the contract are £400,000 as at the 20X8 year end. At the end of December 20X8 materials costing £500,000 have been paid for and are in inventory ready for use in 20X9. The client pays £5 million every quarter after the contract has reached the 20% completion stage in terms of outputs from the contract, and has paid the first instalment on 15 December 20X8. Actual contract costs incurred to date are £10 million.

Harness Technology plc uses an input method based on the contract costs incurred at each year end to measure the progress towards satisfaction of the performance obligation.

Required:

Based on all the information given:

(a) Calculate the total figure for inventory on the 20X8 statement of financial position of Harness Technology plc.

(b) Show the amounts that would be included as revenues and costs in the statement of profit or loss for the year ended 31 December 20X8 for the MidGreen Project.

(c) Explain the basic principles involved in:

(i) the valuation of inventories

(ii) the recognition of contract revenues and costs.

Visit the Online Resource Centre for solutions to all these end of chapter questions plus visual walkthrough solutions. You can test your understanding with extra questions and answers, explore additional case studies based on real companies, take a guided tour through a company report and much more. Go to the Online Resource Centre at **www.oxfordtextbooks.co.uk/orc/maynard2e/**

13

Liabilities

Liabilities encompass many items. These range from normal trade payables for goods that have been delivered and not yet paid for, to accruals for overhead expenses incurred not yet billed, to liabilities under leasing arrangements and pension schemes, and debt instruments. The accounting for some of these liabilities is set out in various financial reporting standards, some of which are the subject of other chapters in this textbook—accounting for current and deferred taxation, and the resulting tax liabilities is discussed in Chapter 9; debt instruments are the subject of Chapter 14; liabilities under leasing arrangements are discussed in Chapter 15, and retirement benefit liabilities are included in Chapter 16.

This chapter deals mainly with a particular subset of liabilities—provisions and contingent liabilities. These arise when there is uncertainty as to the amount or the timing of the settlement of liabilities which are not accounted for under other financial reporting standards. These uncertainties, together with the fact that the settlement is in the future, result in the accounting for these liabilities requiring estimates and much judgement. To ensure there is some consistency of treatment, International Accounting Standard (IAS) 37 *Provisions, Contingent Liabilities and Contingent Assets* specifies when a provision should be recognised, gives guidance as to its measurement and addresses what should happen in increasing cases of uncertainty.

Confirmation of the existence and measurement of liabilities and, in some cases, the measurement of assets and other transactions, may occur after the end of the financial year. A question arises as to what extent a company should change its financial statements as a result of what happens after the statement of financial position date. IAS 10 *Events after the Reporting Period* addresses this and its requirements are discussed at the end of this chapter.

★ Learning objectives

After studying this chapter you will be able to:

- understand the key problems in accounting for liabilities and how these are addressed by financial reporting standards
- understand the relationship between liabilities, provisions and **contingent liabilities**, and explain their accounting treatment
- explain the accounting treatment of **contingent assets**
- understand the impact on the financial statements of events that happen after the financial year end.

✔ Key issues checklist

- ❑ Impact of accounting for liabilities improperly—big bath accounting and prudence.
- ❑ Definition of a liability.
- ❑ Issues with the definition—reliance on estimates and judgement.
- ❑ Criteria for the recognition of a provision.
- ❑ Methods for the measurement of a provision.
- ❑ Accounting for operating losses, restructuring and **onerous contracts**.
- ❑ Contingent liabilities and their relationship to provisions.
- ❑ Contingent assets and their accounting treatment.
- ❑ Disclosures required for provisions, contingent liabilities and contingent assets.
- ❑ IASB discussions of changes to the accounting for provisions and contingent liabilities.
- ❑ The critical period after the end of the financial year before the financial statements are authorised for issue.
- ❑ Adjusting and non-adjusting events, and their treatment in the financial statements.
- ❑ Proposed dividends
- ❑ The going concern assumption.

13.1 Accounting for liabilities

13.1.1 Key issues in accounting for liabilities

The International Accounting Standards Board's (IASB) definition of a liability as given in the 2015 Exposure Draft (ED) to its **Conceptual Framework** is:

> A liability is a present obligation of the entity to transfer an economic resource as a result of past events.

(IASB, 2015a, para. 4.24)

The proposed recognition criteria in the ED are that the information about the liability provided should be relevant and faithfully represented.

One of the key issues in accounting for liabilities is that the transfer of resources is going to happen in the future, after the date of the statement of financial position. By the time the financial statements have been published, the transfer may not yet have occurred. For liabilities such as trade payables this may not present a problem for recognition and measurement; however, this may be less clear-cut for other transactions and situations, and gives rise to a number of questions:

- What exactly is meant by a present obligation?
- How definite does the expectation of the transfer of resources have to be?
- What is meant by an economic resource?

In addition to these definition and recognition issues, there may also be uncertainty surrounding how much will be paid to settle the liability and therefore how the transfer of resources is measured.

Companies have, in the past, accounted for liabilities on the grounds of prudence, which used to be considered one of the fundamental underpinning principles of financial reporting. Management of companies took this further and used the uncertainties of accounting for the future and liabilities to manipulate profits. This is commonly referred to as 'big bath' accounting.

 Example of 'big bath' accounting

In October 20X6, following years of declining profits, a company undergoes a management buy-out (MBO), which is funded by venture capitalists. A period of restructuring is commenced by the new management team, who consider a prudent estimate for restructuring costs to be £2 million. The draft financial statements at 31 December 20X6 show a large loss.

An argument for accounting for this situation on the basis of prudence, which was not unknown in the past, follows:

1   20X6 is a 'bad year' already

2   So it does not matter so much if 20X6's results are made even worse by including large (prudent) provisions for restructuring costs which will be incurred in 20X7:

    Dr   Restructuring expenses   £2 million
      Cr   Provisions (Liability)   £2 million

3   In 20X7, as these costs are actually incurred, they are charged against the provision (assume these amount to £1.5 million):

    Dr   Provisions   £1.5 million
      Cr   Bank   £1.5 million

4   This leaves a large credit balance on the provisions account, which is no longer required at 31 December 20X7

5   This will be written back to profit and loss in 20X7:

Dr	Provisions	£0.5 million	
	Cr	Profit	£0.5 million

The result of this is that the 20X7 financial statements are much improved by this credit to profit, which will please the venture capital firm and demonstrate that the new management team are performing well!

The above accounting is clearly not acceptable if financial statements are to faithfully represent the financial performance and position of a company. The IASB has reintroduced the concept of prudence in the *Conceptual Framework* ED (as discussed in Chapter 2), but this does not mean that the days of 'big bath' accounting or income smoothing as a result of manipulating liabilities will return, as there will be limits to the use of prudence. In addition, the ED contains discussion and clarification of the terms included in its definition of a liability.

13.1.2 Terms used in the definition of a liability

Present obligation

One key characteristic of a liability is that there is a present obligation that arises from past events. A present obligation is a duty or responsibility to act or perform in a certain way. This may be because the company has no practical ability to avoid the obligation. This could arise from a legal obligation which is enforceable as a result of a contract or statutory requirement, for example the purchase of goods or the receipt of a service. However, obligations can also be **constructive**, where usual business custom and practice creates an expectation that a business has accepted certain responsibilities. An example of this could be if a business usually carries out repair work on products it has supplied even after the expiry of the warranty period.

Past event

A past event will give rise to a present obligation when a company has received some economic benefit or conducted activities that establish the extent of the obligation, in other words the amount or the basis for determining the amount, before the date of the statement of financial position. For example, goods must have been received, or a bank loan which will be repaid at some future date must have been received. This past event is termed the obligating event. Future activity or commitments do not give rise to a present obligation.

 Example of a past event versus future commitment

A company's directors decide to acquire a property in the future, which is recorded in board minutes. However, this does not give rise to a present obligation. This is a future commitment only and a contract would need to have been signed for a past event to have occurred.

Obligation to transfer an economic resource

The obligation to transfer an economic resource only requires the potential to make the transfer. In other words, it need not be certain, or even probable, but there must be at least one circumstance in which the company would be required to make the transfer.

The transfer of the economic resource does not have to mean a cash payment. It could refer to:

- the transfer of assets
- the provision of services, e.g. repairs under a warranty
- the replacement of one liability with another, e.g. the rolling over of a loan
- the conversion of a liability to equity, such as convertible debt instruments.

However, the very nature of a liability often leads to uncertainty surrounding the timing and amount of the transfer, and therefore the measurement (or value) of the liability. The transfer of the resource is going to be in the future, and may not have occurred by the time the statement of financial position is drawn up and made available for users. Some liabilities may not be settled for many years and require increased estimation, for example the liabilities for the clean-up of land contaminated by drilling for oil may be settled 20 or 30 years after the drilling commences.

Liabilities where there is uncertainty surrounding timing and amount of the settlement are known as provisions. Note that the term provision is sometimes used in connection with depreciation, impairment and doubtful debts to indicate the amount deducted from the value of the related asset. However, the term provision is to be used in this chapter in connection with the particular type of liability detailed. IAS 37 *Provisions, Contingent Liabilities and Contingent Assets* was issued by the IASB to deal with the issues surrounding the recognition and measurement of provisions.

13.2 Provisions

13.2.1 Recognition of a provision

As a subset of liabilities, the criteria for the recognition of a provision in the financial statements satisfies the definition of and recognition criteria for a liability as given in the 2010 *Conceptual Framework*. (Note that although the definition of a liability in this *Framework* is similar to that proposed in the 2015 ED, discussed in section 13.1.1, the recognition principles are different. The 2010 *Conceptual Framework* recognition criteria for a liability requires that (1) it is probable that any economic benefit associated with the liability will flow from the entity, and (2) the liability can be measured reliably.)

IAS 37 specifies three recognition criteria, all of which must be met, otherwise a provision cannot be included in the statement of financial position.

1   The company has a present obligation as a result of a past event.

2   It is probable that an outflow of resources embodying economic benefits will be required to settle the obligation.

3   A reliable estimate can be made of the amount of the obligation.

(IASB, IAS 37, para. 14)

What is meant by a present obligation and obligating event has already been discussed. A couple of further examples to illustrate this discussion follow.

 Examples of whether obligating events exist

1   A company in the oil industry causes contamination, but cleans up only when required to do so under the laws of the particular country in which it operates. One country in which it operates has had no legislation requiring cleaning up and the entity has been contaminating land in that country for several years. At 31 December 20X0 it is virtually certain that a draft law requiring a clean-up of land already contaminated will be enacted shortly after the year end.
    The obligating event is the contamination of the land.

2   Under new legislation, a company is required to fit smoke filters to its factories by 30 June 20X1. At 31 December 20X0 the company has not fitted the smoke filters.

    There is no obligation because there is no obligating event either for the costs of fitting smoke filters or for fines under the legislation. The company could avoid this future expenditure by its future actions, for example by changing its method of operation.

The second criterion for the recognition of a provision is that the outflow of resources must be probable, in other words more likely than not to occur. In probability terms this means that the probability should be greater than 50%. This clearly introduces subjectivity into the question of recognition, as there are no clear-cut guidelines as to the likelihood of an outflow occurring. The meaning of an outflow of resources embodying economic benefits can be taken to mean the same as the transfer of an economic resource, which was discussed in Chapter 2, section 2.6.5.

The final criterion is that a reliable estimate of the value of the outflow of resources can be made. In most cases this should be possible, as IAS 37 specifies that this amount should be the best estimate at the statement of financial position date. As for the second criterion the uncertainties surrounding this estimate introduce subjectivity which requires management judgement. Experience of similar events and transactions, or independent expert advice, such as legal advice, may have to be called for. Evidence from events that occur after the financial reporting date may also be used. (Note: events after the reporting period are discussed further in section 13.5.)

13.2.2 Measurement of a provision

The best estimate is explained by IAS 37 as the amount a business would rationally pay to settle the obligation. This implies it would take a sensible course of action after considering

Table 13.1 The best estimate for different types of obligation

Obligation	Best estimate	Example
(a) A single obligation	The individual most likely outcome	A company has to carry out repair work in plant it has supplied which it estimates at £1,000. This may be the most likely outcome, but the company should consider additional possible outflows if these initial repairs do not solve the problem. The company may decide to increase the amount of the provision.
(b) A large population of possible obligations	All obligations are weighted by their associated probabilities and an expected value is calculated	A company sells goods with a warranty under which customers are covered for the cost of repairs detected within a year of purchase. Different amounts of repair costs should be weighted by their respective probabilities of occurrence. The provision is the sum of these weighted outcomes.
(c) A continuous range of possible obligations	The mid-point of the range	A company is being sued for damages due to defective products and have been found liable. Lawyers advise the damages may range from £200,000 to £400,000. The company may determine the provision at £300,000.

all factors. However, uncertainties should be taken into consideration. Table 13.1 provides explanations and examples of what is meant by the best estimate for different types of obligation.

The risks and uncertainties surrounding many provisions should be taken into account when determining the best estimate. Risk affects the estimates of the amount(s) of the possible outcome(s). When judgements are made companies should ensure that provisions are not understated—the application of cautious prudence. However, IAS 37 is quite clear in stating that risk should not be overstated and uncertainties should not justify excessive provisions.

In estimating future costs, companies should take into account the effect of future changes in technology or new legislation provided there is sufficient objective evidence that these will alter the costs.

13.2.3 Use of present value

The settlement of some provisions may not arise for a number of years, for example the clean-up of contaminated land by an oil company. IAS 37 specifies that if the time value of money is material, the amount of the provision should be the present value of the expenditures required to settle the obligation. In other words, a discounted cash flow basis is used for measurement purposes. This introduces yet more subjectivity into the measurement of the provision. Firstly, the question of what is meant by material requires judgement by management.

⚠ **Reminder** *Material information is defined in the* Conceptual Framework *as that whose omission or misstatement could influence decisions taken by a user. This is discussed further in Chapter 1. Materiality will be different for different users.*

The second question raised by the discounting requirement is what discount rate should be used to carry out the calculation. IAS 37 specifies that this should be:

> ... a pre-tax rate (or rates) that reflect(s) current market assessments of the time value of money and the risks specific to the liability.

(IASB, 2005, para. 47)

So that the effect of risk is not double-counted, the rate should not reflect risks for which future cash flow estimates have already been adjusted.

 Worked example 13.1: to show a provision involving discounted cash flow

---

At 31 December 20X0 Cleaner Energy plc, a company involved in nuclear activities, estimates that it will incur decommissioning costs of £900 million in 60 years' time. The pre-tax discount rate for this liability has been estimated at 2%.

Required:

(a) Calculate and show the accounting for the provision for decommissioning costs at 31 December 20X0.

(b) Show the effect of small changes in the estimates used in estimating the provision.

(c) Assuming no changes in estimates, show the accounting for the provision for decommissioning costs at 31 December 20X1.

(a) The provision for decommissioning should be recorded at

$$£900 \text{ million} \times \frac{1}{(1.02)^{60}} = £274.3 \text{ million}$$

		£	£
Debit	Decommissioning expenses	274.3 million	
Credit	Provision		274.3 million

(b) Note that only small changes in the discount rate or the estimate of the year of decommissioning lead to significant changes in the provision.

(i) If the discount rate used is 2.5%, the provision would be

$$£900 \text{ million} \times \frac{1}{(1.025)^{60}} = £204.6 \text{ million}$$

(ii) If the activities extend for a further 5 years, the provision would be

$$£900 \text{ million} \times \frac{1}{(1.02)^{65}} = £248.4 \text{ million}$$

(c) Each year the provision is recalculated and, as the provision is nearer in time, it will increase. Assuming no changes in the initial estimates, this unwinding of the discount rate is accounted for as a finance charge in the statement of comprehensive income. This is referred to as the unwinding of the discount rate.

Assuming original estimates, at 31 December 20X1 the provision would be

$$£900 \text{ million} \times \frac{1}{(1.02)^{59}} = £279.8 \text{ million}$$

		£	£
Debit	Finance costs (279.8 – 274.3)	5.5 million	
Credit	Provision		5.5 million

[This can also be calculated as 2% × £274.3 million = £5.5 million]

13.2.4 Particular circumstances included in IAS 37

IAS 37 addresses a number of particular circumstances which may be considered to give rise to provisions and which have been misused by companies in past years (see Example of 'big bath' accounting in section 13.1.1).

Future operating losses

The first of these is future operating losses. The standard is very clear that no provision should be recognised for these. Essentially, these are estimates of the future, not arising as a result of past events, and so they are not liabilities. Forecast operating losses may indicate that certain operating assets are impaired and so companies should be aware of this when considering impairment testing. (See Chapter 10 for a discussion of impairment.)

Restructuring

The second issue that is specifically discussed by IAS 37 concerns costs of restructuring. Restructuring is a general term which could encompass all sorts of activities, including redundancies, relocations, reorganisations and other disruption to normal business activities. IAS 37 defines restructuring as a programme that is planned and controlled by management, and which materially changes either:

(a) the scope of business undertaken by the company

(b) the manner in which the business is conducted.

This could include the sale or termination of part of the business, and closure of business locations, relocations of business activities from one region or country to another and changes in management structures, such as the elimination of a layer of management.

In order to recognise a provision for restructuring costs, the three criteria for the recognition of a provision must be fulfilled. This requires a company to have a constructive obligation to restructure, which, in turn, would require some formal evidence, such as a detailed plan for the restructuring. Such a plan would include details of which part of the business was to be restructured, anticipated and realistic dates for the various stages and estimates of the nature and amount of expenditure. A constructive obligation also requires there to be a valid expectation in those affected that the restructuring will be carried out, so the plan must have been communicated to the relevant employees. A board decision to carry out the restructuring programme is insufficient in itself to give rise to a provision. However, the restructuring activities need not have actually started.

IAS 37 gives guidance as to the costs that may be included in determining the provision for restructuring. These must be necessary costs arising directly from the restructuring and not costs associated with the ongoing activities of the company.

Examples of costs which could be included in the provision are:

- termination of leases
- disposal of surplus inventories
- remuneration of employees engaged in the restructuring activities
- redundancy costs.

Costs specifically excluded are:

- retraining or relocating continuing staff
- marketing
- investment in new systems and distribution networks
- future operating losses.

Onerous contracts

The third item addressed specifically by IAS 37 is the requirement for a provision to be recognised for the obligations under an onerous contract. Many contracts into which businesses enter are for specific lengths of time, and establish rights and obligations for each of the parties involved. Some contracts can be cancelled without compensation being required by any party. An onerous contract is one in which this is not possible and where the resulting unavoidable costs of meeting the terms of the contract exceed any benefits expected to be received under it. In this case a provision is recognised and is measured at the least net cost of exiting from the contract. What this means is that it is assumed a business would take a rational approach to either:

(i) fulfilling the terms of the contract

(ii) not fulfilling the terms and incurring fines or penalties

and would choose the option which had the lower cost.

Example of an onerous contract

A company operates profitably from a factory that it has leased under an operating lease. During December 20X0 the company relocates its operations to a new factory. The lease on the old factory continues for the next four years. It cannot be cancelled and the factory cannot be re-let to another user.
 Consider the criteria for the recognition of a provision.

1 There is a legal obligation on the company to make the lease payments arising from the obligating event which is the signing of the lease contract.

2 When the lease becomes onerous in December 20X0, an outflow of resources embodying economic benefits is probable.

3 The amount of the provision can be estimated as the lower of:

 (a) the best estimate of the unavoidable lease payments

 (b) the penalties to be incurred if the company 'walks away' from the contract.

13.2.5 Disclosures

To assist users' understanding of the amounts included in the financial statements as provisions, companies are required to explain the nature of the provisions recognised and the expected timing of the outflows, together with an indication of the uncertainties surrounding these. This may include details of assumptions which have been made about the future.

 Companies will naturally wish to exercise caution about these disclosures. For example, if a company is required to include a provision for damages because it anticipates losing an ongoing court case, it will clearly wish to minimise the amount of the provision and be very careful about the language used in the provisions note so that admission of liability is not necessarily apparent. In practice, companies will use, and auditors will rely on, legal professionals to assist in the drafting of such information. IAS 37 permits companies not to disclose information if it is considered that it could seriously prejudice the position of the company in a dispute with other parties. However, in this case the company would still be required to disclose the general nature of the dispute together with the fact that, and the reason why, full details have not been disclosed.

 Companies often list provisions as one of the areas where significant estimates have been made and judgement exercised.

Financial reporting in practice 13.1   BP plc, 2010 and 2015

Oil companies, such as BP, will normally have significant provisions relating to the decommissioning of their production facilities and pipelines, and future environmental clean-up costs. BP plc's 2010 Annual Report, its first after the Gulf of Mexico oil spill, which occurred during May to August 2010,

(continued)

(continued)

contains a very lengthy provisions disclosure note, which itself refers to substantial descriptions of the oil spill disaster contained elsewhere in the report.

BP's total provisions at 31 December 2009 of US$14,630 million leapt to a total of US$31,907 million at 31 December 2010. These included provisions relating to the assessment of environmental damage ($809 million), spill response clean-up costs ($1,043 million), litigation and claims ($10,973 million) and US Clean Water Act penalties ($3,510 million).

The explanations of the provisions, particularly in relation to the litigation and claims, were worded in very careful language, to give nothing away. The note indicated that the company has used its previous history and experience to estimate the amounts provided for, but acknowledged that 'actual costs could ultimately be significantly higher or lower than those recorded as the claims and settlement process progresses'. A range of possible outcomes was given as $6 billion to $13 billion.

The impact of this disaster is still apparent in BP's 2015 financial statements. The company acknowledges that total costs relating to the incident accounted for through profit and loss up to 31 December 2015 have been US$55.5 billion. Of the company's total provisions at 31 December 2015 of $41,114 million, $16,507 million relate to the Gulf of Mexico oil spill.

Companies are also required to disclose for each class of provision a reconciliation of the balance at the start of the year to the balance at the end of the year which shows:

(a) Additional provisions made during the year, including increases to existing provisions

(b) Amounts charged against the provision during the year

(c) Any amounts reversed during the year because the provision is no longer required or can be reduced

(d) The increase in any provision included at present value as a result of the outflow being one year closer

(e) The effect of any changes in the discount rate used for provisions which have been included at present value.

This is illustrated by the provisions disclosure note in Marks & Spencer plc's 2015 financial statements.

Financial reporting in practice 13.2 — Marks and Spencer plc, 2015

Note 22 Provisions

	Property £m	Restructuring £m	Other £m	2015 Total £m	2014 Total £m
At start of year	25.1	46.3	4.8	76.2	35.2
Provided in the year	15.2	13.7	4.8	33.7	71.8
Released in the year	(3.6)	(15.6)	(0.1)	(19.3)	(4.3)
Utilised during the year	(15.7)	(15.1)	(2.0)	(32.8)	(25.6)

Exchange differences	(0.6)	(1.4)	–	**(2.0)**	(0.9)
Discount rate unwind	0.3	–	–	**0.3**	–
Reclassification from trade and other payables	22.2	–	–	**22.2**	–
At end of year	42.9	27.9	7.5	**78.3**	76.2
Analysed as:					
Current				**46.2**	44.8
Non-current				**32.1**	31.4

Property provisions relate to onerous lease contracts and dilapidations primarily arising as a result of the closure of stores in the UK, China and the Czech Group (see note 5). These provisions are expected to be utilised over the period to the end of each specific lease.

Restructuring provisions relate to the estimated costs of several strategic programmes including the closure of four stores in Ireland in the prior year and the current restructure of the logistics network (see note 5). These provisions are expected to be utilised within seven years.

13.3 Contingent liabilities

13.3.1 Definition

As discussed earlier, a company will only recognise a provision if the three criteria are met:

1 The company has a present obligation as a result of a past event

2 It is probable that an outflow of resources embodying economic events will be required to settle the obligation

3 A reliable estimate can be made of the amount of the obligation.

Given that the last two criteria in particular are highly subjective, there is scope for companies to 'manage' the inclusion or exclusion of provisions. So what happens if:

● there is some doubt about whether a present obligation exists

● it is less than 50% probable, but there is still some possibility that an outflow of resources will be required

● a reliable estimate of the obligation cannot be made?

If companies could just ignore the possibilities that a liability may exist, this would not provide faithfully representative information of the company's financial position to users. IAS 37 therefore includes another category of liability, a contingent liability, which it defines as:

A possible obligation that arises from past events and whose existence will be confirmed only by the occurrence of one or more uncertain future events not wholly within the entity's control; OR

A present obligation which is not recognised because:

● it is not probable that an outflow of resources will be required to settle the obligation; or

● the amount of the obligation cannot be measured with sufficient reliability.

(IASB, 2005, para. 10)

In other words a contingent liability is a form of provision where there is considerable doubt and uncertainty about its existence or value. Given these uncertainties, contingent liabilities are not recognised in the financial statements, but are required to be disclosed within a separate disclosure note. Only if the possibility of an outflow of resources is considered remote is no disclosure required. What is meant by remote is not defined in IAS 37; no suggested probability percentage is given below which something would be considered remote. However, the use of this word implies that an event would have to be highly unlikely.

13.3.2 Relationship between provisions and contingent liabilities

Clearly, the relationship between provisions and contingent liabilities is close. They are both concerned with the same sorts of issue, with the question of inclusion in the financial statements, or disclosure, or no disclosure resting on how likely a future event may turn out to be, or how certain an estimate of the amount is. The flowchart shown in Figure 13.1 demonstrates

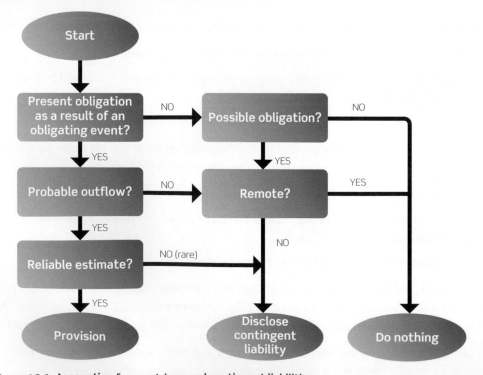

Figure 13.1 Accounting for provisions and contingent liabilities

this. If items are classified initially as contingent liabilities, they must be continually kept under review to determine whether the likelihood of an outflow becomes probable, or the outcome of events makes estimates more reliable. An item that is initially classified as a contingent liability may become a provision in a later accounting period.

Worked example 13.2: to show a provision versus a contingent liability

After a wedding reception held at a hotel, Abbey Park Hotel plc, in December 20X0, ten people died as a result of food poisoning. Legal proceedings are started in December seeking damages from the hotel for supplying the food which caused the poisoning, but the company disputes any liability.

Up to the date of authorisation for the issue of the financial statements for the year to 31 December 20X0, the hotel's lawyers advise that it is probable that the hotel will not be found liable.

However, when the hotel prepares the financial statements for the year to 31 December 20X1, its lawyers advise that, owing to developments in the case, it is probable that the company will be found liable.

Required:

Discuss the accounting treatment of this situation in the financial statements of Abbey Park Hotel plc for the years ended 31 December 20X0 and 20X1.

The obligating event was the wedding reception held in December 20X0. Following the flowchart in Figure 13.1:

At 31 December 20X0

1   Is there a present obligation as a result of the obligating event?

No—although there is an obligating event, there is no present obligation as the company disputes the liability and the lawyers advise it is probable that the hotel will not be found liable.

2   Is there a possible obligation as a result of the obligating event?

Yes—the lawyers advise it is only probable that the hotel will not be found liable, indicating that there may be some possibility.

3   Is the outflow of resources (i.e. payment of damages) considered remote?

As there is no definition of remote, the answer to this will probably rest on the advice of the lawyers.

Unless this is considered very unlikely, the company would have to disclose a contingent liability in a note to its financial statements. If it was sufficiently unlikely, then the company would make no mention of the event at all.

At 31 December 20X1

1   Is there a present obligation as a result of the obligating event?

Yes—events have moved on and the advice of the lawyers has now changed. The hotel company now has an obligation.

2   Is there a probable outflow of resources?

Yes—the lawyers are advising it is probable the hotel company will be found liable and therefore have to pay damages.

3   Can a reasonable estimate be made of the amount?

It is likely that an estimate of the damages could be made and the lawyers would, again, advise.

The company will have to include a provision in its statement of financial position at 31 December 20X1, including a corresponding expense in its statement of profit or loss. The amount would be the best estimate, as discussed earlier in the chapter.

13.3.3 Contingent assets

Although this is a chapter on liabilities, contingent assets are included in IAS 37, and, as the name suggests, relate to contingent liabilities. The definition of a contingent asset mirrors that of a contingent liability.

> A possible asset that arises from past events and whose existence will be confirmed only by the occurrence of one or more uncertain future events not wholly within the entity's control ...
>
> *(IASB, 2005, para. 10)*

Contingent assets arise from unplanned or other unexpected events that give rise to the possibility of an inflow of economic benefits to a company. The inflow may be in the form of cash, but does not have to be. A typical example of a contingent asset is where a company is involved in a legal dispute and is claiming damages from a third party.

If the outcome of the future event is virtually certain, resulting in an inflow of benefits, then the related asset is not a contingent asset, as the criteria for the recognition of an asset as detailed in the 2010 *Conceptual Framework* are met. (Note the criteria for the recognition of an asset in this *Framework* are that (1) it is probable that any economic benefit associated with the asset will flow to the entity, and (2) the asset can be measured reliably.) The accounting for this situation would be:

Debit   Asset (Receivable)

Credit   Income

If the outcome is anything less than virtually certain, then an asset is not recognised, as this may result in the recognition of income that may never be realised. However, if it is considered probable that an inflow of resources will result, the company should include the contingent asset in a disclosure note. The meaning of probable is the same as for provisions above, in other words more than 50% likely.

13.3.4 Contingent liabilities versus contingent assets

Table 13.2 shows that the accounting treatment for contingent liabilities and assets is based on the application of asymmetric prudence (see Chapter 2 for a discussion of prudence) as losses are being recognised and disclosures relating to liabilities are required with lower probability thresholds than gains or assets.

Table 13.2 Comparison of the accounting treatment of contingent liabilities and contingent assets

Likelihood of outflow/inflow	Accounting treatment	
	Liability	Asset
Virtually certain	Recognise	Recognise
Probable	Recognise provision	Disclose contingent asset
Possible	Disclose contingent liability	No disclosure
Remote	No disclosure	No disclosure

 Worked example 13.3: to show the accounting treatment of a contingent liability and a contingent asset

A claim has been made against Delta Construction plc for injury suffered by a pedestrian in connection with building work by the company. The company's legal advisors have confirmed that Delta Construction will probably have to pay damages of £200,000. Legal advisors go on to advise that a claim can be made against the building subcontractors for £100,000.

Required:

Discuss the accounting treatment of these issues.

The claim against the company and the counter-claim made by the company are treated separately following the principle that assets and liabilities should not be offset.

Claim of £200,000 against the company

1   The company has a present obligation as a result of a past event (the injury suffered).

2   Legal advisors are advising that there is a probable outflow of resources.

3   There is a reliable estimate of the amount (£200,000).

The three criteria for the recognition of a provision are met, so the company will record a provision for £200,000:

Debit	Expenses
Credit	Provision

Claim of £100,000 by the company

There is the possibility that the company may recover an amount from the building company (a possible asset). This, however, is contingent upon the company actually making the claim and then the outcome of any legal discussion, or possibly a court case. The outcome is clearly uncertain and not within the control of the company.

This situation therefore gives rise to a contingent asset. The probability of an inflow of resources (the receipt of the £100,000) needs to be estimated. If it is considered probable, i.e. more than 50% likely, the company will disclose this as a note to the financial statements. However, if it is considered less than 50% probable, then no mention will be made in the financial statements.

13.3.5 Disclosures of contingent liabilities and contingent assets

For both contingent liabilities and contingent assets the disclosure notes should provide information about:

1 The nature of the contingent liability or asset

2 An estimate of their financial effect

3 Details relating to the uncertainties.

For contingent assets it is important that the disclosures do not give misleading indications of the likelihood of income arising.

It needs to be made clear where contingent liabilities arise from the same set of circumstances as provisions that have been made.

Financial reporting in practice 13.3   BP plc, 2015

This last point is particularly illustrated in the case of the disclosures made by BP concerning the Gulf of Mexico oil spill, which has been provided as an example for provisions earlier. Not only is there extensive discussion of the provisions the company still has in relation to this event, but the company has also included a lengthy contingent liability note. The contingent liabilities relate mainly to affected businesses' economic losses, further lawsuits which had been brought or may still be brought in the future by holders of American Depositary Shares and individuals and corporations for claims for personal injury, commercial or economic injury, damage to real and personal property, breach of contract and violations of statute as a result of the oil spill. BP states that it has provided for its best estimate of amounts expected to be paid that can be measured reliably. Where it is not possible to measure reliably other obligations arising from the incident, nor practicable to estimate their magnitude or possible timing of payment, no amounts have been provided for these obligations as at 31 December 2015.

13.4 Issues with IAS 37 and its future

As one of its convergence projects with the US Financial Accounting Standards Board (FASB), in 2005 the IASB issued an ED of a new financial reporting standard to replace IAS 37. It had identified three key issues with the standard which it wants to address:

1 Inconsistencies with other IFRS in the treatment of the 'probability of outflows'

Under IAS 37 a provision is recognised only if it is probable (more likely than not) that there will be an outflow of resources. If it is less than likely a contingent liability is disclosed (unless the likelihood is considered remote). These recognition criteria are inconsistent with treatment of liabilities in IFRS 3 *Business Combinations* and IAS 39

Financial Instruments: Recognition and Measurement. Companies may therefore not be recognising some material liabilities in their financial statements.

2   Convergence with FASB

IAS 37 and US generally accepted accounting principles (GAAP) differ in how the costs of restructuring a business are treated. IAS 37 requires a provision to be recorded for the total costs of restructuring when it announces or starts to implement a restructuring plan. In contrast, US GAAP requires a provision to be recorded for the individual costs only when the business has incurred the costs.

3   Improvement in the measurement of liabilities

The IASB considers that the measurement of liabilities in IAS 37 is unclear and there is evidence of different measures being used by businesses. Provisions are required to be measured at the 'best estimate' of the expenditure required to settle the obligation. Companies interpret this in different ways as follows:

- the most likely outcome

- the weighted average cost of all possible outcomes (expected value)

- the minimum or maximum amount in a range of outcomes.

In addition, IAS 37 does not specify the costs the business should include in the measurement which has led companies in practice to include different costs. For example, some companies include only incremental costs, while others include all direct costs, and others a proportion of overheads.

The IASB received many comments on its proposals, in particular that its proposals on the measurement of liabilities lacked clarity. This resulted in the IASB issuing a further ED on *Measurement of Liabilities in IAS 37* in 2010. The proposals in this included the following:

- uncertainty about the amount and timing of the outflow of resources should be included by using a measurement that reflects their expected value, i.e. the probability-weighted average of the outflows for the range of possible outcomes

- the measurement of a liability should be the amount an entity would rationally pay at the measurement date to be relieved of the liability. This would be the lower of:

  - an estimate of the present value of the outflow of resources

  - the amount the entity would pay to cancel the obligation

  - the amount the entity would pay to transfer the obligation to a third party

- clarification of amounts that should be included in provisions for restructuring, legal disputes and the undertaking of a future service (e.g. decommissioning plant at the end of its life).

The IASB also published further details of how the new proposals would relate to lawsuits, an area which particularly concerned respondents to the ED.

These proposals would remove the 'probability of outflows' recognition criterion. In addition, the amount recognised for a liability would not be an estimate of an actual amount that the company would pay, but a probability-weighted figure, as illustrated by the following example.

 Worked example 13.4: to show the measurement of a liability under the ED

Britoil plc, an oil production company, owns and operates an oil rig. Existing environmental laws oblige rig owners to dismantle rigs that have reached the end of their useful lives. Rig owners cannot cancel such obligations, or transfer them to third parties. However, there are contractors that provide dismantling services for rig owners. A contractor would charge $125,000 to dismantle the oil company's rig now, in a way that complies with existing environmental laws. The rig has an estimated remaining useful life of 10–15 years. The current 10- and 15-year risk-free rates of interest are, respectively, 6% and 5.5% each year.

Measurement of the liability is at the present value of the outflows required to fulfil the obligation. The outflows are the amounts the company estimates a contractor would charge at the end of the rig's life to dismantle the rig at that time. This is estimated by taking the current price of $125,000 and estimating future price increases—based on knowledge and experience of the market, and possible technological developments. The estimates are based on existing legal requirements.

Suppose the company identifies six outcomes that represent a reasonable estimate of the distribution of possible outcomes:

Outcome	Useful life	Estimated outflow ($)	Discount rate	Estimated probability
1	10 years	200,000	6%	5%
2	10 years	225,000	6%	25%
3	10 years	275,000	6%	20%
4	15 years	230,000	5.5%	5%
5	15 years	260,000	5.5%	25%
6	15 years	340,000	5.5%	20%

Required:

Calculate the value of the liability for dismantling the oil rig at the end of its estimated useful life.

Probability-weighted average of the present value of the six outcomes would give the measurement of the liability:

Outcome	Estimated outflow ($)	Discounted outflow ($)	Estimated probability	Present value ($)
1	200,000	111,679	5%	5,584
2	225,000	125,639	25%	31,410
3	275,000	153,559	20%	30,712
4	230,000	103,025	5%	5,151
5	260,000	116,463	25%	29,116

6	340,000	152,297	20%	30,459
				132,432
Risk adjustment (rational payment to be relieved of risk of uncertainties in prices)—say 5%				6,622
Liability recognised				139,054

Despite intentions to publish the new standard by the end of 2010, this did not happen and there was no further movement on the project. The IASB has subsequently commenced a research project into IAS 37, which acknowledges problems with the standard including those identified in section 13.4. However, the publication of the ED of the *Conceptual Framework* (see Chapter 2 for discussion of this) is changing and clarifying the recognition criteria for the elements. This may guide any changes to the 'probability of outflows' recognition criterion for provisions—probability criteria have been removed from the recognition principles in the *Conceptual Framework* ED. However, the IASB does indicate that consistency with other standards would not in itself be a reason for removing the 'probable outflows' criterion from IAS 37, and that recognition requirements may need to vary between standards. This is because provisions and contingent liabilities have characteristics that distinguish them from many other liabilities. They typically cannot be measured by reference to an observable transaction price; they tend not to be traded, so do not have an observable current market price; and there is typically no exchange transaction that provides an observable price for the liability. The IASB has indicated it will wait for the *Conceptual Framework* to be finalised before it considers publication of a further ED to change IAS 37.

13.5 Events after the reporting period

In accounting for provisions and contingent liabilities, estimates of the future are required to be made. Information from events and transactions which arise after the date of the statement of financial position is therefore relevant in helping determine these. A question which arises in connection with this is how long after the end of an accounting period should a company have to be aware of events and transactions which may affect amounts or disclosures included in the financial statements? Should details of an unexpected event, such as a fire at the company's premises, be included in the financial statements?

The answer to the last question is yes. If financial statements are to provide relevant information to the users then information about significant or material events which could affect their decisions, even those that occur after the end of the financial year, should be incorporated into the financial statements. To ensure consistent treatment of such items IAS 10 *Events after the Reporting Period* sets out when actual figures in the financial statements should be changed and the disclosures that should be provided.

13.5.1 Definition of events after the reporting period

A typical timeline for the production and publication of a company's financial statements is shown in Figure 13.2.

Figure 13.2 A timeline for the production and publication of financial statements

For listed companies the date that the directors authorise the issue of the financial statements to the shareholders will typically be 2–3 months after the end of the financial year, with the annual general meeting (AGM) held a few weeks after this.

 Example to illustrate the period in which events are required to be noted

Consider the following information for a company:

● year end: 31 December 20X0

● preparation of financial statements completed: 15 February 20X1

● board of directors meeting: 18 February 20X1 (at the meeting the board approve the financial statements and authorise them for issue)

● AGM held: 28 March 20X1 (at the AGM the shareholders approve the financial statements)

● the approved financial statements are filed by the company (as per Company legislation) on 6 April 20X1.

A significant event occurred on 7 March 20X1 which it is considered would alter an investor's opinion on the financial position of the company. Should this be included in the financial statements?

Events after the reporting period are defined in IAS 10 as:

> Those events, both favourable and unfavourable, which occur between the end of the reporting period and the date on which the financial statements are authorised for issue by the board of directors.

> *(IASB, 2004, para. 3)*

There are two types of event after the reporting period, classification of which determines the accounting treatment. These are outlined in Table 13.3.

A condition is a transaction or item that has happened. So an adjusting event may confirm this or provide information that helps determine its measurement. A non-adjusting event is a material transaction or item that occurs in the period after the end of the financial year and before the financial statements are authorised for issue, information about which needs to be provided to the users as it may affect decisions they may make. The disclosures should include the nature of the event and an estimate of its financial effect or, if this is not possible, a statement that such an estimate cannot be made.

Table 13.3 Types of events after the reporting period and their accounting treatment

Type of event	Accounting treatment
Adjusting Events that provide evidence of conditions that existed at the end of the reporting period	Adjust the financial statements to reflect the adjusting event
Non-adjusting Events that are indicative of conditions that arose after the reporting period	Do not adjust the financial statements, but provide details of the event in a disclosure note

 Worked example 13.5: of events after the reporting period

Company Beta has a financial year end of 30 June 20X5 and authorised the issue of its financial statements to shareholders on 31 October 20X5. The following events have occurred.

Required:

Determine whether they are adjusting or non-adjusting and what the relevant accounting treatment should be.

1   On 31 July 20X5 Beta was advised by the liquidator that a customer who owed £150,000 at 30 June 20X5 was insolvent. The liquidator advised that he would be paying all of this customer's creditors 10p for every pound owed and estimated this would be paid in September 20X5.

2   Beta's inventory at 30 June 20X5 includes a line of products valued at cost of £100,000. Owing to declining economic trends in the market, this inventory was not able to be sold during July 20X5. On 10 August 20X5 Beta entered into an agreement to sell the entire line of inventory to a competitor for £80,000.

3   In July 20X5 Beta acquired a factory building for £2 million. Negotiations with the seller had commenced in April 20X0.

4   Beta has a portfolio of investments valued at market value at 30 June 20X5 at £600,000. The market value of these investments fell to £450,000 as of 31 October 20X5 as the stock market declined.

All events have occurred in the period between the end of the financial year and the date of authorisation of the issue of the financial statements. Whether they are adjusting or non-adjusting events and the subsequent accounting treatment therefore has to be determined.

1   This is an adjusting event since the receivable balance of £150,000 was the condition in existence at the end of the financial year. The details from the liquidator provide information about the measurement of the receivable.

Adjustment required is to write off the element of the debt which will not be received (0.9 × £150,000):

		£	£
Debit	Irrecoverable debts expense	135,000	
Credit	Receivables		135,000

2   This is an adjusting event as the inventory was in existence at the end of the financial year. The sale after the end of the year provides information about its net realisable value (NRV).

Adjustment required is to write down the value of this line of inventory to its NRV (i.e. reduce it to £80,000):

		£	£
Debit	Cost of sales	20,000	
Credit	Inventory (SoFP)		20,000

3   The condition is the purchase of the factory building and this happened after the end of the financial year. Although negotiations with the seller had been ongoing before 30 June 20X5, intention to acquire the building does not give rise to a condition that had actually happened. (Beta could always pull out of the negotiations.)

This is a non-adjusting event. The acquisition, however, would be considered a material item and so a note should be provided in the financial statements describing the transaction and its financial effect.

4   The decline in the market value of the investments does not normally relate to their condition at the end of the financial year. It reflects circumstances that have arisen subsequently.

This is a non-adjusting event. The investments remain at their year-end valuation of £600,000. The decline in the value is likely to be considered material and so disclosure about the fall in the market value would be made in a note to the financial statements.

An example of the disclosures relating to a non-adjusting event arising after the end of the financial year is given.

Financial reporting in practice 13.4   Arsenal Holdings plc, 2015

Note 31—Post balance sheet events

Player transactions

Since the end of the financial year a subsidiary company, Arsenal Football Club plc, has contracted for the purchase and sale of various players. The net payment resulting from these transfers, taking into account the applicable levies, is £10.5 million (2014—net payment of £52.5 million). These transfers will be accounted for in the year ending 31 May 2016.

Note—To put this in context, the cost of player registrations in the 2015 year end amounted to £114 million.

13.5.2 Dividends

Final dividends for a financial year which are declared after the end of the year are not liabilities because at the date of the year end there is no obligation for an outflow of resources. This is so even if a final dividend is expected by shareholders. If the dividends are declared before the date the financial statements are authorised for issue to the shareholders, the dividends are disclosed in the notes in accordance with IAS 1 *Presentation of Financial Statements*.

Financial reporting in practice 13.5   J Sainsbury plc, 2015

10 Dividends

	2015 pence per share	2014 pence per share	2015 £m	2014 £m
Amounts recognised as distributions to equity holders in the year:				
Final dividend of prior financial year	12.3	11.9	234	225
Interim dividend of current financial year	5.0	5.0	96	95
	17.3	16.9	330	320

After the balance sheet date, a final dividend of 8.2 pence per share (2014: 12.3 pence per share) was proposed by the Directors in respect of the 52 weeks to 14 March 2015, resulting in a total final proposed dividend of £157 million (2014: £234 million). The proposed final dividend has not been included as a liability at 14 March 2015.

13.5.3 Going concern assumption

The going concern assumption is one of the fundamental principles of financial reporting as detailed in Chapter 2.

🛈 **Reminder** *Going concern means it is assumed an entity will continue in existence for the foreseeable future. If the entity intends to liquidate or materially curtail the scale of its operations, the financial statements may have to be prepared on a different basis, for example, by valuing the assets and liabilities on a break-up basis.*

IAS 1 requires a company to disclose if there are material uncertainties related to events or conditions that may cast significant doubt upon the company's ability to continue as a going concern. These events or conditions may arise after the end of financial year. For example, there may be a sudden deterioration in operating results and financial position caused by economic conditions or the company may fail to renew its overdraft facility with its bank. The directors of the company will need to be alert to this and consider if the going concern assumption is still appropriate. If not, then IAS 10 requires a fundamental change to the basis of accounting, which would mean the assets and liabilities would be valued on a different basis.

Going concern matters have received particular attention since the financial crisis and these together with related disclosures have been discussed in detail in Chapter 4.

Summary of key points

Accounting for liabilities has, in the past, been abused by companies on the grounds of prudence. Although the IASB is likely to reintroduce prudence as an underpinning concept to the preparation of financial statements, circumstances where this is appropriate will be carefully described. The definition and criteria for the recognition of a liability in the ED to its *Conceptual Framework* are also being revised. However, uncertainties about whether there is to be a settlement of an obligation and the amount at which this is to be made always exist for many liabilities, and this requires estimates and judgements about the future. This is the key issue with the accounting for many liabilities.

Certain liabilities are dealt with by specific financial reporting standards. IAS 37 *Provisions, Contingent Liabilities and Contingent Assets* addresses liabilities not the subject of these other standards where there is uncertainty about the timing and the amount of the outflow of resources. It sets out three criteria which have to be met for a provision to be included in the financial statements. However, these criteria themselves are based on judgement. For instance, the probability of a future event happening has to be assessed and estimates about the value also have to be made. The recognition or not of provisions can have a significant impact on a company's financial statements as profit may be reduced, and key liquidity ratios and debt covenants affected.

IAS 37 further explains the treatment and disclosures of potential liabilities which are not yet recognised as a provision because they are contingent upon the outcome of a future event which is not within the control of the company. These contingent liabilities also arise because the probability of an outflow of resources is considered less than likely or because the amount of the outflow cannot be estimated reliably. In these cases financial statements would be rendered unreliable if amounts were included in them. However, users need to know about these potentially large obligations, and so companies are required to make disclosures with sufficient details to provide users with this relevant information.

Contingent assets are also considered by IAS 37, and the asymmetrical treatment of contingent liabilities and contingent assets should be noted.

The current accounting for provisions and contingent liabilities is inconsistent with some other international financial reporting standards' requirements and US standards. The IASB and US FASB had worked on proposals for a new standard and issued an ED in 2010. However, this has now been replaced by an IASB research project, the outcome of which will wait for the revised *Conceptual Framework* to be issued.

Given that so much of the accounting for liabilities and provisions relies on judgements about what may happen after the end of the financial year, the chapter concludes by considering how companies should deal with such events. IAS 10 *Events after the Reporting Period* specifies the critical period in which companies have to be aware of these events, and the definitions and resulting accounting treatment for adjusting and non-adjusting events. Consideration of going concern is a crucial current issue and companies are required to consider this carefully in their review of these events.

 ## Further reading

IASB (International Accounting Standards Board) (2004) IAS 10 *Events after the Reporting Period*. London: IASB.

IASB (International Accounting Standards Board) (2005) IAS 37 *Provisions, Contingent Liabilities and Contingent Assets*. London: IASB.

Bibliography

Arsenal Holdings plc (2015) *Annual Report 2015.* London: Arsenal Holdings.

BP plc (2011) *Annual Report and Form 20-F, 2010.* London: BP.

BP plc (2016) *Annual Report and Form 20-F, 2015.* London: BP.

IASB (International Accounting Standards Board) (2004) IAS 10 *Events after the Reporting Period.* London: IASB.

IASB (International Accounting Standards Board) (2005) IAS 37 *Provisions, Contingent Liabilities and Contingent Assets.* London: IASB.

IASB (International Accounting Standards Board) (2010) *Conceptual Framework.* London: IASB.

IASB (International Accounting Standards Board) (2015a) Exposure Draft *Conceptual Framework for Financial Reporting.* London: IASB.

IASB (International Accounting Standards Board) (2015b) Staff Paper: *Research—Provisions, Contingent Liabilities and Contingent Assets (IAS 37): Project Overview.* London: IASB.

IASB (International Accounting Standards Board) (2015c) Staff Paper: *Research—Provisions, Contingent Liabilities and Contingent Assets (IAS 37): Possible Problems with IAS 37.* London: IASB.

IASB (International Accounting Standards Board) (2015d) Staff Paper: *Research—Provisions, Contingent Liabilities and Contingent Assets (IAS 37): Implications of Conceptual Framework Proposals.* London: IASB.

J Sainsbury plc (2015) *Annual Report and Financial Statements, 2015.* London: J Sainsbury.

Marks and Spencer plc (2015) *Annual Report and Financial Statements, 2015.* London: Marks and Spencer.

Questions

● Quick test

1   The following events occurred before the financial statements were approved for release to shareholders by the directors of the respective companies.

Required:

Discuss whether they should be classified as adjusting or non-adjusting events occurring after the end of the reporting period.

(a) One month after the year end, a company received notification advising that the large balance on a receivable would not be paid as the customer was being wound up. No payments are expected from the customer or receiver.

(b) Before the financial statements of a company are finalised, a defect was found in the material used in some batches of Product X awaiting shipment to an overseas customer. It was discovered that these were the only batches affected and that they were all manufactured in the last week of the financial year. As a result, the customer was offered a 40% discount on the agreed price. This was accepted and the sale proceeded at a value of £60,000. The value placed on the inventory in question in the year end accounts was £80,000.

(c) At the end of the reporting period, a company is negotiating with its insurance provider about the amount of an insurance claim that it had filed. Within 3 weeks of the financial reporting date, the insurance provider agreed to pay £200,000.

(d) A serious fire occurred one week after the end of the financial year for a furniture manufacturing company. The company's entire inventory of recliner chairs were water damaged during this incident and, before the audit of the financial statements was complete, they were sold for £20,000 to an overseas customer. The cost of the chairs was £45,000.

(e) A company took delivery of a new machine from the USA in the last week of the financial year. It was discovered almost immediately afterwards that the supplier of the machine had filed for bankruptcy and would not be able to honour the warranties and repair contract on the new machine. Because the machine was so advanced, it was unlikely that any local entity could provide maintenance cover.

2   Portia plc is currently defending two legal actions:

(a) An employee, who suffered severe acid burns as a result of an accident in Portia's factory, is suing for £20,000, claiming that the directors failed to provide adequate safety equipment. Portia's lawyers are contesting the claim, but have advised the directors that they will probably lose.

(b) A customer is suing for £50,000, claiming that Portia's hair care products damaged her hair. Portia's lawyers are contesting this claim and have advised that the claim is unlikely to succeed.

Required:

Explain whether, and how much, Portia plc should provide for these legal claims in its financial statements.

3   Xanver plc has the following two legal claims outstanding:

● a legal action against Xanver claiming compensation of £200,000, filed in February 20X7. Xanver has been advised that it is probable that the liability will materialise

● a legal action taken by Xanver against another entity claiming damages of £300,000, started in March 20X7. Xanver has been advised that it is probable that it will win the case.

Required:

How should Xanver plc report these legal actions in its financial statements for the year ended 30 April 20X7?

●● Develop your understanding

4   Explain which one(s) of the following would require a provision to be created by Abel plc at the end of its reporting period, 31 October 20X5:

(a) Under new legislation, businesses are required to fit smoke filters to their factories by 30 April 20X5. At 31 October 20X5 Abel has not fitted the smoke filters

(b) Abel makes refunds to customers for any goods returned within 30 days of sale and has done so for many years, even though it has no legal obligation to do so

(c) On 12 October 20X5 the board of Abel decided to close down a division. By 31 October 20X5 the decision was not communicated to any of those affected and no other steps were taken to implement the decision.

Would your answer change if by 20 October 20X5 a detailed plan for closing down the division was agreed by the board, letters were sent to customers warning them to seek an alternative source of supply, and redundancy notices were sent to the staff of the division?

5   Discuss whether the legal requirement for an airline to overhaul its aircraft once every three years means that a provision for the costs of doing so should be recognised?

6   Discuss the treatment of the following items in the respective companies' financial statements.

   (a) Borax plc has always paid bonuses to its two directors based on 5% of profit before tax. The draft financial statements at 31 March 20X1 include a gross bonus amounting to £11,500 each following the resolution to pay a bonus based on the draft figures on 20 March 20X1. This bonus is not paid until the financial statements are approved because of various adjustments that are often incorporated in the final accounts. The accounts are approved by the board of directors four months after the year end and, because of a large write-down of inventory, the profits have reduced to an extent that the gross bonus should only be £4,500 each.

   (b) Carstairs plc is a supermarket that operates four different business divisions: groceries, mobile telephone provision, Internet service provision and domestic appliances. Each division is material to the financial statements of the company. The financial year end is 31 March 20X3 and the financial statements have not yet been authorised for issue. On 30 June 20X3 the company's directors decided that because of extremely difficult trading conditions, and a heavy loss, it would discontinue the domestic appliances division. This announcement was made on 1 July 20X3.

7   Balti plc sells refrigerators and freezers, and provides a one-year warranty against faults occurring after sale. Balti estimates that if all goods with an outstanding warranty at its statement of financial position date of 31 March 20X6 need minor repairs the total cost would be £3 million. If all the products under warranty needed major repairs the total cost would be £12 million. At 31 March 20X7 these amounts have risen to £3.5 million and £13 million respectively.

   Based on previous years' experience, Balti estimates that 85% of the products will require no repairs, 14% will require minor repairs and 1% will require major repairs.

   During the year ended 31 March 20X7 actual costs of repairs under the warranty amounted to £480,000.

   Required:

   Explain the accounting treatment of the warranty in Balti plc's financial statements for the year ended 31 March 20X7, quantifying figures which would appear in the statement of profit or loss and statement of financial position.

●●● Take it further

8   Warwick Refreshments runs a brewing business. In February 20X4, the accounts for the year ended 31 December 20X3 are being finalised. The following issues remain outstanding.

   (a) A customer bought a glass of Warwick Best Beer in a local bar during October 20X3 and became ill. The customer is suing the bar and Warwick Refreshments. The case has not yet come to court and, although the entity's solicitors believe they will win the case, the directors offered an out-of-court settlement of £10,000 as a goodwill gesture. Under the terms of the offer, each side would meet their own costs, which, in the case of Warwick Refreshments, are £1,500 up to December 20X3. This entire amount had been paid by the year end. The customer has not yet formally accepted the offer.

   (b) A consignment of hops costing £95,000 was delivered to the brewery on 20 December 20X3. The supplier has not yet issued an invoice.

   (c) Bottles of the entity's beers are supplied by Bottlebank. Five years ago, in order to secure supplies, Warwick Refreshments gave a guarantee over a £3,000,000 10-year bank loan taken out by Bottlebank. The guarantee is still in force. Bottlebank's latest accounts indicate net assets of £6.8 million, and it has not breached any of the terms and conditions of the loan.

(d) Owing to a faulty valve, a batch of beer was inadvertently discharged into a river instead of into the bottling plant in March 20X3. Warwick Refreshments paid a fine of £20,000 in July 20X3 for an illegal discharge. It is also responsible for rectifying any environmental damage. To 31 December 20X3, £200,000 had been paid. The extent of further expenditure is uncertain, although it is estimated to be between £100,000 and £140,000.

Required:

Explain how each of the above items should be treated in the financial statements of Warwick Refreshments for the year ended 31 December 20X3.

9   On 1 October 20X5, Havant Oil plc acquired a newly constructed oil platform at a cost of £30 million together with the right to extract oil from an offshore oilfield under a government licence. The terms of the licence are that Havant Oil will have to remove the platform (which will then have no value) and restore the sea bed to an environmentally satisfactory condition in 10 years' time when the oil reserves have been exhausted. The estimated cost of this on 30 September 20Y5 will be £15 million. An appropriate discount rate to use for Havant Oil is 10%. Discount factors using this rate at different time periods are as follows:

Time period	Discount factor
7	0.513
8	0.467
9	0.424
10	0.386

On 1 October 20X8 the oil platform suffered an accident and was completely destroyed. The accident caused an oil spill in the approximate area causing significant damages to the environment. As a result of the accident, the government licence was revoked and Havant Oil was informed by authorities that it was unlikely to obtain the licence again for the offshore oilfield. Havant Oil was also ordered to remove the remains of the platform and restore the sea bed within one year.

The finance director of Havant Oil gathered the following information after the accident:

1   The cost of the removal of the platform and restoration of the sea bed is re-estimated at £10 million

2   The engineers have estimated the clean-up of the oil spill will require an additional £50 million

3   Preliminary estimates indicate that £20 million may be recoverable from Havant Oil's insurance policy

4   The fishermen in the nearby area have filed a class action against Havant Oil claiming £300 million of damages. Havant Oil has instructed its lawyers to commence negotiations with the fishermen to try and settle an amount outside of court. The lawyers believe the final compensation may be significantly less than the original claim.

Required:

(a) Discuss the difference between a liability, provision and contingent liability.

(b) In relation to IAS 37 *Provisions, Contingent Liabilities and Contingent Assets*, discuss the accounting treatment of the acquisition of the oil platform under the government licence in the financial statements of Havant Oil plc for the year ended 30 September 20X6, showing amounts which would appear in the statement of financial position and statement of profit or loss for that year as appropriate.

(c) Discuss and quantify, where appropriate, how Havant Oil plc should account for the oil spill and related events in the financial statements for the year ended 30 September 20X9.

 Visit the Online Resource Centre for solutions to all these end of chapter questions plus visual walkthrough solutions. You can test your understanding with extra questions and answers, explore additional case studies based on real companies, take a guided tour through a company report and much more. Go to the Online Resource Centre at **www.oxfordtextbooks.co.uk/orc/maynard2e/**

14

Financial instruments

Financial instruments is a difficult and controversial financial accounting and reporting issue, brought very much to the fore by the financial crisis of 2008, when the accounting methods for and lack of disclosures of the exposure to risks resulting from some instruments were considered by some to be partly responsible for the crisis.

The International Accounting Standards Board (IASB) has been working for many years to produce adequate financial reporting standards in this area, and the resulting standards are International Accounting Standard (IAS) 32 *Financial Instruments: Presentation*, IAS 39 *Financial Instruments: Recognition and Measurement*, which has now been replaced by International Financial Reporting Standard (IFRS) 9 *Financial Instruments*, and IFRS 7 *Financial Instruments: Disclosures*.

This chapter discusses the key issues relating to the classification of financial instruments, their recognition and derecognition, initial and subsequent measurement, impairment and the main disclosure requirements. It does not cover the more complex areas of accounting for financial derivatives or hedging instruments. It focuses on IFRS 9 rather than IAS 39.

★ Learning objectives

After studying this chapter you will be able to:

- understand what the accounting for financial instruments covers and why it is both an important and complex topic
- differentiate between debt and **equity instruments** and account for **compound financial instruments**
- define, classify and account for financial assets and liabilities both on initial recognition and subsequently
- explain the disclosure requirements relating to financial instruments and the risk associated with them.

✔ Key issues checklist

- ❑ Why accounting for financial instruments is such a key issue.
- ❑ Definitions of financial assets, **financial liabilities** and equity instruments.
- ❑ Debt instruments v. equity instruments.
- ❑ Accounting for preference shares.
- ❑ Accounting for compound instruments.
- ❑ Recognition of financial instruments per IFRS 9.
- ❑ **Derecognition** of financial instruments—transfer of risks and rewards of ownership and control.
- ❑ **Securitisation** of financial assets.
- ❑ Classification of financial assets and liabilities per IFRS 9.
- ❑ Initial measurement—including fair value.
- ❑ Subsequent measurement—including effective interest method.
- ❑ Impairment—expected loss model.
- ❑ Disclosures per IFRS 7—statements of financial position and comprehensive income, accounting policies and fair value.
- ❑ Disclosures relating to the significance, nature and extent of risk.
- ❑ Evaluation of IFRS 9.

14.1 Why is accounting for financial instruments important?

The financial crisis of 2008 exposed financial instruments as a major financial reporting issue, particularly for financial institutions. Indeed the accounting methods for and lack of disclosures of the exposure to risks resulting from some financial instruments were considered by some to be partly responsible for the crisis. However, this is not just an accounting issue for financial institutions; nor is it an issue that has only been around since the financial crisis. The increasing diversity of business and the wider development and availability of financial instruments since towards the end of the twentieth century has increased the use of complex financial transactions by all sorts of businesses in order to reduce their exposure to risks. Most major listed companies, whether in retail or telecommunications or manufacturing, will have financial instruments on their statement of financial position. The existence of financial instruments has a major effect on the risk profile of such companies, and can have a significant effect on their profits, solvency and cash flow.

Financial reporting in practice 14.1   Rolls-Royce plc, 2015

Rolls-Royce plc, a major manufacturing company, includes other financial assets and liabilities on its 2015 statement of financial position. The company states that it:

(a) Uses various financial instruments to manage its exposure to movements in foreign exchange rates.

(b) Uses commodity swaps to manage its exposure to movements in the price of commodities (jet fuel and base metals).

(c) Uses interest rate swaps, forward rate agreements and interest rate caps to manage its exposure to movements in interest rates.

The IASB's predecessor, the International Accounting Standards Committee (IASC), produced the first international financial reporting standards dealing with financial instruments in the late 1990s. These were largely based on the many rules-based US accounting standards in this area. Ever since then, the international financial reporting standards have been considered controversial, attracting many criticisms, particularly that of complexity. Many users of financial statements and other interested parties have found the requirements of the standards difficult to understand, apply and interpret.

This stems from the fact that many financial instruments themselves are complex and hard to understand, even with full information about terms and conditions. Preparers of financial statements find it difficult to apply principles and communicate the economic substance of transactions or events involving financial instruments and the resulting financial position and results.

The IASB has responded to the criticisms and, after many amendments and reissues, the current extant standards are:

- IAS 32 *Financial Instruments: Presentation*
- IAS 39 *Financial Instruments: Recognition and Measurement*
- IFRS 9 *Financial Instruments* replaces IAS 39
- IFRS 7 *Financial Instruments: Disclosures*.

14.1.1 The main issues in accounting for financial instruments

Principles-based financial reporting standards require the accounting for financial instruments to be according to their economic substance rather than their legal form. This leads to the main issues addressed by the standards including:

- The classification of debt instruments versus equity instruments
- The categorisation of financial instruments
- The measurement of the different categories of financial instrument
- Derecognition of financial instruments
- Presentation and disclosure
- Derivatives and hedging instruments.

All these issues except for derivatives and hedging instruments are discussed in this chapter.

14.2 What are financial instruments?

Financial instruments vary from straightforward, traditional instruments such as a variable rate bank loan, through to various forms of derivative instruments. The basic definition of a financial instrument is:

> any contract that gives rise to a financial asset of one entity and a financial liability or equity instrument of another entity.

(IASB, IAS 32, para. 11)

Note that there are always two parties to the contract, one of which recognises an asset, and the other of which recognises either a liability or equity or a combination of the two.

A financial asset is any asset that is:

(a) cash;

(b) an equity instrument of another entity;

(c) a contractual right:

    (i) to receive cash or another financial asset from another entity; or

    (ii) to exchange financial assets or financial liabilities with another entity under conditions that are potentially favourable to the entity; or

(d) a contract that will or may be settled in the entity's own equity instruments.

(IASB, IAS 32, para. 11)

Note that under (c) there has to be a *contractual right* to receive cash or another financial asset or to partake in a favourable exchange of financial instruments. The contractual right must be one that cannot be avoided, and is usually enforceable by law.

A financial liability is any liability that is:

(a) a contractual obligation:

    (i) to deliver cash or another financial asset to another entity; or

    (ii) to exchange financial assets or financial liabilities with another entity under conditions that are potentially unfavourable to the entity; or

(b) a contract that will or may be settled in the entity's own equity instruments.

(IASB, IAS 32, para. 11)

Similar to the financial asset definition, note that there has to be a *contractual obligation* to deliver cash or another financial instrument or to partake in an unfavourable exchange of financial instruments. Again, the contractual obligation must be one that cannot be avoided, and is usually enforceable by law.

An equity instrument is any contract that results in a residual interest in the assets of an entity after deducting all of its liabilities.

 Example of the definitions of financial assets and liabilities

Which of the following are financial assets, liabilities or equity instruments?

- Machinery
- Inventories
- Three-year bank deposit
- Trade receivables
- Insurance prepayment
- Bank overdraft
- Equity shares
- Redeemable preference shares

Machinery and inventories are not financial instruments. They are physical assets whose control creates an opportunity to generate an inflow of cash or other assets, and do not give rise to a present right to receive cash or other financial assets.

The insurance prepayment is not a financial instrument. The future economic benefit is the receipt of the insurance cover rather than the right to receive cash or other financial assets.

The three-year bank deposit and trade receivables are financial assets as the business with these assets has contractual rights to receive cash from them.

The bank overdraft is repayable in cash and is therefore a financial liability.

The equity shareholders own the residual interest in a company, but they have no contractual right to demand any of it to be delivered to them, for example by way of a dividend. Equally, the company has issued an equity instrument, not a financial liability, because the company has no contractual obligation to distribute the residual interest.

The redeemable preference shares are a financial liability as there is a contractual obligation to redeem them for cash at some point in the future.

Common financial instruments therefore include:

- Cash and timed deposits
- Trade payables and receivables
- Loans payable and receivable
- Debt and equity investments
- **Derivatives** such as interest rate swaps and foreign exchange contracts
- Redeemable and irredeemable preference shares
- Convertible debt instruments
- Investments in shares issued by other entities.

14.3 Debt and equity instruments

One of the principles underlying accounting for financial instruments is that this should be according to their economic substance rather than their legal form. This principle applies particularly to certain types of financial instrument issued by a company whose legal form is that of an equity instrument but in substance is a liability. Other financial instruments issued may combine features of both equity instruments and financial liabilities. The definitions of financial instruments given in section 14.2 are crucial in determining the substance of the instrument.

The key feature of a liability is the obligation to transfer economic benefits. Therefore, the financial instrument is a financial liability if there is:

- A contractual obligation on the issuer to deliver cash/another financial asset, or
- A contractual right for the holder to receive cash/another financial asset.

If this does not apply then the financial instrument is an equity instrument.

14.3.1 Redeemable preference shares

The example in section 14.2 introduced one of these instruments: redeemable preference shares. Although legally an equity instrument, these must be redeemed by the company issuing them for a fixed or determinable amount at a fixed or determinable future date. In addition, the annual dividend is fixed and not payable at the discretion of the directors. The company therefore has a contractual obligation to deliver cash, and the redeemable preference shares are accounted for as a financial liability. The treatment of the preference dividends corresponds to this classification, and they are accounted for as a finance charge in the statement of profit or loss. Note that most preference shares issued by a company are redeemable.

14.3.2 Irredeemable preference shares

As their name suggests, irredeemable preference shares are not required to be redeemed. However, this does not automatically mean that they are accounted for as equity, as their classification depends on other terms, such as the rights to dividends. If dividends on the irredeemable preference shares are mandatory and cumulative, then the entity has a contractual obligation to pay the dividends to the preference shareholders and therefore the shares should be accounted for as liabilities. If the payment of dividends on the shares is discretionary, there is no mandatory requirement to pay the dividends, and there is therefore no contractual obligation to deliver cash. In this case the irredeemable preference shares should be accounted for as equity.

Therefore, in practical terms preference shares are only treated as part of equity when they will never be redeemed, or the redemption is solely at the option of the issuer and at the time of issue redemption is extremely unlikely, plus the payment of dividends is discretionary.

14.3.3 Compound financial instruments

A compound financial instrument is one which contains both a liability component and an equity component. One of the most common types of compound instrument is convertible debt. This financial instrument creates a financial liability for the issuer as there is an obligation to pay interest and eventually repay the capital. However, there is also the option for the holder of the instrument to convert it into equity shares of the issuer; this is the equity component. The substance of this financial instrument is the issue of non-convertible debt plus an option to acquire shares in the future.

IAS 32 *Financial Instruments: Presentation* requires the component parts of this type of financial instrument to be classified separately. The standard specifies that the value for the liability component should be calculated first at the present value of the interest payments and the eventual capital repayment, assuming the instrument is redeemed. The present value should be discounted at the market rate for an instrument of similar credit status and the same cash flows but without the conversion option. The value of the liability component should then be deducted from the fair value of the instrument as a whole to leave a residual value for the equity component.

Worked example 14.1: to show the measurement of the liability and equity components of a compound financial instrument

On 1 January 20X3 Claycroft plc issues £500,000 of 6% loan stock at par. Interest is payable on 31 December each year. The stock is due for redemption at par on 31 December 20X6, but may be converted into equity shares on that date instead.

The market rate of interest on similar loan stock without the conversion option is 8%.

Required:

Calculate the liability component and the equity component of the loan stock.

The value of liability component is the present value of the cash payments discounted using the market interest rate for similar loan stock without the conversion option.

Date of payment	Payment	Discount factor*	Present value
	£		£
31 Dec 20X3	30,000	$1/1.08$	27,778
31 Dec 20X4	30,000	$1/(1.08)^2$	25,720
31 Dec 20X5	30,000	$1/(1.08)^3$	23,815
31 Dec 20X6	530,000	$1/(1.08)^4$	389,566
Fair value of liability component			466,879

* Discount and annuity tables can be used.

Lenders are willing to pay £500,000 for loan stock whose fair value is £466,879. The additional £33,121 (= 500,000 − 466,879) represents the price the lenders are willing to pay for the option to convert. This therefore is the fair value of the equity component. It is included as a reserve in equity.

The split between the liability and equity components remains the same throughout the term of the instrument even if there are changes in market interest rates, share prices or other events that alter the likelihood that the conversion option will be exercised.

14.3.4 Presentation of interest, dividends, gains and losses

The classification of a financial instrument as a financial liability or an equity instrument determines whether interest, dividends, losses and gains relating to that instrument are recognised as income or expense in profit or loss.

Interest, dividends, losses and gains relating to a financial instrument or a component that is a financial liability are recognised as income or expense in profit or loss. Thus, dividend payments on shares wholly recognised as liabilities are recognised as expenses in the same way as interest on a loan. Similarly, gains and losses associated with redemptions or refinancings of financial liabilities are recognised in profit or loss.

Distributions to holders of an equity instrument are debited directly to equity, net of any related income tax benefit. Transaction costs of an equity transaction are accounted for as a deduction from equity, net of any related income tax benefit. Redemptions or refinancings of equity instruments are recognised as changes in equity.

14.4 Recognition and derecognition of financial instruments

14.4.1 Introduction to IFRS 9 Financial Instruments

IAS 39 *Financial Instruments: Recognition and Measurement* was one of the accounting standards inherited by the IASB when it was formed in 2001. Largely based on the US standards relating to financial instruments in existence at that time, this standard was always particularly problematic due to its complexity and its rules-based nature. Indeed, when the EU made IFRS mandatory for all listed companies from 1 January 2005, this standard was subject to the infamous 'carve-out' to make it acceptable to certain French banks. The 'carve-out' involved modifications to delete certain paragraphs relating to hedge accounting.

The reform of accounting for financial instruments was one of the areas identified in the Norwalk Agreement of 2002 between the IASB and US Financial Accounting Standards Board (FASB). Work on a replacement standard was accelerated in response to the financial crisis of 2008. In particular, interested parties including the G20, the Financial Crisis Advisory Group (a group set up by the IASB and US FASB to advise on how improvements in financial reporting could help enhance investor confidence in financial markets) and others highlighted the timeliness of recognition of expected credit losses, the complexity of multiple impairment models and the effects of changes in banks' creditworthiness as areas in need of revision.

The project was split into three phases which have dealt with:

1. The classification and measurement of financial instruments
2. Impairment of financial instruments
3. Hedge accounting.

Various interim versions have been issued as the project's phases have been completed, and the final version of IFRS 9 *Financial Instruments* was issued in July 2014. It is effective for financial accounting periods beginning on or after 1 January 2018, although, as with all new financial reporting standards, early adoption is permitted. It applies to all types of financial instruments except certain ones specifically excluded, such as investments in subsidiaries, associates, joint ventures and other joint arrangements. It covers recognition and measurement, impairment, derecognition and general hedge accounting.

14.4.2 Recognition of financial instruments

The criteria for the recognition of financial instruments in IFRS 9 are the same as those in IAS 39:

An entity shall recognise a financial asset or a financial liability in its statement of financial position when, and only when, the entity becomes party to the contractual provisions of the instrument.

(IASB, IFRS 9, para. 3.1.1)

Note that this is different from the recognition criteria in the *Conceptual Framework* and in most other standards. It means that derivative instruments must be recognised if a contractual right or obligation exists. For example, if a company purchases a six-month forward contract with a zero fair value at its inception, this exposes the company to risks and rewards due to changes in the value of the **underlying**, and it should therefore be recognised when the contract is initiated.

🛈 **Reminder** *The criteria for recognition of assets and liabilities in the 2010* Conceptual Framework *are:*

- *There is a probable inflow or outflow of resources*
- *The asset or liability has a cost or value that can be measured reliably.*

The proposed criteria in the ED of the new Conceptual Framework *are that assets and liabilities should be recognised if such recognition provides users of financial statements with relevant and faithfully representative information.*

14.4.3 Derecognition of financial instruments

The criteria for the derecognition of financial instruments in IFRS 9 are also the same as those in IAS 39. Derecognition is the removal of a previously recognised financial instrument from an entity's statement of financial position.

An entity should derecognise a financial asset when:

(a) the contractual rights to the cash flows from the financial asset expire, or

(b) the entity transfers substantially all the risks and rewards of ownership of the financial asset to another party.

A financial liability is derecognised when it is extinguished, in other words, when the obligation specified in the contract is discharged or cancelled or expires.

Although these seem fairly straightforward criteria, the complexity of transactions in financial instruments often creates difficulties in establishing whether exposure to risks and rewards or control or other involvement remains even if legal title has been transferred. So the IASB has produced a set of steps to help companies in the derecognition of financial assets, as shown in Figure 14.1. The principle behind these is that of substance over form.

The transfer of risks and rewards is evaluated by comparing the entity's exposure, before and after the transfer, with the variability in the amounts and timing of the net cash flows of the transferred asset. An entity is deemed to have retained substantially all the risks and rewards of ownership of a financial asset if its exposure to the variability in the present value

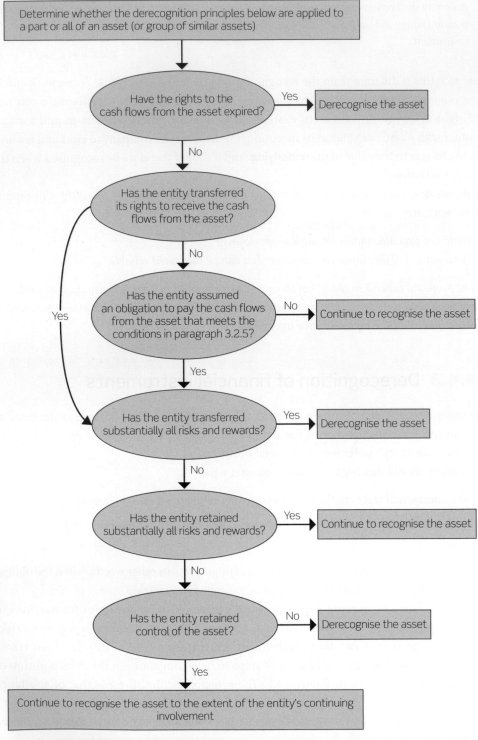

Figure 14.1 Derecognition of a financial asset

(IASB, IFRS 9 Application Guidance, para B3.2.1)

of the future net cash flows from the financial asset does not change significantly as a result of the transfer. An entity has transferred substantially all the risks and rewards of ownership of a financial asset if its exposure to such variability is no longer significant in relation to the total variability in the present value of the future net cash flows associated with the financial asset.

 Examples of transfers of risks and rewards of ownership

Which of the following transactions would result in the transfer of the risks and rewards of ownership?

1. An unconditional sale of a financial asset
2. A sale and repurchase transaction where the repurchase price is at a fixed price
3. A sale of a financial asset together with an option to repurchase the financial asset at its fair value at the time of repurchase.

1 and 3 result in the transfer of the risks and rewards of ownership, and these financial assets would be derecognised. For transaction 3, because any repurchase is at the fair value at the time of repurchase, all risks and rewards of ownership are with the buyer.

Transaction 2 does not transfer the risks and rewards of ownership as these remain with the seller.

The transfer of the risks and rewards of ownership may be subjective. If it is not entirely clear, then a company should determine whether it has retained control of the financial asset. If it has, it continues to recognise the asset to the extent of its continuing involvement. IFRS 9 provides guidance as to whether control is deemed to have been retained. Essentially if the transferee cannot sell the asset or the transferor retains an option to repurchase the asset at a fixed price, then the transferor is considered to have retained control. The passing of control of the asset to the transferee requires an active market to exist and for the transferee to have the practical ability to sell the asset in its entirety with no strings attached.

14.4.4 Securitisation of financial assets

The securitisation of financial assets is particularly relevant to the question of derecognition, particularly where **special purpose entities** (SPEs) are involved. Securitisation is the packaging of pools of financial assets such as loans and receivables and the sale of these packages. Investors buy the repackaged assets by providing finance in the form of securities or loans which are secured on the underlying pool and its associated income stream. This immediately releases cash for the original holder of the financial assets. SPEs are often used to acquire the repackaged assets, with the SPE issuing debt to third parties to raise the finance for the acquisition.

If an SPE is used, the accounting issue is whether the financial assets can be derecognised. This in turn depends on whether the SPE has assumed all the risks and rewards of the ownership of the assets and whether the originator has ceded control of the assets to the SPE. If the SPE is controlled by the originator, then it will be consolidated into (included in) the financial statements of the originator, and the assets will still be included in the consolidated financial statements, in other words, not derecognised.

If the SPE is not controlled by the originator, derecognition of the assets may still not be possible if the risks and rewards of ownership have not been substantially passed to the SPE. This would be the case if the lenders to the SPE had recourse to the originator for security for their loans or if the originator retained the risk of bad debts.

(See Chapter 17 for details of consolidated financial statements.)

 Examples of securitisation

Some football clubs need to raise cash quickly to buy players. They may obtain this by securitising future season ticket sales to the lender.

The 2008 financial crisis was in part caused by the securitisation of American sub-prime mortgages and the use of SPEs. The banks created packages of mortgages, and sold them to SPEs receiving cash, a better asset for credit rating purposes than the packages of mortgages. The SPEs were not consolidated into the banks' financial statements.

14.4.5 Partial derecognition

Derecognition could apply to part of a financial asset or liability. This is only allowable if the part comprises:

(a) specifically identified cash flows, or

(b) a fully proportionate share of the total cash flows.

The profit or loss or loss on derecognition must be calculated and is recognised in profit or loss in the same way as for any non-current asset:

Profit of loss on derecongnition = Proceeds received/paid − Carrying amount of asset/liability transferred

Where only part of a financial instrument is derecognised, the carrying amount should be allocated between the part retained and the part transferred based on their relative fair values on the date of transfer.

 Example of partial derecognition

A company with a financial asset in the form of a bond has the right to two separate sets of cash inflows—those relating to the interest and those relating to the ultimate repayment of the principal.

The company sells the rights to receive the interest to another party while retaining the right to receive the principal.

Any difference between the proceeds received and the carrying amount (measured at the date of derecognition) of the interest cash flows would be recognised in profit or loss. The amount derecognised is calculated by multiplying the carrying amount of the debt instrument by the proportion

$$\frac{\text{Fair value of the interest cash flows}}{\text{Fair value of whole debt instrument}}$$

The principal element of the debt instrument would still be recognised.

14.5 Measurement of financial instruments

The measurement of financial instruments is determined by their classification. One of the major criticisms of IAS 39 related to the complex classification categories, each of which had its own rules for determining which instruments should or could be included and how the financial assets would be tested for impairment. IFRS 9 has simplified these requirements and classification is based on a logical approach that reflects:

1. The business model for managing financial instruments, and

2. The contractual cash flow characteristics of the financial instrument.

The business model refers to how a company manages its financial assets in order to generate cash flows. Cash flows can be generated by receiving contractual cash flows such as dividends and interest, selling the assets or both. The business model should be determined on a level that reflects how financial assets are managed to achieve a particular business objective. It should not be determined for individual assets, but made on a higher level of aggregation, for example, on the basis of a portfolio of financial assets. Although judgement will be necessary when assessing a business model, it can typically be observed through the activities that a company takes, such as the business plans produced, the amount and frequency of sales of assets and how managers are compensated.

The intention is that this approach to the classification will improve the ability of users of financial statements to better understand the information about the amounts, timings and uncertainty of future cash flows, which is one of the objectives of financial reporting as set out in the IASB's *Conceptual Framework*.

14.5.1 Classification of financial assets

The classification of financial assets is summarised in Figure 14.2.

Thus there are two categories for the measurement of a financial asset: fair value and amortised cost. By assessing the business model followed by the cash flow characteristics of the financial instrument, the classification will result in financial assets for which current

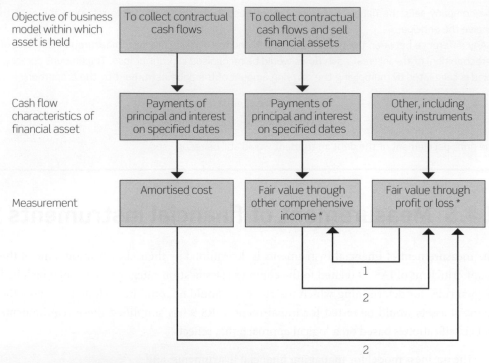

Figure 14.2 Classification of financial assets on initial recognition

* These methods mean the financial asset is measured on the statement of financial position at fair value, with the gains or losses from the changes in fair value being accounted for in other comprehensive income/profit or loss. The income from the investment and any impairment losses are included in profit or loss.

1 Investments in equity instruments may not be classified as measured at amortised cost and must be measured at fair value. This is because contractual cash flows on specified dates are not a characteristic of equity instruments. However, if an equity instrument is not held for trading (for example, it has been acquired for some strategic purpose), an irrevocable election can be made at initial recognition to measure the equity instrument at fair value through other comprehensive income, with the dividend income only being recognised in profit or loss.

2 Instruments that meet the criteria for measurement at amortised cost or fair value through other comprehensive income may be designated at initial recognition as being measured at fair value through profit or loss only if this provides more relevant information. This would be the case if an accounting mismatch would arise from measuring assets or liabilities or from recognising gains and losses on them on different bases.

values are more informative being measured at fair value, and those for which contractual cash flows are more informative generally being measured at amortised cost. This is a cash-flow-based model and is explained in section 14.5.7.

It can be seen from Figure 14.2 that only financial assets with contractual cash flows arising from payments of principal and interest can be measured at amortised cost or fair value through other comprehensive income. This generally applies to debt instruments which are considered basic lending arrangements. These are arrangements where the interest is considered as the return for the time value of money and credit risk. The interest can also encompass a return for, for example, liquidity risk, or amounts to cover expenses or a profit margin. However, contractual terms that introduce exposure to risks or volatility in the contractual cash flows, such as exposure to changes in equity prices or commodity prices, do not give rise to contractual cash flows that are solely payments of principal and interest on the principal amount outstanding. In these cases the measurement methods would not be applicable.

Example of contractual cash flows that are not solely payments of principal and interest on the principal amount outstanding

A financial instrument is a bond that is convertible into a fixed number of equity instruments of the issuer.

The holder of the financial instrument would analyse the convertible bond in its entirety. The contractual cash flows are not payments of principal and interest on the principal amount outstanding because they reflect a return that is inconsistent with a basic lending arrangement. In this example the return is linked to the value of the equity of the issuer.

14.5.2 Classification of financial liabilities

The classification requirements of financial liabilities under IFRS 9 have not changed from IAS 39. A financial liability is classified as measured at amortised cost unless:

1. it is held for trading, or
2. it is designated at fair value through profit or loss on initial recognition.

In these cases it is measured at fair value through profit or loss. The reasons for designating a liability as measured at fair value through profit and loss on initial recognition are the same as the choice for this designation for a financial asset.

Example of the designation of a financial liability at initial recognition at fair value through profit or loss

A financial asset and financial liability may be part of a hedging relationship. The classification requirements can create a measurement or recognition inconsistency (referred to as an 'accounting mismatch') when, for example, the financial asset is classified as subsequently measured at fair value through profit or loss and the liability in the hedging relationship is subsequently measured at amortised cost with changes in its fair value not recognised. In such circumstances, the company may conclude that its financial statements would provide more relevant information if both the asset and the liability were measured as at fair value through profit or loss.

The only new issue which IFRS 9 deals with in relation to the classification of financial liabilities is the volatility in profit or loss caused by changes in the credit risk of financial liabilities that an entity has elected to measure at fair value. The fair value of an entity's own debt is affected by changes in the entity's own credit risk. If an entity's credit risk falls, the fair value of its liabilities falls, and under the previous standard, IAS 39, a gain would have been recognised in profit or loss:

Dr   Financial liability

   Cr   Profit or loss

To many users of financial statements this is counterintuitive and confusing. So IFRS 9 requires changes in the fair value due to changes in the entity's own credit risk to be recognised in other comprehensive income rather than in profit or loss.

14.5.3 Reclassification of financial instruments

IFRS 9 requires financial assets to be reclassified between measurement categories when, and only when, a company's business model for managing them changes. This is a significant event and is expected to be uncommon. Since the business model is determined on a high level of aggregation, if it changes, all affected financial assets should be reclassified.

If reclassification occurs, further disclosures are required.

IFRS 9 does not permit financial liabilities to be reclassified.

14.5.4 Initial measurement of financial instruments

Financial instruments are initially measured at the fair value of consideration given. For instruments which are classified as measured at amortised cost or at fair value through other comprehensive income, transaction costs directly attributable to the acquisition of the asset or issue of the liability are included in this measurement. Transaction costs related to the acquisition of financial instruments classified as measured at fair value through profit or loss are expensed when incurred. Transaction costs typically include fees and commissions.

Trade receivables are measured at their transaction price.

14.5.5 Fair value

As discussed in Chapter 2, fair value, as defined by IFRS 13, is the price that would be received to sell an asset or paid to transfer a liability in an orderly transaction between market participants at the measurement date. IFRS 13 requires that the following are considered in determining fair value:

1. The asset or liability being measured

2. The principal market (i.e. where the most activity takes place), or where there is no principal market, the most advantageous market (i.e. in which the best price could be achieved), in which an orderly transaction would take place for the asset or liability

3. The highest and best use of the asset or liability and whether it is used on a standalone basis or in conjunction with other assets and liabilities

4. Assumptions that market participants would use when pricing the asset or liability.

Having considered these factors, IFRS 13 provides a hierarchy of inputs for arriving at fair value, with level 1 inputs used where possible:

Level 1	Quoted prices in active markets for identical assets that the entity can access
Level 2	Inputs other than quoted prices that are directly or indirectly observable for the asset
Level 3	Unobservable inputs for the asset

If a company has investments in equity instruments that do not have a quoted price in an active market and it is not possible to obtain their fair values reliably, they should be measured at cost.

The fair value on initial recognition is normally the transaction price. However, if part of the consideration is given for something other than the financial instrument, then the fair value should be estimated using a valuation technique.

Worked example 14.2: to show how the initial fair value of an interest-free loan is determined and the subsequent accounting

As part of an agreement to build a closer working relationship with Tocil plc, Garfield plc lends it £15,000 for three years on an interest-free basis. The agreement requires Tocil plc to provide marketing and product promotion for Garfield plc.

The market interest rate for a similar loan to a company with a similar credit rating as Tocil plc is 8%.

Required:

How should the loan be accounted for by Garfield plc?

The initial fair value of the loan should be determined by discounting the £15,000 receivable in three years' time to its present value, using the market interest rate.

$$PV = 15,000 / 1.08^3 = £11,907$$

The difference between the face value of the loan and the fair value to be recorded of 15,000 − 11,907 = £3,093 should immediately be recognised as an expense in profit or loss.

		£	£
Dr	Financial asset	11,907	
Dr	Finance expense	3,093	
Cr	Cash		15,000

Each year Garfield plc should recognise finance income of 8% on the balance of the loan, increasing the loan's carrying amount by the amount recognised in profit or loss.

In year 1 this amounts to 8% × 11,907 = £953

		£	£
Dr	Financial asset	953	
Cr	Finance income		953

In year 2 the finance income amounts to 8% × (11,907 + 953) = £1,029

		£	£
Dr	Financial asset	1,029	
Cr	Finance income		1,029

Similar accounting occurs in year 3

14.5.6 Subsequent measurement of financial instruments

The subsequent measurement of financial assets and liabilities is in accordance with the classification rules specified in Figure 14.2 and section 14.5.2 respectively.

14.5.7 Amortised cost

Many financial assets and liabilities are subsequently measured at amortised cost. The amortised cost of a financial asset is shown in Figure 14.3 and uses the effective interest method.

The effective interest method spreads the financing element of the financial asset over the period to maturity, and is recognised as finance income in the statement of profit or loss. The financing element is the difference between the initial amount recognised for the asset and the amount receivable at maturity. It is calculated using the effective interest rate, which is the rate that exactly discounts estimated future cash payments or receipts over the expected life of the asset to the net carrying amount of the financial asset.

The amortised cost of a financial liability is calculated in a similar manner as shown in Figure 14.4.

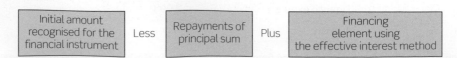

Figure 14.3 Amortised cost of a financial asset

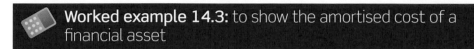

Figure 14.4 Amortised cost of a financial liability

Worked example 14.3: to show the amortised cost of a financial asset

Westwood plc acquires a zero coupon bond with a nominal value of £100,000 on 1 January 20X3 for £94,500. Broker's fees of £1,500 were incurred in relation to the purchase. The bond is quoted in an active market, and is redeemable on 31 December 20X4 at a premium of 10%. The effective rate of interest on the bond is 7.04%.

Required:

Assuming that this financial asset is classified as measured at amortised cost, show the amounts to be included in the financial statements of Westwood plc for the years 20X3 and 20X4.

Year	Carrying amount at start of year	Interest	Carrying amount at end of year
	£	£	£
20X3	96,000	6,758	102,758
20X4	102,758	7,242	110,000

Notes

1. The initial carrying amount includes the broker's fees of £1,500
2. The interest (referred to as amortisation) is calculated by applying the effective interest rate to the carrying amount at the start of the year
3. Amortisation in 20X4 includes a rounding figure of £8.

Finance income of £6,758 and £7,242 will be included in the statement of profit or loss for 20X3 and 20X4 respectively.

The financial asset will be included at a value of £102,758 in the statement of financial position at 31 December 20X3. It will be redeemed, and therefore derecognised, on 31 December 20X4.

Worked example 14.4: to show the amortised cost of a financial liability

Driscol plc issued bonds with a nominal value of £500,000 and coupon rate of 4% on 1 January 20X5 for £394,408. The company is required to pay interest annually in arrears, and will redeem the bonds at par on 31 December 20X9. The effective interest rate on the bonds is 9.5%.

Required:

Show the amounts to be included in the financial statements of Driscol plc for each of the years 20X5 through to 20X9.

Year	Carrying amount at start of year	Interest	Repayment	Carrying amount at end of year
	£	£	£	£
20X5	394,408	37,469	(20,000)	411,877
20X6	411,877	39,128	(20,000)	431,005
20X7	431,005	40,945	(20,000)	451,950
20X8	451,950	42,935	(20,000)	474,885
20X9	474,885	45,115	(20,000)	500,000

Notes:

1. The interest is the financing element calculated by applying the effective interest rate of 9.5% to the carrying amount at the start of the year
2. The repayment is the actual interest payments made by Driscol plc of $4\% \times 500,000 = 20,000$
3. The 20X9 interest includes a rounding figure of £1.

The interest figures will be included as a finance expense in the statements of profit or loss for the respective years.

The financial liability will be included at the year-end carrying amounts in the respective statements of financial position. It will be redeemed, and therefore derecognised, on 31 December 20X9.

14.5.8 Subsequent measurement at fair value

Where a financial asset is classified as measured at fair value, this has to be established at each period end, and IFRS 13 *Fair Value Measurement* applies—see section 14.5.5.

In practice, for some unquoted equity instruments, it can be very difficult, or even impossible, to obtain sufficient information to obtain the fair value without making such extreme subjective judgements that the measurement may be considered not decision-useful. Preparers of financial statements have also indicated that in some cases the cost of gathering information and estimating the fair values could exceed the benefits.

IFRS 9 indicates that in limited circumstances the initial cost of the investment in the equity instrument may be the best estimate of fair value. Generally, though, this will not apply if there are significant changes in the financial affairs of the investee company which would cause the fair value to diverge from the cost.

As indicated in the notes to Figure 14.2, the changes in fair value are recognised either in profit or loss or in other comprehensive income, dependent upon the classification at recognition.

Worked example 14.5: to show the subsequent measurement and accounting for a financial asset

In April 20X2 Cryfield plc purchased 50,000 £1 listed equity shares at a price of £3.50 per share. Transaction costs were £2,500. At 31 December 20X2 these shares were trading at £4.20 per share. A dividend of 6 pence per share was received on 30 September 20X2.

Required:

Show the figures relating to this investment to be included in Cryfield plc's financial statements at 31 December 20X2 on the basis that:

(a) the shares were bought for trading

(b) the shares were bought as a source of dividend income and at their acquisition an irrevocable election was made to recognise them at fair value through other comprehensive income.

(a) Equity instruments held for trading are classified as measured at fair value through profit and loss (see Figure 14.2). Transaction costs on financial instruments so classified are expensed through profit and loss.

Statement of profit or loss		£
Investment income	(change in fair value 50,000 × (4.20 − 3.50))	35,000
Investment income	(dividend received of 50,000 × 0.06)	3,000
Transaction costs		(2,500)
Statement of financial position		
Investments in equity instruments	(50,000 × 4.20)	210,000

(b) Given that Cryfield plc has made an election to recognise the equity instrument at fair value through other comprehensive income, the transaction costs are included in the initial measurement of the asset.

Statement of profit or loss		£
Investment income	(dividend received of 50,000 × 0.06)	3,000
Statement of other comprehensive income		
Gain on investment in equity instruments (change in fair value)	50,000 × 4.20 − ((50,000 × 3.50) + 2,500))	32,500
Statement of financial position		
Investments in equity instruments	(50,000 × 4.20)	210,000

14.6 Impairment of financial assets

IAS 39 used an 'incurred loss' model for the impairment of financial assets. This delayed the recognition of credit losses until there was evidence of a trigger event, which in practice often meant the actual default. It was designed to limit entities' ability to create hidden reserves which could be reversed during less profitable times. However, during the financial crisis of 2008, this delayed recognition of credit losses on loans and other financial instruments was identified as a weakness in the accounting standard as it enabled companies to postpone recognition of losses. In addition, IAS 39, which used multiple impairment models for different financial instruments, was also identified as too complex.

IFRS 9 has addressed these concerns, and it includes one impairment model which applies to all financial assets—those classified as measured at amortised cost and fair value, lease receivables, trade receivables and any commitments to lend money and provide financial guarantees. It is based on providing for 'expected losses'. This means that entities are required to recognise expected credit losses at all times and to update these amounts at each reporting date to reflect changes in the credit risk of financial instruments. The model is forward-looking and eliminates the threshold trigger event to have occurred before credit losses are recognised. In addition, the new model is accompanied by improved disclosures about expected credit losses and credit risk. The financial statements should reflect the general pattern of deterioration or improvement in the credit quality of its financial assets, and thus provide users with more useful information.

14.6.1 Three-stage approach to the impairment model

The IFRS 9 impairment model requires assessment of the credit risk of all financial assets, with the accounting required moving across three stages to reflect any increase in risk, as shown in the following table.

On initial recognition of any financial asset, a credit loss allowance/provision will be accounted for which is equivalent to a 12-month expected credit loss:

Debit   Impairment loss—this is recognised in profit or loss
  Credit   Credit loss allowance

If the credit risk increases, this allowance will be replaced by lifetime expected credit losses and therefore increase. If the credit quality improves, the allowance may revert to the 12-month expected credit loss.

Twelve-month expected credit losses are calculated by weighting the lifetime expected credit losses by the probability of a default event occurring within the next 12 months. This is neither the same as the expected cash shortfalls, nor the same as the credit losses on financial assets which are forecast to actually default in the next 12 months.

	Stage 1	Stage 2	Stage 3
Credit quality	Credit quality has not significantly deteriorated since initial recognition	Credit quality has significantly deteriorated since initial recognition	Credit-impaired
Credit loss allowance	12-month expected credit loss	Lifetime expected credit loss	Lifetime expected credit loss
Interest revenue	Calculated on the gross carrying amount (i.e. without adjustment for expected credit losses)	Calculated on the gross carrying amount (i.e. without adjustment for expected credit losses)	Calculated on the gross carrying amount adjusted for the loss allowance

Lifetime expected credit losses are an expected present value measure of losses that will arise if a borrower defaults on their obligation throughout the life of the financial instrument, in other words the present value of all expected cash shortfalls. Because this considers the time value of cash flows, a credit loss will arise even if the entity expected to be paid in full but later than when contractually due.

Clearly lifetime expected credit losses are a subjective estimate. IFRS 9 does not prescribe particular measurement methods to calculate these, and specifies that the expected credit losses should represent neither a best nor worst-case scenario, and may be a probability-weighted outcome. It states that companies should consider reasonable and supportable information that is available without undue cost or effort. Although the model is forward-looking, historical information is an important base for future predictions, so details of past events, current conditions and forecasts of future conditions should be considered. For example, rather than estimating specific cash flow shortfalls for a particular financial asset, a better estimate may be obtained by considering information such as historical loss rates adjusted for current and forecast conditions for a portfolio of similar assets.

 Example of full lifetime and 12-month expected credit losses

A company sells goods to a customer on 1 September 20X1 with three payments of £10,000 due at annual intervals for the next three years commencing on 1 September 20X2. According to IFRS 15 Revenue from Contracts with Customers, the initial receivable and sale revenue recognised is at a discounted cash flow amount using a market rate of interest that reflects the risks of the customer. Assuming this is 9%, the receivable (the financial asset) would be initially recorded at:

$$10,000/1.09 + 10,000/1.09^2 + 10,000/1.09^3 = £25,313$$

In order to estimate the lifetime expected credit loss, the company would consider previous sales where consideration was received in annual instalments, together with information about the credit-worthiness of this particular customer, for example its financial state of affairs, whether it has cash flow issues, etc.

The lifetime expected credit loss would not be the full £25,313, nor any particular cash flow amount, but probably some proportion of £25,313 using a probability-weight based on previous experiences. Assume this is estimated at £6,500.

On initial recognition of the receivable, the company would also have to consider the probability of a default occurring within the next 12 months, as IFRS 9 requires an allowance for the 12-month credit loss to be accounted for at this point. Assume this is estimated at 20%.

On initial recognition of the receivables, the company would create an allowance for credit losses of $20\% \times 6,500 = £1,300$ which would be offset against the receivable of £25,313.

If it was considered that the credit risk had increased significantly, the allowance for credit losses would be increased to the lifetime figure of £6,500.

Note that for trade receivables which do not have a significant IFRS 15 financing component, IFRS 9 allows a simplified approach to the loss allowance on initial recognition. It is measured at the lifetime expected credit loss. In other words, the additional step of determining the probability of a default in the next 12 months does not have to be considered.

For other trade receivables and lease receivables, a company can choose to apply the three-stage approach (as in the example above) or to recognise an allowance for lifetime expected credit losses from initial recognition. This is an accounting policy choice.

14.6.2 Assessing significant increases in credit risk

When credit is first extended the initial creditworthiness of the borrower and initial expectations of credit losses are usually taken into account in determining acceptable pricing and other terms and conditions. A true economic loss arises when expected credit losses exceed initial expectations, in other words when the exposure to credit risk increases. So recognising lifetime expected credit losses after a significant increase in credit risk better reflects this economic loss in the financial statements.

IFRS 9 does not set a specific probability of default to make the assessment of whether there has been a significant increase in credit risk, and entities may apply various approaches. The guidance in IFRS 9 specifies that entities should consider reasonable and supportable information that is available without undue cost or effort. Credit risk analysis takes into account many factors such as the type of product, characteristics of the financial instrument and the borrower.

The assessment of significant increases in credit risk may be done on a collective basis, for example, on a group or sub-group of financial instruments. This is to ensure that lifetime expected credit losses are recognised even if evidence of the increase in credit risk is not yet available on an individual level. Typically, credit risk increases significantly before contractual payments on a financial instrument become overdue, or modifications or restructurings are required. However, it may not always be possible to identify these increases in credit risk for individual financial instruments. Grouping financial instruments with some similar characteristics may enable an entity to identify information relating to changes in credit risk on a timely basis. For example, identifying geographical regions that have been adversely affected by changing economic conditions.

Note that there is a rebuttable assumption that the credit risk on a financial asset has increased significantly since initial recognition when contractual payments are more than 30 days past due.

Some financial instruments may be determined to have a low credit risk at the reporting date. If this is the case, the company may assume that the credit risk of the financial instrument has not increased significantly since initial recognition. An example of a low credit risk instrument is one that has an investment grade rating.

 Example of assessment of significant increases in credit risk

A company has a portfolio of home loans which originate in a particular country. Twelve-month expected credit losses are recognised for all the loans on initial recognition (stage 1).

At the end of the next reporting period, information emerges that a region in the country is experiencing tough economic conditions. Lifetime expected credit losses are recognised for those loans within that region (stage 2) and 12-month expected credit losses, including any changes in this estimate, continue to be recognised for the other loans (stage 1).

By the end of the next reporting period, more information has emerged and the entity is able to identify the particular loans that have defaulted or are about to default. Lifetime expected credit losses continue to be recognised on these loans, and interest revenue switches to a net interest basis (stage 3).

14.7 Disclosures

14.7.1 Necessity for disclosures

IFRS 7 *Financial Instruments: Disclosures* is the applicable standard which sets out the disclosure requirements for financial instruments. These are extensive. The use of financial instruments by entities is widespread and the risks associated with such instruments can be particularly significant. Over the last 10 to 15 years the techniques used by entities for measuring and managing exposure to risks arising from financial instruments have evolved and new risk management concepts and approaches have gained acceptance. Following the IASB's fundamental review of what information should be disclosed for users, IFRS 7 was issued in 2005 because it was felt that the disclosure requirements in the existing standards needed to be improved. Various amendments to IFRS 7 have been issued subsequently. The standard is based on the principle that users need transparent information concerning an entity's exposure to risk and how the entity manages that risk when assessing an entity's financial position and performance or of the amount, timing and uncertainty of its future cash flows.

IFRS 7 applies to all financial instruments, except those covered by other financial reporting standards, namely:

(a) Interests in subsidiaries, associates and joint ventures

(b) Employers' rights and obligations arising from employee benefit plans

(c) Insurance contracts

(d) Financial instruments under share-based payment transactions.

The IFRS applies to all entities, including entities that have few financial instruments (for example, a manufacturer whose only financial instruments are accounts receivable and accounts payable) and those that have many financial instruments (for example, a financial institution most of whose assets and liabilities are financial instruments). The extent of disclosure required depends on the extent of the entity's use of financial instruments and of its exposure to risk.

The standard applies to both recognised and unrecognised financial instruments. Although IFRS 9 and its predecessor, IAS 39, aim to ensure that all financial instruments, including derivatives, are recognised in the financial statements in accordance with their provisions, there may be some financial instruments, for example, some loan commitments, which fall outside their scope.

14.7.2 Objectives of IFRS 7

IFRS 7 has two main objectives which are to enable users to evaluate:

(a) the significance of financial instruments for the entity's financial position and performance; and

(b) the nature and extent of risks arising from financial instruments to which the entity is exposed during the period and at the end of the reporting period, and how the entity manages those risks.

(IFRS 7, para. 1)

The disclosures provide both qualitative and quantitative information about the entity's use of financial instruments and exposure to risks, including minimum disclosures about credit risk, liquidity risk and market risk.

The main disclosures are detailed below.

14.7.3 Statement of financial position

The carrying amounts of each of the following categories of financial categories, as defined in IFRS 9, must be disclosed in the statement of financial position or in the notes:

(a) financial assets measured at fair value through profit or loss, showing separately:

(i) those designated as such upon initial recognition, and

(ii) those mandatorily measured at fair value through profit or loss in accordance with IFRS 9

(b)   financial liabilities at fair value through profit or loss, showing separately:

    (i)   those designated as such upon initial recognition, and

    (ii)   those that meet the definition of held for trading in IFRS 9

(c)   financial assets measured at amortised cost

(d)   financial liabilities measured at amortised cost

(e)   financial assets measured at fair value through other comprehensive income, showing separately:

    (i)   those measured at fair value through other comprehensive income in accordance with IFRS 9, and

    (ii)   investments in equity instruments designated as such upon initial recognition.

(IASB, IFRS 7, para. 8)

Financial reporting in practice 14.2 — International Airlines Group, 2014

International Airlines Group's 2014 detailed financial instruments disclosure note includes the following summary of its financial assets and liabilities by category. Note that this company applies IAS 39 in its 2014 financial statements, hence some of the categories of financial instrument included, for example, available-for-sale financial assets, are different to those now specified in IFRS 9.

Note 27 Financial instruments

a Financial assets and liabilities by category

The detail of the Group's financial instruments at December 31, 2014 by nature and classification for measurement purposes is as follows:

€ million	Loans and receivables	Derivatives used for hedging	Available for sale	Non-financial assets	Total carrying amount
Non-current assets					
Available-for-sale financial assets	–	–	84	–	84
Derivative financial instruments	–	80	–	–	80
Other non-current assets	167	–	–	21	188
Current assets					
Trade receivables	1,252	–	–	–	1,252
Other current assets	244	–	–	367	611
Non-current assets held for sale	–	–	11	7	18

(continued)

(continued)

Derivative financial instruments	–	178	–	–	178
Other current interest-bearing deposits	3,416	–	–	–	3,416
Cash and cash equivalents	1,528	–	–	–	1,528

	Loans and Payables	Financial liabilities Derivatives used for hedging	Non-financial liabilities	Total carrying amount
Non-current liabilities				
Interest-bearing long-term borrowings	5,904	–	–	5,904
Derivative financial instruments	–	359	–	359
Other long-term liabilities	7	–	219	226
Current liabilities				
Current portion of long-term borrowings	713	–	–	713
Trade and other payables	3,017	–	264	3,281
Deferred revenue on ticket sales	–	–	3,933	3,933
Derivative financial instruments	–	1,313	–	1,313

If an entity has designated a financial asset or a group of financial assets, at fair value through profit or loss on initial recognition, it should disclose:

(a) the maximum exposure to credit risk of the financial asset (or group of financial assets) at the end of the reporting period

(b) the amount by which any related credit derivatives or similar instruments mitigate that maximum exposure to credit risk

(c) the amount of change, during the period and cumulatively, in the fair value of the financial asset (or group of financial assets) that is attributable to changes in the credit risk of the financial asset

(d) the amount of the change in the fair value of any related credit derivatives or similar instruments that has occurred during the period and cumulatively since the financial asset was designated.

(IASB, IFRS 7, para. 9)

If an entity has designated a financial liability as at fair value through profit or loss, it should disclose:

(a) the amount of change, during the period and cumulatively, in the fair value of the financial liability that is attributable to changes in the credit risk of that liability

(b) the difference between the financial liability's carrying amount and the amount the entity would be contractually required to pay at maturity to the holder of the obligation.

(IASB, IFRS 7, para. 10A)

For both financial assets and financial liabilities, the amount of the change in fair value attributable to a change in credit risk can be determined either:

(i) as the amount of change in its fair value that is not attributable to changes in market conditions that give rise to market risk, or

(ii) using an alternative method the entity believes more faithfully represents the amount of change in its fair value that is attributable to changes in the credit risk of the asset.

Changes in market conditions that give rise to market risk include changes in an observed (benchmark) interest rate, commodity price, foreign exchange rate or index of prices or rates.

 Worked example 14.6: to show how the change in the fair value attributable to credit risk can be calculated

On 1 January 20X3, Rootes plc issues a five-year bond with a par value of £100,000 and an annual fixed coupon rate of 7%. The coupon rate reflects the market London Interbank Offered Rate (LIBOR) rate and the credit spread associated with the bond at the time of the issue. At the time of the issue LIBOR was 5%.

Suppose that on 31 December 20X3, the fair value of the bond has decreased to £98,326, as the LIBOR has increased to 5.25%. The yield to maturity for the bond has now risen to 7.50%.

Required:

Calculate the change in the fair value of the bond at 31 December 20X3 attributable to a change in credit risk.

At 1 January 20X3 LIBOR was 5%, hence this implies a credit spread (credit risk) of 2%. The price of the bond will subsequently change either due to change in LIBOR (market risk) or due to a change in the credit spread.

At 31 December 20X3 the credit spread has now increased to 2.25% (7.50% – 5.25%), implying a deterioration in the credit quality of the bond.

The change in the fair value of the bond attributed to credit risk is calculated by subtracting from the total change in the fair value the changes due to market risk (i.e. due to changes in LIBOR).

To calculate the change in the value of the bond due to changes in LIBOR alone, calculate the fair value of the bond, at the new LIBOR of 5.25% assuming that the credit spread has remained at 2%. i.e. Discount the remaining four payments using a discount rate of 7.25%:

$$\frac{7{,}000}{1.0725} + \frac{7{,}000}{1.0725^2} + \frac{7{,}000}{1.0725^3} + \frac{7{,}000+100{,}000}{1.0725^4} = £99{,}158$$

		£
Change in market value	100,000 – 98,326	1,674
Change in market value due to market risk	100,000 – 99,158	(842)
Change in market value due to credit risk		832

If an entity has designated investments in equity instruments to be measured at fair value through other comprehensive income, the following should be disclosed:

(a) which investments in equity instruments have been designated to be measured at fair value through other comprehensive income

(b) the reasons for using this presentation alternative

(c) the fair value of each such investment at the end of the reporting period

(d) dividends recognised during the period, showing separately those related to investments derecognised during the reporting period and those related to investments held at the end of the reporting period

(e) any transfers of the cumulative gain or loss within equity during the period including the reason for such transfers.

(IASB, IFRS 7, para. 11A)

14.7.4 Statement of comprehensive income

The following items of income, expense, gains or losses should be disclosed either in the statement of comprehensive income or in the notes:

(a) net gains or net losses on:

   (i) financial assets or financial liabilities measured at fair value through profit or loss, showing separately those on financial assets or financial liabilities designated as such upon initial recognition, and those on financial assets or financial liabilities that are mandatorily measured at fair value through profit or loss. For financial liabilities designated as at fair value through profit or loss, an entity shall show separately the amount of gain or loss recognised in other comprehensive income and the amount recognised in profit or loss

   (ii) financial liabilities measured at amortised cost

   (iii) financial assets measured at amortised cost

   (iv) investments in equity instruments designated at fair value through other comprehensive income

   (v) financial assets measured at fair value through other comprehensive income, showing separately the amount of gain or loss recognised in other comprehensive income during the period and the amount reclassified upon derecognition from accumulated other comprehensive income to profit or loss for the period

(b) total interest revenue and total interest expense for financial assets that are measured at amortised cost or that are measured at fair value through other comprehensive income (showing these amounts separately); or financial liabilities that are not measured at fair value through profit or loss

(c) fee income and expense arising from:

   (i) financial assets and financial liabilities that are not at fair value through profit or loss, and

(ii) trust and other fiduciary activities that result in the holding or investing of assets on behalf of individuals, trusts, retirement benefit plans, and other institutions.

(IASB, IFRS 7, para. 20)

14.7.5 Accounting policies and fair value disclosures

An entity's accounting policies relating to financial instruments will include the measurement bases of the different categories of financial instrument. Other policies which are relevant to an understanding of the financial statements will include derecognition and impairment.

For financial instruments measured at amortised cost, IFRS 7 includes the following general requirements:

(a) For each class of financial assets and financial liabilities an entity should disclose the fair value of that class of assets and liabilities in a way that permits it to be compared with its carrying amount.

(b) In disclosing fair values, an entity should group financial assets and financial liabilities into classes (in other words, into groups of financial instrument that exhibit similar characteristics).

It also states that disclosure of fair value is not required:

● where the carrying amount is a reasonable approximation of fair value

● for investments in equity instruments that do not have a quoted market price in an active market for an identical instrument, or derivatives linked to such equity instruments.

IFRS 13 *Fair Value Measurement* provides disclosure requirements in respect of the fair value of financial instruments measured at fair values. It requires that information is disclosed to help users assess:

(a) for assets and liabilities measured at fair value after initial recognition, the valuation techniques and inputs used to develop those measurements

(b) for recurring fair value measurements (i.e. those measured at each period end) using significant unobservable (Level 3) inputs, the effect of the measurements on profit or loss or other comprehensive income for the period.

In order to achieve this, the following should be disclosed as a minimum for each class of financial assets and liabilities measured at fair value:

(a) The fair value measurement at the end of the period

(b) The level of the fair value hierarchy within which the fair value measurements are categorised in their entirety

(c) For assets and liabilities measured at fair value at each reporting date, the amounts of any transfers between Level 1 and Level 2 of the fair value hierarchy and reasons for the transfers

(d) For fair value measurements categorised within Levels 2 and 3 of the hierarchy, a description of the valuation techniques and inputs used in the fair value measurement, plus details of any changes in valuation techniques

(e) For recurring fair value measurements categorised within Level 3 of the fair value hierarchy:

(i)   A reconciliation from the opening to closing balances

(ii) The amount of unrealised gains or losses recognised in profit or loss in the period and the line item in which they are recognised

(iii) A narrative description of the sensitivity of the fair value measurement to changes in unobservable inputs

(f) For recurring and non-recurring fair value measurements categorised within Level 3 of the fair value hierarchy, a description of the valuation processes used by the entity.

An entity should also disclose its policy for determining when transfers between levels of the fair value hierarchy are deemed to have occurred.

Financial reporting in practice 14.3 | J Sainsbury plc, 2015

The following extract from the note on financial instruments from Sainsbury's 2015 financial statements shows the disclosures relating to financial instruments which are measured at fair value. Note Sainsbury applies IAS 39, so the classifications of the financial instruments are not the same as IFRS 9.

Note 29 Financial instruments

Fair value measurements recognised in the balance sheet

The following table provides an analysis of financial instruments that are recognised at fair value, grouped into Levels 1 to 3 based on the degree to which the fair value is observable:

- Level 1 fair value measurements are derived from quoted market prices (unadjusted) in active markets for identical assets or liabilities at the balance sheet date. This level includes listed equity securities and debt instrument on public exchanges;

- Level 2 fair value measurements are derived from inputs other than quoted prices included within Level 1 that are observable for the asset or liability, either directly (i.e. as prices) or indirectly (i.e. derived from prices). The fair value of financial instruments is determined by discounting expected cash flows at prevailing interest rates; and

- Level 3 fair value measurements are derived from valuation techniques that include inputs for the asset or liability that are not based on observable market data (unobservable inputs)

	Level 1 £m	Level 2 £m	Level 3 £m	Total £m
At 14 March 2015				
Available-for-sale financial assets				
Interest bearing financial assets	-	37	-	37
Other financial assets	-	-	145	145
Financial assets at fair value through profit or loss				
Derivative financial assets	-	90	-	90
Financial liabilities at fair value through profit or loss				
Derivative financial liabilities	-	(99)	(14)	(113)

Reconciliation of Level 3 fair value measurements of financial assets and liabilities:

52 weeks to 14 March 2015	Available-for-sale financial assets £m	Commodity derivatives £m	Total £m
At 16 March 2014	184	3	187
In finance cost in the Group income statement	-	(17)	(17)
In other comprehensive income	(39)	-	(39)
At 14 March 2015	145	(14)	131

14.7.6 Financial instruments risk disclosures

There are numerous risks associated with transactions in financial instruments. The disclosures relating to risks are designed to show the extent to which an entity is exposed to these different types of risk, and are both qualitative and quantitative.

The definitions of the various types of risk are given in Table 14.1:

The qualitative disclosures for each type of risk arising from financial instruments require details of:

(a) the exposures to risk and how they arise

(b) the entity's objectives, policies and processes for managing the risk and the methods used to measure the risk

(c) any changes in (a) or (b) from the previous period.

Table 14.1 Types of risk associated with financial instruments

Credit risk	The risk that one party to a financial instrument will cause a financial loss for the other party by failing to discharge an obligation.
Currency risk	The risk that the fair value or future cash flows of a financial instrument will fluctuate because of changes in foreign exchange rates.
Interest rate risk	The risk that the fair value or future cash flows of a financial instrument will fluctuate because of changes in market interest rates.
Liquidity risk	The risk that an entity will encounter difficulty in meeting obligations associated with financial liabilities that are settled by delivering cash or another financial asset.
Market risk	The risk that the fair value or future cash flows of a financial instrument will fluctuate because of changes in market prices. Market risk comprises three types of risk: currency risk, interest rate risk and other price risk
Other price risk	The risk that the fair value or future cash flows of a financial instrument will fluctuate because of changes in market prices (other than those arising from interest rate risk or currency risk), whether those changes are caused by factors specific to the individual financial instrument or its issuer or by factors affecting all similar financial instruments traded in the market.

The quantitative risk disclosures specified in IFRS 7 concentrate on credit risk, liquidity risk and market risk; however, disclosures about all financial instrument related risks should be provided. This should be based on the information provided internally to key management personnel.

The disclosures relating to credit risk, which relate to impairment, are particularly extensive and were extended when that part of IFRS 9 dealing with expected credit losses was completed. They are to enable users of financial statements to understand the effect of credit risk on the amount, timing and uncertainty of future cash flows. To achieve this objective, credit risk disclosures shall provide:

(a) information about an entity's credit risk management practices and how they relate to the recognition and measurement of expected credit losses, including the methods, assumptions and information used to measure expected credit losses

(b) quantitative and qualitative information that allows users of financial statements to evaluate the amounts in the financial statements arising from expected credit losses, including changes in the amount of expected credit losses and the reasons for those changes

(c) information about an entity's credit risk exposure (i.e. the credit risk inherent in an entity's financial assets and commitments to extend credit) including significant credit risk concentrations.

(IASB, IFRS 7, para. 35B)

For liquidity risk the following disclosures are required:

(a) A maturity analysis of financial liabilities

(b) A description of the way risk is managed.

For market risk, the disclosures require a sensitivity analysis showing the effects on profit or loss of changes in each market risk. If the sensitivity analysis reflects interdependencies between risk variables, such as interest rates and exchange rates, the method, assumptions and limitations must be detailed.

Financial reporting in practice **14.4**	Next plc, 2015

Next plc provides the following disclosures of the risks associated with its financial instruments.

Note 27. Financial instruments: risk management and hedging activities

NEXT operates a centralised treasury function which is responsible for managing the liquidity, interest and foreign currency risks associated with the Group's activities. As part of its strategy for the management of these risks, the Group uses derivative financial instruments. In accordance with the Group's treasury policy, derivative instruments are not entered into for speculative purposes. Treasury policy is reviewed and approved by the Board and specifies the parameters within which treasury operations must be conducted, including authorised counterparties, instrument types and transaction limits, and principles governing the management of liquidity, interest and foreign currency risks.

The Group's principal financial instruments, other than derivatives, are cash and short term deposits, bank overdrafts and loans, and corporate bonds. The main purpose of these financial instruments is to raise finance for the Group's operations. In addition, the Group has various other financial assets and liabilities such as trade receivables and trade payables arising directly from its operations.

Liquidity risk

The Group manages its cash and borrowing requirements centrally to minimise net interest expense within risk parameters agreed by the Board, whilst ensuring that the Group has sufficient liquid resources to meet the operating needs of its businesses. The forecast cash and borrowings profile of the Group is monitored to ensure that adequate headroom remains under committed borrowing facilities.

Interest rate risk

The Group is exposed to fair value interest rate risk on its fixed rate corporate bonds and cash flow interest rate risk on floating rate bank loans and overdrafts. The forecast cash and borrowings profile of the Group is monitored regularly to assess the mix of fixed and variable rate debt, and the Group uses interest rate derivatives where appropriate to reduce its exposure to changes in interest rates and the economic environment.

Interest rates: fair value hedges

The Group has interest rate swap agreements in place as fair value hedges of part of the interest rate risk associated with the Company's corporate bonds. Under the terms of the swaps, which have the

(continued)

(continued)

same key features as the bonds, the Group receives a fixed rate of interest equivalent to the relevant coupon rate, and pays a variable rate. Details of the effective rates payable are given in Note 20.

Foreign currency risk

The Group's principal foreign currency exposures arise from the purchase of overseas sourced products. Group policy allows for these exposures to be hedged for up to 24 months ahead in order to fix the cost in Sterling. This hedging activity involves, inter alia, the use of spot, forward and option contracts.

The market value of outstanding foreign exchange contracts is reported regularly at Board level, and reviewed in conjunction with percentage cover taken by season and current market conditions in order to assess and manage the Group's ongoing exposure.

The Group does not have a material exposure to currency movements in relation to translation of overseas investments and consequently does not hedge any such exposure. The Group's net exposure to foreign currencies, taking hedging activities into account is illustrated by the sensitivity analysis in Note 30.

Credit risk

Investments of cash surpluses, borrowings and derivative instruments are made through banks and companies which must fulfil credit rating and investment criteria approved by the Board. Concentrations of risk are mitigated by the use of various counterparties at any one time. All customers who wish to trade on credit terms are subject to credit verification procedures. Receivable balances are monitored on an ongoing basis and provision is made for estimated irrecoverable amounts. The concentration of credit risk is limited due to the Directory customer base being large and diverse. The Group's outstanding receivables balances are detailed in Note 14.

Capital risk

The capital structure of the Group consists of debt, as analysed in Note 31, and equity attributable to the equity holders of the parent company, comprising issued capital, reserves and retained earnings as shown in the Consolidated Statement of Changes in Equity. The Group manages its capital with the objective that all entities within the Group continue as going concerns while maintaining an efficient structure to minimise the cost of capital. The Group is not restricted by any externally imposed capital requirements.

As part of its strategy for delivering sustainable long term growth in earnings per share, the Group has been returning capital to shareholders by way of share buybacks in addition to dividends (including special dividends). Share buybacks are transacted through both on-market purchases and contingent contracts for off-market share purchases.

14.8 Evaluation of IFRS 9

IFRS 9 is required to be adopted for accounting periods beginning on or after 1 January 2018, and so the full effects of its application in practice are yet to be seen. Various interested parties such as the European Central Bank and European Banking Authority have indicated that they regard the new standard positively.

Many of the changes included are principally directed at banks as a result of the deficiencies in financial reporting of financial instruments exposed during the financial crisis. According to Hans Hoogervorst, the Chairman of the IASB, the introduction of the expected loss model for credit losses is the most important element of change in IFRS 9. He considers that this new model is an improvement as it will lead to a more timely recognition of inevitable losses and will make it much more difficult for the banks to hide problem loans on their statement of financial position. It is inevitable that the model will result in earlier recognition of credit losses; however, he does not perceive that the requirements will result in banks having to account for large up-front losses when no losses have actually occurred—a fear that would discourage banks from making longer-term loans. Many commentators, though, expect banks' loan loss provisions in their financial statements to increase by around 50% on average. This will vary depending on the type of loan, with long-term lending such as mortgage portfolios expected to have higher increases in related provisions. Higher risk lending, including lending to SMEs, may also see larger increases. Some banks will therefore be affected more than others.

IFRS 9 will also reduce banks' regulatory capital which is already under pressure and great scrutiny. The users of financial statements will want to know whether banks will need to raise additional capital and about their continued ability to pay dividends.

The credit loss model will require significantly more judgement and assumptions as it relies on more forward-looking information. In part to address this, significantly more disclosures are required, and these will contribute to the length and complexities of financial reports. For preparers, costs of implementing the new model are expected to be significant as different information will be required to be gathered to make the required estimates.

Hoogervorst, however, considers that the implementation of IFRS 9 will contribute to economic growth, because banks will be forced to clean up their bad loans sooner. This should allow credit to flow to healthier companies with growth opportunities. Ultimately IFRS 9 may contribute to a safer, more resilient financial system—one which is demanded by all.

 ## Summary of key points

Financial instruments range from straightforward items such as receivables and payables and variable rate bank loans, through to various forms of complex derivative instruments. The issues arising from their accounting derive from their complexities. In 2001 the IASB inherited mainly rules-based financial reporting standards relating to financial instruments, and have spent 10 to 15 years amending these to be more principles-based. The 2008 financial crisis exacerbated the need for the accounting and disclosures, particularly relating to associated risks, to be improved.

The principle of substance over form leads to financial instruments, which according to their legal form are equity instruments, being accounted for according to their economic substance as debt instruments. This also results in financial instruments, which exhibit both equity and debt characteristics, having to be split, with each element accounted for separately. The accounting for the associated dividends follows this treatment.

IFRS 9 is the financial reporting standard which deals with the bulk of the accounting issues to do with financial instruments. The recognition of a financial instrument is required when there is a contractual right or obligation. Derecognition is only permitted when all risks and rewards of owner-ship and control have been transferred. The determination of this for some complex financial instru-ment transactions may not be straightforward; therefore careful judgement has to be exercised.

Measurement of financial instruments is the main area which was changed by IFRS 9. All financial instruments are initially measured at fair value of consideration given. Their subsequent measurement depends on their classification on initial recognition. The classification is determined by assessing firstly the business model for managing financial instruments, followed by the contractual cash flow charac-teristics of the financial instrument. The result is that financial assets are measured at either amortised cost or fair value, but companies may elect to measure those classified as measured at amortised cost as measured at fair value. Changes in fair value pass through either profit or loss or other comprehensive income depending on the contractual cash flows. The default subsequent measurement of financial liabilities is amortised cost, but again an election may be made to measure these at fair value.

Impairment is a major issue for financial assets, and IFRS 9 changed the model for this to one of accounting for expected credit losses. This addresses one of the main concerns which was identified in the financial crisis—when and how banks recognised credit losses. The accounting now follows a three-stage process. A 12-month expected credit loss has to be accounted for on initial recognition of any financial asset. If the credit quality is considered to significantly deteriorate, then the provi-sion for the credit loss increases to a lifetime credit loss. Further deterioration leads to the interest revenue being based on the carrying amount of the asset adjusted for the loss allowance. As with impairment of other assets, significant estimates and judgement are required.

Disclosures relating to financial instruments are extensive. The aims of IFRS 7, which covers the disclosure requirements, are to enable users to evaluate the significance of financial instruments for the entity's financial position and performance, and the nature and extent of risks relating to financial instruments to which the entity is exposed, and how the entity manages those risks. The disclosures are both quantitative and qualitative.

 ## Further reading

IASB (International Accounting Standards Board) (2003a) IAS 32 *Financial Instruments: Presentation*. London: IASB.

IASB (International Accounting Standards Board) (2005) IFRS 7 *Financial Instruments: Disclosures*. London: IASB.

IASB (International Accounting Standards Board) (2014a) IFRS 9 *Financial Instruments*. London: IASB.

IASB (International Accounting Standards Board) (2014b) *IFRS 9 Financial Instruments Project Summary*. London: IASB.

 ## Bibliography

Deloitte, *IAS 32—Financial Instruments: Presentation*. Available from http://www.iasplus.com/en-gb/standards/ias/ias32 (accessed 8 August 2016).

Hoogervorst, H., (2016) *Introductory Comments to the European Parliament*, Speech to the European Parliament, January 2016. Brussels. Available from http://www.ifrs.org/Alerts/Conference/Documents/2015/Hans-Hoogervorst-speech-Jan-2016.pdf (accessed 8 August 2016).

IASB (International Accounting Standards Board) (2003a) IAS 32 *Financial Instruments: Presentation*. London: IASB.

IASB (International Accounting Standards Board) (2003b) IAS 39 *Financial Instruments: Recognition and Measurement*. London: IASB.

IASB (International Accounting Standards Board) (2005) IFRS 7 *Financial Instruments: Disclosures*. London: IASB.

IASB (International Accounting Standards Board) (2014a) IFRS 9 *Financial Instruments*. London: IASB.

IASB (International Accounting Standards Board) (2014b) *IFRS 9 Financial Instruments Project Summary*. London: IASB.

International Airlines Group (2014) *Annual Report and Accounts*. Madrid: IAG.

J Sainsbury plc (2015) *Annual Report and Financial Statements*. London: J Sainsbury.

Next plc (2015) *Annual Report and Accounts*. Leicester: Next.

Patel, K. (2015) Expect the Unexpected, *By All Accounts*, January 2015. London: ICAEW.

Rolls-Royce plc (2016) *Annual Report, 2015*. London: Rolls-Royce.

 ## Questions

● Quick test

1 Identify whether the following financial instruments should be classified as a financial liability or as part of equity explaining the reasons for your choice.

   (a) Redeemable preference shares with a coupon rate of 5%.

   (b) Share options granted to senior executives. The options may be exercised after a period of 3 years.

2 Which of the following should be recognised as a financial instrument under IFRS 9?

   (a) A guarantee to replace or repair goods sold by a business in the normal course of business

   (b) The placing of a purchase order for a specific quantity of raw sugar beet for use in manufacturing

   (c) A forward contract to purchase a raw sugar beet at a specified quantity and price on a specific date

3 On 1 January 20X2 Moran plc issued £500,000 6% convertible redeemable preference shares. Issue costs of £20,000 were incurred and the preference shares are redeemable at par for cash on 31 December 20X6 or are convertible into 100,000 new £1 equity shares at that date. The preference dividend is paid on 31 December each year. The interest rate on similar preference shares without the conversion option is 8%.

   Required:

   Show how the convertible preference shares will be accounted for in the financial statements of Moran plc for the year ended 31 December 20X2.

4 Beresford plc raises finance by issuing zero coupon bonds at par on 1 April 20X4 with a nominal value of £100,000. The bonds will be redeemed after two years at a premium of £14,490. The effective rate of interest is 7%.

   Required:

   Assuming that it is not held for trading, nor designated at fair value through profit or loss on initial recognition, explain and illustrate how the loan is accounted for in the financial statements of Beresford plc.

●● Develop your understanding

5 Squab plc raises finance by issuing £200,000 6% four-year loan notes on 1 January 20X0. The loan notes are issued at a discount of 10%, and will be redeemed after four years at a premium of £10,146. The effective rate of interest is 12%. The issue costs were £10,000.

Required:

Explain and illustrate how the loan is accounted for in the financial statements of Squab plc.

6 On 1 January 20X4 Lysander plc buys £250,000 6% loan stock for £234,825. Interest will be received on 31 December each year, and the stock will be redeemed at par on 31 December 20X8. As with other similar investments, the company intends to hold the stock until maturity and calculates the effective interest rate to be 7.5%.

Required:

Explain and show how this financial instrument will be accounted for in the financial statements of Lysander plc for the years ended 31 December 20X4–20X8.

7 On 1 January 20X1 Dyke plc issued three-year 5% £300,000 loans notes at nominal value when the effective rate of interest is also 5%. The loan notes will be redeemed at par. The liability is classified at fair value through profit or loss. At 31 December 20X1 market interest rates have risen to 6%.

Required:

Explain and illustrate how the loan is accounted for in the financial statements of Dyke plc in the year ended 31 December 20X1.

8 Bishop plc anticipates capital expenditure in a few years. The company invests its excess cash in short- and long-term financial assets so that it can fund the expenditure when the need arises. Many of the financial assets have contractual lives that exceed the entity's anticipated investment period. Bishop's policy is to hold financial assets to collect the contractual cash flows and, when an opportunity arises, to sell assets to re-invest the cash in financial assets with a higher return. The managers responsible for the portfolio are remunerated based on the overall return generated by the portfolio.

Required:

Explain which business model Bishop plc will apply for classifying its financial assets.

9 Tucker plc is a company which holds a few financial assets. It generally holds the assets to generate revenue until their maturity date (if any). The company made the following acquisitions:

(a) On 22 August 20X3 Tucker acquired 500,000 shares in Greswold plc, a listed entity, for £3.50 per share. The costs associated with the purchase were £15,000 and were included in the cost of the investment. The directors plan to realise this investment before the end of 20X3. There has been no further adjustment made to the investment since the date of purchase. The shares were trading at £3.65 each on 30 September 20X3.

(b) On 1 October 20X2 Tucker purchased a bond with a par value of £5 million. The bond carries a 5% coupon, payable annually in arrears, and is redeemable on 30 September 20X7 at £5.8 million. Tucker fully intends to hold this bond until the redemption date. The bond was purchased at a 10% discount. The effective interest rate on the bond is 10.26%. The interest due for the year was received and credited to investment income in the statement of profit or loss.

Required:

Explain how financial instruments (a) and (b) should be classified, initially measured and subsequently measured in the financial statements of Tucker plc. Prepare any journal entries required to correct the accounting treatment for the year to 30 September 20X3.

●●● Take it further

10 Braemar plc issued 8 million 5% five-year convertible £1 bonds on 1 January 20X6. The proceeds of £8 million were credited to non-current liabilities and debited to bank. The 5% interest paid has been charged to finance costs in the year to 31 December 20X6. The market rate of interest for a similar bond with a five-year term but no conversion terms is 7%.

Required:

Explain and demonstrate how this convertible instrument would be initially measured in accordance with IAS 32 *Financial Instruments: Presentation* and subsequently measured in accordance with IFRS 9 *Financial Instruments* in the financial statements for the year ended 31 December 20X6.

11 During the year ended 31 December 20X7, Aslan plc entered into the following transactions:

(a) On 1 July Aslan sold to a third party the right to receive the interest cash flows on a fixed maturity debt instrument it holds and will continue to legally own up to the date of maturity. The debt instrument is quoted in an active stock market. Aslan has no obligation to compensate the third party for any cash flows not received.

(b) On 1 September Aslan acquired 80,000 shares in a stock market quoted company. The shares were purchased at £4.54 per share. The broker charged a commission of 1% on the transaction. Aslan elected to measure the shares at fair value through other comprehensive income. Aslan decided to 'bed and breakfast' the shares on 31 December 20X7 to realise a tax loss, and therefore sold the shares at market price and bought them back on 2 January 20X8, the next day of trading. The market price did not change on 2 January 20X8. The broker charged a 1% commission on both transactions. The quoted share price on 31 December 20X7 was £4.22–£4.26.

Required:

Discuss the accounting treatments of these transactions in Aslan plc's financial statements for the year ended 31 December 20X7 in accordance with IFRS 9 *Financial Instruments*, including calculations as appropriate.

12 Micawber plc, a manufacturer, operates only in one geographical region. The customer base consists of a large number of small clients and the trade receivables are categorised by common risk characteristics that are representative of the customers' abilities to pay all amounts due in accordance with the contractual terms. The trade receivables do not have a significant financing component in accordance with IFRS 15 *Revenue from Contracts with Customers*. In accordance with IFRS 9, the loss allowance for trade receivables is always measured at an amount equal to lifetime time expected credit losses.

To determine the expected credit losses for the portfolio, Micawber uses a provision matrix. The provision matrix is based on its historical observed default rates over the expected life of the trade receivables and is adjusted for forward-looking estimates. At every reporting date the historical observed default rates are updated and changes in the forward-looking estimates are analysed. At 31 December 20X1 trade receivables total £30 million, and it is forecast that economic conditions will deteriorate over the next year.

On this basis, Micawber estimates the following provision matrix:

	Current	1–30 days past due	31–60 days past due	61–90 days past due	More than 90 days past due
Default rate	0.3%	1.6%	3.6%	6.6%	10.6%

The trade receivables at 31 December 20X1 have been aged as follows:

Total	Current	1–30 days past due	31–60 days past due	61–90 days past due	More than 90 days past due
£30m	£15m	£7.5m	£4m	£2.5m	£1m

Required:

Explain and calculate the provision for expected credit losses which would be included in the financial statements of Micawber plc at 31 December 20X1.

13 On 15 December 20X0 Maxime plc purchases a debt instrument at par value of £1,000,000 and elects to measure the instrument at fair value through other comprehensive income. The instrument has an interest rate of 5% over the contractual term of 10 years, and has a 5% effective interest rate. At initial recognition the entity determines that the asset is not purchased or originated credit-impaired.

On Maxime's year end of 31 December 20X0, the fair value of the debt instrument has decreased to £950,000 as a result of changes in market interest rates. The company determines that there has not been a significant increase in credit risk since initial recognition and that expected credit losses should be measured at an amount equal to 12-month expected credit losses, which amounts to £30,000.

On 1 January 20X1, Maxime decides to sell the debt instrument for £950,000, which is its fair value at that date.

Required:

Show and explain the accounting entries at 15 December 20X0, 31 December 20X0 and 1 January 20X1.

 Visit the Online Resource Centre for solutions to all these end of chapter questions plus visual walkthrough solutions. You can test your understanding with extra questions and answers, explore additional case studies based on real companies, take a guided tour through a company report and much more. Go to the Online Resource Centre at **www.oxfordtextbooks.co.uk/orc/maynard2e/**

15

Leases

The exclusion of certain long-term liabilities from a company's statement of financial position, commonly called off balance sheet financing, has been a continuing issue for companies, the users of their financial statements and accounting standard-setters for a number of decades. Over the years companies have sought to structure transactions involving debt to ensure that their accounting treatment was in line with current accounting practice, but in a way to enable the debt to be kept off the statement of financial position. To counter this, accounting standard-setters have issued and revised various standards to ensure that financial statements faithfully reflect the commercial substance of all financial transactions and items.

One of the major areas that has given rise to off balance sheet financing is leasing, whereby companies acquire the use of non-current assets for a period of time in return for a series of payments. Prior to the issue of financial reporting standards on leases, companies argued that because they did not own the assets neither the assets nor the obligations for the payments appeared on their statements of financial position. International Accounting Standard (IAS) 17 *Leases* partially addressed this by requiring leases to be classified as either finance or operating. If an asset was acquired under a finance lease, the asset should be recognised on the statement of financial position together with the related obligation for the payments. Operating leases remained 'off balance sheet' and payments under the lease agreement were accounted for like rental expenses.

The IASB has been working for many years on a new financial reporting standard to bring all leases onto the statements of financial position of companies and thus enable users to have a complete and understandable picture of a company's leasing activities. It finally issued IFRS 16 *Leases* in early 2016, with implementation required from 1 January 2019. The single lessee accounting model takes a right-of-use approach to the recognition of the leased asset and requires recognition of a liability representing the companies' obligation to make lease payments.

Because of the length of time before companies are required to report under IFRS 16, this chapter considers both leasing standards, IAS 17 and IFRS 16. It explains and discusses the accounting methods for both lessees and lessors.

★ Learning objectives

After studying this chapter you will be able to:

- understand what off balance sheet financing is and its implications for financial reporting
- explain the distinction between **finance and operating leases**, and be able to demonstrate the accounting methods for the two different types of lease for both lessees and lessors in accordance with IAS 17
- understand what a lease agreement is and the single **right-of-use asset** model under IFRS 16, and be able to demonstrate the accounting for leases for both lessees and lessors in accordance with this standard
- explain what a sale and leaseback transaction is, and its accounting treatment under both IAS 17 and IFRS 16

✔ Key issues checklist

- ❏ What is off balance sheet financing and its effect on financial statements.
- ❏ What is a lease.
- ❏ The approach to accounting for leases as given in IAS 17:
  - ❏ The distinction between finance leases and operating leases.
  - ❏ Significant lease terminology definitions—lease term, the inception and commencement of a lease, **minimum lease payments**, **guaranteed and unguaranteed residuals**, discount rates.
  - ❏ Accounting for a finance lease for a lessee.
  - ❏ Accounting for an operating lease for a lessee.
  - ❏ Disclosures in the financial statements of lessees.
  - ❏ Accounting for a finance lease for a lessor.
  - ❏ Accounting for an operating lease for a lessor.
  - ❏ Disclosures in the financial statements of lessors.
  - ❏ Sale and leaseback transactions where the lease is a finance lease or an operating lease.
- ❏ The problems IAS 17 left unresolved.
- ❏ The reasons for and principles behind IFRS 16.
  - ❏ Identification of a lease.
  - ❏ The lease term.
  - ❏ Exceptions to the lease accounting model.
  - ❏ The single accounting model for lessees.
  - ❏ Initial and subsequent measurement of the lease liability and right-of-use asset.
  - ❏ **Reassessments**.
  - ❏ **Modifications**.

❑ Disclosures for the lessee.

❑ Accounting for leases by the lessor.

❑ Sale and leaseback transactions.

❑ The impact on the financial statements of a lessee under IFRS 16.

15.1 Off balance sheet financing

15.1.1 Why is off balance sheet financing an issue?

Off balance sheet financing refers to situations where some, or all, of a business's debt obligations are not recognised on its statement of financial position. If a company has obligations which are not recognised, then its financial statements cannot be said to be faithfully representative, are misleading and, at worst, fraudulent. The statement of financial position is used by users to evaluate the financial health of a business. A company with lower levels of debt may look more attractive to potential investors than one with high debt. As discussed in Chapter 5, debt balances are included in key financial ratios, such as return on capital employed and gearing. If debt can be excluded from the statement of financial position these ratios will appear improved.

❗ **Reminder** *Return on capital employed (ROCE) is a key measure of return to investors. Gearing measures the balance of debt and equity financing and is an indicator of risk for an equity investor.*

 Example of the effect of off balance sheet finance on accounting ratios

Assume a company's summarised statements of financial position including and excluding £1,500 of long-term debt are as follows. From the rules of double-entry if the debt (a credit balance) is not recognised, then a debit balance (which could be an asset or a loss) is also not recognised. Assume, in this case, a corresponding asset is also excluded.

	Including debt £	*Excluding debt* £
Non-current assets	4,000	2,500
Current assets	2,500	2,500
	6,500	5,000
Equity	1,800	1,800
Long-term debt	1,700	200
Current liabilities	3,000	3,000
	6,500	5,000

Assume the company's profit before interest and tax for the year then ended was £400.

ROCE $\dfrac{\text{PBIT}}{\text{Equity}+\text{LT debt}}$ $\dfrac{400}{3,500}=11.4\%$ $\dfrac{400}{2,000}=20\%$

Gearing $\dfrac{\text{Debt}}{\text{Equity}}$ $\dfrac{1,700}{1,800}=94.4\%$ $\dfrac{200}{1,800}=11.1\%$

The company's ROCE is higher and its gearing is lower when the debt and corresponding asset are excluded from the statement of financial position.

15.1.2 Transactions involving off balance sheet finance

The collapse of the US energy giant, Enron, in 2001 revealed substantial off balance sheet financing. An outline of the case is given in Chapter 3. Enron used rules based US financial reporting standards to avoid consolidating (in other words, including) special purpose entities (SPEs) in its financial statements. The SPEs, which Enron essentially controlled, had been used by the company to hide huge losses and debts.

The issue of control of one entity by another is at the heart of the question of which entities' results and net assets should be included in a company's consolidated financial statements. The IASB completed a major programme of work in this area in 2011, and issued a new suite of financial reporting standards dealing with consolidated financial statements and other business combinations. IFRS 10 *Consolidated Financial Statements* addresses the key question of control, which is discussed in Chapter 17.

Other arrangements that have given rise to off balance sheet finance include sale and leaseback arrangements, inventories sold under consignment, debt factoring and the securitisation of assets. Broadly, all of these involve the 'sale' of assets by a company, with related obligations being incurred to re-acquire the assets in the future. The IASB has addressed the issue of the potential for an asset and obligation to be off balance sheet from these types of transactions by considering what constitutes a sale and when revenue from a sale should be recognised. Accounting for revenue is spelt out in IFRS 15 *Revenue from Contracts with Customers*. This takes a principles-based approach, with the recognition of revenue being based on the transfer of control. This is now consistent with the approach to consolidated financial statements. These matters are discussed in detail in Chapters 7 and 17.

Other complex transactions in financial instruments are evolving continuously and some of these may result in companies being able to avoid recognising all their debts on their statements of financial position. IFRS 9 *Financial Instruments* deals with such transactions, some of which have been discussed in Chapter 14.

15.1.3 Leases

The main topic of this chapter which has given rise to off balance sheet financing is leases, where one company (the lessee) gains access to an asset for a period of time in return for a payment or series of payments to another company (the lessor), which retains legal ownership of the asset. Leasing as a means of obtaining the use of assets grew enormously in the latter half of the twentieth century. Prior to any standards dealing with this, the accounting treatment followed the legal form, and the asset remained on the books of the lessor. The lessee's financial statements showed neither the asset nor the obligation for the payments, and the payments were accounted for as rental expenses.

It is reported that in the USA, in the 1970s, billions of dollars of leased items were not shown on the books of companies, a situation of which investors began to be increasingly critical. In the UK, the issue received particular attention after the collapse of a major tour operator, Court Line, in 1974. This revealed that the company had undisclosed aircraft lease obligations of £millions; obligations which were much greater than the failed company's reported net assets.

IAS 17 *Leases* which partially addressed this off balance sheet issue was based on financial reporting standards which had been introduced in both the USA in the 1970s and the UK in the 1980s. Under IAS 17 the accounting treatment of certain lease arrangements, termed finance leases, requires the assets and the related obligations to be recognised on the statement of financial position. However, this still leaves many lease arrangements, termed operating leases, off balance sheet. The IASB has worked for many years to address this, and issued a new financial reporting standard, IFRS 16 *Leases*, to replace IAS 17 in January 2016. This requires substantially all leases to be brought on balance sheet. Given the significant changes that this brings for many companies, the final implementation date is some time after the issue of the standard, and is for accounting periods starting on or after 1 January 2019. Most companies will be reporting under IAS 17 until 31 December 2018.

This chapter therefore considers the financial accounting and reporting under both IAS 17 and IFRS 16.

15.1.4 Principles-based approach

As seen from the earlier discussion, off balance sheet financing may arise from a variety of items and transactions, and different financial reporting standards have been developed and then revised, sometimes a number of times, to deal with these different areas. The IASB's approach is to produce standards which are based on the principles contained in its *Conceptual Framework*, including substance over form.

🛈 **Reminder** *Substance over form, as discussed in Chapter 2, means that accounting should be in accordance with the economic or commercial reality of a transaction rather than its legal form. This will help ensure that financial statements convey information that is faithfully representative of the underpinning transactions and items.*

Principles-based standards should ensure that no 'rules' or 'bright lines' are created either side of which an obligation would be recognised or not recognised, respectively, and which would have the effect of actually influencing the way a transaction is set up. Financial reporting standards should reflect the transactions of businesses and not influence their structure.

Consistency between standards is also important. As discussed, new standards that have been issued are addressing this. The issue of control of an asset (which has a related liability) is crucial in ensuring this consistent approach.

🛈 **Reminder** *The definition of an asset given in both the 2010* Conceptual Framework *and the Exposure Draft (ED) to the new Framework includes the term control. (Note that control does not mean ownership.)*

15.2 Leases

Companies acquire assets for long-term use in different ways. A company may purchase an asset outright, in which case legal ownership passes to it from the seller. The company can then do what it wishes with the asset as it obtains all the risks and rewards that come with ownership, and the asset is accounted for as a non-current asset.

However, for various reasons, including lack of available cash, or tax efficiency, a company may hire or lease an asset for a period of time by making regular payments over the period of the hire or lease. Legal ownership remains with the hirer or lessor, but the company gains economic benefits from the use of the asset. In a hire purchase agreement, ownership passes to the company at the end of the agreement, once the final payment has been made.

The commercial substance of this transaction is that the company has, over the period of the agreement, acquired the use of a non-current asset and may acquire some, or all, of the risks and benefits as if the company owned the asset. The asset is used in a similar manner to other non-current assets, even though, legally, it belongs to the hirer or lessor.

The substance over form principle implies that an asset acquired under a hire or lease arrangement should be capitalised. This accounting treatment also follows from the IASB's definition of an asset in the ED to its revised *Conceptual Framework*:

> An asset is a present economic resource controlled by the entity as a result of past events
>
> *(IASB, 2015: para. 4.4)*

15.3 Accounting for leases under IAS 17

15.3.1 Classification of leases

When the first financial reporting standards requiring the capitalisation of leases were produced, the accounting standard-setters at the time recoiled from introducing a requirement for the capitalisation of all leases. To reduce the impact on the thousands of affected companies' statements of financial position and accounting ratios, a distinction was drawn between a finance lease and an operating lease with different accounting treatments for each. Thus in the predecessor standards and then finally in IAS 17, finance leases were required to be on balance sheet and operating leases remained off balance sheet. (The impact of this at the time was still dramatic, with subsequent falls in share prices of the affected companies.)

The definition of a finance lease is given in IAS 17 as one which

... transfers substantially all the risks and rewards incidental to ownership [to the lessee].

(IASB, 2005: para. 4)

All other leases are classified as operating leases.

The commercial substance of a lease agreement needs to be considered carefully to differentiate between a finance lease and an operating lease. As with many other areas in financial reporting, this leads to judgement needing to be exercised. The risks of owning an asset include possible losses resulting from the asset lying idle or because it has become technologically obsolete, or variable returns from the use of the asset as economic conditions alter. Rewards resulting from owning an asset include profitable returns or gains from an appreciation in value. So if these result from using an asset, then it is considered similar to owning the asset and the asset should be included in the statement of financial position.

To help in the classification, IAS 17 provides examples of certain typical conditions in lease agreements, which may indicate that a lease is a finance lease. These generally indicate that the leased asset will be used only by one lessee, who will probably retain the asset at the end of the lease term:

(a) the lease transfers ownership of the asset to the lessee by the end of the lease term;

(b) the lessee has the option to purchase the asset at a price that is expected to be sufficiently lower than the fair value at the date the option becomes exercisable for it to be reasonably certain, at the inception of the lease, that the option will be exercised;

(c) the lease term is for the major part of the economic life of the asset even if title is not transferred;

(d) at the inception of the lease the present value of the minimum lease payments amounts to at least substantially all of the fair value of the leased asset; and

(e) the leased assets are of such a specialised nature that only the lessee can use them without major modifications.

Operating leases, however, are much more like rental agreements, with the probability that an individual asset will be leased to a number of different lessees under agreements covering shorter time frames.

Not all the above conditions have to be present in a lease arrangement; indeed, only one may be, but all clauses in the agreement need to be considered together. Other factors which may indicate the lease should be classified as a finance lease are:

(a) if the lessee can cancel the lease, the lessor's losses associated with the cancellation are borne by the lessee;

(b) gains or losses from the fluctuation in the fair value of the residual accrue to the lessee (for example, in the form of a rent rebate equalling most of the sales proceeds at the end of the lease); and

(c) the lessee has the ability to continue the lease for a second period at a rent that is substantially lower than market rent.

 Examples of classification of leases

1 A company leases the machine tools it uses in its manufacturing processes. Legal title is transferred to the company after three years.

This may be a finance lease because title is transferred, and the company enjoys the risks and rewards of ownership as it uses the tools.

2 A company leases a car for a salesman for a five-year period, after which the car will be returned to the lessor and scrapped.

This may be a finance lease as the lease term is for the full useful economic life of the asset.

3 A company leases a photocopier. The present value of the minimum lease payments is £3,000, but the fair value of the asset is £12,000.

This may be an operating lease as the fair value of the asset is much higher than the minimum lease payments.

4 A company acquires some equipment made bespoke to its specifications. If the equipment were to be sold to a third party it would require substantial modification.

This may be a finance lease as only the lessee can use the equipment without major modifications.

The lease classification is made at the inception of the lease, which is when the terms of the lease, including the financial settlement, are agreed. This may be the contract signing date or, if earlier, the date when the main terms were agreed. The date of inception of a lease may be different from the date of commencement of the lease; and the difference between these two dates is important. The lease is classified at the date of inception and, in the case of a finance lease, values for the asset and liability are determined at this date. The date of commencement is the date when the lessee is able to use the leased asset. For example, a company leasing a building may move in several months after the lease contract was agreed. Values determined at inception are not recognised in the financial statements until the commencement date. In many cases, the dates are not far apart.

15.3.2 Minimum lease payments

One of the most persuasive conditions used to indicate a lease is a finance lease is that the present value of the minimum lease payments amounts to at least substantially all of the fair value of the leased asset (condition (d) in the first list in section 15.3.1). The use of the words 'substantially all' is interesting here. IAS 17 was written after the UK's accounting standard on leases was issued and is based largely on this standard. The UK standard at the time included a similar condition, but included a precise 90% cut-off instead of the words 'substantially all'. However, the use of a 'bright line', such as this 90% cut-off, is contrary to principles-based international financial reporting standards, and so rather looser terminology requiring judgement is included instead. However, in practice in the UK, companies often apply this 90% rule to determine whether a lease agreement is a finance or operating one, and, indeed, structure the terms of lease agreements so that perhaps only 89% is reached, meaning the lease can be treated as operating.

Minimum lease payments require careful definition as the nature of payments does vary from lease to lease. Minimum lease payments are defined in IAS 17 as the payments over the lease term that the lessee is required and it (or any party related to the lessee) guarantees to make, but the following are excluded:

- **contingent rentals** (i.e. payments that are not fixed in amount, but are based on a future factor which may change, e.g. a percentage of future sales)

- costs for services and taxes to be paid by, and reimbursed to, the lessor.

The lease term also requires definition, as leases may be extended after an initial period. The lease term here means the non-cancellable period for which the lessee has contracted to lease the asset, plus any further period in which the lessee has the option to extend the lease, provided that at the start of the whole arrangement it is reasonably certain that the lessee will take this option.

In practice during the initial lease period the lease will either be non-cancellable or will be cancellable only under certain conditions, for example on the payment of a heavy settlement figure. During this period the amounts payable will be sufficient to repay to the lessor the cost of the equipment plus interest thereon. During any subsequent extension period the lease may be cancellable at any time at the lessee's option. The rentals during this period will probably be of a nominal amount (sometimes referred to as a 'peppercorn rent').

 Worked example 15.1: to show a minimum lease payments calculation

Jana plc enters into an agreement to lease a machine for five years at an annual rent of £1,000 payable at the end of each year. The cash price for the machine if purchased would be £3,650.

(Assume the machine has zero residual value at the end of the five years and also assume a discount rate of 12%.)

Required:
Calculate the present value (PV) of the minimum lease payments and use this to determine the type of lease.

The present value of the minimum lease payments is calculated as:

Payment £		Discount factor	PV £
1,000	×	$1/(1.12)$	893
1,000	×	$1/(1.12)^2$	797
1,000	×	$1/(1.12)^3$	712
1,000	×	$1/(1.12)^4$	636
1,000	×	$1/(1.12)^5$	567
			3,605

(Alternatively, discount or annuity tables could be used.)

The present value of the minimum lease payments at £3,605 is compared with the fair value of the asset at the inception of the lease, which is given by the cash price of the machine of £3,650.

In this example, these amount to 'substantially all' of the fair value of the asset, and (in the absence of information about other clauses in the lease agreement) the lease would be accounted for as a finance lease.

15.3.3 Leases of property

When property is leased, separate consideration needs to be given to the land and the buildings. A characteristic of land is that it usually has an indefinite economic life and legal title to the land may not pass to the lessee at the end of the lease term. If this is the case, the lease of the land will be treated as an operating lease because the lessee is not receiving substantially all of the risks and rewards incidental to ownership. If title to the land does pass to the lessee at the end of the lease term, it is likely that the land lease would be classified as a finance lease. The lease of the buildings will be classified as finance or operating according to the criteria discussed previously.

However, in practice this often results in the land lease being treated as an operating lease, while the buildings lease is treated as a finance lease. The minimum lease payments will then need to be allocated between the two leases. This is done in proportion to the relative fair values of the leasehold interests in the land element and the buildings element at the inception of the lease. If this cannot be done, then both elements are treated as finance leases unless it is clear that both leases are operating leases.

15.4 Accounting for leases under IAS 17 in lessees' financial statements

Figure 15.1 summarises the accounting treatments of finance and operating leases specified in IAS 17. These are discussed in detail below.

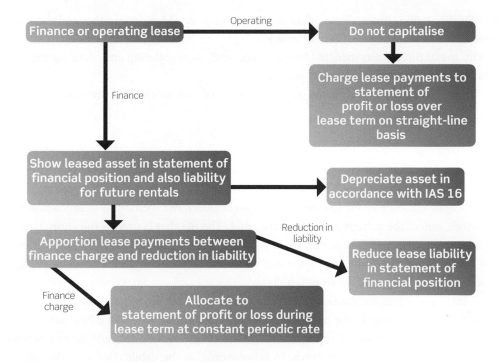

Figure 15.1 Accounting treatment of finance and operating leases for lessees

15.4.1 Finance leases

The commercial substance of a finance lease is that the lessee is acquiring the economic benefits of the leased asset for the major part of its economic life in return for a entering into an obligation to make a series of payments to the lessor. The asset is therefore capitalised, just as any other asset for which legal title has been obtained is capitalised, and a liability is recognised for the future lease payments. The value at which the asset and liability are initially recognised is the same, and is measured at the inception of the lease. It is given by the lower of:

● the fair value of the leased asset, and

● the present value of the minimum lease payments.

In order to calculate the present value of the minimum lease payments, a discount rate is required. If it is possible to determine this, this should be the **interest rate implicit in the lease**, in other words the discount rate that ensures:

> Present value of (minimum lease payments + unguaranteed residual value)
>
> = fair value of leased asset + initial direct costs of lessor

(Note: The value remaining in the asset at the end of the lease term is termed the residual value, and this may be guaranteed by the lessee or unguaranteed. See section 15.5.1 for further discussion. In the above calculation the unguaranteed residual value and the initial direct costs of the lessor are taken as zero.)

Any initial direct costs incurred by the lessee, such as negotiating and securing the lease arrangement, are added to the asset amount.

The double-entry required at the commencement of a finance lease is therefore:

Debit   Non-current asset

Credit   Lease obligation

As with any other non-current asset, once it has started to be used, depreciation has to be accounted for. To be consistent with all other owned assets, this is applied in accordance with IAS 16. (See Chapter 10 for full details of depreciation.) The method of depreciation will, therefore, reflect the pattern of usage of the asset. The life that is used is the shorter of the lease term and the useful economic life of the asset. If it is reasonably certain that the lessee will obtain ownership of the asset at the end of the lease term, then the expected useful life is used for the calculation of depreciation.

As lease payments are made, these are not expensed, but are apportioned between the finance charge inherent in the payments and the reduction of the outstanding liability. IAS 17 requires that the finance charge is calculated so as to give a constant periodic rate of interest on the remaining liability balance. In other words, as the liability reduces, the interest expense reduces. Payments on a lease are a constant amount each payment period, so this will mean that the split between interest portion and the capital portion will change over the lease term, with higher interest charges in earlier periods. Calculations to show this using the **effective interest method** (sometimes called the actuarial method) are given in Worked example 15.2, but, in practice, a lessee may use some form of approximation to simplify the calculations, such as the sum-of-digits method.

The double-entry for accounting for the lease payments is as follows:

Debit   Lease obligation   }   with full payment

Credit   Bank   }

Debit   Finance charge   }   with interest element

Credit   Lease obligation   }

Any payments made for contingent rents are charged as expenses in the year they are incurred:

Debit   Lease expense

Credit   Bank

 Worked example 15.2: to show the finance lease accounting

Able plc leases a computer from TG Finance plc from 1 January 20X3. The terms of the lease are that Able plc pays four annual rental payments of £10,000 each, with the first payment being made on 1 January 20X3. Thereafter, the computer can be rented indefinitely for a nominal sum of £1 per year. The cost of the computer new would be £34,868, and the interest rate implicit in the lease is 10% per year.

Required:

(a) Determine whether the lease is a finance lease or an operating lease

(b) If relevant, compute the amount of the lease obligation to be shown at the end of each year in the statement of financial position

(c) Show how the lease would be accounted for in Able plc's financial statements for the year ended 31 December 20X3.

(a) The determination of whether the lease is a finance or operating lease should look for indications that the risks and rewards of ownership have passed to the lessee. Here, the lease term can be extended indefinitely for a minimal sum, which IAS 17 states is an indication of a finance lease.

In addition, the present value of the minimum payments is 4 × £10,000 discounted using a 10% discount rate = £34,868, which is equal to (i.e. substantially all of) the fair value of the computer.

The asset is therefore capitalised and a liability recognised for £34,868, the fair value of the computer, which is the same as the present value of the minimum lease payments.

(b) The calculation of the finance charge and the amount by which the lease obligation is reduced each year is achieved by drawing up a table tracking the lease obligation balance as follows:

Year	Obligation at start of year £	Instalment £	Obligation after instalment £	Interest @ 10% £	Obligation at end of year £
20X3	34,868	(10,000)	24,868	2,487	27,355
20X4	27,355	(10,000)	17,355	1,736	19,091
20X5	19,091	(10,000)	9,091	909	10,000
20X6	10,000	(10,000)	–		

(c) The accounting at the commencement of the lease to capitalise the asset and recognise the lease obligation is:

		£	£
Debit	Asset	34,868	
Credit	Lease obligation		34,868

The first payment is accounted for as:

		£	£
Debit	Lease obligation	10,000	
Credit	Bank		10,000

At the end of the year, the finance charge is calculated and accounted for as:

		£	£
Debit	Finance charge	2,487	
Credit	Lease obligation		2,487

Depreciation would also be accounted for. Given that there is no indication whether the asset would be used for a period different to the lease term, the asset would be depreciated over the lease term of 4 years (£34,868/4 = £8,717):

		£	£
Debit	Depreciation expense	8,717	
Credit	Accumulated depreciation		8,717

The resulting figures in the financial statements at 31 December 20X3 are therefore as follows:

Statement of financial position at 31 December 20X3

Non-current assets	£
Asset cost	34,868
Accumulated depreciation	(8,717)
Net book value	26,151

Lease liability

The total balance remaining at the end of the year is given in the table in part (b) as £27,355. This is split between the amount due within one year (current liability) and the amount due after more than one year (non-current liability). These figures can be obtained from the table.

Look at the figures in the next year line (i.e. the 20X4 line). The payments on this lease are being made in advance each year. Once the payment has been made, the balance on the obligation is £17,355. This figure is the amount due after one year, the non-current liability. The current liability is therefore the difference between the total £27,355 and £17,355, in other words £27,355 − £17,355 = £10,000.

(Note the calculation has been spelt out this way, so that the similarity between leases where payments are made in advance and those where payments are made in arrears can be seen—see Worked example 15.3.)

	£
Current liability	10,000
Non-current liability	17,355

Statement of profit or loss for the year ended 31 December 20X3

There are two figures relating to this lease which will be included in the statement of profit or loss:

	£
Finance charge (from table)	2,487
Depreciation expense	8,717

Contrast Worked example 15.2 with one where the lease payments are made in arrears.

Worked example 15.3: to show a finance lease liability with payments in arrears

On 1 January 20X0, at the start of its financial year, Jones plc enters into an agreement to lease a cutting machine for a period of four years. Assume that this is a finance lease and that the relevant figures are given as follows:

- annual payment of £20,000 made on 31 December each year
- interest rate implicit in lease 8%
- fair value of machine at inception of lease £66,244 (which is equivalent to the present value of the minimum lease payments).

Required:
Calculate the total lease obligation at 31 December 20X0, and show the split of this into current and non-current liabilities.

The lease obligation table is drawn up as follows. Note the order of the columns which follows the sequence of items to be accounted for—interest for the year is charged before the annual payment is made.

Year	Obligation at start of year	Interest @ 8%	Obligation after interest	Payment	Obligation at end of year
	£	£	£	£	£
20X0	66,244	5,300	71,544	(20,000)	51,544
20X1	51,544	4,124	55,668	(20,000)	35,668
20X2	35,668	2,853	38,521	(20,000)	18,521
20X3	18,521	1,482	20,003*	(20,000)	–

* Rounding difference.

At 31 December 20X0 the total lease obligation is £51,544. In order to calculate the split of this between current and non-current, as before, look at the figures in the 20X1 line. The obligation after the payment is £35,668. This is the non-current liability. The balance of £51,544 – £35,668 = £15,876 is the current liability. (Note this is because of the £20,000 payment to be made in 20X1, £4,124 will be taken as the finance charge.)

15.4.2 Finance lease disclosures

Amounts capitalised as non-current assets and the lease obligations are not netted off on the statement of financial position, as this would defeat the purpose of the accounting treatment and not be faithfully representative.

In the property, plant and equipment disclosure note, details of the carrying amount of assets held under finance leases must be indicated, often by a footnote such as:

Of the total carrying amount of £X, £Y relates to assets held under finance leases.

Other than this, all disclosures relating to property, plant and equipment required by IAS 16 are applicable to assets leased under finance leases.

For the liability IAS 17 requires disclosure of future lease payments, split between amounts due:

● within 1 year
● within 2–5 years
● after more than 5 years.

This disclosure must be given in two ways:

● on a gross basis—this shows gross future lease payments for each of the three time-period categories and then deducts as a single figure the future periods' finance charges. The resulting figure is the total lease obligation figure included in liabilities
● on a present value basis—this excludes from each of the three time-period categories the finance charges allocated to future periods.

If there are contingent rentals these need to be disclosed along with details of the basis on which these have been calculated. Other details of lease agreements, such as renewal or purchase options and any restrictions imposed should be provided to enable users to understand the implications of the company entering into the agreements.

 Example of disclosures of finance lease liabilities

Based on Worked example 15.2 of a finance lease, the disclosures relating to the lease liability at 31 December 20X3 would be as follows.

Gross basis

	£
Finance lease liabilities include gross lease payments due within:	
1 year	10,000
2–5 years	20,000
	30,000
Less: finance charges allocated to future periods (£1,736 + £909)	(2,645)
	27,355

Present value basis

	£
Finance lease liabilities include amounts due within:	
1 year	10,000
2–5 years (balancing figure)	17,355
	27,355

Financial reporting in practice 15.1 | International Airlines Group, 2014

The 2014 annual report of International Airlines Group discloses the following in relation to finance leases.

Note 13: Property, plant and equipment

€ million	Fleet	Property	Equipment	Total
Net book amounts				
31 December 2014	**9,974**	**1,260**	**550**	**11,784**
31 December 2013	8,515	1,218	495	10,228
Analysis at 31 December 2014				
Owned	4,290	1,173	411	**5,874**
Finance leased	5,398	5	32	**5,435**
Progress payments	286	82	107	**90**
Assets not in current use	121			**475**
	9,974	**1,260**	**550**	**11,784**

Details of the finance lease obligations are included within the long-term borrowing note.

Note 23: Long-term borrowings

a Current

€ million	2014	2013
Bank and other loans	**164**	183
Finance leases	**549**	404
	713	587

b Non-current

€ million	2014	2013
Bank and other loans	**1,069**	1,169
Finance leases	**4,835**	3,366
	5,904	4,535

e Obligations under finance leases

The Group uses finance leases principally to acquire aircraft. These leases have both renewal options and purchase options, at the option of the Group. Future minimum lease payments under finance leases are as follows:

(continued)

(continued)

€ million	2014	2013
Future minimum payments due:		
Within one year	676	492
After more than one year but within five years	2,463	1,893
In five years or more	3,100	1,858
	6,239	4,243
Less: Finance charges	(855)	(473)
Present value of minimum lease payments	5,384	3,770
The present value of minimum lease payments is analysed as follows:		
Within one year	549	404
After more than one year but within five years	2,079	1,650
In five years or more	2,756	1,716
	5,384	3,770

The Group's finance lease for one Airbus A340-600 is subject to financial covenants which are tested annually. The lease is part of a syndicate family. The Group has informed the syndicate that it had failed to meet the covenants for the year to 31 December 2014. As a result of these covenant breaches, the finance lease has technically become repayable on demand and $79 million (€65 million) has been classified as current. The institutions formally waived the breach on 25 February 2015.

15.4.3 Operating leases

As discussed previously, under IAS 17 an operating lease is any lease other than a finance lease. The accounting for these leases is straightforward as it follows the legal form. In other words, the lease payments are recognised as an expense and IAS 17 specifies that this should be on a straight-line basis over the lease term unless another systematic basis is more representative of the lessee's use of the asset. Payments may follow a different pattern, in which case normal accounting for accruals and prepayments will ensue.

Given that these leases are off balance sheet, no amounts are recognised in the financial statements for the obligations. However, disclosures of these commitments are required to help users evaluate the financial obligations of companies under these lease arrangements. As for finance leases the future minimum lease payments are broken down into amounts due:

- within 1 year
- within 2–5 years
- after more than 5 years.

Further disclosures include amounts expensed in profit and loss, and a general description of the company's significant leasing arrangements.

Financial reporting in practice 15.2 | Air France–KLM, 2015

As with many airlines, Air France–KLM finances its acquisition of aircraft through lease arrangements. At its financial year end of 31 December 2015, the company's financial statements disclosed the following obligations under these lease agreements.

37.2 Operating lease commitments

The minimum future payments on operating leases are as follows:

In € millions	Minimum lease payments	
As of December 31	2015	2014
Flight equipment		
Due dates		
Y+1	1,131	1,041
Y+2	1,099	1,009
Y+3	952	960
Y+4	804	818
Y+5	640	704
Over 5 years	1,360	1,727
Total	5,986	6,259
Buildings		
Due dates		
Y+1	210	210
Y+2	153	159
Y+3	127	132
Y+4	111	111
Y+5	92	94
Over 5 years	707	768
Total	1,400	1,474

This example serves to illustrate large amount of off balance sheet financing present in companies such as airlines.

15.5 Accounting for leases under IAS 17 in lessors' financial statements

Under IAS 17, accounting for leases in the financial statements of lessors is more or less a mirror image of the accounting by lessees. The same definitions and guidance for the classification of a lease as finance or operating apply to lessors. For finance leases, the asset is

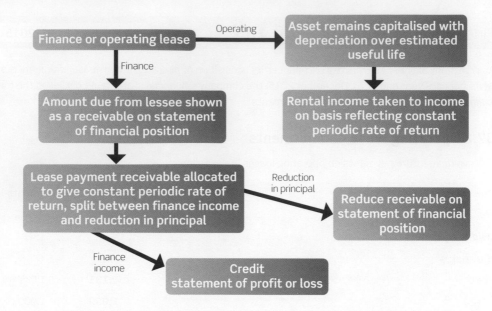

Figure 15.2 Accounting treatment of finance and operating leases for lessors

derecognised (in other words sold to the lessee) and a profit or loss on sale is recognised at this point. The entitlement to receive lease payments is recognised as a receivable. For operating leases, the asset remains in the financial statements of the lessor and the receipt of the lease payments is recognised as income on a straight-line basis over the period of the lease.

Figure 15.2 summarises the IAS 17 requirements.

15.5.1 Finance leases

Under a finance lease substantially all the risks and rewards incidental to ownership are transferred by the lessor to the lessee and, therefore, the asset is derecognised (i.e. removed from the lessor's statement of financial position). The lease payment receivable is treated as a repayment of principal together with finance income to reimburse and reward the lessor for its investment and services. The lease payment receivable is recognised initially at an amount equal to the net investment in the lease. The net investment in a lease is the present value of the gross investment in the lease, which is defined as:

> Present value of (minimum lease payments receivable by the lessor plus any unguaranteed residual value accruing to the lessor).

At the end of the lease term, the lessee may guarantee that the asset will have a certain value. This is a guaranteed residual value. However, the lease arrangement may also include a figure for the residual value based, say, on expected market values. This is an unguaranteed residual value as it may never be realised; however, it is taken into account by the lessor when the lease is settled and in calculating the lease payment receivable.

The discount rate to be used in calculating the present value is based on the interest rate implicit in the lease. This has the same definition as for lessee accounting (see section 15.4.1).

The double-entry at the commencement of the lease is therefore as follows.

Derecognition of asset:

| Debit | Cost of sales | } | with carrying amount of asset |
| Credit | Asset | } | |

Sale of asset under finance lease agreement:

| Debit | Lease payment receivable | } | at net investment in lease |
| Credit | Sales revenue | } | |

A lessor will probably incur initial direct costs, for example commission, legal fees and other costs of negotiating and setting up a lease. For lessors other than manufacturers and dealers, which are discussed in section 15.5.2, these initial costs are included in the initial measurement of the finance lease receivable and therefore reduce the amount of income recognised over the lease term.

As lease payments are received they are apportioned between a reduction in the lease receivable and finance income on a systematic and rational basis, so that a constant periodic rate of return on the lessor's net investment in the lease is achieved. This is done by carrying out the same form of calculation as for lessees in allocating their payments under a finance lease between a reduction in the lease liability and the finance charge. The actuarial method is the one which will achieve this.

The double-entry for this is as follows:

Debit	Bank	}	with full receipt
Credit	Lease payment receivable	}	
Debit	Lease payment receivable	}	with interest element
Credit	Finance income	}	

 Worked example 15.4: to show the accounting for a finance lease in the financial statements of a lessor

Crystal Finance plc leased an asset to Bengal Ltd with the following terms:

Lease term	4 years
Inception of lease	1 January 20X1
Annual payments in advance	£10,000
Residual value of asset guaranteed by lessee	£6,000
Expected residual value at end of lease	£8,000
Fair value of the asset	£38,966
Interest rate implicit in the lease	10%

The unguaranteed residual value is £2,000 (i.e. £8,000 – £6,000).

Required:

Assuming this is a finance lease, show the accounting treatment of the lease in the financial statements of Crystal Finance plc for the year ended 31 December 20X1.

The net investment in the lease is calculated as follows:

Date		Gross investment	Discount factor (10%)	Net investment
		£		£
1.1.X1	Instalment 1	10,000	1	10,000
1.1.X2	Instalment 2	10,000	1/1.1	9,091
1.1.X3	Instalment 3	10,000	$1/1.1^2$	8,264
1.1.X4	Instalment 4	10,000	$1/1.1^3$	7,513
31.12.X4	Guaranteed residual value	6,000	$1/1.1^4$	4,098
Minimum lease payments		46,000		38,966
31.12.X4	Unguaranteed residual value	2,000	$1/1.1^4$	1,366
		48,000		40,332

A lease receivable table can be drawn up similar to the one drawn up for the lease obligation in the lessee's books:

Year	Receivable at start of year	Instalment	Receivable after instalment	Interest @ 10%	Receivable at end of year
	£	£	£	£	£
20X1	40,332	(10,000)	30,332	3,033	33,365
20X2	33,365	(10,000)	23,365	2,337	25,702
20X3	25,702	(10,000)	15,702	1,570	17,272
20X4	17,272	(10,000)	7,272	727	7,999*

* At the end of the lease term, the balance on the receivable equates to the expected residual value of the lease of £8,000 (ignore the rounding difference of £1).

Detailed bookkeeping for the first year is as follows. At the commencement of the lease, the lease payment receivable is set up as the net investment in the lease:

		£	£
Debit	Lease payment receivable	40,332	
Credit	Revenue		40,332

The first receipt reduces the lease payment receivable:

		£	£
Debit	Bank	10,000	
Credit	Lease payment receivable		10,000

At the end of the year, interest is accounted for:

		£	£
Debit	Lease payment receivable	3,033	
Credit	Finance income		3,033

Financial statement extracts for 20X1

	£
Statement of profit or loss	
Finance income	3,033
Statement of financial position	
Non-current assets	
Finance lease receivable (read from the 20X2 line in the table)	23,365
Current assets	
Finance lease receivable (£33,365—£23,365)	10,000

Note: the solution has separated the amount receivable according to the normal non-current/current asset definition. In practice, lessors, if they are financial institutions, will usually present their statement of financial position on a liquidity basis and the receivable will be a single figure, with further analysis in the notes.

15.5.2 Manufacturers or dealers

The accounting treatment of finance leases by a manufacturer or a dealer who acquires assets to lease to others is slightly different to that described previously. The reason for this is that such companies often offer artificially low interest rates on the lease arrangement to attract customers. If the accounting was carried out using the methods described earlier, the net investment in the lease would be inflated and the company would recognise an artificially high profit on the sale of the asset at the commencement of the lease. This would also not be consistent with profits earned if the lessor made an outright sale of the asset.

So IAS 17 requires the following figures to be used in the accounting:

1 The revenue recognised at the lease commencement should be the lower of the fair value of the asset and the present value of the minimum lease payments computed using a market interest rate

2 The cost of sale recognised at the lease commencement should be the lower of the cost of the asset, or its carrying amount if different, less the present value of any unguaranteed residual value

3 Costs incurred in negotiating and setting up the lease are accounted for as an expense at the lease commencement because these costs are mainly related to earning the selling profit.

Worked example 15.5: to show the accounting for a finance lease for a car dealer

On 1 January 20X2 a dealer sold a car for £30,000, payable either in full on delivery or by three annual payments in advance at 0% finance. Each payment was therefore £10,000. The dealer had purchased the car from the manufacturer for £24,000. The market rate of interest was 6%. The purchaser chose the interest-free option.

(Assume zero residual values.)

Required:

What amounts should the dealer recognise in its statement of profit or loss for the year ended 31 December 20X2 and in its statement of financial position at that date?

The car dealer has an asset with a carrying amount of £24,000.

The present value of the minimum lease payments is calculated as:

	Payment	Discount	
	£	factor (6%)	£
1.1.X2	10,000	1	10,000
1.1.X3	10,000	1/1.06	9,434
1.1.X4	10,000	$1/1.06^2$	8,900
			28,334

At the commencement of the lease, the following are recognised in the statement of profit or loss:

	£
Revenue	28,334
Cost of sales	(24,000)
Gross profit	4,334

The lease payment receivable will be recognised at 1 January 20X2 at £28,334. The first two years of the receivable can be tracked as follows:

Year	Receivable at start of year	Instalment	Receivable after instalment	Interest @ 6%	Receivable at end of year
	£	£	£	£	£
20X2	28,334	(10,000)	18,334	1,100	19,434
20X3	19,434	(10,000)	9,434		

Also recognised in the 20X2 statement of profit or loss is finance income of £1,100.

In the statement of financial position at 31 December 20X2, the car dealer will have a lease receivable of £19,434 split £9,434 non-current asset and £10,000 current asset.

15.5.3 Finance lease disclosures

Again, the IAS 17 disclosures for finance leases for lessors mirror the disclosures required by lessees. For the receivable, the future lease payments to be received should be split between amounts receivable:

- within 1 year
- within 2–5 years
- after more than five years.

This disclosure must be given both:

- on a gross basis, i.e. showing gross future lease receipts for each of the three time-period categories, then deducting as a single figure the future periods' finance income to arrive at the total lease receivable
- on a present value basis, which excludes from each of the three time-period categories the finance income allocated to future periods.

The future periods' finance income is useful to users as it provides an indication of future income.

Additional disclosures include:

- the unguaranteed residual values accruing to the benefit of the lessor
- contingent rentals which have been included as income in the year
- a general description of the lessor's material leasing arrangements.

Financial reporting in practice 15.3   Lloyds Banking Group, 2015

The annual report and accounts of Lloyds Banking Group include finance lease receivables in loans and advances to customers. Details of these are provided in the disclosure note relating to this balance.

Loans and advances to customers include finance lease receivables, which may be analysed as follows:

	2015 £m	2014 £m
Gross investment in finance leases, receivable:		
Not later than 1 year	497	573
Later than 1 year and not later than 5 years	1,225	1,214
Later than 5 years	2,407	3,136
	4,129	4,923

(continued)

(continued)

Unearned future finance income on finance leases	(1,316)	(1,837)
Rentals received in advance	(62)	(73)
Net investment in finance leases	2,751	3,013

The net investment in finance leases represents amounts recoverable as follows:

	2015	2014
	£m	£m
Not later than 1 year	319	339
Later than 1 year and not later than 5 years	859	763
Later than 5 years	1,573	1,911
Net investment in finance leases	2,751	3,013

Equipment leased to customers under finance leases primarily relates to structured financing transactions to fund the purchase of aircraft, ships and other large individual value items. During 2015 and 2014 no contingent rentals in respect of finance leases were recognised in the income statement. There was no allowance for uncollectable finance lease receivables included in the allowance for impairment losses (2014: £1 million).

15.5.4 Operating leases

For an operating lease the lease term is, by definition, shorter than the asset's useful life. As for lessees the accounting for an operating lease for a lessor is very straightforward. The asset remains in the financial statement of the lessor according to its nature. If it is an item of property, plant and equipment it is depreciated in accordance with IAS 16 and is subject to impairment reviews as per IAS 36.

The receipts are accounted for as income and recognised on a straight-line basis over the period of the lease term, even if receipts are not made on this basis. If another systematic and rational basis is more representative of the time pattern in which the benefit from the leased asset is receivable, this should be used. The initial direct costs incurred by lessors in negotiating and arranging an operating lease should be added to the carrying amount of the leased asset and recognised as an expense over the lease term through depreciation.

Disclosure should be made of the future minimum lease payments split between amounts due:

- within 1 year
- within 2–5 years
- after more than 5 years.

15.6 Sale and leaseback transactions

A sale and leaseback transaction involves the owner of an asset selling it, usually to a finance house or bank, and simultaneously leasing it back. These arrangements provide companies with the opportunity to release capital tied up in the business's assets to enable investment in other opportunities or to return it to shareholders. In essence, a company acquires cash in exchange for a commitment to make regular lease payments without losing use of the asset.

A sale and leaseback transaction can result in either a finance lease or an operating lease, as determined by applying the principles contained in IAS 17. As the accounting treatment of the transaction depends on this categorisation, this decision is critical.

15.6.1 Finance leases

If the lease part of a sale and leaseback transaction results in a finance lease, the risks and rewards of ownership remain with the company that made the original sale and the transaction is effectively a means of this company obtaining finance using the asset as security. The recognition of a profit on the sale of the asset would therefore not faithfully represent the transaction. Any excess of sales proceeds over the carrying amount of the asset is therefore deferred and amortised over the lease term. The finance lease is then accounted for in the usual way.

> **Worked example 15.6:** to show the accounting for a sale and leaseback transaction as a finance lease

Gradgrind plc owns an asset with a carrying amount of £79,000 that it sells to Beta Finance plc on 1 January 20X4 for its fair value of £100,000. Gradgrind immediately leases the asset back from Beta Finance for its remaining economic life of 3 years at £36,000 per year payable in advance. Assume an interest rate of 8%.

Required:
Show the accounting treatment of this transaction in the financial statements of Gradgrind plc for the year ended 31 December 20X4.

On sale of the asset, the following accounting entries are made:

		£	£
Debit	Bank	100,000	
Credit	Asset		79,000
	Deferred revenue		21,000

The present value of the minimum lease payments totals £100,197 (i.e. £36,000 + £36,000/1.08 + £36,000/1.08²), so this lease is accounted for as a finance lease in the usual way. At the commencement of the lease the accounting entries are:

		£	£
Debit	Asset	100,000	
Credit	Lease liability		100,000

(Note: amount is the lower of the present value of the minimum lease payments and the fair value of the asset.)

The first payment under the lease is made:

		£	£
Debit	Lease liability	36,000	
Credit	Bank		36,000

At the end of the year, 31 December 20X4, depreciation and the interest are accounted for:

		£	£
Debit	Depreciation (100,000/3)	33,333	
Credit	Asset		33,333
Debit	Finance charge (see working)	5,120	
Credit	Lease liability		5,120

In addition, the deferred income is amortised to profit and loss:

		£	£
Debit	Deferred revenue (21,000/3)	7,000	
Credit	Profit and loss		7,000

Statement of profit or loss for the year ended 31 December 20X4

	£
Depreciation expense	(33,333)
Finance charge	(5,120)
Release of deferred income	7,000

Statement of financial position at 31 December 20X4

	£
Non-current assets:	
Cost	100,000
Accumulated depreciation	(33,333)
	66,667
Non-current liabilities:	
Lease obligation (see working)	33,120
Deferred income	7,000

Current liabilities:		
Lease obligation		36,000
Deferred income		7,000

Working

Year	Obligation at start of year	Instalment	Obligation after instalment	Interest @ 8%	Obligation at end of year
	£	£	£	£	£
20X4	100,000	(36,000)	64,000	5,120	69,120
20X5	69,120	(36,000)	33,120		

The effect of this is that the asset has effectively been revalued to its fair value of £100,000, with the accounting treatment of this rather different to that permitted under IAS 16 for the revaluation of property, plant and equipment (see Chapter 10 for full details). The new depreciation expense net of the deferred income release (£33,333 − £7,000 = £26,333) is the same as the original depreciation expense (£79,000/3 = £26,333).

The effective commercial transaction of the company receiving a loan based on the security of the asset is reflected by the accounting set out in IAS 17.

15.6.2 Operating leases

The commercial reality of a sale and leaseback involving an operating lease is that a real sale has taken place as the risks and rewards of ownership pass to the finance company, and the seller's intentions are to continue to use the asset for only a portion of its remaining useful life. For example, a business may sell its current premises and then lease them back for a year while it builds new premises, using the sale proceeds to finance this. Thus, a profit or loss on sale (sale proceeds minus carrying amount) should be recognised. However, the accounting for this becomes more complex depending on the sale value of the asset.

If the sale price is at fair value, the profit or loss on sale should be recognised immediately in profit or loss. If the sale price is different from fair value, different rules apply:

1   If the sale price is below fair value and future lease payments are at market levels, any profit or loss is recognised immediately.

    Even though lease payments are set at market levels, the sale price might be below fair value because the company is desperate for cash and so accepts a low sale price to alleviate its liquidity problems. Under these circumstances it is appropriate that the whole loss on disposal should be recognised immediately.

2   If the sale price is below fair value and the loss is compensated for by future lease payments at below market levels, the loss is deferred and amortised in proportion to the lease payments over the period for which the asset is expected to be used.

3   If the sale price is above fair value, the excess over fair value is deferred and amortised over the period for which the asset is expected to be used.

15.7 Future accounting for leases

15.7.1 Issues with IAS 17

As discussed at the start of this chapter, one of the intentions of IAS 17 was to prevent off balance sheet financing resulting from leasing arrangements. However, the distinction was drawn between finance and operating leases, leaving the latter off balance sheet. In 2014 listed companies using IFRS or US GAAP disclosed almost US$3 trillion of off balance sheet lease commitments, representing over 85% of lease agreements. Although companies are required to make disclosures of such future obligations arising under operating leases, this is not a substitute for actual recognition of the assets and liabilities of these agreements. The distinction between the classification of a lease as operating or finance therefore has a considerable impact on the financial statements. Investors have to make arbitrary adjustments to include the assets and liabilities of operating leases in their calculations of a company's indebtedness and financial ratios, such as gearing, return on capital and interest cover, which can then be used in company comparisons. However, these adjustments can only ever be estimates, and it is difficult to perform a clear comparison between companies that lease assets versus companies that acquire assets financed by other forms of loans.

Companies have also structured lease agreements in order to avoid the 'substantially all' transfer of risks and rewards, resulting in similar leases being accounted for differently from company to company. The US Securities and Exchange Commission even expressed concerns about lack of transparency of information about lease obligations. Sir David Tweedie, former chairman of the IASB, is reputed to have said that he wished to fly in an airplane that was actually reflected in the financial statements of the airline company!

It is also argued that the treatment of operating leases under IAS 17 is inconsistent with the definitions of assets and liabilities in the *Conceptual Framework*. An operating lease contract confers a right to use a leased item. This right meets the definition of an asset, and the obligation of the lessee to pay rentals meets the definition of a liability.

15.7.2 Background to IFRS 16 *Leases*

The IASB began work on a new leasing standard to replace IAS 17 as part of its convergence project with the US Financial Accounting Standards Board (FASB). It issued an ED in August 2010, which triggered an unprecedented number of comment letters many of which criticised some of the proposals. Following public meetings and global outreach work the IASB re-exposed its proposals in 2013, receiving yet more feedback and requiring much analysis. Different models for accounting for leases for both lessees and lessors were proposed in these EDs which many respondents considered added too much complexity. IFRS 16 *Leases* was finally issued in January 2016, and is applicable for accounting periods beginning on or after 1 January 2019. Earlier application is permitted, but only if companies also apply IFRS 15 *Revenue from Contracts with Customers*, as there is some relationship between these two new financial reporting standards. The IASB and other professional accountancy bodies and firms are holding many explanatory and training sessions in the period before implementation as the new standard requires such a big change in accounting affecting so many companies. It should be noted that at the time of writing, the EU has not yet **endorsed** IFRS 16.

Although convergence has been a priority for both the IASB and US FASB throughout the leases project, and the boards have reached the same conclusions on many areas, there are some areas on which they could not reach agreement. Accordingly, the lease accounting model for lessees under US GAAP now differs from the IFRS 16 model principally in relation to some presentation and disclosure requirements for leases which had been classified as operating leases under IAS17.

15.8 Accounting for leases under IFRS 16

The main change to lease accounting and reporting is that a single model will be used by lessees with the distinction between finance and operating leases no longer applicable and substantially all leases brought on balance sheet. The IASB and most respondents to its EDs agree that leases create assets and debt-like liabilities for a lessee. However for lessors, the dual model with different accounting treatment for finance and operating leases will remain and not change substantially from the accounting specified in IAS 17. These issues are now discussed in more detail below.

15.8.1 Definition of a lease

The definition of a lease in IFRS 16 together with the application guidance is much more extensive than in IAS 17. This perhaps reflects the more complex leasing contracts that are now prevalent and the fact that the IASB did not wish to create any more bright lines which would encourage companies to consider structuring their contracts to avoid bringing leases onto the statement of financial position. The definition takes a right-of-use approach:

> A contract is, or contains, a lease if the contract conveys the right to control the use of an identified asset for a period of time in exchange for consideration.
>
> *(IASB, 2016a, para. 9)*

The right to control the use of an asset means the customer (the lessee) must have the right to obtain substantially all of the economic benefits from the use of the asset and the right to direct the use of the identified asset. For many lease contracts, the lessee obtains substantially all the economic benefits by having exclusive use of the asset, but the lessee could sub-lease the asset and still meet this requirement. If the supplier of the asset can choose to substitute alternative assets throughout the period of use, and would benefit from doing this, then the lessee would not be considered to have the right to direct the use of the identified asset.

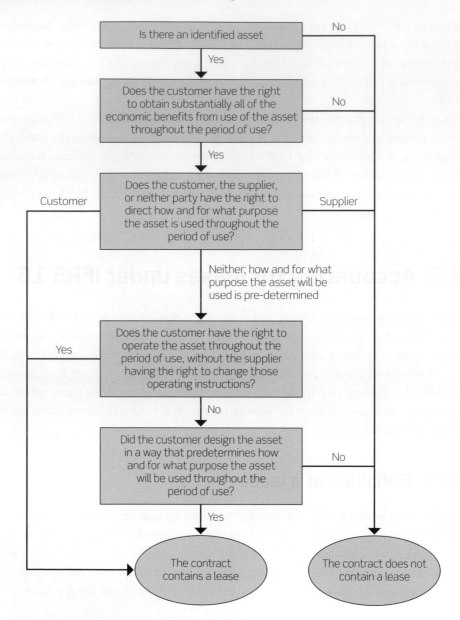

Figure 15.3 Assessment of whether a contract contains a lease (IASB, 2016a, para. B31)

IFRS 16 contains a flowchart to help companies determine whether a contract contains a lease which is shown in Figure 15.3:

 Example of identifying whether a contract contains a lease

A company enters into a contract with a property owner to use an explicitly specified retail unit for a five-year period. The unit is part of a larger retail space with many retail units. The property owner can require the company to relocate to another retail unit, in which case, the property owner is required to provide the company with a retail unit of similar quality and specifications to the original unit and to pay for company's relocation costs. The property owner would benefit economically from relocating the company only if a major new tenant were to decide to occupy a large amount of retail space at a rate sufficiently favourable to cover the costs of relocating the company and other tenants in the retail space. However, at inception of the contract, it is not likely that those circumstances will arise.

The contract requires the company to use the retail unit to sell its goods during the hours that the larger retail space is open. The company makes all of the business decisions about the use of the retail unit during the period of use. The company also controls physical access to the unit throughout the five-year period of use.

The contract requires the company to make fixed payments to the property owner, as well as a percentage of sales.

Is there an identified asset?

The retail unit is explicitly specified in the contract. The property owner has a right to substitute the retail unit, but could benefit economically from substitution only in specific circumstances. The property owner's substitution right is not substantive because, at inception of the contract, those circumstances are not considered likely to arise.

The retail unit is an identified asset.

Has the customer the right to obtain substantially all of the economic benefits from the use of the retail unit?

The company has exclusive use of the retail unit throughout the period of use. Although a portion of the cash flows derived from sales from the retail unit will be passed to the property owner as consideration, this does not prevent the company from having the right to obtain substantially all of the economic benefits from the use of the retail unit.

Has the customer the right to direct the use of the retail unit?

During the period of use, all decisions on how and for what purpose the retail unit is used are made by the customer. The contractual restriction that goods can only be sold during the opening hours of the larger retail space defines the scope of the contract, but it does not limit the company's right to direct the use of the retail unit.

Conclusion

The contract contains a lease of retail space.

Some contracts may contain leases of more than one asset, and also include non-lease components. For example, a company may lease a fleet of motor vehicles with maintenance and servicing also included. Provided the lessee can benefit from the use of each asset separately and they are not interrelated, each lease component should be accounted for individually and separated from the service contract element (which would not be a lease). The basis on which this is done is similar to the allocation of the contract price to the performance obligations in a revenue contract (see Chapter 7 for further details of this). So the consideration in a contract that contains one or more leases is allocated to each lease component on the basis of the relative stand-alone prices of the lease components and the aggregate stand-alone price of the non-lease components. The stand-alone price is the price the lessor would charge the lessee for that component separately. This may have to estimated. For practical expediency, a company could elect not to separate out the leased assets if they are all of the same class, nor to separate any non-lease component.

The lease term is important for purposes of the measurement of the lease liability, and is defined as:

Non-cancellable period of lease	plus	Optional renewal period, if the lessee is reasonably certain to extend the lease	plus	Periods covered by an optional termination, if the lessee is reasonably certain not to terminate the lease early

This has to be determined at the start of a lease, and judgement will have to be exercised to determine whether the company is likely to extend or cancel the lease at some point in the future. The lease term will have to be reassessed if there is a significant event or change in circumstances that affects these estimates, and this will affect the measurement of the lease liability at this point—see section 15.8.3.

15.8.2 Exceptions to lease accounting model

IFRS 16 exempts some leases of right-of-use assets from its requirements. These include leases for the exploration of oil, gas and other non-regenerative resources, biological assets, service concessions and licences for intellectual property and rights for media-related intangible assets such as films, recordings and manuscripts.

In developing the standard, the IASB listened to many respondents who had expressed concerns about the costs of applying the requirements of IFRS 16 to leases that are large in number but low in value. They had suggested that the costs of the application would outweigh any improvement in reported information. Accordingly IFRS 16 allows a lessee to elect not to account for the following leases on its statement of financial position:

1. Short-term leases

    A short-term lease is one that has a lease term of 12 months or less. A lease that has a purchase option, however, is not a short-term lease. This exception may be adopted for a class of similar assets.

2. Leases where the **underlying asset** is of low value

    A low value asset is one where typically the value of an equivalent new asset is less than US$5,000. To be classified as such, the asset has to be independent of other assets, and is one which will not be sub-leased. Low value does not necessarily mean the asset is immaterial to the lessee. Examples of low value assets suggested by the IASB include tablets and personal computers, small items of office furniture and telephones.

The lease payments associated with these two types of lease are recognised as an expense in operating profit or loss on a straight-line basis over the lease term, or on another systematic basis if this is more representative of the pattern of the lessee's benefit.

15.8.3 Lessee accounting

Accounting for leases by the lessee under IFRS 16 is very similar to the accounting for finance leases under IAS 17.

Measurement of lease liability and right-of-use asset

At the commencement of the lease a non-current right-of-use asset and a lease liability are recognised. The lease liability is initially measured as follows:

| Present value of lease rentals | plus | Present value of expected payments at end of lease |

The lease rentals include only those payments that are unavoidable:

- All fixed payments
- Variable payments which are based on an index or rate
- Amounts expected to be payable under residual value guarantees
- The price of a purchase option that the lessee is reasonably certain to exercise.

The variable payments based on an index or rate include, for example, payments linked to a consumer price index or benchmark interest rate such as LIBOR. They are measured initially using the index or rate at the commencement date of the lease. They exclude variable payments which are based on, for example, sales achieved or mileage driven. These latter variable payments are expensed in profit or loss.

The payments are discounted using the interest rate implicit in the lease. This has the same definition as in IAS 17, in other words the discount rate that ensures the present value of the minimum lease payments plus unguaranteed residual value is equal to the fair value of leased asset plus the initial direct costs of lessor. If it cannot be determined, than the lessee's incremental borrowing rate should be used.

The asset is initially measured at cost which is defined here as:

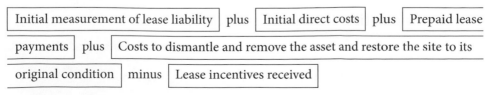

IAS 16 *Property, Plant and Equipment* and IAS 36 *Impairment of Assets* apply for the subsequent measurement of the asset. In other words the asset is depreciated over its useful life, the lessee can elect to use the revaluation model, and the usual impairment requirements and accounting apply. For depreciation, the useful life is taken as:

● the estimated useful life of the asset—for arrangements where the lessor will transfer ownership of the asset to the lessee by the end of the lease term, or where the cost of the asset includes the exercise of a purchase option, or

● the earlier of the estimated useful life of the asset and the end of the lease term—for all other arrangements.

The lease liability is subsequently measured by adding interest on the lease liability and deducting the lease payments made—essentially the effective interest method as described and illustrated in section 15.4.1 is used.

Worked example 15.7: to show the accounting for a lease under IFRS 16

On 1 July 20X3, Chudleigh plc enters into an agreement to lease an item of machinery which will produce specialised units of a product for four years. Payments under the agreement are as follows:

1. Annual payment on 1 July each year. On 1 July 20X3 this is £100,000 and will then rise by 2% compound each year to take account of inflation.

2. Further payment on 1 July each year of £5,000 for every additional 10,000 units produced in excess of 50,000 in the preceding year.

On 1 July 20X3, Chudleigh plc estimates it will produce the following number of units:

y/e 30 June 20X4	40,000
y/e 30 June 20X5	70,000
y/e 30 June 20X6	100,000
y/e 30 June 20X7	120,000

Chudleigh plc incurs cost of £8,000 to install the machine.

The interest rate implicit in the lease is not readily determinable. Chudleigh estimates that it could borrow an amount similar to the value of the machinery being leased for four years at an interest rate of 6% per annum.

Required:
Show how this lease would be accounted for in the financial statements of Chudleigh plc for the financial years ending 30 June 20X4–20X7.

Step 1—Calculation of initial lease liability

Initial lease liability = PV of lease rentals + PV of expected payments at end of lease

The lease rentals would include the 2% inflationary rise (since this is a variable payment based on an index).

The variable payments based on the number of units produced would not be included.

Date	Lease rental		Discount factor	Present value
	£			£
1 July 20X3		100,000	1	100,000
1 July 20X4	100,000 × 1.02 =	102,000	1/1.06	96,226
1 July 20X5	102,000 × 1.02 =	104,040	$1/1.06^2$	92,595
1 July 20X6	104,040 × 1.02 =	106,121	$1/1.06^3$	89,101
Initial lease liability				377,922

Step 2—Apply effective interest rate method to determine the lease liability at the end of each of the financial years, and the finance charge each year

Note that this table is the same as for a finance lease under IAS 17—see Worked example 15.2.

Year-end 30 June	Liability at start of year	Instalment	Liability after instalment	Interest @ 6%	Liability at end of year
	£	£	£	£	£
20X4	377,922	(100,000)	277,922	16,675	294,597
20X5	294,597	(102,000)	192,597	11,556	204,153
20X6	204,153	(104,040)	100,113	6,007	106,120
20X7	106,120	(106,120)	–	–	–

Step 3—Calculate the cost of the asset and the annual depreciation

Cost of right-to-use asset recognised = Initial lease liability + Direct costs

= 377,922 + 8,000 installation costs

= £385,922

Annual depreciation = £385,922/4 = £96, 481

The lease would be accounted for for each of the years ended 30 June 20X4–20X7 as follows:

	20X4	20X5	20X6	20X7
	£	£	£	£
Statement of profit or loss				
Depreciation expense	96,481	96,481	96,480	96,480
Finance charge	16,675	11,556	6,007	–

Statement of financial position

Non-current asset—Right-of-use asset:

Cost	385,922	385,922	385,922	385,922
Accumulated depreciation	(96,481)	(192,962)	(289,442)	(385,922)
Carrying amount	289,441	192,960	96,480	–
Current liability:				
Finance lease obligation	102,000	104,040	106,120	–
Non-current liability:				
Finance lease obligation	192,597	100,113	–	–

Reassessment

Adjustments need to be made for remeasurements to reflect any reassessment of the payments. These can arise from changes to:

- The fixed lease payments
- The lease term
- The rate used to discount the payments
- The assessment of an option to purchase the underlying asset
- The amounts expected to be paid under a residual value guarantee, or
- The index or rate used in the determination of future lease payments.

Reassessment of variable and optional payments does not have to be carried out at each financial year end. The measurement of inflation-linked payments is only reassessed when cash payments change, and of optional payments only on the occurrence of a significant event that is within the control of the lessee.

Any change (debit or credit) to the lease liability will be an adjustment (credit or debit respectively) to the right-of-use asset, and ultimately subsequent depreciation. If the adjustment is a reduction in (debit to) the liability, and the amount exceeds the carrying value of the asset, the excess is accounted for in profit or loss.

 Worked example 15.8: to show the accounting for the subsequent measurement following reassessment

On 1 January 20X1 Fingal plc enters into a four-year lease for an item of machinery, with an option to extend for a further two years. Lease payments are £100,000 per year for the first four years, and £60,000 per year during the optional two years, all payable at the beginning of each year. At the start of the lease, Fingal has no intention of extending the lease.

The interest rate implicit in the lease is not readily determinable. Fingal estimates that it could borrow an amount similar to the value of the machinery being leased for four years at an interest rate of 5% per annum.

On 1 January 20X4 Fingal decides it will take up the option to extend the lease until 31 December 20X6. At this date, the company's incremental borrowing rate has increased to 6% per annum.

Required:

Show how this lease would be accounted for over the years 20X1 to 20X6.

At the commencement of the lease, it is not reasonably certain that Fingal plc will extend the lease, and so the lease term is taken as the initial four years. The impact of the change in circumstances on 1 January 20X4 will be accounted for as a reassessment on this date. The lease liability and right-of-use asset are therefore initially measured at

$$100,000 \times (1 + 1/1.05 + 1/(1.05)^2 + 1/(1.05)^3) = £372,300$$

The lease liability over the first three years is as follows:

Year	Liability at start of year £	Instalment £	Liability after instalment £	Interest @ 5% £	Liability at end of year £
20X1	372,300	(100,000)	272,300	13,615	285,915
20X2	285,915	(100,000)	185,915	9,296	195,211
20X3	195,211	(100,000)	95,211	4,761	99,972

Usual rules as illustrated in Worked example 15.7 apply to determine the split between the current and non-current portions of the liability.

The right-of-use asset is initially depreciated over four years, the length of the lease term at the commencement of the lease.

Annual depreciation expense = 372,300/4 = £93,075

Year	Cost of asset £	Depreciation expense £	Accumulated depreciation £	Net book value £
20X1	372,300	93,075	93,075	279,225
20X2	372,300	93,075	186,150	186,150
20X3	372,300	93,075	279,225	93,075

At 1 January 20X4, the lease is reassessed and the liability is remeasured at

$$100,000 + 60,000 \times (1/1.06 + 1/(1.06)^2) = £209,800$$

The difference between this and the liability at 31 December 20X3 of 209,800 − 99,972 = £109,828 is accounted for as follows:

		£	£
Debit	Right-of-use asset	109,828	
Credit	Lease liability		109,828

The right-of-use asset now has a carrying value of 93,075 + 109,828 = £202,903 which will be depreciated over the three remaining years of the lease at 202,903/3 − £67,634 per year. (The bookkeeping for the remeasurement of the asset at 1 January 20X4 will probably result in the cost account being adjusted to carry the remeasured value of £202,903, with the accumulated depreciation being adjusted to zero.)

The lease liability for the remaining three years is as follows:

Year	Liability at start of year	Instalment	Liability after instalment	Interest @ 6%	Liability at end of year
	£	£	£	£	£
20X4	209,800	(100,000)	109,800	6,588	116,388
20X5	116,388	(60,000)	56,388	3,383	59,711
20X6	59,711	(59,711)*	–		

* Rounding difference

The right-of-use asset will be accounted for as follows:

	Value of asset	Depreciation expense	Accumulated depreciation	Net book value
	£	£	£	£
20X4	202,903	67,634	67,634	135,269
20X5	202,903	67,634	135,268	67,635
20X6	202,903	67,635	202,903	–

Modifications

The reassessment of a lease should be distinguished from the modification of a lease, as the accounting treatment may be different. A modification to a lease changes its scope or the consideration to introduce different terms and conditions. For example, a lease might be shortened or extended (and the option to do so was not in the original conditions), or the asset leased might change, for example where a lessee already leases two floors of a building and the parties agree to add a third floor.

The accounting for the modification depends on how the contract is modified. If the lease is reduced as a result of the modification (for example, only one floor of a building is leased instead of the original two), effectively part of the asset has been sold, and so a gain or loss on the disposal has to be accounted for. This is determined by proportionately reducing both the carrying values of the asset and the lease liability, with the net difference taken to profit or loss as the gain or loss. Next the lease liability is remeasured, and the resulting difference between this and the adjusted lease liability is accounted for as for a reassessment—as in Worked example 15.8.

If the lease increases as a result of the modification (for example, an extra floor of a building is leased) and the change to the payments is commensurate with the stand-alone price for the increased lease, then the modification would be accounted for as a separate lease contract. If the change in payments is not considered commensurate with the stand-alone price for the increased lease, then this would be considered more like a reassessment, and the accounting would remeasure the lease liability and adjust the right-of-use asset as in Worked example 15.8.

Disclosures

The objective of the disclosures for lessees is to enable users of financial statements to assess the effect that leases have on the financial position, financial performance and cash flows of the lessee. Essentially, most items and balances relating to leases are separated out from other items and balances either on the face of the financial statements, or in notes. These include:

(a) The depreciation charge for right-of-use assets by class of underlying asset

(b) The interest expense on lease liabilities

(c) The expense relating to short-term leases and low value assets

(d) The expense relating to **variable lease payments** not included in the measurement of lease liabilities

(e) Income from subleasing right-of-use assets

(f) Total cash outflow for leases

(g) Additions to right-of-use assets

(h) Gains or losses arising from sale and leaseback transactions

(i) The carrying amount of right-of-use assets at the end of the reporting period by class of underlying asset.

Since the lease liability is a financial liability, the disclosure requirements of IFRS 7 Financial Instruments: Disclosure apply to this balance (see Chapter 14 for further details). Essentially, a maturity of lease liabilities based on undiscounted gross cash flows is shown, with the company determining the most appropriate time bands.

The disclosures should also include qualitative information about the nature of the company's leasing activities and any exposure to future cash flows that are not reflected in the measurement of lease liabilities, for example from variable lease payments, short-term leases, or commitments to future leases not yet commenced.

There are no practical company examples to illustrate the application of IFRS 16 yet available. Some companies' accounting policies contained in their 2015 financial statements make mention of forthcoming changes that will result from the future application of IFRS 16, and that they are carrying out an evaluation of these.

15.8.4 Lessor accounting

The two EDs produced by the IASB in the development of IFRS 16 included changes to lessor accounting which provided some symmetry with the changes to lessee accounting. This would have resulted in lessors having to recognise a lease receivable for most leases. The feedback received to these proposals from many investors and analysts indicated that the requirements of lessor accounting under IAS 17 were well understood and, unlike lessee accounting, were not fundamentally flawed. Most users do not currently adjust lessors' financial statements for the effects of leases, indicating that the lessor accounting model of IAS 17 already provides users with the information that they need. Respondents suggested that although it might seem appropriate to have symmetrical lessee and lessor accounting models, this was not essential. As a result, the IASB came to the conclusion that the costs of changing the lessor model seemed to outweigh the benefits. Accordingly IFRS 16 has not changed the essential requirements of the IAS 17 lessor model as described and illustrated in section 15.5.

With increased focus on the reporting of a lessor's exposure to risk, however, there are additional disclosures about a lessor's leasing activities, and in particular its exposure to residual value risk, in other words, how it manages the risk relating to the rights it retains in the assets it leases. This risk can be minimised by, for example, buy-back agreements, residual value guarantees or variable lease payments for use in excess of specified limits. These sorts of strategies require disclosure.

15.8.5 Sale and leaseback arrangements

Accounting for sale and leaseback transactions changes for the lessee under IFRS 16 as the distinction between finance and operating leases has gone. Although most sale and leaseback arrangements are negotiated as one transaction, the accounting is determined by whether the transfer of the asset is a sale as defined by IFRS 15 *Revenue from Contracts with Customers* (see Chapter 7 for details). Essentially control of the asset must have been transferred to the buyer-lessor.

If the transfer of the asset does not meet IFRS 15's requirements, then no sale is recognised by the seller-lessee and no purchase is recognised by the buyer-lessor. The transaction represents in substance a financing arrangement (a loan is being made by the buyer-lessor with security provided by the asset which is being retained by the seller-lessee) and will be accounted for as such. So the seller-lessee and buyer-lessor will account for any amounts received or paid relating to the leaseback as a financial asset or a financial liability, and apply the requirements of IFRS 9 *Financial Instruments* (see Chapter 14 for details).

If the transfer of the asset is classified as a sale:

● On leaseback, the seller-lessee measures the right-of-use asset at the proportion of the previous carrying amount of the asset that relates to the right of use retained by the seller-lessee. This means that on the sale the seller-lessee recognises only the amount of any gain or loss that relates to the rights transferred to the buyer-lessor. Even though from a legal point of view the whole asset may have been sold and leased back, from an economic view, the leaseback only gives the seller-lessee rights to use the asset for the duration of the lease.

● The buyer-lessor accounts for the purchase of the asset by applying applicable financial reporting standards, and for the lease by applying the lessor accounting requirements in IFRS 16.

Prices negotiated in sale and leaseback transactions are not always at market values, and so for comparability with other sales or leases, adjustments need to be made. The gain on sale uses the fair value in its calculation, and the following further adjustments are made:

1. If the sale proceeds are below market (fair) value, typically this will mean that the leaseback payments will be reduced compared to market prices. So the difference between the fair value of the sale and the actual sale price is treated as a prepayment of lease payments.

2. If the sale proceeds are greater than market (fair) value, typically this will mean that leaseback rental payments will be above market rates. Consequently the difference between the fair value of the sale and the actual sale price is treated as additional financing provided by the buyer-lessor.

 Worked example 15.9: to show the accounting for a sale and leaseback transaction with transaction prices different from market prices

Dussek plc sells a building to Global Financing plc for cash of £2,000,000. The fair value of the building at that time is £1,800,000; the carrying amount immediately before the transaction is £1,000,000. At the same time, Dussek enters into a contract with Global Financing for the right to use the building for 18 years, with annual payments of £120,000 payable at the end of each year. The interest rate implicit in the lease is 4.5%, which results in a present value of the annual payments of £1,459,200. The terms and conditions of the transaction are such that the transfer of the building by Dussek to Global Financing meets the definition of a sale under IFRS 15 *Revenue from Contracts with Customers*. Global Financing classifies the lease of the building as an operating lease.

Required:
Show the accounting for this transaction in the financial statements of both Dussek plc and Global Financing plc in accordance with IFRS 16.

Dussek and Global Financing will account for the transaction as a sale and leaseback.

Accounting by Dussek plc

Since the consideration for the sale of the building is not at fair value, Dussek makes adjustments to measure the sale proceeds at fair value. The amount of the excess sale price of £200,000 (£2,000,000 − £1,800,000) is recognised as additional financing provided by Global Financing to Dussek.

		£	£
Debit	Cash	200,000	
Credit	Lease liability		200,000

The sale and leaseback is accounted for as follows.

Dussek plc recognises a right-of-use asset as the proportion of the previous carrying amount (£1,000,000) that reflects the right of use retained. The proportion is the present value of the lease payments divided by the fair value of the building. The value of the right-of use asset is therefore calculated as 1,259,200*/1,800,000 × 1,000,000 = £699,555.

*Note that the present value of the lease payments is not the full £1,459,200, because part of this (£200,000) represents the repayment of the additional financing granted to Dussek.

Given that only a proportion of the asset has been retained, there is a gain or loss on the sale of the remaining portion:

Total gain on sale = fair value of asset on sale − carrying amount = 1,800,000 − 1,000,000
= £800,000.

Portion of gain on sale recognised as such = (1,800,000 − 1,259,200)/1,800,000 × 800,000
= £240,355

The accounting for the sale and leaseback transaction is:

		£	£
Debit	Cash	1,800,000	
	Right-of-use asset	699,555	
Credit	Building		1,000,000
	Lease liability		1,259,200
	Gain on sale		240,355

Accounting by Global Financing plc

At the commencement date of the lease the accounting will be:

		£	£
Debit	Building	1,800,000	
	Financial asset	200,000	
Credit	Cash		2,000,000

Note that the financial asset of £200,000 represents 18 payments of £16,447 discounted at 4.5%. (£16,447 = 200,000/1,459,200 × £120,000).

The financial asset will be accounted for in accordance with IFRS 9 *Financial Instruments at amortised cost*.

So the lease receipts of £120,000 will be split: £16,447 which will accounted for in the subsequent measurement of the financial asset, and £103,553 (£120,000 – £16,447) which will be accounted for as lease rental income.

15.9 Impact of IFRS 16 *Leases*

Without doubt the introduction of IFRS 16 will have a considerable impact on the financial statements of many companies. Research conducted by the IASB in 2014 has resulted in estimates of the understatement of long-term liabilities ranging from 22% by North American companies to 45% by Latin American companies. The statement of financial position impact is obvious, with an increase in non-current assets and liabilities (both current and non-current). Financial position ratios that measure gearing and liquidity will be significantly affected, plus debt covenants and returns on capital employed or on net assets.

For the statement of profit or loss, IRFS 16 changes the nature of expenses related to operating leases which will be brought on balance sheet. Figure 15.4 summarises this.

The operating lease expense under IAS 17 is typically accounted for on a straight-line basis within operating costs. The application of IFRS 16 will mean this expense is replaced by a depreciation charge in operating costs and an interest expense on the lease liability in finance charges. The depreciation expense is usually straight-line over the life of the lease, but the interest expense reduces over the life of the lease, front-loading the expense and reducing as the lease matures. It is anticipated that this difference in expense over the years of a lease between IAS 17 and IFRS 16 will be insignificant for companies holding portfolios of leases

	IAS 17		IRFS 16
	Finance leases	Operating leases	All leases
Revenue	X	X	X
Operating costs (excluding depreciation and amortisation)	–	Single expense	–
EBITDA			⇧⇧
Depreciation and amortisation	Depreciation	–	→ Depreciation
Operating profit			⇧
Finance costs	Interest	–	→ Interest
Profit before tax			⇔

Figure 15.4 The impact of IFRS 16 on the statement of profit or loss

that start and end in different reporting periods. However, there are differences in key performance metrics such as EBITDA (earnings before interest, tax, depreciation and amortisation) and operating profit, and this will also affect key performance ratios such as return on capital employed and profit margin. Interest cover will also change.

 Example of the effect of the accounting for a lease under IAS 17 and IFRS 16 on the statement of profit or loss

Prior to IFRS 16, suppose the lease shown in Worked example 15.7 was accounted for as an operating lease under IAS 17. The annual lease rentals would have been included as an operating expense, and there would be no balances relating to the lease on the statement of financial position.

The expenses charged to profit and loss under the different methods of accounting for the lease would be as follows:

	20X4		20X5		20X6		20X7	
Year end 30 June	IAS 17 £	IFRS 16 £	IAS 17 £	IFRS 16 £	IAS 17 £	IFRS 16 £	IAS 17 £	IFRS 16 £
Operating costs								
Lease rentals	100,000	–	102,000	–	104,040	–	106,121	–
Depreciation	–	96,481	–	96,481	–	96,480	–	96,480
Finance charges	–	16,675	–	11,556	–	6,007	–	–
	100,000	113,156	102,000	108,037	104,040	102,487	106,121	96,480

For cash flows, the change in accounting does not alter the amount of cash transferred between the lessee and lessor. Total reported cash flows will not alter. However, operating cash outflows will reduce because the IAS 17 operating lease payments will not be included as an operating activity. Instead the repayments of the lease liability will be classified as financing cash outflows. The interest element of the payments may be included as operating or financing activities.

Companies leasing large assets such as aircraft, ships and properties typically account for these as operating leases, and the application of IFRS 16 will bring these items on balance sheet together with the associated liabilities. Industries that will see significant changes are therefore transport, logistics, airline, mining and retail.

Whilst there may be some concern amongst companies about the costs of the change in accounting, its impact on the key financial ratios mentioned earlier, and potential consequential changes on their credit ratings, the business benefits of leasing and the overall cash flows are unchanged. The lead time to implementation of IFRS 16 is long, allowing companies and their investors to fully understand and evaluate the impact on future financial statements. The enhanced transparency and comparability of companies' financial transactions, performance and position are considered worthy goals.

 ## Summary of key points

Off balance sheet accounting, one of the most significant financial accounting problems of the later twentieth and early twenty-first centuries, is when financing obligations do not appear on companies' statements of financial position. The types of financial transaction and arrangement which give rise to this are various, but the result is that companies' financial positions, and gearing and return on capital ratios appear better than they would if the debt were recognised.

Leasing arrangements are one of the main contributors to off balance sheet financing. The current accounting standard, IAS 17 *Leases*, classifies leases as either finance or operating. Operating leases remain off balance sheet, although disclosures of obligations under this type of lease do have to be made. A transfer of risks and rewards of ownership model is used to distinguish between the two types of lease; if these are transferred to the lessee then the lease is a finance lease, otherwise the lease is an operating lease. This inevitably involves a subjective judgement, so a key method by which this may be determined is to evaluate whether the present value of the minimum lease payments is at least substantially all of the fair value of the asset. Many companies have taken substantially all to mean around 90%, thus creating a 'bright line', which is contrary to the intentions of principles-based standards.

For lessees, under IAS 17, the accounting for finance leases requires the asset and liability to be included on the statement of financial position at the lower of the present value of the minimum lease payments and the fair value of the asset. The asset is depreciated and the payments are split between a repayment of the liability and an interest charge. The interest is calculated so as to provide a constant periodic rate of interest on the remaining liability balance.

Operating leases are accounted for as hire arrangements with all lease payments being expensed in profit or loss.

The accounting treatment of lease agreements for lessors is virtually a mirror image of that for lessees. For finance leases the asset is sold to the lessee, so it is removed from assets and a receivable is recognised at the present value of the minimum lease payments receivable plus any unguaranteed residual value accruing to the lessor. As lease payments are received these are split between a reduction of the receivable and finance income, which is calculated so as to provide a constant periodic rate of interest on the remaining receivable balance.

For operating leases, the risks and rewards of ownership remain with the lessor, and so the asset remains in the lessor's books, with the receipt of lease payments being accounted for as rental income in the statement of profit or loss.

The IASB and the US FASB have worked for many years on a revised standard which removes the distinction between finance and operating leases and, for lessees, requires them all to be accounted for the same way and brought onto balance sheets. IFRS 16 was finally issued in January 2016, with an implementation date of 1 January 2019, to enable companies to start the necessary preparation for this significant change in accounting methods. For lessees a single right-of-use model applies to all their leases, except for short-term and low-value leases, with the accounting similar to the accounting for finance leases under IAS 17. For lessors, despite some alternative models being put forward in the standard's exposure drafts, it was decided to leave the accounting substantially the same as it currently is in IAS 17. This means the distinction between finance and operating leases still exists for these companies. There is additional detail in IFRS 16, and increased disclosures.

The impact of IFRS 16 on all financial statements of lessees will be significant, but particularly for certain industries where leasing of large assets is prevalent. However, it is considered that the increased transparency and comparability will be of great benefit to users, once they have understood the resulting changes in key figures and metrics.

 ## Further reading

IASB (International Accounting Standards Board) (2005) IAS 17 *Leases*. London: IASB.

IASB (International Accounting Standards Board) (2016a) IFRS 16 *Leases*. London: IASB.

 ## Bibliography

Air France–KLM (2016) *Annual Report 2015*. Tremblay-en-France: Air France–KLM.

Anon. (2010) Lease of strife, *Financial Times* (4 August 2010).

Hogarth, P. (2016) The Nightmare Before Christmas?, *By All Accounts*, January 2016. London: ICAEW.

Hughes, J. (2009) Leasing: Attempt to close a false divide, *Financial Times* (4 February 2009).

Hussey, R. and Ong, A. (2011) IAS 17: Is it fatally flawed?, *International Accountants*, May: 12–15.

IASB (International Accounting Standards Board) (2005) IAS 17 *Leases*. London: IASB.

IASB (International Accounting Standards Board) (2015) Exposure Draft ED/2015/3 *Conceptual Framework for Financial Reporting*. London: IASB.

IASB (International Accounting Standards Board) (2016a) IFRS 16 *Leases*. London: IASB.

IASB (International Accounting Standards Board) (2016b) IFRS 16 *Leases Basis for Conclusions*. London: IASB.

IASB (International Accounting Standards Board) (2016c) IFRS 16 *Leases Illustrative Examples*. London: IASB.

IASB (International Accounting Standards Board) (2016d) IFRS 16 *Leases Project Summary and Feedback Statement*. London: IASB.

IASB (International Accounting Standards Board) (2016e) IFRS 16 *Leases Effects Analysis*. London: IASB.

ICAEW (Institute of Chartered Accountants in England and Wales) (2016a) IFRS 16 *Leases FAQ*. London:

ICAEW (Institute of Chartered Accountants in England and Wales) (2016b) Webinar: *The New IFRS on Leases* (listened to on 22 March 2016).

International Airlines Group (2015) *2014 Annual Report and Accounts*. Madrid: IAG.

Kabureck, G. (2015) Little to Fear in New World of Lease Accounting, *Compliance Week*, December 2015. Boston: ComplianceWeek.

Lloyd, S. (2016) A New Lease of Life, *Investor Perspectives*, January 2016. London: IFRS.

Lloyds Banking Group (2016) *Annual Report and Accounts, 2015*. Edinburgh: Lloyds Banking Group.

Poole, V. (2010) No pain, no gain. Available at: http://www.accountancyage.com (accessed 18 December 2012).

PwC (PricewaterhouseCoopers) (2016) In Depth: *IFRS 16—A New Era of Lease Accounting!* London: PwC.

 # Questions

Quick test

1   (a) Explain what 'off balance sheet financing' is and how IAS 17 *Leases* addresses this issue.

    (b) Dawlish plc entered into a lease for its computer system commencing 1 April 20X6. The terms of the lease are that Dawlish pays four annual rental payments of £150,000 each, with the first payment made on 1 April 20X6. Thereafter, the computer can be rented indefinitely for a nominal sum of £1 per year. The cost of the computer new would have been £523,028 and the finance cost implicit in the lease is 10% per year. Dawlish expects to use the computer system for five years.

    Required:

    Discuss the accounting treatment of this transaction in the accounts of Dawlish plc for the years ended 31 March 20X7 and 20X8 under IAS 17, and calculate the relevant statement of financial position and statement of profit or loss values to be shown.

2   On 1 January 20X0, Power Tools plc acquired use of a machine that normally sells for £3,000,000. Owing to cash flow constraints Power Tools entered into a lease agreement with the machine supplier to pay six semi-annual instalments of £700,000 over the next three years starting on 30 June 20X0. The half-yearly interest rate implicit in the lease is 10%. The machine would normally be expected to last three years. Power Tools is required to insure the machine and cannot return it to the lessor without severe penalties.

    Required:

    (a) Describe whether the lease should be classified as an operating or finance lease according to IAS 17.

    (b) Show the effect of the lease on the statement of profit or loss and statement of financial position of Power Tools plc for the year ended 31 December 20X0 in accordance with IAS 17.

3   Conex plc is the lessee of an asset on a non-cancellable lease contract with a primary term of three years from 1 January 20X7. The rental is £5,404 per quarter, payable in advance. The lessee has a right after the end of the primary period to continue to lease the asset as long as the company wishes at a rent of £1 per year. The lessee bears all maintenance and insurance costs. The leased asset could have been bought for cash at the start of the lease for £55,404. The rate of interest implicit in the lease is 3% per quarter. The company expects to continue to employ the asset for one year after the end of the primary term and uses the straight-line method of depreciation.

Required:

Assuming Conex plc applies IAS 17 *Leases*, show the amounts relating to this agreement to be included in the financial statements of the company for the relevant years.

4   (a) Discuss the difference between a finance lease and an operating lease as given in IAS 17, and explain why this distinction is important in this accounting standard.

(b) Nottingham plc, whose year end is 31 March 20X4, manufactures shoes. On 1 April 20X3 the company entered into an agreement with Capital Finance plc for the lease of a new machine. Terms of the lease include:

(i)   Neither party can cancel

(ii) Nottingham plc is to have responsibility for maintenance

(iii) Six instalments of £45,000 are payable half-yearly in advance.

The cash price of the machine on 1 April 20X3 was £240,000 and the machine is expected to have a life of five years. The rate of interest implicit in the lease is 5% semi-annually.

Required:

In accordance with IAS 17, discuss the accounting treatment of this transaction in the accounts of Nottingham plc for the year ended 31 March 20X4, and calculate the relevant statement of financial position and statement of profit or loss values to be shown.

●● Develop your understanding

5   IAS 17 *Leases* is used to prevent off balance sheet financing abuses for leasing transactions.

Discuss what off balance sheet financing is, why it is important that this issue is tackled, and how the international accounting standard-setters have addressed the issue to date.

(You should use leases and other transactions giving rise to off balance sheet financing as examples to illustrate your answer.)

6   (a) IAS 17 *Leases* distinguishes between two types of lease: finance and operating; and stipulates different accounting treatments for each.

Discuss the requirements of IAS 17 in relation to the principle of 'substance over form'.

(b) Ferrars plc, which has an accounting year end of 31 December 20X7, entered into the following lease agreements with other companies in 20X7:

(i)   On 1 January 20X7 Ferrars leased a specialised machine (Machine X) on a non-cancellable lease contract from Willoughby plc. On that date the machine had a fair value of £503,030. Ferrars estimates that the useful life of the machine is six years.

Details of the lease are:

- term of lease—six years
- six-monthly lease payment, payable in arrears on 30 June and 31 December—£60,000
- six-monthly implicit interest rate—6%
- Ferrars to bear all maintenance and insurance costs.

(ii) Ferrars leased another machine (Machine Y) from Darcy plc on 1 January 20X7. The lease term is three years with three instalments of £84,000 payable to Darcy on 1 January each year. The expected useful life of this machine is six years. At the end of the lease period Machine Y will be transferred back to Darcy. The fair value of the machine at 1 January 20X7 was £300,000 and the annual interest rate implicit in this lease is 12%.

Ferrars plc uses the straight-line method of depreciation for its machinery and estimates the residual value of all machines as zero.

Required:

(a) Discuss the accounting treatment of the two leases in the financial statements of Ferrars plc in accordance with IAS 17.

(b) Show the relevant statement of profit or loss and statement of financial position figures for the two leases for Ferrars plc for the year ended 31 December 20X7.

7   Alpha plc has entered into the following sale and leaseback transactions, details of which are provided as follows.

(i)   Alpha sold an asset with carrying amount of £8,000 to Beta plc at £10,000 and immediately leased back the asset under a finance lease. The fair value of the asset is £10,000.

(ii) Alpha sold an asset with carrying amount of £8,000 to Gamma plc at £10,000 and immediately leased back the asset under an operating lease. The fair value of the asset is £10,000.

(iii) Alpha sold an asset with carrying amount of £12,000 to Delta at £10,000 and immediately leased back the asset under an operating lease. The fair value of the asset is £15,000.

(iv) Alpha sold an asset with carrying amount of £8,000 to Epsilon at £15,000 and immediately leased back the asset under an operating lease. The fair value of the asset is £10,000.

Required:

Explain how Alpha plc should account for each sale and leaseback transaction under IAS 17.

8   Discuss whether the following contracts are leases or contain a lease according to IFRS 16:

(a) A coffee company enters into a contract with an airport operator to use a space in the airport to sell its goods for a three-year period. The contract states the amount of space and that the space may be located at any one of several boarding areas within the airport. The airport operator has the right to change the location of the space allocated to the coffee company at any time during the period of use. There are minimal costs to the airport operator associated with changing the space for the coffee company. The coffee company uses a kiosk (that it owns) that can be moved easily to sell its goods. There are many areas in the airport that are available and that would meet the specifications for the space in the contract.

(b) Mediterranean Air Group enters into a contract with an aircraft owner for the use of an explicitly specified aircraft for a two-year period. The contract details the interior and exterior specifications for the aircraft.

There are contractual and legal restrictions in the contract on where the aircraft can fly. Subject to those restrictions, Mediterranean Air Group determines where and when the aircraft will fly, and which passengers and cargo will be transported on the aircraft. The aircraft owner is responsible for operating the aircraft, using its own crew. Mediterranean Air Group is prohibited from hiring another operator for the aircraft or operating the aircraft itself during the term of the contract.

The aircraft owner is permitted to substitute the aircraft at any time during the two-year period and must substitute the aircraft if it is not working. Any substitute aircraft must meet the interior and exterior specifications in the contract. There are significant costs involved in outfitting an aircraft in the aircraft owner's fleet to meet Mediterranean Air Group's specifications.

(c) Plantagenet plc enters into a contract with Telcom plc for network services for two years. The contract requires Telcom to supply network services that meet a specified quality level. In order to provide the services, Telcom installs and configures servers at Plantagenet's premises—Telcom determines the speed and quality of data transportation in the network using the servers. Telcom can reconfigure or replace the servers when needed to continuously provide the quality of network services defined in the contract. Plantagenet does not operate the servers or make any significant decisions about their use.

●●● Take it further

9   On 1 January 20X8, Shilton plc sold a machine that had a carrying amount in its financial statements of £400,000 to Bucknor plc for its fair value of £497,000. Shilton immediately leased the machine back under the following conditions:

(i)   The term of the lease is four years non-cancellable

(ii) The annual rental is £125,000 payable at the beginning of the year

(iii) The future economic life of the equipment is estimated to be five years

(iv) The machine is to be sold to Shilton for £50,000 at the end of the lease term

(v) The interest rate implicit in the lease is 8%

(vi) Shilton depreciates all its equipment on a straight-line basis.

Required:

(a) Discuss how the lease should be classified for both the lessor and the lessee in accordance with IAS 17.

(b) Prepare the journal entries and show how this lease transaction should be reported in the statement of profit or loss and statement of financial position of Shilton plc for the year ended 31 December 20X8.

10 On 1 January 20X4 Carston plc acquired an asset for its fair value of £75,979 and immediately leased it out to Bollington Ltd for four years under a finance lease with the following lease terms:

● annual payments of £20,000 paid on 1 January each year

● residual value of asset guaranteed by the lessee £7,500

● expected residual value at end of lease £9,000

● interest rate implicit in the lease 10%

● direct costs incurred by lessor at start of lease £500.

Carston's depreciation policy for similar assets is 40% per annum on a reducing balance basis.

Required:

(a) In accordance with IAS 17, show the figures which would appear in the financial statements of Carston plc in relation to this lease agreement for the year ended 31 December 20X4.

(b) Also in accordance with IAS 17, if there were significant restrictions on what the lessee was allowed to do with the asset, the lease would be classified as an operating lease. Using the same figures, show how the lease would be presented in the financial statements of Carston plc for the year ended 31 December 20X4.

11 Surefast plc owns the office building it occupies. The company intends to move into newer premises which are to be built on a nearby site. In order to finance the construction, the company is negotiating a sale and leaseback agreement with Goodrich plc for its current office building. Goodrich has offered Surefast two options.

	Option 1	Option 2
Period of leaseback	3 years	3 years
Purchase price payable by Goodrich	£2.73 million	£3 million
Annual rental payable by Surefast	£210,000	£300,000

The current market value of the office building is approximately £2.85 million and the current carrying amount of the depot in Surefast's statement of financial position is £2.4 million. The market rental for Surefast's offices is estimated to be £250,000 per year.

Required:

Show how each of the above options would impact Surefast's profit or loss for the next three years under IAS 17.

12 On 1 January 20X3 Alton plc enters into a 10-year lease of property with annual lease payments of £50,000, payable at the beginning of each year. The contract specifies that lease payments will increase every two years on the basis of the increase in the Consumer Price Index (CPI) for the preceding 24 months. The CPI at 1 January 20X3 is 125. Ignore any initial direct costs.

The rate implicit in the lease is not readily determinable. Alton's incremental borrowing rate is 5% per annum, which reflects the fixed rate at which the company could borrow an amount similar to the value of the right-of-use asset, in the same currency, for a 10-year term, and with similar collateral.

On 1 January 20X5 the CPI has increased to 135.

Required:

Show how this lease would be accounted for in the financial statements of Alton plc for the years ended 31 December 20X3, 20X4 and 20X5 in accordance with IFRS 16.

13 On 1 January 20X1 Grafton plc enters into a 10-year lease for 5,000 square metres of office space. On 1 January 20X6, Grafton and the lessor agree to amend the original lease for the remaining five years to reduce the lease payments from £100,000 per year to £95,000 per year. The interest rate implicit in the lease cannot be readily determined. Grafton's incremental borrowing rate at the commencement date is 6% per annum. Grafton's incremental borrowing rate at 1 January 20X6 is 7% per annum. The annual lease payments are payable at the end of each year.

Required:

In accordance with IFRS 16, show how this lease would be accounted for in Grafton plc's financial statements in the years ended 31 December 20X1 and 20X6.

14 On 1 July 20X3 Howarth plc enters into a 10-year lease for 5,000 square metres of office space. The annual lease payments are £50,000 payable at the end of each year. The interest rate implicit in the lease cannot be readily determined. Howarth's incremental borrowing rate at the commencement date is 6% per annum. On 1 July 20X8, Howarth and the lessor agree to amend the original lease to reduce the space to only 2,500 square metres of the original space starting from 30 September 20X8. The annual fixed lease payments (from 1 July 20X8 to the end of the lease) are also reduced to £30,000. Howarth's incremental borrowing rate on 1 July 20X8 is 5% per annum.

Required:

In accordance with IFRS 16, show how this lease would be accounted for in Howarth plc's financial statements over the life of the lease.

 Visit the Online Resource Centre for solutions to all these end of chapter questions plus visual walkthrough solutions. You can test your understanding with extra questions and answers, explore additional case studies based on real companies, take a guided tour through a company report and much more. Go to the Online Resource Centre at **www.oxfordtextbooks.co.uk/orc/maynard2e/**

16

Employee benefits and share-based payments

➤ Introduction

This chapter covers accounting and reporting for both short- and long-term employee benefits, with particular emphasis on the key issues of defined benefit pension plans and share-based payments. The huge liabilities for companies caused by their final salary defined benefit schemes has resulted in many such schemes being closed to new entrants; however, the obligations for companies remain. It is important for users to be able to understand the impact of these schemes on the financial performance and position of a company, and the inherent risks that arise from their existence. International Accounting Standard (IAS) 19 *Employee Benefits* is the financial reporting standard which deals with all employee remuneration, except for share-based remuneration, and focuses particularly on defined benefit plans.

Share-based payment schemes form part of many standard remuneration packages in large companies, especially for directors and senior management. International Financial Reporting Standard (IFRS) 2 *Share-based Payment* introduced the recognition of the expense of such schemes, and sets out how the expense is measured and the disclosures required for the many different types of scheme that exist.

★ Learning objectives

After studying this chapter you will be able to:

- Understand how short-term **employee benefits** are accounted for
- Understand the two types of **retirement benefit plans**, the accounting issues arising from them, and how to account for and the disclosures required for **defined benefit plans**
- Understand the different share-based payment arrangements that companies enter into, and how they are accounted for and disclosed in financial statements.

✔ Key issues checklist

- ❏ Short-term employee benefits including bonuses, holiday pay and sick pay.
- ❏ The different types of retirement benefit plan.
- ❏ Principles behind accounting for retirement benefit plans.
- ❏ Accounting for **defined contribution plans**.
- ❏ Accounting for defined benefit plans—statement of financial position balance.
- ❏ Basis and calculation of defined benefit obligation—**projected unit credit method**.
- ❏ Measurement of defined benefit plan assets.
- ❏ Actuarial gains and losses.
- ❏ Statement of comprehensive income expense calculations.
- ❏ Remeasurements.
- ❏ Disclosures for defined benefit plans.
- ❏ Issues relating to the accounting for defined benefit plans.
- ❏ Types of share-based payment schemes.
- ❏ Principles underpinning the accounting for **share-based payment transactions**.
- ❏ Measurement and recognition of the expense and equity balance for **equity-settled share-based arrangements**.
- ❏ Non-market and market **vesting conditions**.
- ❏ Other variations in vesting conditions.
- ❏ Modifications, cancellations and settlements.
- ❏ Measurement and recognition of the expense and liability for **cash-settled share-based arrangements**.
- ❏ Share-based transactions with a choice of settlement method—recipient or company.
- ❏ IFRS 2 disclosures.

16.1 Employee remuneration

A significant proportion of businesses' expenses is taken up by employment costs. The proportion varies from industry to industry and company to company, with it generally being higher in service and retail organisations. There are many elements that make up remuneration to employees, for example:

- Short-term benefits—wages, salaries, bonuses, paid holidays, private health care
- Post-employment benefits—pensions, post-retirement health cover
- Other long-term benefits—sabbatical and long-service leave
- Termination benefits—redundancy and severance pay
- Share-based remuneration.

Companies Act 2006 requires some minimal disclosure of total employee costs (staff costs) in companies' financial statements, and many more disclosures are required of directors' remuneration, as discussed in Chapter 3. However, the accounting for all employee benefits is rather complex. In particular, accounting issues arise in cases where valuations linked to some forms of employee benefits are needed, and where the timing of benefits awarded is not always in the same period as the one in which the employee's services are provided.

The International Accounting Standards Board (IASB) has issued two financial reporting standards to deal with these accounting issues. IFRS 2 *Share-based Payment*, issued in 2004, applies to benefits which are share-based. IAS 19 *Employee Benefits*, the latest version of which was issued in 2011, is the catch-all standard dealing with all other forms of benefits.

16.2 Short-term employee benefits

Short-term employee benefits are those that fall due within twelve months from the end of the period in which the employees provide their services. They include:

- Wages, salaries and social security contributions
- Holiday pay, paid sick leave and paid maternity/paternity leave
- Profit sharing and bonuses payable within twelve months of the end of the period
- Non-monetary benefits such as private health care, company cars and housing.

The accounting treatment is generally straightforward. It recognises the benefits to be paid in exchange for the employees' services in the period they are provided on an accruals basis, and amounts are not discounted. How this applies to short-term compensated absences and profit sharing and bonus plans is discussed and illustrated in more detail in the next two sections.

16.2.1 Short-term compensated absences

There are two categories of short-term compensated absences:

1. **Accumulating absences** are benefits that accrue over an employee's period of service and may be able to be carried forward and used in future periods. Typically, holiday pay falls in this category. The cost of providing these benefits are recognised as an expense as the employee provides the service on which the entitlement to the benefits accrues. If an employee has an unused entitlement at the end of an accounting period, and the company expects to provide this, a liability should be created.

2. **Non-accumulating absences** are benefits that an employee is entitled to, but are not normally capable of being carried forward to the following period if they are unused during the period. Paid sick leave and maternity/paternity pay fall in this category. The cost of providing these benefits is expensed as the absences occur.

 Worked example 16.1: to show the accounting for paid vacation

Blaze plc has 100 employees, all of whom have worked for the company for the full year ended 31 December 20X6. Each is entitled to 20 days' paid vacation per year, at a rate of £80 per day. Unused vacation is carried forward to the following year.

At 31 December 20X6, 95 of the employees have used their full holiday entitlement; and the remaining five have 18 days between them to carry forward.

Required:

How should the expense be recognised in the financial statements of Blaze plc for the year ended 31 December 20X6?

An expense should be recognised as part of staff costs in profit or loss for the year ended 31 December 20X6 for:

100 employees × 20 days × £80 = £160,000

(100 employees × 20 days − 18 days to carry forward) × £80 = £158,560 has been paid during the year.

A liability is recognised in the statement of financial position at 31 December 20X6 for the unused paid vacation entitlement carried forward:

18 days × £80 = £1,440

16.2.2 Profit sharing and bonus plans

A company recognises the expected cost of profit sharing and bonus payments when:

(a) it has a present legal or constructive obligation to make such payments as a result of past events; and

(b) a reliable estimate of the obligation can be made.

A present obligation exists when the company has no realistic alternative but to make the payments. A constructive obligation arises where past performance has led to the expectation that benefits will be payable.

It is often the case that conditions attach to bonus payments—for example, the employee must still be in the company's employment when the bonus becomes payable. In order to make a reliable estimate, the profit sharing and bonus plan should have formal terms setting out how the benefits are to be calculated, or the amount payable is determined before the financial statements are authorised for issue to the shareholders.

 Worked example 16.2: to show the calculation of an annual bonus

Tripod plc has no contractual obligation to pay a bonus to its employees, but past practice shows it has paid a bonus of typically 5% of pre-tax profits into a bonus pool. Employees who remain in employment three months after the end of the financial year are then allocated and paid a bonus in proportion to their salaries. Past data shows that employees representing 10% of annual salaries leave in this three-month window.

For the year ended 30 September 20X3, Tripod plc's pre-tax profits are £1.2 million.

Required:

Calculate the bonus to be recognised in the financial statements for the year ended 30 September 20X3.

Despite Tripod having no contractual obligation to pay bonuses, there is a constructive obligation arising from past practice. The bonus will be recognised as an accrued expense in the financial statements for the year ended 30 September 20X3, calculated as:

$5\% \times £1,200,000 \times (100 - 10)\% = £54,000$

16.3 Post-retirement issues

Many developed economies have ageing populations. This is as a result of many factors, including increased life expectancy, fewer births leading to a decline in the proportion of young people in the total population and the post-World War II baby-boomer generation reaching retirement age. The funding of state-provided pensions is consequently under severe pressure, and governments of these economies therefore have been taking steps to encourage private funding of pensions. In the UK in the early 2000s the government tried to encourage more long-term saving for retirement, particularly among those on low to moderate earnings, by introducing a Stakeholder pension scheme; however, workers had to opt into this scheme and the take-up was not as high as hoped for. New auto-enrolment schemes have more recently been introduced requiring employers to provide a savings scheme for all their employees unless they opt out, and to which employers have to contribute.

Private pension providers, though, also face pressures. As major investors in stock markets, the value of their assets are subject to all market fluctuations. In the UK in the late 1990s, the ability of private pension schemes to reclaim the tax credit on dividends was abolished, reducing funds invested in the schemes. Statutory funding requirements have also been imposed.

16.4 Types of retirement benefit plans

A retirement benefit plan (also referred to as a pension scheme) is a separate legal entity, usually set up as a form of trust by a business, into which the business and employees make contributions over the period of the employment. There are tax benefits for both employee and employer from making contributions to pension schemes. The pension scheme invests the monies contributed, and administers the final pension payments. There are two main types of scheme: defined contribution (or money purchase) schemes and defined benefit schemes, also referred to as final salary schemes.

16.4.1 Defined contribution plans

As its name suggests, under a defined contribution scheme the contributions from both the employees and the employer are fixed, normally at a percentage of the employees' salaries. The amount of pension paid to the former employees is not guaranteed, and will depend on the performance of the scheme's investments. The risk that the final pension will be lower than expectations is carried entirely by the employees.

These schemes are fairly simple to operate and common amongst all, and particularly smaller, companies. They have become increasingly popular with larger companies as these organisations have closed their defined benefit schemes, as discussed in section 16.4.2.

16.4.2 Defined benefit plans

These are defined in IAS 19 as all pension schemes other than defined contribution schemes. Under this type of scheme, the amount of pension paid to the former employees is guaranteed and determined by the employees' lengths of service and salary levels—it is generally linked to salaries paid in the later years of employment. Contributions into the scheme are variable and depend on how the scheme is performing in relation to the expected obligations. Since the employees usually make fixed contributions into the scheme, it is the employer's contributions that will vary, and the employer therefore bears the risk of insufficient funds being available, but can also gain if the scheme is considered to be in surplus.

A formal **actuarial valuation** is carried out at regular intervals to determine a scheme's obligations—which will depend on **actuarial assumptions** such as employee turnover, future salary levels and life expectancy—and the value of the assets in the scheme. (Note—an **actuary** is a professional who deals with the measurement and management of risk and uncertainty, generally using probability and mathematical and economics-based statistical models.) The employer's contributions may vary as a result—the business will be required to increase contributions to make up a shortfall or deficit; alternatively the business may take a contribution holiday to eliminate a surplus.

There are two types of defined benefit scheme. Funded schemes are the type most common in the UK and USA and are separate legal entities from the business, usually managed by independent trustees, and as described earlier. Unfunded schemes are not separate legal entities, so the assets remain those of the business and are not ring-fenced for the payment of benefits. This is the usual type of scheme for many continental European countries, for example France and Germany.

As a result of the post-retirement issues described in section 16.3, many defined benefit pension schemes have found they do not have sufficient funding to meet the demands on them. Consequently the businesses have huge liabilities to make up the deficits. As an illustration of this, the aggregate deficit of all pension funds at 31 December 2015 in the UK's Pension Protection Fund was £222.4 billion, and at the end of 2014 the combined deficits on pension schemes operated by FTSE 350 companies totalled £65 billion. These vast deficits have been around for many years—and this is an issue which has no immediate remedy.

The vast majority of businesses operating defined benefit schemes have therefore closed them to new employees. If they offer a pension as part of a remuneration package, they now offer a defined contribution scheme, or contributions into a personal scheme.

Financial reporting in practice **16.1**

Tata Steel and British Home Stores, 2016

Two major British companies which were both in financial difficulties in 2016, Tata Steel's Port Talbot business and British Home Stores, have revealed enormous defined benefit pension scheme deficits of £700 million and £570 million respectively. These deficits have caused much debate in the discussions about the companies' futures.

16.5 Accounting for retirement benefit plans

IAS 19 specifies the accounting for retirement benefit plans for companies. The accounting methods flow from the principles of this part of the standard, which are as follows:

● The financial statements of a company with a retirement benefit plan should reflect at fair value the assets and liabilities arising from its retirement benefit obligations and any related funding.

- The operating costs of providing retirement benefits to employees should be recognised in the accounting period(s) in which the benefits are earned by the employees.

- Related finance costs and any other changes in value of the assets and liabilities should be recognised in the accounting periods in which they arise.

- The financial statements should contain adequate disclosure of the cost of providing retirement benefits and the related gains, losses, assets and liabilities.

16.5.1 Accounting for defined contribution plans

Accounting for defined contribution plans is straightforward. The contributions made by the employer are in return for the services provided by the employee during the relevant period. The employer has no further obligation for the value of the assets in the plan or the benefits payable.

As a result, the employer's contribution is accounted for as a remuneration expense in the period for which the services are provided by the employee. This is on an accruals basis, so that any amounts unpaid at the end of a period are a liability. If the employer has overpaid contributions, these are accounted for as a prepayment, but only to the extent that there will be a reduction of future contributions or a refund.

 Worked example 16.3: to show the accounting for a defined contribution plan

Florestan plc operates a defined contribution benefit plan for its employees, and is required to contribute 6% of employees' total remuneration into the plan.

During the year ended 31 March 20X4, the company paid total salaries of £20.8 million. A bonus of £4 million based on the profits of the year ended 31 March 20X4 was paid to the relevant employees in May 20X4. The company had paid £1.1 million into the retirement plan by 31 March 20X4.

Required:

Show the effect of the above transactions on the financial statements of Florestan plc for the year ended 31 March 20X4.

		£000
Salaries		20,800
Bonus		4,000
		24,800
Pension contribution for year	6% × 24,800,000	1,488

(continued)

(continued)

Contribution paid	1,100
Owing at 31 March 20X4	388

Statement of profit or loss for the year ended 31 March 20X4

Employees' remuneration expenses will include:

Salaries and bonus	24,800
Pension contribution	1,488

Statement of financial position at 31 March 20X4

Accruals will include:

Bonuses	4,000
Pension contribution	388

16.5.2 Accounting for defined benefit plans

The accounting for a defined contribution plan is inappropriate for a defined benefit plan. This is because, as described in section 16.4.2, the contributions to the plan vary depending on actuarial valuations of the plan's obligations and the value of its assets and expected returns. This approach would lead to misleading figures on the statement of financial position.

IAS 19 takes an approach from the perspective of the statement of financial position by considering what the company's obligations are to provide the agreed benefits to current and former employees, and whether the pension plan's assets are sufficient to meet these. The value of the plan is therefore established as:

	£
Present value of defined benefit obligation at reporting date	X
Fair value of plan assets at reporting date	(X)
Plan deficit/(surplus)	X/(X)

The plan's net deficit or surplus will be reported as a non-current liability or asset respectively in the company's statement of financial position at the reporting date. If the plan is in surplus, the asset recognised is the lower of:

1. the surplus as calculated above, and

2. the **asset ceiling**, which is the present value of any economic benefits available in the form of refunds from the plan or reductions in future contributions to the plan.

16.5.3 Measurement of defined benefit plan assets

The assets are those held by the separate legal entity fund. They are measured at fair value, as defined by IFRS 13:

> Fair value is the price that would be received to sell an asset in an orderly transaction between market participants at the measurement date.
>
> *(IASB, IFRS 13, para. 9)*

Fair value has been discussed in Chapter 2. It is a market-based exit price taking into account market conditions at the measurement date. Generally, the types of assets held by pension schemes will be quoted and unquoted securities, property and insurance policies. Companies should maximise the use of relevant observable inputs and minimise the use of unobservable inputs to determine the fair value of the assets, and so market values will be used where available, and financial models used if market values are not readily available.

16.5.4 Measurement of defined benefit plan obligation

The defined benefit plan obligation is defined as:

> the present value of all expected future payments required to settle the obligation resulting from employee service in the current and prior periods.
>
> *(IASB, IAS 19, para. 8)*

A number of issues relating to this definition need clarifying.

Expected future payments refer to the actual future payments under the plan that employees have earned based on the service they have given. The payments are based on a number of assumptions and estimates, such as future salaries, since the level of benefits are often related to employees' final salaries; and the number of members who will actually draw benefits from the plan, which in turn will depend on estimates of employee turnover and mortality rates.

It is calculated using what is called the projected unit credit method, which sees each period of service as giving rise to an additional unit of benefit entitlement. It measures each unit separately to build up the total obligation. As retirement approaches, the value of each unit of benefit entitlement increases as its discount factor reduces.

The future payments are discounted to their present value using a discount rate that is the market yield on high quality fixed-rate corporate bonds. In some countries this may not be available, so the rate used is the market yield on government bonds.

Worked example 16.4: to show how the obligation is calculated using the projected unit credit method

A lump sum benefit is payable on termination of service and equal to 1% of final salary for each year of service. An employee's salary in year 1 is £10,000 and is assumed to increase at 7% (compound) each year. The employee is expected to leave after five years. Assume the market yield on high quality fixed-rate corporate bonds is 10%.

Required:

Show the obligation at the end of each year for the employee, assuming that there are no changes in the actuarial assumptions given.

Final salary in year 5 = $10,000 \times 1.07^4 = £13,108$

Year	1	2	3	4	5
	£	£	£	£	£
Benefit attributed to:					
–current year (1% of final salary)	131	131	131	131	131
–prior years	0	131	262	393	524
–current and prior years	131	262	393	524	655

The obligation is the present value of the benefit attributed to current and prior years and is calculated by discounting the accrued benefit at each year end assuming the expected length of service of 5 years as follows:

Year	1	2	3	4	5
	£	£	£	£	£
	$\dfrac{131}{1.1^4}$	$\dfrac{262}{1.1^3}$	$\dfrac{393}{1.1^2}$	$\dfrac{524}{1.1}$	$\dfrac{655}{1}$
	= 89	= 196	= 324	= 476	= 655

This can be broken down as follows:

Year	1	2	3	4	5
	£	£	£	£	£
Opening obligation[1]	–	89	196	324	476
Interest at 10%[2]	–	9	20	33	48
Current service cost[3]	89	98	108	119	131
Closing obligation	89	196	324	476	655

Notes:

1 The opening obligation is the present value of the benefit attributed to prior years.

2 The interest is calculated at 10% of the opening obligation.

3 The current service cost is the present value of the benefit attributed to the current year (discounted over the five years of expected service), i.e. $131/1.1^n$.

(Note: this example ignores any additional adjustment needed to reflect the probability that the employee may leave the company at an earlier or later date.)

It can be seen from this example how complex the calculation of the total obligation of a defined benefit plan obligation is for a large company with thousands of employees who may receive benefits in the form of lump sums on retirement and/or annual pensions. The calculations are based on actuarial assumptions which can be split into two main categories: demographic assumptions and financial assumptions. These should be unbiased, in other words, neither too cautious nor too imprudent. They should also be based on market expectations of the periods during which the obligations will be settled—which may be well into the future. Demographic assumptions are concerned with issues such as mortality rates before and after retirement, the rate of employee turnover and early retirements. Financial assumptions relate to future salary levels, which have to take into account seniority, promotions and inflation.

16.5.5 Accounting for a defined benefit plan in the statement of comprehensive income

The rules of double-entry mean that any changes in the measurements of the obligations and assets of a defined benefit plan over an accounting period will affect total comprehensive income for that period. For instance, if the value of the plan's assets changes:

Debit	Plan assets	for an increase
Credit	Comprehensive income	

Debit	Comprehensive income	for a decrease
Credit	Plan assets	

Similarly, if the measurement of the plan's obligations changes:

Debit	Comprehensive income	for an increase
Credit	Plan obligation	

Debit	Plan obligation	for a decrease
Credit	Comprehensive income	

An analysis of the changes is required, with the different elements from this analysis being shown separately either in profit or loss or in other comprehensive income or expense. The change in the measurements of the obligations and assets showing these elements can be presented as follows:

	PV of defined benefit obligation £	FV of plan assets £
Value at start of year (actuarial value)	(X)	X
Retirement benefits paid out	X	(X)
Contributions paid into plan		X
Interest on plan assets		X
Interest cost on obligation	(X)	
Current service cost	(X)	
Past service costs	(X)	
Gain or loss on settlements	X/(X)	
	(X)	X
Remeasurements	X/(X)	X/(X)
Value at end of year (actuarial value)	(X)	X

An explanation of the different elements follows.

Retirement benefits paid out These payments are made by the retirement plan itself and do not pass through the accounting records of the company. The amounts paid out reduce both the plan's obligations and assets.

Contributions paid into the plan These are the employees' and employer's contributions paid in during the year. The accounting is:
Debit Plan assets
 Credit Bank

Interest on plan assets This is an assumed return on the plan's assets. It is calculated as:
Interest rate × plan assets at start of the year
The interest rate used is the market yield on high quality corporate bonds.

Interest cost on obligation This represents the unwinding of the discount rate used to measure the obligation as the obligation for the benefits becomes one year closer.
It can be seen in Worked example 16.1 that this is the interest on the opening obligation, which uses the market yield on high quality corporate bonds as the interest rate.

Current service cost This is the increase in the present value of the plan's obligation resulting from employees' service in the current year. It can be seen as part of the breakdown of the obligation in Worked example 16.1.

Past service cost This is the change in the present value of the plan's obligation for employee service in past periods, resulting from a plan amendment or a **curtailment**. For example, a plan might decide to introduce a medical benefits scheme for former employees. This will create an additional obligation. A curtailment occurs when a company significantly reduces the number of employees covered by a plan as a result of, for example, the closure of a plant or the discontinuance of an operation.

Settlements A settlement occurs when an employer decides to eliminate part or all of its post-employment obligations other than in a way that is set out in the terms of the plan and is included in the actuarial assumptions. A gain or loss on settlement is the difference between the settlement price and the present value of the obligation being settled.

Remeasurements These are balancing figures in the above reconciliations and are discussed in more detail in section 16.5.6.

Returning to the rules of double-entry, it follows that the entries which will appear in total comprehensive income are:

- Interest on plan assets } These are netted off, so the calculation becomes
- Interest cost on obligation } the net interest on the opening net liability/asset
- Current service cost
- Past service cost
- Gain or loss on settlements
- Remeasurements.

A net remeasurement figure from the reconciliations of both the obligation and the assets is included in other comprehensive income; the other figures will appear in profit and loss.

16.5.6 Remeasurements

Remeasurements occur because of changes in the many estimates required. IAS 19 classifies these as:

(a) **Actuarial gains and losses**

(b) **Return on plan assets**

(c) Any change in the effect of the asset ceiling.

At the end of every accounting period, a new actuarial valuation, using updated assumptions, should be carried out for the obligation. This gives rise to actuarial gains and losses which will arise for the following reasons:

- Actual events, for example, employee turnover and salary increases, differ from the estimates made
- Assumptions relating to benefit payment options change
- Estimates are revised—for example, future employee turnover, salary increases, mortality rates, etc.
- Changes to the discount rate used.

The return on plan assets refers to the difference between the recognition of the changes to the plan assets (the opening balance, plus interest, and the cash payments into or out of the plan) and the valuation of the assets at fair value at the end of the accounting period.

Previous versions of IAS 19 allowed companies choice as to how the actuarial gains and losses and differences between the actual and expected return on plan assets were accounted for. Companies could choose to recognise these amounts in profit or loss, or in other comprehensive income and expense, or an alternative '10% corridor' method was available allowing deferral of the recognition of some of these amounts. However, these choices resulted in lack of comparability between companies, potential large fluctuations in profit or loss and the potential for a plan to be recorded as an asset when in reality it was in deficit.

In 2011, IAS 19 was revised. Actuarial gains and losses were redefined as remeasurements as described earlier, and the requirement introduced that they should be recognised immediately in other comprehensive income or expense. The aim is to ensure that the financial effects of the underlying economic events are recorded in the periods in which they occur, thus providing a more faithfully representative picture. The impact is that remeasurements bypass the all-important performance measure of profit after tax, earnings per share and other key investor ratios, but do so for all companies.

 Worked example 16.5: to show the figures which would appear in the financial statements for a defined benefit plan

Hadrill plc, which prepares annual accounts to 31 December, has operated a defined benefit pension scheme for many years. The scheme is non-contributory (i.e. employees are not required to make contributions). At 31 December 20X2, the company's statement of financial position showed a defined benefit liability of £575,000, made up as follows:

	£000
Present value of defined benefit obligation	2,430
Fair value of plan assets	1,855
Defined benefit liability	575

The following figures relate to the year to 31 December 20X3:

	£000
Employer contributions	450
Benefits paid	375
Current service cost for the year	415
Present value of defined benefit obligation at 31 December 20X3	2,810
Fair value of plan assets at 31 December 20X3	2,190
Interest rate on high quality corporate bonds	8%

Required:

Calculate the amounts which should be shown in Hadrill plc's statement of comprehensive income for the year ended 31 December 20X3 and the defined benefit liability (or asset) which should be shown in the company's statement of financial position at that date.

Step 1: Calculate the change in the PV of the obligation

	£000
PV of obligation at start of year	2,430
Add: Interest cost (8% × 2,430)	194
Current service cost	415
Less: Benefits paid in year	(375)
	2,664
Remeasurement (balancing figure)	146
PV of obligation at end of year	2,810

Step 2: Calculate the change in FV of plan assets

	£000
FV of plan assets at start of year	1,855
Add: Interest (8% × 1,855)	148
Contributions received from employer	450
Less: Benefits paid in year	(375)
	2,078
Remeasurement * (balancing figure)	112
FV of plan assets at end of year	2,190

* Equals difference between interest on plan assets and actual return

Statement of comprehensive income	£000
In profit or loss	
Current service cost for year	415
Net interest cost for year (194 – 148)	46
Total expense	461
In other comprehensive income	
Remeasurement expense (146 – 112)	34
Statement of financial position	**£000**
Present value of defined benefit obligation	2,810 Cr
Less: Fair value of plan assets	(2,190) Dr
Defined benefit liability	620

16.5.7 Disclosures for defined benefit plans

The 2011 revision of IAS 19 enhanced the disclosures, as many users had considered the disclosures in the previous version did not adequately highlight the risks arising from defined benefit plans. The disclosures now aim to:

- explain the characteristics of the defined benefit plans and the risks associated with them
- identify and explain the amounts in the financial statements arising from the plans
- describe how the plans may affect the amount, timing and uncertainty of the company's cash flows.

The disclosures include:

(a) a description of the defined benefit plan

(b) a reconciliation of the fair value of plan assets from the opening to the closing position

(c) the actual return on the plan assets

(d) a reconciliation of the movements in the present value of the defined benefit obligation during the period

(e) an analysis of the total expense recognised in profit or loss

(f) the principal actuarial assumptions made.

Financial reporting in practice 16.2	Marks and Spencer plc, 2015

At 28 March 2015 M&S plc had a defined benefit plan asset on its statement of financial position. The following information has been extracted from the retirement benefits note in the group's 2015 financial statements. The extensive disclosures are explained below.

11 Retirement benefits

M&S provides some details of the different pension schemes it operates for its employees.

The Group provides pension arrangements for the benefit of its UK employees through the Marks & Spencer UK Pension Scheme (a defined benefit arrangement which was closed to new entrants with effect from 1 April 2002) and Your M&S Pension Saving Plan (a defined contribution arrangement which has been open to new members with effect from 1 April 2003).

The defined contribution plan is a pension plan under which the Group pays contributions to an independently administered fund, such contributions are based upon a fixed percentage of employees' pay. The Group has no legal or constructive obligations to pay further contributions to the fund once the contributions have been paid. Members' benefits are determined by the amount of contributions paid by the Group and the member, together with investment returns earned on the contributions arising from the performance of each individual's chosen investments and the type of pension the member chooses to buy at retirement. As a result, actuarial risk (that benefits will be lower than expected) and investment risk (that assets invested in will not perform in line with expectations) fall on the employee.

The defined benefit arrangement operates on a final salary basis and at the year end had some 12,000 active members (last year 13,000), 54,000 deferred members (last year 55,000) and 51,000 pensioners (last year 51,000). At the year end, the defined contribution arrangement had some 38,000 active members (last year 38,000) and some 6,000 deferred members (last year 5,000). The scheme is governed by a Trustee board which is independent of the Group.

The Group also operates a small funded defined benefit pension scheme in the Republic of Ireland. This scheme closed to future accrual from 31 October 2013. Retirement benefits also include a UK post-retirement healthcare scheme and unfunded retirement benefits.

Financial details of the defined benefit plan are next provided, and information about how M&S has addressed the plan's deficit since March 2012:

Within the total Group retirement benefit cost of £74.9m (last year £53.5m), £33.7m (last year £27.0m) relates to the UK defined benefit scheme, £36.4m (last year £39.2m) to the UK defined contribution scheme and £4.8m (last year £12.7m) to other retirement benefit schemes.

The most recent actuarial valuation of the UK Defined Benefit Pension Scheme was carried out at 31 March 2012 and showed a deficit of £290m. As a result, a funding plan of £112m cash contributions was agreed with the Trustees. The Group contributed payments of £28m to the UK defined benefit scheme in March 2014 and March 2015 in the current financial year, and expects to contribute an additional £28m each year until March 2017. The difference between the valuation and the funding plan is expected to be met by better than expected investment returns on the scheme's assets. Future contributions to meet the cost of accruing

(continued)

(continued)

benefits to the UK scheme are made at the rate of 23.4% of pensionable salaries up to the next full actuarial valuation.

The financial risks associated with the defined benefit plan are detailed:

By funding its defined benefit pension schemes, the Group is exposed to the risk that the cost of meeting its obligations is higher than anticipated. This could occur for several reasons, for example:

● Investment returns on the schemes' assets may be lower than anticipated, especially if falls in asset values are not matched by similar falls in the value of the schemes' liabilities.

● The level of price inflation may be higher than that assumed, resulting in higher payments from the schemes.

● Scheme members may live longer than assumed, for example due to unanticipated advances in medical healthcare. Members may also exercise (or not exercise) options in a way that leads to increases in the schemes' liabilities, for example through early retirement or commutation of pension for cash.

● Legislative changes could also lead to an increase in the schemes' liabilities.

In addition, the Group has an obligation to the UK defined benefit scheme via the interest in the Scottish Limited Partnership (refer to note 12), through which the Group is exposed to additional risks. In particular, under the legal terms of the Partnership, a default by the Group on the rental payments to the Partnership or a future change in legislation could trigger earlier or higher payments, or an increase in the collateral to be provided by the Group.

Note A shows the overall value of its pension schemes' assets and liabilities:

A. Pensions and other post-retirement liabilities

	2015 £m	2014 £m
Total market value of assets	8,596.5	6,729.4
Present value of scheme liabilities	(8,135.8)	(6,528.7)
Net funded pension plan asset	460.7	200.7
Unfunded retirement benefits	(0.7)	(0.7)
Post-retirement healthcare	(11.0)	(11.0)
Net retirement benefit asset	449.0	189.0
Analysed in the statement of financial position as:		
Retirement benefit asset	460.7	200.7
Retirement benefit deficit	(11.7)	(11.7)
	449.0	189.0

The asset recognised for the UK Defined Benefit Scheme is based on the assumption that the full surplus will ultimately be available to the Group as a future refund of surplus.

Notes B and C include details of assumptions that the actuaries have used in their calculations of the values of the schemes' assets and liabilities, with note D providing some sensitivity analysis of these assumptions. Users require this information to assess how faithfully representative the pension scheme figures are.

B. Financial assumptions

The financial assumptions for the UK scheme and the most recent actuarial valuations of the other post-retirement schemes have been updated by independent qualified actuaries to take account of the requirements of IAS 19 'Employee Benefits' in order to assess the liabilities of the schemes and are as follows:

	2015	2014
	%	%
Rate of increase in salaries	1.0	1.0
Rate of increase in pensions in payment for service	1.9–3.0	2.2–3.3
Discount rate	3.10	4.45
Inflation rate	3.1	3.4
Long-term healthcare cost increases	7.1	7.4

The inflation rate of 3.1% reflects the Retail Price Index (RPI) rate. Certain benefits have been calculated with reference to the Consumer Price Index (CPI) as the inflationary measure and in these instances a rate of 2.1% (last year 2.4%) has been used.

C. Demographic assumptions

Apart from post-retirement mortality, the demographic assumptions are in line with those adopted for the last formal actuarial valuation of the scheme performed as at 31 March 2012. The post-retirement mortality assumptions are based on an analysis of the pensioner mortality trends under the scheme for the period to March 2012 updated to allow for anticipated longevity improvements over the subsequent years. The specific mortality rates used are based on the VITA life tables, adjusted to allow for the experience of scheme pensioners.

The life expectancies underlying the valuation are as follows:

		2015	2014
Current pensioners (at age 65)	– males	22.7	22.4
	– females	24.4	24.1
Future pensioners (at age 65)	– males	22.4	21.8
	– females	25.1	24.6
Deferred pensioners (at age 65)	– males	23.2	22.6
	– females	26.0	25.4

(continued)

(continued)

D. Sensitivity analysis

The table below summarises the estimated impact of changes in the principal actuarial assumptions on the pension scheme surplus:

	2015 £m	2014 £m
(Decrease)/increase in scheme surplus caused by an increase in the discount rate of 0.25% (last year 0.5%)	(70.0)	50.0
Increase/(decrease) in scheme surplus caused by an increase in the inflation rate of 0.25%	30.0	(50.0)
Increase in scheme surplus caused by a decrease in the average life expectancy of one year	330.0	230.0

This sensitivity analysis is based on a change in one assumption while holding all others constant. Therefore interdependencies between the assumptions have not been taken into account within the analysis.

Note E provides a breakdown of the nature of the investments held by the defined benefit scheme, and explains the rationale for this.

E. Analysis of assets

The investment strategy of the UK defined benefit pension scheme is driven by its liability profile, in particular its inflation-linked pension benefits. In addition to its interest in the Scottish Limited Partnership (refer to note 12), the scheme invests in different types of bonds (including corporate bonds and gilts) and derivative instruments (including inflation, interest rate, cross-currency and total return swaps) in order to align movements in the value of its assets with movements in its liabilities arising from changes in market conditions. Broadly the scheme has hedging that covers 90% of interest rate movements and 85% of inflation movements, as measured on the Trustee's funding assumptions which use a discount rate derived from gilt yields.

The fair value of the plan assets at the end of the reporting period for each category are as follows:

	2015 £m	2014 £m
Debt investments		
– government	4,180.0	2,319.0
– corporate bonds	1,211.0	1,255.7
– asset backed securities and structured debt	363.9	232.0
Scottish Limited Partnership interest (see note 12)	531.3	574.7
Equity investments—quoted	1,131.8	998.1
Equity investments—unquoted	178.0	110.1

Property	**327.1**	278.6
Derivatives		
– interest and inflation rate swap contracts	**(127.5)**	51.3
– foreign exchange contracts and other derivatives	**190.9**	123.3
Hedge and reinsurance funds	**313.6**	329.8
Cash and cash equivalents	**306.2**	444.1
Other	**(9.8)**	12.7
	8,596.5	6,729.4

The fair values of the above equity and debt investments are determined based on publicly available market prices wherever available.

Unquoted investments, hedge funds and reinsurance funds are stated at fair value estimates provided by the manager of the investment or fund. Property includes both quoted and unquoted investments. The market value of the Scottish Limited Partnership interest is based on the expected cash flows and benchmark asset-backed credit spreads. It is the policy of the Scheme to hedge a proportion of interest rate and inflation risk. The Scheme reduces its foreign currency exposure using forward foreign exchange contracts.

At year end, the UK scheme indirectly held 199,032 (last year 199,523) ordinary shares in the Company through its investment in UK Equity Index Funds.

Note F shows the different elements of the pension scheme expense changed to profit or loss, as detailed in section 16.5.5. Note the remeasurements are broken down according to the different type of assumption behind them.

F. Analysis of amounts charged against profits

Amounts recognised in comprehensive income in respect of retirement benefit plans are as follows:

	2015 £m	2014 £m
Current service cost	**82.4**	88.7
Administration costs	**2.0**	3.0
Past service costs—curtailment charge	**1.0**	1.0
UK and Ireland one-off pension credits	**–**	(27.5)
Net interest income	**(10.5)**	(11.7)
Total	**74.9**	53.5
Remeasurement on the net defined benefit surplus:		
–actual return on scheme assets excluding amounts included in net interest income	**1,722.4**	(322.0)
–actuarial gain/(loss)—experience	**33.7**	(17.4)

(continued)

(continued)

–actuarial loss—demographic assumptions	**(83.9)**	–
–actuarial (loss)/gain—financial assumptions	**(1,478.5)**	254.1
Components of defined benefit cost recognised in other comprehensive income	**193.7**	(85.3)
Total	**268.6**	(31.8)

Notes G and H provide the required reconciliations of the opening balances of the schemes' assets and liabilities to the closing balances, as shown in section 16.5.5.

G. Scheme assets

Changes in the fair value of the scheme assets are as follows:

	2015	2014
	£m	£m
Fair value of scheme assets at start of year	**6,729.4**	6,930.0
Interest income based on discount rate	**293.0**	294.0
Actual return on scheme assets excluding amounts included in net interest income[1]	**1,722.4**	(322.0)
Employer contributions	**143.0**	92.1
Benefits paid	**(276.5)**	(261.2)
Administration costs	**(2.0)**	(3.0)
Exchange movement	**(12.8)**	(0.5)
Fair value of scheme assets at end of year	**8,596.5**	6,729.4

1. The actual return on scheme assets was a gain of £2,015.4m (last year loss of £27.9m).

H. Pensions and other post-retirement liabilities

Changes in the present value of retirement benefit obligations are as follows:

	2015	2014
	£m	£m
Present value of obligation at start of year	**6,540.4**	6,694.0
Current service cost	**82.4**	88.7
Curtailment charge	**1.0**	1.0
One-off UK and Ireland pension credit (note 5)	–	(27.5)
Interest cost	**282.5**	282.3
Benefits paid	**(276.5)**	(261.2)

Actuarial (gain)/loss—experience	**(33.7)**	17.4
Actuarial loss—demographic assumptions	**83.9**	–
Actuarial loss/(gain)—financial assumptions	**1,478.5**	(254.1)
Exchange movement	**(11.0)**	(0.2)
Present value of obligation at end of year	**8,147.5**	6,540.4
Analysed as:		
Present value of pension scheme liabilities	**8,135.8**	6,528.7
Unfunded pension plans	**0.7**	0.7
Post-retirement healthcare	**11.0**	11.0
Present value of obligation at end of year	**8,147.5**	6,540.4

The average duration of the defined benefit obligation at 28 March 2015 is 18 years (last year 18 years).

16.5.8 Appraisal of the IAS 19 accounting for defined benefit plans

Although the 2011 revision of IAS 19 was designed to make it easier for users of financial statements to understand how defined benefit plans affect an entity's financial position, financial performance and cash flows, a number of issues in relation to the accounting methods remain. Firstly, plan assets are measured at fair value. These will fluctuate, and may be quite volatile, leading to significant changes passing through other comprehensive income. The current fair value at the financial year end may be considered irrelevant for a pension scheme given pension scheme assets are held for the long term.

Despite the changes in the 2011 version of IAS 19, the figures being accounted for in the statement of comprehensive income are complex, and may not be easily understood by users of the financial statements. Some might argue that given the elements in the calculations are so interrelated, the distinction between what passes through profit or loss and the remeasurements, which pass through other comprehensive income, is artificial. Use of a standard interest rate to calculate the net interest is inevitably going to differ from actual returns on assets. In addition, it may not be the most appropriate figure to discount the obligation to present value. The interest figure in profit or loss therefore is not a faithful representation of any finance expense or income.

The IASB has indicated that there are matters relating to pensions and related benefits that need to be addressed. The body intends to carry out a fundamental and broad-based review of these, with the ultimate aim of developing a model that provides sound financial reporting of plans that range from pure defined contribution to pure defined benefit, including accounting for contribution-based promises. There is a growing range of hybrid plan designs that incorporate features of both defined contribution and defined benefit plans. Such plans were not envisaged when IAS 19 was developed and problems are observed when IAS 19 requirements are applied. However, this is considered a long-term project, and it is unlikely that there will be any significant changes for some time.

16.6 Share-based payment

Share-based payment awards (such as share options and shares) are common features of employee remuneration for directors, senior executives and other employees. Some entities also issue shares or share options to pay suppliers, such as providers of professional services.

Financial reporting in practice 16.3   J Sainsbury plc, 2016

Sainsbury's operates a number of different share-based remuneration schemes as the company details in its 2016 annual report.

Deferred Share Award 2016/17 policy

The Deferred Share Award ('DSA') is used to drive performance against a diverse range of key financial and strategic scorecard measures and rewards Executive Directors for achieving the short-term objectives that will directly lead to building the sustainable, long-term growth of the Company. These awards are made in shares to ensure further alignment of Executive Directors' interests with shareholders.

The DSA covers broadly the top 40 senior leaders in the Company, including Executive Directors. Performance is assessed in the round based on the Committee's judgement of performance achieved against a number of measures within four broad categories. The categories and examples of the measures that will be reviewed for 2016/17 are set out below.

Financial performance	Profit, earnings per share, sales
Returns to shareholders	Total shareholder return, dividend yield
Relative performance against peers	Market share, industry profit pool
Strategic goals	Products, services, price, customers, colleagues, values

Long-term incentives 2016/17 policy

The long-term incentive vehicle in use at Sainsbury's is known as Future Builder. Around 200 senior managers participate in this arrangement. A core award of shares is granted, calculated as a percentage of salary and scaled according to level of seniority. Vesting of the core award is dependent upon performance against specific measures (common for all participants) tested at the end of a three-year performance period.

All-employee share plans

The Company encourages share ownership and operates two all-employee share plans for colleagues, namely the Savings-Related Share Option Plan ('Sharesave') and the All-Employee Share Ownership Plan, of which the Sainsbury's Share Purchase Plan ('SSPP') is a part. As these are all-employee plans there are no performance conditions.

Prior to the issue of IFRS 2 *Share-based Payment*, there was no accounting standard covering the recognition and measurement of these types of transactions. This became a key issue for companies, given the increasing prevalence of share-based payment awards in many countries. It was also anomalous, in that payments to employees for their services in cash were recorded as an expense, whereas payments in share options were not. As share-based payment awards became a larger component of employee and particularly executive compensation in the late 1990s, standard-setters came to believe that share-based payment awards are an integral component of a total compensation package. As such, they concluded that an entity should recognise an expense for share-based payments, just as it does for cash compensation. This would ensure financial statements provided more transparent and faithfully representative information for investors and the business community.

IFRS 2 was issued in February 2004, and prescribes the measurement and recognition principles for all share-based payment awards within scope of the standard. The standard applies to share-based payment transactions with employees and other third parties, whether settled in cash, equity instruments or other less common assets (e.g. gold). The standard has been amended several times since it was issued.

The introduction of IFRS 2 had a significant impact on some companies' reported profits. For example, GlaxoSmithKlein plc, the pharmaceutical giant, adopted IFRS 2 in 2005 in line with all other EU listed companies and restated its 2004 and 2003 results. The effect of the application of IFRS 2 on the pre-tax profits of these years was: in 2004 a decrease of £309 million (5.0%); and in 2003 a decrease of £368 million (5.8%). Since 2004, some companies have been re-evaluating the use of share options as part of employee remuneration.

16.7 Basic principles

16.7.1 Types of share-based transactions

IFRS 2 applies to all share-based payment transactions. The standard recognises three types of transaction, according to the method of settlement:

1. Equity-settled share-based payment transactions

    The company receives goods or services in exchange for equity instruments of the company which could be shares or share options.

2. Cash-settled share-based payment transactions

    These are sometimes referred to as liability awards. The company receives goods or services in exchange for amounts of cash that are based on the price or value of the company's shares or other equity instruments of the company.

3. Transactions with a choice of settlement

    The company receives goods or services and either the company or the supplier has a choice as to whether the company settles the transaction in cash or other assets or by issuing equity instruments.

Goods and services referred to in this list can be received from external suppliers or employees. Goods include inventories, consumables, property, plant and equipment, intangibles and other non-financial assets.

Transactions falling outside the scope of IFRS 2 are those in financial assets which are within the scope of IAS 32 *Financial Instruments: Presentation* and IFRS 9 *Financial Instruments*; those with shareholders acting solely in their capacity as shareholders; and goods and services received by a company that are settled by companies or shareholders not within the group. The acquisition of goods in a business combination, and transfers of assets in certain group restructurings are also excluded.

16.7.2 Accounting for share-based transactions

The general principle of IFRS 2 is that the company recognises an expense or asset for the goods or services received, with the credit entry recognised either in equity or as a liability, depending on how the share-based payment award is required to be settled, as shown in Figure 16.1.

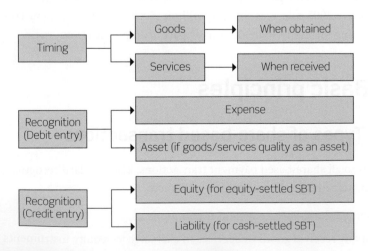

Figure 16.1 Recognition of share-based transactions (SBT)

16.7.3 Measurement at fair value

The measurement of the transaction is at the fair value of either the goods or services received or the equity instruments granted (which is discussed in section 16.8). However, the definition of fair value used here is not the current IFRS 13 definition because IFRS 13 does not apply to transactions within the scope of IFRS 2. The definition used by IFRS 2 is:

> The amount for which an asset could be exchanged, a liability settled, or an equity instrument granted could be exchanged, between knowledgeable, willing parties in an arm's length transaction.

> *(IASB, IFRS 2, Appendix A)*

The difference between this definition and that discussed in Chapter 2 is not significant for the purposes of the coverage of IFRS 2 in this chapter.

As shall be seen, the majority of share-based transactions with employees require fair values of the company's shares or of share options to be used. The fair value should be based on market prices where available. If market prices are not available, the fair value should be estimated using a suitable valuation technique. The actual valuation techniques are outside the scope of this textbook, but IFRS 2 discusses some general issues relating to the techniques selected.

In particular, share options granted to employees do not generally have a readily available market price because the conditions attached to the options usually make them different from other options that a company may trade on the open market. So option pricing models, such as the Black-Scholes model or the Binomial model, have to be used to calculate fair value. Various factors have to be considered in the use of these models:

(a) The exercise price of the option.

This is given in the agreement.

(b) The life of the option

Employee options often have long lives with a range of dates in which the option can be exercised. An estimate of the expected life of an individual option will have to be obtained.

(c) The current price of the underlying shares

This will be readily available for listed companies.

(d) The expected volatility of the share price

This is an estimated measure of the amount by which a share price is expected to fluctuate during a period, and is typically expressed in terms of the percentage variation in price that is expected to arise over a period of time.

(e) The dividend expected

This should only be included where the employee is not entitled to dividends on the options granted.

(f) The risk-free interest rate

'The implied yield currently available on zero-coupon government issues of the country in whose currency the exercise price is expressed' is typically used.

The determination of fair value, the date of its measurement and the accounting for subsequent changes in fair value is determined by the different types of share-based transactions as discussed further in the sections which follow.

16.7.4 Share-based transaction terminology

Before the accounting for the different types of share-based transactions is discussed in detail, some relevant terminology needs to be explained.

Grant date	The date at which the entity and the other party agree to the share-based payment arrangement. This is when the parties have a shared understanding of the terms and conditions of the arrangement. At this date the entity agrees to pay cash, other assets or equity instruments to the other party provided that specified vesting conditions, if any, are met. If the agreement is subject to an approval process, the approval date becomes the grant date.
Vesting conditions	The conditions that must be satisfied for the other party to become entitled to receive the share-based payment. Vesting conditions are service or **performance conditions**, with the performance conditions being either non-market based or market based.
Service condition	A vesting condition which requires the other party to complete a specified period of service during which services are provided to the entity.
Performance condition	A vesting condition which requires the other party to complete a specified period of service and meet specified performance targets while rendering the service.
Non-market-based condition	A non-market-based condition not connected to the market price of the entity's shares. Examples include achievement of a specific level of sales or profit, or completion of a particular project.
Market-based condition	A market-based condition is linked to the market price of the shares in some way. Examples of such a condition include a minimum increase in the share price, a minimum increase in shareholder return or achieving a target share price.
Vesting period	The period during which the vesting conditions are to be satisfied. This could be a number of years.
Vesting date	The date on which all vesting conditions have been met and the third party becomes entitled to the share-based payment.

If the vesting conditions are met immediately, the grant date and vesting date are the same.

Some conditions may be part of the agreement, but are essentially non-vesting conditions. IFRS 2 does not specifically define a non-vesting condition, but uses the term to describe a condition that is neither a service condition nor a performance condition. A performance condition is distinguished from a non-vesting condition by having a service requirement, whereas a non-vesting condition does not. This means that if an employee is entitled to an award on the grant date and is not required to provide any future services to the entity, such a condition is referred to as a non-vesting condition. Examples of non-vesting conditions include non-compete clauses, targets based on a commodity index or the employee paying contributions towards the exercise price of a share-based payment award.

The determination of whether there is a shared understanding of the terms and conditions of the arrangement may require the exercise of significant judgement. This may be the case, for example, when the formula for determining the number of awards to employees is not clearly defined; or final substantive approvals are required; or the number of shares ultimately received will not be known until the vesting date. All terms of the award and the specific facts and circumstances will have to be examined by entities in order to make this assessment.

16.8 Equity-settled share-based payment transactions

If goods or services are received by an entity in exchange for shares or share options, the transaction is accounted for as follows:

Debit   Expense/asset
  Credit   Equity

IFRS 2 does not stipulate which account within equity should be credited, although in practice, many companies set up a separate reserve account.

The measurement is at fair value, and this is determined by whether the transaction is with employees or other third parties as shown in Figure 16.2.

16.8.1 Allocation of expense to financial periods

If the instruments granted **vest** immediately, in other words the vesting conditions are met at the grant date, the transaction is accounted for in full on the grant date. This also applies to awards with non-vesting conditions.

If the entitlement to the shares or share options requires vesting conditions to be met over a vesting period, the expense is spread over the vesting period. Where the vesting conditions are non-market based, only the number of shares or share options expected to vest will be

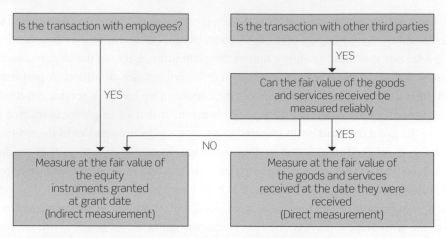

Figure 16.2 Measurement of equity-settled share-based transactions

accounted for. This estimate must be revised as necessary at each accounting period end which falls within the vesting period. On the vesting date, the estimate is revised to the actual number of shares or share options that do actually vest.

The allocation of the expense to the periods covered by the vesting period is illustrated in Worked example 16.6 and Worked example 16.7.

Worked example 16.6: to show the accounting for an equity-based share-based transaction with a third party

Bramble plc has been paying for services provided by its lawyers, Carter & Co., at the rate of £500 per hour. Carter & Co. has informed Bramble that it will be increasing its fees by 5% per annum from 1 January 20X1 for the foreseeable future. Bramble plc is currently experiencing some cash flow difficulties, and agrees with Carter & Co. that it will make payments in the form of shares from 1 January 20X1. The arrangement is for the years 20X1 and 20X2. Bramble plc will issue 5,000 of its £1 equity shares to Carter & Co. every six months in exchange for Carter & Co. providing 300 hours of advice over each six-month period.

Required:

What is the expense recognised in profit or loss and the corresponding increase in equity in 20X1 and 20X2?

Carter & Co. is another third party, so the services received and shares issued by Bramble plc are measured at the fair value of the services received. These can be reliably measured using the fees information.

In 20X1

Expense included in profit or loss = $(2 \times 300) \times (1.05 \times £500) = £315,000$

10,000 £1 equity shares are issued, so the credit to equity is split £10,000 to share capital and £305,000 (315,000 − 10,000) to share premium.

In 20X2

Expense included in profit or loss $= (2 \times 300) \times (1.05^2 \times £500) = £330,750$

10,000 £1 equity shares are issued, so the credit to equity is split £10,000 to share capital and £320,750 (330,750 − 10,000) to share premium.

Worked example 16.7: to show the accounting for an equity-based share-based transaction with employees

On 1 January 20X5 Blaze plc grants 100 share options to each of its 500 employees. Each grant is conditional upon the employee working for the entity over the next three years. The entity estimates that the fair value of each share option at grant date is £15.

On the basis of a weighted average probability, Blaze plc estimates that 20% of employees will leave during the three-year period and therefore forfeit their rights to the share options.

Required:

Calculate the expense to be recognised in profit or loss for each of the years 20X5, 20X6 and 20X7:

(a) On the basis that the actual numbers of employees leaving over the three-year period is 20%

(b) On the basis that at the financial year ends the estimates of the numbers of employees leaving is revised in light of the actual numbers leaving, as follows:

	Number leaving	Estimate of total departures over the three-year period
20X5	20	15%
20X6	22	12%
20X7	15	

(a) The expense will be spread over the vesting period as follows:

Year		Cumulative expense £	Expense for year £
20X5	$100 \times 500 \times 80\% \times £15 \times \frac{1}{3}$	200,000	200,000
20X6	$100 \times 500 \times 80\% \times £15 \times \frac{2}{3}$	400,000	200,000
20X7	$100 \times 500 \times 80\% \times £15$	600,000	200,000

(b) The expense will be spread over the vesting period. However the change in estimate of total departures has to be accounted for. At the end of 20X7 it is known how many share options will vest. The calculations are as follows:

Year		Cumulative expense £	Expense for year £
20X5	100 × 500 × 85% × £15 × 1/3	212,500	212,500
20X6	100 × 500 × 88% × £15 × 2/3	440,000	227,500
20X7	100 × (500 − 57) × £15	664,500	224,500

16.8.2 Market-based vesting conditions

If the vesting conditions are market based, then these conditions are taken into account when calculating the fair value of the equity instruments at the grant date. However, they are not taken into account when estimating the number of shares or share options likely to vest at each period end. So even if the market condition is not satisfied, for example, the share price appears unlikely to achieve the target price, the expense will still be recorded over the vesting period. At the vesting date, if the target price has not been reached, the shares or share options will not vest. However, no subsequent adjustment is made to the financial statements—there is no write-back of the expense, and the increase in equity remains.

 Example of an equity-based share-based transaction with non-market and market vesting conditions

Suppose a company grants share options to a senior employee with two conditions:

1. The employee must work for the company for three years; and

2. The share price must increase at 20% per annum compound over the three years.

The share price growth is a market condition and will be taken into account in estimating the fair value of the options at grant date. However, no adjustment is made for changes in the market price of the shares over the vesting period. It is only the non-market condition that will be considered.

So, for years 1 and 2, if the employee continues to work for the company, and it is likely they will for the full three years, the company will estimate that the vesting conditions will be met. Any changes in the market price of the shares over this time are ignored. The accounting for the expense and increase in equity will follow along the lines as shown in Worked example 16.7 using the fair value of the share options at grant date.

Suppose at the end of the year 3 the employee is still working for the company, but the share price increase has failed to reach the target of 20% per annum compound. This market-based condition is still ignored for the purposes of recording the expense and the increase in equity in this year.

The share options have not vested, but there is no write-back of expenses or adjustments to the equity reserve.

16.8.3 Variable and multiple vesting periods

If an employee is granted share options conditional upon the achievement of both a performance condition and remaining in the company's employment until that performance condition is satisfied, the length of the vesting period will vary depending on when that performance condition is satisfied. The company will have to estimate the length of the expected vesting period at grant date, based on the most likely outcome of the performance condition.

If the performance condition is a market condition, the estimate of the length of the expected vesting period needs to be consistent with the assumptions used in estimating the fair value of the options granted, and it is not subsequently revised. If the performance condition is not a market condition, the estimate of the length of the vesting period should be revised, as necessary, if subsequent information indicates that the length of the vesting period differs from previous estimates.

> **Worked example 16.8:** to show the accounting for a share-based transaction with market and non-market performance conditions

Compeyson plc issued 10,000 share options to certain employees that will vest once revenues reach £1 billion and the company share price is £20. The employees will have to be employed with Compeyson plc at the time the share options vest in order to receive the options. The share options had a fair value of £12 each at the grant date and will expire in 10 years.

Required:

What expense should be calculated and how would it be accounted for under each of the following different scenarios?

(a) Revenues reach £1 billion, all employees are still employed and the share price is £25.

(b) Revenues reach £1 billion, all employees are still employed and the share price reaches only £19.

(c) The share price is greater than £20, all employees are still employed, but revenues have not yet reached £1 billion.

(d) Revenues reach £1 billion, the share price is greater than £20 and half of the employees who received options left the company prior to the vesting date.

The three vesting conditions are defined as follows:

- Revenue target—non-market-based performance condition
- Share price target—market-based performance condition
- Employee remaining in employment—service condition.

Compeyson plc will have to estimate the vesting period, in other words how long will it be before both revenues have reached £1 billion and the share price has reached £20. This cannot exceed 10 years. The total expense calculated for each of the scenarios will be spread over this period.

(a) All vesting conditions have been met

Total expense = 10,000 × £12 = £120,000

(b) The market-based performance condition has not been met. This does not affect the recording of the expense which totals £120,000 and is spread over the estimated vesting period. The award will not vest, but the expense and increase in equity remain accounted for.

(c) The non-market-based performance condition has not been met. In the year that it is assumed this will not be met, the total expense is recorded as zero, causing a credit to profit or loss in that year, and the reversal of the equity balance which has been created.

(d) The service condition has not been met for half the employees. Over the estimated vesting period, Compeyson plc should be revising its estimate of how many employees will remain employed which will affect the cumulative expense recorded. Once the other conditions have been met, the vesting period has ended, and at this point the total expense will be ½ × 10,000 × £12 = £60,000

Share-based payment awards frequently have one grant date and different vesting periods. If this is the case, the company must separately determine the fair value of each award with a different vesting period and recognise the expense over the relevant vesting period. This is illustrated in the following example.

 Example of an award with multiple vesting periods

On 1 January 20X3, a company grants an award to an executive for 40,000 share options, such that 10,000 share options vest in each of the next four years depending on whether the executive is employed at the end of that year.

There is one grant date—1 January 20X3 (and, therefore, one measurement date) for multiple service periods. This award has a vesting pattern whereby the 20X3 portion has a one-year vesting period, the 20X4 portion has a two-year vesting period, the 20X5 portion has a three-year vesting period, and the 20X6 portion has a four-year vesting period. Each portion of the total award is accounted for as a separate share-based award and accounted for separately.

Suppose the example were varied such that performance targets were set on 1 January of each respective year. In this case there would be multiple grant dates. Each respective year would represent an award of 10,000 options, each of which has a 1 January grant date and a one-year vesting period.

16.8.4 Modifications in equity-settled share-based awards

The terms of an agreement for an equity-settled share-based award may be modified before the award vests. This may be as a result of changes in the market price of the company's share due to circumstances outside the company's immediate control. For example, a general downturn in the equity market may mean that the original share option exercise price set is no longer attractive. In such circumstances the agreement may be modified and the exercise price reduced to make it valuable again. Note that this will also affect the fair value of the option.

The accounting treatment of modifications and repricing is as follows:

1. Continue to recognise the original fair value of the instrument even where the later modification has reduced the fair value.

2. Recognise the increase in the fair value of the instrument measured immediately before and after the modification, or any increase in the number of instruments granted as a result of modification. These increases are recognised over the period between the modification date and the vesting date.

3. If modification occurs after the vesting date, then the additional fair value must be recognised immediately.

 Worked example 16.9: to show the accounting for the repricing of share options

Bilbo plc granted 1,000 share options at an exercise price of £50 to each of its 30 key management personnel on 1 January 20X4. The options only vest if the managers were still employed on 31 December 20X7. The fair value of the share options was estimated at £20 and the entity estimated 10 managers would leave before 31 December 20X7. This estimate was confirmed on 31 December 20X4.

The entity's share price collapsed early in 20X5. On 1 July 20X5 the entity modified the share options scheme by reducing the exercise price to £15. It estimated that the fair value of an option was £2 immediately before the price reduction and £11 immediately after. It retained its estimate that options would vest with 20 managers.

Required:

How should the modification be recognised?

Total cost of the original option scheme = 1,000 shares × 20 managers × £20 = £400,000

This is recognised at the rate of £100,000 each year.

Cost of the modification = 1,000 × 20 managers × (£11−£2) = £180,000

This additional cost should be recognised over the period from 1 July 20X5 to 31 December 20X7, i.e. 30 months.

Total cost in year ended 31 December 20X5 = £100,000 + (£180,000 × 6/30) = £136,000

Note that this seems counterintuitive, since a reduction in the fair value of the options (£20 to £15) would seem to imply that there should be a reduction in the expense.

16.8.5 Cancellations and settlements

A company may settle or cancel an equity-based award during the vesting period. The principle behind the accounting is that the cancellation or settlement does not avoid the total expected expense; it just brings the recognition forward to earlier periods. However, an adjustment will need to be made to the equity balance that has been created. The accounting is as follows:

1. On the date of cancellation or settlement, the remaining fair value of the instruments that has not yet been recognised over the vesting period is immediately recognised.

2. Any amount paid to the employees on settlement is treated as a share buy-back and is recognised as a reduction of equity. If the payment amount is greater than the fair value of the instruments, measured at the settlement date, the excess is recognised immediately in profit or loss.

 Worked example 16.10: to show the accounting for the cancellation of a share-based transaction

Weller plc granted 1,000 share options at an exercise price of £15 to each of its 20 key management personnel on 1 January 20X0. The options only vest if the managers are still employed by the entity on 31 December 20X2. The fair value of the options was estimated at £28 and the entity estimated that 16 managers would still be employed at 31 December 20X2. This estimate remained the same on 31 December 20X0.

In 20X1 Weller decided to abolish the existing scheme, for which the only vesting condition was being employed over a particular period, and replace it with an alternative performance target-related scheme. The scheme was cancelled on 30 June 20X1 when the fair value of the options was £48 and the market price of the entity's shares was £55. Compensation was paid to the 18 managers in employment at that date, at the rate of £50 per option.

Required:

How should the entity recognise the cancellation?

Original cost of share option scheme

= 1,000 shares × 16 managers × £28 = £448,000

This is recognised at the rate of £149,333 in each of the three years.

At 30 June 20X1 Weller recognises the total cost based on the amount of options it estimates would have vested, using the actual no. of employees at that date

= 1,000 × 18 managers × £28 = £504,000

20X1 charge to profit or loss = 504,000–149,333 = £354,667

At 30 June 20X1 compensation paid = 1,000 × 18 × £50 = £900,000

Of this, the amount attributable to the fair value of the options cancelled

$= 1,000 \times 18 \times £48$ (the fair value of the option, not of the underlying share) $= £864,000$

This is deducted from equity as a share buy-back. The remaining £36,000 (900,000 − 864,000) is charged to profit or loss.

16.9 Cash-settled share-based payment transactions

Cash-settled share-based payment transactions are transactions where the settlement of the liability for goods and services received is in cash, and the amount is based on the value of the company's equity instruments. Examples of such transactions include:

- **Share appreciation rights (SARs)** whereby the employees become entitled to a future cash payment (rather than an equity instrument) based on the increase in the company's share price over a specified period of time
- Rights to redeemable shares—these will be convertible to cash on redemption

16.9.1 Accounting for cash-settled share-based payment transactions

Many of the principles and accounting for cash-settled share-based payment transactions are similar to that for equity-settled share-based payment transactions. The basic accounting a transaction is:

Debit   Expense/asset
    Credit   Liability

The expense is recognised in profit or loss as services are provided. For example, if share appreciation rights do not vest until the employees have completed a specified period of service, the company should recognise the expense and the related liability over that period. When determining the rights to payment that will vest, any vesting conditions are taken into account in a similar way as for equity-settled transactions.

However, the measurement of the transaction is at the fair value of the liability. In addition, the fair value of the liability is remeasured at each reporting period end and at the date of settlement. Any changes in fair value are recognised in profit or loss.

Worked example 16.11: to show the accounting for a cash-settled share-based payment award

On 1 January 20X1 Griffin plc grants 100 cash share appreciation rights (SARs) to each of its 300 employees, on condition they continue to work for the company until 31 December 20X3.

During 20X1, 20 employees leave. At 31 December 20X1, Griffin estimates that a further 40 will leave during 20X2 and 20X3.

During 20X2, 10 employees leave. At 31 December 20X2, Griffin estimates that a further 20 will leave during 20X3.

During 20X3, 10 employees leave.

At 31 December 20X3 60 employees exercise their SARs. Another 120 exercise their SARs at 31 December 20X4, and the remaining employees exercise them at the end of 20X5.

The fair values of a SAR at each year end, together with the intrinsic values at the date of exercise are as follows:

	Fair value of SAR £	Intrinsic value £
20X1	10.00	
20X2	12.00	
20X3	15.00	11.50
20X4	18.50	17.00
20X5		22.50

Note—the intrinsic values are the amount of cash actually paid at the date of exercise.

Required:

Calculate the amount to be recognised in profit or loss for each of the five years ended 31 December 20X1 to 20X5 and the liability to be recognised in the statements of financial position at these dates.

For the three years to the vesting date of 31 December 20X3, the expense is based on Griffin's estimate of the number of SARs that will actually vest. However, the value of the liability is remeasured at each year end.

		Liability at year end £		Expense for year £
20X1	Expected to vest (300 – 20 – 40)			
	$240 \times 100 \times £10 \times {}^{1}/_{3}$	80,000		80,000
20X2	Expected to vest (280 – 10 – 20)			
	$250 \times 100 \times £12 \times {}^{2}/_{3}$	200,000		120,000

20X3	SARs exercised				
	60 × 100 × £11.50			69,000	
	Not yet exercised (270 – 10 – 60)				
	200 × 100 × £15	300,000		100,000	169,000
20X4	SARs exercised				
	120 × 100 × £17			204,000	
	Not yet exercised (200 – 120)				
	80 × 100 × £18.50	148,000		(152,000)	52,000
20X5	SARs exercised				
	80 × 100 × £22.50			180,000	
		Nil		(148,000)	32,000

16.10 Share-based transactions with a choice of settlement

The accounting for a share-based transaction with a choice of settlement depends on which party has the choice.

16.10.1 Choice of employee or other provider of goods or services

If the employee or other provider of goods or services has the right to choose the choice of settlement, the company has issued an instrument with a debt component in so far as the recipient may demand settlement in cash, and an equity component to the extent that the recipient may demand settlement in shares. So IFRS 2 treats the transaction as an issue of a compound financial instrument, where the debt element and the equity element are split.

Reminder *One of the most common types of compound instrument is convertible debt. This financial instrument creates a financial liability for the issuer as there is an obligation to pay interest and eventually repay the capital. However, there is also the option for the holder of the instrument to convert it into equity shares of the issuer; this is the equity component. The substance of this financial instrument is the issue of non-convertible debt plus an option to acquire shares in the future.*

(See Chapter 14 for further details.)

$$\boxed{\text{Fair value of goods or service}} = \boxed{\text{Fair value of debt component}} + \boxed{\text{Equity component (residual)}}$$

Figure 16.3 Measurement of the components of an instrument where the employee has the choice of settlement

The measurement applies similar principles to IAS 32 *Financial Instruments: Presentation* in that the debt component is measured first as if it were a cash-settled transaction. The equity component is measured as the residual between the value of the instrument as a whole and the value of the debt component, as shown in Figure 16.3.

The fair value of the goods and services is measured as follows:

(a) For goods and services measured directly, usually where the provider is not an employee, it is the fair value of those goods and services.

(b) For other transactions, usually with employees, where the fair value of the services provided is measured indirectly by reference to the fair value of the equity instruments granted, it is the value of the instrument as a whole.

 Worked example 16.12: to show the accounting for a share-based transaction where the employee has the choice of settlement

On 1 January 20X4 Finching plc granted an employee a right under which she can, if she is still employed on 31 December 20X6, elect to receive either 8,000 shares or cash to the value, on that date, of 7,000 shares.

The market price of the entity's shares is £21 at the date of grant, £27 at the end of 20X4, £33 at the end of 20X5 and £42 at the end of 20X6, at which time the employee elects to receive the shares. Finching estimates the fair value of the share route to be £19.

Required:

Show the accounting for the above transaction for the years 20X4–20X6.

The employee has the choice as to how this arrangement is settled, so it is accounted for as a compound financial instrument.

Fair value of debt component (cash route) = 7,000 × £21 = £147,000

Fair value of share route = 8,000 × £19 = £152,000

Fair value of equity component is therefore 152,000 − 147,000 = £5,000

The share-based payment is recognised as follows:

		Liabilities	Equity	Expense
		£	£	£
20X4	$1/3 \times 7,000 \times £27$	63,000		63,000
	$£5,000 \times {}^1/_3$		1,667	1,667
20X5	$2/3 \times 7,000 \times £33$	154,000		91,000
	$£5,000 \times {}^2/_3$		3,334	1,667
20X6	$7,000 \times £42$	294,000		140,000
	£5,000		5,000	1,666

As the employee elects to receive shares rather than cash, £294,000 is transferred from liabilities to equity at the end of 20X6. The final balance on equity is 294,000 + 5,000 = £299,000.

16.10.2 Choice of company

Where a company has the right to choose what form the settlement will take, it should recognise a liability to the extent that it has a present obligation to deliver cash. Such circumstances arise where, for example, the company is prohibited from issuing shares or where it has a stated policy, or past practice, of issuing cash rather than shares.

Where a present obligation exists, the company should record the transaction as if it is a cash-settled share-based payment transaction. If no present obligation exists, the company should treat the transaction as if it was purely an equity-settled transaction. On settlement, if the transaction was treated as an equity-settled transaction and cash was paid, the cash should be treated as if it was a repurchase of the equity instrument by a deduction against equity.

16.11 Disclosures

The disclosures required for share-based payment schemes are extensive. They are designed to enable users to understand:

(a) the nature and extent of share-based arrangements that existed during the accounting period

(b) how the fair value of the goods and services received, or of the equity instruments granted was determined

(c) the effect of share-based payment transactions on the entity's profit or loss for the period and on its financial position.

Full details of each separate share-based arrangement are required to be disclosed, together with information about all movements in share options and the prices at which the options have been exercised or are offered. Full details of how all fair values used in the measurement of the arrangements have been determined need to be shown, plus details of option pricing models used, and how market conditions and volatility have affected the values used.

The total expense recognised for the period arising from share-based payment transactions is required to be disclosed, including separate disclosure of that portion of the total expense that arises from transactions accounted for as equity-settled share-based payment transactions. For liabilities arising from share-based payment transactions, further disclosures are required of the total carrying amount and the total intrinsic value at the end of the period.

Financial reporting in practice 16.4   J Sainsbury plc, 2016

J Sainsbury plc operates a number of different share-based payment arrangements as described in the accounting policy in its 2016 financial statements.

Share-based payments

The Group provides benefits to employees (including Directors) of the Group in the form of equity-settled and cash-settled share-based payment transactions, whereby employees render services in exchange for shares, rights over shares or the value of those shares in cash terms.

For equity-settled share-based payments the fair value of the employee services rendered is determined by reference to the fair value of the shares awarded or options granted, excluding the impact of any non-market vesting conditions. All share options are valued using an option-pricing model (Black-Scholes or Monte Carlo). This fair value is charged to the income statement over the vesting period of the share-based payment scheme.

For cash-settled share-based payments, the fair value of the employee services rendered is determined at each balance sheet date and the charge recognised through the income statement over the vesting period of the share-based payment scheme, with the corresponding increase in accruals.

The value of the charge is adjusted in the income statement over the remainder of the vesting period to reflect expected and actual levels of options vesting, with the corresponding adjustments made in equity and accruals.

For illustration purposes, the disclosures relating to one of the schemes is shown below:

Note 31 Share-based payments

The Group recognised £21 million (2014: £33 million) of employee costs (note 7) related to share-based payment transactions made during the financial year. Of these, £nil (2014: £nil) were cash-settled.

National insurance contributions are payable in respect of certain share-based payments transactions and are treated as cash-settled transactions. At 14 March 2015, the carrying amount of national insurance contributions payable was £6 million (2014: £7 million) of which £nil (2014: £1 million) was in respect of vested grants.

The Group operates a number of share-based payment schemes as set out below:

(a) Savings-Related Share Option Scheme (Sharesave)

The Group operates a Savings-Related Share Option Scheme, which is open to all UK employees with more than three months' continuous service. This is an approved HMRC Scheme and was established in 1980. Under Sharesave, participants remaining in the Group's employment at the end of the three-year or five-year savings period are entitled to use their savings to purchase shares in the Company at a stated exercise price. Employees leaving for certain reasons are able to use their savings to purchase shares within six months of their leaving.

At 14 March 2015, UK employees held 25,016 five-year savings contracts (2014: 21,445) in respect of options over 22.6 million shares (2014: 20.4 million) and 39,675 three-year savings contracts (2014: 24,950) in respect of options over 32.4 million shares (2014: 27.9 million). A reconciliation of option movements is shown below:

	2015 Number of options	2015 Weighted average exercise price	2014 Number of options	2014 Weighted average exercise price
	million	pence	million	pence
Outstanding at the beginning of the year	48.3	279	47.1	261
Granted	23.5	213	13.7	332
Forfeited	(9.2)	288	(5.4)	277
Exercised	(7.6)	247	(6.9)	266
Expired	–	261	(0.2)	257
Outstanding at the end of the year	**55.0**	**254**	48.3	279
Exercisable at the end of the year	**5.8**	**253**	3.3	260

The weighted average share price during the period for options exercised over the year was 290 pence (2014: 346 pence). The weighted average remaining contractual life of share options outstanding at 14 March 2015 was 2.4 years (2014: 2.3 years).

Details of options at 14 March 2015 are set out below:

Date of grant	Date of expiry	Exercise price pence	2015 Options outstanding million	2014 Options outstanding million
17 December 2008 (5-year period)	31 August 2014	224	–	1.7
10 December 2009 (5-year period)	31 August 2015	273	2.5	3.1
10 December 2010 (3-year period)	31 August 2014	297	–	1.6

(continued)

(continued)

10 December 2010 (5-year period)	31 August 2016	297	**2.8**	3.3
9 December 2011 (3-year period)	31 August 2015	238	**3.5**	8.7
9 December 2011 (5-year period)	31 August 2017	238	**4.1**	4.7
12 December 2012 (3-year period)	31 August 2016	267	**6.4**	8.0
12 December 2012 (5-year period)	31 August 2018	267	**3.1**	3.7
11 December 2013 (3-year period)	31 August 2017	332	**6.7**	9.5
11 December 2013 (5-year period)	31 August 2019	332	**2.9**	4.0
12 December 2014 (3-year period)	31 August 2018	213	**15.8**	–
12 December 2014 (5-year period)	31 August 2020	213	**7.2**	–
			55.0	48.3

Options granted during the year were valued using the Black-Scholes option-pricing model. No performance conditions were included in the fair value calculations. The fair value per option granted during the year and the assumptions used in the calculation are as follows:

		2015	**2014**
Share price at grant date (pence)		**265**	415
Exercise price (pence)		**213**	332
Expected volatility	–3-year period (%)	**21.9**	18.8
	–5-year period (%)	**21.2**	20.8
Option life	–3-year period (years)	**3.2**	3.2
	–5-year period (years)	**5.2**	5.2
Expected dividends (expressed as dividend yield %)		**5.6**	4.5
Risk-free interest rate	–3-year period (%)	**1.6**	2.2
	–5-year period (%)	**2.1**	3.5
Fair value per option	–3-year period (pence)	**43**	74
	–5-year period (pence)	**41**	87

The expected volatility is based on the standard deviation of the Group's share price for the period immediately prior to the date of grant of award, over the period identical to the vesting period of the award, adjusted for management's view of future volatility of the share price.

The resulting fair value is expensed over the service period of three or five years, as appropriate, on the assumption that 25% of options will be cancelled over the service period as employees leave the Sharesave Scheme.

16.12 The future of IFRS 2

The application of IFRS 2 involves difficult classification and complex valuation issues and is sometimes counterintuitive. Clearly the measurement techniques for share options are based on estimation models requiring subjective judgement. Some users have expressed opinions that the standard is overly complex.

The variations in awards and conditions are numerous, and users should be aware of how the various vesting conditions affect the expense charged to the income statement differently. For example, if an option has a market vesting condition, a company might still recognise an expense even if that condition is not met and the option does not vest. By contrast, an award subject only to a non-market vesting condition does not result in an expense under IFRS 2 if the condition is not met.

In 2014 the IASB issued an exposure draft of a few changes and clarifications to the standard, classified as narrow-scope amendments. This has addressed three issues:

1. The effects of vesting conditions on the measurement of a cash-settled share-based payment. The proposals clarify that the accounting for the effects of vesting and non-vesting conditions on the measurement of a cash-settled share-based payment should follow the approach used for measuring equity-settled share-based payments.

2. How companies should account for the situation where a company is obliged by law to withhold tax from share-based payment awards granted to employees.

3. The accounting for a modification to the terms and conditions of a share-based payment that changes the classification of the transaction from cash-settled to equity-settled.

There are no other substantial changes proposed at present.

 ## Summary of key points

Employee remuneration comes in many forms including immediate cash, benefits, deferred awards and share-based remuneration. There are two accounting standards which deal with the accounting issues arising from the myriad of arrangements that exist—IAS 19 *Employee Benefits* and IFRS 2 *Share-Based Payment*.

Short-term employee benefits are generally straightforward to account for, based on accruals. Non-share-based long-term benefits take the form of retirement benefit plans, the financial significance of which depends on the type of plan offered by companies. Defined contribution plans, where the company has no obligation beyond the amounts it agrees to pay into the scheme as the employee provides their services, are again accounted for on a straightforward accruals basis.

Defined benefit plans, however, are far more complex and, due to increasing longevity of their members, these schemes have created huge liabilities for companies, as their obligations have increased. The complexity of the accounting stems from the measurement of the plans' assets and liabilities and how the changes in these have arisen and are presented. A company with a defined benefit plan will include a net asset or liability on its statement of financial position, being the difference between the fair value of the plan's assets and the estimated obligations. These figures are based on actu-arial valuations, with the measurement of the obligation requiring many assumptions and estimates. Changes in the measurement of the asset and liability from one period end to the next are split between various estimated or actual costs and income earned, and these are shown in the statement of profit or loss. Given the changes in the underlying assumptions and estimates that inevitably occur, there will always be differences between what has been charged to profit or loss and the change in the net asset or liability. These differences are termed remeasurements, and are presented in other comprehensive income or expense.

Share-based remuneration, as a proportion of employee remuneration, has increased enormously over the past 30 to 40 years, particularly for senior employees and executives. However, it was only in 2004 that IFRS 2 was issued, requiring recognition of the expense of this type of remuneration in financial statements. The standard also covers share-based payments to other third parties, but its main focus is on those to employees. The key issue is how the expense should be measured.

There are two main types of arrangement: those settled through the issue of equity shares, and those settled in cash, although various hybrid arrangements are also entered into. Equity-settled share-based arrangements use the fair value of the share or share option at grant date to measure the expense. This is then spread over the vesting period, with adjustments made at each report-ing period end for changes in estimates of service and non-market-based performance conditions. Market-based performance conditions are not accounted for, even where the share options do not actually vest. The basic accounting requires an amount to be recognised in equity as the expense is recognised. IFRS 2 sets out how the many changes in these types of arrangement which may occur over the vesting period are accounted for.

Cash-settled share-based arrangements create an expense and a liability. For these arrangements, the liability is measured at its fair value, and this is adjusted (increased) at each accounting period end over the vesting period. The expense is therefore the increase in the liability.

Share-based arrangements where there is a choice whether they are settled in shares or in cash can exist. In these circumstances, the accounting depends on who has the choice of the settlement method: the employee or the company.

For all main issues dealt with by these two financial reporting standards, the disclosures are exten-sive. Full details of all retirement benefit schemes and share-based payment arrangements have to be described, together with information about how the numerous estimates have been derived, plus the impact of all transactions arising from the schemes on the financial statements needs to be clear. The ultimate objective is to ensure that users are able to understand the nature of these schemes, the effect of them on the financial performance and position of an entity, and any exposure to risks.

 ## Further reading

IASB (International Accounting Standards Board) (2013) IAS 19 *Employee Benefits*, revised 2013. London: IASB.

IASB (International Accounting Standards Board) (2009) IFRS 2 *Share-Based Payment*, revised 2009. London: IASB.

 ## Bibliography

Ernst and Young (2015) *Accounting for Share-based Payments under IFRS 2—the Essential Guide*. London: EY.

Eurostat (2015) Statistics Explained: *Population Structure and Ageing*. Available from: http://ec.europa.eu/eurostat/statistics-explained/index.php/Population_structure_and_ageing (accessed 26 January 2016).

Evans, J. (2015) *UK pension deficits widen as contributions drop*. Available from: http://www.ft.com/cms/s/0/7f284e26-3e9b-11e5-9abe-5b335da3a90e.html#axzz3yMa1wGbq (accessed 26 January 2016).

IASB (International Accounting Standards Board) (2009) IFRS 2 *Share-Based Payment*, revised 2009. London: IASB.

IASB (International Accounting Standards Board) (2011) IFRS 13 *Fair Value Measurement*. London: IASB.

IASB (International Accounting Standards Board) (2013) IAS 19 *Employee Benefits*, revised 2013. London: IASB.

IASB (International Accounting Standards Board) (2014) Exposure Draft ED/2014/5 *Classification and Measurement of Share-based Payment Transactions Proposed amendments to IFRS 2*. London: IASB.

ICAEW (Institute of Chartered Accountants in England and Wales) (2015) *IFRS Factsheet: IAS 19 Employee Benefits—Revised*. London: ICAEW.

Pension Protection Fund news. Available from: http://www.pensionprotectionfund.org.uk/News/Pages/details.aspx?itemID=412 (accessed 26 January 2016)

Questions

● Quick test

1. Delft plc's agreed contributions to a defined contribution plan for 20X5 are £770,000. Of this sum the company had paid £704,000 by the end of the year. It is becoming clear that the pension fund assets will be insufficient to finance the expected level of employee benefits and that the company would have to increase its annual contributions by 35% if employee expectations were to be met.

   Required:

   In relation to this plan, calculate the expense which should be shown in Delft plc's statement of profit or loss for the year ended 31 December 20X5 and the amount of the liability which should appear on the company's statement of financial position at this date.

2. When accounting for share-based payment arrangements, explain:
   (a) The difference between a non-vesting condition and a performance condition
   (b) The main differences in the treatment of an equity-settled arrangement and a cash-settled arrangement.

3. On 1 January 20X1 Dawson plc grants 10,000 share options to a director on the condition that the director remains in employment for three years and the market price of the related shares increases from £50 at this date to above £65 at 31 December 20X3. On 1 January 20X1 Dawson plc determines the fair value of the options taking into account the possibility that the share price will exceed £65 at the end of three years (and therefore become exercisable), and the possibility that the share price will not exceed £65 at the end of three years (and hence the options will be forfeited). The company estimates the fair value of the share options with this market condition to be £24 per option.

Required:

Show how the grant of these options will be accounted for in the financial statements of Dawson plc in the years 20X1, 20X2 and 20X3.

4. Bayliss plc grants share options to a director on the condition that the director does not compete with the reporting entity for a period of three years. The fair value of the award at the date of grant, including the effect of the non-compete clause, is £150,000.

    Required:

    Explain how and why the grant of these options would be accounted for in the financial statements of Bayliss plc.

5. Dylan plc established a share appreciation scheme on 1 January 20X6. Each of the company's 100 employees was granted a bonus to be paid on 1 January 20X8. The bonus is calculated as £100 for every £1 increase in the company's share price over its market value on 1 January 20X6, which was £15.

    The employees must remain in continuous employment with the company until the vesting date.

    Dylan plc's share price at each year end is as follows:

31 December 20X6:	£18
31 December 20X7:	£25

    Dylan plc has a record of excellent staff retention, and estimated that no members of staff would leave during the period of the scheme. In actuality, no staff left in 20X6, and only two members of staff left in 20X7.

    Required:

    Show how this scheme is accounted for in Dylan plc's financial statements for the years ended 31 December 20X6 and 20X7.

6. Sparrow plc's defined benefit plan net liability at 31 December 20X2 and 20X3 is measured as follows.

	20X2 £	20X3 £
Defined benefit obligation	1,140,000	1,380,000

    The discount rates used for calculating the defined benefit obligation were 4.5% at 31 December 20X2 and 4% at 31 December 20X3.

    Required:

    (a) Calculate the interest cost to be charged to profit or loss for 20X5.

    (b) How should the discount factor that is used to discount post-employment benefit obligations be determined?

    (c) What elements should the discount rate specifically not reflect according to IAS 19?

●● Develop your understanding

7. Distinguish between a defined contribution retirement plan and a defined benefit retirement plan, and explain why the accounting for the latter is more difficult.

8. On 1 January 20X7 Woakes plc granted options over 10,000 of its shares to one of its senior employees. One of the conditions of the share option scheme was that the employee must work for Woakes plc for three years. The employee continued to be employed by Woakes plc during 20X7, 20X8 and 20X9.

    A second condition for vesting is that the costs for which the employee is responsible should reduce by 10% per annum compound over the three-year period. At the date of grant, the fair value of each share option was estimated at £21.

    At 31 December 20X7 the employee's costs had reduced by 15% and therefore it was estimated that the performance condition would be achieved.

    Due to a particularly tough year of trading for the year ended 31 December 20X8, the employee had only reduced costs by 3% and it was thought at that time that she would not meet the cost reduction target by 31 December 20X9.

    At 31 December 20X9, the end of the performance period, the employee did meet the overall cost reduction target of 10% per annum compound.

    Required:

    How should this transaction be recognised in the financial statements of Woakes plc for the years 20X7, 20X8 and 20X9?

9. At 1 January 20X2, Warwick plc grants 100 shares each to 500 employees, conditional upon the employees remaining in the entity's employ during the vesting period. The shares will vest at the end of 20X2 if the entity's earnings increase by more than 18%; at the end of 20X3 if the entity's earnings increase by more than an average of 13% per year over the two-year period; and at the end of 20X4 if the entity's earnings increase by more than an average of 10% per year over the three-year period. The shares have a fair value of £30 per share at 1 January 20X2, which equals the share price at grant date. No dividends are expected to be paid over the three-year period.

    By 31 December 20X2, the entity's earnings have increased by 14%, and 30 employees have left. The entity expects that earnings will continue to increase at a similar rate in 20X3, and therefore expects that the shares will vest at 31 December 20X3. The entity expects, on the basis of a weighted average probability, that a further 30 employees will leave during 20X3.

    By 31 December 20X3, the entity's earnings have increased by only 10% and therefore the shares do not vest at the end of 20X3. 28 employees have left during the year. The entity expects that a further 25 employees will leave during 20X4, and that the entity's earnings will increase by more than 6%, thereby achieving the average of 10% per year.

    By 31 December 20X4, 23 employees have left and the entity's earnings had increased by 8%, resulting in an average increase of 10.64% per year. The remaining employees each received 100 shares at this date.

    Required:

    Show the expense and equity figures which will appear in the financial statements of Warwick plc in each of the three years, 20X2, 20X3 and 20X4.

10. At 1 January 20X0, Hagrid plc grants share options to each of its 100 employees working in the sales department. The share options will vest at the end of 20X2, provided that the employees remain in Hagrid plc's employ, and provided that the volume of sales of a particular product increases by at least an average of 5% per year. If the volume of sales of the product increases by an average of between 5% and 10% per year, each employee will receive 100 share options. If the volume of sales increases by an average of between 10% and 15% each year, each employee

will receive 200 share options. If the volume of sales increases by an average of 15% or more, each employee will receive 300 share options.

On grant date, Hagrid plc estimates that the share options have a fair value of £20 per option. The company also estimates that the volume of sales of the product will increase by an average of between 10% and 15% per year, and therefore expects that, for each employee who remains in service until the end of 20X2, 200 share options will vest. Hagrid plc also estimates, on the basis of a weighted average probability, that 20% of employees will leave before 31 December 20X2.

By 31 December 20X0, seven employees have left and Hagrid plc still expects that a total of 20 employees will leave by the end of 20X2. Product sales have increased by 12% and the entity expects this rate of increase to continue over the next two years.

By 31 December 20X1, a further five employees have left. Hagrid plc now expects only three more employees will leave during 20X2. Product sales have increased by 18%, resulting in an average of 15% over the two years to date. The company now expects that sales will average 15% or more over the three-year period, and hence expects each sales employee to receive 300 share options at the end of 20X2.

By 31 December 20X2, a further two employees have left. Hagrid plc's sales have increased by an average of 16% over the three years. Therefore, each of the remaining employees receives 300 share options.

Required:

Show the expense and equity figures which will appear in the financial statements of Hagrid plc in each of the three years, 20X0, 20X1 and 20X2.

11. The financial controller of Hawk plc has prepared the following reconciliation of the company's defined benefit scheme's assets:

	£000
Scheme assets at 1 April 20X7	15,520
Interest @ 8%	1,242
Net contributions received	320
Actuarial deficit	(922)
Scheme assets at 31 March 20X8	16,160

Required:

(a) Explain each of the items in the above reconciliation and how they would be presented in the financial statements of Hawk plc for the year ended 31 March 20X8.

(b) Identify the benefits to Hawk plc of moving from a defined benefit to a defined contribution scheme.

12. At 1 July 20X3, Copperfield plc grants 10,000 share options with a 10-year life to each of 10 senior executives. The share options will vest and become exercisable immediately if and when the Copperfield plc's share price increases from £5 to £7, provided that the executive remains in service until the share price target is achieved.

Copperfield plc applies a binomial option pricing model, which takes into account the possibility that the share price target will be achieved during the 10-year life of the options, and the possibility that the target will not be achieved. Copperfield plc estimates that the fair value of the share options at grant date is £2.50 per option. From the option pricing model, the company determines that the mode of the distribution of possible vesting dates is five years. In other words, of all the possible outcomes, the most likely outcome of the market condition is that the share price target will be achieved at 30 June 20X8. Copperfield plc also estimates that two executives will have left by this date.

Throughout the years ended 30 June 20X4–20X7, Copperfield plc continues to estimate that a total of two executives will leave by 30 June 20X8. However, in total three executives leave, one in each of years ended 30 June 20X6, 20X7 and 20X8. The share price target is achieved at 30 June 20X9. Another executive leaves during this year, before the share price target is achieved.

Required:

Show the expense and equity figures which will appear in the financial statements of Copperfield plc in each of the years ended 30 June 20X4–20X8.

●●● Take it further

13. On 1 January 20X0 Marley plc grants 100 cash share appreciation rights (SARs) to each of its 500 employees, on condition that the employees remain in its employment for the next three years.

    During 20X0, 35 employees leave. Marley plc estimates that a further 60 will leave during 20X1 and 20X2. During 20X1, 40 employees leave and Marley plc estimates that a further 25 will leave during 20X2. During 20X2, 22 employees leave. At 31 December 20X2, 150 employees exercise their SARs, another 140 employees exercise their SARs at 31 December 20X3 and the remaining employees at 31 December 20X4.

    Marley plc estimates the fair value of the SARs at the end of each year in which a liability exists as shown below. At 31 December 20X2, all SARs held by the remaining employees vest. The intrinsic values of the SARs at the date of exercise at the end of 20X2, 20X3 and 20X4 are also shown below:

Year	Fair value	Intrinsic value
	£	£
20X0	14.40	
20X1	15.50	
20X2	18.20	15.00
20X3	21.40	20.00
20X4		25.00

    Required:

    Calculate the amount to be recognised in Marley plc's statement of profit or loss for each of the five years ended 31 December 20X0–20X4 and the liability to be recognised in the statements of financial position at these dates.

14. At 1 April 20X5, Rashid plc grants 100 share options to each of its 500 employees. Each grant is conditional upon the employee remaining in service over the next three years. Rashid plc estimates that the fair value of each option is £15. On the basis of a weighted average probability, Rashid plc estimates that 100 employees will leave during the three-year period and therefore forfeit their rights to the share options.

During the year ended 31 March 20X6, 40 employees leave. By this date, Rashid plc's share price has dropped, and Rashid plc reprices its share options. The repriced share options will vest at 31 March 20X8. Rashid plc estimates that a further 70 employees will leave during the years ended 31 March 20X7 and 20X8.

During the year ended 31 March 20X7, a further 35 employees leave and Rashid plc estimates that a further 30 employees will leave during the year ended 31 March 20X8. During this year, a total of 28 employees actually leave. For the remaining employees, the share options vest at 31 March 20X8.

Rashid plc estimates that, at the date of repricing, the fair value of each of the original share options granted (i.e. before taking into account the repricing) is £5 and that the fair value of each repriced share option is £8.

Required:

What are the amounts that should be recognised in the financial statements for the years ended 31 March 20X6, 20X7 and 20X8?

15. At 1 October 20X1, Havers plc grants 10,000 shares with a fair value of £33 per share to a senior executive, conditional upon the completion of three years' service. By 30 September 20X3, the share price has dropped to £25 per share. At that date, the entity adds a cash alternative to the grant, whereby the executive can choose whether to receive 10,000 shares or cash equal to the value of 10,000 shares on vesting date. The share price is £22 on vesting date.

Required:

Show how this transaction would be accounted for in the financial statements of Havers plc for the years ended 30 September 20X2, 20X3 and 20X4.

16. Bodega plc operates a defined benefit pension scheme. The following information relates to the scheme for the financial year ended 31 December 20X8.

	At 1 January 20X8 £000	At 31 December 20X8 £000
Fair value of plan assets	7,875	6,960
Present value of obligations	9,375	10,480
Interest rate on high quality corporate bonds	7%	6%
For year-ended 31 December 20X8		
Employer contributions	65	
Employee contributions	40	
Current service cost	200	
Benefits paid	213	
Past service cost	375	

Required:

In relation to this scheme, and in accordance with IAS 19 *Employee Benefits*, calculate the amounts that will be recognised in Bodega plc's statement of comprehensive income for the year ended 31 December 20X8 and in the statement of financial position at that date.

Visit the Online Resource Centre for solutions to all these end of chapter questions plus visual walkthrough solutions. You can test your understanding with extra questions and answers, explore additional case studies based on real companies, take a guided tour through a company report and much more. Go to the Online Resource Centre at **www.oxfordtextbooks.co.uk/orc/maynard2e/**

Part 5

Consolidated financial statements

17

Subsidiaries

➤ Introduction

Today, the modern global economy is driven by complex, multi-entity organisations which have their shares listed on multiple international stock markets. Investors in these markets require information about the organisation as a whole, and thus need financial statements which represent fairly the combination of the different entities.

Arguably, the rise of consolidated financial reporting may be considered one of the most important accounting developments of the twentieth century. Consolidated financial statements have developed since the early 1900s to combine the financial statements of more than one entity so that they reflect the entities' investments in each other and combinations of their businesses. The financial results and position of the combined entities are therefore presented as those of a single entity.

This chapter examines accounting for simple parent and subsidiary business combinations, where one company acquires control of another. In 2011 the International Accounting Standards Board (IASB) concluded its work on accounting for consolidated financial statements with the issue of the following accounting standards in this area:

● International Financial Reporting Standard (IFRS) 10 *Consolidated Financial Statements*
● IFRS 12 *Disclosure of Interests in Other Entities*

In this chapter these standards are discussed, together with the requirements of the other accounting standards that are still applicable for this subject:

● International Accounting Standard (IAS) 27 *Separate Financial Statements*
● IFRS 3 *Business Combinations.*

The focus of the chapter is on the techniques of preparation of the consolidated statement of financial position, the consolidated statement of profit or loss, the consolidated statement of comprehensive income and the consolidated statement of changes in equity. The preparation of the consolidated statement of cash flows is discussed in Chapter 18.

★ Learning objectives

After studying this chapter you will be able to:

● understand the need for consolidated financial statements

● understand the different categories of investment by one company in another and how different accounting treatments result

● explain when a parent/subsidiary relationship exists, and how and why the question of **control** is central to this

● prepare a consolidated statement of financial position, statement of comprehensive income, and statement changes of equity for a simple group structure, including a parent company and one or more subsidiaries, using the acquisition method

● discuss the disclosures required by reporting companies.

✔ Key issues checklist

❏ Categories of investments by one company in another.

❏ The need for consolidated financial statements.

❏ The single entity concept.

❏ The definition of a subsidiary.

❏ The key question—control—and issues relating to how this is determined:

    ❏ power

    ❏ substantive and protective rights

    ❏ power with minority shareholding

    ❏ potential voting rights.

❏ Exemptions from consolidation.

❏ The **acquisition method** of preparing consolidated financial statements for a simple group structure of a parent plus one or more subsidiaries:

    ❏ consolidated statement of financial position

    ❏ consolidated statement of profit or loss and statement of comprehensive income

    ❏ consolidated statement of changes in equity.

❏ Consideration and its valuation.

❏ Goodwill on acquisition.

❏ Subsidiary fair values in acquisition accounting.

❏ The two alternative methods for the valuation of non-controlling interest (NCI) in the consolidated financial statements.

❏ Pre- and post-acquisition reserves.

❏ Preference shares and other debt instruments acquired by the parent company.

❏ Intragroup transactions and balances.

❏ **Unrealised profit in inventories**.

❑ Acquisition of a subsidiary part-way through the latest accounting period.

❑ Disclosures required by IFRS 12.

17.1 Categorisation of investments

It is normal commercial practice for businesses to make investments in other businesses as part of their overriding strategies. Investments can be in corporations or unincorporated businesses and range from minor investments to earn some investment income to full purchase or takeover. Mergers and acquisitions (M&A) activity is on a vast scale—in 2015, global M&A activity totalled US$4.3 trillion in volume. Given the size of this activity it is therefore imperative that accounting for the resulting business combinations is based on sound principles, is consistent and faithfully represents the relationships of the combined businesses.

Broadly, there are three categories of investment of one company in another according to the degree of influence, or interest, that the investing company (the investor) has over the company in which it invests (the investee), as shown in Table 17.1. The degree of influence often arises through the percentage of equity shares that are held by the investor, since equity shares provide the investor with votes—usually one vote per share held. As discussed in later sections, other factors may also have to be taken into account to determine the degree of influence exercised. The categorisation of the investee determines the resulting accounting.

17.1.1 Limited influence

The simple investment is, as its name suggests, the simplest to account for. This situation arises where one company invests in another company by acquiring a small proportion of the equity shares (usually less than 20%) and holding them for investment purposes. The investor is only concerned with the operations and financial results of the investee to the extent of the investment income (dividends) that it receives, and the effect on the investee's share price. It plays no part in the management of the investee company, and thus its interest in the investee is said to be passive.

Table 17.1 Categories of investment of one company in another

Degree of influence	Limited		Partial	Total
Nature of interest	Acquirer has a *passive interest* in acquiree	Acquirer exercises *significant influence* over acquiree	Acquirer *shares control* of acquiree *jointly* with others	Acquirer *controls* acquiree
Resulting category	Simple investment	Associate	Joint arrangement	Subsidiary

The accounting for this investment follows the commercial substance of this situation, in that the investor shows the investment as a financial asset on its statement of financial position. This is measured in accordance with IFRS 9 *Financial Instruments* (IAS 39 *Financial Instruments: Recognition and Measurement* before IFRS 9 is adopted). See Chapter 14 for a full discussion of IFRS 9.

In the statement of profit or loss, dividends are recognised as finance income when the right to receive the dividend has been established.

17.1.2 Partial influence

Partial influence can be obtained either by the investor acquiring a certain proportion of equity shares (usually 20% or more, but less than 50%) in the investee to give it **significant influence** over the investee, or by the investor acquiring its investment with other investors and control of the investee company being shared amongst all the investors. The investor has more than merely a passive interest in the operations and financial results of the investee, and the accounting treatment of either the associate or the joint arrangement reflects this. This is the subject of Chapter 18.

17.1.3 Total influence

Total influence is the topic of this chapter. The investor, in this case called the parent company, obtains control over the investee, which is termed a subsidiary. What is meant by control, which is at the heart of this categorisation, is discussed in section 17.2. Where control exists, consolidated financial statements are prepared which incorporate the subsidiary's financial results, assets, liabilities and cash flows with the parent's. These financial statements are sometimes referred to as group accounts. The method of accounting used is called the acquisition method, and is set out in IFRS 3 *Business Combinations*.

17.1.4 The need for consolidated financial statements

 Worked example 17.1: to show the need for consolidated financial statements

Suppose Company P owns 100% of the equity share capital of company S, which gives it control. In the first year of trading of both companies the following transactions occur:

- P buys goods for £2,000 and sells them to S for £4,000
- P requires S to mark up the goods by 100% and sell them back to P for £8,000
- P then gets S to distribute all its profit by dividend.

These transactions can be represented as shown in Figure 17.1.

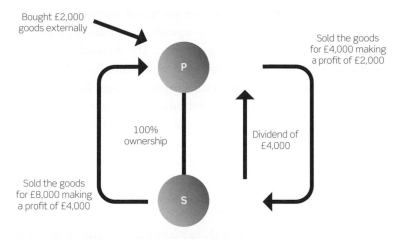

Figure 17.1 Transactions between the two companies

P and S are two separate companies, and are legally required to prepare their own individual financial statements. The statements of profit or loss of these companies will appear as follows:

	P		S	
	£	£	£	£
Sales		4,000		8,000
Purchases	10,000		4,000	
Closing inventory	(8,000)		—	
Cost of sales		(2,000)		(4,000)
Net profit		2,000		4,000
Dividends received		4,000		—
Dividends paid		—		(4,000)
Retained profit		6,000		—

If the shareholders in company P received P's individual financial statements only, they may anticipate a dividend of up to £6,000 as a result of these transactions. If company P marked up the goods again, sold them on to S, which did the same and sold them back to P, and so on, company P could appear to make an ever increasing amount of profit! Clearly, this is misleading and does not represent the economic reality of the situation.

The faithful representation of the scenario is that company P has bought some goods and still has them at the end of the financial period. The financial statements that the shareholders in company P receive should reflect this position and not show bogus profits. As company P controls company S, consolidated financial statements, which include the financial transactions of the two companies taken together as if they were one, would reflect the commercial reality and be faithfully representative of this.

Consolidated financial statements are therefore designed to extend the reporting entity, in other words, the parent company, to include other entities which are subject to its control. This means that the assets, liabilities and activities of subsidiary companies are treated as if they were part of the parent company's own net assets and activities. The overall aim is to present the financial results and position of the reporting entity and its subsidiaries, in other words, the group, as if they were those of a single entity. The shareholders in the parent company are the group shareholders, and are interested in the consolidated financial statements. The financial results and position of the individual parent company become mainly irrelevant.

However, the parent company and all its subsidiary companies are separate legal entities, and are required by UK legislation to prepare and file individual financial statements. When a group annual report is prepared, the consolidated financial statements and the parent company's individual financial statements are both included. The subsidiaries' individual financial statements are not part of this. However, the consolidated financial statements are required to include a list of and information about the subsidiary companies so that the users understand the composition of the group.

Many listed groups will consist of a publicly listed parent company and private limited subsidiary companies.

Financial reporting in practice 17.1 — J Sainsbury plc, 2015

J Sainsbury plc has four principal operating subsidiaries, details of which are provided in the notes to its group financial statements. This extract from the group's 2015 financial statements shows how the group or consolidated balance sheet and the parent company balance sheet are presented side by side.

Balance sheets

At 14 March 2015 and 15 March 2014

| | | Group | | Company | |
| | | 2015 | 2014 | 2015 | 2014 |
	Note	£m	£m	£m	£m
Non-current assets					
Property, plant and equipment	11	9,648	9,880	1	16
Intangible assets	12	325	286	–	–
Investments in subsidiaries	13	–	–	7,630	7,562
Investments in joint ventures and associates	14	359	404	18	6
Available-for-sale financial assets	15	184	255	37	37
Other receivables	17a	83	26	1,363	1,229
Amounts due from Sainsbury's Bank customers	17b	1,412	1,292	–	–
Derivative financial instruments	29	21	28	33	23
		12,032	12,171	9,082	8,873

Current assets					
Inventories	16	**997**	1,005	–	–
Trade and other receivables	17a	**471**	433	**1,399**	1,428
Amounts due from Sainsbury's Bank customers	17b	**1,599**	1,283	–	–
Derivative financial instruments	29	**69**	49	**44**	48
Cash and bank balances	26b	**1,285**	1,592	**92**	136
		4,421	4,362	**1,535**	1,612
Non-current assets held for sale	18	**84**	7	**15**	–
		4,505	4,369	**1,550**	1,612
Total assets		**16,537**	16,540	**10,632**	10,485

17.2 Control

17.2.1 Ownership versus control

The definition of a subsidiary company is fundamental to the preparation of consolidated financial statements. When consolidated financial statements were originally introduced in the early part of the twentieth century, the companies that were consolidated were determined by reference to legal ownership. If the investor owned more than 50% of the voting share capital of the investee, it was deemed to control the investee, as resolutions at the annual general meeting (AGM) are passed by simple majority.

This ownership model generally sufficed for determining control until the 1970s. However, from this time, it became more common for companies to set up other entities in which they had little or no legal ownership interest, but which they effectively controlled. These entities, referred to as special purpose entities (SPEs), could be used to undertake borrowings, and because the entities were not 'controlled' according to the legal ownership model, they would not be consolidated into the financial statements of the parent company. The result was a case of off balance sheet financing, an illustration of which is provided in Figure 17.2.

In the situation illustrated in Figure 17.2, the sponsor may hold a minority of the equity of the SPE or none of it, and may or may not retain a beneficial interest. However, if the sponsor retains the right to modify decision-making powers and liquidate the SPE, then effective control is present.

The case of Enron is a classic illustration of this form of off balance sheet financing. Enron hid its losses and vast debts in various entities in which it owned a minimal proportion of shares, but which it effectively controlled. According to the narrowly drawn rules contained in the US accounting standards at the time, which were based on the concept of legal ownership,

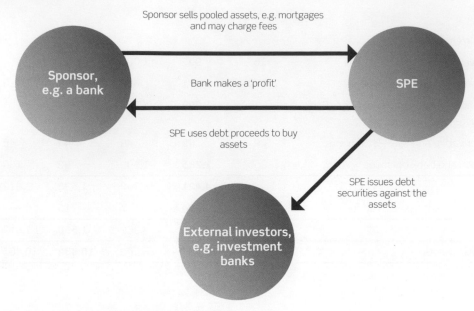

Sponsor sells pooled assets, e.g. mortgages and may charge fees

Sponsor, e.g. a bank

SPE

Bank makes a 'profit'

SPE uses debt proceeds to buy assets

SPE issues debt securities against the assets

External investors, e.g. investment banks

Figure 17.2 Example of a special purpose entity

the entities were not consolidated in Enron's financial statements, with the result that Enron's financial results and position appeared much better than they really were. Once Enron had collapsed, its SPEs came to light, leading to questions being raised about the rules-based nature of the accounting standards. Critics at the time claimed that this type of disaster could not have happened within a principles-based regulatory environment where the issue of ownership and control would have been resolved by following the substance over form approach.

17.2.2 IASB business combinations project

From when it was formed in 2001, the IASB started work on a consolidations project to improve the quality of accounting for business combinations and address the diversity that had existed in practice. The project was conducted in a number of phases, which, over the years, resulted in many revisions to the international financial reporting standards dealing with business combinations. IFRS 3 *Business Combinations*, which addresses how consolidated financial statements are prepared, was issued in 2004 and IAS 27 *Separate Financial Statements*, a standard assumed by the IASB in 2001, has been revised a number of times. The project was given impetus by the global financial crisis of 2007–8, and culminated in the issue of three new IFRS in May 2011:

- IFRS 10 *Consolidated Financial Statements*
- IFRS 11 *Joint Arrangements*
- IFRS 12 *Disclosure of Interests in Other Entities*.

The relationship of the various financial reporting standards is shown in Figure 17.3.

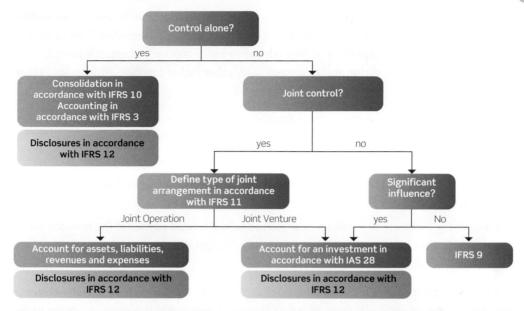

Figure 17.3 Relationship between different categories of investment and the relevant financial reporting standards (ICAEW, 2012). Reproduced with the kind permission of ICAEW.

IFRS 10 addresses the definition of control and requires the same control criteria to be applied to all entities. It replaced those parts of IAS 27 that dealt with control and SIC-12 *Consolidation—Special Purpose Entities*. IFRS 12 requires enhanced disclosures of the composition of group structures, the relationships a reporting company has with other entities, specifically special purpose or **structured entities**, and the risks companies are exposed to from their involvement with such entities.

For the vast majority of companies with straightforward interests in other companies, the new standards have not altered whether they are consolidated or not. However, other companies with more complex interests have had to consider the revised requirements carefully. These latter situations are largely outside the scope of this textbook.

17.2.3 Definition of control

The definition of control has three elements, all of which must be present:

- power over the investee from existing rights
- exposure, or rights, to variable returns from the investee
- the ability to use power to affect the amount of the investor's returns that the investor receives.

Power is the ability of the investor to direct those activities which significantly affect the investee's returns—termed the relevant activities. Relevant activities are the day-to-day activities of a business and include selling and purchasing goods or services, managing financial assets and determining financing structures or obtaining finance. Power arises from rights, which may be straightforward to identify (e.g. through holding more than 50% of voting rights) or may be more complex (e.g. through one or more contractual arrangements).

Even if a majority of voting shares are not held, other rights can give an investor power over its investee. Examples include:

(a) rights to appoint, reassign or remove members of an investee's key management personnel who have the ability to direct the relevant activities—usually the board of directors

(b) rights to dominate the nominations process for electing members of the board of directors

(c) rights to direct the investee to enter into, or veto, significant transactions for the benefit of the investor

(d) where the investee's key management personnel are related parties of the investor, for example, the chief executive officer of the investee and the chief executive officer of the investor are the same person.

For rights to give power, they must be substantive. In other words, even if contractual rights to carry out the relevant activities do not exist, if the investor has the practical ability to do so, then this would provide some evidence of power. Substantive rights differ from protective rights. Protective rights are designed to protect the interests of their holder, but they do not give the holder power over the investee to which those rights relate.

 Example of protective rights

An investee company enters into a loan arrangement with a bank that contains several covenants. If a covenant is breached, the bank has the right to veto major business decisions which are considered to be the relevant activities of the operating entity, and to call in the loan. In this case the bank's rights are considered to be protective. The investor continues to consolidate the investee company.

Control also requires the investor to be exposed to or have rights to the variable returns of the investee. Returns include dividends, interest, fees and changes in the value of the investor's investment; they may be positive or negative and, for control, the amounts the investor will receive must have the potential to vary with the investee's performance. Note that although only one investor will control an investee, more than one party can share in the returns of an investee.

The third criterion for control to be present requires the interaction between the first two criteria.

As indicated, a company which holds less than the majority of voting rights of the investee may still have control, which would lead to the consolidation of the investee. All facts and circumstances would need to be considered and in many cases, significant judgement exercised. In addition to the examples given earlier of where the investor may be deemed to have power over the investee, other factors could be:

- a contractual arrangement between the investor and other vote holders
- rights arising from other contractual arrangements
- where the investee is a structured entity, in other words one which has been designed so that voting rights are not the dominant factor in deciding who controls the entity— e.g., voting rights may relate only to administrative matters and the key activities which affect returns are directed by means of contractual arrangements
- where the investor has substantive potential voting rights
- in certain circumstances, where the investor is an agent and its principal has delegated decision-making authority to the agent.

IFRS 10 contains extensive application guidance to assist companies in determining whether they control and have power over another entity. One area that is addressed is where the investor holds less than the majority of the voting rights, but it has the practical ability to direct the relevant activities unilaterally owing to the size and dispersion of the other shareholders' holdings.

 Examples of power with a significant minority shareholding

Consider the following situations:

1 Company A holds 45% of the voting rights of company B. The remaining voting rights are held by many other shareholders, none individually holding more than 1% of the voting rights.

2 Company A holds 45% of the voting rights of company B. Two other investors each hold 26% of the voting rights of B. Three other shareholders own 1% each.

3 Company A holds 45% of the voting rights of company B. Eleven other shareholders each hold 5% of the voting rights of B.

Does company A have power over company B?

1 On the basis of the absolute size of its holding and the relative size of the other shareholdings, company A has a sufficiently dominant voting interest to give it power. It would be unlikely that the other dispersed shareholders would have arrangements where they would consult each other or be able to make collective decisions.

2 In this case, the two shareholders holding 26% of the voting rights could easily cooperate at the AGM, and prevent company A from directing the relevant activities of company B. Company A could therefore not be said to have power over company B.

3 Here, the absolute and relative sizes of the various shareholdings are less conclusive. In practice, if there are no arrangements in place whereby the 11 shareholders each holding 5% of the voting rights could consult each other or make collective decisions, then it may be difficult for them to do so and prevent company A from being able to direct the relevant activities.

However, the fewer the parties that would need to act together to outvote company A, the more reliance needs to be placed on other facts and circumstances to determine whether A has power over B. The history of the pattern of voting by these other shareholders could be examined to see whether they do turn up and vote at all, or whether they always vote in a particular way. IFRS 10 does not provide any bright lines in terms of percentages that would have to be held, or minimum numbers of small minority shareholders. Professional judgement would have to be exercised in this sort of case.

Potential voting rights (see Figure 17.4) are also addressed by the application guidance to IFRS 10. If the potential rights are substantive, they need to be considered in assessing control. Substantive here means that the holder of the rights must have the practical ability to exercise that right.

 Example of potential voting rights

Does B plc control C Ltd in this situation?

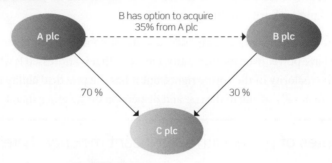

Figure 17.4 Example of potential voting rights

Deciding whether potential voting rights are substantive often requires judgement. The terms of the potential voting rights will need to be examined to determine how soon it is likely that the option will be exercised, whether the price is fixed or variable, and whether the current market value of the potential voting rights gives an indication of whether the option is likely to be exercised. For example, an option that is exercisable in the near future and is in-the-money (i.e. is at a price less than market price) is more likely to be considered substantive.

17.3 Exemptions from the preparation of consolidated financial statements

There are certain situations where the investor, which has subsidiary companies, does not have to prepare consolidated financial statements. For this to apply, all of the following criteria must be fulfilled:

1   The parent is a wholly-owned or partially-owned subsidiary of another entity itself, and all its other owners do not object to consolidated financial statements not being prepared

2   The parent's ultimate or any intermediate parent produces financial statements that comply with IFRS and are available for public use

3   The parent's debt or equity instruments are not traded in a public market

4   The parent does not file its financial statements with a securities commission or other regulatory organisation for the purpose of issuing any class of instruments in a public market.

Companies that qualify as investment entities are also exempt from preparing consolidated financial statements. Instead, in their financial statements, all subsidiaries are required to be measured at fair value, with changes in fair value passing through profit or loss. An investment entity is a company whose business purpose is to invest funds solely for returns from capital appreciation, investment income or both, and which evaluates the performance of its investments on a fair value basis. Private equity or venture capital organisations, pension funds, sovereign wealth funds and other investment funds are likely to be classed as investment entities.

17.4 Consolidation techniques

Financial reporting in practice 17.2 | Tesco plc, 2015

The accounting policies of Tesco contain various notes relating to the basis of consolidation:

Basis of consolidation

The consolidated Group financial statements consist of the financial statements of the ultimate Parent Company ('Tesco PLC'), all entities controlled by the Company (its subsidiaries) and the Group's share of its interests in joint ventures and associates.

Subsidiaries

Subsidiaries are consolidated in the Group's financial statements from the date that control commences until the date that control ceases.

Business combinations and goodwill

The Group accounts for all business combinations by applying the acquisition method. All acquisition-related costs are expensed.

On acquisition, the assets (including intangible assets), liabilities and contingent liabilities of an acquired entity are measured at their fair value. Non-controlling interest is stated at the non-controlling interest's proportion of the fair values of the assets and liabilities recognised.

Goodwill arising on consolidation represents the excess of the consideration transferred over the net fair value of the Group's share of the net assets, liabilities and contingent liabilities of the acquired subsidiary, joint venture or associate and the fair value of the non-controlling interest in the acquiree. If the consideration is less than the fair value of the Group's share of the net assets, liabilities and contingent liabilities of the acquired entity (i.e., a discount on acquisition), the difference is credited to the Group Income Statement in the period of acquisition.

At the acquisition date of a subsidiary, goodwill acquired is recognised as an asset and is allocated to each of the cash-generating units expected to benefit from the business combination's synergies and to the lowest level at which management monitors the goodwill. Goodwill arising on the acquisition of joint ventures and associates is included within the carrying value of the investment. On disposal of a subsidiary, joint venture or associate, the attributable amount of goodwill is included in the determination of the profit or loss on disposal.

Tesco's accounting policy note includes some important terminology which refers to the methods used in consolidation:

- acquisition method
- fair value measurement of subsidiary's assets and liabilities
- goodwill
- goodwill allocation to cash-generating units.

These will be discussed and illustrated in detail together with other techniques of consolidation in the remainder of this chapter. The method for consolidating a subsidiary company set out in IFRS 3 *Business Combinations* is called the acquisition method.

17.4.1 Consideration

To acquire shares in another company from existing shareholders, the investor gives consideration in return. This consideration can be in the form of cash or its own shares, or possibly some other assets, or a combination of these. If there is a cash element to the consideration, this may be deferred or be based on some future performance criteria. The underpinning principle is that the consideration, whatever its type, is measured at fair value.

If cash is given at the date of acquisition then the fair value is the amount of cash. The fair value of deferred cash is its discounted present value. The fair value of any shares given will be the market value of the shares, which will exist for a listed company, and may have to be estimated if not readily available.

Costs incurred by the acquiring company which are directly attributable to the acquisition, such as due diligence or legal costs, are required to be expensed. They do not form part of the consideration.

 Worked example 17.2: to show the accounting for the consideration

The summarised statement of financial position of Dukes plc at 1 January 20X0 is set out as follows:

	£000
Non-current assets	
Property, plant and equipment	500
Current assets	250
Total assets	750
Equity	
Share capital (£1 shares)	300
Retained earnings	260
	560

	190
Current liabilities	
Total equity and liabilities	750

On 1 January 20X0 Dukes acquired 100% of the shares of Spring Ltd for £150,000 and gained control.

Required:

Prepare the statement of financial position of Dukes immediately after the acquisition if:

(a) Dukes acquired the shares for cash

(b) Dukes issued 50,000 equity shares of £1 each. At the date of issue the market value of these shares was £3 each.

Dukes plc

Statement of financial position at 1 January 20X0

	(a) Cash acquisition £000	(b) Share exchange £000
Non-current assets		
Property, plant and equipment	500	500
Investment in Spring	150	150
Current assets	100^1	250
	750	900
Equity		
Share capital (£1 shares)	300	350^2
Share premium	–	100^2
Retained earnings	260	260
	560	710
Current liabilities	190	190
	750	900

Notes

1 Cash has decreased by £150,000.

2 The fair value of the 50,000 shares issued is £3 per share. The shares are therefore being issued at a premium of £2 per share.

17.4.2 Date of acquisition

The date of acquisition is the date on which the investor obtains control of the subsidiary and is generally the date on which the investor legally transfers the consideration, acquires the assets and assumes the liabilities of the subsidiary—sometimes referred to as the closing date. However, an investor might obtain control on a date that is either earlier or later than the closing date if, for example, there is a written agreement which provides that the acquisition date precedes the closing date. All facts and circumstances need to be considered in identifying the acquisition date.

17.4.3 Acquisition method

Consolidated financial statements present the financial information about the group as a single economic entity. The basic rules of preparation are as follows:

1 The parent company combines the financial statements of itself and its subsidiaries line by line by adding together like items of assets, liabilities, income and expenses.

2 The carrying amount of the parent's investment in each subsidiary and the parent's portion of equity of each subsidiary are netted off on consolidation, which will usually result in a figure for goodwill on acquisition.

3 Non-controlling interests (NCI) in the profit or loss of consolidated subsidiaries for the reporting period are identified. (Non-controlling interest is explained in section 17.4.5.)

4 NCI in the net assets of consolidated subsidiaries are identified separately from the parent's ownership interests in them.

5 Measurement of the subsidiaries' assets and liabilities are at their fair value at the date of acquisition.

6 Transactions and balances between the group companies are eliminated.

17.4.4 Consolidated statement of financial position

The chapter initially deals with consolidated statements of financial position, as many consolidation techniques will be addressed in the preparation of this statement. Taking the simplest case first where the investor acquires 100% of the equity share capital of the investee, the rules given in section 17.4.3 may be presented as shown in Figure 17.5.

The consolidated statement of financial position in final form shows the total net assets controlled by the group, including 100% of the net assets of the subsidiary, which are valued at fair value as at the date of acquisition. The ownership interest in the group's net assets is only that of the shareholders of P—the group shareholders.

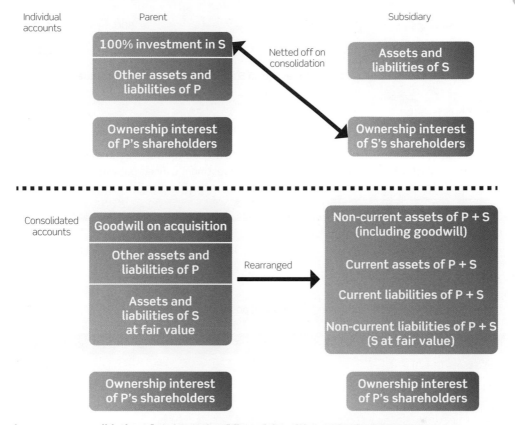

Figure 17.5 Consolidation of statements of financial position: 100% investment

Worked example 17.3 illustrates how the consolidated statement of financial position is drawn up from the separate statements of financial position of the parent and the subsidiary.

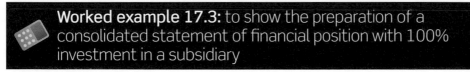

Worked example 17.3: to show the preparation of a consolidated statement of financial position with 100% investment in a subsidiary

P plc has just bought 100% of the shares of S Ltd. The two statements of financial position are as follows:

	P plc	S Ltd
	£	£
Investment in S Ltd	600	
Net assets	400	600
	1,000	600
Share capital	500	200

Retained earnings	500	400
	1,000	600

(Assume that the book values of the net assets in S are equivalent to their fair values.)

Required:

Prepare the consolidated statement of financial position at the date of acquisition.

The investment can be considered as P paying £600 to acquire control of £600 worth of net assets of S. S's net assets equate to its equity, so the investment cancels out with S's equity:

	£
Consideration	600
S's equity	600
	—

The resulting consolidated statement of financial position is as follows:

	£
Net assets (P + S)	1,000
Equity	
Share capital (P only)	500
Retained earnings (P only)	500
	1,000

The parent company controls net assets valued at £1,000 and the ownership interest in these is all the group shareholders.

17.4.5 Non-controlling interest (NCI)

As discussed previously, a parent–subsidiary relationship will result if the investor acquires more than 50% of the voting rights, which means more than 50% of the equity share capital. So if the investor acquires a proportion of equity shares in the investee which is less than 100%, but more than 50%, there will remain a group of shareholders of the subsidiary which owns a minority of the shares, and who do not have control, as illustrated by Figure 17.6.

The consolidated statement of financial position will still include all net assets controlled by the parent company, including 100% of the net assets of the subsidiary at fair value as at the date of acquisition, and the ownership interest in these net assets. This ownership interest, however, will now include that of the non-controlling shareholders in the subsidiary. This can be represented by Figure 17.7.

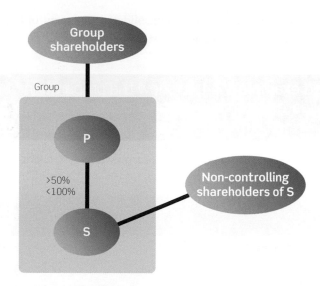

Figure 17.6 Illustration of non-controlling interest

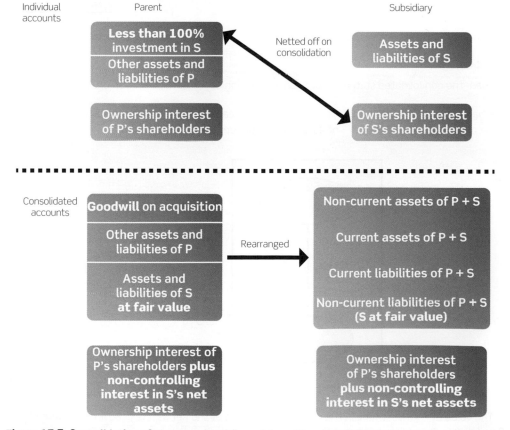

Figure 17.7 Consolidation of statements of financial position: less than 100% investment

Worked example 17.4 illustrates how the consolidated statement of financial position is drawn up where there is non-controlling interest in the subsidiary.

Worked example 17.4: to show the preparation of a consolidated statement of financial position with less than 100% ownership of the shares in the subsidiary

The statements of financial position of P plc and S Ltd are as follows, immediately after P has acquired the shares in S:

	P plc £	S Ltd £
Investment in S Ltd (800 shares)	2,400	
Net assets	2,300	3,000
	4,700	3,000
Share capital (£1 equity shares)	2,000	1,000
Retained earnings	2,700	2,000
	4,700	3,000

(Assume that the book values of the net assets in S are equivalent to their fair values.)

Required:

Prepare the consolidated statement of financial position at the date of acquisition.

P has acquired 80% (800/1,000) of the equity share capital of S. P still controls S, but there is a non-controlling interest (NCI) in S of 20%. This can be represented as follows:

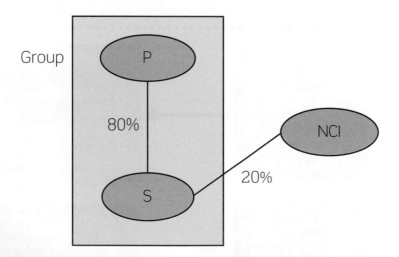

The value of P's investment in S is compared with 80% of the net assets (= 80% of the equity) of S as follows:

	£
Consideration	2,400
Net assets acquired (80% × 3,000)	2,400
	–

The ownership interest of the non-controlling shareholders in the net assets of S needs to be shown in the consolidated statement of financial position as:

NCI = 20% of net assets (= 20% of equity)
    = 20% × £3,000
    = £600

The resulting consolidated statement of financial position is as follows:

	£
Net assets (P + S)	5,300
	5,300
Equity	
Share capital (P only)	2,000
Retained earnings (P only)	2,700
	4,700
NCI	600
	5,300

The parent company controls net assets valued at £5,300, and there is ownership interest in these from the group shareholders valued at £4,700 and from the 20% non-controlling shareholders in S valued at £600.

17.5 Goodwill arising on acquisition

As demonstrated in Worked example 17.4, on the acquisition of a subsidiary, the fair value of the investment is compared with the parent's share of the fair value of the assets acquired. In this example the two amounts are the same. However, the acquirer is usually prepared to pay a premium for its investment and thus there will be a resulting excess—a debit balance. This premium represents a payment made by the acquirer in anticipation of future economic benefits from the subsidiary's net assets that it now controls, but that are not identified individually and recognised separately in the subsidiary company's own financial statements. It is termed **goodwill arising on acquisition**.

The treatment of goodwill arising on acquisition has undergone many changes in the history of consolidated financial statements. The alternatives are writing it off (as an expense or against reserves) or capitalising it as an asset. If it is capitalised, another question arises: should it be amortised over its useful life or considered for impairment? It is generally accepted now that this excess consideration fulfils the definition of an asset given in the IASB's *Conceptual Framework* and can thus be recognised as a non-current intangible asset in the consolidated financial statements. Note that goodwill arising on acquisition is a figure which arises from the consolidation process. Even though it is presented as an intangible non-current asset, it is specifically excluded from IAS 38 *Intangible Assets*.

🛈 **Reminder—goodwill annual impairment test** *Goodwill acquired in a business combination is never amortised, but is tested each year for impairment. For the purpose of its impairment testing, goodwill is allocated to the cash-generating units (CGUs) expected to benefit from the combination, which are then tested for impairment. Any impairment loss is allocated first to goodwill and then to the net assets of the CGU. Any impairment loss passes through the consolidated statement of profit or loss. (See further example in Chapter 11.)*

17.5.1 Goodwill per IFRS 3 *Business Combinations*

IFRS 3 defines goodwill as follows:

> The acquirer shall recognise goodwill as of the acquisition date measured as the excess of (a) over (b) below:
>
> **(a)** the aggregate of:
>
> (i) the consideration transferred measured in accordance with this IFRS, which generally requires acquisition-date fair value;
>
> (ii) the amount of any non-controlling interest in the acquiree measured in accordance with this IFRS; and
>
> (iii) in a business combination achieved in stages, the acquisition-date fair value of the acquirer's previously held *equity interest* in the acquiree.
>
> **(b)** the net of the acquisition-date amounts of the identifiable assets acquired and the liabilities assumed measured in accordance with this IFRS.

(IASB, 2012, para. 32)

Note: (a) (iii) is outside the scope of this textbook, so will be ignored in all future calculations. This is illustrated in the following worked example.

 Worked example 17.5: to show goodwill arising on acquisition

P plc acquires 600 shares in S Ltd and the following statements of financial position are drawn up immediately:

	P plc	S Ltd
	£	£
Investment in S Ltd	1,500	
Net assets	2,500	2,000
	4,000	2,000

Share capital (£1 equity shares)	1,000	1,000
Retained earnings	3,000	1,000
	4,000	2,000

(Assume that the book values of the net assets in S are equivalent to their fair values.)

Required:

Prepare the consolidated statement of financial position at the date of acquisition.

P has acquired 60% (600/1,000) of S's equity share capital.

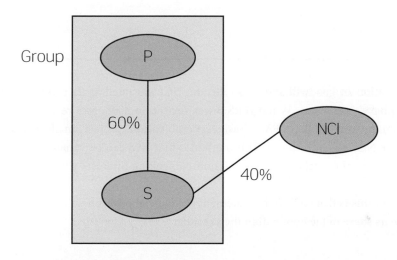

The calculation of goodwill arising on acquisition is as follows:

	£
Consideration	1,500
Plus: NCI in the net assets of S at acquisition (40% × 2,000)	800
	2,300
Less: Net assets at acquisition (100% × 2,000)	(2,000)
Goodwill on acquisition	300

P has paid a premium for its investment in S because it must expect to gain future benefits from this investment.

The NCI in S Ltd is calculated in the same way as before:

NCI = 40% of net assets of S (= 40% of equity)
      = 40% × £2,000
      = £800

The resulting consolidated statement of financial position is as follows:

	£
Intangible assets	
Goodwill	300
Other net assets (P + S)	4,500
	4,800
Equity	
Share capital (P only)	1,000
Retained earnings (P only)	3,000
	4,000
NCI	800
	4,800

In the calculation of goodwill shown so far, the NCI is valued at its proportionate share of the subsidiary's net assets. When IFRS 3 was revised in 2008, as a result of conclusions reached from the joint IASB/US FASB business combinations project, an alternative method of valuing the NCI was introduced. This method is that NCI can be valued at fair value—in other words using the market value of the non-controlling interest's shares—if this can be determined.

The effect of this is that NCI in the statement of financial position will be a different value and include its share of the goodwill in the subsidiary.

 Worked example 17.6: to show non-controlling interest (NCI) valued at fair value

P plc acquired 60% of the equity shares of S plc and gained control. At the date of acquisition the summarised statements of financial position of the two companies were as follows:

	P plc £000	S plc £000
Investment in S	90	
Other net assets	270	80
	360	80
Equity		
Share capital (£1 shares)	200	50
Share premium	–	20
Retained earnings	160	10
	360	80

Note

The total of the fair value of the net assets of S plc at acquisition was £120,000. The market value of a £1 share in S at the date of acquisition was £2.75.

Required:

Calculate goodwill arising on acquisition if P values the NCI at:

(a) the fair value of the separable net assets

(b) fair value.

The group structure is as follows:

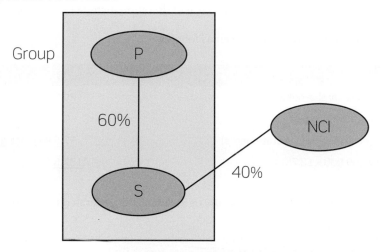

(a)

	£000
Consideration	90
Plus: NCI at acquisition (40% × £120,000)	48
	138
Less: Net assets at acquisition (100% × £120,000)	(120)[1]
Goodwill on acquisition	18

(b)

	£000
Consideration	90
Plus: NCI at acquisition (40% × 50,000 × £2.75)	55
	145
Less: Net assets at acquisition (100% × £120,000)	(120)[1]
Goodwill on acquisition	25

Notes

1   Note this figure in the goodwill calculation is the same under both methods.

So what gives rise to the difference in the two NCI values?

(a) Under method (a), the net assets of S are identified and fair valued separately. A total of these separate fair value figures is calculated and the NCI's share of this total is used in the consolidated financial statements.

(b) Under method (b), the fair value of company S as a whole is used, which is what is reflected in the market price of its shares. The valuation of a company as a whole will include assets which cannot be recognised separately in S's financial statements, in other words internally generated goodwill. So the NCI, calculated as its proportion of the fair value of the company as a whole, will therefore include its share of S's goodwill.

In Worked example 17.6, this can be seen as follows:

	£000
Fair value of S's separable net assets	120.0
Internally generated goodwill	
(not recognised in S's financial statements)	17.5 (balancing figure)
Fair value of S (50,000 × £2.75)	137.5

Under method (b) the NCI includes 40% of S's internally generated goodwill:

40% × £17,500 = £7,000

which is the difference between the NCI figures in (a) and (b) (£55,000 – £48,000 = £7,000).

Since this latter option of valuing NCI was introduced by a revision to IFRS 3 only in 2008, it is not used by many UK companies—it is more common in the USA. It may require a valuation technique to be applied if there is no active market in the shares not held by the investor. It should also be noted that the value of the acquirer's stake and the NCI may differ on a per-share basis. This is because the acquirer's controlling share may include a control premium, whereas the per-share value of the non-controlling stake may need to be discounted to reflect lack of control. Most examples in this textbook require NCI to be valued at the fair value of the separable net assets of the subsidiary.

17.5.2 Negative goodwill

Although not very common, goodwill on acquisition may be negative. In this case the consideration plus the measurement of the non-controlling interest in the subsidiary is less than the measurement of the identifiable net assets of the subsidiary. (Effectively, the parent company has paid less than the value of its share of the net assets of the subsidiary.) This is termed a 'bargain purchase' and may arise in practice through a forced sale of the subsidiary. The resulting credit balance of goodwill is a gain and is recognised in the consolidated statement of profit or loss in the year in which the acquisition occurs, and therefore increases consolidated profit and retained earnings.

17.5.3 Multiple investments

A separate goodwill calculation is performed for each investment in a subsidiary—in practice the investments will be on different dates. Negative goodwill is never netted off with positive goodwill. The different NCI balances from different investments will be calculated separately, but combined to give one balance in the consolidated financial statements.

17.5.4 Other issues relating to the goodwill calculation

As part of accounting for the acquisition process, the investor is encouraged to identify and value intangible assets in the subsidiary, even if these are not permitted to be recognised in the subsidiary's own individual financial statements under IAS 38 *Intangible Assets*. For example, internally generated assets not meeting the recognition criteria of IAS 38 or the subsidiary's own brands may be identified as separable assets and be able to be measured reliably at fair value. These assets will be recognised in the consolidated financial statements and subsequently accounted for according to IAS 38. Note that they will continue to be excluded from recognition in the subsidiary's own financial statements. (See Chapter 11 for further details of accounting for intangible assets.)

The intentional effect of this is to reduce the value given to goodwill arising on acquisition. Rather than having a large goodwill balance, which incorporates various intangible items, the identification and inclusion of exactly what assets are now controlled in the consolidated financial statements should increase their transparency. Users are better informed and the faithful representation of the financial statements is enhanced.

IFRS 3 details some further exceptions to the recognition and measurement of other assets and liabilities of the acquired company at acquisition. Most of these concern items which are outside the scope of this textbook; however, there are a couple which should be noted.

(1) Where the subsidiary company has contingent liabilities and they are present obligations that arise from past events and their fair value can be measured reliably, they are recognised as an identifiable liability of the subsidiary in the goodwill calculation and consolidated financial statements. This is contrary to IAS 37 *Provisions, Contingent Liabilities and Contingent Assets*, as the liability is being recognised, even when it is not probable that an outflow of resources embodying economic benefits will be required to settle the obligation.

🔔 **Reminder** *A contingent liability is in IAS 37 defined as:*
  (a) *a possible obligation that arises from past events and whose existence will be confirmed only by the occurrence or non-occurrence of one or more uncertain future events not wholly within the control of the entity; or*
  (b) *a present obligation that arises from past events but is not recognised because:*
     (i) *it is not probable that an outflow of resources embodying economic benefits will be required to settle the obligation; or*
     (ii) *the amount of the obligation cannot be measured with sufficient reliability.*

It is not recognised in the financial statements, but is disclosed in a note to the financial statements. (See Chapter 13 for full details of contingent liabilities.)

(2) Assets classified as held for sale in the subsidiary at the date of acquisition are valued at fair value less costs to sell, in accordance with IFRS 5 *Non-current Assets Held for Sale and Discontinued Operations*.

17.5.5 Post-implementation review of IFRS 3

The IASB concluded its post-implementation review of IFRS 3 in June 2015. A number of issues, which have been discussed in the previous sections, were raised by users, preparers, auditors and regulators. The subsequent accounting for goodwill arising on acquisition was considered particularly important to many, in other words, whether an impairment model is the most appropriate. The practicalities of performing an impairment test for this goodwill are complex, time-consuming and expensive, and involve significant judgements, especially in determining the assumptions used in the value in use calculation and in allocating goodwill to cash-generating units. The alternative of amortising goodwill over a period of time was considered by some to be more faithfully representative, as goodwill on acquisition is replaced by internally generated goodwill over time. Many analysts ignore any figures relating to this intangible asset in their assessment of consolidated financial statements, whilst others considered that the impairment model was useful as an indication of whether an acquisition was working as intended.

The separate recognition of intangible assets in the subsidiary was supported by some users because it could provide an insight on why the acquirer purchased another company. However, again it is highly subjective, with lack of availability of sufficiently reliable and observable information for fair values. In particular, measuring the fair value of contingent consideration and contingent liabilities is highly judgemental.

The IASB has commenced a research project into these areas.

17.6 Consolidated statement of financial position after acquisition date

In all examples considered so far, the consolidated statement of financial position has been drawn up at the date of acquisition. However, investors need to present consolidated financial statements at all subsequent financial year ends.

17.6.1 Post-acquisition fair value adjustments

The consolidated statement of financial position will include the subsidiaries' net assets as of the date the financial statements are drawn up, but these values will incorporate any adjustments which were made at the date of acquisition to the subsidiaries' net assets to fair value. This may include:

● increases or decreases in the values of property, plant and equipment, and other assets which are still held

● increases or decreases in the property, plant and equipment depreciation figures as a result of the revaluation to fair value.

17.6.2 Pre- and post-acquisition reserves

The consolidated reserves (including consolidated retained earnings) will only include only changes in the subsidiaries' reserves which have arisen after the date of acquisition. **Pre-acquisition reserves**, which are netted off in the calculation of goodwill, are not available for distribution to the group shareholders.

Adjustments to the consolidated retained earnings will have to be made to account for:

● increased or decreased depreciation on revalued property, plant and equipment

● the realisation of profits or losses from inventories which were revalued to fair value at acquisition and which have subsequently been sold.

The NCI will take its share of any fair value adjustments as they affect values of assets and liabilities of the subsidiary.

 Worked example 17.7: to show the accounting for pre- and post-acquisition retained earnings

On 1 January 20X3 P plc acquired 80% of the equity share capital of S Ltd for £150,000 cash. The statements of financial position of the two companies at 31 December 20X3 were as follows:

	P plc £000	S Ltd £000
Property, plant and equipment (PPE)	400	70
Investment in S	150	
Other net assets	220	40
	770	110
Equity share capital (£1 shares)	200	30
Retained earnings	570	80
	770	110

On 1 January 20X3 the retained earnings of S were £50,000. On this date the fair value of S's PPE was £20,000 in excess of the book values. S depreciates its PPE using the straight-line method and, at 1 January 20X3, these assets had a remaining useful life of ten years.

Required:

Prepare the consolidated statement of financial position at 31 December 20X3.

The group structure is as follows:

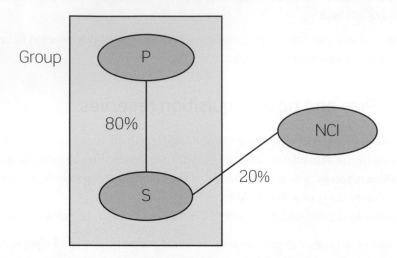

If S had included the revaluation of its PPE to fair value in its financial statements, it would have made the adjustment:

		£000	£000
Debit	PPE	20	
Credit	Revaluation reserve		20

The goodwill calculation incorporates this and becomes:

	£000
Consideration	150
Add: NCI share of [*FV of net assets* of subsidiary]	
[= Share capital + reserves including notional revaluation reserve *at date of acquisition*]	
20% × [30 + 50 + 20]	20
	170
Less: FV of net assets of subsidiary (30 + 50 + 20)	(100)
Goodwill	70

The fair value adjustment to S's PPE means that additional annual depreciation of £20,000/10 = £2,000 has to be accounted for in the consolidated financial statements:

- in consolidated PPE—in this example one year's additional accumulated depreciation
- in consolidated retained earnings
- and it affects the NCI balance.

Working 1—PPE

	£000
P	400
S	70
Fair value adjustment	20
Less: additional depreciation	(2)
	488

Working 2—Consolidated retained earnings

	£000
P	570
P's share of post-acquisition retained earnings of S	
adjusted for additional depreciation	
80% × [(80–50)—2]	22.4
	592.4

Working 3—NCI

	£000
S's net assets at 31 December 20X3	110
Fair value adjustment	20
Additional depreciation	(2)
	128
NCI share 20% × 128	25.6

Consolidated statement of financial position

	£000
Goodwill	70
Property, plant and equipment	488
Other net assets (P + S)	260
	818
Equity share capital	200
Retained earnings	592.4
	792.4
NCI	25.6
	818

17.7 Acquisition of preference shares and other financial instruments in the subsidiary

17.7.1 Preference shares

The acquisition of preference shares of the subsidiary does not affect the question of control, as preference shares (usually) do not carry voting rights or possess rights to reserves. However, the consideration for the preference shares may not equate to their par value and therefore goodwill on acquisition may arise. If the preference shares are acquired at the same time as the equity shares, the calculation of this goodwill is subsumed within the calculation of goodwill on the purchase of the equity shares.

The proportion of preference shares not held by the parent company forms part of NCI and is measured at the appropriate percentage of the par value of the shares. This is amalgamated with other NCI balances.

Any other reserves in the subsidiary's accounts are divided between the parent's share and the NCI's share according to the percentage ownership of the equity shares.

 Worked example 17.8: to show preparation of a consolidated statement of financial position including preference shares

P plc has purchased 800 equity shares and 40 preference shares in S Ltd. S Ltd's issued share capital comprises £200 in equity 20p shares and £100 in £1 irredeemable preference shares. The statements of financial position of the two companies immediately after the acquisition of the shares by P are as follows:

	P plc £	S Ltd £
Investment in S Ltd	950	
Net assets	50	600
	1,000	600
Equity		
Equity shares	450	200
Preference shares	50	100
Retained earnings	500	300
	1,000	600

At the date of acquisition, the fair values of S Ltd's net assets were £750.

Required:

Prepare the consolidated statement of financial position at the date of acquisition.

% shareholdings

Equity shares	800/(200 × 5*)	80%
Preference shares	40/100	40%

* S Ltd's equity shares are 20p shares, so £1-worth of share capital equates to 5 shares. S Ltd has issued £200-worth of equity shares.

The shareholdings can be represented as shown in Figure 17.8.

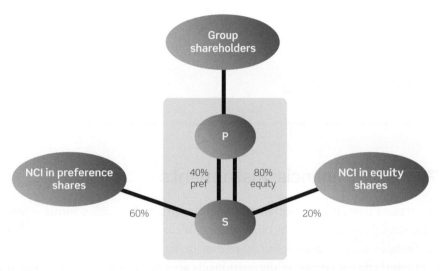

Figure 17.8 Group structure

Working—goodwill

	£	£
Consideration		950
Add: NCI in fair value of net assets of S		
Equity share capital	200	
Retained earnings	300	
Fair value adjustment	150	
	20% × 650	130
Preference share capital	60% × 100	60
		1,140
Less: Fair value of net assets of S		750
Goodwill		390

Consolidated statement of financial position

	£
Goodwill	390
Other net assets (50 + 600 + 150 FV adjustment)	800
	1,190
Equity	
Equity shares (P only)	450
Preference shares (P only)	50
Retained earnings (P only)	500
	1,000
NCI (130 + 60 from goodwill working)	190
	1,190

17.7.2 Other financial instruments

Like preference shares, the acquisition of debentures or bonds or other forms of long-term debt in the subsidiary does not affect the question of control. That part of the investment in the parent's statement of financial position relating to the consideration for these debt instruments (an asset) and the portion of the instruments acquired in the subsidiary's statement of financial position (a liability) will be cancelled out in the consolidated statement of financial position (see section 17.8). Any portion of the debt instruments not acquired by the parent at the date of acquisition is not part of NCI. This remains as a liability in the consolidated statement of financial position.

17.8 Intragroup transactions and balances

It is very common for companies within the same group to trade with each other. For example, a group may comprise a manufacturing company, a distribution company and a retailer. Other assets may be bought and sold between the group companies, and it is also usual for the parent company to charge management fees to the subsidiary companies it controls, possibly to reflect the time the directors and senior management personnel of the parent have spent directing and controlling the operations of the subsidiary.

As seen in Worked example 17.1, which demonstrated the need for consolidated financial statements, transactions between group companies should not be reflected in the consolidated accounts. Given that each company records the transactions in their own individual financial statements, the consolidation process requires adjustments to cancel these out.

A sale from one group company to another is a purchase in this other company's accounts; thus, for consolidated financial statements purposes, the sale will cancel out with the purchase. Any management charge will be recorded as fee income in the parent's accounts, which will cancel out on consolidation with the management fee expenses in the subsidiaries' accounts.

These transactions are likely to be on credit terms, and so receivable and payable balances will exist between the group companies. In the statement of financial position these intragroup balances are cancelled out. The consolidated financial statements will therefore show the transactions and resulting balances of the group as a single entity.

 Example of intragroup receivables and payables

P plc owns 75% of the equity share capital of S Ltd.

1 P plc sells goods to S Ltd and at the financial year end S owes P £50,000.

   P plc will show the balance of £50,000 in its trade receivables and S Ltd will have a corresponding £50,000 in its trade payables.

   When the consolidated statement of financial position is drawn up, £50,000 will be deducted from both trade receivables and trade payables.

2 Suppose just before the year end, S Ltd sends a payment to P plc for £20,000 as part settlement of its liability, but P does not receive this until a few days into the new financial year.

   P will still have a balance of £50,000 included in its trade receivables, but the trade payables balance in S's accounts will now be £30,000. The two balances will not fully cancel each other out.

   This situation is referred to as **cash-in-transit**. The cash is accounted for in the consolidated financial statements as if it had been received by P plc by the financial year end. So consolidated bank balances are increased by £20,000 and P's trade receivables are reduced by £20,000:

   Debit   Bank

   Credit   Trade receivables

The resulting intragroup trade receivable and trade payable of £30,000 now cancel out on consolidation.

17.8.1 Unrealised profit in inventories

The cancellation of the transactions just described will not affect consolidated profits. However, consider the situation where one group company makes a profit from the sale of goods to another and some of these goods are on hand in the buyer's inventories at the consolidated statement of financial position date. The profit element included in the value of these inventories needs to be eliminated on consolidation as it has not yet been realised by selling the goods on outside the group.

Example of unrealised profit in inventories

Company S is a subsidiary of company P. During the year, P purchases goods for £160. P sells these goods onto S for £280. By the end of the year S has sold three-quarters of these goods to customers outside the group.

This may be represented by Figure 17.9.

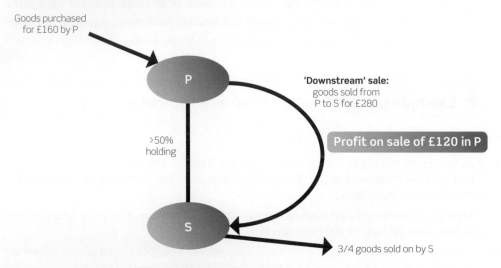

Figure 17.9 Intragroup trading and unrealised profit in inventories

At the year end one-quarter of the goods remain in S's inventories. These had cost S $1/4 \times 280 = £70$.

The concept of the group being a single entity means that the consolidated financial statements should reflect the cost of the goods to the group, which is $1/4 \times 160 = £40$.

The profit element of £30 (£70 – £40) is therefore eliminated from consolidated inventories. As unrealised profit, it is also eliminated from P's profits.

Now consider the situation using the same figures, but reversing the direction of the sale so that it is an **upstream sale** from S to P, with the inventories in P's accounts and S having made the profit. The profit element of £30 is still eliminated from consolidated inventories. The unrealised profit has to be eliminated from S's profits, which means that the NCI in S take its share of this unrealised profit.

Note: care should be taken when calculating the unrealised profit on inventories. Details may be provided in the form of a gross profit/margin percentage or a mark-up. Gross profit/margin is a percentage based on selling price, while mark-up is a percentage based on cost.

 Example of gross margin versus mark-up

1 Goods are sold for £600 at a mark-up of 25%

Profit included = **25/125** × £600 = £120

2 Goods are sold for £1,000 giving a gross margin of 25%

Profit included = **25/100** × £1,000 = £250

 Worked example 17.9: to show the accounting for intragroup balances and unrealised profit in inventories

P plc acquired 60% of the equity shares of S Ltd on 31 December 20X5. The two statements of financial position at 31 December 20X6 are as follows:

	P plc		S Ltd	
	£	£	£	£
Non-current assets		280		150
Investment in S Ltd		160		
		440		
Current assets				
Inventories	240		220	
Receivables	200		130	
Bank	60		30	
		500		380
Total assets		940		530
Equity				
Share capital		200		100
Retained earnings		400		160
		600		260
Payables		340		270
Total equity and liabilities		940		530

At the date of acquisition the retained earnings of S Ltd were £70. At this date, the fair values of S's non-current assets were determined as £50 greater than their carrying amounts with an estimated remaining useful life of 10 years. S uses the straight-line method of depreciation.

During 20X6 P plc sold goods which had cost £160 to S Ltd for £280. Of these goods, S had sold three-quarters by 31 December 20X6.

At 31 December 20X6 S Ltd owed P plc £50.

Required:

Prepare the consolidated statement of financial position at 31 December 20X6.

Workings

The group structure is as follows:

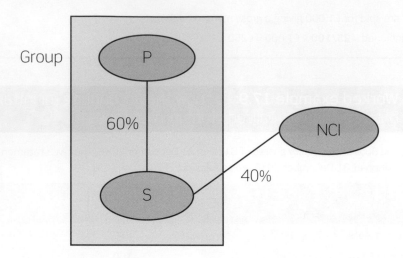

Working 1—goodwill

	£
Investment	160
Add: NCI in fair value of net assets of S at acquisition	
= 40% × (share capital + reserves + fair value adjustment at date of acquisition)	
= 40% × (100 + 70 + 50)	88
	248
Less: Fair value of net assets of S at acquisition	(220)
Goodwill	28

Working 2—unrealised profit in inventories

Sale from P to S—'downstream' sale.
Eliminate unrealised profit of £30 from closing inventories and consolidated retained earnings.

Working 3—intercompany debt

Intercompany debt of £50 eliminated from consolidated receivables and payables.

Working 4—non-current assets

	£
P	280
S	150
Plus: fair value adjustment	50
Less: additional fair value depreciation (£50/10)	(5)
	475

Working 5—consolidated retained earnings

	£
P plc	400
Less: unrealised profit in inventories	(30)
Plus: share of S's post-acquisition retained earnings adjusted for	
fair value depreciation 60% × (160–70–5)	51
	421

Working 6—non-controlling interest (NCI)

	£
NCI share of S's net assets at 31 December 20X6 adjusted for fair values	
40% × (260 + 50–5)	122

Consolidated statement of financial position at 31 December 20X6

		£	£
Non-current assets			475
Goodwill			28
			503
Current assets			
Inventories	(240 + 220 – 30)	430	
Receivables	(200 + 130 – 50)	280	
Bank	(60 + 30)	90	
			800
Total assets			1,303
Equity			
Share capital	(P only)		200
Retained earnings			421
			621
NCI			122
Payables	(340 + 270 – 50)		560
Total equity and liabilities			1,303

17.9 Consolidated statement of profit or loss

As discussed earlier, the consolidated financial statements for a parent and its subsidiary companies are prepared using the acquisition method. For the statement of profit or loss this means that all like items of income and expenses are added together line by line. Note, as for assets and liabilities, 100% of the subsidiaries' income and expenses are included, irrespective of whether the shareholding of the parent in the subsidiaries is less than 100%. Remember the parent controls its subsidiaries, so it controls their profits completely.

Intragroup activities as described in section 17.8 have to be eliminated so that the results of the group as a single entity are shown. This will also include elimination of dividends received by the parent from the subsidiaries.

Consolidation items that have been seen so far in this chapter as adjustments to consolidated retained earnings will be included under an appropriate heading in the consolidated statement of profit or loss. These will include:

- the unrealised profit in closing inventories
- additional depreciation on the subsidiaries' non-current assets revalued to fair value at the date of acquisition
- goodwill impairment.

The NCI in the profit or loss of consolidated subsidiaries for the reporting period is calculated and shown at the foot of the statement of profit or loss. The balance of the consolidated profit is attributable to the group shareholders.

If a subsidiary company is acquired part-way through the reporting period, the income and expenses of the subsidiary are included only from the date of acquisition. This may require time-apportionment of these items.

 Worked example 17.10: to show the preparation of a consolidated statement of profit or loss

P plc purchased 80% of the equity shares in S Ltd on 1 January 20X1. Statements of profit or loss of the companies for the year ended 31 December 20X2 are as follows:

	P plc		S Ltd	
	£000	£000	£000	£000
Revenue		640		330
Cost of sales		410		200
Gross profit		230		130
Distribution costs	35		20	
Administrative expenses	70	105	55	75
Profit from operations		125		55
Income from investments		28		–
Profit before tax		153		55
Tax		26		10
Profit for the year		127		45

Notes

1 During 20X2 S sold goods, which had cost it £20,000, to P. S marked up these goods by 50%.
2 By the year end 30% of these goods had not been sold by P.
3 During 20X2 S paid total dividends of £35,000.
4 At the date of acquisition the fair values of S's non-current assets were £100,000 greater than their book values. The assets were considered to have a remaining useful life of 10 years. S uses a straight-line depreciation policy.

Required:

Prepare the consolidated statement of profit or loss for the year ended 31 December 20X2.

The group structure is as follows:

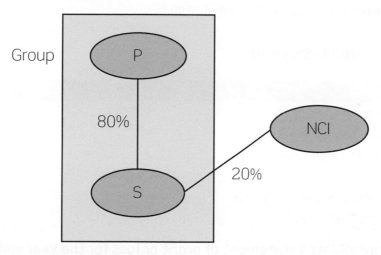

Working 1—investment income

The first item to check is whether the investment income in P's statement of profit or loss is completely from dividends received from S or whether there is any other investment income from sources external to the group.

Intragroup dividend	= 80% × S's dividend
	= 80% × £35,000
	= £28,000

This is equivalent to the investment income in P's statement of profit or loss. Hence, P's income from investments is cancelled out on consolidation.

Working 2—intragroup sales

	£
Cost of intragroup sales	20,000
Mark-up	10,000
Selling price	30,000

£30,000 is eliminated from both sales and purchases (S's sale is P's purchase).

Working 3—unrealised profit in inventories

P's closing inventories must be reduced to the cost to the group.

Thirty per cent of the £10,000 profit from the intragroup sales is deducted from closing inventories. This has the effect of *increasing* consolidated cost of sales by £3,000.

The sale is an 'upstream' sale from S to P. Thus, the NCI in S takes its share of the elimination of this profit element.

Working 4—fair value depreciation

The additional depreciation on the larger fair values of S's non-current assets is included in the consolidated statement of profit or loss.

Additional depreciation = $10\% \times £100,000 = £10,000$

Working 5—NCI in S's profit

	£000
S's profit after tax	45
Less: unrealised profit in inventories	(3)
Less: additional FV depreciation	(10)
	32

NCI in S's profit = $20\% \times 32,000 = £6,400$

P plc's consolidated statement of profit or loss for the year ended 31 December 20X2

		£000	£000
Revenue	(P + S – intragroup W2)		
	(640 + 330 – 30)		940
Cost of sales	(P + S – intragroup W2 + unrealised profit in inventories W3)		
	(410 + 200 – 30 + 3)		583
Gross profit			357
Distribution costs	(35 + 20)	55	
Administrative expenses	(70 + 55 + FV depreciation 10 W4)	135	
			190
Profit before tax			167
Tax	(26 + 10)		36
Profit for the year			131

Attributable to:	
Shareholders of the group (balancing figure) *	124.6
NCI W5	6.4
	131

* Note that the NCI in S's net profit is calculated first. The profit attributable to the group shareholders is the balancing figure.

17.9.1 Consolidated statement of comprehensive income

As discussed in Chapter 4, the statement of profit or loss is either presented on its own with a statement of other comprehensive income and losses as an additional statement, or the statement of profit or loss forms part of the statement of comprehensive income. The main items of other comprehensive income within the scope of this textbook relate to the surpluses or deficits on revaluations of property, plant and equipment (see Chapter 10 for details of these) and actuarial remeasurements from defined benefit retirement plans (see Chapter 16 for further details).

For the purpose of this textbook, consolidated statements of comprehensive income will be limited to only including items arising from property, plant and equipment revaluations in the parent company. Note that if this were to be included, the interest in the group's profit for the year and in the group's total comprehensive income from the group's shareholders and the NCI should be disclosed, as shown by the example in Chapter 4.

17.10 Consolidated statement of changes in equity

⏺ **Reminder** *The consolidated statement of changes in equity shows the changes in the equity balances over the course of the financial year. The closing balances on this statement are transferred to the equity section of the statement of financial position.*

Chapters 1 and 4 discuss this statement in detail.

The consolidated statement of changes in equity requires a column showing the changes in NCI over the year. If a subsidiary has been acquired during the financial year this column will also have to include any NCI valued at the date of acquisition. A pro forma consolidated statement of changes in equity is shown in the Example statement.

Example statement

Company XXX

Consolidated statement of changes in equity for the accounting period

	Share capital £000	Share premium £000	Retained earnings £000	NCI £000	Total £000
At start of year	XX	XX	XX	XX	XX
On acquisition of subsidiary				XX	XX
Profit for year[1]			XX	XX	XX
Dividends paid[2]			(XX)	(XX)	(XX)
At end of year	XX	XX	XX	XX	XX

[1] The figures for the profit for the year are the figures from the bottom section of the consolidated statement of profit or loss.

[2] The dividends deducted from consolidated retained earnings are dividends paid to the group shareholders. The dividends deducted from the NCI column are the NCI's share of dividends paid by the subsidiaries.

 Worked example 17.11: to show the preparation of a consolidated statement of changes in equity

Using the details given in the statement of profit or loss in Worked example 17.10, further information is as follows.

1   The equity account balances of P and S at 31 December 20X1 were as follows:

	P plc £000	S Ltd £000
Equity share capital	150	80
Share premium	60	–
Retained earnings	129	140
	339	220

2   At the date of acquisition S's retained earnings were £90,000.

3   During the year ended 31 December 20X2 P paid total dividends of £50,000.

Required:

Prepare the consolidated statement of changes in equity for the year ended 31 December 20X2.

A reminder that the group structure is as follows:

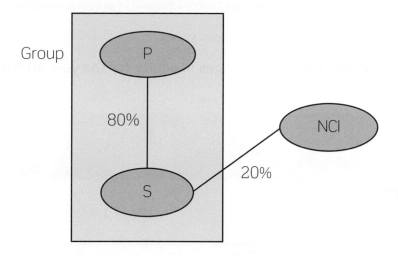

Working 1—consolidated retained earnings at 1 January 20X2

Remember, this is a statement of financial position balance, so the workings are as detailed in section 17.6.2.

	£000
P	129
P's share of S's post-acquisition retained earnings *at 1 January 20X2*	
adjusted for accumulated fair value depreciation	
80% × (140 − 90 − 1 year × 10)	32
	161

Working 2—NCI at 1 January 20X2

Remember, this is also a statement of financial position balance, so the workings are as detailed in section 17.4.5.

	£000	£000
NCI share of S's net assets at fair value *at 1 January 20X2*		
[Remember net assets at fair value = equity + fair value adjustment]		
Share capital	80	
Retained earnings	140	
Fair value adjustment	100	
Fair value accumulated depreciation (1 year × 10)	(10)	
	20% × 310	62

Working 3—dividends paid

Dividends paid to the group shareholders of £50,000 will be deducted from consolidated retained earnings.

Dividends paid to the NCI in S = 20% × £35,000 = £7,000

Consolidated statement of changes in equity for the year ended 31 December 20X2

	Share capital £000	Share premium £000	Retained earnings £000	NCI £000	Total £000
At 1 January 20X2	150	60	161	62	433
Profit for year			124.6	6.4	131
Dividends paid			(50)	(7)	(57)
At 31 December 20X2	150	60	235.6	61.4	507

The balances at 31 December 20X2 are the balances which will be transferred to the statement of financial position.

These balances can be checked as follows.

Working 4—retained earnings at 31 December 20X2

	P £000	S £000
Retained earnings at 1 January 20X2	129	140
Profit for the year	127	45
Dividends paid	(50)	(35)
Retained earnings at 31 December 20X2	206	150

Consolidated retained earnings at 31 December 20X2

	£000	£000
P W4		206
P's share of S's post-acquisition retained earnings *at 31 December 20X2* adjusted for unrealised profit in inventories and accumulated fair value depreciation:		
Post-acquisition retained earnings (150 W4–90)	60	
Unrealised profit in inventories	(3)	
Fair value accumulated depreciation (2 years × 10)	(20)	
	80% × 37	29.6
		235.6

NCI at 31 December 20X2

	£000	£000
NCI share of S's net assets at fair value *at 31 December 20X2*		
Share capital	80	
Retained earnings	150	
Unrealised profit in inventories	(3)	
Fair value adjustment	100	
Fair value accumulated depreciation (2 years × 10)	(20)	
	20% × 307	61.4

17.11 Disclosures in the financial statements

The financial reporting standards relating to consolidations issued in 2011 included a separate standard specifically addressing disclosures—IFRS 12 *Disclosure of Interests in Other Entities*. This details the disclosures required for all categories of investments by one company in another, except for simple investments, which are dealt with by IFRS 7 *Financial Instruments: Disclosures*. Users of financial statements had been constantly requesting improvements to the disclosure of a company's interests in other entities to help identify the profit or loss and cash flows available to the investing company, and to determine the value of a current or future investment. The 2007 global financial crisis also highlighted a lack of transparency about the risks to which a company was exposed from its involvement with special purpose and structured entities.

IFRS 12 therefore combines disclosure requirements for interests in subsidiaries, associates, joint arrangements and unconsolidated structured entities. Those relating to associates and joint arrangements are discussed further in Chapter 18.

Importantly for users, the significant judgements and assumptions a company has made in determining the nature of its interest in another entity or arrangement, and in determining the type of joint arrangement in which it has an interest must be disclosed. The impact of this is that where the determination of control, in other words the question of whether an investee is a subsidiary and should be consolidated, is not straightforward, the reporting company has to explain the basis for its decisions.

If a company has interests in a structured entity that it does not consolidate, then it must provide sufficient information to enable users:

(a) to understand the nature and extent of its interests in unconsolidated structured entities

(b) to evaluate the nature of, and changes in, the risks associated with its interests in unconsolidated structured entities.

Quantitative and qualitative information is required to explain the interest in the entities, together with the company's maximum exposure to losses which may arise from the investments.

17.11.1 Disclosures of interests in subsidiary companies

Disclosures of interests in subsidiary companies are required to enable users of the consolidated financial statements:

(a) to understand:

    (i)   the composition of the group; and

    (ii) the interest that non-controlling interests have in the group's activities and cash flows; and

(b) to evaluate:

    (i)   the nature and extent of significant restrictions on the parent company's ability to access or use assets, and settle liabilities, of the group;

    (ii) the nature of, and changes in, the risks associated with the parent's interests in consolidated structured entities;

    (iii) the consequences of changes in the ownership interest in a subsidiary that do not result in a loss of control; and

    (iv) the consequences of losing control of a subsidiary during the reporting period.

This will include factual information about a subsidiary and a summary of its financial information. However, there is again a focus on the provision of information about the risks arising from the investments.

Financial reporting in practice 17.3	Barclays plc, 2015

Barclays includes extensive disclosures about its subsidiaries and structured entities in its 2014 financial statements. Extracts from these disclosures are shown to illustrate the type of information now required to be provided.

Accounting policy—Consolidation

Barclays applies IFRS 10 *Consolidated Financial Statements*.

   The consolidated financial statements combine the financial statements of Barclays PLC and all its subsidiaries. Subsidiaries are entities over which Barclays PLC has control. The Group has control over another entity when the Group has all of the following:

1)   power over the relevant activities of the investee, for example through voting or other rights;

2)   exposure to, or rights to, variable returns from its involvement with the investee; and

3)   the ability to affect those returns through its power over the investee.

The assessment of control is based on the consideration of all facts and circumstances. The Group reassesses whether it controls an investee if facts and circumstances indicate that there are changes to one or more of the three elements of control.

Intra-group transactions and balances are eliminated on consolidation and consistent accounting policies are used throughout the Group for the purposes of the consolidation.

Changes in ownership interests in subsidiaries are accounted for as equity transactions if they occur after control has already been obtained and they do not result in loss of control.

Barclays provides lists of its principal subsidiaries and its ownership interest.

Note 36—Significant judgements and assumptions used to determine the scope of the consolidation

Determining whether the Group has **control of an entity** is generally straightforward based on ownership of the majority of the voting capital. However, in certain instances this determination will involve significant judgement, particularly in the case of structured entities where voting rights are often not the determining factor in decisions over the relevant activities. This judgement may involve assessing the purpose and design of the entity. It will also often be necessary to consider whether the Group, or another involved party with power over the relevant activities, is acting as a principal in its own right or as an agent on behalf of others.

There is also often considerable judgement involved in the ongoing assessment of control over structured entities. In this regard, where market conditions have deteriorated such that the other investors' exposures to the structure's variable returns have been substantively eliminated, the Group may conclude that the managers of the structured entity are acting as its agent and therefore will consolidate the structured entity.

An interest in equity voting rights exceeding 50% would typically indicate that the Group has control of an entity. However certain entities are excluded from consolidation because the Group does not have exposure to their variable returns. These entities are controlled by external counterparties rather than the Group. Where appropriate, interests relating to these entities are included in Note 37 Structured entities.

Note 37—Consolidated structured entities

A structured entity is an entity in which voting or similar rights are not the dominant factor in deciding control. Structured entities are generally created to achieve a narrow and well defined objective with restrictions around their ongoing activities. Depending on the Group's power over the activities of the entity and its exposure to and ability to influence its own returns, it may consolidate the entity. In other cases it may sponsor or have exposure to such an entity but not consolidate it.

The Group has contractual arrangements which may require it to provide financial support to the following types of consolidated structured entities:

- Securitisation vehicles
- Commercial paper (CP) and medium term note conduits
- Fund management entities
- Covered bonds
- Employee benefit trusts.

(continued)

(continued)

Unconsolidated structured entities in which the Group has an interest

An interest in a structured entity is any form of contractual or non-contractual involvement which creates variability in returns arising from the performance of the entity for the Group. Such interests include holdings of debt or equity securities, derivatives that transfer financial risks from the entity to the Group, lending, loan commitments, financial guarantees and investment management agreements.

Interest rate swaps, foreign exchange derivatives that are not complex and which expose the Group to insignificant credit risk by being senior in the payment waterfall of a securitisation and derivatives that are determined to introduce risk or variability to a structured entity are not considered to be an interest in an entity and have been excluded from the disclosures below.

The disclosure note continues with details of Barclays interests in the assets and liabilities of the unconsolidated structured entities. Barclays' maximum exposure to losses, both on and off-balance sheet is also provided.

 ## Summary of key points

With one or two exceptions, consolidated financial statements are required to be drawn up for a parent company and its subsidiary companies—the group—as if the group were a single entity. The key issue in determining whether the investee company is a subsidiary or not, and therefore whether it should be consolidated or not, is that of control. The issue of control has been the subject of much deliberation by the IASB and is the main subject of IFRS 10 *Consolidated Financial Statements*, in which it is defined as having three elements for the investor:

- power over the investee
- exposure or rights to variable returns from the investee
- ability to use power to affect the reporting company's returns.

In the vast majority of situations within the scope of this textbook, control is present through the investor holding more than 50% of the voting or equity share capital of the subsidiary. However, a principles-based definition of control is very important, not least to eliminate the possibilities of entities which are controlled not being consolidated, which could lead to off balance sheet financing and financial statements not being faithfully representative.

The chapter has discussed and provided examples of the preparation of a consolidated statement of financial position, statement of profit or loss, statement of comprehensive income and statement of changes in equity. The techniques of consolidation follow the acquisition method and require all assets, liabilities, income and expenses of the parent company and its subsidiaries to be combined, line-by-line, with the subsidiaries' figures being incorporated at their fair value at the date of acquisition. The effects of intragroup trading and other activities are eliminated, and if the acquisition is made part-way through the most recent accounting period, only the post-acquisition profit and loss elements of the subsidiary are included. If the parent company holds less than 100% of the voting share capital of a subsidiary company, then there is NCI in this company, which is shown in all consolidated statements.

At the date of acquisition, if the fair value of the consideration plus the NCI in the subsidiary exceeds the fair value of the identified separable net assets of the subsidiary, then goodwill on acquisition arises. This fulfils the definition of an intangible asset and it is recognised in the consolidated financial statements. It is not amortised, but is tested annually for impairment.

The latest financial reporting standards require that investing companies explain the judgements they made in determining whether to consolidate or exclude from consolidation their interest in other entities. In addition, they should evaluate and disclose their exposure to risk from their consolidated subsidiaries and interests in unconsolidated structured entities.

Note—a full summary of the methods used in preparing consolidated financial statements as demonstrated in this textbook is included in the online resources.

 ## Further reading

IASB (International Accounting Standards Board) (2011a) IAS 27 *Separate Financial Statements*. London: IASB.

IASB (International Accounting Standards Board) (2011b) IFRS 10 *Consolidated Financial Statements*. London: IASB.

IASB (International Accounting Standards Board) (2012) IFRS 3 *Business Combinations*. London: IASB.

 ## Bibliography

Barclays plc (2015) *Annual Report, 2014*. London: Barclays.

Bloomberg, *Global M&A Market Review: Financial Rankings*, 2015.

Boulton, J. (2011) *Profit alert!,* ICAEW By All Accounts.

Bryer, R. (2011a) *Consolidated Accounts I: Theory and Regulations*. Working paper. Coventry: Warwick Business School.

Bryer, R. (2011b) *Consolidated Accounts II: Fair Value Accounting for Acquisitions and Investments*. Working paper. Coventry: Warwick Business School.

Bryer, R. (2012) *Consolidated Accounts III: IFRS 10 and the Problem of Control*. Working paper. Coventry: Warwick Business School.

Davies, A. (2011) A weighty subject *Accountancy* 148 (1420). Available online by subscription only at http://www.accountancylive.com.

IASB (International Accounting Standards Board) (2011a) IAS 27 *Separate Financial Statements*. London: IASB.

IASB (International Accounting Standards Board) (2011b) IFRS 10 *Consolidated Financial Statements*. London: IASB.

IASB (International Accounting Standards Board) (2011c) IFRS 12 *Disclosure of Interests in Other Entities*. London: IASB.

IASB (International Accounting Standards Board) (2011d) *Effect Analysis: IFRS 10 Consolidated Financial Statements and IFRS 12 Disclosure of Interests in Other Entities*. London: IASB.

IASB (International Accounting Standards Board) (2011e) *Project Summary and Feedback Statement: IFRS 10 Consolidated Financial Statements and IFRS 12 Disclosure of Interests in Other Entities*. London: IASB.

IASB (International Accounting Standards Board) (2012) IFRS 3 *Business Combinations*. London: IASB.

IASB (International Accounting Standards Board) (2015) *Post-implementation Review of IFRS 3 Business Combinations*. London: IASB.

ICAEW Institute of Chartered Accountants in England and Wales (2015a) IFRS Factsheet: *IFRS 3 revised*. London: ICAEW.

ICAEW Institute of Chartered Accountants in England and Wales (2015b) IFRS Factsheet: *Interest in Other Entities*. London: ICAEW.

IFRS Foundation (2013) Staff Paper: *IFRS 10 Consolidated Financial Statements Effect of Protective Rights on an Assessment of Control*. London: IFRS.

J Sainsbury plc (2015) *Annual Report and Financial Statements, 2015*. London: J Sainsbury.

Tesco plc (2015) *Annual Report and Financial Statements 2015*. London: Tesco.

 Questions

Quick test

1 Explain whether consolidated financial statements are required in the following situations:

(a) A plc obtained control over the net assets of B Ltd by making a direct purchase of those net assets.

(b) A plc acquired 6,000 of the 10,000 £1 equity shares of B Ltd but none of its 10,000 £1 preference shares.

(c) A plc acquired 4,000 of the 10,000 £1 equity shares and had a signed agreement giving it the power to appoint or remove any or all of the directors of B Ltd

(d) A plc acquired 4,500 of the 10,000 £1 equity shares of B Ltd and none of the 10,000 £1 preference shares, but had an agreement with a pension fund which held 600 £1 equity shares that it would have proxy powers in all voting matters.

2 P plc acquires all the shares in S Ltd and the following statements of financial position are immediately drawn up. Prepare the consolidated statement of financial position. You may assume that the fair values of S Ltd's net assets are equivalent to their book values.

	P plc £	S Ltd £
Investment in S Ltd	29,000	
Non-current assets	5,000	12,000
Current assets		
Inventories	4,000	6,000
Receivables	3,000	4,000
Cash and cash equivalents	1,000	2,000
	8,000	12,000
Total assets	42,000	24,000

Equity		
Equity share capital (£1 shares)	25,000	15,000
Retained earnings	14,000	3,000
	39,000	18,000
Current liabilities	3,000	6,000
Total equity and liabilities	42,000	24,000

3   P plc buys 100% of the equity share capital of S Ltd when S has a credit balance on its retained earnings of £300. The statements of financial position of the two companies at a later date are as follows:

	P plc	S Ltd
	£	£
Investment in S Ltd	1,800	
Net assets	1,500	1,500
	3,300	1,500
Equity share capital	2,000	1,000
Retained earnings	1,300	500
	3,300	1,500

Prepare the consolidated statement of financial position at this later date. You may assume that the fair values of S Ltd's net assets were equivalent to their book values at the date of acquisition.

4   Marks plc acquired 10,000 shares in Spencer Ltd on 1 January 20X2 when the retained earnings of Spencer were £5,000. At 31 December 20X4 the statements of financial position of the two companies are as follows:

	Marks plc	Spencer Ltd
	£	£
Non-current assets		
Property, plant and equipment	85,000	11,000
Investment in Spencer Ltd	17,000	
	102,000	
Current assets	214,000	33,000
Total assets	316,000	44,000
Share capital (£1 equity shares)	100,000	10,000
Retained earnings	40,000	9,000
	140,000	19,000
Current liabilities	176,000	25,000
Total equity and liabilities	316,000	44,000

Prepare the consolidated statement of financial position of Marks plc at 31 December 20X4. You may assume that the fair values of Spencer Ltd's net assets were equivalent to their book values at the date of acquisition.

5 P plc acquired 2,750 shares in S Ltd on 1 April 20X3 when the retained earnings of S Ltd were £2,200. The statements of financial position at 31 March 20X5 are as follows:

	P plc £	S Ltd £
Investment in S Ltd	4,850	
Net assets	26,650	7,700
	31,500	7,700
Share capital (£1 equity shares)	30,000	5,000
Retained earnings	1,500	2,700
	31,500	7,700

Prepare the consolidated statement of financial position at 31 March 20X5. You may assume that the fair values of S Ltd's net assets were equivalent to their book values at the date of acquisition.

●● Develop your understanding

6 Two investors, Ash plc and Beech plc, form a company, Chestnut plc, to develop and market a medical product. Ash plc is responsible for developing and obtaining regulatory approval of the medical product—that responsibility includes having the unilateral ability to make all decisions relating to the development of the product and to obtaining regulatory approval. Once the regulator has approved the product, Beech plc will manufacture and market it—this company has the unilateral ability to make all decisions about the manufacture and marketing of the product. Discuss which company, Ash plc or Beech plc, would have power over Chestnut plc in accordance with IFRS 10 *Consolidated Financial Statements*.

7 Marlow plc holds 35% of the voting shares in Nexus plc. Three other shareholders each hold 5% of the shares. The remaining shares are held by numerous other shareholders, none individually holding more than 1% of the voting rights. None of the shareholders has arrangements to consult any of the others or make collective decisions. Decisions about the relevant activities of the investee require the approval of a majority of votes cast at relevant shareholders' meetings—75% of the available votes have been cast at recent relevant shareholders' meetings. Discuss whether Marlow plc has power over Nexus plc.

8 Bimex plc has annual shareholder meetings at which decisions about operating and financing activities are made. The next scheduled shareholder meeting is in six months. However, a special shareholder meeting can be called by shareholders that individually or collectively hold 5% of the voting rights, provided a notice period of 21 days is given. Policies over operating and financing activities can be changed at either annual or special shareholder meetings. Amex plc holds 40% of the voting share capital of Bimex plc. It also holds an option to acquire a further 20% of the voting shares. This option is exercisable in 14 days. Discuss the implications of the potential voting rights that Amex plc holds in Bimex plc in determining the relationship between the two companies:

(a) If the option is deeply in the money, and

(b) If the option is out of the money.

9   The following statements of financial position have been prepared at 31 December 20X8.

	Smith plc	Jones Ltd
	£	£
Non-current assets		
Property, plant and equipment	85,000	18,000
Investment: 120,000 shares in Jones	60,000	
	145,000	
Current assets	160,000	84,000
Total assets	305,000	102,000
Equity share capital (20p shares)	100,000	30,000
Retained earnings	70,000	25,000
	170,000	55,000
Current liabilities	135,000	47,000
Total equity and liabilities	305,000	102,000

Smith plc acquired its holding in Jones Ltd on 31 December 20X7, when Jones' retained earnings stood at £20,000. At this date, the fair value of items of property, plant and equipment was estimated as being £10,000 higher than their book value. The remaining life of these assets at 31 December 20X7 was estimated at five years and Jones uses the straight-line method of depreciation.

Prepare the consolidated statement of financial position of Smith plc at 31 December 20X8.

10 Morecombe plc acquired 8,000 equity shares and 6,000 preference shares in Wise Ltd on 31 December 20X3 when the retained earnings of Wise Ltd were £25,000. The following statements of financial position were prepared at 31 December 20X6:

	Morecombe plc	Wise Ltd
	£	£
Investments: shares in Wise Ltd		
Preference shares	5,000	
Equity shares	35,000	
	40,000	
Sundry net assets	160,000	70,000
	200,000	70,000
Called up share capital		
Equity shares of £1 each	20,000	10,000
Preference shares of £1 each	100,000	20,000
Retained earnings	80,000	40,000
	200,000	70,000

Prepare the consolidated statement of financial position of Morecombe plc at 31 December 20X6. You may assume that the fair values of Wise Ltd's net assets were equivalent to their book values at the date of acquisition.

11 On 30 June 20X4, Ant plc acquired 60% of the equity share capital and 20% of the irredeemable preference share capital of Dec Ltd for £95,000 and £15,000 respectively. At the date of acquisition the fair values of Dec's property, plant and equipment, which had a carrying value of £160,000, was estimated at £200,000. Dec Ltd depreciates its property, plant and equipment on the straight-line method, and the assets' remaining useful lives were estimated at 8 years. Also, at the date of acquisition the balance on Dec's retained earnings was £50,000 and the balance on the share premium account was £9,000.

The following statements of financial position have been prepared at 30 June 20X8:

	Ant plc £	Dec Ltd £
Non-current assets		
Property, plant and equipment	220,000	170,000
Investment: shares in Dec Ltd	110,000	
	330,000	
Current assets	270,000	186,000
Total assets	600,000	356,000
Equity		
Equity shares of £1 each	200,000	90,000
Preference shares of £1 each	–	40,000
Share premium account	25,000	9,000
Retained earnings	150,000	80,000
	375,000	219,000
Current liabilities	225,000	137,000
Total equity and liabilities	600,000	356,000

Prepare the consolidated statement of financial position of Ant plc at 30 June 20X8.

12 P plc bought 40,000 shares in S1 Ltd and 27,000 shares in S2 Ltd on 31 December 20X2. The following statements of financial position were drafted at 31 December 20X3.

	P plc £	S1 Ltd £	S2 Ltd £
Investments in subsidiaries			
S1 Ltd 40,000 shares	49,000		
S2 Ltd 27,000 shares	30,500		
Non-current assets	90,000	38,200	31,400
Net current assets	80,500	19,200	14,600
	250,000	57,400	46,000

Share capital (£1 equity shares)	200,000	50,000	36,000
Retained earnings			
At 1 January 20X3	11,000	3,000	4,800
Profit/(loss) for 20X3	16,000	(1,600)	3,400
	27,000	1,400	8,200
General reserve	23,000	6,000	1,800
	250,000	57,400	46,000

Draw up the consolidated statement of financial position for P plc at 31 December 20X3. You may assume that the fair values of both S1 Ltd's and S2 Ltd's net assets were equivalent to their book values at the date of acquisition.

13 Draw up a consolidated statement of financial position at 31 December 20X5 from the following:

	P plc £	S Ltd £
Investment in S Ltd		
6,000 shares acquired 31/12/20X4	9,700	
Other non-current assets	9,000	5,200
	18,700	5,200
Current assets		
Inventories	3,100	7,200
Receivables	4,900	3,800
Bank	1,100	1,400
	9,100	12,400
Total assets	27,800	17,600
Equity share capital (£1 shares)	20,000	10,000
Retained earnings		
At 31 December 20X4	6,500	3,500
(Loss)/profit for 20X5	(2,500)	2,000
	4,000	5,500
Current liabilities	3,800	2,100
Total equity and liabilities	27,800	17,600

At 31 December 20X5 S Ltd owes P plc £600.

During 20X5 P plc sold goods to S Ltd for £500. P had marked up these goods by £200. Twenty-five per cent of these goods were still in inventory at the statement of financial position date.

You may assume that the fair values of the net assets of S Ltd at the date of acquisition were equivalent to their book values.

14 You are presented with the following information from the Seneley group of companies for the year ended 30 September 20X6:

	Seneley £000	Lowe £000	Wright £000
Non-current assets	225	300	220
Investments—shares in group companies:			
Lowe Ltd	450		
Wright Ltd	130		
	580		
Current assets			
Inventories	225	150	45
Trade receivables	240	180	50
Cash and cash equivalents	50	10	5
	515	340	100
Total assets	1320	640	320
Equity share capital	800	400	200
Retained earnings	200	150	50
	1,000	550	250
Current liabilities	320	90	70
Total equity and liabilities	1,320	640	320

Additional information:

(a) The authorised, issued, and fully paid share capital of all three companies consists of £1 equity shares

(b) Seneley purchased 320,000 shares in Lowe on 1 October 20X3 when Lowe's retained earnings were £90,000

(c) Seneley purchased 140,000 shares in Wright on 1 October 20X5 when Wright's retained earnings were £60,000

(d) During the year to 30 September 20X6 Lowe had sold goods to Seneley for £15,000. These goods had given Lowe a gross profit of 40%, and Seneley still had half these goods in inventories at 30 September 20X6. For all other intragroup trading, the inventories had been sold on outside the group by 30 September 20X6

(e) Included in the respective trade payable and trade receivable balances at 30 September 20X6 were the following intercompany debts:
- Seneley owed Wright £5,000
- Lowe owed Seneley £20,000
- Wright owed Lowe £25,000.

Required:

Prepare the Seneley group's consolidated statement of financial position at 30 September 20X6.

You may assume that the fair values of the net assets of Lowe and Wright at the date of acquisition were equivalent to their book values.

●●● Take it further

15   B plc acquired 200,000 of the equity shares of A Ltd on 30 November 20X2 when the retained earnings of A amounted to £15,000. The statements of financial position of the two companies at 30 November 20X4 are as follows:

	B plc	A Ltd
	£	£
Non-current assets		
Property, plant and equipment		
Cost	140,000	100,000
Accumulated depreciation	(32,000)	(34,390)
	108,000	65,610
200,000 shares in A Ltd (cost)	63,000	
	171,000	
Current assets		
Inventories	17,000	13,390
Receivables	10,000	11,000
Bank	2,000	–
	29,000	24,390
Total assets	200,000	90,000
Equity		
Equity share capital (20p shares)	100,000	50,000
Retained earnings	80,000	30,000
	180,000	80,000
Current liabilities		
Bank overdraft	–	3,000
Payables	20,000	7,000
	20,000	10,000
Total equity and liabilities	200,000	90,000

The fair value of A's property, plant and equipment at 30 November 20X2 was £86,000, when its book value was £81,000. (A depreciates its assets at an average rate of 10% on the reducing balance method.)

During the year ended 30 November 20X4 B purchased goods from A for £30,000. A had marked up these goods by 25%. B had sold two-thirds of these goods to external customers by the statement of financial position date. At 30 November 20X4 A had a receivable of £2,500 in its books representing the amount due from B. B had paid this on 28 November.

The impairment review at 30 November 20X4 estimated the recoverable amount of goodwill to be £3,000. There had been no impairment at 30 November 20X3.

Required:

Prepare the consolidated statement of financial position at 30 November 20X4.

16 The following information relates to the Brodick group of companies for the year to 30 April 20X7:

	Brodick plc £000	Lamlash Ltd £000	Corrie Ltd £000
Revenue	1,100	500	130
Cost of sales	(630)	(300)	(70)
Gross profit	470	200	60
Administrative expenses	(105)	(150)	(20)
Investment income	30	–	–
Profit before tax	395	50	40
Tax	(65)	(10)	(20)
Profit after tax	£330	£40	£20

Additional information:

1 The issued share capital of the group is as follows:

Brodick plc: £5,000,000 (£1 ordinary shares)

Lamlash Ltd: £1,000,000 (£1 ordinary shares)

Corrie Ltd: £200,000 (50p ordinary shares).

2 Brodick plc purchased 800,000 shares in Lamlash Ltd on 1 May 20X0 when the retained earnings of Lamlash amounted to £56,000. At 1 May 20X6 Lamlash's retained earnings were £106,000.

3 Brodick plc purchased 240,000 shares in Corrie Ltd on 1 May 20X4 when the retained earnings of Corrie amounted to £20,000. At 1 May 20X6 Corrie's retained earnings were £30,000.

4 Lamlash and Corrie trade with Brodick and, during the year, intercompany sales totalled £40,000 and £10,000 respectively. One-quarter of the goods sold by Lamlash to Brodick is still in Brodick's inventories at the year end. Lamlash earns a 30% gross margin on its intercompany sales.

5 Adjustment to the fair values of the net assets of Lamlash and Corrie was required on their respective dates of acquisition, but the adjustments were not put through the books. Lamlash's net assets' fair value was £100,000 greater than their book value and Corrie's net assets' fair value was £50,000 greater than their book value. Additional depreciation expense each year of £10,000 and £5,000 in Lamlash and Corrie, respectively, is required as a result of this.

6   The companies paid the following dividends during the year ended 30 April 20X7:

Brodick: £200,000

Lamlash: £30,000

Corrie: £10,000.

7   Brodick's retained earnings at 1 May 20X6 were £460,000.

8   No company has any reserve accounts other than retained earnings.

Required:

Prepare the Brodick group of companies' consolidated statement of profit or loss and consolidated statement of changes in equity for the year ended 30 April 20X7.

17 You are presented with the following summarised information for Norbreck plc and its subsidiary, Bispham Ltd:

Statements of comprehensive income for the year ended 30 September 20X7

	Norbreck plc	Bispham Ltd
	£000	£000
Revenue	1,700	450
Cost of sales	(920)	(75)
Gross profit	780	375
Administrative expenses	(300)	(175)
Investment income	40	–
Profit before tax	520	200
Tax	(30)	(20)
Profit after tax	£490	£180

Statements of financial position at 30 September 20X7

	Norbreck plc	Bispham Ltd
	£000	£000
Non-current assets		
Property, plant and equipment	1,280	440
Investments: shares in group company	500	–
	1,780	440
Current assets		
Inventories	300	250
Receivables	200	150
Cash and cash equivalents	40	30
	540	430
Total assets	2,320	870

Equity

Equity share capital (£1 shares)	900	400
Retained earnings	720	220
	1,620	620
Current liabilities		
Trade payables	80	160
Other creditors	160	70
	240	230
Provisions for liabilities and charges	460	20
	700	250
Total equity and liabilities	2,320	870

Additional information:

1 Norbreck plc acquired 320,000 shares in Bispham Ltd on 1 October 20X4 when Bispham's retained earnings were £40,000.

2 At this date, the fair values of Bispham's property, plant and equipment were agreed as £150,000 greater than their book values. These values were not incorporated into Bispham's books. Bispham has a 10% straight-line depreciation policy.

3 Bispham has sold goods to Norbreck during the year for £50,000, which included a 25% mark-up on cost. At the year end one-fifth of these inventories are still held by Norbreck.

4 The review for impairment of goodwill arising on acquisition made at 30 September 20X7 revealed that there was an impairment loss of £8,000. There had been no previous impairment loss.

5 Retained earnings at 30 September 20X6 for Norbreck and Bispham were £320,000 and £90,000 respectively.

6 Dividends paid by the companies during the year ended 30 September 20X7 were Norbreck £90,000 and Bispham £50,000.

Required:

Prepare Norbreck plc's consolidated statement of comprehensive income and statement of changes in equity for the year ended 30 September 20X7, and a consolidated statement of financial position at that date.

18 The following financial statements have been drawn up for Old plc, Field Ltd and Lodge Ltd

Statements of profit or loss for the year ended 30 April 20X6

	Old plc	Field Ltd	Lodge Ltd
	£000	£000	£000
Revenue	1,250	875	650
Opening inventories	90	150	80

Purchases	780	555	475
Closing inventories	(110)	(135)	(85)
Cost of sales	760	570	470
Gross profit	490	305	180
Distribution costs	(125)	(85)	(60)
Administrative expenses	(28)	(40)	(72)
Profit from operations	337	180	48
Investment income	(88)	–	–
Profit before tax	425	180	48
Tax	(125)	(75)	(20)
Profit for the year	£300	£105	£28

Statement of changes in equity for the year ended 30 April 20X6—retained earnings

	Old plc	Field Ltd	Lodge Ltd
	£000	£000	£000
At 1 May 20X5	30	40	50
Profit for the year	300	105	28
20X5 final dividend paid	(45)	(35)	(15)
20X6 interim dividend paid	(68)	(44)	(15)
At 30 April 20X6	£217	£66	£48

Other information:

(a) The share capital of the companies is as follows:

	Old plc	Field Ltd	Lodge Ltd
Equity shares of £1 each	£450,000	£350,000	£200,000

(b) Old plc acquired the whole of the equity shares in Field Ltd many years ago when Field's retained earnings were £6,000, and 120,000 shares in Lodge Ltd on 1 August 20X5.

(c) Profits of all three companies are deemed to accrue evenly throughout the year.

(d) Field Ltd paid its interim dividend on 31 July 20X5.

(e) Lodge Ltd paid its 20X5 final dividend on 30 June 20X5 and its 20X6 interim dividend on 14 November 20X5.

(f) Field Ltd sells goods for resale to Old plc. The following goods purchased from Field are included in Old's inventories:

At 1 May 20X5	£36,000
At 30 April 20X6	£40,000

The gross profit for Field Ltd on sales of these goods is 25%.

Total sales in the year by Field Ltd to Old plc were £150,000.

Required:

Prepare the consolidated statement of profit or loss for Old plc and its subsidiaries for the year ended 30 April 20X6 and the consolidated retained earnings column as it would appear in the consolidated statement of changes in equity for the year ended 30 April 20X6.

Assume the fair values of the net assets of Field Ltd and Lodge Ltd were equivalent to their book values at the date of acquisition.

19 The following financial statements have been drawn up for Gold plc and Silver Ltd at 31 December 20X8.

Statements of profit or loss for the year ended 31 December 20X8

	Gold plc £000	Silver Ltd £000
Revenue	4,250	900
Cost of sales	(2,300)	(150)
Gross profit	1,950	750
Administrative expenses	(750)	(350)
Investment income	170	–
Profit before tax	1,370	400
Tax	(275)	(40)
Profit for the year	1,095	360

Statement of changes in equity for the year ended 31 December 20X8—retained earnings

	Gold plc £000	Silver Ltd £000
At 1 January 20X8	300	100
Profit for the year	1,095	360
Dividends paid: equity	(270)	(100)
preference	–	(120)
At 31 December 20X8	1,125	240

Statements of financial position at 31 December 20X8

	Gold plc £000	Silver Ltd £000
Non-current assets		
Property, plant and equipment	3,200	980
Investments	1,250	–
	4,450	980
Current assets		
Inventories	750	500
Receivables	500	300
Cash and cash equivalents	100	60
	1,350	860
Total assets	5,800	1,840
Equity		
Equity share capital (£1 shares)	2,250	700
6% Preference share capital (£1 shares)	–	200
Retained earnings	1,125	240
	3,375	1,140
Current liabilities		
Trade payables	1,075	320
Other payables	200	340
	1,275	660
Provisions for liabilities and charges	1,150	40
Total equity and liabilities	5,800	1,840

Additional information:

(a) The cost of Gold's investment in Silver is made up as follows:

	£000
560,000 equity shares	1,000
150,000 preference shares	250
	1,250

(b) The shares were acquired on 1 January 20X6 when the retained earnings of Silver amounted to £112,000.

(c) At this date the fair values of Silver's property, plant and equipment were £100,000 greater than their book values. Silver uses an average depreciation policy of 30% reducing balance on its non-current assets.

(d) A review for impairment of goodwill at 31 December 20X8 requires goodwill to be written down to £300,000. No previous write-downs have been required.

(e) Gold and Silver do not trade with each other, but included in Gold's revenue and Silver's administrative expenses is a management charge of £200,000. £50,000 is owing from Silver to Gold at 31 December 20X8.

Required:

Prepare Gold plc's consolidated statement of profit or loss and consolidated statement of changes in equity for the year ended 31 December 20X8 and a consolidated statement of financial position at that date.

Visit the Online Resource Centre for solutions to all these end of chapter questions plus visual walkthrough solutions. You can test your understanding with extra questions and answers, explore additional case studies based on real companies, take a guided tour through a company report and much more. Go to the Online Resource Centre at www.oxfordtextbooks.co.uk/orc/maynard2e/

18

Associates, joint arrangements and statements of cash flow

This chapter examines the accounting methods required when an investor exerts partial influence over its investee company. It can do this individually or enter into an arrangement with other investors whereby they jointly control the investee. Individually, the investor does not control the investee and thus consolidation is not appropriate; however, its investment is more than just a passive one. Alternative methods of accounting to demonstrate this are required.

If the investor individually can demonstrate significant influence over the investee company, this latter company is classified as an associate and the equity method of accounting for the investment is used. If the investor has entered into a joint arrangement with other investors, the arrangement needs to be classified as either a joint operation or a joint venture, and different accounting methods follow. A joint venture uses the equity method of accounting.

The 2011 issue of new accounting standards in the area of consolidated financial statements included a replacement standard for joint arrangements—International Financial Reporting Standards (IFRS) 11 *Joint Arrangements*—and resulted in a revision to International Accounting Standard (IAS) 28, which deals with associates. This latter standard is now entitled *Investments in Associates and Joint Ventures*. Disclosures for associates and joint arrangements are contained in IFRS 12 *Disclosure of Interests in Other Entities*.

The focus of the chapter is on the techniques of accounting for associates and joint ventures in the consolidated statement of profit or loss, the consolidated statement of comprehensive income, the consolidated statement of changes in equity and the consolidated statement of financial position by the equity method. The accounting for other joint operations is also discussed. In addition the techniques for the preparation of a consolidated statement of cash flows are included to complete the consolidated financial statements.

18.1 Associate companies

18.1.1 Categorisation of investments

Chapter 17 discussed the categorisation of an investment by one company in another according to the degree of influence or interest that the investing company (the investor) has over or in the investee company (the company invested in). A reminder of the categories is given in Table 18.1.

Chapter 17 demonstrated how consolidated financial statements are prepared for a simple group of companies consisting of a parent and one or more subsidiary companies.

This chapter deals with the situations where the investor has partial, not total, influence over the investee. For an individual investor this is where it has significant influence. If this is the case, then the investee is termed an associate and the equity method of accounting is used for the investment.

Table 18.1 Categories of investment of one company in another

Degree of influence	Limited	Partial		Total
Nature of interest	Acquirer has a *passive interest* in acquiree	Acquirer exercises *significant influence* over acquiree	Acquirer *shares control* of acquiree *jointly* with others	Acquirer *controls* acquiree
Resulting category	Simple investment	Associate	Joint arrangement	Subsidiary

18.1.2 Significant influence

Significant influence is defined in IAS 28 *Investments in Associates and Joint Ventures* as:

> … the power to participate in the financial and operating policy decisions of the investee, but is not control or joint control of those policies.

(IASB, 2011, para. 3)

Significant influence is presumed if the investor holds 20% or more of the voting share capital of the investee, unless it can clearly be demonstrated that this is not the case. The holding can be direct or indirect, for example through a subsidiary company, as illustrated in Figure 18.1.

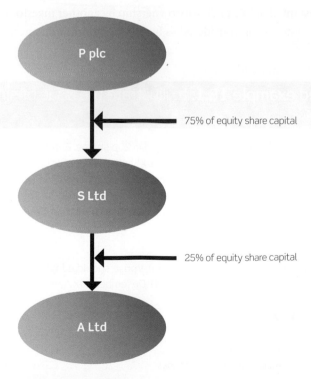

Figure 18.1 Indirect holding of an associate

In this situation P plc's effective ownership of A Ltd is only 19% (75% × 25%). However, the 25% holding in A Ltd by S Ltd would be presumed to give S significant influence over A. As P controls S, it therefore controls this 25% investment in A. The P plc group's consolidated financial statements therefore include the parent, P, and subsidiary, S, with A included in the consolidated accounts as an investment in an associate.

Conversely, if the investor holds less than 20% of the voting share capital, it is presumed that significant influence does not exist, unless this can be demonstrated clearly. Evidence of significant influence could be from one or more of the following:

(a) representation on the board of directors

(b) participation in policy-making processes, including participation in decisions about dividends or other distributions

(c) material transactions between the investor and investee

(d) interchange of managerial personnel

(e) provision of essential technical information.

Similar to the question of control and whether one company is a subsidiary of another as discussed in Chapter 17, management's judgement may have to be exercised to determine whether significant influence does exist. If the investor holds convertible financial instruments that give it potential voting rights which are currently exercisable, these will also need to be taken into account in the determination of whether significant influence exists.

In addition, the distribution of the shareholding of the remaining voting shares should be considered. A substantial or even majority ownership by another investor does not necessarily preclude the investor being considered as having significant influence.

 Worked example 18.1: to illustrate the issue of significant influence

Sefi Ltd has issued equity share capital of £10 million in 25p shares. Enterprise plc has held 12 million of these shares since it acquired them on 1 April 20X5 when a director of Enterprise was appointed to the board of Sefi. At 31 December 20X7 the remaining equity shares in Sefi were owned by many separate investors. In March 20X8 Rocket plc, a company unrelated to Enterprise plc, bought 22 million shares from these shareholders. From this date the director of Enterprise lost her seat on Sefi's board.

Required:
Explain, with reasons, the accounting treatment Enterprise should adopt for its investment in Sefi in its financial statements for the two years ending 31 December 20X7 and 20X8.

31 December 20X7

Total no. of equity shares of Sefi = 10 million × 4 = 40 million

Enterprise's holding = 12 million/40 million = 30%

There is a presumption that Enterprise plc exercises significant influence over Sefi Ltd This is enhanced by a director of Enterprise sitting on the board of Sefi. Sefi would be accounted for as an associate of Enterprise plc.

31 December 20X8

The position from March 20X8 is that although Enterprise still owns 30% of Sefi's shares, Sefi has become a subsidiary of Rocket, as this company has acquired more than 50% of Sefi's shares (22 million/40 million = 55%). Sefi is now under the control of Rocket; therefore, it is difficult to see how Enterprise can now exert significant influence over Sefi. The fact that Enterprise has lost its seat on Sefi's Board appears to reinforce this point. Unless Enterprise can provide evidence that it still has significant influence over Sefi, it is likely that the investment in Sefi would no longer be accounted for as an associate, but would be treated as a financial asset under IFRS 9 *Financial Instruments*. It will cease to be equity accounted from the date of loss of significant influence. It will be measured at that date at fair value. The difference between this fair value and the carrying amount of the investment as an associate will be recognised in profit or loss.

18.1.3 Exemptions from accounting for an associate

An investor will not account for its investment in an associate using the equity method if all of the following conditions apply. Note—these are the same conditions which apply to an investor not accounting for its investment as a subsidiary, as discussed in Chapter 17.

1   The investor is a wholly or partially owned subsidiary of another entity itself and all its other owners do not object to consolidated financial statements not being prepared

2   The investor's ultimate or any intermediate parent produces financial statements that comply with IFRS and are available for public use

3   The investor's debt or equity instruments are not traded in a public market

4   The investor does not file its financial statements with a securities commission or other regulatory organisation for the purpose of issuing any class of instruments in a public market.

There are also alternative accounting methods where the investment in an associate is held by an entity that is a venture capital organisation or a mutual fund, unit trust or other similar entity. These are outside the scope of this textbook.

18.1.4 The equity method of accounting

As the investor has significant influence over the investee, the investor has an interest in the associate's performance and return on its investment, which extends beyond the receipt of dividends. The distributions received may, in any event, bear little relation to the performance of the associate. The equity method of accounting for an associate therefore extends the scope of the investor's financial statements to include its share of the associate's profits or losses. This provides more informative reporting of the investor's net assets and profit or loss.

In practice this means the following for the preparation of financial statements:

(a) On the statement of financial position the investment in the associate is recognised initially at cost, and the carrying amount is then adjusted to include the investor's accumulated share of the profits or losses, and other comprehensive income of the associate since the date of acquisition. Dividends received from the associate reduce the carrying amount of the investment.

Retained earnings includes the investor's accumulated share of the profits or losses of the associate since the date of acquisition. Other reserves, such as a revaluation reserve, will include the investor's share of the changes in the associate's reserves since the date of acquisition.

(b) In the statement of comprehensive income, the investor's share of the associate's profit or loss after tax for the accounting period is included in one line, prior to the subtotal of profit before tax. The associate's profit or loss after tax is adjusted:

(i) for the elimination of unrealised profit in inventories resulting from an upstream sale from the associate to the investor

(ii) for additional, or a reduction in, depreciation based on the fair values of property, plant and equipment (PPE) at the acquisition date

(iii) if the investment in the associate was made during the year. In this instance only the investor's share of the profit or loss after tax which has arisen since the acquisition date is included. This may be done on a time-apportionment basis.

Partial elimination of unrealised profits on transactions between associates and other group companies is required. This means the investor's share of unrealised profit in inventories remaining at the financial year end from sales of goods between the investor and other group companies and the associate, is eliminated. (See Chapter 17 for a full discussion of unrealised profit in inventories.)

Any impairment losses are also included in profit and loss—see further discussion in section 18.1.5.

The investor's share of any other comprehensive income of the associate is included in other comprehensive income.

(c) In the statement of changes in equity the retained earnings figures will include the investor's share of the post-acquisition profits and losses of the associate. Note that non-controlling interest (NCI) figures are unaffected by any investment in associates.

18.1.5 Goodwill and impairment losses

Goodwill relating to an associate is not accounted for separately under the equity method of accounting. If, at the date of acquisition, there is an excess of the cost of the investment over the investing company's share of the fair value of the net assets of the associate then this 'goodwill' is not accounted for separately. It is included in the carrying amount of the investment as it is inherent within the cost of the investment.

However, if there is an excess of the investing company's share of the fair value of the net assets of the associate over the cost of the investment, this is added to the net profit or loss of the associate in the year of acquisition. It therefore increases the investing company's share of the associate's profit (or reduces the investing company's share of the associate's loss) in this year.

As goodwill is not recognised separately, it is not tested for impairment. However, the carrying amount of the investment as a whole is considered for impairment. Impairment will have occurred if, and only if, there is evidence that a loss event has occurred, in other words some event that will have an impact on the estimated future cash flows from the investment in the associate. It may not be possible to identify a single event that causes impairment, but it is more likely that the combined effect of several events cause impairment. It should be noted that expected accounting losses, no matter how likely, are not automatically recognised as impairment losses. Loss events which give rise to impairment are likely to arise from the associate having significant financial difficulties, and could include:

(a) a breach of contract, such as a default in payments by the associate

(b) the investor, for economic or legal reasons relating to its associate's financial difficulty, granting to the associate a concession that it would not otherwise consider

(c) the probability that the associate will enter bankruptcy or other financial reorganisation, or

(d) the disappearance of an active market for the trading of the associate's shares because of its financial difficulties.

Significant changes that have taken place in the technological, market, economic or legal environment in which the associate operates, and which will have an adverse effect on the associate, could also be an indication that impairment has occurred.

Any impairment is accounted for in accordance with IAS 36 *Impairment of Assets*. Thus, if there are indications that the investment may be impaired, its recoverable amount (the higher of value in use and fair value less costs to sell) has to be determined and compared with the carrying amount. IAS 28 gives some guidance as to how the value in use should be estimated as follows:

(a) The investor's share of the present value of the estimated future cash flows expected to be generated by the associate, including the cash flows from its operations, plus the proceeds from the ultimate disposal of the investment, or

(b) The present value of the estimated future cash flows expected to be received from dividends paid to the investor, plus the proceeds from the ultimate disposal of the investment.

Helpfully, IAS 28 advises that if appropriate assumptions are made, these two methods should give the same result. As for all impairment testing, there is a huge reliance on management's estimates and assumptions.

18.1.6 Classification as held for sale

If an investment in an associate, or a portion thereof, meets the criteria to be classified as held for sale, then the investing company is required to apply the accounting set out in IRFS 5. This is discussed in detail in Chapter 6.

🕛 **Reminder** *An asset or a disposal group is classified as held for sale if there is a formal commitment to disposal with evidence of positive steps taken towards this before the year end. The sale must be expected to be completed within a year. If classified as held for sale, the asset or disposal group is valued at the lower of carrying amount and fair value less costs to sell.*

 Worked example 18.2: to show the accounting for an associate in consolidated financial statements

Alpha plc is a company with subsidiary undertakings. It also has 25% of the equity share capital of Beta Ltd This was bought for £100,000 on 1 January 20X0 when Beta had retained earnings of £20,000 and when the fair value of Beta's PPE was £30,000 in excess of its carrying amount. The PPE had a remaining useful life of 10 years at this date.

The following are the financial statements of the Alpha group and Beta Ltd Note that the Alpha group financial statements have already consolidated Alpha plc and its subsidiaries.

Statements of profit or loss for the year ended 31 December 20X3

	Alpha plc and subsidiaries (consolidated)	Beta Ltd
	£000	£000
Revenue	540	200
Cost of sales	(370)	(130)
Gross profit	170	70
Distribution costs	(20)	(3)
Administrative expenses	(40)	(8)
Investment income from Beta Ltd	10	–
Profit before tax	120	59
Tax	(28)	(16)
	92	43
Attributable to:		
Owners of Alpha	80	
NCI	12	
	92	

Extracts from statements of changes in equity for the year ended 31 December 20X3

	Alpha plc and subsidiaries (consolidated)		Beta Ltd
	Retained earnings	NCI	Retained earnings
	£000	£000	£000
At 1 January 20X3	35	44	53
Profit for year	80	12	43
Dividends paid	(40)	(6)	(40)
At 31 December 20X3	75	50	56

Statements of financial position at 31 December 20X3

	Alpha plc and subsidiaries (consolidated)	Beta Ltd
	£000	£000
PPE	115	142
Investment in Beta Ltd (at cost)	100	–
Goodwill	30	–
Other net assets	180	114
	425	256
Share capital	300	200
Retained earnings	75	56
	375	256
NCI	50	–
	425	256

Required:

Prepare the full consolidated financial statements of the Alpha group at 31 December 20X3.

The group can be represented as shown in Figure 18.2.

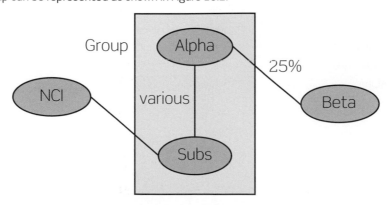

Figure 18.2 Representation of the Alpha group

Workings

(a) The investment income from Beta Ltd is eliminated on consolidation.

(b) Share of profit of associate for statement of profit or loss

	£000
Beta profit after tax	43
Fair value depreciation (£30/10)	(3)
	40

Alpha's share = 25% × £40,000 = £10,000

(c) Investment in associate

	£000
Cost	100
Plus: share of post-acquisition adjusted retained earnings of Beta	
25% × ((56 – 20) – 4 years × 3)	6
	106

(d) Retained earnings at 1 January 20X3

	£000
Alpha plus subsidiaries	35
Plus share of post-acquisition adjusted retained earnings of Beta	
25% × ((53 – 20) – 3 years × 3)	6
	41

Consolidated statement of profit or loss for the year ended 31 December 20X3

			£000
Revenue	)		540
Cost of sales	)		(370)
Gross profit	)	(Alpha and subsidiaries only)	170
Distribution costs	)		(20)
Admin expenses	)		(40)
			110
Share of profit of associate (W(b))			10
Profit before tax			120
Tax		(Alpha + subsidiaries only)	28
Profit for the year			92
Attributable to:			
Owners of Alpha		(Balancing figure)	80
NCI			12
			92

Consolidated statement of changes in equity for the year ended 31 December 20X3

	Share capital	Retained earnings	NCI	Total
	£000	£000	£000	£000
At 1 January 20X3	300	41 (W(d))	44	385
Profit for year		80	12	92
Dividends paid		(40)	(6)	(46)
At 31 December 20X3	300	81	50	431

Consolidated statement of financial position at 31 December 20X3

		£000
Goodwill		30
PPE	(Alpha + subsidiaries only)	115
Investment in associate (W(c))		106
Other net assets	(Alpha + subsidiaries only)	180
		431
Share capital		300
Retained earnings		81
		381
NCI		50
		431

18.1.7 Disclosure requirements

The disclosure requirements for associates are included in IFRS 12 *Disclosure of Interest in Other Entities*. The investor is required to disclose information that enables the users to evaluate:

(a) the nature, extent and financial effects of its interests in associates, including the nature and effects of any contractual relationships with the other investors in the associates, and

(b) the nature of, and changes in, the risks associated with these interests.

Note that, as for disclosures relating to subsidiaries, there is now an emphasis on disclosing the risks associated with the investments.

The disclosure requirements, again as for subsidiaries, include factual information about material associate companies, including whether the nature of the activities conducted by these associates are strategic to the investing company's activities. Summarised financial information of the associates should be shown and the method of accounting disclosed.

Financial reporting in practice 18.1

Nestlé includes the following information about its associates in its 2014 financial statements. It has one associate which it considers significant enough for separate disclosures to be made.

Accounting policy—Associates

Companies where the Group has the power to exercise a significant influence but does not exercise control are accounted for using the equity method. The net assets and results are adjusted to comply with the Group's accounting policies. The carrying amount of goodwill arising from the acquisition of associates is included in the carrying amount of investments in associates.

Note 15—Associates and joint ventures

		In millions of CHF		2014
	L'Oréal	Other associates	Joint ventures	Total
At 1 January	9,525	1,156	1,634	**12,315**
Currency retranslations	(160)	(2)	13	**(149)**
Investments	–	154	200	**354**
Divestments [a]	(2,585)	–	(167)	**(2,752)**
Share of results	934	(63)	(43)	**828**
Impairment	–	(211)	–	**(211)**
Share of other comprehensive income	(13)	–	(57)	**(70)**
Dividends and interest received	(543)	(58)	(115)	**(716)**
Other [b]	33	23	(1,008)	**(950)**
At 31 December	7,191	1,001	457	**8,649**

[a] Relate to the 48.5 million of L'Oréal shares sold to L'Oréal (see note 15.1)
[b] Relate mainly to the derecognition of the joint venture Galderma when the Group brought its ownership form 50% to 100%.

Income from associates and joint ventures

	In millions of CHF	
	2014	2013
Share of results	828	1,264
Impairment [a]	(211)	–
Profit on partial disposal of L'Oréal shares [b]	4,569	–
Revaluation gain on the 50% shareholding already held in Galderma [c]	2,817	–
	8,003	**1,264**

[a] A number of small associated companies have been impaired based on recent financial information and developments in their business environments, none of which are individually significant.
[b] Includes a cumulative gain of CHF 436 million recognised by L'Oréal in its other comprehensive reserves and a cumulative loss of CHF 625 million recognised by the Group inn its currency translation reserve that have been recycled to the income statement.
[c] Includes a cumulative currency translation loss of CHF 56 million that has been recycled to the income statement.

15.1 L'Oréal

The Group holds 129,881,021 shares in L'Oréal, the world leader in cosmetics, representing a 23.4% participation in its equity after elimination of its treasury shares.

On 8 July 2014, the Group sold 48,500,000 shares to L'Oréal for CHF 7342 million for cancellation. As a result, the participation in its equity after elimination of its treasury shares was reduced from 29.7% to 23.5%.

At 31 December 2014, the market value of the shares held amounts to CHF 21.8 billion.

Summarised financial information

	In billions of CHF	
	2014	2013
Total current assets	10.6	11.4
Total non-current assets	28.0	26.9
Total assets	**38.6**	38.3
Total current liabilities	11.2	8.1
Total non-current liabilities	3.1	2.5
Total liabilities	**14.3**	**10.6**
Total equity	**24.3**	**27.7**
Total sales	**27.4**	**28.2**
Profit from continuing operations	3.4	3.5
Profit from discontinued operations [a]	2.6	0.1
Other comprehensive income	(0.1)	0.4
Total comprehensive income	**5.9**	**4.0**

[a] Relate mainly to the profit on disposal of Galderma.

Reconciliation of the share of results

	In billions of CHF	
	2014	2013
Share held by the Group in the profit from continuing operations of L'Oréal	0.9	1.1
Share held by the Group in the profit from discontinued operations of L'Oréal [a]	0.6	–
Elimination of the profit on disposal of Galderma	(0.6)	–
Share of results of L'Oréal	0.9	1.1

[a] Relate mainly to the profit on disposal of Galderma.

(continued)

(continued)

Reconciliation of the carrying amount

	In billions of CHF	
	2014	2013
Share held by the Group in the equity of L'Oréal	5.7	8.2
Goodwill and other adjustments	1.5	1.3
Carrying amount of L'Oréal	7.2	9.5

15.2 Other associates

The Group holds a number of other associates that are individually not material.

18.2 Joint arrangements

For a variety of reasons companies may enter into contractual arrangements with other companies to work together. Reasons may include the production of a particular product, or the exploration of whether oil and gas resources exist, or the delivery of a government contract. In some instances the companies party to the arrangement may set up another entity for the purpose of carrying out the work. Irrespective of the structure or legal form of such an arrangement, the principle behind the accounting for joint arrangements set out in IFRS 11 *Joint Arrangements* is that it should reflect the rights and obligations that the companies have as a result of the arrangement.

IFRS 11 changed the approach to the accounting for joint arrangements as set out in its predecessor standard. The old IAS 31 *Interests in Joint Ventures* was considered unsatisfactory by the International Accounting Standards Board (IASB) and not faithfully representational of many joint arrangements. Choices in accounting methods were also allowed by the standard, which had led to similar arrangements being accounted for differently, thus making comparisons difficult for users.

IRFS 11 defines a joint arrangement as an arrangement in which two or more parties have joint control. Joint control is a contractually agreed sharing of control by the parties and requires the unanimous consent of all the parties sharing control in decisions that are made about the arrangement's activities. The unanimity of the consent of all the parties is important when considering the issue of control—if this is not unanimous this would raise questions about whether there was a parent/subsidiary relationship with one party in essence controlling the decision-making.

In practice, joint arrangements can take very many different forms, but for accounting purposes two different types are defined which lead to different accounting methods being applied. The two types are joint operations and joint ventures.

18.2.1 Joint operations

A joint operation is defined as a joint arrangement whereby the parties that have joint control have rights to the assets and obligations for the liabilities that relate to the arrangement.

The parties to the arrangement are called joint operators. The assets and liabilities of a joint operation may be legally acquired and incurred, respectively, by a separate entity set up by the joint operators; however, if the details of the arrangement specify the parties' rights to the assets and obligations for the liabilities, then the arrangement will still be classified as a joint operation.

A joint operator accounts for a joint operation by including in its own individual financial statements:

(a) its share of any assets held jointly

(b) its share of any liabilities incurred jointly

(c) its share of the revenue from the sale of the output by the joint operation

(d) its share of any expenses incurred jointly.

If a joint operator enters into a transaction with the joint operation, then, as for the accounting for associate companies, interoperation profits must be eliminated so that the commercial reality of the transaction is reflected. So, for example, if the joint operator sells or contributes assets to the joint operation, the commercial reality of this is that the joint operator is conducting this transaction with the other joint operators. The joint operator recognises any gains and losses only to the extent of the other parties' interests in the joint operation.

There may be parties that participate in a joint operation and have rights to the assets and obligations for liabilities, but which do not have joint control. These parties should also account for their share of the operation's assets, liabilities, revenue and expenses in their own financial statements.

18.2.2 Joint ventures

The other type of joint arrangement is a joint venture. This is defined by IFRS 11 as a joint arrangement whereby the parties that have joint control have rights to the net assets of the arrangement. The implication of the term 'net assets' in this definition is that the parties, referred to as joint venturers, have rights to an investment in the arrangement rather than for specific assets and liabilities.

It might appear that a consequence of this definition, together with the definition of a joint operation, would lead to an arrangement being classified as a joint venture if the joint arrangement's activities were conducted through a separate entity. However, this is not necessarily the case, and the IASB has been careful to emphasise the principle of the accounting methods for joint arrangements, namely that it should reflect the rights and obligations that the investors have as a result of the arrangement.

The difference may be summarised by Figure 18.3.

If an arrangement is classified as a joint venture, then the accounting treatment follows the definition. An investor's interest in the net assets of an investee is faithfully represented by using the equity method in accordance with IAS 28 *Investments in Associates and Joint Ventures*. Thus, the accounting for joint venture is the same as accounting for an associate, as detailed in section 18.1. Critics have pointed out that having significant influence over an

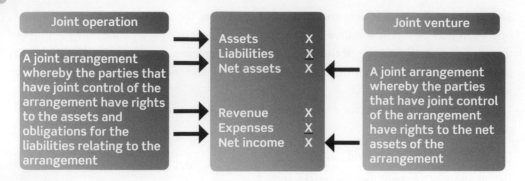

Figure 18.3 The difference between a joint operation and a joint venture

investee is different to having joint control, although both now result in the same accounting method. The IASB's response was that the equity method of accounting reflects a company's interest in the net assets of an investee which represents the relationship between an investor and a joint venture.

 Example of the classification of a joint arrangement

Alpha and Beta are two companies whose businesses are the provision of many types of public and private construction services. They set up a contractual arrangement to work together for the purpose of fulfilling a contract with a government for the design and construction of a road between two cities. The contractual arrangement determines how Alpha and Beta will share participation, and establishes joint control of the arrangement.

The parties set up a separate company, Zeta, through which to conduct the arrangement. Zeta, on behalf of Alpha and Beta, enters into the contract with the government. In addition, the assets and liabilities relating to the arrangement are held in Zeta. The main feature of entity Zeta's legal form is that Alpha and Beta, not Zeta, have rights to the assets and obligations for the liabilities of this company.

The contractual arrangement between Alpha and Beta additionally establishes that:

(a) The rights to all the assets needed to undertake the activities of the arrangement are shared by Alpha and Beta on the basis of the share of their participation in the arrangement

(b) Alpha and Beta have several, and joint, responsibilities for all operating and financial obligations relating to the activities of the arrangement on the basis of the share of their participation

(c) The profit or loss resulting from the activities of the arrangement is shared by Alpha and Beta on the basis of the share of their participation.

For the purposes of coordinating and overseeing the activities, Alpha and Beta appoint an operator, who will be an employee of one of the companies. After a specified time, the role of the operator will rotate to an employee of the other company. Alpha and Beta agree that the activities will be executed by the operator's employees on a 'no gain or loss' basis.

In accordance with the terms specified in the contract with the government, Zeta invoices the construction services to the government on behalf of Alpha and Beta.

Required:

Discuss whether this arrangement should be classified as a joint operation or a joint venture, and explain the consequential accounting method.

The joint arrangement is carried out through a separate company, Zeta, but the legal form of Zeta does not confer separation between Alpha and Beta and Zeta. In other words, the assets and liabilities held in Zeta are the assets and liabilities of Alpha and Beta. This is reinforced by the terms agreed by Alpha and Beta in their contractual arrangement, which state that these companies have rights to the assets, and obligations for the liabilities, relating to the arrangement that is conducted through Zeta. The joint arrangement is therefore a joint operation.

Alpha and Beta each recognise in their financial statements their share of the assets (e.g. PPE, and accounts receivable) and their share of any liabilities resulting from the arrangement (e.g. accounts payable to third parties) on the basis of their agreed participation share. Each also recognises its share of the revenue and expenses resulting from the construction services provided to the government through Zeta.

18.2.3 Disclosure requirements

The disclosures for interests in joint arrangements, in other words both joint operations and joint ventures, are set out in IFRS 12, and are identical to those for associates. These have been detailed in section 18.1.7.

Financial reporting in practice 18.2 — Tesco plc, 2015

In its 2015 Annual Report and Financial Statements, Tesco describes its accounting policy for its joint ventures, and lists its principal joint ventures, all except one of which are in property investment. It describes the judgements it has exercised in determining that the investees are joint ventures, and also provides summarised financial information about them (although this is not reproduced).

Accounting policy—Joint ventures and associates

The Group has assessed the nature of its joint arrangements under IFRS 11 'Joint arrangements' and determined them to be joint ventures. This assessment required the exercise of judgement as set out in Note 13.

The Group's share of the results of joint ventures and associates is included in the Group Income Statement and Group Statement of Other Comprehensive Income using the equity method of accounting. Investments in joint ventures and associates are carried in the Group Balance Sheet at cost plus post-acquisition changes in the Group's share of the net assets of the entity, less any impairment in value. The carrying values of investments in joint ventures and associates include acquired goodwill.

If the Group's share of losses in a joint venture or associate equals or exceeds its investment in the joint venture or associate, the Group does not recognise further losses, unless it has incurred obligations to do so or made payments on behalf of the joint venture or associate.

Unrealised gains arising from transactions with joint ventures and associates are eliminated to the extent of the Group's interest in the entity.

(continued)

(continued)

Note 13—Interests in joint ventures and associates
Principal joint ventures and associates

The Group's principal joint ventures and associates are:

	Nature of relationship	Business activity	Share of issued share capital, loan capital and debt securities	Country of incorporation	Principal area of operation
Shopping Centres Limited	Joint venture	Property investment	50%	England	United Kingdom
BLT Properties Limited	Joint venture	Property investment	50%	England	United Kingdom
The Tesco British Land Property Partnership(b)	Joint venture	Property investment	50%	England	United Kingdom
Tesco BL Holdings Limited	Joint venture	Property investment	50%	England	United Kingdom
The Tesco Red Limited Partnership	Joint venture	Property investment	50%	England	United Kingdom
The Tesco Aqua Limited Partnership	Joint venture	Property investment	50%	England	United Kingdom
The Tesco Coral Limited Partnership	Joint venture	Property investment	50%	England	United Kingdom
The Tesco Blue Limited Partnership	Joint venture	Property investment	50%	England	United Kingdom
The Tesco Atrato Limited Partnership	Joint venture	Property investment	50%	England	United Kingdom
The Tesco Property Limited Partnership	Joint venture	Property investment	50%	England	United Kingdom

The Tesco Passaic Limited Partnership	Joint venture	Property investment	50%	England	United Kingdom
The Tesco Navona Limited Partnership	Joint venture	Property investment	50%	England	United Kingdom
The Tesco Sarum Limited Partnership	Joint venture	Property investment	50%	England	United Kingdom
The Tesco Dorney Limited Partnership	Joint venture	Property investment	50%	England	United Kingdom
Arena (Jersey) Management Limited	Joint venture	Property investment	50%	Jersey	United Kingdom
The Tesco Property (No. 2) Limited Partnership	Joint venture	Property investment	50%	Jersey	United Kingdom
Tesco Mobile Limited	Joint venture	Telecommunications	50%	England	United Kingdom
Tesco Underwriting Limited	Joint venture	Financial services	49.9%	England	United Kingdom
Gain Land Limited	Associate	Retail	20%	British Virgin Islands	People's Republic of China/ Hong Kong
Tesco Lotus Retail Growth Freehold and Leasehold Property Fund	Associate	Property investment	25%	Thailand	Thailand
Trent Hypermarket Limited	Joint venture	Retail	50%	India	India

The Group holds a 22% investment stake in Lazada Group GMBH ('Lazada'). This investment is not treated as an associate because the Group does not have the power to participate in key management decisions.

(continued)

(continued)

The accounting period end dates of the joint ventures and associates consolidated in these financial statements range from 31 December 2014 to 28 February 2015. The accounting period end dates of the joint ventures differ from those of the Group for commercial reasons and depend upon the requirements of the joint venture partner as well as those of the Group. The accounting period end dates of the associates are different from those of the Group as they depend upon the requirements of the parent companies of those entities.

There are no significant restrictions on the ability of the joint ventures and associates to transfer funds to the parent, other than those imposed by the Companies Act 2006.

Summarised financial information for joint ventures and associates

The summarised financial information for UK Property joint ventures has been aggregated in order to provide useful information to users without excessive detail since these entities have similar characteristics and risk profiles largely based on the nature of their activities and geographic market.

The UK Property joint ventures involve the Group partnering with third parties in carrying out property investments in order to enhance returns from property and access funding whilst reducing risks associated with sole ownership. These property investments generally cover shopping centres and standalone stores. The Group enters into operating leases for some or all of the properties held in the joint ventures. These leases provide the Group with some rights over alterations and adjacent land developments. Some leases also provide the Group with options to purchase the other joint venturers' equity stakes at a future point in time. In some cases the Group has the ability to substitute properties in the joint ventures with alternative properties of similar value, subject to strict eligibility criteria. In other cases, the Group carries out property management activities for third party rentals of shopping centre units.

The property investment activities are carried out in separate entities, usually partnerships or limited liability companies. The Group has assessed its ability to direct the relevant activities of these entities and impact Group returns and concluded that the entities qualify as joint ventures since decisions regarding them require the unanimous consent of both equity holders. This assessment included not only rights within the joint venture agreements, but also any rights within the other contractual arrangements between the Group and the entities.

The Group made a number of judgements and assertions in arriving at this determination, the key ones being:

- since the provisions of the joint venture agreements require the relevant decisions impacting investor returns to be either unanimously agreed by both joint venturers at the same time, or in some cases to be agreed sequentially by each venturer at different stages, there is joint decision making within the joint venture;

- since the Group's leases are priced at fair value, and any rights embedded in the leases are consistent with market practice, they do not provide the Group with additional control over the joint ventures or infer an obligation by the Group to fund the settlement of liabilities of the joint ventures;

- any options to purchase the other joint venturers' equity stakes are priced at market value, and only exercisable at future dates, hence they do not provide control to the Group at the current time;

- where the Group has a right to substitute properties in the joint ventures, the rights are strictly limited and are at fair value, hence do not provide control to the Group; and

- where the Group carries out property management activities for third party rentals in shopping centres, these additional activities are controlled through joint venture agreements or lease agreements, and do not provide the Group with additional powers over the joint venture.

The summarised financial information below* reflects the amounts presented in the financial statements of the relevant joint ventures and associates, and not the Group's share of those amounts. These amounts have been adjusted to conform to the Group's accounting policies where required.

*This information has not been reproduced, as the type of information provided is the same as for associate companies, as seen in Financial reporting in practice 18.1.

18.3 Future of the equity method of accounting

The equity method of accounting attempts to provide information about an investor's interest in other entities in which it has more than a passive interest, and yet does not have control. It is an intermediate form of accounting between accounting only for the receipt of investment income and full consolidation. Despite the fact that the basic mechanics of the equity method have been followed for decades, IAS 28, which sets out the accounting, has been criticised for not fully making clear what it is trying to portray. It can be seen as a quasi-consolidation approach (a one-line consolidation) through the incorporation of the investor's share of the associates' or joint ventures' profits or losses and the elimination of the investor's share of profits from upstream and downstream transactions. On the other hand, the equity method can be considered to be more about the measurement of the investment in the associates and joint ventures on the statement of financial position. However, the methods used result in a figure that does not really apply the concepts underpinning the measurement of an asset.

Over the years, the IFRS interpretations committee has received numerous requests for clarification on certain aspects of IAS 28. The IASB has finally commenced a research project to address application problems with the equity method of accounting for associates and joint ventures, including the elimination of profits or losses in transactions between the investor and the associates and joint ventures, and to consider the role of equity accounting for subsidiaries in separate financial statements.

18.4 Consolidated statements of cash flow

These two chapters on consolidated financial statements conclude by considering the final financial statement, the consolidated statement of cash flows. IAS 7 *Statement of Cash Flows* governs the preparation and presentation of a statement of cash flows, and this applies equally to individual company and consolidated statements of cash flow. The aim of a consolidated statement of cash flows is to show the cash inflows and outflows of the group with third parties.

The statement of cash flows for an individual company is discussed in detail in Chapter 4 and an example of its preparation demonstrated. This preparation is from the two statements of financial position at the beginning and end of the financial year and this same approach will be taken for consolidated financial statements.

🛈 **Reminder** *A statement of cash flows shows the historical changes in cash and cash equivalents, classifying cash flows as arising from:*

- *operating activities*
- *investing activities*
- *financing activities.*

It reconciles opening and closing cash and cash equivalents balances, where cash equivalents are defined as short-term, highly liquid investments that are readily convertible to known amounts of cash and which are subject to an insignificant risk of changes in value.

Used in conjunction with the rest of the financial statements, a statement of cash flows provides information about:

- *the changes in the net assets of an entity*
- *an entity's financial structure (including its liquidity and solvency)*
- *its ability to affect the amounts and timing of cash flows in order to adapt to changing circumstances and opportunities.*

Cash flow information is useful in assessing the ability of the entity to generate cash and cash equivalents.

For consolidated statements of cash flows the following additional items need to be considered:

1 Dividends paid to the NCI in subsidiaries are disclosed separately and classified as financing activities

2 Any impairment of goodwill arising on the acquisition of a subsidiary is added back in the reconciliation of profit before tax to cash flows from operating activities

3 The net cash effect of the acquisition (or disposal) of a subsidiary is disclosed separately under investing activities. The net cash effect is the cash paid (or received) net of the cash balances the subsidiary has at the date of acquisition or disposal.

If there are investments in associates or joint ventures accounted for by the equity method, the cash flows shown in the consolidated statement of cash flows are restricted to the cash flows between the investor and the investee, in other words to dividends and advances. So, additional items are:

4 Dividends received from associates that are disclosed separately and classified as investing activities

5 Cash payments (and receipts) to acquire (and dispose of) associates, respectively, that are classified under investing activities.

Example of how cash flows from an investment in an associate would be included in the consolidated statement of cash flows

The following is an extract from the consolidated statement of profit or loss of the Baxter plc group for the year ended 31 December 20X7:

	£000
Group profit from operations	273
Share of profit of associates	60
Profit before tax	333
Income tax expense	(63)
Profit for the year	270

The consolidated statements of financial position at 31 December 20X7 and 20X6 show the following:

	20X7	20X6
	£000	£000
Non-current assets		
Investment in associate	552	528

Baxter plc has only one associate company, in which it has invested since 20X3.

Required:

In relation to the investment in the associate, what figure(s) will be included in the consolidated statement of cash flows for the Baxter plc group for the year ended 31 December 20X7?

The share of profit of the associate of £60,000 does not represent a cash flow, so must be subtracted in the reconciliation of profit before tax to cash flows from operating activities.

The only cash flow from holding the investment in the associate is from any dividends paid by the associate and received by the investor. This is calculated from reconciliation:

	£000	
Opening investment in associate	528	
Add: Share of profit of associate	60	
Less: Dividend received from associate	(36)	Balancing figure
Closing investment in associate	552	

A separate line item, dividends received from associate £36,000, will be included in the consolidated statement of cash flows—under cash flows from investing activities.

18.4.1 Acquisition or disposal of subsidiaries

As indicated in section 18.4 the net cash effect of acquisition or disposal of a subsidiary is shown as a separate line item under investing activities.

Example of the cash effect of the acquisition of a subsidiary

P plc acquired 75% of S Ltd by issuing 250,000 £1 shares at their fair value of £2.50 per share and £200,000 in cash. At the date of acquisition the cash and cash equivalents in S Ltd's statement of financial position amounted to £30,000.

Required:

What figure would be included for the acquisition of a subsidiary under investing activities in P plc's consolidated statement of cash flows?

Acquisition of subsidiary S Ltd, net of cash acquired = £200,000 − £30,000

$$= £170,000$$

This would be shown as a cash outflow, i.e. the figure would be in brackets, under investing activities.

Care should be taken when calculating the movements in individual asset and liability balances not to double-count the effects of the acquisition or disposal of a subsidiary during the accounting period. The consolidated asset or liability balances may have increased or decreased, not from any cash flow, but because the subsidiary's assets or liabilities were added to or deducted from the consolidated figures.

Subsidiary *acquired* in the period	*Subtract* PPE, inventories, receivables, payables, etc. at the date of acquisition from the movement on these items.
Subsidiary *disposed of* in the period	*Add* PPE, inventories, receivables, payables, etc. at the date of acquisition from the movement on these items.

 Example of the calculation of additions to property, plant and equipment (PPE)

An extract from the consolidated statement of financial position of P plc at 31 December is as follows:

	20X7	20X6
	£000	£000
PPE	500	400

During 20X7 P plc acquired 80% of the equity share capital of S Ltd At the date of acquisition, S Ltd's assets included PPE with an estimated fair value of £75,000.

There were no disposals of PPE in the year. Depreciation of £25,000 was charged to the consolidated statement of profit or loss.

Required:

Calculate the amount to be disclosed as 'Purchase of property, plant and equipment' under cash flows from investing activities in the consolidated statement of cash flows.

If there had been no acquisition of S during the year, the purchase of PPE would have been obtained from the reconciliation:

	£000	
Opening balance	400	
Add: purchases	125	Balancing figure
Less: depreciation	(25)	
Closing balance	500	

However, £75,000 of the PPE at 31 December 20X7 is from S's acquired PPE—this is not a cash flow. So the reconciliation becomes:

	£000	
Opening balance (P only)	400	
Add: acquisition of S's PPE	75	
Add: purchases	50	Balancing figure
Less: depreciation	(25)	
Closing balance	500	

A cash outflow of £50,000 would be shown for 'Purchases of property, plant and equipment' under cash flows from investing activities in the consolidated statement of cash flows.

18.4.2 Worked example of a consolidated statement of cash flows

 Worked example 18.3: to show the preparation of a consolidated statement of cash flows

On 1 October 20X8 P plc acquired 90% of S Ltd by issuing 100,000 shares at their fair value of £2 per share and paying £100,000 in cash. At that time the fair values of the net assets of S Ltd were as follows:

	£000
PPE	190
Inventories	70
Trade receivables	30
Cash and cash equivalents	10
Trade payables	(40)
	260

The consolidated statements of financial position of P plc at 31 December were as follows:

	20X8	20X7
	£000	£000
Non-current assets		
PPE	2,500	2,300
Goodwill	66	–
	2,566	2,300
Current assets		
Inventories	1,450	1,200
Trade receivables	1,370	1,100
Cash and cash equivalents	76	50
	2,896	2,350
Total assets	5,462	4,650
Equity attributable to owners of the parent		
Equity share capital (£1 shares)	1,150	1,000
Share premium account	650	500
Retained earnings	1,791	1,530
	3,591	3,030
NCI	31	–
	3,622	3,030
Current liabilities		
Trade payables	1,690	1,520
Income tax payable	150	100
	1,840	1,620
	5,462	4,650

The consolidated statement of profit or loss for the year ended 31 December 20X8 was as follows:

	£000
Revenue	10,000
Cost of sales	(7,500)
Gross profit	2,500
Administrative expenses	(2,080)
Profit before tax	420
Income tax expense	(150)
Profit for the year	270

Profit attributable to:

Owners of P plc	261
NCI	9
	270

The retained earnings in the consolidated statement of changes in equity for the year ended 31 December 20X8 were as follows:

	Retained earnings
	£000
Balance at 1 January 20X8	1,530
Profit for the period	261
Balance at 31 December 20X8	1,791

You are also given the following information:

1 Depreciation charged to the consolidated statement of profit or loss amounted to £210,000.

2 There were no disposals of PPE during the year.

Required:

Prepare a consolidated statement of cash flows for P plc for the year ended 31 December 20X8 under the indirect method in accordance with IAS 7 *Statement of Cash Flows*. Provide the note which shows he reconciliation of profit before tax to cash generated from operations.

Workings

1 Check whether there is any impairment of goodwill.

On the acquisition of S Ltd, goodwill would have been calculated as

	£000
Consideration	300
Add: NCI in fair value of net assets of S Ltd 10% × 260	26
	326
Less: fair value of net assets of S Ltd	(260)
	66

This is the balance in the statement of financial position at 31 December 20X8, hence there has been no impairment of goodwill.

2 Net cash paid for the acquisition of the subsidiary.

	£000
Total consideration	300
Less: non-cash consideration (100,000 × £2)	(200)
Less: cash of S at acquisition	(10)
Cash out flow for acquisition	90

3 Cash paid for the purchase of PPE.

	£000
Balance at 31 December 20X7	2,300
On acquisition	190
Less: depreciation	(210)
	2,280
Additions (balancing figure)	220
Balance at 31 December 20X8	2,500

4 Proceeds from the issue of share capital.

	£000
Ordinary share capital at 31 December 20X8	1,150
Share premium at 31 December 20X8	650
	1,800
Ordinary share capital at 31 December 20X7	1,000
Share premium at 31 December 20X7	500
	1,500
Difference (1,800 – 1,500)	300
Shares issued on acquisition of subsidiary	(200)
Other shares issued during year for cash	100

5 Dividend paid to NCI.

It is helpful to think of the NCI column of statement of changes in equity column.

	£000
NCI on acquisition	26
NCI for the year—from consolidated statement of profit or loss	9
	35
Dividend paid to NCI (balancing figure)	(4)
Balance at 31 December 20X8	31

Reconciliation of profit before tax to cash generated from operations

		£000
Profit before taxation		420
Add back: Depreciation		210
		630
Increase in trade receivables	(1,370 – 1,100 – 30)	(240)
Increase in inventories	(1,450 – 1,200 – 70)	(180)
Increase in trade payables	(1,690 – 1,520 – 40)	130
Cash generated from operations		340

Consolidated statement of cash flows for the year ended 31 December 20X8

		£000	£000
Cash flows from operating activities		340	
Income taxes paid	(100 + 50 − 150)	(100)	
Net cash from operating activities			240
Cash flows from investing activities			
Acquisition of subsidiary S Ltd, net of cash acquired		(90)	
Purchase of PPE		(220)	
Net cash used in investing activities			(310)
Cash flows from financing activities			
Proceeds from issue of share capital		100	
Dividend paid to NCI		(4)	
Net cash from financing activities			96
Net increase in cash and cash equivalents			26
Cash and cash equivalents at beginning of year			50
Cash and cash equivalents at end of year			76

18.4.3 Disclosures

The disclosures for statements of cash flow are discussed in Chapter 4. Where there have been acquisitions or disposals of subsidiaries during an accounting period, the following additional disclosures are required:

(a) Total purchase price/disposal consideration

(b) Portion of purchase price/disposal consideration discharged by means of cash and cash equivalents

(c) Amount of cash and cash equivalents in subsidiary acquired or disposed of

(d) Amount of other assets and liabilities in subsidiary acquired or disposed of, summarised by major category.

The separation of cash flows arising from acquisitions and disposals of subsidiaries assists users in distinguishing these amounts from the cash flows arising from the other operating, investing and financing activities.

Financial reporting in practice **18.3**	IAG, 2013

An extract from IAG's statement of cash flows (which is a consolidated statement of cash flows) for the year ended 31 December 2013 includes the following highlighted items relating to group cash flows:

(continued)

(continued)

	2013 € million	2012 € million
Cash flows from investing activities		
Acquisition of property, plant and equipment and intangible assets	(2,196)	(1,239)
Sale of property, plant and equipment and intangible assets	525	46
Cash acquired on Business combination (net of consideration)	**293**	**(1)**
Interest received	27	43
(Increase)/decrease in other current interest-bearing deposits	(593)	246
Dividends received	3	14
Other investing movements	6	3
Net cash flows from investing activities	(1,935)	(888)
Cash flows from financing activities		
Proceeds from long-term borrowings	1,529	534
Proceeds from equity portion of convertible bond issued	72	–
Repayment of borrowings	(275)	(338)
Repayment of finance leases	(402)	(331)
Acquisition of own shares	(42)	–
Acquisition of non-controlling interest	**(24)**	**–**
Distributions made to holders of perpetual securities and other	(20)	(21)
Net cash flows from financing activities	838	(156)

Note 3—Business combinations

On April 26, 2013, the Group acquired a further 44.66 per cent of the issued share capital of Vueling for €9.25 per share, therefore bringing the IAG Group shareholding in Vueling to 90.51 per cent. The Group already indirectly owned 45.85 per cent of Vueling through its subsidiary Iberia.

The acquisition will contribute to the geographic diversification of the Group. Through Vueling's leading position in Barcelona and growth in the rest of Europe, IAG expects incremental synergies primarily from purchasing and financing; additionally Vueling incorporates a low-cost platform for the Group.

Transaction costs related to the acquisition of Vueling totalling €5 million were recognised within Property, IT and other costs in the Income statement for the year to December 31, 2013.

From April 26, 2013, Vueling's contribution to the consolidated Group results was revenue of €1,130 million, and an operating profit of €168 million. Had Vueling been consolidated from January 1, 2013, the Group would have reported total revenue of €18,851 million and an operating profit after exceptional items of €496 million for the year to December 31, 2013.

The assets and liabilities arising from the acquisition are as follows:

	Fair value
	€ million
Property, plant and equipment	3
Intangible assets Brand	35
Landing rights[1]	89
Other	16
Other non-current assets	171
Cash and cash equivalents	417
Other current interest-bearing deposits	13
Trade receivables[2]	70
Other current assets	120
Trade and other payables	(436)
Provision for liabilities and charges	(223)
Deferred tax liability	(26)
Net identifiable assets/(liabilities) acquired	249

[1] Landing rights have been assessed as having indefinite lives and will be tested annually for impairment.

[2] The gross contractual amount for trade receivables is €70 million, 100 per cent which is expected to be collected.

The goodwill is recognised as follows:

	€ million
Cash consideration for obtaining control[1]	124
Fair value of pre-existing interest in Vueling	127
Purchase price representing IAG's 90.51 per cent ownership in Vueling	251
Non-controlling interest[2]	26
Fair value of identifiable net assets	249
Goodwill	28

[1] There is no deferred or contingent consideration.

[2] The non-controlling interest at April 26, 2013 has been valued at €9.25 per share.

🔑 Summary of key points

An investor can exert partial influence over an investee either on its own, through having the power to participate in the financial and operational decisions of the investee, or by entering into a contractual arrangement with other investors and forming a joint arrangement. In order for the financial statements of the investor to faithfully represent these situations, they need to reflect more than just the cost of the investment and the distributions received from the investee company.

In the first case the investor is presumed to have significant influence over the investee if the holding of equity shares is more than 20%, although there are other indicators. The investee is termed an associate and the equity method of accounting is used. This means the investor's financial statements will include its share of the associate's profits or losses, and the investment on the statement of financial position will include the investor's share of the cumulative profits and losses of the associate since the date of acquisition.

A joint arrangement requires the parties to the arrangement to have joint control. This means they have to reach unanimous agreement over decisions about the running of the arrangement. There are two types of joint arrangement for accounting purposes, and different accounting results depending on the categorisation. The first is a joint arrangement where the parties have rights to the assets and obligations for the liabilities of the arrangement. A joint operator includes in its financial statements its share, as specified in the agreement, of the specific assets, liabilities, income and expenses of the operation.

A joint venture is the other type of joint arrangement. This is where the parties have rights to the net assets of the arrangement and thus is more like an investment in the arrangement. A joint venturer accounts for this investment by the equity method.

The final section of the chapter demonstrates the preparation of a consolidated statement of cash flows, indicating how cash flows of a group consisting of subsidiaries and associates are accounted for and presented.

 ## Further reading

IASB (International Accounting Standards Board) (2004) IAS 7 *Statement of Cash Flows*. London: IASB.

IASB (International Accounting Standards Board) (2011a) IAS 28 *Investments in Associates and Joint Ventures*. London: IASB.

IASB (International Accounting Standards Board) (2011b) IFRS 11 *Joint Arrangements*. London: IASB.

 ## Bibliography

EFRAG (European Financial Reporting Advisory Group) (2014) *The Equity Method: A Measurement Basis or One-Line Consolidation?* Brussels: EFRAG.

IASB (International Accounting Standards Board) (2004) IAS 7 *Statement of Cash Flows*. London: IASB.

IASB (International Accounting Standards Board) (2011a) IAS 28 *Investments in Associates and Joint Ventures*. London: IASB.

IASB (International Accounting Standards Board) (2011b) IFRS 11 *Joint Arrangements*. London: IASB.

IFRS Foundation (2015) Staff Paper *The Equity Method of Accounting: Approach to the Project*. London: IFRS.

International Airlines Group (2014) *2013 Annual Report and Accounts*. Madrid: IAG.

Nestlé (2015) *Financial Statements 2014*. Vevey: Nestlé.

Tesco plc (2015) *Annual Report and Financial Statements, 2015*. Cheshunt: Tesco.

Questions

Quick test

1   The draft statements of financial position at 31 December 20X6 of three companies are set out as follows:

	Lanchester Ltd	Norman Ltd	Thorne Ltd
	£000	£000	£000
PPE	300	100	160
Investments at cost			
18,000 shares in Norman	100	–	–
18,000 shares in Thorne	30	–	–
Other net assets	320	160	80
	750	260	240
Equity			
Equity shares of £1 each	250	30	60
Retained earnings	400	180	100
	650	210	160
Long-term loans	100	50	80
	750	260	240

The shares in Norman Ltd were acquired on 1 January 20X4 when its retained earnings were £70,000. At this date the fair value of its PPE was £40,000 greater than the book value and the average life of these assets remaining was 8 years.

The shares in Thorne Ltd were acquired on 1 January 20X6 when its retained earnings were £30,000. At this date the fair value of its PPE was £20,000 greater than the book value and the average life of these assets remaining was 5 years.

Both companies use the straight-line method of depreciation.

Required:

Prepare the consolidated statement of financial position at 31 December 20X6.

2   Aroma plc, a company with 100% owned subsidiaries, purchased 30% of Therapy Ltd on 1 July 20X0. At all times, Aroma participates fully in Therapy's financial and operating policy decisions.

The equity of Therapy Ltd at acquisition was as follows:

	£000
Share capital	1,000
Revaluation reserve	100
Retained earnings	450
	1,550

Statements of profit or loss for the year ended 30 June 20X4

	Aroma plc group £000	Therapy Ltd £000
Revenue	5,000	3,000
Cost of sales	(3,000)	(1,500)
Gross profit	2,000	1,500
Expenses	(790)	(440)
Profit from operations	1,210	1,060
Investment and interest income	55	–
Finance charges	(50)	(10)
Profit before tax	1,215	1,050
Tax	(400)	(350)
Profit after tax	815	700

Aroma plc and Therapy Ltd paid total dividends of £300,000 and £50,000, respectively, during the year.

Statements of financial position at 30 June 20X4

	Aroma plc group £000	Therapy Ltd £000
Non-current assets		
Goodwill	800	
PPE	3,200	3,500
Investment in Therapy Ltd	1,000	
	5,000	
Current assets		
Inventories	670	430
Receivables	500	395
Cash and cash equivalents	130	215
	1,300	1,040
Total assets	6,300	4,540
Equity		
Equity share capital	2,000	1,000
Revaluation reserve	1,000	500
Retained earnings	2,550	2,470
	5,550	3,970
Current liabilities	750	570
Total equity and liabilities	6,300	4,540

Therapy's revaluation reserve at 1 July 20X3 was £400,000.

Required:

Prepare the consolidated statements of profit or loss and changes in equity for the year ended 30 June 20X4 and the consolidated statement of financial position at this date.

3   Two property management companies, Hafford plc and Lysters plc, set up a separate company, Fairfax Ltd, for the purpose of acquiring and operating a shopping centre. The contractual arrangement between Hafford and Lysters establishes joint control of the activities that are conducted in Fairfax. The main feature of Fairfax's legal form is that the company, not Hafford and Lysters, has rights to the assets, and obligations for the liabilities, relating to the arrangement. These activities include the rental of the retail units, managing the car park, maintaining the centre and its equipment, such as lifts, and building the reputation and customer base for the centre as a whole.

The terms of the contractual arrangement are such that:

(a) Fairfax owns the shopping centre. The contractual arrangement does not specify that Hafford and Lysters have rights to the shopping centre.

(b) Hafford and Lysters are not liable in respect of the debts, liabilities or obligations of Fairfax. If Fairfax is unable to pay any of its debts or other liabilities, or to discharge its obligations to third parties, the liability of each party to any third party will be limited to the unpaid amount of that party's capital contribution.

(c) Hafford and Lysters have the right to sell or pledge their interests in Fairfax.

(d) Hafford and Lysters each receive a share of the income from operating the shopping centre (which is the rental income net of the operating costs) in accordance with its interest in Fairfax.

Required:

Discuss whether this arrangement should be classified as a joint operation or a joint venture, and explain the consequential accounting method.

●● Develop your understanding

4   The abbreviated financial statements of three companies are as follows.

Statements of profit or loss for the year ended 31 December 20X6

	Hartleys plc	Samuel Smith Ltd	Adnams Ltd
	£000	£000	£000
Profit from operations	26	30	20
Investment income from Samuel Smith Ltd	6		
Investment income from Adnams Ltd	4		
Profit before tax	36	30	20
Tax	9	11	7
Profit after tax	27	19	13

Retained earnings columns from statements of changes in equity for the year ended 31 December 20X6

	Hartleys plc	Samuel Smith Ltd	Adnams Ltd
	£000	£000	£000
Balance at 1 January 20X6	20	16	10
Profit for the year	27	19	13
Dividends paid	(10)	(8)	(10)
Balance at 31 December 20X6	37	27	13

Statements of financial position at 31 December 20X6

	Hartleys plc	Samuel Smith Ltd	Adnams Ltd
	£000	£000	£000
Non-current assets			
PPE	163	74	11
30,000 shares in Samuel Smith Ltd	45		
4,000 shares in Adnams Ltd	7		
	215		
Current assets	11	36	25
Total assets	226	110	36
Equity			
Called up share capital (£1 shares)	100	40	10
General reserve	60	–	–
Retained earnings	37	27	13
	197	67	23
Current liabilities			
Payables	20	32	6
Tax payable	9	11	7
	29	43	13
Total equity and liabilities	226	110	36

The following additional information is provided:

(a) Hartleys plc purchased its investments 2 years ago when the retained earnings of Samuel Smith Ltd and Adnams Ltd were £12,000 and £8,000 respectively.

(b) The companies do not trade with each other.

(c) The book values and fair values of the non-current assets of the investee companies at the respective dates of acquisition were as follows:

	Book value	Fair value
Samuel Smith Ltd	£62,000	£66,000
Adams Ltd	£10,000	£12,000

The fair values have not been incorporated into the companies' accounts. Both companies use a 10% straight-line depreciation method.

Assume the fair values of the other net assets of these companies were not materially different from their book values at the time of the acquisitions.

Required:

Prepare the consolidated statements of comprehensive income and changes in equity for the year ended 31 December 20X6, and a consolidated statement of financial position at that date.

5   The statements of profit or loss and the retained earnings columns from the statements in changes in equity for the year ended 31 March 20X6, and the statements of financial position at 31 March 20X6 of three companies, Worcester plc, Pershore Ltd and Evesham Ltd, are as follows.

Statements of profit or loss for the year ended 31 March 20X6

	Worcester plc	Pershore Ltd	Evesham Ltd
	£000	£000	£000
Revenue	10,630	4,260	5,870
Cost of sales	7,760	3,200	4,110
Gross profit	2,870	1,060	1,760
Distribution costs	730	275	590
Administrative expenses	1,290	405	760
	2,020	680	1,350
Profit from operations	850	380	410
Income from investments	77	–	–
Finance costs	(231)	(15)	(94)
Profit before tax	696	365	316
Income tax	160	80	70
Profit for the year	536	285	246

Statements of changes in equity—retained earnings for the year ended 31 March 20X6

	Worcester plc	Pershore Ltd	Evesham Ltd
	£000	£000	£000
At 1 April 20X5	4,863	975	2,430
Profit for the year	536	285	246
Dividends paid	(144)	(90)	(66)
At 31 March 20X6	5,255	1,170	2,610

Statements of financial position at 31 March 20X6

	Worcester plc £000	Pershore Ltd £000	Evesham Ltd £000
Assets			
Non-current assets			
PPE	8,400	2,070	3,810
Investments	3,975		
	12,375		
Current assets			
Inventories	1,860	645	1,440
Trade and other receivables	1,785	960	1,875
Cash and cash equivalents	450	–	675
	4,095	1,605	3,990
Total assets	16,470	3,675	7,800
Equity			
Equity shares (£1 shares)	3,000	750	2,400
6% Irredeemable preference shares (£1 shares)	900	–	300
Share premium	1,840	195	–
Retained earnings	5,255	1,170	2,610
	10,995	2,115	5,310
Liabilities			
Current liabilities			
Bank overdraft	–	375	–
Trade and other payables	1,725	1,185	1,290
	1,725	1,560	1,290
Non-current liabilities			
Debentures	3,750	–	1,200
Total liabilities	5,475	1,560	2,490
Total equity and liabilities	16,470	3,675	7,800

Additional information:

(a) The balance on Worcester plc's Investment account is made up as follows:

	£000
450,000 shares in Pershore Ltd	1,725
840,000 equity shares in Evesham Ltd	2,250
	3,975

(b) Worcester plc purchased its investment in Pershore Ltd on 1 April 20X4 when the balance on Pershore's retained earnings was £810,000. At this date the fair value of Pershore's PPE was £2,100,000, while the book value was £1,500,000.

(c) Worcester plc purchased its investment in Evesham Ltd on 1 April 20X5, when the balance on Evesham's retained earnings was £2,430,000. At this date the fair values of Evesham's PPE was £5,400,000, while the book value was £4,500,000.

(d) The fair values of all other net assets in Pershore and Evesham at the respective dates of acquisition can be assumed to be equal to their book values.

(e) Assume Pershore and Evesham use an average depreciation method of 10% straight-line.

(f) Pershore Ltd issued its preference shares when it was first formed. Since 1 April 20X4 and 1 April 20X5 there have been no movements in share capital in Pershore Ltd and Evesham Ltd respectively.

(g) Worcester, Pershore and Evesham trade with each other. During the year ended 31 March 20X6 Worcester and Evesham purchased goods from Pershore for £2,450,000 and £85,000, respectively, which Pershore had marked up by 25%. At the year end, Worcester's inventories included some of these goods, which had cost it £780,000.

(h) Worcester and Evesham's accounts payable include amounts owing to Pershore of £180,000 and £45,000 respectively. Pershore's accounts receivable show £320,000 due from Worcester and £45,000 from Evesham.

Required:

Prepare Worcester plc's consolidated statement of profit or loss and consolidated statement of changes in equity for the year ended 31 March 20X6, and its consolidated statement of financial position at that date.

6   Companies Fyfield plc and Gresham plc have set up a strategic and operating agreement (the framework agreement) in which they have agreed the terms according to which they will conduct the manufacturing and distribution of a product (product P) in different markets.

The companies have agreed to conduct manufacturing and distribution activities by establishing joint arrangements, described as follows.

(1) *Manufacturing activity*: Fyfield and Gresham have agreed to undertake the manufacturing activity through a joint arrangement (the manufacturing arrangement). The manufacturing arrangement is structured in a separate company, Mixit Ltd, whose legal form causes it to be considered in its own right (i.e. the assets and liabilities held in Mixit are the assets and liabilities of Mixit and not the assets and liabilities of Fyfield and Gresham). In accordance with the framework agreement, Fyfield and Gresham have committed themselves to purchasing the whole production of product P manufactured by the manufacturing arrangement in accordance with their ownership interests in Mixit. Fyfield and Gresham subsequently sell product P to another arrangement, jointly controlled by the two parties themselves, that has been established exclusively for the distribution of product P, described as follows. Neither the framework agreement nor the contractual arrangement between Fyfield and Gresham dealing with the manufacturing activity specifies that Fyfield and Gresham have rights to the assets, and obligations for the liabilities, relating to the manufacturing activity.

(2) *Distribution activity*: Fyfield and Gresham have agreed to undertake the distribution activity through a joint arrangement (the distribution arrangement). The companies have structured the distribution arrangement in a separate company, Donna Ltd, whose legal form causes it

to be considered in its own right (i.e. the assets and liabilities held in Donna are the assets and liabilities of Donna, and not the assets and liabilities of Fyfield and Gresham). In accordance with the framework agreement, the distribution arrangement orders its requirements for product P from Fyfield and Gresham according to the needs of the different markets where the distribution arrangement sells the product. Neither the framework agreement nor the contractual arrangement between Fyfield and Gresham dealing with the distribution activity specifies that these companies have rights to the assets, and obligations for the liabilities, relating to the distribution activity.

In addition, the framework agreement establishes:

(a) That the manufacturing arrangement will produce product P to meet the requirements that the distribution arrangement places on Fyfield and Gresham

(b) The commercial terms relating to the sale of product P by the manufacturing arrangement to Fyfield and Gresham. The manufacturing arrangement will sell product P to Fyfield and Gresham at a price agreed by Fyfield and Gresham that covers all production costs incurred. Subsequently, Fyfield and Gresham sell the product to the distribution arrangement at a price agreed by Fyfield and Gresham

(c) That any cash shortages that the manufacturing arrangement may incur will be financed by Fyfield and Gresham in accordance with their ownership interests in Mixit.

Required:

Discuss whether this arrangement should be classified as a joint operation or a joint venture, and explain the consequential accounting method.

●●● Take it further

7 The financial statements for the year ended 30 June 20X5 of Strauss plc, Cook Ltd and Anderson Ltd at are given as follows.

Statements of profit or loss for the year ended 30 June 20X5

	Strauss plc	Cook Ltd	Anderson Ltd
	£000	£000	£000
Revenue	5,090	2,650	1,530
Cost of sales	2,955	2,075	1,105
Gross profit	2,135	575	425
Distribution and administration expenses	1,775	415	195
Profit from operations	360	160	230
Income from investments	66	–	–
Profit before tax	426	160	230
Income tax expense	168	35	50
Profit after tax	258	125	180

Extracts from the statements of changes in equity for the year ended 30 June 20X5

	Strauss plc	Cook Ltd	Anderson Ltd
	Retained earnings		
	Strauss plc	Cook Ltd	Anderson Ltd
	£000	£000	£000
Balance at 1 July 20X4	472	165	510
Profit for the year	258	125	180
Dividends paid	(100)	(20)	(200)
Balance at 30 June 20X5	630	270	490

Statements of financial position at 30 June 20X5

	Strauss plc	Cook Ltd	Anderson Ltd
	£000	£000	£000
Non-current assets			
PPE	1,580	1,090	820
Investments			
In Cook Ltd	950		
In Anderson Ltd	370		
	2,900		
Current assets			
Inventories	830	450	390
Accounts receivable	970	410	370
Cash and cash equivalents	70	–	150
	1,870	860	910
Total assets	4,770	1,950	1,730
Equity			
Share capital	2,000	600	500
Share premium	800	100	–
Retained earnings	630	270	490
	3,430	970	990
Current liabilities			
Bank overdraft	–	30	–
Accounts payable	780	750	580
Corporation tax	560	200	160
	1,340	980	740
Total equity and liabilities	4,770	1,950	1,730

Additional information:

(a) The investments in Cook and Anderson were made as follows:

	Nominal value of ordinary share capital	No. of shares acquired	Date of acquisition	Retained earnings at date ofacquisition
Cook	£1	480,000	1.7.20X3	£110,000
Anderson	20p	625,000	1.7.20X4	£510,000

Since 1 July 20X3 and 1 July 20X4 there have been no movements in share capital in Cook Ltd and Anderson Ltd respectively.

(b) The book values and fair values of the PPE of Cook at the date of acquisition of its shares by Strauss were £810,000 and £960,000 respectively. At this date the expected remaining useful life of these assets was estimated at five years. The fair values of all other net assets in Cook can be assumed to be equivalent to their book values.

(c) During the year ended 30 June 20X5 Cook and Anderson purchased goods from Strauss for £375,000 and £150,000 respectively. Strauss earned a gross margin of 40% from these transactions. At the year end Cook had one-third of the goods it had purchased in its inventories and owed Strauss £75,000. Anderson had one-quarter of the goods it had purchased in its inventories.

(d) At 30 June 20X5 a review for impairment found that the recoverable amount of the goodwill arising on the acquisition of Cook was £100,000. In all other reviews for impairment of goodwill, no adjustments to goodwill values had been necessary.

(e) Assume that Strauss values the non-controlling interest using the proportion of net assets method.

Required:

Prepare the following financial statements for the Strauss plc group:

(i) The consolidated statement of profit or loss for the year ended 30 June 20X5

(ii) The retained earnings and non-controlling interest columns of the consolidated statement of changes in equity for the year ended 30 June 20X5

(iii) The consolidated statement of financial position at 30 June 20X5.

8 (a) In the context of accounting for business combinations, discuss the difference between an acquiring company having:

(i) significant influence

(ii) control

over the acquiree company and explain the different accounting treatments that result.

(b) The statements of profit or loss of three companies, Hexham plc, Colwell Ltd and Alston Ltd, for the year ended 30 June 20X7 and their statements of financial position at that date are as follows.

Statements of profit or loss for the year ended 30 June 20X7

	Hexham £000	Colwell £000	Alston £000
Revenue	5,268	1,950	1,449
Cost of sales	(3,531)	(1,458)	(1,173)
Gross profit	1,737	492	276
Distribution costs	(846)	(243)	(153)
Administrative expenses	(417)	(90)	(87)
Profit from operations	474	159	36
Income from shares in group companies	42	–	–
Finance charges	(45)	–	(12)
Profit before tax	471	159	24
Taxation	(96)	(36)	(6)
Profit for the year	375	123	18

Statements of financial position at 30 June 20X7

	Hexham £000	Colwell £000	Alston £000
Non-current assets			
PPE	705	198	222
Investment in Colwell Ltd	378		
Investment in Alston Ltd	75		
	1,158		
Current assets			
Inventories	435	120	168
Receivables	603	156	183
Cash and cash equivalents	166	96	–
	1,204	372	351
Total assets	2,362	570	573
Equity			
Equity shares of £1 each	450	90	150
Share premium	195	60	–
Retained earnings	472	195	(57)
	1,117	345	93

Non-current liabilities	450	–	150
Current liabilities			
Bank overdraft	–	–	108
Payables	795	225	222
	795	225	330
Total equity and liabilities	2,362	570	573

Additional information

(a) Hexham plc acquired 63,000 shares in Colwell Ltd on 1 July 20X5 when Colwell's retained earnings were £126,000 and the balance on its share premium was £60,000.

(b) At 1 July 20X5 the fair values of Colwell's non-current assets were £240,000 whereas the net book values were £180,000. The assets had an estimated remaining useful life of 10 years at this date. The fair values of all other net assets were equivalent to their book values.

(c) Hexham plc acquired 60,000 shares in Alston Ltd on 1 January 20X7. Alston's profits for the year ended 30 June 20X7 may be assumed to have arisen evenly over the year.

(d) At 1 January 20X7 the fair values of Alston's net assets can be assumed to be equal to their book values.

(e) During the year ended 30 June 20X7 Hexham sold goods to Colwell for £75,000, earning a 40% gross profit on this transaction. One quarter of these goods was still in Colwell's inventories at the year end.

(f) At 30 June 20X7 Hexham's trade receivables include an amount owing from Colwell of £30,000.

(g) The review for impairment of goodwill at 30 June 20X7 indicated that goodwill on acquisition should be written down to £100,000.

(h) During the year ended 30 June 20X7 Hexham and Colwell paid dividends of £80,000 and £60,000 respectively. Alston did not pay any dividends during the year.

Required:

Prepare Hexham plc's consolidated statement of profit or loss and statement of changes in equity for the year ended 30 June 20X7 and a consolidated statement of financial position at that date.

9 The following are extracts from the consolidated financial statements of Tahir plc and one of its wholly owned subsidiaries, Amex Ltd, the shares in which were acquired on 31 October 20X8.

Statements of financial position at:

	Tahir plc Group		Amex Ltd
	31 December 20X8	31 December 20X7	31 October 20X8
ASSETS	£000	£000	£000
Non-current assets			
PPE	4,764	3,685	694
Goodwill	42	–	–

Investments in associates	2,195	2,175	–
Current assets			
Inventories	1,735	1,388	306
Receivables	2,658	2,436	185
Cash and cash equivalents	43	77	7
Total assets	11,437	9,761	1,192
EQUITY AND LIABILITIES			
Equity			
Equity share capital	4,896	4,776	400
Share premium account	216	–	–
Retained earnings	2,477	2,000	644
Non-current liabilities			
Loans	1,348	653	–
Current liabilities			
Payables	1,915	1,546	148
Bank overdrafts	239	406	–
Taxation	346	380	–
Total equity and liabilities	11,437	9,761	1,192

Consolidated statement of profit or loss for the year ended 31 December 20X8

	£000
Profit before interest and tax	546
Share of profit of associates	120
Profit before tax	666
Income tax expense	126
Profit for the period	540
Profit attributable to:	
Owners of Tahir plc	540
Non-controlling interest	–
	540

The following information is also given:

(a) The consolidated figures at 31 December 20X8 include Amex Ltd

(b) Depreciation charged on PPE during the year was £78,000. Additions to PPE, excluding PPE acquired on the acquisition of Amex Ltd, were £463,000. There were no disposals.

(c) The cost on 31 October 20X8 of the shares in Amex Ltd was £1,086,000. This was satisfied by Tahir plc issuing £695,000 unsecured loan stock at par, 120,000 ordinary shares of £1 each at a value of 280p each and £55,000 in cash.

(d) No write down of goodwill was required during the period.

(e) Total dividends paid by Tahir plc during the period amounted to £63,000.

Required:

Prepare the following:

(i) A consolidated statement of cash flows for Tahir plc for the year ended 31 December 20X8 using the indirect method

(ii) A note reconciling profit before tax to cash generated from operations

(iii) A note showing the effect of the subsidiary acquired in the period.

 Visit the Online Resource Centre for solutions to all these end of chapter questions plus visual walkthrough solutions. You can test your understanding with extra questions and answers, explore additional case studies based on real companies, take a guided tour through a company report and much more. Go to the Online Resource Centre at www.oxfordtextbooks.co.uk/orc/maynard2e/

Part 6
Conclusion

19

Interpretation of financial statements revisited

> ➤ **Introduction**

For a user to understand companies' financial statements a sound approach to their interpretation using all relevant information is required. This chapter revisits interpretation of financial statements, the techniques of which were introduced in Chapter 5. It uses the basic analytical tools discussed in this chapter together with details of what constitutes published financial statements, and knowledge of the accounting methods used in the recognition and measurement of many of the key figures in the financial statements. This is material that has been covered in all previous chapters.

A model for interpretation which uses all of this information, the CORE approach (context, overview, ratios and evaluation), is discussed and illustrated by use of a full example of the interpretation of a single company, J Sainsbury plc.

Much of the approach to this interpretation will apply to company-to-company comparisons also. If this is the interpretation being performed, the contextual information is vital to an understanding of the differences between the companies.

After studying this chapter you will be able to:

● understand and perform an interpretation of companies' published financial statements using a variety of techniques and information.

❑ The CORE approach to the interpretation of financial statements.

❑ Context

    ❑ external and internal environments.

❑ Overview

    ❑ horizontal and trend analyses

    ❑ other significant information in the annual report.

❑ Ratio calculations

    ❑ categories of ratios

    ❑ companies' key performance indicators (KPIs)

    ❑ operating segments.

❑ Indicators of financial distress.

❑ Evaluation.

❑ The effect of recognition and measurement methods.

❑ The effect of and changes in accounting policies.

❑ Comprehensive case study.

❑ Use of databases.

19.1 Interpretation of financial statements in the context of material covered in the textbook

Chapter 5 provided details of some analytical techniques that can be used in the interpretation of the financial statements of a company. The methods covered in that chapter were horizontal analysis, vertical analysis and ratio analysis. It was emphasised there that these were techniques to be used as part of an interpretation, and that a full interpretation of financial statements requires an understanding of far more than some line-by-line comparisons and ratio calculations. The bases for the recognition and measurement of different figures need to be understood, and to be meaningful; any interpretation must be set in the context of the company's internal and external environments.

If all previous chapters have been studied, readers should now have knowledge and understanding of what constitutes published financial statements, and the accounting methods used in the recognition and measurement of many of the key figures in the financial statements. The information contained in accounting policies and disclosure notes, which explain, enhance and provide a breakdown of the aggregated figures on the face of the financial statements, has also been discussed throughout the textbook.

An annual report of a company, however, does not just contain financial statements and related notes. A UK company publishes a wealth of narrative information in the first half of its annual report, which includes its own interpretation of the company's financial performance and position. There is also much information about how the financial results and position have been achieved, the company's governance regime, and its environmental and social policies. All of this is to enable the users to assess the long-term success of the business. Details of these issues have been discussed in detail in Chapter 3.

19.2 A CORE approach

A framework for the interpretation of the financial statements of a company can be represented as shown in Figure 19.1.

This four-stage CORE (context, overview, ratios and evaluation) approach ensures that any interpretation will focus on areas that are important, and take into account external and internal influences on the financial data presented in the financial statements. The stages are discussed in more detail in the following sections.

As highlighted in Chapter 5, it is crucial that the purpose of the interpretation and the user's needs are used to direct the interpretative techniques employed and the areas investigated.

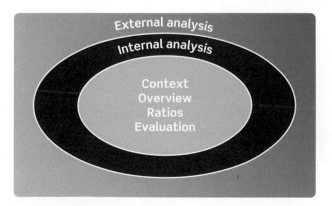

Figure 19.1 CORE analysis in strategic performance appraisal. Adapted from *Management Accounting Research*, vol.4, Moon and Bates, 'Core analysis in strategic performance appraisal', pp.139–152, Copyright (1993), reproduced with permission from Elsevier.

19.2.1 Context

Before any meaningful interpretation of financial statements can be performed, it is essential to understand the context in which the company is operating. Context here means the external and internal environments, and events that could influence the financial performance and position of a company.

Many external factors and influences can be identified by consideration of the following:

- What does the company do?
- In which markets does it compete?
- What is its position in its markets?
- What are the market structures?
- How do the main players compete?
- Recent industry/sector performance
- Recent economic and political developments, e.g. inflation, interest and exchange rates
- Review of specific 'news' about the company being analysed.

By identifying the company and the sectors in which it operates, some broad expectations about what the financial statements might look like can be derived. A review of the actual financial statements against these expectations could then highlight anomalies or areas requiring investigation. For example, a retail chain would be expected to have high property assets and/or property lease expenses, high inventories, and relatively low receivables. An international airline company would be expected to have high values for plant and equipment (aircraft, although many of these will be off balance sheet under IAS 17, spare parts, etc.), some property, average receivables and low inventories. Note that companies operate in many different sectors and provide details of which it identifies as its main ones in the segmental information it discloses. See Chapter 6 for further details of the disclosure requirements of operating segments.

Internal factors are things a company controls and relate to developments in the company's own strategic positioning within its sector, and steps it takes which influence its performance. To identify these factors the following questions need to be considered:

- What is the company's strategy?
- How does the company compete?
- What changes have occurred recently?
  - Changes in activities might include the mix of business, major new contracts, new products or processes, acquisitions, or disposals
  - Changes in strategy might include market positioning, or taking a balanced scorecard approach
- Review of specific 'news' about the company and its competitors.

Again, the actual effect of any of these on the financial performance and position should be compared with the expected effect, which will help confirm figures or identify areas requiring further investigation.

 Examples of external and internal context

How might the following factors affect the financial performance and position of a company?

1 A competitor starts selling a new, upgraded product.

This external factor might cause the sales revenue from the company's existing product to be affected. If the improved product's selling price is set too high, then revenues may not suffer; however, if the new product's selling price is set carefully, sales may be taken away from the company and revenues fall.

2 A company takes the decision to close the data processing function and outsource this operation, possibly overseas.

This internal factor will have implications for the financial performance and position of the company, as property, plant and equipment is disposed of affecting assets and capital; higher profit margins are achieved from lower salary costs; and the influence of exchange rates may have to be accounted for.

19.2.2 Overview

Before plunging into detailed ratio analysis, this stage provides an overview of the financial performance and the position the company is in at the end of the financial year. It is about reviewing trends in key figures in the financial statements through horizontal and trend analyses—techniques that were discussed in Chapter 5.

🔵 **Reminder**

1   Horizontal analysis compares key figures in the financial statements with the comparative year's figures, selecting those which are of particular interest for the purposes of the analysis. The aim of this is to gain a 'feel' for the financial performance and position of the company at least for the later year compared with the previous year and to direct attention to areas which require additional investigation. The key figures will usually include revenue, operating profit, profit before tax, certain key assets and liabilities and cash flow subtotals from the different activities.

2   As conclusions drawn from an overview of just two years' worth of figures may be distorted by one-off figures in either year, trend analysis extends horizontal analysis to more years of data to establish a longer trend in changes. Companies publish key figures for the past five years (sometimes ten years) in their annual report.

It is essential to be aware of significant, one-off events within any period under review as these can distort comparisons or trends. Examples of these could include mergers or acquisitions, share issues, reorganisations and natural catastrophes, such as floods. Some companies may disclose the financial effect of these separately on the face of the statement of comprehensive income under the heading of exceptional items, as discussed in Chapter 6; however, this would be a voluntary disclosure method. Other companies may refer to the effect in the notes.

In performing the overview, any changes in accounting policies need to be taken into account, as, again, the comparison or trend may be distorted if this has occurred. Changes in accounting policy are highlighted in financial statements and are discussed in more detail in Chapter 4. For company-to-company comparisons, it is essential to take into account the differences in accounting policies. Further discussion of how different accounting policies may affect the financial data to be analysed is included later in this chapter.

An overview of financial statements should also include an overview of other significant information contained in the annual report. For example:

- Is the audit opinion unqualified, in other words clean?

- Have there have been changes in key personnel?

- What does the company identify as its principal risks?

- Where have significant estimates or judgements been made?

19.2.3 Ratios

The third stage in the interpretation of a set of financial statements is to calculate financial ratios. Not all ratios need to be calculated for every analysis. As detailed in Chapter 5, the categorisation of ratios will help different groups of users determine which will be relevant for the purposes of their particular analysis. The ratios explained in Chapter 5 are summarised in Table 19.1.

This is a typical set of financial ratios; however, there will be other ratios which may be calculated to meet the aims of the interpretation. For example, for companies in the pharmaceutical or telecommunications industries, ratios of intangible non-current assets to tangible non-current assets can reveal information about the underlying stability of the companies' capital. Ratios which incorporate non-financial data may also be relevant, for example the ratio of sales revenue to number of employees or sales revenue to floor area may be relevant in a retail company.

Interpreters should also look at the KPIs that companies themselves define in their annual report and how these are calculated. Clearly, these ratios have significance for the company.

The actual figures to be used in the numerator and denominator of ratios should be considered carefully. For example, a company may have different categories of non-current liability on its statement of financial position, including provisions, deferred tax, pension fund liabilities and long-term borrowings. In determining the denominator of the ratio return on capital employed (profit before interest and tax/equity + long-term debt), care must be taken that only the appropriate figure for long-term debt is included and that also any current portion of the debt, which will be included in current liabilities, is also included.

In addition, ratios can be calculated for the different operating segments that the company has defined. This is discussed in more detail in Chapter 6.

Table 19.1 Typical financial ratios used in interpretation

Ratio category	Ratios
Profitability Effectiveness in generating profits	● Return on capital employed (ROCE) ● Asset turnover ● Net profit margin ● Gross profit margin ● Expenses as a percentage of sales
Liquidity Ability to meet liabilities when they fall due	● Current ratio ● Liquid ratio
Efficiency/activity Effectiveness of use of business assets	● Asset turnover ● Inventory turnover ● Receivables collection period ● Payables payment period
Gearing Financial structure	● Gearing ● Financial leverage ● Interest cover
Investor/stock market Returns to investors	● Return on equity (ROE) ● Earnings per share (EPS) ● Price/earnings ratio (PE ratio) ● Dividend per share ● Dividend cover ● Dividend yield ● Total shareholder returns
Cash flow ratios Availability of cash to meet demands	● Cash return on capital employed ● Cash from operations / Profit from operations ● Cash interest cover ● Cash flow per share ● Cash dividend cover

19.2.4 Ratios to indicate financial distress

A number of the ratios given in section 19.2.3 taken together may indicate that a company is in financial difficulties. Falling profitability ratios do not in themselves mean a company is struggling, but, collectively with other ratios, there may be indicators of future problems. For example, if profitability and liquidity, or cash availability, are both falling, gearing increasing, and interest cover falling, the company may have difficulties meeting future debt servicing requirements. This could mean renegotiations with debt providers are needed or, worse, the company is put into administration or liquidators are called in.

There have been a number of attempts to develop a scoring system which would indicate that a company was in financial difficulties—a score below a certain target providing this indication. The original Z-score was developed by Professor Altman in 1968 and combines a number of weighted financial ratios as follows:

$$Z = 0.012R_1 + 0.014R_2 + 0.033R_3 + 0.006R_4 + 0.999R_5$$

where:

R_1 = working capital/total assets

R_2 = retained earnings/total assets

R_3 = earnings before interest and tax/total assets

R_4 = market capitalisation/book value of debts

R_5 = sales/total assets.

A score of 3.0 and above is considered to be a sign of a healthy company, whereas a score of below 1.8 is considered to mean the company is very likely to fail. The range in the middle is a 'grey area'.

A number of alternative Z-scores have subsequently been developed, but there are limitations to all of these models arising from different measurement and classification methods used by companies and the fact that they are based on historical data. In practice they are not widely used.

Other non-financial information should be considered, together with the financial ratios, and, collectively, these may give indications of a company in difficulties. Non-financial information could include:

- changes in senior management, particularly if unexpected
- high staff turnover
- recent unexpected changes in auditors or other financial advisors
- renewal of bank overdraft facilities with less favourable terms and conditions
- applications for loans from other than mainstream lenders
- a reduction in the company's credit rating.

A-scores have been developed that attempt to quantify non-financial indicators by weighting them and producing an overall score out of 100. An A-score will group the indicators under three headings—defects, mistakes and symptoms. Defects relate to management structure, decision-making, accounting systems and response to change. Mistakes are concerned with gearing and trading levels. Symptoms are poor financial ratios. A score above 25 indicates a company in difficulties.

19.2.5 Evaluation

The evaluation stage is the interpretation of all the information gathered in the previous three stages. Consistency between the data collected, ratios calculated and conclusions reached in each stage needs to be checked, together with ensuring that areas highlighted as requiring investigation in one stage have been followed through.

As comparisons of ratios from one period to another, or from one company to another, are made, the bases of the figures used in the ratios have to be considered. For example, what figures are included in the numerator and denominator, what changes/differences have occurred in these figures, and what effect will these have on the ratios? Knowledge of the valuation basis of the figures included in the ratio may affect the interpretation, and this is discussed in section 19.3. It is also important to understand the relationship between ratios, such as given by the Du Pont pyramid of operating ratios; one ratio may give one interpretation of the state of the business, but it needs to be supported by other ratios.

The business and financial reviews included in the narrative sections of a company's annual report will often provide some useful evaluation of the company's financial performance and position. Although the reliability of this information could be questioned, as it has been produced by the company, it will have been reviewed by the external auditors to provide assurance that it is at least consistent with the financial statements.

19.3 The effect of recognition and measurement issues and accounting policies on interpretation

The bases of the figures which are used in analytical techniques and ratios must be fully understood so that an appropriate interpretation is made. This means that the accounting methods concerning recognition and measurement issues of all figures used should be considered in the evaluation. This will also encompass understanding the accounting policies the company or companies have used. Significant changes in accounting policies will affect comparative figures and trends, but this information should be available as these changes are required to be disclosed.

It is now a number of years since the 2005 requirement for all European Union (EU) companies to use International Financial Reporting Standards (IFRS). Although companies at the time produced one year's financial statements according to both IFRS and their national generally accepted accounting principles (GAAP), they were not required to adjust all figures in their five-year data, so a good trend analysis was difficult. However, it should be remembered that other countries have adopted IFRS more recently, and also that the IASB is continually updating and reissuing financial reporting standards. The first time a company uses a new or reissued standard there may be a significant effect on comparative figures. For example, IFRS 16 requires virtually all leases to be capitalised, and the application of this standard will have an enormous effect on companies' asset and liability figures and many ratios (see Chapter 15 for further discussion of this).

A summary of the recognition and measurement issues included in this textbook which may affect the interpretation of financial statements is given in this section. It should always be remembered that many figures are based on management's best estimates or judgement, and so the interpretation of these figures may be more suggestive than absolute. Companies are required to disclosure the areas where significant estimates and judgement have been applied, and the audit report now also draws attention to these in its discussion of the areas giving rise to material mis-statement. See Chapters 3 and 6 for further discussion of this topic.

The summary also includes some reminders of information included in financial statements which may be useful in an interpretation.

19.3.1 Statement of profit or loss and statement of comprehensive income

Revenue

- This will be an aggregate figure from many different sources, activities, and companies in a group.

- The accounting policy should provide details of the bases for the recognition of the different revenue streams.

- Revenue from the different operating segments is disclosed (IFRS 8).

Discontinued operations

- The financial result from discontinued operations is disclosed separately on the face of the statement of comprehensive income. This comprises the net profit/loss from the operation plus any profit or loss from the sale of the operation or impairment loss from revaluation of the net assets if still held at the year end. A breakdown of these figures is included in a disclosure note.

- The exclusion of discontinued operations figures may be useful for predictions of future results.

One-off or exceptional items

- As discussed previously these will distort comparatives and trends.

- Companies are required to disclose these separately if they are considered material and relevant to an understanding of the company's financial performance.

- Companies may elect to disclose them separately on the face of the statement of comprehensive income, or details may be in a note.

Operating segments

- The disclosures for operating segments are very useful to break down the aggregate figures included on the face of the main financial statements.

- From the information required to be disclosed, certain financial ratios on a segment-by-segment basis can be calculated and compared.

- The segments are chosen by management to fit in with how they organise and manage their business, so will not necessarily be comparable from one company to another.

Adjustments to the fair value measurement of assets and liabilities, including impairment losses

- Certain assets and liabilities, mainly financial instruments, are measured each year end at fair value with the changes passing through profit or loss. Arguably, these changes have little to do with the financial performance of a business.

- Some changes in fair value of financial instruments pass through other comprehensive income.

- Impairment losses and their reversal will mainly be included in profit or loss. These may arise from external factors which have little to do with the financial performance of the business.

Earnings per share

- Remember, basic and diluted earnings per share (EPS) are disclosed on the face of the statement of profit or loss, and a disclosure note provides details of its calculation. There is no need to recalculate these figures!

19.3.2 Statement of changes in equity

All changes in equity balances are shown in this statement, including all transactions with the shareholders. It is therefore useful in understanding ratios that use equity in their denominator, for example return on capital employed, return on equity and gearing.

19.3.3 Statement of financial position

Property, plant and equipment

- The accounting policy will disclose information about depreciation methods and rates used for the different classes of assets. Remember these are based on estimates. This information will help in an understanding of the depreciation expense in profit and loss, assets' ages and when assets are expected to be replaced.

- Decreases in the estimates of the useful economic life of non-current assets will lower the reported carrying amount. Although such a change in estimate would imply the assets of the business are wearing out faster than expected (which may be of concern and raise questions about when and how they will be replaced), ratios with net assets in the denominator would improve owing to the lower asset value.

- If the business replaces failing assets with new ones, increasing its operating capacity or using improved technology, such ratios will decline.

- A comprehensive disclosure note shows all movements in non-current assets by class over the year, so significant acquisitions and disposals can be identified.

- There are two alternative measurement models available, and although most UK companies use the historic cost model, some may choose the revaluation model for some classes of assets. If the latter method is used, the depreciation expense and profit will be affected. Various disclosures are required which enable comparison to the historic cost model.

- Whether the companies are property-owning or not needs to be established for company-to-company comparisons.

- If a company applies IAS 17, property, plant and equipment will include assets capitalised under finance leases, but not assets held under operating leases. Once companies implement IFRS 16, virtually all leased assets will be capitalised, increasing the value of assets—and for many industries this will be substantial. The initial measurement of leased assets under IFRS 16 is essentially at the present value of the lease payments, so this will not be comparable to the measurement in companies that purchase comparable assets.

Intangible assets

- Companies that can recognise intangible assets through direct purchase or acquisition of companies in which intangible assets can be identified are not directly comparable to companies that generate their own intangible assets where the recognition criteria may not be satisfied.

- Goodwill included in financial statements only arises from the acquisition of a subsidiary. Thus, companies that grow organically are not directly comparable to those that grow through acquisitions.

- Much judgement is required in determining when internally generated intangible assets can be recognised.

- As for property, plant and equipment, two alternative measurement models are available—historic cost or revaluation.

- Accounting for amortisation varies according to the type of intangible asset.

Financial assets

- The measurement of financial assets is determined by the classification on acquisition, which in turn reflects the business model used and the cash flow characteristics of the asset. Companies can make certain elections as to classification which would be disclosed. The accounting policies are important if company comparisons are being made.

- Impairment is based on an expected loss model, and again the accounting policy or other disclosures will provide the detail of how companies have applied this.

Inventories

- Inventories will include materials, work-in-progress and finished goods, and this breakdown is disclosed.

- Companies will have many different inventory lines subject to different internal purchasing policies. This information will not necessarily be disclosed.

- The accounting policy will disclose the measurement method which will be the lower of cost and net realisable value.

Receivables

- Management's attitude to credit risk will affect the amount included as an allowance for irrecoverable debts; this may change over time.

Contract assets and liabilities

- These balances apply particularly to construction companies, and they may be assets or liabilities.

- Disclosures of how a company recognises contract revenue and the related costs and thus how the resulting balance has been derived are required, but these policies may vary from company to company.

Current liabilities

- Current liabilities will include various balances including bank overdrafts, accounts payable, accruals, provisions, deferred income, tax payable, construction contract balances and the current portion of any long-term liabilities, such as long-term borrowings and finance leases. All these are very different in their nature.

- Management's judgement has to be exercised, particularly in the recognition and measurement of provisions.

Debt

- The current portion of long-term debt should be included in any ratio which includes debt.

- Companies often use the term 'net debt', which is interest-bearing loans less cash and bank balances and marketable securities. The reason for this is that net debt is the figure that represents the outcome of treasury management policies.

Financial liabilities

- The measurement methods of financial liabilities can vary from company to company and the accounting policy should disclose the methods used.

- The accounting policy disclosures and those relating to risk are important in evaluating the financial stability of a company and in company comparisons.

Defined benefit pension plan liability or asset

- The net liability or asset balance may be substantial and is based on actuarial valuations. It can have an impact on and assessment of the long-term viability of a company.

- Consideration should be given to whether it forms part of the long-term capital of a company when calculating ratios such as return on capital employed (which is discussed further in the case study below).

Non-controlling interest

- This should not be included in the figure of equity which is used in various ratios.

19.3.4 Statement of cash flows

- This should be used in any interpretation of liquidity and availability of cash and cash equivalents.

- The reconciliation of profit before tax to cash flows generated from operating activities is particularly useful in the interpretation of the management of working capital.

- Horizontal and trend analysis is less meaningful for this statement as some cash inflows and outflows will not be regularly recurring items and will vary in amount from year to year, e.g. cash outflows to acquire property, plant and equipment or proceeds from the issue of shares.

- Some further financial ratios use cash flows in their calculation, and have been discussed in Chapter 5.

19.4 Case study

A comprehensive analysis of the 2015 financial statements of J Sainsbury plc now follows, which will demonstrate many of the techniques discussed in this chapter and in Chapter 5. Note that this is not the only approach to the interpretation that could be taken. It is principally for an equity investor or a potential investor, but, for completeness, assesses all areas.

J Sainsbury is one of the leading UK supermarkets with stores solely in the UK. The financial statements are available from their website at www.j-sainsbury.co.uk. For convenience the main financial statements for the group (income statement, statement of comprehensive income, balance sheet and cash flow statement) have been included at the end of the chapter.

Some of the analysis, however, uses information contained in other parts of the annual report and financial statements for 2015.

19.4.1 External environment

For the purposes of this exercise a full analysis of the external environment has not been performed. However, the period covered by the financial statements (52 weeks ended 14 March 2015 and the comparative 52 weeks ended 15 March 2014) was one of major change for the supermarket industry. Consumers have significantly adjusted their grocery shopping habits, shopping more often online and more frequently, but buying fewer items on each visit. Large out-of-town supermarkets are therefore seeing a reduction in their sales, and in-town convenience stores are proving more popular. The Big 4 supermarkets, Sainsbury's, Tesco, Asda and Morrisons, have all experienced increased competition and pressure on their prices from the discount stores such as Aldi and Lidl.

One key external factor that affects one of Sainsbury's major products is the impact of oil prices and fuel taxes on petrol sales. Over the period covered by the financial statements oil prices fell substantially.

19.4.2 Internal environment

An assessment of this will start from identifying exactly what Sainsbury's strategic and business objectives are, and if there have been any significant changes to these in 2015. This information is gathered principally from the narrative reports contained in the company's annual report, but quality newspaper and magazine reports can be used.

Sainsbury's strategic objectives are not defined in these terms in the annual report. However, the company's business model defines five areas of focus for its business and the company reviews its operations under these headings:

- great products and services at fair prices
- being there for our customers
- colleagues making a difference
- knowing our customers better than anyone else
- our values making us different—these encompass being best for food and health, sourcing with integrity, respecting the environment, making a positive difference to the community and providing a great place to work

The products offered by Sainsbury's are groceries, clothing, general merchandise and financial services (through Sainsbury's Bank). Non-food products and services are available in many of the stores, and have performed well, with the general merchandise business growing by 7% in the 2015 year and clothing by 12%. Sainsbury's has identified opportunities for further growth in this area. As demand for online shopping grows, the company has invested in technology to expand the products available through these channels and enhance the overall customer experience. More choice is available in how goods are delivered through increasing the number of stores offering click and collect. Sainsbury's Bank is now 100% owned by J Sainsbury plc, and has performed well in 2015. This is a service Sainsbury wishes to grow.

During the 2015 year Sainsbury's entered into a joint venture with Netto, a discount store chain, to enable to the company to gain insight into this side of the grocery business. It has plans to open further Netto stores in future years.

At the end of the 2015 year the company operated a total of 1,304 stores of varying sizes and locations. This included net additions of 5 new supermarkets and 96 new convenience stores. Sales from the larger supermarkets fell by over 2% in the 2015 year, whereas the convenience business grew by 16% and the online business by 7%. Overall trading intensity (sales divided by sales area) has continued to decline though. Following a strategic review, Sainsbury's is reducing its new store opening programme, and this will now predominantly focus on convenience stores. The strategic review also resulted in a significant impairment charge, which is discussed in more detail in Worked example 19.2, where the financial results are analysed.

Sainsbury's has made significant investment in the retail price of its products in 2015 to improve its competitiveness, and as a result of lowering prices, volumes have increased. The overall effect was to reduce operating profit. This investment will, however, continue into 2016.

Sainsbury's continues to keep a tight control on operating costs and managed to achieve savings of £140 million in 2015 which more than offset inflationary rises.

19.4.3 Summary of Sainsbury's context

What do we expect the financial statements to show from this review of the external and internal environments?

A supermarket, by its nature, is likely to have:

- high levels of land and buildings
- a negative working capital cycle
- low receivables
- fairly low levels of inventories
- low margins and high turnover
- relatively stable profit/revenue patterns.

Sales in 2015 should have grown from the addition of the new stores, but the year has been difficult for the large supermarket companies with the intense competition from the discount supermarkets. Sainsbury's has cut grocery prices to remain competitive, but has also focused on cost savings that have countered inflationary pressures. There have also been increased sales from clothing and general merchandise which may cause increased margins, but the price of petrol has fallen. Overall, the picture of profit margins is mixed.

Large additions to property are expected, but there will be a reduction in value due to the impairment review. The funding of the additions will need to be analysed. The company's statement of financial position will include significant financial assets and liabilities relating to Sainsbury's Bank.

19.4.4 Overview

Changes in key figures in the financial statements from 2014 to 2015 are now calculated and reviewed.

Worked example 19.1: to show the selection and calculation of changes in key figures in Sainsbury's financial statements from 2014 to 2015

	2015 £m	2014 £m	Change
Revenue	23,775	23,949	−0.7%
Operating profit (PBIT)	81	1,009	−92.0%
Underlying operating profit[1]	782	879	−11.0%
(Loss)/Profit before tax	(72)	898	−108%
Underlying profit before tax[1]	681	798	−14.7%
(Loss)/Profit after tax	(166)	716	−123%
Shareholders' funds (equity)	5,539	6,003	−7.7%
Net debt (as defined by Sainsbury's)	2,343	2,384	−1.7%
Capital employed (defined here as equity plus net debt)	7,882	8,387	−6.0%
Non-current assets	12,032	12,171	−1.1%
Current assets	4,505	4,369	+3.1%
Current liabilities	6,923	6,765	+2.3%
Net cash and cash equivalents movement (net decrease/ increase as a percentage of opening balance)	−19%	+213%	
No. of shares	1,919 m	1,907 m	+0.6%
Closing share price[2]	259p	333p	−22.2%

(Note: closing 2013 share price was 363p.)

[1] Sainsbury's breaks down profit before tax on the face of its income statement into 'underlying profit before tax' plus other items. All profit measures included in Sainsbury's KPIs also use this measure of profit.

Underlying profit before tax is defined as profit before tax before any profit or loss on the disposal of properties, investment property fair value movements, retail financing fair value movements, impairment of goodwill, IAS 19 pension financing element, defined benefit pension scheme expenses, acquisition adjustments and one-off items that are material and infrequent in nature. In other words, Sainsbury's is stripping out of its key profit measure all items that do not relate to its core (underlying) retailing activity.

[2] Share price is not available from the financial statements.

Five year data

	2015	2014	2013	2012	2011
Sales[3] (including VAT, including fuel, including Bank) (£m)	26,122	26,353	25,632	24,511	22,943
(Decrease)/Increase on previous year (%)	(0.9)	2.8	4.6	6.8	7.1[4]
Indexed[5]	122	123	120	114	107
Underlying operating profit—retailing (£m)	720	873	831	789	738
(Decrease)/Increase on previous year (%)	(17.5)	5.1	5.3	6.9	10.0[4]
Indexed[5]	107	130	124	118	110
Underlying profit before tax (£m)	681	798	758	712	665
(Decrease)/Increase on previous year (%)	(14.7)	5.3	6.5	7.1	9.0[4]
Indexed[5]	117	131	124	117	109
Earnings per share					
Underlying basic (pence)	26.4	32.8	30.8	28.1	26.5
(Decrease)/Increase on previous year (%)	(19.5)	6.5	9.6	6.0	10.9[4]
Proposed dividend per share (pence)	13.2	17.3	16.7	16.1	15.1
Number of outlets at financial year end	1,304	1,203	1,106	1,012	934
Sales area (000 sq. ft)	22,819	22,160	21,265	20,347	19,108
Net increase on previous year (%)	3.0	4.2	4.5	6.5	7.7[4]
Indexed[5]	129	125	120	115	108
No. of new stores	106	104	101	92	68
Sales intensity (including VAT)					
Sales per sq. ft (£ per week)	18.24	18.93	19.27	19.47	20.04

[3] Note that Sainsbury's narrative reports discuss a number of different sales measures:

- sales including value added tax (VAT) and including fuel
- sales including VAT and excluding fuel
- like-for-like sales (which excludes sales from new stores which were not in operation in the previous year).

Its KPIs include like-for-like sales (which includes VAT, excludes fuel, and excludes Bank), retail sales growth (which measures year-on-year growth in retail sales including VAT, excluding fuel and excluding Bank), and trading intensity per week (which is sales per week divided by sales area, with sales including VAT, excluding fuel and excluding Bank).

Sales, as reported in the income statement, would be total sales, including fuel and Bank, but excluding VAT.

[4] The 2010 financial statements have had to be obtained in order to calculate the 2011 increase on the previous year. These show:

sales	£21,421 million
underlying operating profit—retailing	£671 million
underlying profit before tax	£610 million
earnings per share—underlying basic	23.9 pence
sales area	17,750,000 sq. ft.

[5] Indexation is explained in Chapter 5. The base year used here is 2010.

Preliminary comments

The overview confirms the changes in and difficult trading conditions for Sainsbury's referred to in the internal review. Revenues and all profit figures have fallen in 2015, and in particular this has resulted in an overall loss before tax. To gain a fuller understanding of these figures it is necessary to break down the profit figures into underlying profit and overall profit, as many of the performance measures use underlying profit, and this is a very different figure from the overall profit/(loss).

 Worked example 19.2: to show the break-down of Sainsbury's profit into underlying profit and other items

Underlying profit was defined in worked example 19.1. The relevant figures for 2015 and 2014, taken from the face of the income statement and note 4, are as follows:

	£m	£m
Underlying operating profit	782	879
Underlying finance income	19	20
Underlying finance costs	(126)	(131)
Underlying share of post-tax profit/(loss) from joint ventures and associates	6	30
Underlying profit before tax	681	798
Profit on disposal of properties	7	52
Investment property fair value movements	7	–
Retail financing fair value movements	(30)	(8)
IAS 19 pension financing charge	(31)	(23)
Defined benefit pension scheme expenses	(6)	(7)
Acquisition adjustments	13	18
One-off items	(713)	68
(Loss)/profit before tax	(72)	898

It is clear to see that, although the 2015 underlying operating profit fell by over £100 million or 11%, the main cause of the overall loss before tax is the £713 million one-off items. Note 3 and the chief financial officer's report provide further information about this. As a result of Sainsbury's reassessing its store pipeline and the potential to achieve an appropriate return on capital, the company made the decision that some sites would no longer be developed, and the value of unprofitable or only marginally profitable trading stores needed reviewing for impairment. An impairment review was carried out, with the result that there has been a significant impairment charge, plus provisions made for onerous contracts (see Chapter 13 for a discussion of this item), totalling £628 million. The recoverable amount of the property, plant and equipment was calculated for each store on the basis of value in use (see Chapter 10 for further details of accounting for impairment). In addition costs of £53 million were incurred in relation to transitioning Sainsbury's Bank (which was fully acquired only in 2014) to a new banking platform.

An analysis of Sainsbury's underlying retailing supermarket business, which is the bulk of its business, should therefore use underlying profit figures as the profit performance measures. The 2015 impairments affect only the 2015 figures, and the remaining less significant reconciling items are not directly connected to the supermarket business. Inclusion of these items, whilst not being ignored in the overall interpretation, would distort the analysis of the company's core business and any conclusions drawn.

The five-year data puts the 11% fall in underlying operating profit in context. It can be seen from the trends that rates of increase in both sales and underlying profit have been declining over the five years until 2015 when they suffered a reduction. This links to the trading changes and competition that supermarkets have been facing over the past few years. Although the number of new stores has been increasing over the five years, again the rate of increase of sales area has decreased. However, increases in sales did not match the additional store space as the sales intensity has actually been falling each year over the five years. This does indicate that there is spare capacity, which, as Sainsbury's specifies, is to be put to better use. It would be useful to see this last statistic split between the larger supermarkets and the convenience stores.

The overall fall in underlying profitability has resulted in the fall in underlying earnings per share, and it is not surprising that Sainsbury's has cut the proposed dividend per share. The inevitable conclusion is the significant fall in share price over the 2015 year.

The changes in the balance sheet figures tie in with the comments above. Although Sainsbury's continued to invest in new stores in 2015, which would increase non-current assets, the impairment has caused the overall value of these to fall. Current assets and current liabilities show modest increases partly from the increased Sainsbury's Bank business. Equity has decreased in value as a loss has been made and the company has continued to pay a dividend. However, debt has not changed significantly.

There appears to be a significant fall in cash and cash equivalent balances of 19%, partly caused by less cash flow from operating activities. Although this looks like a dramatic fall compared to the 2014 increase in cash and cash equivalents, the previous year's figures included the acquisition of the remaining Sainsbury's Bank business which would have significantly boosted cash inflows.

Further detailed analysis using ratios is required to draw full conclusions.

Other information obtained from an overview of the annual report reveals that there was a change in chief executive officer in July 2014; however, this had been announced well in advance and the new CEO had served on the board of directors for many years previously as the company's commercial director. The performance of the company is unlikely to have been affected by this. The audit report is unqualified.

There have been no changes in accounting policies and the company considers that the impact on the financial statements of new financial reporting standards applicable for 2015 is not significant. The areas which Sainsbury's details as requiring significant judgement and estimates are as follows:

- goodwill impairment—goodwill is immaterial
- impairment of assets other than goodwill—see discussion in Worked example 19.2
- post-employment benefits—comprise 17% (2014: 20%) of non-current liabilities
- provisions—immaterial amounts in current and non-current liabilities
- income taxes
- supplier income—which includes supplier incentives, rebates and discounts—these represent a material deduction to cost of sales.

19.4.5 Ratios

The calculation of a set of financial ratios from a published set of financial statements is more complex than for financial statements presented in an exam question. Questions always arise about which figures to include or exclude under a particular heading. It should be remembered that there are no absolute definitions of ratios. Consistency in calculation from one period to the next, or from company to company, or from ratio to ratio should be maintained as far as possible, and the interpretation should be of the ratios that have been calculated. Basic explanations of the ratios are included in Chapter 5—they have not been repeated here. In the calculation of the following ratios, various questions have been asked to illustrate this, and although the ratios have been calculated in a particular way, these are not the only solution.

Any of the 2015 ratios using overall profit figures will be unrepresentative of the underlying business due to the one-off impairment charges and other non-supermarket business related figures. These ratios will therefore be rather meaningless and mask any conclusions which could be drawn. Sainsbury's, in its KPIs, uses underlying profit as its measure of earnings, and it would be better to use this, as this will also tie into the analysis which the company provides in its Business Review. The EPS note (note 9) provides details of the underlying profit after tax which Sainsbury's has used in its underlying EPS calculations. These figures will be used in the following ratios.

19.4.6 Shareholder ratios

Return on equity	$\dfrac{\text{Profit attributable to equity holders}}{\text{Equity}}$

- Using underlying profit after tax

$$2015 \quad \frac{505}{5,539} = 9.1\% \qquad 2014 \quad \frac{623}{6,005} = 10.4\%$$

EPS	$\dfrac{\text{Profit attributable to equity holders}}{\text{No. of equity shares}}$

- This is disclosed on the face of the income statement, but should basic or fully diluted be used in an analysis?
- Basic EPS is usually used for trend analysis of performance, and incorporates all elements of profit and loss. Diluted EPS is a theoretical figure based on the maximum number of shares that could be in issue if all options are converted.
- All EPS calculations are shown here including those using underlying profit after tax.

2015	Basic	(8.7)p	2014	Basic	37.7p
	Diluted	(8.7)p		Diluted	36.9p
	Underlying basic	26.4p		Underlying basic	32.8p
	Underlying diluted	25.7p		Underlying diluted	32.2p

Dividend per share	$\dfrac{\text{Dividends}}{\text{No. of equity shares}}$

- Should this ratio use dividends paid, which comprises the previous year's final dividend and the current year's interim, or dividends for the current year?

Dividends recognised in the statement of changes in equity are dividends paid in the financial year, i.e. the 2014 final dividend and the 2015 interim dividend. It is more usual to calculate this ratio using the 2015 dividends—both interim and final—the latter is disclosed in note 10. This is also what the company has done in its headline financial summary figure on page 1.

- At what point should the number of shares be taken? The number of shares has varied over the year, so in calculating this ratio the weighted average has been used as disclosed in note 9 to the financial statements.

$$2015 \quad 5.0 + 8.2 = 13.2p \qquad 2014 \quad 5.0 + 12.3 = 17.3p$$

Dividend cover	$\dfrac{\text{Profit attributable to equity holders}}{\text{Total dividends}}$

- Which dividends should be included?

As mentioned above, it is more usual to include the same year's interim and final dividends in calculating this ratio. The ratio provides information about how well these dividends are covered by the 2015 profits and what proportion is being paid out as a dividend as opposed to being reinvested in the business.

$$2015 \quad \frac{505}{(96+157)} = 2.0 \qquad 2014 \quad \frac{623}{(95+234)} = 1.9$$

PE ratio	$\dfrac{\text{Market price per share}}{\text{Earnings per share}}$

- Using underlying basic EPS

$$\frac{259.1}{26.4} = 9.8 \qquad \frac{333.2}{32.8} = 10.2$$

Total shareholder returns	$\dfrac{\text{Change in share price} + \text{dividend}}{\text{Opening share price}}$

- The share price may be volatile and opening or closing share price may be affected by an abnormal event that was not prevalent throughout the year. If the share price is volatile at the year end and the effect seems to be temporary, then it might be necessary to use share price at a different point, which is considered more representative of the long-term picture.

$$2015 \quad \frac{(259.1-333.2)+13.2}{333.2} = -18.3\% \qquad 2014 \quad \frac{(333.2-362.8)+17.3}{362.8} = -3.4\%$$

19.4.7 Profitability

Return on capital employed	$\dfrac{\text{Profit before interest and tax (PBIT)}}{\text{Capital employed}}$

- Given the nature of the impairment charge and the other one-off items, it is better to use underlying operating profit. Sainsbury's uses this in its financial review and KPIs. However, there is an argument for including profits and losses from property transactions as a core part of a supermarket's activities are concerned with transactions in and valuations of property. Changes in the valuation of other assets (the fair value movements) are not connected to a supermarket's key business, and Sainsbury's has little control over these, so it would be appropriate to exclude these figures.

- Although immaterial, there is a question over whether the share of profits from joint ventures should be included or excluded. This depends on two things. Firstly, what is the nature of the joint ventures? Are their operations similar enough to the parent company's for it to make sense to include them and does the management of Sainsbury's have enough control over the operations to hold them accountable for the results? Secondly, to what are the ratios to be compared and to what use are the ratios to be put? Are results from joint ventures included in the comparative figures?

Is this ratio about assessing the return from the company's core business or is it about assessing the performance of the group as a whole?

● Why does this ratio exclude the finance income/costs?

As discussed in Chapter 5, this is to ensure that the numerator and denominator are consistent. Most companies, such as Sainsbury's, will have equity and debt funding for their operations, and therefore a ratio including both of these in the denominator has more meaning. The numerator should be a profit figure before any returns to the providers of funding are deducted.

● How should capital employed be defined? Capital employed is Equity + Debt.

● How should debt be defined?

The notes to the financial statements show that borrowings consist of loans, loan notes, bonds, bank overdrafts and finance lease obligations, so the current and non-current figures for borrowings would be a reasonable figure to use. Note that the Chief Financial Officer's definition of capital employed in the financial review is 'average of opening and closing net assets before net debt', where:

Net assets = Total assets minus total liabilities (or equity)

'Before net debt' means add back net debt. Net debt is defined in the financial statements (note 27) as:

Borrowings, bank overdrafts, finance lease obligations and financial derivative liabilities net of cash and cash equivalents, financial derivative assets and interest-bearing financial assets and deposits.

In other words Sainsbury's own definition of capital is the average of opening and closing equity plus net debt.

An alternative ratio to return on capital employed is return on net assets.

Return on net assets	$\dfrac{\text{Profit before interest and tax (PBIT)}}{\text{Total assets} - \text{current liabilities}}$

This raises further questions:

● Should net assets include intangible assets? Many analysts exclude intangible assets on the grounds that their valuation is subjective and they are not recognised consistently from company to company. In some cases these assets have a very different character to the other assets included in capital employed.

● Should net assets include investment in joint ventures? Here, consistency with the numerator should be maintained. If the share of profits from joint ventures is included in the numerator profit, then the investment in joint ventures must be included in the denominator. Otherwise, both should be excluded. Arguments are detailed previously as to whether profit from joint ventures should be included or not.

- Should net assets include financial assets and derivative financial instruments? Again, consistency with the numerator should be maintained. If income from the financial assets and derivatives is included in the numerator, the asset should be included in the denominator.

- Should net assets include deferred tax assets? This comes down to whether we want to class tax assets as an income-generating asset. However, deferred tax largely represents a timing difference in tax cash flows which does not really fit in with the idea of an asset which generates income, as in operating profits.

- Should net assets include non-current assets held for sale? This depends on whether the ratio is being used to look backwards, i.e. what return was generated from all net assets held by the business in the year which includes assets held for sale, or forwards, i.e. the ratio is to be used to forecast future returns when these assets are likely to be held no longer.

One further question for Sainsbury's in the comparison of 2015 to 2014 is how much this ratio is impacted by the acquisition of the remaining 50% of Sainsbury's Bank which occurred close to the end of the 2014 year. The assets and liabilities of the bank are consolidated in the 2014 balance sheet figures, and yet only a few weeks of results are included in the 2014 underlying operating profit. Sainsbury's adjusts the 2014 figures it uses in its KPI to compensate, as discussed below.

Return on capital employed	$\dfrac{\text{Profit before interest and tax (PBIT)}^{1}}{\text{Capital employed}^{2}}$

Using:

1 Underlying operating profit, which excludes underlying share of post-tax profit/(loss) from joint ventures and associates.

2 Equity plus current and long-term borrowings. 2014 figures include 100% of Sainsbury's Bank assets and liabilities.

$$2015 \quad \frac{782}{(5,539+260+2,506)}=9.4\% \qquad 2014 \quad \frac{879}{(6,005+534+2,250)}=10.0\%$$

Alternative:

Return on capital employed	$\dfrac{\text{Profit before interest and tax (PBIT)}^{3}}{\text{Capital employed}^{4}}$

Using:

3 Underlying operating profit.

4   NCA + CA – CL, excluding intangible assets, investments in joint ventures, financial assets and liabilities, assets held for sale. 2014 figures include 100% of Sainsbury's Bank assets and liabilities.

$$2015 \quad \frac{782}{[(12,032-325-359-184-21)+(4,421-69)-(6,923-75)]}=9.0\%$$

$$2014 \quad \frac{879}{[(12,171-286-404-255-28)+(4,362-49)-(6,765-65)]}=10.0\%$$

Per the financial review in Sainsbury's annual report, ROCE is defined as:

$$\frac{\text{Underlying profit before interest and tax}^5}{\text{Average capital employed}^6}$$

5   Includes underlying share of post-tax profit from joint ventures.

6   Average of opening and closing net assets before net debt. Note the closing capital employed for 2014 is reduced by 50% of Sainsbury's bank consolidated net assets (£243 million) to reflect the fact the bank was consolidated for only four weeks of this year.

$$2015 \quad \frac{782+6}{8,136}=9.7\% \qquad 2014 \quad \frac{879+30}{8,073}=11.3\%$$

$$\textbf{Asset turnover} \qquad \frac{\text{Revenue}}{\text{Net assets}^7}$$

● The same issues identified earlier apply to the definition of net assets. Should assets that do not directly generate revenue, such as financial instruments and joint ventures, be excluded?

7   Using same definition as in the above second calculation of ROCE:

$$2015 \quad \frac{23,775}{8,647}=2.7 \qquad 2014 \quad \frac{23,949}{8,811}=2.7$$

$$\textbf{Net profit margin} \qquad \frac{\text{Profit before interest and tax (PBIT)}}{\text{Revenue}}$$

● The same issues arise for this ratio as identified earlier in relation to defining the profit figure. Underlying operating profit is used.

$$2015 \quad \frac{782}{23,775}=3.3\% \qquad 2014 \quad \frac{879}{23,949}=3.7\%$$

Gross profit	$\dfrac{\text{Gross profit}}{\text{Revenue}}$

$$2015 \quad \frac{1,208}{23,775} = 5.1\% \qquad\qquad 2014 \quad \frac{1,387}{23,949} = 5.8\%$$

19.4.8 Liquidity

Current ratio	$\dfrac{\text{Current assets}}{\text{Current liabilities}}$

Liquid ratio	$\dfrac{\text{Current assets} - \text{inventories}}{\text{Current liabilities}}$

● These ratios assume that all current assets can be liquidated at their statement of financial position values in order to settle all current liabilities in a short time frame. Is this reasonable here?

Sainsbury's current assets include derivatives, which it may not be possible to liquidate immediately. The best way to judge liquidity is usually to study the cash flow statement. In the case of Sainsbury's, overall cash and cash equivalent balances decreased from £1,579 million to £1,276 million, a decrease of 19%, whereas in the previous year they increased by £1,075 million.

$$2015 \quad \text{Current} \quad \frac{4,505}{6,923} = 0.65 \qquad\qquad 2014 \quad \text{Current} \quad \frac{4,369}{6,765} = 0.65$$

$$2015 \quad \text{Liquid} \quad \frac{4,505 - 997}{6,923} = 0.51 \qquad\qquad 2014 \quad \text{Liquid} \quad \frac{4,369 - 1,005}{6,765} = 0.50$$

19.4.9 Management efficiency

● Should year-end or average inventories be used?

Year-end inventory may not be representative of usual inventory levels because of the time of year or the company deliberately running down inventories at the year end (to assist with inventory checks). Average inventory is a far better measure to use for this ratio; however, it is not available from the financial statements. The average of inventory at the beginning and end of the year may be better than just year-end inventory, but with only two years' worth of financial statements available, a comparative calculation for 2014 will not be possible.

$$2015 \quad \frac{997}{22,567} \times 365 = 16\,\text{days} \qquad 2014 \quad \frac{1,005}{22,562} \times 365 = 16\,\text{days}$$

Payables payment period	$\dfrac{\text{Trade payables}}{\text{Credit purchases}} \times 365$

- Care should be taken as to which payables figure is used. The figure on the face of the balance sheet includes trade payables, other payables (such as amounts owing for wages, VAT, employment taxes) and accruals. The ratio is giving users an indication of the time Sainsbury's takes to pay its suppliers for goods, hence only trade payables are relevant. The figure should be taken from the notes to the financial statements (note 19).

- Is credit purchases able to be derived?

  Credit purchases is not available from the financial statements. Provided opening and closing inventory levels are not significantly different, purchases may be able to be approximated by cost of sales. However, other direct costs will also be included in cost of sales, since administrative expenses per the income statement does not include all staff costs. Without knowing the allocation of expenses to the different line items in the income statement, the ratio, as calculated, is not completely representative of the length of time taken to pay suppliers.

$$2015 \quad \frac{2,089}{22,567} \times 365 = 34\,\text{days} \qquad 2014 \quad \frac{1,846}{22,562} \times 365 = 30\,\text{days}$$

Note that the receivables collection period has not been calculated as it is not significant for a retailer. Although there is a sizeable receivables figure on the face of the statement of financial position, and there are some trade receivables, the balance consists mainly of other receivables, and prepayments and accrued income.

19.4.10 Gearing

Gearing ratio	$\dfrac{\text{Debt}^{8\,\text{or}\,9}}{\text{Equity}}$

- The question of how debt is defined has been discussed previously in relation to capital employed. Borrowings from the face of the statement of financial position could be used or, alternatively, Sainsbury's provides its own definition and calculation of net debt.

8   Using current and non-current borrowings:

$$2015 \quad \frac{260+2,506}{5,539} = 49.9\% \qquad 2014 \quad \frac{534+2,250}{6,005} = 46.4\%$$

9   Using Sainsbury's definition of net debt:

$$2015 \quad \frac{2,343}{5,539} = 42.3\% \qquad\qquad 2014 \quad \frac{2,384}{6,005} = 39.7\%$$

Financial leverage	$\dfrac{\text{Total capital employed (net assets)}^{10}}{\text{Shareholders' funds}}$

- This ratio is intended to measure what proportion of Sainsbury's net assets is financed by equity and, by implication, what proportion by debt. It provides a measure of the exposure of the company to the risk of fixed return and fixed-term finance. However, is it reasonable to regard everything that is not equity as debt?
- Should all assets be included?

See earlier discussion relating to return on capital employed.

10 Using net assets as total assets minus current liabilities:

$$2015 \quad \frac{16,537-6,923}{5,539} = 1.74 \qquad\qquad 2014 \quad \frac{16,540-6,765}{6,005} = 1.63$$

Interest cover	$\dfrac{\text{Profit before interest and tax}^{11}}{\text{Interest (finance costs)}}$

11 PBIT has been taken from the income statement, i.e. including all one-off items and fair value movements, as this ratio is measuring the ability of the company to pay its finance expenses from its profit. Finance income has been added to PBIT.

$$2015 \quad \frac{81+19}{180} = 0.56 \qquad\qquad 2014 \quad \frac{1,009+20}{159} = 6.5$$

19.4.11 Cash flow

Ratios based on cash flows are calculated to aid in the interpretation of the overall financial results and particularly liquidity. These are the ratios discussed in Chapter 5.

Cash return on capital employed	$\dfrac{\text{Cash return}^{12}}{\text{Capital employed}^{13}}$

12 This is defined as: cash generated from operations + interest received + dividends received.

13 The definition used here is the one used in the second calculation of ROCE above.

$$2015 \quad \frac{1,136}{8,647}=13.1\% \qquad 2014 \quad \frac{1,227}{8,811}=13.9\%$$

Cash to profit from operations	$\dfrac{\text{Cash generated from operations}}{\text{Profit from operations}^{14}}$

14 Using underlying profit from operations.

$$2015 \quad \frac{1,136}{782}=1.45 \qquad 2014 \quad \frac{1,227}{879}=1.40$$

Liquidity	$\dfrac{\text{Cash generated from operations}}{\text{Current liabilities}}$

$$2015 \quad \frac{1,136}{6,923}=0.16 \qquad 2014 \quad \frac{1,227}{6,765}=0.18$$

Cash interest cover	$\dfrac{\text{Cash return}}{\text{Interest paid}}$

$$2015 \quad \frac{1,136}{180}=6.3 \qquad 2014 \quad \frac{1,227}{159}=7.7$$

Cash flow per share	$\dfrac{\text{Cash flow for equity shareholders}^{15}}{\text{No. of equity shares}^{16}}$

15 This is defined as: cash return – interest paid – tax paid.

16 Using the weighted average number of shares used in the EPS calculation.

$$2015 \quad \frac{1,136-134-91}{1,911.0}=0.48 \qquad 2014 \quad \frac{1,227-148-140}{1,896.8}=0.50$$

Cash dividend cover	$\dfrac{\text{Cash flow for equity shareholders}}{\text{Equity dividends paid}}$

$$2015 \quad \frac{911}{330}=2.8 \qquad 2014 \quad \frac{939}{320}=2.9$$

Free cash flow	Cash flow from operating activities – capital expenditure

$$2015 \quad 911-(951+78)=(118) \qquad 2014 \quad 939-(916+13)=10$$

19.4.12 Other KPIs

Sainsbury's includes two other KPIs in its annual report which are not included in any of the aforementioned figures:

Core retail capital expenditure

2015	£947 million	*2014*	£888 million

Operating cash flow

2015	£1,136 million	*2014*	£1,227 million

19.4.13 Segmental analysis

Sainsbury's operating segments are 'determined on information provided to the operating board to make operational decisions on the management of the group'. They are given as:

- retailing (supermarkets and convenience)
- financial services (Sainsbury's Bank)
- property investments (joint ventures with the British Land Company plc and Securities Group plc).

Their comparative sizes and importance to the company's operating performance are as follows:

	Retailing	*Financial services*	*Property investments*
	%	%	%
Assets	72	26	2
Revenue	99	1	–
Underlying profit before tax	89	9	2

Clearly, retailing is the dominant segment, although one-quarter of the company's assets relate to Sainsbury's Bank. This will have affected the ROCE and return on net assets ratios calculated above for the whole company.

Profit margin and return on assets ratios (using underlying profit before tax as the profit measure) for the different operating segments shows:

		Retailing		*Financial services*		*Property investments*	
Profit margin	*2015*	604/23,443	2.6%	62/332	18.7%	–	
	2014	758/23,921	3.2%	24/28	85.7%	–	
Return on assets	*2015*	604/11,916	5.1%	62/4,270	1.5%	15/351	4.3%
	2014	758/12,026	6.3%	24/4,113	0.6%	16/401	4.0%

Remember the ratios for the financial services segment for 2014 are not fully representative as Sainsbury's Bank was only fully consolidated a few weeks prior to the end of this financial year. However, the effect of the differences between the returns of these segments on the overall financial statements is minimal given the overwhelming size of the retailing segment.

19.4.14 Evaluation

Summary of ratios	2015	2014
Return on equity *	9.1%	10.4%
(Loss)/earnings per share—basic	(8.7)p	37.7p
Earnings per share—underlying basic *	26.4p	32.8p
Dividend per share	13.2p	17.3p
Dividend cover *	2.0	1.9
PE ratio *	9.8	10.2
Total shareholder returns	(18.3)%	(3.4)%
Return on capital employed (using equity and borrowings) *	9.4%	10.0%
Return on net assets *	9.0%	10.0%
Asset turnover (using net assets)	2.7	2.7
Underlying net profit margin *	3.3%	3.7%
Gross profit	5.1%	5.8%
Gearing (using Sainsbury's definition of net debt)	42.3%	39.7%
Financial leverage	1.74	1.63
Interest cover	0.56	6.5
Current ratio	0.65	0.65
Liquid ratio	0.51	0.50
Inventory holding period	16 days	16 days
Payables payment period	34 days	30 days
Cash return on capital employed	13.1%	13.9%
Cash/profit from operations	1.45	1.40
Cash liquidity	0.16	0.18
Cash interest cover	6.3	7.7
Cash flow per share	0.48	0.50
Cash dividend cover	2.8	2.9

* Using underlying profit figures

Evaluation

Sainsbury's overarching business is the supermarket retail business in which it sells groceries, clothing, general merchandise, petrol and financial services. Sainsbury's revenues, profits and returns to shareholders had been growing for the past few years to 2014, although the rate of growth had been slowing. This reflected the increasing pressure in the supermarket industry with changing consumer patterns and the growth of competition from discount stores. In 2015 revenues and underlying profits fell, with some profit figures back at 2012 levels, and this was despite continued expansion of store space. Falls in oil and therefore petrol prices over 2014–15 will also have contributed to the decline in sales revenue. However, Sainsbury's has recognised that growth in grocery retail will now come from its online services and convenience stores, and also from non-grocery products and Sainsbury's Bank business, which was fully acquired in 2014. Thus the company is reassessing its store pipeline, and future expansion will be in convenience stores and other shopping channels.

The company's strategic evaluation of its stores resulted in a significant one-off impairment charge and provision for onerous lease contracts of £628 million in 2015. This caused very large reductions in all reported profit figures, with a final loss before tax being reported. Due to the exceptional nature of these charges, further analysis using ratios has used profit figures from the underlying supermarket business, otherwise this will be hidden.

A more detailed evaluation of 2015 compared with 2014 follows.

Shareholders' perspective

As a shareholder looking for healthy returns and growth, 2015 was not a good year. Despite this, return on equity has only fallen by just over one percentage point. However this masks the large fall in underlying profits after tax which was mitigated by the reduction in equity of 7.7%. Given that there was minimal change in issued share capital, underlying basic earnings per share decreased by 20%. Due to the reported loss after tax, there is a basic loss per share as calculated in accordance with IAS 33.

Sainsbury's has decided that its dividend should be affordable and, in the context of the decreased profits, has cut it to 13.2p per share, a reduction of 24%. However the company states that it plans to maintain this at levels to give a dividend cover of 2.

Sainsbury's reduced revenues and profits are not unusual in this period, as all the large supermarkets have suffered similarly. Share prices in all the major supermarkets have fallen, so the decreases in Sainsbury's PE ratio and total shareholder returns, caused by the fall in the company's share price, should be set in this context.

Profitability

The return ratios (ROCE and RONA) are very similar and have decreased by only up to one percentage point in 2015 compared to 2014. However, as for ROE above, this hides the fact that underlying operating profit fell by 11% because there was also a reduction in capital. Whilst net debt remained similar over the two years, the value of equity reduced from the losses retained in 2015. An examination of the significant changes in net assets shows a reduction in non-current assets mainly from the impairment loss, increases in assets and liabilities relating to Sainsbury's Bank, a reduction in cash balances and an increase in trade and other payables. The reduction in cash balances is explained by the statement of cash flows. This shows a reduction in operating cash flows, which is partly caused by less cash flowing in from lower revenues, and loans made to Sainsbury's Bank customers. These are mitigated by increases in trade payables.

Investors and the company should be slightly encouraged by the operating profitability ratios, which, in a poor year, have only declined a little in 2015. Despite pressure on selling prices, Sainsbury has managed to keep costs of sales in line with these, resulting in a fall in gross profit margin of only 0.4 percentage points. The company's continuing programme of cost reductions and improvements has continued and the underlying net profit margin is only marginally lower than 2014.

Asset turnover has remained the same, meaning that the decreases in both revenues and net assets are proportionately the same. The fall in return on capital employed can therefore be seen to be caused by the reduction in profit margins.

Gearing

Although it appears that Sainsbury's gearing and exposure to debt has increased in 2015, the increase in the ratio has been caused by the reduction in equity. Net debt has actually marginally decreased. The company's definition of net debt has netted off cash and cash equivalent balances with its borrowings, and since cash has decreased significantly, this further indicates that borrowings have fallen. Although there have been changes in some borrowings—some repayments and new borrowings taken out—the overall debt financing position of the company has not materially changed.

The finance charges related to borrowings have fallen. Although the interest cover is less than one in 2015, this ratio has been calculated using reported profit before interest, in other words including the one-off impairment charge and other non-underlying business items. The company has sufficient operating cash flow to make the interest payments.

Liquidity

As with all supermarkets, Sainsbury's has net current liabilities, and current and liquid ratios well below 1. This does not necessarily indicate liquidity problems as cash pours into the retail outlets every day and Sainsbury's, like other large supermarkets, may require long payment terms from many of its suppliers. The liquidity ratios are the same in both 2015 and 2014, although there have been some changes in individual balances. Amounts due both from and to Sainsbury's Bank customers in current assets and current liabilities respectively have increased as this business grows, cash and cash equivalents have decreased, trade payables have increased and the current portion of long-term borrowings has decreased.

The inventory holding period is the same in 2015 and 2014, probably as one would expect. However, the payables payment period has increased as trade and other payables has increased. Has Sainsbury's negotiated longer credit periods with suppliers to manage cash flows from operating activities? Is the company deliberately taking longer to pay, or does it have different suppliers and/or contracts? The chief finance director, in his report, refers to this as 'operational efficiencies'.

The ratios based on cash flows all show small reductions confirming the decline in cash generated from operations, except for the ratio of cash flow to profit from operations. Despite the overall reduction in cash and free cash flow, these ratios do not indicate cash or liquidity issues.

Risks

Grocery retail is generally not a risky business sector, despite the changes in consumer behaviour and pressures for the large supermarkets of the past few years. Sainsbury's does not have significant risky investments. The company appears to have considered its principal risks and uncertainties and has adjusted its strategy accordingly as described previously. It was able to do this from a position of strong brand, broad customer base and financial stability.

Conclusion

- A relatively low-risk business which is having to adapt to significant changes in the market.

- Reduced financial performance from its core business, exacerbated by one-off financial accounting impairment losses, leading to overall losses.

- Large decreases in shareholder returns.

- Despite this, strength in the balance sheet maintained.

- Announcements of changes in future company strategy.

An investor only interested in the short term may consider the decreased financial performance in 2015 does not meet their requirements. However, Sainsbury's is a very successful company which has a sound financial base and an excellent track record of increased returns for shareholders year on year. The company's annual report appears to indicate that it is reacting to the changes in the industry and adapting its future strategy to take advantage of its areas of strength. It may, however, take time for results to return to 2014 levels. An investor looking for a company advocating sustainability issues should also note that Sainsbury's prides itself on its focus on its corporate responsibility commitments and claims they are at the heart of its policies and decision-making.

19.5 Industry statistics—use of databases

There are a number of databases which contain company and average industry sector financial ratios, such as FAME and DataStream. While these are undoubtedly very useful in the interpretation of the financial statements of companies, care should be exercised in the use of the ratios included therein. It is important to understand how the database has defined the ratios and also which figures have been used in their calculation. As can be seen from the discussion for Sainsbury's, there are alternative definitions and ways of calculating many ratios.

 ## Summary of key points

Interpretation of financial statements requires more than an analysis of financial data. This chapter has set out an approach which starts with a review of the external environment in which a company is operating, followed by a review of internal factors that may affect its financial performance and position. Interpretation can only be meaningful if set in these contexts.

The next stage in interpretation is to carry out an overview of the financial data through horizontal and trend analyses, taking into account one-off or exceptional items and events that could affect an individual year's figures. If the interpretation is using published annual reports of companies, this overview stage should also consider the effect of other significant information which is contained in the narrative reports.

The calculation and analysis of financial ratios are at the heart of any interpretation, but this should be directed towards the required interpretation for the particular user. To properly interpret ratios, the user must take into account the changes or differences in the individual figures that make up a ratio, the bases of valuation and any changes or differences in these, and the relationships between ratios. This interpretation should be set in the context of the information gathered from the review of the external and internal environments and the overview of the financial statements themselves.

 ## Further reading

Moon, P. and Bates, K. (1993) 'Core analysis in strategic performance appraisal', *Management Accounting Research*, 4, 139–152. Why read? This expands upon the approach to financial statement analysis taken in this chapter.

 ## Bibliography

J Sainsbury plc (2015) *Annual Report and Financial Statements, 2015*. London: J Sainsbury. [Reproduced by kind permission of Sainsbury's Supermarkets Ltd. The opinions expressed are those of the author.]

Moon, P. and Bates, K. (1993) Core analysis in strategic performance appraisal, *Management Accounting Research*, 4, 139–152.

 ## Questions

●●● Take it further

1   Pink plc and Goldie plc are competing companies operating UK mobile phone networks for personal and business customers. There is increased regulatory pressure on the pricing of mobile phone tariffs within the telecommunications industry and, with the strong competition between companies, this leads to competitive pricing structures.

Extracts from the annual reports of the two companies are as follows:

Statements of profit or loss for the latest financial years

	Pink	Goldie
	£m	£m
Revenue	2,695	5,220
Cost of sales	(1,595)	(2,990)
Gross profit	1,100	2,230
Selling and distribution costs (see note 1)	(190)	(430)
Administrative expenses	(150)	(290)
Impairment losses (see note 2)	(1,000)	–
(Loss)/profit from operations	(240)	1,510
Finance costs	(75)	(160)
(Loss)/profit before taxation	(315)	1,350
Tax	(195)	(460)
(Loss)/profit for the year	(510)	890

Final dividends of 6.5p per share (Pink) and 6.2p per share (Goldie) were disclosed in the financial statements.

Statements of financial position at the year ends

	Pink		Goldie	
	£m	£m	£m	£m
ASSETS				
Non-current assets				
Property, plant and equipment		1,600		3,060
Intangibles		4,615		10,780
		6,215		13,840
Current assets				
Inventories	15		30	
Trade receivables	460		990	
Cash and cash equivalents	620		450	
		1,095		1,470
Total assets		7,310		15,310
EQUITY & LIABILITIES				
Equity				
Issued capital—£1 equity shares		1,335		2,660

Share premium		2,600	5,180
Other reserves		270	470
Retained earnings		115	1,580
Shareholders' equity		4,320	9,890
Non-current liabilities			
Borrowings	2,060		4,070
Provisions	20		30
		2,080	4,100
Current liabilities			
Trade payables	565		700
Taxation and other liabilities	345		620
		910	1,320
Total equity and liabilities		7,310	15,310

Note 1

Pink plc spent £10 million in this financial year on new advertising and sports sponsorship to boost brand awareness.

Note 2

The impairment losses of £1,000 million included in the operating profit of Pink plc arise from a fall in the estimated fair values of the company's goodwill and other intangible assets, such as operating licences. The estimation of fair values is an issue involving significant management judgement.

Required:

Produce a report for a potential equity investor which compares the financial performance, financial position and liquidity of Pink plc and Goldie plc.

Your report should include:

● an overview of the financial information provided

● calculations of appropriate ratios

● an evaluation of the financial performance, financial position, and liquidity of the two companies in comparison with each other

● conclusions and recommendations for the potential investor, which should also include details of further information that you consider should be obtained to enhance the analysis.

2   Hawtons plc is a long established and well-known producer and retailer of luxury confectionery, specialising in chocolate. The company supplies its products through 379 shops and cafés, 250 franchises, plus Internet and mail order services. The annual report states that the company's long-term goals are:

● to re-establish Hawtons as the undisputed leading premium chocolate brand in the UK

● to increase its share of the UK chocolate market by more than 50%

● to increase all year round business to reduce dependency on Christmas and Easter

● to improve operating profit margins

● the selective development of export sales.

The statements of financial position, comprehensive income and cash flows for Hawtons are shown as follows:

Hawtons plc: statements of financial position at 30 June

	20X8 £000	20X7 £000
Non-current assets		
Intangible assets	4,786	5,950
Property, plant and equipment	64,084	66,378
	68,870	72,328
Current assets		
Inventories	24,307	18,202
Trade and other receivables	15,155	12,628
Cash and cash equivalents	1,088	2,858
	40,550	33,688
Total assets	109,420	106,016
Equity		
Ordinary shares	6,835	6,811
Share premium account	13,750	13,551
Retained earnings	14,450	14,524
	35,035	34,886
Non-current liabilities		
Borrowings	5,295	6,692
Deferred tax liabilities	2,750	2,512
Retirement benefit obligations	15,965	15,417
Other non-current liabilities	2,612	1,996
Provisions	586	478
	27,208	27,095
Current liabilities		
Borrowings	24,057	22,577
Trade and other payables	22,014	19,859
Tax payable	984	1,418
Provisions	122	181
	47,177	44,035
Total equity and liabilities	109,420	106,016

Hawtons plc: Statements of profit or loss for the years ended 30 June

	20X8 £000	20X7 £000
Revenue	208,122	185,989
Cost of sales	(103,017)	(86,022)
Gross profit	105,105	99,967
Operating expenses	(95,918)	(91,923)
Other operating income	1,139	808
Operating profit	10,326	8,852
Finance income	45	61
Finance costs	(1,901)	(1,832)
Profit before taxation	8,470	7,081
Taxation	(2,402)	(1,785)
Profit for the year	6,068	5,296
Earnings per share		
Basic	9.1p	8.0p
Diluted	9.0p	7.9p

Hawtons plc: statements of other comprehensive income and expense for the years ended 30 June

	20X8 £000	20X7 £000
Profit for the year	6,068	5,296
Other comprehensive income/expense		
Actuarial (loss)/gain in the defined benefit pension scheme	(2,148)	1,510
Movement of deferred tax on actuarial (loss)/gain in the defined benefit pension scheme	601	(453)
Effect of reduction in tax rate	–	(342)
Net other comprehensive (expense)/income	(1,547)	715
Total comprehensive income for the year	4,521	6,011

Hawtons plc: statements of cash flow for the years ended 30 June

	20X8	20X7
	£000	£000
Cash flows from operating activities	11,481	14,600
Cash flows from investing activities		
Proceeds from sale of property, plant and equipment	262	400
Purchase of property, plant and equipment	(5,680)	(5,030)
Net cash used in investing activities	(5,418)	(4,630)
Cash flows from financing activities		
Net proceeds from issue of ordinary shares	223	748
Interest paid	(1,831)	(1,849)
Interest received	37	25
Capital element of finance lease rental payments	(3,712)	(4,526)
Borrowings advanced	2,000	3,000
Dividends paid	(4,550)	(4,512)
Net cash used in financing activities	(7,833)	(7,114)
Net (decrease)/increase in cash and cash equivalents and bank overdrafts	(1,770)	2,856
Cash and cash equivalents at beginning of period	2,858	2
Cash and cash equivalents at end of period	1,088	2,858

Notes to the financial statements

(i)   The intangible assets of the company are pieces of computer software, some of which have been acquired externally and some of which were generated internally. The amortisation charge for these assets, which amounted to £2.018 m in 20X8 and £1.973 m in 20X7, is recognised in cost of sales within the statements of profit or loss.

(ii) The dividends paid by the company were a 1.95p per share interim dividend and a 4.85p final dividend in both years.

(iii) The mid-market price of the ordinary shares at 29 June 20X7 (the last dealing day prior to 30 June 20X7) was 175p and at 27 June 20X8 (the last dealing day prior to 28 June 20X8) was 114p. The range for the period was from 112p to 200p.

(iv) The number of shares in issue was 6.835m at 30 June 20X8 and 6.811m at 30 June 20X7.

Required:

You are considering including Hawtons plc in your investment portfolio. Analyse the performance of the company during the two years 20X8 and 20X7 and assess whether it is likely to be a worthwhile investment.

3   Obtain the 2015 Annual Report and Accounts for Next plc, which are available from www.nextplc.co.uk.

Required:

Using the analysis of the financial performance of Next plc as completed for Question 9 in Chapter 6, which used the company's segmental information, carry out a full interpretation of Next plc's financial statements for the year ended 24 January 2015.

4   Obtain the most recent financial statements of two companies operating in the same business sector. Carry out a comparative analysis of the two companies' financial statements, paying particular attention to the effect of any significant differences in the companies' recognition and measurement policies.

Case Study: To assist with your understanding of the Case Study in Chapter 19, extracts from the main financial statements of Sainsbury's *Annual Report and Financial Statements, 2015* are reproduced here.

Financial reporting in practice 19.1 — J Sainsbury plc, 2015

Group income statement for the 52 weeks to 14 March 2015

	Note	2015 £m	2014 £m
Revenue	4	23,775	23,949
Cost of sales		(22,567)	(22,562)
Gross profit		1,208	1,387
Administrative expenses		(1,132)	(444)
Other income		5	66
Operating profit	5	81	1,009
Finance income	6	19	20
Finance costs	6	(180)	(159)
Share of post-tax profit from joint ventures and associates	14	8	28
(Loss)/profit before tax		(72)	898
Analysed as:			
Underlying profit before tax		681	798
Profit on disposal of properties	3	7	52
Investment property fair value movements	3	7	–
Retail financing fair value movements	3	(30)	(8)
IAS 19 pension financing charge	3	(31)	(23)
Defined benefit pension scheme expenses	3	(6)	(7)
Acquisition adjustments	3	13	18
One-off items	3	(713)	68

		(72)	898
Income tax expense	8	**(94)**	(182)
(Loss)/profit for the financial year		**(166)**	716
(Loss)/earnings per share	9	**pence**	pence
Basic		**(8.7)**	37.7
Diluted		**(8.7)**	36.9
Underlying basic		**26.4**	32.8
Underlying diluted		**25.7**	32.2

Group statement of comprehensive income for the 52 weeks to 14 March 2015

	Note	2015 £m	2014 £m
(Loss)/profit for the period		**(166)**	716
Items that will not be reclassified subsequently to the income statement			
Remeasurements on defined benefit pension scheme	30b	**(19)**	(326)
Current tax relating to items not reclassified	8	**6**	34
Deferred tax relating to items not reclassified	8	**(1)**	19
		(14)	(273)
Items that may be reclassified subsequently to the income statement			
Currency translation differences	24	**3**	(2)
Available-for-sale financial assets fair value movements			
Group		**(39)**	34
Items reclassified from available-for-sale assets reserve	24	**1**	–
Cash flow hedges effective portion of fair value movements:			
Group	24	**(13)**	(43)
Joint ventures and associates	24	**3**	2
Items reclassified from cash flow hedge reserve	24	**21**	4
Current tax relating to items that may be reclassified	8	**–**	(1)
Deferred tax relating to items that may be reclassified	8	**9**	(2)
		(15)	(8)
Total other comprehensive loss for the financial year (net of tax)		**(29)**	(281)
Total comprehensive (loss)/income for the financial year		**(195)**	435

(continued)

(continued)

Group balance sheets at 14 March 2015 and 15 March 2014

	Note	2015 £m	2014 £m
Non-current assets			
Property, plant and equipment	11	9,648	9,880
Intangible assets	12	325	286
Investments in joint ventures and associates	14	359	404
Available-for-sale financial assets	15	184	255
Other receivables	17a	83	26
Amounts due from Sainsbury's Bank customers	17b	1,412	1,292
Derivative financial instruments	29	21	28
		12,032	12,171
Current assets			
Inventories	16	997	1,005
Trade and other receivables	17a	471	433
Amounts due from Sainsbury's Bank customers	17b	1,599	1,283
Derivative financial instruments	29	69	49
Cash and cash equivalents	26b	1,285	1,592
		4,421	4,362
Non-current assets held for sale	18	84	7
		4,505	4,369
Total assets		16,537	16,540
Current liabilities			
Trade and other payables	19a	(2,961)	(2,692)
Amounts due to Sainsbury's Bank customers and banks	19b	(3,395)	(3,245)
Borrowings	20	(260)	(534)
Derivative financial instruments	29	(75)	(65)
Taxes payable		(188)	(189)
Provisions	22	(44)	(40)
		(6,923)	(6,765)
Net current liabilities		(2,418)	(2,396)

Non-current liabilities

Other payables	19a	**(265)**	(204)
Amounts due to Sainsbury's Bank customers and banks	19b	**(266)**	(302)
Borrowings	20	**(2,506)**	(2,250)
Derivative financial instruments	29	**(38)**	(21)
Deferred income tax liability	21	**(215)**	(227)
Provisions	22	**(77)**	(29)
Retirement benefit obligations	30	**(708)**	(737)
		(4,075)	(3,770)
Net assets		**5,539**	6,005
Equity			
Called up share capital	23	**548**	545
Share premium account	23	**1,108**	1,091
Capital redemption reserve	24	**680**	680
Other reserves	24	**146**	127
Retained earnings	25	**3,057**	3,560
Equity attributable to owners of parent		**5,539**	6,003
Non-controlling interests		**-**	2
Total equity		**5,539**	6,005

Group cash flow statement for the 52 weeks to 14 March 2015

		2015	2014
	Note	£m	£m
Cash flows from operating activities			
Cash generated from operations	26a	**1,136**	1,227
Interest paid		**(134)**	(148)
Corporation tax paid		**(91)**	(140)
Net cash generated from operating activities		**911**	939
Cash flows from investing activities			
Purchase of property, plant and equipment		**(951)**	(916)
Purchase of intangible assets		**(78)**	(13)
Proceeds from disposal of property, plant and equipment		**40**	335

(continued)

(continued)

Acquisition of subsidiaries, net of cash acquired		**(6)**	1,016
Investment in joint ventures		**(12)**	(13)
Proceeds from repayment of loan to joint venture		**17**	4
Interest received		**20**	20
Dividends and distributions received		**70**	–
Net cash (used in)/generated from investing activities		**(900)**	426
Cash flows from financing activities			
Proceeds from issuance of ordinary shares		**19**	19
Proceeds from short-term borrowings		**–**	200
Repayment of short-term borrowings		**(381)**	(200)
Proceeds from long-term borrowings		**674**	250
Repayment of long-term borrowings		**(240)**	(206)
Purchase of own shares		**(18)**	–
Repayment of capital element of obligations under finance lease payments		**(29)**	(25)
Interest elements of obligations under finance lease payments		**(9)**	(8)
Dividends paid	10	**(330)**	(320)
Net cash used in financing activities		**(314)**	(290)
Net (decrease)/increase in cash and cash equivalents		**(303)**	1,075
Opening cash and cash equivalents		**1,579**	504
Closing cash and cash equivalents	26b	**1,276**	1,579

Visit the Online Resource Centre for solutions to all these end of chapter questions plus visual walkthrough solutions. You can test your understanding with extra questions and answers, explore additional case studies based on real companies, take a guided tour through a company report and much more. Go to the Online Resource Centre at **www.oxfordtextbooks.co.uk/orc/maynard2e/**

TERMINOLOGY CONVERTER

Term used in this book	Equivalent terms	Explanatory note
Statement of financial position	Balance sheet	The term statement of financial position is the one used by international accounting standards, but IAS 1 does permit entities to use the alternative name, balance sheet.
Statement of comprehensive income	Statement of profit or loss and other comprehensive income	The latest name for this statement is the statement of profit or loss and other comprehensive income. IAS 1 does permit entities to use the alternative name, statement of comprehensive income.
Statement of profit or loss	Income statement Profit and loss account	The term statement of profit or loss is the one used in IAS 1 for companies that choose to present this as a separate statement, but IAS 1 does permit entities to use alternative names. Most UK listed companies use income statement.
Statement of cash flows	Cash flow statement	A minor change to the IAS 1 name. IAS 1 does permit the alternative cash flow statement.
Property, plant and equipment	Tangible fixed assets	
Carrying amount	Book value	
Equity shares	Ordinary shares	
Nominal value	Par value	
Liquid ratio	Acid test ratio, or Quick ratio	
Nominal ledger	General ledger	Alternative terms widely used.
Inventories	Stock	
Receivables	Debtors	
Payables	Creditors	
Irrecoverable debt	Bad debt	
Allowance for irrecoverable debts	Allowance for doubtful debts	
Revenue	Turnover	

GLOSSARY

Accounting policies The specific principles, bases, conventions, rules and practices applied by an entity in preparing and presenting financial statements.

Accounting standards/Financial reporting standards Generic term to describe authoritative statements issued by independent standard-setting bodies detailing how transactions and other events should be reflected in the financial statements. (See Financial Reporting Standards and International Financial Reporting Standards.)

Accrual accounting/accruals principle The effects of transactions and other events and circumstances on a business's economic resources and claims are accounted for in the periods in which those effects occur, even if the resulting cash receipts and payments occur in a different period.

Accumulating compensated absences Compensated absences by an employee that are carried forward and can be used in future periods if the current period's entitlement is not used in full.

Acquisition method The method of accounting used to account for the acquisition of subsidiaries by an investor company.

Active market A market in which all the following conditions exist: (a) the items traded in the market are homogeneous; (b) willing buyers and sellers can normally be found at any time; and (c) prices are available to the public.

Actuarial assumptions The unbiased best estimates of the demographic and financial variables that will determine the ultimate cost of providing pension benefits.

Actuarial gains and losses Changes in the present value of a defined benefit plan obligation resulting from (a) experience adjustments (the effects of differences between the previous actuarial assumptions and what has actually occurred); and (b) the effects of changes in actuarial assumptions.

Actuarial valuation A full financial review of a defined benefit pension fund conducted by an actuary. The fund's assets are valued and the liabilities measured using actuarial

assumptions. All defined benefit pension schemes are required to have a full actuarial valuation every three years.

Actuary A business professional who deals with the measurement and management of risk and uncertainty. Actuaries work in the health, pensions and insurance industries amongst others.

Amortisation The term used for depreciation of intangible assets. (See depreciation.)

Amortised cost A method of measurement for financial assets and financial liabilities. It uses the effective interest method. (See Effective interest method.)

Asset A present economic resource controlled by the entity as a result of past events. An economic resource is a right that has the potential to produce economic benefits. Assets are classified as non-current (held for long-term use) or current (continuously changing as business is conducted).

Asset ceiling A cap on the amount a defined benefit plan, which is in surplus, can be recognised in the statement of financial position. It is the present value of any economic benefits available in the form of refunds from the plan or reductions in future contributions to the plan.

Associate A company over which its investor company can demonstrate significant influence. This is usually evidenced by a shareholding of 20–50% of its equity shares.

Association of Chartered Certified Accountants (ACCA) A global professional accountancy body offering a professional accountancy qualification. A member of the Consultative Committee of Accountancy Bodies.

Asymmetric prudence Losses are recognised at an earlier stage than gains are recognised. (See Prudence.)

Audit An examination of the financial and other related statements of a company by an independent member of a Recognised Supervisory Body in order to express an opinion whether the statements are prepared, in all material respects, in accordance with an applicable financial reporting framework.

Authorised share capital The maximum share capital a company may issue as detailed in its Memorandum of Association.

Basic earnings per share (EPS) Profit or loss attributable to equity shareholders (i.e. profit or loss after tax and after preference dividends) divided by the number of equity shares outstanding during the period.

Breakage (relating to a contract with a customer) The contractual rights under a contract not exercised by the customer.

Call option (a type of repurchase agreement) The entity has a right to repurchase the asset. (See Repurchase agreement.)

Capital The residual interest in the assets of an entity after deducting all its liabilities. It represents the owners' investment in the entity.

Carrying amount The value of an asset or liability recognised in the financial statements.

Cash and cash equivalents The term used for bank and cash balances in a statement of financial position. Cash is cash on hand and demand deposits. Cash equivalents are short-term, highly liquid investments that are readily convertible to known amounts of cash and which are subject to an insignificant risk of changes in value.

Cash-generating unit The smallest identifiable group of assets that generates cash inflows which are largely independent of cash inflows from other assets or groups of assets.

Cash-in-transit A payment by one entity to another at the financial year end which has been recorded as cash out by the paying entity, but which has not been recorded as cash in by the receiving entity.

Cash-settled share-based payment transaction The entity receives goods or services in exchange for amounts of cash that are based on the price or value of the entity's shares or other equity instruments. (See Share-based payment transaction.)

Cautious prudence (See Prudence.)

Chartered Institute of Management Accountants (CIMA) A global professional accountancy body offering a professional accountancy qualification especially for management accountants.

Close family member Those family members who may be expected to influence, or be influenced by, that person in their dealings with the entity and include: (a) that person's children and spouse or domestic partner; (b) children of that person's spouse or domestic partner; and (c) dependants of that person or that person's spouse or domestic partner. (See Related party.)

Company An entity with a separate legal identity from the owners, where the owners' liability is limited to the amount they have invested. Ownership is evidenced by the holding of shares in the limited liability company.

Comparable information An enhancing qualitative characteristic of financial information. Information is more useful if it can be compared from year to year and from business to business.

Component of an entity Operations and cash flows that can be clearly distinguished, operationally and for financial reporting purposes, from the rest of the entity.

Compound financial instrument A financial instrument that, from the issuer's perspective, contains both a liability and an equity element.

Conduct Committee A committee of the FRC, one role of which is to ensure that the provision of financial information by public and large private companies complies with relevant reporting requirements. It does this through the Corporate Reporting Review Committee which enquires into cases where it appears that the requirements, primarily CA 2006 requirements, have not been followed. This sub-committee calls on the Financial Reporting Review Panel to assist in this work. (See Financial Reporting Council (FRC) and Financial Reporting Review Panel (FRRP).)

Consolidated financial statements The financial statements of a parent and its subsidiaries presented as those of a single economic entity.

Construction contract A contract negotiated specifically for the construction of an asset or a combination of assets that are closely interrelated or interdependent in terms of their design, technology and function, or their ultimate purpose or use. Contracts often last for more than one year.

Constructive obligation An obligation that exists because of an established pattern of past actions by an entity or published policies, and as a result the entity has created a valid expectation that it will discharge the obligation.

Contingent asset A possible asset that arises from past events and whose existence will be confirmed only by the occurrence or non-occurrence of one or more uncertain future events not wholly within the control of the entity.

Contingent liability A possible obligation that is not recognised in the statement of financial position because of uncertainties surrounding its existence or measurement.

Contingent rent Payments under an IAS 17 finance lease agreement that are not fixed in amount, but are based on some factor which may change other than the passage of time.

Control The ability to direct the use of and obtain substantially all of the benefits from the economic resource and prevent other parties from doing so.

Control (of an entity) The power to govern the financial and operating policies of an entity, together with exposure or rights to variable returns from the entity, together with the ability to influence the returns.

Credit risk The risk that one party to a financial instrument will cause a financial loss for the other party by failing to discharge an obligation.

Creditor UK GAAP term for account payable. A creditor is a third party to whom an entity has an outstanding obligation.

Currency risk The risk that the fair value or future cash flows of a financial instrument will fluctuate because of changes in foreign exchange rates.

Current service cost The increase in the present value of a defined benefit plan's obligation resulting from employees' service in the current year.

Current tax The amount of income taxes payable or recoverable in respect of the taxable profit (taxable loss) for an accounting period.

Current value A measurement base for assets and liabilities which uses information that is updated to reflect conditions at the measurement date. The base includes fair value or value in use for assets and fulfilment value for liabilities. (See Fair value, Value in use and Fulfilment value.)

Curtailment A reduction in the number of employees covered by a defined benefit plan.

Debit and credit The type of bookkeeping entry made to an account or the nature of the balance on an account at the end of an accounting period.

Decision-usefulness The principal objective of financial accounting and reporting advocated by the IASB, which is to provide financial information about the reporting entity that is useful to existing and potential investors, lenders and other creditors in making decisions about providing resources to the entity.

Debtor The UK GAAP term for account receivable. A debtor is a third party from whom resources are receivable.

Deferred tax An accounting measure representing income taxes payable or recoverable in the future relating to transactions which have already taken place.

Defined benefit plan Retirement benefit plan other than a defined contribution plan. The amount of pension paid to the former employees is guaranteed and determined by the employees' lengths of service and salary levels.

Defined contribution plan Retirement benefit plan under which an entity pays fixed contributions into a fund. It has no legal or constructive obligation to pay further contributions or direct benefit payments to employees if the fund does not hold sufficient assets to pay all employee benefits relating to the employee service in the current and past periods.

Depreciable amount The cost of an asset, or other amount substituted for cost, less its residual value.

Depreciation The systematic allocation of the depreciable amount of an asset over its useful life.

Derecognition The removal of a previously recognised asset or liability from an entity's statement of financial position.

Derivative A financial instrument or other contract with all three of the following characteristics: (a) its value changes in response to the change in the underlying (such as a specified interest rate, financial instrument price, commodity price, foreign exchange rate or other variable); (b) it requires no initial net investment or an initial net investment that is smaller than would be required for other types of contracts that would be expected to have a similar reaction to changes in market factors; and (c) it is settled at a future date. (See Underlying.)

Development The application of research findings or other knowledge to a plan or design for the production of new or substantially improved materials, devices, products, processes, systems or services before the start of commercial production or use.

Diluted earnings per share (EPS) An alternative EPS ratio using figures which assume that convertible instruments are converted, that options or warrants are exercised, or that equity shares are issued upon the satisfaction of specified conditions.

Directors The individuals appointed by the shareholders to run and manage a company.

Discontinued operation A component of an entity that either has been disposed of or is classified as held for sale and (a) represents a separate major line of business or geographical area of operations; (b) is part of a single co-ordinated plan to dispose of a separate major line of business or geographical area of operations; or (c) is a subsidiary acquired exclusively with a view to resale.

Disposal group A group of assets to be disposed of together in a single transaction, together with the liabilities directly associated with those assets that will be transferred in the transaction. The group includes goodwill arising on acquisition if the group is a cash-generating unit to which goodwill has been allocated. (See Cash-generating unit and Goodwill arising on acquisition.)

Distributable profits A company's accumulated, realised profits (which have not previously been distributed or capitalised) less its accumulated, realised losses (which have not previously been written off in a reduction or reorganisation of its share capital), and which are available for a distribution, such as a dividend, to shareholders. Generally distributable profits comprise revenue reserves.

Dividends A distribution to shareholders as a return to them for their investment in the company. Dividends may be interim, which are paid part way through the financial year, or final (also called proposed dividends), which are proposed by the directors after the end of the financial year and paid during the following year.

Double-entry bookkeeping The method used to record financial transactions in a financial accounting system. Every transaction has an effect on two (or more) accounts and is recorded so that the total of account(s) debited equals the total of account(s) credited. This ensures the balance of the statement of financial position.

Downstream and upstream sales Sales of items from a parent company to its subsidiary companies (downstream) or from the subsidiary companies to the parent (upstream).

Economic resource A right that has the potential to produce economic benefits.

Effective interest method The method used to apportion payments made by entities with financial liabilities measured at amortised cost, lessees under IAS 17 finance leases and all leases under IFRS 16 between the finance charge and the reduction of the outstanding liability so as to produce a constant periodic rate of interest on the remaining balance of the liability. The method is also used to apportion amounts received by holders of financial assets measured at amortised cost between the finance income and the reduction of the principal sum. (See Amortised cost.)

Elements Assets, liabilities, equity, income and expenses—the building blocks of financial statements. All financial transactions are expressed as changes to one or more of these items.

Employee benefits All forms of consideration given by an entity in exchange for services rendered by an employees.

Endorsement by the European Commission New financial reporting standards or amendments to standards issued by the IASB cannot be applied by companies listing on EU stock markets until they have been adopted by the EU.

Enhancing qualitative characteristics Characteristics that will improve the usefulness of relevant and faithfully represented financial information. The enhancing characteristics are comparability, verifiability, timeliness and understandability.

Equity The term for capital for a company comprising share capital and reserves. Equity is the residual interest in the assets of the entity after deducting all its liabilities.

Equity instrument Any contract that results in a residual interest in the assets of an entity after deducting all of its liabilities.

Equity method of accounting The method of accounting used by an investor company to include its share of and associate's or a joint venture's profits or losses.

Equity-settled share-based payment transaction The entity receives goods or services in exchange for equity instruments of the entity which could be shares or share options. (See Share-based payment transaction.)

Equity shares Shares that are not preference shares and do not have any predetermined dividend amounts. An equity share entitles the owner to a vote in matters put before shareholders in proportion to their percentage ownership in the company.

Exceptional items Financial transactions or items which are unusual owing to their nature or their size, and which an entity may wish to present separately in its financial statements.

Executive director A managing director involved in the day-to-day operation of a company. The role also includes designing, developing and implementing strategic plans.

Expectations gap The lack of understanding by a user of an assurance report (such as an audit report) of the assurances actually being provided or the work done in making the assurances.

Expenses Decreases in assets or increases in liabilities that result in decreases in equity, other than those relating to distributions to holders of equity claims.

Fair value The price that would be received to sell an asset or paid to transfer a liability in an orderly transaction between market participants at the measurement date.

Faithfully representative information A fundamental qualitative characteristic of information. Faithfully representative information should be as complete as possible, neutral and free from error.

Finance lease A type of lease defined by IAS 17 that transfers substantially all the risks and rewards incidental to ownership of an asset.

Financial Accounting Standards Board (FASB) The accounting standard-setting body in the USA. Accounting standards issued by the FASB are applicable to all US non-governmental entities. The standards are officially recognised as authoritative by the Securities and Exchange Commission (SEC).

Financial asset Cash; or an equity instrument in another entity; or any other asset that gives a contractual right to receive cash or another financial asset from another entity, or to exchange financial assets or financial liabilities with another entity under conditions that are potentially favourable to the entity.

Financial Conduct Authority (FCA) An independent body that regulates financial firms providing services to consumers and maintains the integrity of the UK's financial markets. It has a wide range of rule-making, investigatory and enforcement powers.

Financial instrument Any contract that gives rise to a financial asset of one entity and a financial liability or equity instrument of another entity.

Financial liability Any liability that is a contractual obligation to deliver cash or another financial asset to another entity, or to exchange financial assets or financial liabilities with another entity under conditions that are potentially unfavourable to the entity.

Financial Reporting Council (FRC) The UK's independent audit regulator responsible for audit quality in the UK and contributing to the international debate on the future of the audit market. In June 2016 it became the 'competent authority' for audit in the UK under new legislation following the implementation of the EU Audit Regulation and Directive. The FRC promotes high quality corporate governance and reporting by issuing financial reporting standards for use by non-public companies in the UK and corporate governance and stewardship codes. It has responsibilities for monitoring and enforcing these financial reporting and auditing standards. It also oversees the regulatory activities of the professional accountancy bodies and operates independent disciplinary arrangements for public interest cases involving accountants. (See Conduct Committee and Financial Reporting Review Panel (FRRP).)

Financial Reporting Review Panel (FRRP) A body of individuals drawn from commerce and the accountancy professions who are called on by the FRC's Conduct Committee to carry out reviews of public and large listed company reports and accounts. (See Conduct Committee.)

Financial Reporting Standards (FRSs) Accounting standards for use by UK non-listed companies issued by the UK's Financial Reporting Council (FRC).

First-in, first-out (FIFO) A method of valuing inventory which assumes that oldest inventories are used or sold first, thus leaving the newest inventories on hand.

Forward contract (a type of repurchase agreement) The entity has an obligation to repurchase the asset. (See Repurchase agreement.)

Fulfilment value The present value of the cash flows that an entity expects to incur as it fulfils a liability.

Fundamental qualitative characteristics Qualitative characteristics which make financial information useful to users. The fundamental characteristics are relevance and faithful representation.

Gains Increases in economic benefits that meet the definition of income, but are not revenue. (See Income and Revenue.)

Generally accepted accounting principles (GAAP) The standard framework of accounting guidelines used in any given jurisdiction. It includes statutory requirements, mandatory guidelines, such as accounting standards, and underpinning principles.

Going concern An underlying assumption of financial statements. It assumes the reporting entity will continue in operation for the foreseeable future and that it has neither the intention nor the need to liquidate or cease trading. If such an intention or need exists, the financial statements may have to be prepared on a different basis which is disclosed in the financial statements.

Goodwill Intangible items that are not recognised in an entity's financial statements and which contribute to the value of an entity as a whole being greater than the carrying amounts of its net assets.

Goodwill arising on acquisition The only goodwill recognised in financial statements, and only in consolidated financial statements. It is an asset representing the future economic benefits arising from other assets acquired in a business combination that are not individually identified and separately recognised.

Grant date The date at which the entity and the other party agree to the share-based payment arrangement.

Group A parent company and all its subsidiaries.

Guaranteed residual value The value, guaranteed by the lessee, of a leased asset at the end of the lease term.

Hedging instrument A financial instrument used to minimise the risks of changes in expected fair values or future cash flows of financial transactions and items.

Historic cost A measurement basis for assets and liabilities. It uses the amount of cash paid or the fair value of the consideration given to acquire an asset at its acquisition, or the amount of proceeds received in exchange for an obligation, or the amounts of cash or cash equivalents expected to be paid to satisfy a liability.

Horizontal analysis An analytical technique involving the calculation and comparison of changes in line items in the financial statements over successive years.

Impairment loss The amount by which the carrying amount of an asset or a cash generating unit exceeds its recoverable amount. (See Recoverable amount.)

Income Increases in economic benefits in the form of inflows or increases of assets or decreases of liabilities that result in an increase in equity, other than those relating to contributions from equity shareholders.

Income tax All domestic and foreign taxes that are based on taxable profits.

Input methods For long-term contracts with customers, methods used to measure the progress towards the performance obligation on the basis of the selling company's efforts.

Institute of Chartered Accountants in England and Wales (ICAEW) A professional accountancy body providing financial knowledge and guidance to the global accountancy and finance profession. The body offers a professional accountancy qualification, the ACA. A member of the Consultative Committee of Accountancy Bodies.

Intangible asset An identifiable non-monetary asset without physical substance.

Interest rate implicit in the lease (imputed interest rate) The discount rate that, at the inception of a lease, causes the aggregate present value of (a) the minimum lease payments and (b) the unguaranteed residual value to be equal to the sum of (i) the fair value of the leased asset and (ii) any initial direct costs of the lessor.

Interest rate risk The risk that the fair value or future cash flows of a financial instrument will fluctuate because of changes in market interest rates.

International Accounting Standards (IASs) Accounting standards that were issued by the International Accounting Standards Committee (IASC), the predecessor of the IASB, and which were adopted by the IASB upon its formation.

International Accounting Standards Board (IASB) The independent international body with responsibility for setting international financial reporting standards.

International Ethics Standards Board for Accountants (IESBA) An independent standard-setting board, facilitated by IFAC, that develops and issues, in the public interest, high-quality ethical standards and other pronouncements for professional accountants worldwide. Through its activities, the IESBA develops the *Code of Ethics for Professional Accountants*, which establishes ethical requirements for professional accountants. (See IFAC)

International Federation of Accountants (IFAC) A New York-based global organisation for the accountancy profession which develops and promotes international standards in the areas of auditing and assurance, quality control, ethics, accounting education, and public sector accounting, and has as members national accountancy organisations.

International Financial Reporting Standards (IFRSs) Accounting standards issued by the International Accounting Standards Board since its formation.

Inventories Assets held for sale in the ordinary course of business; or in the process of production for such sale; or in the form of materials or supplies to be consumed in the production process or in the rendering of services.

Investment property Property held by the owner or by the lessee under a finance lease to earn rentals or for capital appreciation or both.

Irredeemable preference shares Preference shares which cannot be redeemed during the lifetime of the company.

Joint arrangement An arrangement, usually in connection with two or more parties working together to invest in a business venture, of which the parties have joint control. Joint arrangements can be joint operations or joint ventures.

Joint control The contractually agreed sharing of control of an arrangement, which exists only when decisions about the relevant activities require the unanimous consent of the parties sharing control.

Joint operation A joint arrangement whereby the parties that have joint control of the arrangement have rights to the assets, and obligations for the liabilities, relating to the arrangement.

Joint venture A joint arrangement whereby the parties that have joint control of the arrangement have rights to the net assets of the arrangement.

Lease An agreement whereby a lessor conveys to a lessee in return for a payment or series of payments the right to use an asset for an agreed period of time.

Lease rentals A term used in IFRS 16 to represent payments made by a lessee that are unavoidable. It includes all fixed payments, variable payments which are based on an index or rate, amounts expected to be payable under residual value guarantees and the price of a purchase option that the lessee is reasonably certain to exercise.

Liability A present obligation of the entity to transfer an economic resource as a result of past events. Liabilities are classified as current (due for settlement within one year of the date of the statement of financial position) and non-current (due after one year). (See Economic resource.)

Liquidity The ability of an entity to meet its debts as they fall due.

Liquidity risk The risk that an entity will encounter difficulty in meeting obligations associated with financial liabilities that are settled by delivering cash or another financial asset.

Market-based condition A performance condition linked to the market price of the shares in some way. (See Performance condition.)

Market risk The risk that the fair value or future cash flows of a financial instrument will fluctuate because of changes in market prices. Market risk comprises three types of risk: currency risk, interest rate risk and other price risk. (See Currency risk, Interest rate risk and Other price risk.)

Market-to-book ratio A ratio comparing the market value of a company (no. of shares × market price per share) to its book value (total assets minus total liabilities).

Market value The price at which an asset would trade in a competitive auction setting such as on a stock market.

Materiality An aspect of relevance that relates to the nature or size or both of information. Information is material if its omission or misstatement influences the decision made by a user.

Measurement The valuation of an item.

Minimum lease payments A term used in IAS 17 to mean the payments over the lease term that the lessee is required to make, excluding contingent rent, costs for services and taxes to be paid by and reimbursed to the lessor. (See Contingent rent.)

Modification (of a lease under IFRS 16) Changes in the scope or the consideration of a lease to introduce different terms and conditions.

National Insurance A system of contributions paid by employees and employers in the UK towards the cost of certain state benefits. It is an employment tax.

Net book value The cost of an asset, or other amount substituted for cost, minus its accumulated depreciation or amortisation.

Net realisable value The estimated selling price of an asset in the ordinary course of business less the estimated costs of completion and the estimated costs necessary to make the sale.

Nominal ledger Part of the financial accounting system which comprises all the accounts of the entity in which are recorded all the individual financial transactions.

Nominal value The unit value of a share which is determined when a company is first formed. Also called the par value.

Non-accumulating compensated absences Compensated absences by an employee that are not able to be carried forward to future periods if the current period's entitlement is not used in full.

Non-controlling interest The ownership interest in a subsidiary not attributable, directly or indirectly, to the parent company which controls the subsidiary.

Non-executive director A member of the board of directors of a company who does not form part of the executive management team. A non-executive director acts in an advisory capacity, typically attending board meetings to offer their advice and serving on sub-committees such as the audit committee and remuneration committee. He or she is not an employee of the company but does have the same legal duties, responsibilities and potential liabilities as executive directors, and is usually paid a fee for their services. (See Executive director.)

Non-market-based condition A performance condition not connected to the market price of the entity's shares. (See Performance condition.)

Off balance sheet financing The practice by which transactions involving debt are structured to ensure that their accounting treatment is in line with current accounting practice but the debt is kept off the statement of financial position.

Onerous contract A contract under which the unavoidable costs of meeting the obligations exceed the economic benefits expected to be received.

Operating lease Under IAS 17 this is any lease other than a finance lease.

Operating segment An operating segment is a component of an entity: (a) that engages in business activities from which it may earn revenues and incur expenses; and (b) whose operating results are regularly reviewed by the entity's chief operating decision maker to make decisions about resources to be allocated to the segment and assess its performance; and (c) for which discrete financial information is available.

Ordinary shares See Equity shares.

Other comprehensive income Items of income and expense that are not recognised in profit and loss (i.e. in the statement of profit or loss), as required or permitted by IFRSs, are included in the statement of comprehensive income.

Other price risk The risk that the fair value or future cash flows of a financial instrument will fluctuate because of changes in market prices (other than those arising from interest rate risk or currency risk), whether those changes are caused by factors specific to the individual financial instrument or its issuer or by factors affecting all similar financial instruments traded in the market.

Output methods For long-term contracts with customers, methods used to measure the progress towards the performance obligation on the basis of the value to the customer of the goods or services transferred.

Parent An entity that has one or more subsidiaries. (See Subsidiary.)

Past service cost The change in the present value of a defined benefit plan's obligation for employee service in past periods, resulting from a plan amendment or a curtailment. (See Curtailment.)

PAYE Pay-as-you-earn is a tax payment method in which an employer deducts income tax (and National Insurance, if applicable) from an employee's taxable wages or salary and pays it directly to the tax authorities.

Performance condition A vesting condition which requires the recipient of a share-based payment transaction to complete a specified period of service and meet specified performance targets while rendering the service. (See Vesting condition, Market-based condition and Non-market-based condition.)

Performance obligation A separate element of a contract with a customer, which promises to transfer a distinct good or a service to the customer.

Permanent differences Differences between an entity's taxable profits and its total comprehensive income other than temporary differences. (See Temporary differences.)

Post-employment benefits Employee benefits (other than termination benefits) that are payable after the completion of employment. (See Employee benefits and Termination benefits.)

Pre-acquisition reserves The reserves of a subsidiary or associate company at the date of the acquisition of their shares by the investor company.

Preference shares Shares that have a predetermined dividend amount. A preference share does not entitle the owner to a vote in matters put before shareholders.

Present value A measurement basis for assets and liabilities. It uses the present discounted value of the future net cash inflows or outflows that the asset is expected to generate or that are expected to be required to settle the liability in the normal course of business.

Primary user group Existing and potential investors, lenders, and other creditors.

Principles based financial reporting standards Financial reporting standards based on a conceptual framework that consists of a hierarchy of underpinning principles. The accounting methods specified by the standards reflect the economic reality of transactions and items and require the balanced exercise of judgement in their application.

Private and public limited companies A public limited company (plc) is one whose shares may be traded publicly on stock markets. A private limited (Ltd) company's shares are not able to be traded publicly.

Projected unit credit method An actuarial valuation method that recognises each period of an employee's service as giving rise to an additional unit of benefit entitlement. It measures each unit separately to build up the final obligation.

Property, plant and equipment Tangible items that are held for use in the production or supply of goods or services, for rental to others, or for administrative purposes, and are expected to be used during more than one period.

Prospective adjustments to financial statements A prospective adjustment is one which is made in the current accounting period even if it relates to changes to estimates made in previous accounting periods.

Provision A liability of uncertain timing or amount.

Prudence (cautious prudence) An accounting principle which means that, when judgements and estimates are made under conditions of uncertainty, a degree of caution is exercised so that assets or income are not overstated, and liabilities or expenses are not understated. (See Asymmetric prudence.)

Put option (a type of repurchase agreement) The entity has an obligation to repurchase the asset at the customer's request. (See Repurchase agreement.)

Qualifying asset An asset that necessarily takes a substantial period of time to get ready for its intended use or sale.

Reassessment (of a lease under IFRS 16) Changes in the payments made under a lease.

Recognition The process of incorporating in the statement of financial position or statement of profit or loss an item that meets the definition of an element and satisfies the criteria for recognition.

Recoverable amount The amount the company could recover through either the use or the sale of the asset. The recoverable amount is the higher of the value in use of the asset, and the fair value less costs to sell of the asset. (See Fair value and Value in use.)

Redeemable preference shares Preference shares which can be redeemed (i.e. the company can buy them back from the shareholder) on, or after, a period fixed for redemption under the terms of issue.

Related party A person or entity that is related to the entity that is preparing its financial statements (the reporting entity):

(a) A person or a close member of that person's family is related to a reporting entity if that person:

   (i)   has control or joint control of the reporting entity;

   (ii) has significant influence over the reporting entity; or

   (iii) is a member of the key management personnel of the reporting entity or of a parent of the reporting entity.

(b) An entity is related to a reporting entity if any of the following conditions applies:

   (i)   The entity and the reporting entity are members of the same group (which means that each parent, subsidiary and fellow subsidiary is related to the others).

   (ii) One entity is an associate or joint venture of the other entity (or an associate or joint venture of a member of a group of which the other entity is a member).

(iii) Both entities are joint ventures of the same third party.

(iv) One entity is a joint venture of a third entity and the other entity is an associate of the third entity.

(v) The entity is a post-employment benefit plan for the benefit of employees of either the reporting entity or an entity related to the reporting entity. If the reporting entity is itself such a plan, the sponsoring employers are also related to the reporting entity.

(vi) The entity is controlled or jointly controlled by a person identified in (a).

(vii) A person identified in (a)(i) has significant influence over the entity or is a member of the key management personnel of the entity (or of a parent of the entity).

(viii) The entity, or any member of a group of which it is a part, provides key management personnel services to the reporting entity or to the parent of the reporting entity.

(See Close members of the family of a person.)

Related party transaction A transfer of resources, services or obligations between a reporting entity and a related party, regardless of whether a price is charged.

Relevant information A fundamental qualitative characteristic of information. Relevant information affects the decisions made by users and will either confirm evaluations or be used in making predictions about an entity.

Remeasurements Differences in the reconciliation of opening and closing defined benefit plan assets and liabilities valuations. They arise from actuarial gains and losses and the return on plan's assets. (See Actuarial gains and losses and Return on plan assets.)

Repurchase agreement A contract in which an entity sells an asset to a customer and also promises or has the option to repurchase the asset.

Research The obtaining of new knowledge, the search for application of this knowledge, and the search for, and design of, possible alternative materials, devices, products, processes, systems or services.

Reserves Any part of shareholders' equity, except for share capital. Reserves represent amounts that are retained in the company and not distributed to the shareholders.

Residual value The estimated amount that an entity would currently obtain from the disposal of an asset, after deducting the estimated costs of disposal, if the asset were already of the age and in the condition expected at the end of its useful life.

Restructuring A programme that is planned and controlled by management, and materially changes either: (a) the scope of a business undertaken by an entity; or (b) the manner in which that business is conducted.

Retained earnings A reserve representing the amount of net profits (or losses) not paid out as dividends, but retained by a company to be reinvested in its business.

Retirement benefit plan (pension scheme) An arrangement where an entity provides benefits for its employees on or after termination of service (either in the form of an annual income or a lump sum). The plan is a separate legal entity, and the benefits, or the contributions towards them, can be determined or estimated in advance of retirement.

Retrospective adjustments to financial statements A retrospective adjustment is one where the financial statements are drawn up as if the adjustment had always been applied. All affected previous and comparative figures are restated. It only arises from a change in accounting policy or the correction of a material error.

Return on plan assets The difference between the recognition of the changes to a defined benefit plan's assets (the opening balance, plus interest, and the cash payments into or out of the plan) and the valuation of the assets at fair value at the end of the accounting period.

Revaluation reserve A reserve that records the surplus created when assets are revalued to fair value.

Revenue Income that arises in the course of the ordinary activities of a business. (See Income.)

Right-of-use asset An asset leased by the lessee under a lease contract. The lessee must have the right to obtain substantially all of the economic benefits from the use of the asset and the right to direct the use of the asset.

Rules based financial reporting standards Financial reporting standards containing numerous specific requirements and much detailed implementation guidance in an attempt to address as many potential contingencies as possible.

Securitisation (of financial assets) The packaging of pools of financial assets and the sale of these packages.

Separate business entity An underpinning concept of financial reporting which requires that whatever form a business entity takes, or whatever its legal status, it reports the financial affairs of itself only.

Service condition A vesting condition which requires the recipient of a share-based payment transaction to complete a specified period of service during which services are provided to the entity. (See Vesting conditions.)

Settlement The elimination of part or all of an entity's post-employment obligations other than in a way that is set out in the terms of the plan and is included in the actuarial assumptions.

Share appreciation rights (SARs) Arrangements whereby employees of an entity become entitled to a future cash payment (rather than an equity instrument) based on the increase in the company's share price over a specified period of time.

Share-based payment transaction A transaction in which an entity receives goods and services in return for its own equity instruments (including shares or share options) or by incurring liabilities to the supplier the value of which is based on the price of the entity's equity instruments.

Share capital The portion of a company's equity that is obtained by selling shares to a shareholder. The statement of financial position share capital line item shows the sum of the nominal values of all shares issued.

Share option A contract that gives the holder the right to subscribe to the entity's shares at a fixed or determinable price for a specific period of time.

Share premium The excess of the market value of a share over its nominal value. Share premium is a reserve on the statement of financial position.

Shareholders The investors in a company.

Significant influence The power to participate in the financial and operating policy decisions of an associate, but is not control over those policies. (See Associate and Control.)

Special purpose entities (SPEs) A legal entity of some type created to fulfil narrow, specific, or temporary objectives, such as to finance a large project. SPEs are used typically by companies to isolate themselves from financial risk.

Standard cost The planned cost of the products, components or services produced in a period.

Statement of cash flows The financial statement which shows the inflows and outflows of cash and monetary assets deemed to be equivalent to cash over the accounting period. The inflows and outflows are classified under operating, investing and financing activities.

Statement of changes in equity The financial statement which shows all changes in the equity balances over the accounting period.

Statement of comprehensive income The financial statement which shows the changes in equity that have arisen from the transactions of a company other than with the owners in their capacity as owners. It is in two parts and includes profits and losses, shown in the statement of profit or loss part, and other comprehensive income.

Statement of financial position The financial statement showing the assets, liabilities and capital (equity) of an entity at a particular point in time.

Statement of profit or loss The financial statement which shows the total of income less expenses (i.e. profit or loss) excluding items in other comprehensive income. The statement of profit or loss may be presented separately or as part of the statement of comprehensive income.

Stewardship An objective of financial accounting and reporting which is to provide financial information about the reporting entity in order to assess how efficiently and effectively the entity's management and governing board have discharged their responsibilities to use the entity's resources.

Structured entities An entity that has been designed so that voting rights are not the dominant factor in deciding who controls the entity.

Subsidiary An entity that is controlled by another entity. This is usually evidenced by a shareholding of more than 50% of its equity shares. (See Control of an entity.)

Substance over form An underpinning concept of a principles based financial reporting system which requires that items and transactions are accounted for according to their economic or commercial substance, rather than their legal form.

Sum-of-digits method A method to apportion depreciation or interest on a financial instrument or lease which apportions higher depreciation or interest in earlier years. The method takes the asset's expected life or life of the lease and adds together the digits for each year. Each digit is then divided by this sum to determine the proportion by which the asset should be depreciated or interest should be charged or credited each year, starting with the highest number in the first year.

Tax base The amount attributed to an asset or liability for tax purposes and which reflects the tax consequences that will occur when the carrying amount of the asset or liability is recovered or settled.

Taxable profit (loss) The profit or loss for a reporting period upon which income taxes are payable or recoverable, determined in accordance with the rules established by the taxation authorities.

Temporary differences The difference between the carrying amount of an asset and its tax base which gives rise to a deferred tax liability or asset. Temporary differences can be taxable or deductible.

Termination benefits Employee benefits provided in exchange for the termination of an employee's employment as a result of either: (a) an entity's decision to terminate an employee's employment before the normal retirement date; or (b) an employee's decision to accept an offer of benefits in exchange for the termination of employment. (See Employee benefits.)

Timely information An enhancing qualitative characteristic of financial information. The more recent the information, the more useful it is.

Transaction costs Incremental costs that are directly attributable to the acquisition, issue or disposal of a financial asset or financial liability. An incremental cost is one that would not have been incurred if the entity had not acquired, issued or disposed of the financial instrument.

Transaction price (for a contract with a customer) The amount of consideration to which an entity expects to be entitled in exchange for transferring promised goods or services to a customer, excluding amounts collected on behalf of third parties.

Trial balance A list of all the balances drawn from the nominal ledger accounts at a particular point in time.

Underlying A financial phenomenon, such as a specified interest rate, financial instrument price, commodity price, foreign exchange rate, index of prices or rates, credit rating or credit index, which underpins a derivative, changes in which cause changes in the value of the derivative. (See Derivative.)

Underlying asset An asset that is the subject of a lease, for which the right to use that asset has been provided by a lessor to a lessee.

Understandable information An enhancing qualitative characteristic of financial information. Information which is classified, characterised and presented clearly and concisely is more useful.

Unguaranteed residual value The residual value of a leased asset at the end of the lease term which may be specified in the lease arrangement and be based, say, on expected market values. It may never be realised, however it is taken into account by the lessor when the lease is settled and in calculating the lease payment receivable.

Units of production A method to apportion depreciation to a non-current asset, usually machinery. The method takes the estimate of the total number of units to be produced from using the asset and calculates an accounting period's depreciation by apportioning the asset's depreciable amount in relation to the proportion of units produced in one accounting period compared to the total number.

Unrealised profit in inventories The profit element included in the value of inventories remaining in a parent, subsidiary or associate company at the end of the accounting period which were purchased from another group company.

Upstream sale See Downstream and upstream sales

Unwinding of a discount rate The effect of the change in the discount factor applied to the measurement of a liability using a discounted cash flow basis from the beginning of a year to the end of the year.

Useful life The period over which an asset is expected to be available for use by an entity; or the number of production or similar units expected to be obtained from the asset by an entity.

Value in use The present value of the future cash flows expected to be derived from the use of an asset.

Variable lease payments The portion of payments made by a lessee to a lessor under IFRS 16 for the right to use the leased asset during the lease term that varies because of changes in facts or circumstances occurring after the commencement date, other than the passage of time.

VAT (Value added tax) The tax added to the sales price of goods and services.

Verifiable information An enhancing qualitative characteristic of financial information. The better the evidence supporting a transaction or item, the more reliable the information.

Vertical analysis An analytical technique involving the comparison of financial statements which have been expressed in a common size (i.e. in percentages of a key figure taken from the statements).

Vest Become an entitlement.

Vesting conditions The conditions that must be satisfied for the recipient to become entitled to receive the share-based payment. (See Service condition and Performance condition.)

Vesting date The date on which all vesting conditions have been met and the recipient of the share-based payment transaction becomes entitled to the payment.

Vesting period The period during which the vesting conditions are to be satisfied.

Weighted average cost method A method of valuing inventory where the cost of each item is the weighted average of the cost of similar items at the beginning of a period and the cost of similar items purchased or produced during the period.

Working capital Net current assets or liabilities (i.e. current assets minus current liabilities).

INDEX